THE TIDE AT SUNRISE

A History of the Russo-Japanese War, 1904–1905

by

DENIS *and* PEGGY WARNER

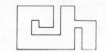

CHARTERHOUSE
New York

༺༊༺༊༺༊

THE TIDE AT SUNRISE
A History of the Russo-Japanese War, 1904–1905
Copyright © 1974 by Denis and Peggy Warner

LIBRARY OF CONGRESS CATALOG CARD NUMBER: 73–89339
ISBN: 0–88327–031–5
MANUFACTURED IN THE UNITED STATES OF AMERICA
DESIGNED BY JACQUES CHAZAUD

PHOTO CREDITS

1/ Melbourne *Herald* 2/ *Collier's Weekly* 3/ *Cassell's History of the Russo-Japanese War* 4/ *Cassell's* 5/ *Cassell's* 6/ *Cassell's* 7/ *Cassell's* 8/ *Cassell's* 9/ *Cassell's* 10/ *Cassell's* 11/ *Cassell's* 12/ *Cassell's* 13/ *Cassell's* 14/ *Cassell's* 15/ Kyodo News Agency 16/ Kyodo News Agency 17/ Kyodo News Agency 18/ Kyodo News Agency 19/ Kyodo News Agency 20/ Imperial War Museum 21/ United States Naval Institute 22/ *Cassell's* 23/ Kyodo News Agency 24/ *Cassell's* 25/ United States Naval Institute 26/ *Cassell's* 27/ United States Naval Institute 28/ Underwood and Underwood 29/ Underwood 30/ Underwood 31/ Underwood 32/ Magic Lantern Slide 33/ Magic Lantern Slide 34/ Underwood 35/ *Cassell's* 36/ *Collier's Weekly* 37/ Magic Lantern Slide 38/ Magic Lantern Slide 39/ Underwood 40/ *Collier's Weekly* 41/ Underwood 42/ *Cassell's* 43/ Underwood 44/ Underwood 45/ Underwood 46/ Underwood 47/ *Cassell's* 48/ *Cassell's* 49/ *Cassell's* 50/ Underwood 51/ Underwood 52/ Underwood 53/ Underwood 54/ Underwood 55/ Underwood 56/ Vickers, Ltd. 57/ Vickers, Ltd. 58/ Underwood 59/ United States Naval Institute

Maps by Don Coutts.

THE TIDE AT SUNRISE

By the same authors

Denis Warner
OUT OF THE GUN
HURRICANE FROM CHINA
THE LAST CONFUCIAN

Peggy Warner
DON'T TYPE IN BED
ASIA IS PEOPLE

For Shelley, Nick, and Annabel

Contents

IV. Elusive Victory

V. The Aftermath

Introduction

ONE HUNDRED TWENTY-ONE YEARS AGO an American squadron dropped anchor in Tokyo Bay and confounded the world. Europe and America regarded the Japanese as ignorant, heathen, semi-barbarous, and sanguinary. Few expected the expedition to succeed. Some thought it was as absurd as a journey to outer space, and the Baltimore *Sun*, when the ships were on the high seas, called on Washington to abandon the "humbug," which, it said, had become a matter of ridicule at home and abroad.

Spacemen might indeed have landed, so momentous was the effect of the Americans' arrival on the Japanese. Even the fire bombs that American Superfortresses rained on Tokyo in the winter of 1944–1945 with crippling loss of life failed to cause anything like the dismay and despair that gripped the city in 1853 when the temple bells tolled to warn of the "invasion."

The million people who lived in Tokyo, or Edo, as it was then called, fled their homes and ran into the streets, wailing, crying, and abjectly afraid. They had no idea what to do or where to go. Rumor of an imminent battle added to the terror of a people who for two centuries had shut themselves off from the world and had no wish to renew its acquaintance now. Provisions became scarce, the price of a suit of armor quadrupled, and normal city life came to a standstill as the people waited tremulously for each messenger to arrive. War horses trampling through the streets and the jangle of men in armor brought no reassurance to those facing the unknown.

Days passed before the tension eased and the shogun's officials, calming their own fears, got down to the serious business of trying to cope with these hairy barbarians who brazenly steamed past the forts at the entrance to Edo

Bay, ignominiously dispelling the fiction that the Japanese guns were so powerful no ship could pass without permission.

All the Americans wanted was trade and coaling facilities, and these by bluff and hint of force they eventually got. In the process, they fired history's most remarkable industrial and national revolution. Within fifty years, to the continued astonishment of the world, Japan was ready to go to war with Russia, which had been drawn to the East by the prospect of trade and the imperial ambitions of the tsars.

It is with this war and its causes and effects that we are concerned here. It was fought in the waters of the Yellow Sea and in the Straits of Tsushima that divide Japan from Korea, and in the mountains and plains of Manchuria, borrowed without permission from China for the occasion. It was the biggest, most stunning war the world had ever known.

Fleets had moved from sail to steam when the Japanese flexed their muscles and fought the Chinese in 1894, but this was the first time that armored battleships with twelve-inch guns had met in anything like equal conflict. Though the dreadnoughts of the First World War were more powerful, the Battle of Tsushima, which brought the two fleets into dramatic and climactic action, was bigger and much more decisive than Jutland.

The land actions were bloody and vast also, vaster in terms of numbers of men involved than Gettysburg, Waterloo, or Borodino. The battle of Liaoyang in Manchuria in August 1904 was second only to Sedan in the numbers of men thrown into action. Six months later at Mukden the Russians committed 275,000 infantrymen, 16,000 cavalry, and 1,219 artillery pieces—the greatest force that any army had ever assembled. Slightly more than 200,000 Japanese took the offensive against it. Breech-loading rifles, machine guns, and new quick-firing artillery pieces added their merciless contribution to the land war. The torpedo and the mine were put to effective use at sea.

The explosion of each new defeat and victory burst with even greater impact in the capitals of the world. Japanese money and Japanese agents quickened the pace of revolution in Russia and fired the tinder of Asian nationalism. To some extent, every war changes the world, but to many Asians who think of the First World War as primarily a European civil war, the war between Russia and Japan in 1904–1905 was the most important of our times. Coolie could be master and master, coolie.

Today, bloodied by the Vietnam War, the United States has taken a step back from Asia and the situations that it helped to shape. It has established a *modus vivendi* with China, is in alliance with Japan, and has begun to improve relations with Russia. Yet Japan, whose trade the United States once sought, is now its biggest competitor, and Russia and China watch each other with undisguised and dangerous enmity across the Ussuri River, which became their common border at the time when Japan was throwing off its isolation.

Forty-five divisions, a quarter of the entire Russian army, man the Sino-Soviet frontier. They are reported to be equipped with nuclear weapons. Vladivostok is home base for more than a hundred submarines, more formidable than the force available to Adolf Hitler in the Atlantic when he went to war in 1939. On the airfields north of the China border the Russians have deployed more than 2,000 aircraft. The build-up has been massive and rapid. In 1968 there were only fifteen Russian divisions in the Far East. Six more arrived in 1969, and in the next two years the number more than doubled.

Russia's ambitions to become a global world power have not been eroded by ideological change since the days of Tsar Nicholas II, or by time. Ironically, the Vietnam War—which saw the floodtide, and also the ebbtide, of American involvement in Asia—attracted an increasing, and no doubt permanent, Russian presence in the waters of the Indian and Pacific oceans.

Japan is surging ahead again and by the end of the century seems likely to challenge the United States for the industrial leadership of the world. China, unified for the first time in the modern era, has three million men under arms and is continuing the development of nuclear weapons.

How will the giants of northeast Asia resolve their differences? By taking this long look at the past, we hope we may help to explain the present and perhaps to anticipate the future.

Denis Warner
Peggy Warner

I

OPENING ROUND

CHAPTER 1

ಶಿಖಿಶಿಖಿಶಿಖಿ

The First Pearl Harbor

THE BRITISH MERCHANT steamer *Foochow* threaded its way through the narrow and shallow entrance of Port Arthur harbor on the morning of February 8, 1904. On its passenger list was Mizuno Kokichi, the Japanese consul in Cheefoo, a Chinese port on the Shantung Peninsula ninety miles away. With him was his "valet," Commander Mori Gitaro of the Japanese navy.

To the visitor approaching the Russian fortress on a day like this, Port Arthur had a distinct charm. The narrow entrance opened into a handsome, landlocked bay, with bare, rugged hills rising sharply on all sides and glowing in the dazzling winter sunshine. The town with its 56,000 inhabitants nestled below the surrounding hills, with a line of white-painted houses and gray-roofed workshops stretching along the waterfront. Squat Quail Hill, topped with a fire observation tower, faced the entrance. To the right were the naval basin, dockyard, and telegraph station, under the shelter of Golden Hill, where the Russian flag flew proudly over the forts and batteries.

To the left was the Tiger's Tail, a long, narrow peninsula that sheltered the calm water moorings for the torpedo boats. Close to the tip of the tail was a white-painted lighthouse, and farther down the peninsula at Laotieh-shan ("Old Iron Mountain") was another, larger lighthouse with search-lights.

Immediately behind the town, crowning the hills and stretching in a protective arc, were more forts, with Fort Erh-lung-shan ("Two Dragon Hill") due north and a double peak that the Russians called High Hill. The double peak was the tallest on the plateau north of Port Arthur and looked

[3]

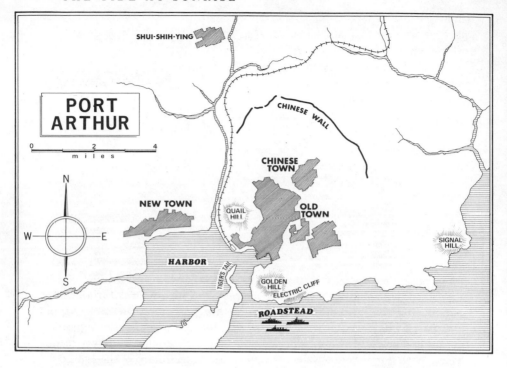

down on all parts of the harbor and the town. It was soon to be known around the world as 203 Meter Hill, or, as the Japanese called it, Nireisan.

It was not the topography of Port Arthur but the whereabouts of its fleet that Commander Mori needed to know. Outside the harbor the "valet" counted the big Russian ships swinging at anchor in three lines, with four cruisers on the outer line, three more cruisers and two battleships in the middle line, and five battleships in a third line about 500 yards from shore.

The Japanese consul had other business in Port Arthur. In the inner harbor he hired a boat to take him to the shore. As his boat, propelled by six Chinese oarsmen, hurried him toward the jetty it passed another, smaller boat heading in the same direction. On board was Ernest Brindle, of the London *Daily Mail,* who had been in quarantine for three days. The sky was clear and cloudless and the sun bright and Brindle was invigorated by the crispness in the air, the sparkling sea, and the view of the town. He recognized the Japanese consul, alert and smiling and looking around with the keenest of interest.

"Good morning," called Brindle. "Where are you going? This doesn't look much like war."

The consul greeted Brindle warmly, still smiling. "I am going to see

[4]

Admiral Alexeiev and arrange to bring away the Japanese residents," he said. "Our minister has been recalled from St. Petersburg and the Japanese government instructed me to come here and look after our people."

Brindle's boatman urged his sampan through the smooth water with long, leisurely strokes of the single, flat-ended oar notched between two spikes at the stern. His breath exhaled like steam in the cold air as the small craft made its way toward the landing stage. By the time it had reached the landing, the Japanese consul was already climbing up the rough wooden ramp to the shore. Brindle watched as he made his way up the hill behind the dockyard to the two-story viceregal lodge, where Viceroy Eugene Ivanovitch Alexeiev, the Tsar's representative in the Far East, lived in solitary splendor, overlooking the harbor, the forts, and the fleets.*

News had reached Port Arthur that Japan had broken off negotiations in St. Petersburg, severed diplomatic relations, and announced that it reserved the right "to take such independent action" as was deemed necessary. Detachments were under orders to leave for the Yalu River on the Korean border to protect the Russian timber concessions there. But no one inside Port Arthur appeared to take the threat of war seriously—no one except the Japanese shopkeepers and merchants who, together with women and children, waited apprehensively for the *Foochow* to take them to Japan. They were well dressed for the most part, some in curly astrakhan caps, fur coats, and fur-lined suede gloves. Many of the women had babies strapped to their backs and their luggage stood beside them: wooden boxes and wicker baskets, sheets and blankets, parasols, bottles of beer and saké, and innumerable pet dogs.

Forty-four years earlier Lieutenant William Arthur, of the Royal Navy, had come to this place at the tip of the Kwantung Peninsula, aboard *H.M.S. Algerine,* a screw-steamer gunboat, with a smaller ship in tow. The ships were part of an Anglo-French force that had cleared the boom obstructions on the Pei River, which guarded the river approaches to the Chinese city of Tientsin; there, at the point of the gun, the British and the French were intent on negotiating new trade treaties with the Chinese. Lieutenant Arthur maneuvered the two boats through the narrow entrance to the harbor, superbly sheltered from the storms of the Yellow Sea, and hoisted the Union Jack. The little Manchurian village of Lushun then became Port Arthur, and, through a succession of tenants, so it remained.

Maimed by the Japanese in the battle of the Yalu River, the Chinese fleet limped into Port Arthur in 1894, only to be forced out by Japanese ground

---

*Alexeiev did not receive the consul, who was passed on to the admiral in charge of the port, Rear-Admiral Nikolai Romonovitch Grevé.

forces which marched down the peninsula, seized the forts that ringed the hills behind the harbor, and celebrated their victory with a poetry-writing contest, a cherry-tree-planting ceremony, and an unpleasant little massacre of Chinese civilians and soldiers. For the Japanese, Port Arthur became a foothold in Manchuria from which they did not intend to be dislodged.

It was a hollow victory. The Japanese had reckoned without the French, the Germans, and the Russians, all of whom had ambitions of their own. They "advised" the Japanese not to insist on including any part of China in the spoils of their well-won war. In 1895, when the Chinese were about to cede Port Arthur to the Japanese, Russian gunboats demonstrated in the Straits of Tsushima, between Japan and Korea. Tokyo, not yet ready to challenge a European power, though itching to take on all of the foreign powers that had cheated her of victory, reluctantly abandoned her claims and in rage and humiliation withdrew.

In time, perhaps, the Japanese might have forgotten Port Arthur, but the Russians moved in two years later, arousing anew half-forgotten angers and inflaming national pride.

Peter the Great had wanted a window to the West. When Nicholas II seized Port Arthur, he got a window to the East. Vladivostok, 1,220 miles to the north, could not adequately serve as the guardian of the eastern empire that Nicholas planned to build. It was ice-bound for more than three months each year, while its sea approaches were watched over from the islands of Japan. Port Arthur met the military need, and Talien, soon to be renamed Dalny,* would become a great Russian commercial center. In 1898 Russia demanded the formal lease of Port Arthur, Talien, and the rest of the Kwantung Peninsula from China. A demonstration of force at Port Arthur and a large bribe for the Chinese negotiators won the lease for Russia, together with the right to connect Port Arthur to the Trans-Siberian Railway, and to the Chinese railway, which ran from Tientsin to the Great Wall.

Port Arthur in early 1904 was like Chicago at its worst—rough, immoral, and vulgar. A Kansas barnyard, one visitor called it. Instead of chickens, the motley collection of western and Oriental citizens jostled with the horses, donkeys, goats, and cattle. From the bay, Port Arthur looked picturesque, but it was derelict and decaying, a collection of jerrybuilt stone houses, temporary warehouses, and equally temporary administrative buildings. By June it was planned that all of Old Town and the Chinese quarter behind it would be torn down to make way for government build-

---

*Dairen, the Japanese reading of the Chinese name.

ings, and when this happened everything else would move to New Town, still going up alongside Quail Hill.

The railway station in Port Arthur was made conspicuous by an immense pile of tens of thousands of cases of vodka. Quail Hill separated the Old Town from New Town, the latter to be the wonder of the East with broad, tree-lined avenues, banks and houses and shops, a grand administrative building, and a grander palace for the viceroy. A large park had been laid out and the foundations set for a cathedral surmounted by the Greek Cross —to be worthy of God and the Tsar. There would be a theater and a sumptuous hotel that would outdo in splendor the Grand in Yokohama, the best in the East.

A garrison of 18,000 soldiers, a similar number of sailors, and about 20,000 dock workers and civilians, Chinese and Russian, and adventurers from all round the world, a plentiful supply of women—one at least for every officer—and the mountain of vodka provided the ingredients for raw frontier life.

With the exception of the viceregal lodge, set in a park and surrounded by a high fence and ornamental trees, the mayor's house, the exclusive Navy Club, and the residences of senior officers, most of old Port Arthur was a slum. Apart from the waterfront there was only one other good roadway in town—a military road leading to the hill forts and the stores and army barracks. The rest of the streets were unpaved tracks. In the winter of 1904, when they were not frozen hard, these tracks became troughs of mud through which horses splashed and jinrickshas had to be dragged by a pair of men. The buildings were filled either with mud or dust.

Entertainment was not lacking. Baratovski's great traveling circus had come all the way from Europe and was established as a semi-permanent institution in a large building on Pushkin Street, the main thoroughfare. The show offered trained tigers and lions, performing horses and monkeys, and numerous acrobats and tightrope dancers. The Viceroy, Admiral Alexeiev, came regularly and sat in a box reserved for him opposite the orchestra.

Between the circus and the navy yards there were music halls, gambling parlors, an ice rink, a circulating library, Chinese theaters, grog shops, and bars with girls who sang and danced and others staffed with prostitutes.

The hotels were grim, about the meanest, so one traveler said, ever provided for civilized man. Effiemov's in the Old Town had twenty-four rooms in a one-story, shedlike building, dark, dingy, and filthy, with cubicles for bedrooms. A typical room contained a broken-down table, a camp stretcher with no bedding (visitors to Port Arthur wisely preferred to bring their own), a pitcher, a bentwood chair, and a washstand made from a wooden packing case with a chipped enamel bowl perched on its top. An advertisement for an American beer was the only wall decoration. There was no carpet on the floor, and the only window was permanently sealed.

The leading restaurant in the town was Saratov's, named after the hospitable, bearded proprietor. The restaurant, in an old Chinese building on a point of land overlooking the harbor, though sleazy and dirty, served a good vodka aperitif followed by a steaming bowl of meat soup thick enough for customers to eat it with a knife and fork—which many did.

At Dalny ("Far Away"), Port Arthur's commercial counterpart forty miles away by train, Russian architects had built imaginatively on the dreams of Nicholas II. Laid out like Washington, D.C., with wide avenues branching off from the municipal park in the center of the city, Dalny had literally been carved out of rock as a monument to Russian commercial determination in the Far East. Acres of warehouses surrounded an immense granite pier, and a breakwater wall half a mile long sheltered the broad, deep bay from the winds that blew in from the East. The park contained tennis courts, bowling greens, a swimming pool, and a zoo. Every type of European architecture was represented. Swiss cottages nestled together with Italian loggias; Elizabethan houses with black beams competed with Spanish mansions.

Dalny had much that Port Arthur lacked, but most Russians in the Far East thought longingly of Port Arthur, despite its squalor. Traffic was heavy between the two towns. The carriages of the trains were magnificently upholstered in leather and finished in stained wood. Each compartment accommodated two people and the seats could be converted into beds. The lines were too light to carry the richly furnished train in safety, and it lurched and rocked along at fifteen miles an hour through the rough, hilly countryside, dotted with bright Chinese shrines and ornate family tombs. Port Arthur was the garrison town, gayer than dull, pretty Dalny. When Alexeiev became Viceroy and in command of all Russian interests in the Far East, civil and military, with his headquarters in Port Arthur, Dalny began to wither.

An Armenian and a bachelor, Viceroy Eugene Ivanovitch Alexeiev was born in the Crimea in 1843, of good though not noble family. His father managed estates in southern Russia for an aristocratic family well connected with the navy. Through the influence of the nobleman young Alexeiev had been admitted to the naval school in St. Petersburg, which at that time excluded all but the sons of aristocrats.

Alexeiev was intelligent, if impulsive, popular with the naval officers and civilians but less highly regarded by the army. His administration of Russian interests in the Far East came in bursts of furious activity, followed by periods of apparent apathy. Sometimes he was very busy, issuing instructions to army, navy, and civilian authorities. At other times, he seemed overwhelmed and overawed by his multitudinous tasks and retired to his lodge, whereupon the Port Arthur fortress went on its merry, inefficient way. Before he took command of the Pacific squadron in 1895 he had spent four years as a naval attaché in Paris and five years in command of the cruiser *Kornilov,* on which he earned himself a reputation as a strict disciplinarian. In 1900, during the Boxer Rebellion, General Alexei Nicolaievitch Kuropatkin, the Russian war minister, made him an army corps commander. He had some claim, therefore, to both army and navy experience.

His chief asset was the confidence of Tsar Nicholas II, who named him governor of Kwantung Territory after the acquisition of Port Arthur in 1897 and commander-in-chief of all navy forces in the Pacific. His elevation to the post of Viceroy in August 1903 caused great alarm in Japan, which viewed his appointment as further evidence that Russia was preparing for war.

Many of Alexeiev's more astute contemporaries felt that the Viceroy's ambitions far outstripped his capabilities. When his appointment had been announced on the recommendation of Captain A. M. Bezobrazov, the state secretary and protagonist of Russia's forward policy in the Far East, it was received with "doubt, hesitation, and pain" by statesmen in Russia. This was the first time an admiral had been appointed to such a high civil office. Serge Yulevitch Witte, the finance minister, whose bitter opposition to the Tsar's militant Far Eastern policy resulted in his own dismissal, thought that Alexeiev was a nincompoop. "He was not an army man," he wrote. "He could not even ride on horseback. Nor did he in any way distinguish himself in the naval service." Witte insisted that Alexeiev had won advantage only by having once stood in for the Grand Duke Alexis Alexandrovitch, uncle of Tsar Nicholas II, after a drunken brawl in Marseilles. Alexeiev had persuaded the authorities that it was he, not the grand duke, who was guilty of the offense, paid the fine, and was rewarded thereafter with undeserved promotion.

The governor and commander of the Port Arthur fortress, Lieutenant-General Baron Anatole Mikailovitch Stoessel, a strict disciplinarian, was a strongly built, uncouth-looking man with a stentorian voice. He had been in two wars: as a staff captain in the Russo-Turkish war, in which he had been wounded, and in the Boxer Rebellion in 1900 as commander of an allied force of 2,000 men, including 1,500 Russians. After penetrating the Boxer lines, he relieved the Russian legation at Tientsin. The house at Port Arthur where he lived with his buxom wife contained many golden ornaments from the ten cases of loot he carried off with him after the Boxer campaign.

The troops hated Stoessel. He terrified officers and men as he rode through the town like a whirlwind, shouting orders in his great voice. Soldiers ran into side streets or hid behind warehouses to get out of his way. If war ever came to Port Arthur, it was said, he would be shot in the back by his own soldiers.

The civilians in Port Arthur frequently caused trouble, and Stoessel used brutal measures in an effort to control them. Since he was known to use his riding whip if they crossed his path, coolies fled at his approach. He told the correspondent of the official newspaper, *Novoye Krai,* the only newspaper in Port Arthur, that he would rather command troops in the field than run a fortress; but while he remained at Port Arthur he, the commander, was both God and tsar. So much money had been spent on the fortress, he said, that the yellow-skinned little Japanese devils would never be able to get into it.

For the Russian navy Stoessel had a particular contempt, perhaps with cause. With some notable exceptions, officers and men of the fleet were poorly trained and indolent. Many naval officers were drawn from the Russian nobility. The Grand Duke Cyril Vladimirovitch, second in line to the Russian throne in 1904, and assigned to the Pacific squadron, took a cabaret singer–prostitute to Port Arthur with him. His brother Boris and other naval officers of the Russian aristocracy knew little about the sea. Telescopic sights, telegraphic equipment, and signal books were all new, but few officers found time to study them. Few of the big ships had practiced with their heavy guns. The men followed the example set by their officers. Most regarded service in the Far East as exile.

Vice-Admiral Oscar Victorovitch Stark, elderly, popular, gregarious and absent-minded, commanded the fleet. He lived with his family in a simple, pleasant house overlooking the harbor. Miss K. A. Massey, an English nurse, cared for the children, and the Starks, as their position required, were among the social leaders of the Far Eastern station. They entertained generously, both at home and on board the flagship *Petropavlovsk,* and Admiral Stark was often criticized abroad for the attention he gave to the social round. The fleet was best known for its drunken sailors lying on the wharves after a night of dissipation ashore and the petticoats swarming up the gangplanks and down the companionways.

Admiral Stark may have paid too much attention to social affairs, but he had his own private reservations about the Japanese. On several occasions he had pleaded with the Viceroy for permission to prepare the fleet for action. Alexeiev, who had been warned by the Tsar not to take any action to aggravate the situation, or to precipitate war, said there was no need for hurry. "This is premature," was his usual reply.

Alexeiev, now sixty-one, heavily bearded, and usually courteous and affable to visiting consuls and other outsiders, privately respected the Japanese whom he had seen in action at Tientsin in the Boxer Rebellion. Publicly, he maintained a firm stand, refusing to be cowed by Japan, which he referred to as the beggar among the great powers. He was fond of saying that he was a self-made man and at the beginning of February kept very much to himself inside his lodge with its antique furniture, Oriental silk screens decorated with dragons and flowers, and a magnificent writing desk with a solid jade top. He would talk of military matters only to his staff.

De Plancton, his diplomatic adviser and secretary, was the most readily accessible member of Alexeiev's staff. Like most of the Viceroy's subordinates, he pooh-poohed the possibility of war with Japan. "Russia has been very patient—magnanimous," he replied to a correspondent's queries. "Now, if Japan will not be quiet, Russia will smash her," and he brought his hand crashing down on the table to make his point. "There will be no war," he said.

Few in Port Arthur disagreed with him: if Russia wanted war, there would be war, but not before. The editor of the *Novoye Krai,* which appeared three times a week, told correspondents it was true that several Russian warships had left harbor with sealed orders in search of Japanese ships. He was, however, more than hopeful that war would be avoided, adding that Japan was not a country that could give an ultimatum to Russia. Russia would certainly not receive one from such a country. The Russians in Port Arthur scarcely considered the Japanese to be people.

The boasting cloaked the growing apprehension among the Viceroy's subordinates. Alexeiev had been informed of Japanese preparations, including the massing of transports and troops near Hiroshima during the early days of January. On January 6 he had asked the Tsar's permission to mobilize his own troops in the Far East and to move detachments to the Yalu. "We can allow Japanese occupation to the mountains forming the watershed of the Yalu and the Tiumen [*i.e.,* to the Korean–Manchurian border]," Nicholas telegraphed on January 27.

Understandably, Alexeiev was tense. A troop of Cossacks now guarded his house. He was said to be unwell and spraying the doors and windows of his house with eau de Cologne to keep germs at bay. In fact, he had more urgent business. A telegram from St. Petersburg read:

It is desirable that the Japanese and not we shall commence military action. Therefore, if they do not start action against us, you must not hinder their landing in southern Korea, or on the eastern shore up to and including Wonsan [about halfway up the eastern Korean coast]. But, if on the western side of Korea their fleet carries out a landing, then you may attack them without waiting the first shot from their side. I have confidence in you. God help you.

It was signed by Tsar Nicholas II.

For reasons that no one knew, Port Arthur's telegraphic link with Korea had failed the day before. No one seemed to associate the breakdown with the threat of war. Only Admiral Stark seemed concerned. The *Varyag*, one of Russia's biggest and best-protected cruisers, was at Chemulpo (Jinsen or Inchon) in Korea, and he would have preferred to have had this new American-built ship under his command at Port Arthur.

It was a risk for the ship to be operating alone. Alexeiev, however, ordered that *Varyag* was on no account to leave Chemulpo without instructions, which would be transmitted by one means or another. Now that the telegraph cable had been cut, the immediate means had ceased to exist, and in Port Arthur no one knew what events were taking place off the Korean coast.

Several hundred Russian naval recruits arrived by train on the afternoon of February 8. They seemed frightened and confused and appeared to have come straight from peasant villages and farms. As they shuffled into line to march to the harbor, people in the streets laughed at them, but at the same time felt pity because of their youth. The crooked streets and lanes of Old Town, behind the waterfront, swarmed with horse-, donkey-, and mule-drawn carts, and jinrickshas. Two-horse droshkies dashed along the waterfront, or Bund, the drivers muffled up in thick fur coats and lashing at their Mongol ponies with long whips. Troops filled the streets, some in full marching order, others slouching along singing popular songs. Now and then there was the sound of military bands and bugle calls rang out from the ring of coastal forts on Tiger's Tail, Golden Hill, and Electric Cliff. The inner harbor was all bustle, with steamers and junks, destroyers and gunboats crowded together near Old Town as Chinese-manned sampans unloaded cargo. There was little efficiency in all the commotion.

Coal stores in the town were full to overflowing, as English tramp steamers and Norwegian ships brought in more and more supplies. All over town piles of coal lay on footpaths, and some had been dumped in rocky fissures near the railway station.

There was the smell of snow in the air that afternoon, but the people of "Arthur," as the inhabitants affectionately called it, still basked in the winter sunshine. Restaurateur Saratov welcomed his fur-clad guests as they came in from the cold. Saratov's, both a restaurant and an unofficial club, was crowded at noon with army and navy officers, girls from the circus and from elsewhere who had found their way to the Far East in search of men and adventure. The click of billiard balls sounded above the chatter in the bar and the four glassed-in dining rooms overlooking the street and the harbor.

The mayor, Colonel Alexander I. Veishinin, was proud of Port Arthur that sunny winter's day. He was an established force in the town, having taken up residence six years before the Russians took it over, when it was mostly pasture land for Chinese farmers. He was a scholarly Cossack, an archaeologist, a student of Oriental art (he had also been in the sacking of Tientsin and his house on the foreshore was stocked with treasures from the city), and a friend of the Viceroy. With great pride he showed visitors around New Town. Port Arthur was the best town on earth, he said. And it was going to be better. Even now there were more places to go and more things to do.

That evening a new restaurant, Nicobadze's, on the edge of New Town, had a fresh collection of chorus girls as the main dish. The restaurant with its up-to-date furnishings was a forerunner of the new Port Arthur that soon would be the wonder of the East. Saratov's was also busy, despite the enormous pile of coal that had been dumped on the waterfront at its front entrance earlier in the day.

All was quiet in the roadstead outside Port Arthur. Among the seven battleships at anchor was the flagship *Petropavlovsk*. Built in St. Petersburg in 1894, she had a displacement of more than 12,000 tons, a complement of 900 men, and mounted four twelve-inch and twelve six-inch guns. With her were *Sevastopol; Poltava; Peresvyet* (which carried the flag of Rear-Admiral Prince Ukhtomski); *Pobyeda; Tsarevitch* ("Royal Prince"), the largest and most heavily armored of the Russian battleships, built in France; and *Retvizan*, armed with four twelve-inch guns, twelve six-inch guns, and twenty twelve-pounders. *Retvizan*'s armor consisted of a belt of steel at the waterline (to deflect torpedoes) 250 feet long and varying between seven and nine inches in width and an armored deck three inches thick. The cruisers *Bayan, Askold, Diana, Pallada, Novik,* and *Boyarin,* and a transport, *Angara,* were also in the roadstead. All the battleships and cruisers, painted white with black funnels and surrounded by a froth of small boats busy fueling them, were still in the positions where Commander Mori had taken note of them that morning.

By late evening the restaurants were crowded with men and women glad to be out of the cold, eating and drinking, singing and playing billiards. Among the numerous private parties given to celebrate the feast day of St. Maria was a dinner at the home of Lady Sonnenbrin, wife of the ranking doctor in the Tenth Regiment. There was also said to be a party at the house of the commander of the fleet, Admiral Stark, whose wife and daughter were named Maria. The streets of Old Town were deserted and dark with only a few oil lamps, set at long distances apart on the roads; but in some houses and restaurants lights shone through tightly closed windows.

Two tall guide lights on Quail Hill lit the narrow entrance to the channel, and the lighthouses on Tiger's Tail and Golden Hill showed dimly through the gloom. At 10:30 P.M. the band was playing aboard the Russian battleship *Tsarevitch,* and the seamen were singing an evening hymn, their voices coming over the water toward the town. The moon had not yet risen. It was a bleak, raw night, with light snow falling on the houses along the quay, slanting down on the smaller ships tucked in the tiny harbor, and sending its filmy white blanket over the close-packed hills that surrounded the town, the forts that capped them, and the battleships and cruisers, their lights just visible, in the roadstead beyond. The harbor was peaceful. All the daytime clamor had gone, together with the haze of smoke from the ships of the fleet and the cargo boats.

Searchlights played lazily across the water from the cruisers *Pallada* and *Askold* in the roadstead. This was Admiral Stark's latest order. He had instructed the fleet to put out their torpedo nets and to be ready to meet any attack. As part of his preparations, he had also taken the battleships and cruisers and some mine layers to sea for tactical exercises on February 3. The orders were not taken seriously by his subordinates. Several ships ignored the instruction to put out their nets and had failed to take any other precautions.

The searchlights from the two duty cruisers did not penetrate a rolling mist far out to sea where the two Russian destroyers, *Rastoropni* and *Bezstrashni,* were on patrol. The Russians had been ordered to cruise with their lights on and not to prepare for action until directed. They were to search the sea to a distance of twenty miles and then to report back to the duty ship.

Their mission accomplished, they were heading without reluctance back to harbor when lookout men on both destroyers saw a long, shadowy line moving through the water ahead. Dim white lights showed at intervals through the mist, and slender trails of froth made patterns on the dark sea. To the Russians, peering through the mist and snow, it was an eerie sight.

The long line of moving lights, like fireflies, stretched for a considerable distance over the sea, and the watching Russians stared in shocked disbelief as they closed the gap on the phantom ships sliding slowly through the night. Suddenly, the lights disappeared and only the long, dim shapes and the lacy white wakes remained. The Russian destroyers quickly made for home, cutting through this line of strange vessels in their haste to report to the duty ship at Port Arthur.

For the ten ships of the First, Second and Third Japanese destroyer flotillas this was the second reverse of the night. Earlier in the evening they had met two other Japanese flotillas on their way to Dalny. Alarmed when the other ships crossed his bows, the commander reduced speed. His line became broken, and it was not until 8:40 P.M. that he had reorganized his three flotillas and continued on his way.

The ten long, lean 300-ton Japanese ships, all built in England between 1899 and 1902, painted dark gray and carrying about fifty men, were cruising at thirteen knots. At this speed, no spark showed from their funnels, and their wakes, though clearly visible to the Russians, were small. The ships' names had been blacked out, and each showed only one screened white tail light.

Seeing two white lights ahead, *Sazanami* ("Ripples"), one of the smallest and oldest of the Japanese destroyers, steamed straight for them, only to find herself alongside the Russian destroyers. Bewildered by this encounter, the ship turned quickly and searched for her consorts but could not find them. All the white tail lights of the other ships had gone out and there was no sound of their engines. Other ships became lost, and two, *Oboro* ("Spring Mist") and *Ikazuchi* ("Thunderbolt"), collided.

Just before midnight, Captain Asai Shojiro on *Shiragumo* saw the lights on Old Iron Mountain and the faint glow of Port Arthur over the water. With his four ships, *Shiragumo* ("White Cloud"), *Asashio* ("Morning Tide"), *Kasumi* ("Mist") and *Akatsuki* ("Daybreak"), the newest and fastest of the ten, he steamed slowly toward the entrance and the lines of Russian ships riding peacefully at anchor. The Japanese destroyers were all capable of thirty-one knots and armed with two twelve-pound guns, four six-pounders, and two torpedoes fitted with net cutters, but they were still throttled back and moving slowly, silently, and cautiously.

Through the dark and the snow the searchlights from the Russian squadron wheeled across the sea, holding the ships for a second and exposing them, the Japanese felt sure, to every pair of eyes on every battleship and cruiser.

There were moments of panic on the Japanese destroyers. If the Russians opened fire, if they gave the alarm, surprise, the vital element in the Japanese plans, would be lost. Time after time the long fingers of light scanned the sea. Once a finger stopped moving and pointed accusingly at the Japanese. After agonizing moments the searchlights passed on, leaving the Japanese sailors confident that the gods were with them. And so they were.

Pallada ("Goddess of the Skies") had seen the Japanese destroyers but thought they were the Russian scouts, returning home. The Japanese saw the lines of fourteen Russian ships and recognized some by their funnels and sidelights. "We silently observed the whole line," Captain Asai noted.

He signaled, "Make the attack." Ten minutes before midnight Port Arthur time,* the four Japanese ships turned to port and churned in at full speed, discharging their first torpedoes at six hundred meters. Captain Asai saw his two torpedoes explode close together near the Russian ships. The three other destroyers followed, and each fired two torpedoes at what they believed to be the Russian battleships *Peresvyet* and *Retvizan* and a cruiser of the *Pallada* class. *Rastoropni* and *Bezzstrashni,* after scuttling back to harbor, were still reporting when the first torpedoes struck.

The battleship *Retvizan* lurched as if she had been struck by an express train as the first torpedo blew a hole in her side. Her searchlight spun out of control and water poured in through the hole. Officers flung from their bunks groped their way to the decks as the call to quarters sounded. No one knew what was happening. If the searchlights found anything, boarding parties were supposed to investigate. There were no orders to fire, and none was officially given now. Officers looking to the flagship for a signal looked for a long time in vain, even after firing had begun. Frantic officers, preparing to fire, were still unsure whether they should do so. Some thought that a training exercise was going on, others that the Russian destroyers were firing.

Pallada was struck amidships in her coal bunkers and heeled over. Fire swept up her side, dispelling any notion that this was an exercise. Even now no one knew what they were shooting at.

The last ship of the Japanese first line, *Akatsuki,* ran in with the Russian lights full on her. Dead ahead her captain saw a huge ship with two masts and three funnels. "The great moment had arrived," he noted in his diary. The destroyer shook violently and the four tall funnels, conning tower, and bridge vibrated with the speed. Guessing the ship ahead to be the *Retvizan,* the captain steamed closer and at six hundred meters fired a torpedo at the stern of the battleship. Still running wildly westward, still with the searchlights hunting her, she approached another ship with two masts and three funnels and swung the helm to fire from her after tube. A towering pillar of smoke rose around the Russian ships, and *Akatsuki,* with shots now bursting about her, followed the three other destroyers to the south.

The "Arthur" squadron was a sitting duck. As rockets soared into the sky around Golden Hill and the batteries on Electric Cliff fired their salvoes, the Japanese ships of the Second and Third flotillas ran in, fired their torpedoes and sped off into the darkness. *Sazanami,* which had lost her sister ships after the encounter with the two Russian destroyers, made a desperate line for Golden Hill lighthouse, fired two torpedoes in quick

---

*12:20 A.M., February 9, Tokyo time.

succession at the Russian ships, turned to starboard, and went off to the southwest at top speed. *Oboro,* crippled earlier by the collision with one of the other Japanese destroyers and failing to respond properly to her helm, fired two torpedoes as she ran drunkenly toward the Russian lines.

Only one Russian ship was not caught entirely napping. On the cruiser *Novik,* Commander Andrew Petrovitch Steer, who had the middle watch from midnight till 4 A.M., shouted to his drummer to "beat to quarters" as the first shot rang out. By the time the flagship had finally and belatedly given instructions for a counterattack, *Novik* had steam up and was preparing to take to sea.

Three of Russia's biggest ships had been badly damaged. The cruiser *Pallada* had an enormous hole by her coal bunker. *Retvizan,* which was hit forward, had a hole measuring 220 square feet in her side. *Tsarevitch,* the most powerful battleship in the fleet, had her bulkhead and armored deck shattered and her steering compartment flooded. *Pallada,* with her coal bunker afire, grounded close to the Tiger's Tail lighthouse, and *Tsarevitch* and *Retvizan* stuck ignominiously in the entrance to the inner harbor. *Novik,* the only Russian ship to give chase, returned at five in the morning to find the squadron battered and the fortress stunned.

As bugles sounded in the night, soldiers tumbled over each other as they ran to the forts. Telephone bells jangled to alert official Port Arthur that war had begun. Officers and men trying to find their way to the forts became hopelessly lost. Siege guns and guns from the ships in the roadstead fired blindly into the darkness. Many of the forts contained neither food nor ammunition. Some siege guns even fired blanks; many others were still wrapped in tarpaulins and coated with grease to protect them from the winter.

The first sound of gunfire brought people from houses and restaurants, but many danced on, some drank on, some slept blissfully throughout the ensuing battle. The *Times* correspondent, asleep in his ship in the harbor, knew nothing of the attack till the next morning, and this was the case also with many people inside the town. A few people stepped outside their houses but, unconcerned, went back inside where it was warmer. It was known that the fleet had been carrying out exercises, and few people expected that the first attack by the Japanese—or any attack at all—would take place at Port Arthur. Anyone awake or able to hear above the noise of his own particular diversion thought that there was a practice alert outside the harbor.

Within hours of the attack, the Japanese destroyers made their rendezvous and vital messages flashed to the flagship *Mikasa,* where Vice-Admiral Togo Heihachiro was anxiously awaiting the news. On the outcome of this

[17]

action hung the movement of the armies that Japan had assembled to march into Korea and Manchuria. For many months military headquarters in Tokyo and Vice-Admiral Togo had prepared for this day.

Both Imperial General Headquarters and the Admiral had wanted to "deliver a severe blow" to the Russians before they had time to prepare, but the government hesitated to risk international censure by a surprise attack. Togo had fewer scruples. He realized that the Russians were well supplied with ships in their two fortified Far Eastern bases, Vladivostok and Port Arthur. He could not afford to blockade these ports simultaneously. Though he would have dearly liked to have attacked with his battle squadron at Port Arthur, he knew that each of his ships, from the battleship *Mikasa* to the smallest sloop and gunboat, was precious. Apart from two armored cruisers, *Nisshin* and *Kasuga*, both displacing more than 7,000 tons, which had been built for Argentina, turned down by Russia, and secretly bought by Japanese agents, Japan had no reserves of armored ships at all and no shipyards for building them. By a stroke of luck, or well-timed diplomacy, the two cruisers left Singapore on February 6, the day diplomatic relations with Russia were broken off. Two battleships were also being built in England but were not delivered.*

Japan's hopes in the war now so dramatically begun depended on the command of the sea. Apart from ships at Vladivostok and Port Arthur, Russia also had a new first-class battleship, *Oslyabya*, and two first-class cruisers on the way to the Far East. "To expose my fleet to the fire of the extremely powerful coast forts of the enemy is from the strategical point of view to be done only as a last resort," Togo reported. "I shall not use the battle squadron but shall send the destroyers to make a night attack."

Peevishly, he asked Tokyo whether it was not possible to take the proper diplomatic steps to insure that the Russians would be taken unaware. A telegram from Tokyo on February 4 made his instructions clear. The main fleet was to escort the destroyers to an area close by the enemy base and then to give the destroyer captains freedom of action. "It is decided to give sailing orders to the fleet at the same time as we break off diplomatic relations," Togo was told.

Early on the morning of February 6 he had called his admirals and captains on board *Mikasa* as she lay at moorings in Sasebo naval base in southern Japan. Togo, a short, stocky man of fifty-six, with a stubbly King George V beard, a thin, graying moustache, and gray-streaked hair that was to turn white before the year was out, received the officers of the fleet in

---

*Clause 8 of the Foreign Enlistment Act in force in Britain prohibited the delivery of any warship to a belligerent power.

his day cabin with its heavy furniture and a coal fire glowing in the grate. Short even for a Japanese—he was only five feet three inches tall—the Vice-Admiral was dwarfed by most of his officers, and his attitude was correspondingly modest and unassuming. His face was expressionless and glum, but the glowering black eyes missed little. Behind the almost uneasy exterior, there was a dogged, unyielding determination.

Born in Satsuma at the southern tip of the island of Kyushu, he had been trained from childhood in the tradition of the warrior gentry *samurai*. In his youth he had seen the ruthlessness of the British when they shelled his own hometown, and he was among those who later turned to the British to learn their technical skills.

The Japanese military were careless of the lives of those who were not with them. They ruled Formosa with an iron hand and were equally ruthless in their dealings with the Chinese and the Koreans. Togo was fully in this tradition. He was stubborn and merciless—a killer. Chinese might drown and he would not lift a hand to rescue them. The Russians might want to surrender, but he had no qualms about continuing to fire. "Treat the white flag as a thing of no meaning," he once told his officers and men. International law also meant little to him. It was never a question with Togo of whether it was legally correct or morally proper to act. His needs dictated his response.

Surprise at Port Arthur was so vital that any thought of the need to declare war never entered his head. The situation demanded that the Russian squadron in Port Arthur be held in check so that the Japanese troops could land at Chemulpo in Korea and march north as quickly as possible to Manchuria. To have signaled his intentions in advance by a declaration of war would have been, in Togo's estimation, an act of criminal folly. He gave no quarter, and, though the occasion had never arisen where he needed it, he is unlikely ever to have expected it himself. The end was always the justification of the means. In this war the Japanese could afford to give the Russians no advantage, no concessions. It was not to be a sporting encounter but a matter of life and death. In the iron-willed, not very intelligent little man in the *Mikasa* Japan had an appropriately ruthless officer to lead the fleet.

Japan was going to war with Russia, Togo told the assembled officers on *Mikasa*. Maps and charts were spread out on the tables and candles burned at a small wooden shrine as the forty admirals and captains began a council of war that lasted all night. After they had made their preparations and Togo had read the Emperor's command to attack the Russian ships, he called a steward and the officers were each given a glass of champagne.

"The thoughts of victory or defeat belong, properly, to the time before the fighting takes place," Togo told them. "Once you cross fire with the enemy, you should never think of victory or defeat. Those who are desirous of not being defeated shall undoubtedly be defeated."

Later that morning Togo took his ships from Sasebo, sailed around the south of Korea, passing Ninepin Rock on the southwest coast, skirted a tiny islet named Cow's Ear Island, and proceeded into the dark blue waters of the Yellow Sea. By 6 P.M. on February 8 the fleet was off Round Island, fifty-one miles southeast of Port Arthur. Through Commander Mori, who had visited Port Arthur with the Japanese consul, Togo knew exactly how many Russian ships were in the roadstead and inside the harbor. He had also been informed that the Japanese residents had left Port Arthur.

The destroyer flotillas were dispatched. "I pray for your complete success," Togo signaled. The remainder of the fleet manned the sides and gave three *banzais* as the destroyers headed for Port Arthur.

Surprise had played the greatest part in the Japanese triumph. Togo had also used shock tactics at the beginning of the war against China in 1894. And thirty-seven years later Japan launched a surprise attack on Pearl Harbor; this time the shock came from the air. Commander Fuchida Mitsuo, who led the Japanese attack on the unready American fleet, was amazed to see the perfect target waiting below. "Had these Americans never heard of Port Arthur?" he asked.

At Pearl Harbor 350 planes destroyed the American ships. At Port Arthur ten small Japanese destroyers, using a new weapon, the Whitehead torpedo, played havoc with the equally unprepared Russian fleet. Those three hits on the Russian ships at Port Arthur had a tremendous bearing on the course of the war. In the months ahead, the hills overlooking the harbor ran with blood, Japanese and Russian, but neither Port Arthur nor the Russian fleet ever recovered from the superficial wounds and the initial shock they suffered just before midnight on February 8, 1904.

They also had a major impact on future Japanese military thinking. Thirty years later a lecturer at the Imperial War College, addressing a specially selected group of officers in a course so secret that its nature was known only to a handful of senior officers, deplored the six months that Japan had spent negotiating with Russia. In future wars, he said, Japan would shorten the negotiating period to prevent a hostile power from seizing the initiative. Pearl Harbor was conceived at Port Arthur, and the flag that flew from the masthead of *Akagi,* the Japanese carrier flagship when the planes were launched to destroy the United States Pacific fleet in 1941, had flown also on *Mikasa* thirty-seven years before.

II

THE MOMENTUM OF DECISION

𝕒𝕒𝕒𝕒𝕒

Rising Sun Rising

HALF A CENTURY BEFORE the Japanese destroyers sprang from the night to attack the Russian fleet in Port Arthur, Japan lived in feudal isolation, its shutters drawn, its face unseen. Russia, yet to be humbled by the Crimean War, was still the world's preeminent military power; Japan was not even a pygmy among the giants.

Yet by 1904 Japan had cast off her feudalism, abandoned her isolation, and catapulted onto the world stage with the same national will to succeed that she exhibited after the Second World War. In the decade between 1893 and 1903 her industries took a gigantic leap forward. The value of her imports more than trebled, the tonnage of her merchant marine grew fourfold, railway receipts increased more than fivefold, the combined deposits in all the banks grew more than sixfold, and the financial transactions at the Tokyo clearing house grew more than tenfold. Six first-class battleships and six armored cruisers from British yards gave authority to her naval voice; her army boasted thirteen divisions; and an alliance with Britain protected her flanks.

At the turn of the century, Tokyo was the most exciting city in Asia. Horse-drawn street cars laid on tracks provided public transport, racing through the crowded streets, horns tooting, bells ringing. "It is a source of terror to ride by any mode of conveyance down some of these narrow Tokyo streets," *Keeling's Guide to Japan* advised. "Every coach and other vehicle carries a horn in order to keep people on the look-out, and the streets are in an interminable crush of stages, cars, jinrickshas and portable groceries. Blockades are frequent and sometimes disastrous." The well-to-do traveled by brougham, a closed, horse-drawn carriage, which was always accompanied by a *betto,* or groom who, as a substitute for the more humble horn, ran through the streets shouting loudly to warn off pedestrians. The streets teemed with people from morning to night, and traffic regulations were almost totally lacking. Teams of horses drove at breakneck speeds over the city's shaky wooden bridges. Sidewalks were unknown and the pedestrian used the streets at his peril. Nor were the risks noticeably reduced in 1903 with the introduction of electric trams.

Tails, white tie, and top hat were de rigueur at palace functions, and there are some happy photographs still in existence of gentlemen in top hats and morning coats fishing for carp in the palace moat. One traveler returned from Europe to report to the Emperor that all royal households there had an office exclusively devoted to the hunt, and that he himself had shot a deer in Germany. The imperial household ministry immediately established its own hunt section.

By conscious effort, Tokyo tried to become the Paris of the Orient. People started to eat beef, a habit that had been abandoned more than a thousand years earlier during the heyday of Buddhism, and to read Rousseau, Mill, Spencer, de Maupassant, Tolstoy, and Dostoevsky. The samurai lost their right to wear their swords in public. And the ancient custom of torturing political and criminal suspects was put to an end.

Westernization came in two waves. It began, appropriately, with the construction of eighty-three public lavatories, the first in Japanese history, in Yokohama. Women began to make their appearance in public life during the 1870s. They dressed in décolleté, wore corsets, and danced to modern music. The Empress led the way, wearing satin and brocade dresses made in Paris and European jewelry studded with diamonds. In a rose-colored dress with a long train and surrounded by her retinue of court ladies, she was even permitted to stand in a corner of the great hall of the imperial palace (with its throne modeled after that of Louis XV) when the Emperor handed the country's first constitution to Prime Minister Kuroda Kiyotaka, marking the first occasion in many years that a woman had attended an important official public function. Kuroda's wife was also present, and foreign diplomats watched them closely, since a few years earlier Kuroda had murdered his first wife and married a young woman known for her promiscuity.

Often the men compromised in their dress for special occasions, dispensing with the trousers of the morning suit and wearing tails over the traditional kimono. Most Japanese did not like western clothing, which they found unattractive and uncomfortable. They accepted it for protective reasons, as some animals change color during different seasons.

Painting, athletics, science, medicine, and technology came with the second wave of westernization of 1885–1887. Bricks had been unknown before then, and part of the adaptation of western techniques included the construction of the first brick and plaster buildings. The government hired Thomas Walters, an Englishman, to build the barracks for the imperial guards in brick. About the same time, the household department in the palace was also rebuilt in brick in the western fashion. The *shoji,*—sliding timber framework doors covered with paper—were replaced with plate glass, which bared the imperial family's secrets to the view of gardeners and others on the grounds.

"An air of garishness is perceptible, and one is startled to think that salons and banqueting halls can all be looked through from end to end," *Keeling's Guide* complained. As a compromise, some of the plate glass was replaced by doors of black lacquer and festooning silk curtains. Though the palace had been equipped with electric light, the Emperor would not allow it to be used.

Lovers of the ancient beauty of the palace, with its brocaded walls and milk-white, unpainted pillars, regarded the western additions as incongruous. The imported chairs, tables, and divans were in poor taste and the new steam heating was expected to play havoc with the equally new parquet floors and the traditional soaring white wooden pillars.

This was a period of iconoclasm. The adoption of western dress and western institutions was not simply flattery, but a conscious effort to take advantage of western systems and institutions and to create a state that would be as modern as the rest and second to none, whatever the consequences. A post and telegraph office opened in 1871. The first railway, with an imported Englishman to drive the train, linked Tokyo and Yokohama in 1872.

This was a memorable occasion. The Emperor performed the opening ceremony, wearing a combination of western and Japanese dress: red trousers, a white kimono, and the old-fashioned high black cap. It was the first time most of the Japanese spectators had seen the Emperor. Some passengers accustomed to removing their shoes before entering a house also removed them before boarding the train. They watched in dismay as the train pulled out, leaving their neatly arranged shoes behind. In the same year the government introduced universal conscription and banned public nudity in the cities.

The following year Japan adopted the European solar calendar, causing confusion among farmers whose success or failure with their crops was based on almanacs linked with moon festivals. Many Japanese still adhered to the old beliefs. Others merely accepted compromises. The red-haired, long-nosed foreigners had been called orangutans or green-eyed monsters who drank to excess. In isolation days they were portrayed in bright-colored prints as queerly shaped creatures, with hairy bodies, more animal than human. Let a Japanese woman cohabit with one of these creatures and her reward could be a baby complete with beard. Large jars of saké left on the beaches, it was said, would lure the drink-loving foreigners to capture. Their long red hair and blood could then be used to make a magnificent scarlet dye. Apart from their drinking habits, the foreigners were also malodorous, and the Japanese, as everyone knew, had no smell.

Largely as a reaction to the evangelical zeal and disruptive effects of the Roman Catholic missionaries, and the opportunism of other Europeans who flocked to its rewarding shores after its discovery in the early 1540s by the Portuguese, Japan had begun two centuries of self-imposed isolation in the seventeenth century. By 1641 its isolation was all but complete. A century of foreign intercourse had brought to its shores gunpowder, firearms, tobacco, cholera, and venereal diseases but nothing worse, in the prevailing view, than Christianity.

Francis Xavier, the apostle of the new order, arrived at Kagoshima at the southern tip of the island of Kyushu in 1549 on a mission remarkable for a succession of miracles. Xavier spoke little or no Japanese, but, according to his biographers, he engaged in long and successful debates with Buddhist theologians (who spoke nothing but Japanese), raised the dead and planted the seeds of faith that flourished for a time despite privation and persecution. Missionaries adapted the teaching of the Church to Japanese interest in ritual and spectacle, but much of the new religion confused the people. Xavier found the questions of the Zen Buddhists especially difficult to answer. "Who created the Creator?" they asked. The story of Adam and Eve evoked gales of laughter. The man and woman in the Garden of Eden should have been protected by God when they were tempted by the devil to eat the apple. Instead, this strange God seemed to look on with amusement, driving them out of Paradise and condemning not only Adam and Eve but all mankind to Hell. What kind of creature was this God? they wondered.

Especially on the island of Kyushu, however, feudal barons saw trade opportunities to be gained by embracing Roman Catholicism and the Portuguese who brought it. This new-found enthusiasm led to attacks on Buddhist temples and outrages against Buddhist monks and to retaliatory attacks against the Christians. Thirty-three years after Xavier's landing in Japan, converts numbered about 150,000, of whom 125,000 were in Kyushu.

To the bewilderment of the Jesuits, Toyotomi Hideyoshi, who ruled as regent and planned to conquer Asia, broke off a long period of apparent friendliness with the Catholics, and in 1587 signed an order banning all missionaries. One Christian explanation of this step was that Hideyoshi had difficulty in obtaining recruits for his seraglio from the Nagasaki area of

Kyushu, celebrated both for its converts and for the beauty of its women, and he issued the order in a fit of drunken and frustrated fury when the Christian women he admired did not respond to his overtures. This may have been one reason, but others included his desire to assert his power over the whole of Kyushu, his objection to the meat-eating habits of the Europeans (who destroyed useful animals), the Christians' anti-Buddhist attitudes, and the kidnaping of Japanese by the Portuguese.

The Jesuits closed the churches but continued to preach in private, and in time the order might have been forgotten but for the commercial rivalries between the Jesuits and the Dominicans and Franciscans; and the intrusion of the Protestant Dutch and English, who did all they could to discredit the Catholic missionaries with the Japanese. The wreck of a Spanish galleon bound for Acapulco from Manila contributed to Hideyoshi's anger with the Christians. The ship was carrying a rich cargo and officials favored seizing her as a derelict. They backed their arguments with claims that Franciscan friars, having been allowed to enter the country as ambassadors of the Spanish governor of Manila, were openly engaging in missionary work. Hideyoshi was outraged when the pilot of the galleon naïvely produced a map of the world to impress local officials with the might of Spain and its colonial possessions and added that the sword followed the Book. "What!" cried Hideyoshi. "My states are filled with traitors and their numbers increase every day." Six Franciscans, three Jesuits, and seventeen Japanese Roman Catholics were arrested. With their noses and ears cut off, they were paraded through the streets of Kyoto and Osaka before being crucified in Nagasaki.

The death of Hideyoshi delayed the final martyrdom or expulsion of other Christians, but only briefly. In 1614 Shogun Tokugawa Iyeyasu issued a further edict enforcing the banishment of priests and missionaries of the Catholic faith and the renunciation of the faith by all Japanese converts. "So long as the sun warms the earth, let no Christian be so bold as to come to Japan; and let all know that if the King of Spain, or the Christians' God, or the Great God of all violate this command he shall pay for it with his head." Catholic children were burned to death in their mothers' arms and thrown over cliffs into the sea. Catholics of all ages who refused to recant were beheaded, hanged, raped, or sprinkled with boiling spa water. Others were wrapped in straw sacks, piled in heaps of human fuel and set on fire.

By prayer the Christians tried to fight back. Infants at breast were allowed to nurse only once a day in the hope that God would be moved by their cries. Christians who would not recant were forced to trample on the cross engraved with the picture of the "Christian criminal God." Many continued to practice Christianity in private and some of the Japanese Christians today are their descendants. All over the country, however, huge notice boards denounced Christ and warned the people of the tortures that awaited them if they returned to Christianity.

Nagasaki had once been a Catholic city. By 1621 its 40,000 converts had either recanted or been executed or banished. Since Japanese sailors, contaminated by contact with the outside world, had proved themselves susceptible to Roman Catholic influence, the ban not only applied to foreigners entering Japan but to Japanese going abroad. To insure that no Japanese would stray away from the home islands, the locally built boats were now required by law to have only one mast and to be so small that they would be unsafe for ocean-going travel.

During the early nineteenth century, Russian and other travelers attempted to establish contact with the Japanese; but except for the Dutch and the Chinese, who were allowed limited access through the port of Nagasaki, and the Koreans, who maintained some contact across the Straits of Tsushima, the door remained tightly closed.

The knocking soon grew louder and more insistent. With the opening of China to foreign trade in the 1840s, pressure mounted in the United States to force the Japanese to do business, and on July 8, 1853, Commodore Matthew Calbraith Perry, bearing a letter to the Emperor from President Millard Fillmore in an ornate gold box worth $1,000, arrived off the entrance to Tokyo Bay, or Edo Bay ("Gate of the Waters"), as it was then called. President Fillmore made known his desire to trade, suggested a trial period of five or ten years to test relations, appealed to the Emperor for generous treatment for shipwrecked whalers, and asked for coaling and bunkering facilities for American ships in Japanese waters.

Since the beginning of the nineteenth century the whaling industry in the North Pacific had been big business. American capital investment ran to $17 million, and American whalers, who made their headquarters in the Hawaiian islands, fretted against the restrictions that denied them the use of Japanese ports. Shipwrecked American sailors in Japanese waters found themselves caged and transported like animals to Nagasaki, where they were handed over to the Dutch to be sent out of the country.

The original plans called for Perry to lead a squadron of twelve ships. Instead, his squadron consisted only of the steamer *Mississippi,* the steam frigate *Susquehanna* (the flagship), and the sloops-of-war *Saratoga* and *Plymouth,* both of which were under sail. Of the two steamships, the *Susquehanna,* the largest, was only 2,450 tons, with an armament of sixteen small guns, scarcely formidable but enough to fill the ill-armed Japanese with despair. In a message to Tokyo the commander of the local defense forces explained urgently that an American attack on the forts at the entrance to the bay would at once expose the whole system of coast defense, with disastrous consequences for the empire. His troops manning the guns in the forts had less than ten rounds of ammunition.

Perry was approaching sixty years of age when he led his squadron along the coast of Japan. He conveyed at all times a sense of authority, and it was this characteristic, above all others, that served him so well in his dealings with the Japanese. The audacity amounting almost to irresponsibility in attempting to break down with so small a force two centuries of firmly ingrained Japanese opposition to all contact with foreigners was a cliffhanging venture that could have led, despite the inadequacy of the Japanese defenses, to disaster for Perry and all of his men. He was far from popular with his contemporaries and his preference for seclusion became in the minds of many synonymous with arrogance and pride. Yet his aloofness and unapproachability now proved invaluable. Among the Japanese there were many ultranationalists who looked for any excuse to use force. If the chance had been provided, the expedition would have had results of an altogether different character.

As Perry's ships approached the entrance to the bay, the steamers towing the sailing craft, the American sailors caught their first glimpse of Fuji's superb cone, still capped with snow, an exquisite treasure set against the foreground of gnarled pines and gray tiled houses in the fishing villages along the soft curve of the coast. To the Japanese who had climbed the hills along the coastline the two steamships trailing their long black scarves of smoke were an awesome sight. Some people thought at first that the ships were on fire and their alarm when they saw they were moving without any assistance from sail or wind knew no bounds.

The news threw the *bakufu** into uproar. The Council of Elders met in emergency session. Many men were too afraid even to speak, though eventually the order went out to mobilize the defenses. That night beacon fires were laid to keep watch along the shoreline. Guard boats, though they kept their distance, surrounded the squadron. In the temples the faithful prayed for a *kamikaze* ("divine wind") to drive away the barbarians, as it had driven off Kublai Khan six centuries before.

When it became obvious that Perry meant business, the Council of Elders divided bitterly about the nature of the reception that should be arranged for him. A few advocated making a show of friendship, thereby gaining time to equip the country with the means of meeting force with force.

The letter delivered, Perry took off, leaving the government to digest his

---

*The Tokugawa shogunate. Literally, it means "Tent City." It was so-called in the early days of feudal government, the "tent" being that used by the shogun in wartime.

threat that he would return in the spring with a larger force to get the reply. Perry had grand ambitions. He wanted to take possession of the Bonin Islands, five hundred miles southeast of Japan, Okinawa, and even Formosa, as advance bases for the major trade offensive he envisaged in competition with the European powers on the China coast.

President Franklin Pierce, who had taken office after Perry's departure, was lukewarm about the expedition in the first place, but as an old friend of Perry he allowed it to continue. He had no interest, however, in the expansive plans that Perry set in motion when, after leaving Tokyo, he took possession of the Bonins and laid down a coaling base in Okinawa.

For the Japanese the problems were piling up. On August 21, 1853, a little more than a month after Perry's departure, four Russian men-of-war under the command of Admiral Effimi Vasilievitch Putiatin dropped anchor at Nagasaki. Japanese clans charged with the port defenses mobilized the troops and the shores were quickly lined with soldiers. Unlike Perry, on whose orders the Japanese had been kept at arm's length, Putiatin welcomed the officials who came out to greet his ships. Well briefed on the so-called "ancestral law" that had taken Japan into isolation, he assured the officials that the only reason for his visit was to deliver an important letter to the government in Tokyo.

The governors at Nagasaki responded promptly. Putiatin's request was sent to Tokyo for consideration by the Great Council, which agreed to receive the letter. After its experience with Perry, however, the Council was determined to keep Putiatin away from Tokyo and contrived many reasons to delay him at Nagasaki.

The shogunate had already decided that Perry, when he returned, should be sent away with an inconclusive answer to his demands. If necessary, it would use force. Merchants in the principal cities had been pressured into making donations for defense and the forts at the entrance of Tokyo Bay were to be strengthened and re-equipped. But the weaknesses caused by two centuries of isolation could not be overcome in a matter of months. The government was all but bankrupt. At best, it could hope only to defer the American and Russian confrontation.

Suspecting that the Japanese were indulging in delaying tactics and aware that Putiatin was in Nagasaki, Perry returned to Tokyo on February 13, 1854, with three steamers, three sailing vessels, and a store ship. He anchored close by the spot where an Englishman, Will Adams, and his Japanese wife had been buried more than two hundred years earlier. Adams, a pilot who came to Japan in 1607, had been scorned by the Jesuits but welcomed by the ruling shogun for whom he built ships and to whom he taught the art of seamanship. He had left a wife and family in England, and, though he was not permitted to leave Japan, he was made an officer and given a house where he lived with his Japanese wife and two children until his death.

This time Perry decided to make a determined show of force. When he passed the forts at the entrance to the bay and clearly had no intention of stopping, Japanese envoys set out from shore in their long boats to plead with him to go no farther. They said that high officials were waiting at the entrance of the bay to receive him, but Perry remained adamant and, in the face of renewed protestations, later moved his squadron to Kanagawa beyond the fishing village of Yokohama ("The Beach Across the Way"), which then had a population of about ten thousand. At this point, the government agreed to negotiate.

Perry came armed with presents, including eight baskets of Irish potatoes, a case of American wine, a hundred gallons of whisky, several casks of champagne, four volumes of Audubon's *Birds of America,* bales of cloth, agricultural implements, a locomotive with tender and passenger cars (one fourth the ordinary size and complete with a circular track), and a miniature magnetic telegraph.

In need of fresh food on his ships, he asked the Japanese for sixty head of cattle and four hundred chickens. When the Japanese learned that the Americans wanted to eat them, they were shocked. Cattle, irreplaceable beasts of burden, were part of the family, and chickens were kept only for their eggs.

Perry repeated the threat that he had been sent by his government to make a treaty and that, if he did not succeed, more ships would come. The Japanese hoped to satisfy him with small concessions, including coal, wood, water, provisions, and the saving of ships and their crews in distress; but Perry wanted all that President Fillmore's letter had asked for. When the Japanese suggested that only Nagasaki could be used by American vessels in quest of supplies, Perry replied that he would not think of accepting Nagasaki as one of the ports he wanted opened.

Having agreed that the Americans should be permitted to bunker at two ports, the Japanese insisted that visiting ships should bring no women with them. The fear that the Americans might attempt to make a permanent settlement persisted, and the Japanese wanted no repetition of their early experiences with the Portuguese. "Great Heavens, if I were to permit any such stipulation as that in the treaty, when I got home all the women would pull all the hair out of my head," Perry exclaimed. Almost a century passed before the Japanese understood what he meant.

The Japanese were no less afraid of the clergy and what influence it might have. These fears were reinforced when the chaplain of the *Susquehanna* made a dash to see Tokyo. Stopped at the River Rokugo outside the city, he was flourishing his sword at the ferryman when messengers from Perry caught up with him and ordered him to return at once. "It is rather a novel thing for an American clergyman to resort to his 'carnal weapon' instead of relying on the 'sword of spirit,' " Townsend Harris, America's first consul in Japan, subsequently observed when, on November 28, 1857, on his way to negotiate a new and much wider treaty, he paused at the scene of the clergyman's exploit.

Item by item the Japanese gave way. On March 31, 1854, to the surprise of the expedition's many critics in Europe and America, the treaty was signed, only to result in further criticism on the ground that Perry's achievements fell far short of the hopes of the commercial world.

Although some members of the *bakufu* were inclined to favor the less pushing Russians and to extend to them concessions that they were not willing to grant the Americans, Putiatin left Nagasaki still empty-handed on February 5, 1854, threatening that his next visit might be to Tokyo. By this time, however, he had other business on his hands. The Crimean War had broken out, and English and French squadrons were prowling the North Pacific, looking for Putiatin and other opportune targets. Putiatin was back in Nagasaki for a brief visit in April 1854 and on the island of Sahkalin to the north of Japan in June, evacuating some Russian troops in anticipation of French and British military action.

In November of the same year, to the utter dismay of the Emperor and his functionaries, who feared a Russian attack against the palace in Kyoto, then the imperial seat, Putiatin arrived in nearby Osaka aboard the schooner *Diana*. Always seemingly more pliable than Perry, he responded this time to palace pleas and left for Shimoda, sixty miles west of the entrance to Tokyo Bay and one of the two ports designated under the treaty with Perry as a place where American vessels could be bunkered.

Negotiations had just begun when, on December 23, Japan was struck by a major earthquake which destroyed the town of Shimoda and spun the *Diana* on the end of her anchor chain. With her fifty-two guns and 250 men she made forty-three complete gyrations in the space of thirty minutes. The tidal wave raced ashore, where the inhabitants of the town, still pulling their dead and injured from the wreckage, were overwhelmed by a wall of water. Putiatin and his men came swiftly to the help of the town authorities. With the hull badly weakened by the strain, the *Diana,* this time with sympathetic Japanese approval, set sail for a new anchorage forty miles away and sank in a sudden storm. The Russians spent the winter ashore building two new schooners and instructing the Japanese in an art in which they were soon to excel.

Again with diplomatic shrewdness, Putiatin presented the *Diana*'s salvaged guns to the *bakufu,* and on February 7, 1855, the Japanese and the Russians signed a treaty basically similar to Perry's Treaty of Kanagawa.

There were, however, important differences. In addition to the ports of Shimoda and Hakodate, the Russians won extraterritorial privileges and were also free to visit Nagasaki.

The Japanese signature on the treaty was a coup for Putiatin. Getting the treaty back to Russia for ratification was another. The Japanese still lacked ocean-going vessels, and the English and French squadrons were determined to catch their elusive quarry when he ventured out aboard one of his newly made schooners. Putiatin solved this problem by sending the treaty home aboard an American ship, the *Caroline Le Foote*. Then he made a dash for Petropavlovsk on the Kamchatka Peninsula, safely avoiding the two English ships and the French corvette that thought they had him trapped.

This breaking down of Japan's barriers by the Americans and Russians may have been good for the cause of international trade, but there were few early signs that it had been good for the Japanese. The uproar that had greeted the arrival of the Americans and Russians continued after the signing of the treaties, especially among members of the samurai.

As the Europeans began to buy goods in the treaty ports, inflation swept the country. Foreigners, who often behaved arrogantly, were both admired and hated. The Japanese coveted their material possessions and blamed them for the sharp rise in prices and for the unstable conditions that followed their arrival. As economic conditions became worse and political frustrations increased, attacks on foreigners became frequent. Eventually these conditions led to a series of rebellions that threw out the shogun's military government, restored the power, prestige, and divinity of the emperor, and inspired the country paradoxically into a frantic scramble to copy and improve everything western.

An "expel-the-barbarians" party won strong support. Foreigners, the party claimed, behaved like barbarians, treated women with too much deference, and interfered with nature, peering at the stars through telescopes, treating the heavens like playthings and generally interfering with nature in a manner likely to cause harm. Some Japanese even doubted that the westerners, with their modern weapons, could defeat Japan, for without spirit and the will to fight they would be easily overthrown. Others believed more realistically that they would have to arm themselves, even if it meant melting down the bronze Buddhas and bells to make guns.

One thing was clear: The "barbarians" were determined to stay. They built their own strange-looking settlements on Japanese soil, rode drunkenly through the streets, and paid little respect to the people. Japanese extremists killed a Russian officer and two sailors in Yokohama in July 1859. Henry Heusken, Townsend Harris's young Dutch interpreter, was one of the next to go. A band of "expel-the-barbarians" fanatics fell on him with their swords on New Year's Eve when he was returning to his home from a visit to the Prussian Embassy. Armed only with his whip, he fought back, but was slashed in the throat and fell dead from his horse.

Even Harris was not immune from threat. An attempt on his life was made when he visited the capital to negotiate the new treaty of amity and commerce. Plans to behead him were thwarted when the ringleaders of the assassination group were imprisoned.* The government provided Harris with protection, but he thought it was suspicious that his would-be assassins should have remained so inactive during his long stay in the capital and yet be prepared to kill him just as the treaty was about to be signed. He called the Japanese the greatest liars in the world. "They never hesitate at uttering a falsehood, even when the truth would serve the same purpose," he wrote.

His life in Japan, complicated by attacks of what he thought to be cholera and liver disease, was far from happy. The Japanese tried desperately to please him, offering him girls and annoying him with their repeated questions about American women. "I will not soil my paper with the greater part of them," he wrote in disgust.

American and other foreign sailors descended on Japanese seaports, demanding rum and women. Often they did not distinguish between Japanese women of low repute and those from good families. They conducted horseraces in the streets and hunted wherever they wished, scattering pedestrians and knocking down the flimsy shops in the narrow streets. To the samurai, whose code of conduct demanded that the lower ranks prostrate themselves when they met their seniors, this loutish behavior violated all the rules of propriety and decency. Hating a foreigner became a duty and a measure of loyalty. In June 1862, the Emperor in Kyoto dispatched special envoys to announce his will to expel all the "barbarians." June 25, 1863, was fixed as the day for final expulsion. Although the shogun dutifully concurred, he conceded subsequently that he was in no position to comply with the sacred order. Others were nevertheless willing to try to carry it out.

At this time in Japan there were about 270 *daimyōs,* or lords of "great name," who ruled their own feudal fiefs. The lowest owned land assessed at ten thousand bales of rice a year, the richest was worth more than a million bales. Around them the *daimyōs* gathered their samurai, who were closely bound to him by ties of loyalty.

Among all the clans, the greatest warriors, and the second richest, were the members of the Satsuma clan. One in every three of its people were

---

*The shogunate's chief minister, who signed the unequal treaty with Harris, was assassinated for having failed to obtain permission from the Emperor.

regarded as of the samurai class. The city of Kagoshima, far off at the southern end of Kyushu and headquarters for the clan, bred a race of warrior-scholars. After Japan closed its doors they were left with no enemies to fight and nowhere to go. No one could leave without permission. For years small groups plotted to overthrow the shogun's military government in Tokyo. For years, also, they made no progress, but now with Japan in a state of turmoil and the shogun clearly unable to meet the new challenges that faced the land, there rose here a remarkable group of Satsuma men who, in collaboration with their former enemies in the Choshu clan, were destined to lead Japan from feudalism to war with Russia.

One incident involving the Satsumas and the foreigners was especially important. In August 1862 a party of three Englishmen and an Englishwoman, out riding at Namamugi on the outskirts of Yokohama, crossed the path of the *daimyō* of Satsuma. Insulted by the foreigners' customary lack of courtesy, the *daimyō's* retinue attacked the group. A Shanghai merchant named Charles Lennox Richardson fell from his horse, seriously wounded, and was finished off with a stab in the neck by a Satsuma retainer. The other two men, both seriously wounded, called to the Englishwoman to gallop to Yokohama.

The English demanded an indemnity of £110,000 from the government in Edo and £25,000 from the fief of Satsuma. Since Japan's total exports at the time were worth only £4 million a year, and a traveler could live comfortably in an hotel for a couple of cents a day, these were crippling demands. The government nevertheless paid up; the Satsumas held out.

On August 8, 1863, a British squadron sailed from Yokohama for Kagoshima with four gunboats, a corvette, and two sloops. The Satsumas were unimpressed by the show of force and declined either to pay the indemnity or to release Richardson's murderers. The British thereupon seized three Satsuma boats which the *daimyō* had bought after the lifting of the restrictions on the size of Japanese ships in 1854. While they were being towed off, the Satsuma batteries opened fire. Among their gunners were the fifteen-year-old Togo Heihachiro and Oyama Iwao, seven years his senior. Both were destined to play major parts in the war that came forty years later.

Togo was dressed in a tight-fitting uniform with a divided skirt, a wooden helmet bearing the Satsuma crest, and two swords at his waist. He carried a musket. His mother watched her husband and three sons go off to the battle and returned to the house to cook a thick bean-paste soup for the fighting men, carrying it to the forts along the seafront herself.

In the ensuing battle, fought during a violent storm, the Satsumas killed thirteen of the attacking British force and wounded fifty. But the British gunners, with guns that could fire for four miles compared with the one-mile

[35]

range of the Satsuma guns, retaliated with overwhelming force. When the fighting ended, the Satsumas' batteries, and factories, and many of the houses in the town had been leveled.

The incident changed the course of history in Japan—and in the world. The youthful Oyama and young Togo now plotted with a man who did not live to see Japan plunge into the Russo-Japanese War but who remained the guiding spirit for many of those who fought in it. His name was Saigo Takamori, a man of immense physique (he weighed over 240 pounds and stood six feet tall) and remarkable qualities of leadership. Under his direction, a group of young Satsuma samurai, and including Oyama and Togo, created a secret society known as the *Seichu-gumi*, or "Loyalty Group." Their plan was to escape from the province and to organize a revolution against the shogunate in Tokyo.

Two years after the bombardment of Kagoshima, in retaliation for interfering with foreign shipping, nine English vessels, three French, four Dutch, and one American bombarded Shimonoseki, the headquarters of the fiefdom of Choshu on the southern extremity of the island of Honshu, and demanded the opening of the straits between Honshu and Kyushu. So determined were the Choshu to resist this and all other foreign intrusions that they abandoned the class distinction which permitted only the samurai to wear the long sword and, for the first time in the history of Japan, had plans for arming the entire populace—peasants, priests, shopkeepers, and even the *eta* (Japan's "untouchables").

Until they saw their forts reduced and their capitals burned, Satsuma and Choshu had been among the leaders of the antiforeign group. Men of arms, they were much impressed by power, and, in this respect, it was clear that the foreigners had much to teach. While they were marshaling their forces and preparing their plans, however, attacks against foreigners continued. Two British officers lost their lives in 1864 when they were attacked by *ronin,* or freelance warriors.

Sir Henry Parkes, the British minister, much respected by the Japanese, was attacked in Kyoto on his way to visit the Emperor. He was guarded by British soldiers and Goto Shojiro, a trusted samurai. When Parkes was attacked, Goto decapitated his would-be assassin and presented the head to the British minister. Parkes saw the Emperor a few weeks later and Goto was presented with a magnificently mounted sword as a reward, with the inscription, "From Victoria, Queen of England, in remembrance of the 23rd. of March, 1868." Thereafter, all Japanese who attacked foreigners were punished.

This did not prevent an officer of a small *daimyō* from ordering an attack on the foreign settlement at Kobe after some Frenchmen had crossed the path of the clan leader in 1868. The Japanese were all armed with new

American rifles but had not learned to adjust the sights, and so the bullets passed over the heads of the foreigners. A Frenchman was nicked by a sword blade, however, and the *daimyō* delivered the leader of the attacking force to the government.

Sir Henry Parkes instructed his second secretary, Lord Redesdale, to attend the death of the condemned man, together with representatives of all other foreign legations. It was the first time foreigners had seen hara-kiri (or *seppuku*) performed. They bowed gravely as the condemned man apologized for his action before raising his short sword above his head with both hands. Carefully tucking the sleeves of his kimono under his knees so that he would not fall backwards, he stabbed himself just below the waist on the left side and then once more slowly across the right side. "It was horrible," Lord Redesdale wrote. But he agreed with other foreign diplomats that the punishment fitted the crime.

The shogun had died in 1866, and the following year saw the death from smallpox of the Emperor Komei. A fifteen-year-old boy, Mutsuhito, known to history as the Emperor Meiji (Meiji was the period of "Enlightened Government"), succeeded him and in November 1867 received full governing powers from the new shogun, Tokugawa Yoshinobu, who surrendered his powers to the Emperor. An initially peaceful transfer of power came to an end when the Satsuma and Choshu clans, with 6,000 rifles provided by Thomas Glover, a Scottish merchant, agreed to cooperate, instead of fighting each other to bring about the restoration.*

The shogun's armies rallied to his side but were defeated after a number of long, bitter, and devastating battles. In the summer of 1868 the imperial capital moved from Kyoto to Edo, the traditional seat of government, which now became known as Tokyo ("Eastern Capital"). As the Emperor's cortege passed by the outskirts of Yokohama, it was greeted by the band of a British regiment that guarded the foreign settlement. Since no Japanese national anthem existed, the band saluted the Emperor with *The British Grenadiers*. On March 5, 1869, all but five of the *daimyōs* agreed to relinquish their rights. They were granted generous compensation and for a time acted as governors of their former provinces. With the early introduction of centralized government from Tokyo, however, the prefectural system was adopted and feudalism came to an end.†

---

*The word "restoration" is essentially a western interpretation which fails to do full justice to the reforms of the period. To the Japanese the end of the shogunate did not mean the restoration of imperial power, because they believed it had always existed.

†In 1868, an American trader and self-styled consul named Van Reed sent several hundred indentured Japanese laborers, including some samurai, to California. They

This was the golden age of youth in Japan. Though there were numerous bitter factional rifts, a group of authoritarian young men, some in their late twenties and early thirties, emerged to guide the even more youthful Emperor. Their influence on Japan's development and progress was to remain paramount for almost half a century.

The Emperor was above mortal question or reproof. Though they were careful to conceal from the public their own wide powers, the Emperor's advisers were more important policy-makers than the man they advised. Foremost among them was Ito Hirobumi, creator of the modern god-emperor myth, several times prime minister, and, until the eleventh hour, a strong opponent of the war with Russia.

Ito was born in 1841 in the remote Choshu village of Tsukari. The village was sixty miles from the prefectural capital, and the population consisted mostly of destitute farmers who scratched a beggarly subsistence from the grudging earth. A less likely spot for the birthplace of a restoration giant* can scarcely be imagined. Nor were the circumstances of his birth more propitious. His father was a poor farmer, tilling no more than three acres of difficult hill land, his mother an even more humbly born woman. She believed in rigorous discipline and needed to exert it with her headstrong son, whose precocious behavior at an early age shocked the not easily shocked villagers. They regarded him as a mixture of genius and devil, for whom it was predicted that he would become either a great national figure or a scoundrel.

Ito lived up to best expectations, though he accomplished many "little feats of wickedness," as the villagers described it, that might have been the envy of men half his age. He believed that Shintoism was good for Japan, but he failed to observe the formalities, having prayed, he said, only three times in his life.

Lord Redesdale, a gifted Japanologist, remembered him in London at the age of twenty-two as wild as a hawk. He smoked and drank heavily and was an inordinate lover of beautiful women. In his youth, he could consume saké by the gallon. Later, he graduated to claret. When he became prime minister, his official residence was remarkable for the number of good-looking girls who found their way there. Even at the age of sixty-five, when he was Resident-General in Korea, four twenty-year-old Japanese beauties, O-Kane, O-Take, O-Ryu, and O-Koto, competed for his favors. According to the *Chosen Koron (Korea Review)*, the "government house was no different

___

were among the forebears of America's *nisei*. Others went to America from the Okayama–Hiroshima area. The first actual immigrants left Japan for Hawaii in 1868. When Hawaii was annexed they went to California.

*Giant in capacity, not size; he was only five feet three inches tall.

from a cheap house of assignation on the outskirts of the town. Singing girls, well known and not so well known in Keijo [Seoul], freely entered it and there ensued scenes of uproarious high jinks."

As a youth he was in the thick of the hue and cry against the foreigners. He was credited with one murder, that of a scholar named Hanawa Jiro. Yet Ito was also a man of rare judgment, immense ability, great foresight, and unusual sensitivity. He was also impetuous. A maidservant who hid him in the dust hole of a Japanese house from *bakufu* searchers in his revolutionary days was rewarded with marriage.

When Ito was still a child, his peasant father—for whom Hamada Kenji, his biographer, discovered links with the Emperor Korei (290 B.C.–213 B.C.) —was adopted by the Choshu samurai, abandoned his family name, Hayashi, and took the name of his foster father, Ito. The family left their native village, and, after some years, brilliant young Hirobumi was sent by the Choshu clan to Nagasaki to study the manufacture of firearms.

In May 1863 Ito, with four samurai companions, fled from the wrath of the shogunate after burning down the new British legation. Dressed in second-hand British sailor's clothes, with shoes many times too big, they hid in the coal hatch of a foreign freighter bound for Shanghai. They went with the approval of the Choshu clan, this time to learn the techniques of operating steam-driven vessels so that the Choshu people, who were violently opposed to the entry of foreigners, could free themselves from dependance on expatriate engineers.

In Shanghai the group split up, and Ito and an almost equally famous companion, Inoue Kaoru, sailed for London aboard a 300-ton freighter carrying a cargo of tea for the big Far Eastern commercial firm, Jardine, Matheson and Company. The master of the ship treated them as deckhands, and Ito's feelings toward the English were always tainted with memories of the nightmare journey to London.

He spent little time there. Jardine, Matheson had arranged for his studies, but after only six months civil war broke out in Japan and Ito hurried back to offer his advice to the Choshu forces threatened alike by English, French, and American punitive expeditions to Shimonoseki and by the resurrected shogunate army coming overland.

Dressed in a pair of tight blue Japanese trousers, a frockcoat, and a sailor's cap, he hoped to pass as a Portuguese. One of his first calls in Yokohama was at the British legation, which he had once tried to burn down. He looked more like a clown than a Portuguese sailor, but Sir Rutherford Alcock, cheerfully unaware of his part in the attack on the legation, was happy to receive him.

Ito's advice to Alcock was that he should help in the overthrow of the shogun and make a treaty with the Emperor at Kyoto. He and Inoue spoke with great bitterness of the tycoon's dynasty, Alcock recalled. "They [the shogunate] kept all the trade, not only foreign but native also, to themselves, by seizing all places where trade was likely to develop, such as Niigata and Nagasaki, and they told me that those feelings were shared by most of the people of the country."

Because they were convinced that it was fruitless for Choshu to attempt to fight the allied force, Alcock sent the two young men to Shimonoseki aboard the *Barossa,* one of the eighteen warships assembling for the attack. The clan was not yet ready to listen to Ito. His advice rejected, the bombardment went ahead.

When Shimonoseki lay in ruins, Ito helped to arrange the treaty between the Choshu clan and the allies. After the restoration he became a councilor of state; drew up the document which the *daimyōs* signed, abandoning their feudal fiefs; and, in a succession of important official posts, helped to reorganize and westernize the government. He managed with only an hour or two of sleep each night. "Never mind," he used to say to those who reproached him, "when I go to sleep it is the time of my death."

After studying the constitutions of Austria and Germany, Ito went to work with Inoue to draw up a constitution for Japan. This was delivered by the Emperor on February 11, 1889, the legendary anniversary of the day on which Emperor Jimmu is said to have proclaimed his kingdom in Yamato in 660 B.C.

Ito's constitution, which allowed the election of a national Diet, followed the model of Bismarck's Germany, the symbol of material modernization and industrialization and was much satirized by critics; but for the Emperor, the constitution reserved an entirely unwestern place. He was declared to be sacred and inviolable.

Though it served to consolidate power in the hands of the Emperor's advisers, the constitution met with popular acclaim. It was also attended by an event of significance in the psychological development of the new Japan. Viscount Mori Arinori, the education minister, whose duties included responsibility for the Shinto religion, was said to have visited the shrines at Ise,* where Amaterasu the Sun Goddess is enshrined, and there he had been observed inspecting the courtyard of the inner sanctum of the shrines by the simple expedient of raising the screening sheet of calico with his walking stick. The story is probably apocryphal; it is nevertheless important. For Mori was a rationalist who

---

*The beauty of the Ise shrine is in the simplicity of its plain, unpainted wood. Entry to the inner parts of the temple was denied to all but shrine officials and the emperor and his entourage.

had even gone so far as to propose that English be used to teach all subjects in schools.*

He was killed by a chauvinist on Constitution Day. After plunging his dagger into Mori, the assassin then killed himself, only to become the idol of the masses, especially when the story about the Ise shrines gained currency. Though the doctrine of emperor-worship is newer than the 1890s, as far as its spread and national acceptance are concerned, Mori's death, and the alleged reasons for it, helped to establish the divine right of the Emperor in the minds of the people. Thereafter, the era of modernization acquired even stronger ultranationalistic backing, with material progress stimulated by heady religion in which the living god dwelt among the people and for whom no act in his name, or for the cause of patriotic duty, was too much to ask.

Accounts vary but most philologists agree that the mythology (or myth history) of Japan held that there were five generations of special heavenly gods, headed by the Creator, the God Lord of the Center (of the universe). They were joined by seven generations of ordinary heavenly gods, among them Prince Izanagi and Princess Izanami, who begat Amaterasu Omikami ("Sky-Shining Great Goddess") and her two brothers. Amaterasu's grandson, Prince Ninigi, descended on Mount Takachiho, near the borders of Kagoshima and Miyazaki prefectures. The mountain has a spearlike head of vegetation and is regarded as a phallic symbol. Here, Prince Ninigi built a palace and established the dynasty. The probability is that Prince Ninigi came not from the heavens but from Taiwan, but the myth history developed and with it Shintoism, "the way of the gods." Scholars studying the ancient history of Japan saw Buddhism and Confucianism as alien and therefore corrupting influences and sought a return to the old ways, the restoration of the monarchy (which traced its line of descent from Amaterasu Omikami) and with it the restoration of Shintoism.

The restoration was therefore accompanied by the widespread construction of Shinto shrines and by ritual festivals in May and November for the souls of all those who had fought for the emperor during and after the restoration. The ministry of divine rituals became an organ of government in 1872, and Shinto was established as the state ethic, and thus above religion—which, by imperial rescript, could no longer be taught in schools after 1889. Activities in the shrines were specifically directed toward the celebration of festivals designed to foster the national spirit. Any ideas of reward or punishment after death were scorned. Buddhism offered salvation

---

*Dwight Whitney, the distinguished Yale linguist, wrote to Mori to tell him that his plan was unthinkable.

in nirvana. The Sun Goddess was the goddess of every living thing. The dead did not really die but lived on in spirit as guardians of their families. The souls of men killed in wars returned to fight alongside the living.

In his *Commentaries on the Constitution,* Ito wrote:

> The Sacred Throne was established at the time when the heavens and earth became separated. The Emperor is Heaven descended, divine and sacred. He is preeminent above all his subjects. He must be reverenced and is inviolable. He has indeed to pay respect to law, but the law has no power to hold Him accountable to it. Not only shall there be no irreverence for the Emperor's person, but also He shall not be made a topic of derogatory comment, nor one of discussion.

Few Japanese peasants had ever heard of the Emperor until the restoration. Now they were required to believe that this son of the deities, who had created the whole earth, was divinely inspired to rule it all. In the beginning, the islands of Japan were formed when Prince Izanagi reached down from the heavens and plunged his glistening spear into the sea. The rest of the world came from the drops that fell from the spear. If it were not for Japan, therefore, the other nations of the world would not exist.

An imperial rescript on education published on October 20, 1890, to complement the rescript on religious training in schools, enjoined the Japanese to be ready in an emergency to "offer yourselves courageously to the state and thus guard and maintain the prosperity of Our Imperial Throne coeval with heaven and earth. . . . The way here set forth is indeed the teaching bequeathed by Our Imperial Ancestors, to be observed by their descendants and the subjects, infallible for all ages, and true in all places." All schools now had to exhibit pictures of the Emperor. These were unveiled and solemnly saluted on national holidays when the education rescript was also recited.

Along with this careful cultivation of the national spirit was an equally conscious move to give it tangible expression. If the British had trailed the Americans and the Russians in pushing the Japanese out of their isolation, they quickly made up for lost time in helping Japan to arm. The Emperor had scarcely been installed in Tokyo when the Duke of Edinburgh, a naval officer, made a formal visit to Japan. That he was the first member of any foreign royal family to make such a visit was not lost on the Japanese, and it led the following year to a visit by a British naval mission. Only ten years after the bombardment of Kagoshima, British naval officers began to teach gunnery and navigation at the newly established Japanese Naval College, and Japanese increasingly took to the sea in British-built ships.

By taking possession of the private fleets built up by the feudal lords after 1854 when the government ended its ban on ocean-going vessels, Japan already had the nucleus of a small navy. The Emperor gave a large portion of his private income for the purchase of warships, and government employees were required to donate one tenth of their salaries for the same purpose.

The first Japanese-built warship in the new fleet was brig-rigged with a wooden hull. Built for the shogun in 1861 and acquired for the imperial navy after the restoration, she took her place with the *Azuma,* an iron-clad ram, which had been built for the Confederate navy. The *Azuma,* which was small enough to fight in the Mississippi River and heavily enough armored to resist fifteen-inch shells, was sold to the Japanese by the Washington Navy Yard after the end of the American Civil War.

The Dutch provided the first steam-driven warship in 1855. An early preference for French boats changed after one disappeared on its way from Singapore to Japan. Though the Japanese continued to build paddle corvettes and barques with graceful swan bows and to arm them later with 4.7-inch Krupp breech-loaders, they placed most of their orders for steam warships with British yards.

Japanese cadets went off to Britain for training. Among the first to go was Lieutenant Togo Heihachiro, who studied at Greenwich Naval College and spent some time aboard Nelson's flagship, *Victory.* He was a pale, thin, conscientious young man whose one concern in England was the scarcity of food. He complained that the English did not eat as well as the Japanese. After he had finished his meager rations on board the training ship *Worchester,* he would soak lumps of bread in his tea cup while the English cadets looked on in horror. Captain Henderson Smith, his instructor, remembered him as an apt pupil. It took him a long time to learn anything, but once learned it was not forgotten. "He was not what one would call smart but he was diligent and painstaking," Smith recalled. "He was usually quiet, but inside he was like a lion."

Japanese enthusiasm and skill deeply impressed the British. They studied and trained with desperate energy. They used so much ammunition practicing with the new quick-firing guns and moving targets that the instructors thought their ammunition supplies would run out. At Portsmouth, F. T. Jane, author of *The Imperial Japanese Navy,* found the Japanese officers interested in nothing but their course of instruction. There was no time for leisure. Off duty, they read Captain A. T. Mahan, the American writer whose works had a profound impact on naval thinking everywhere, and worked on battle tactics. Occasionally Japanese officers would take a holiday, but this usually took the form of a dockyard inspection, followed by a visit to Jane's house, where they played naval war games into the early hours. "Mostly, though not invariably, they are descendants of the old fighting men, the *samurai,*" Jane wrote. "Whatever he may do, in whatever position he may be placed, the Japanese officer never forgets his dignity, and further, is always a gentleman. I believe this is the first impression that he creates: it is also the last."

Under the leadership of General Yamagata Aritomo, a Choshu, who was born in 1838, the army was also quickly reorganized after the restoration. In a population of about thirty-four million, nearly two million belonged to the samurai class. Many found jobs in government, but tens of thousands became unemployed. Their belief was that, as warrior gentry, they should form the new elite army. Against furious opposition, Yamagata sounded the death knell for the samurai when he introduced universal conscription in 1873.

Yamagata did not flinch. When Perry first dropped anchor in Tokyo Bay he had stripped and with a knife in his teeth swam out to the flagship determined to fight the entire ship's company if need be. At nineteen he had been sent to Kyoto as a clan spy. At twenty-one he was wounded when the allied warships bombarded Shimonoseki. Thereafter he worked with Saigo Takomori, of the Satsuma clan, to build an imperial force strong enough to beat the shogunate. This goal achieved, he went to Europe to study the French and Prussian armies, returning to Japan to establish the military academy and to introduce French military instructors. Under his direction, Japan got its first arsenal and numerous military schools, including one for doctors and surgeons.

Only ten years after the restoration, Yamagata had introduced a general staff along the lines of the Prussian general staff, a step forward in military organization not then achieved by the United States. This led to the further modernization of the army in 1883, when it was reorganized into six national divisions, with an additional division, the Guards, acting as imperial bodyguard.

The work that Yamagata, the Choshu, began, Oyama Iwao continued. By the early 1880s Oyama had become the foremost member of the Satsuma clan. He was born at Shimo Kajiya-cho, on the outskirts of Kagoshima. A prince, four marquises, and a count sprang from this little district. Waterloo may have been won on the playing fields of Eton, but the war to restore the emperor, the Sino-Japanese War in 1894–1895, and the Russo-Japanese War were all won in the straw-thatched cottages of Shimo Kajiya-cho, where, under the influence of Oyama's cousin, the great Saigo Takamori, the children were more concerned with revolution than with battledore and shuttlecock.

At the age of ten Oyama began his military training. At seventeen he was a renowned spear fighter. The affinity between poetry, painting, and the martial arts is peculiarly Oriental. Vietnam's Ho Chi Minh spent his leisure hours writing poetry or practicing Chinese calligraphy. Along with his

[44]

spear-fighting, Oyama learned classical Chinese poems derived from the tenets of Zen Buddhism. At eighteen he became one of the hundred members of Saigo's Loyalty Group.

After the Satsuma clan agreed to pay the English indemnity in 1863, Oyama went to Tokyo, where he entered a school run by a progressive military scientist named Egawa, who had studied the Dutch system of gunnery and strategy. Oyama was attached to the Satsuma headquarters when the shogunate forces attacked the Choshu clan in 1864 and later went to Kyoto where he joined Saigo's staff as a gunnery instructor and staff officer, working all the time on the plan to overthrow the shogunate. Part of his job was to secure weapons which came from a Yokohama watchmaker named Favre Bland.

When the restoration battles began, Oyama fought with Saigo behind the "brocade banners," the standard of the loyalist forces, so named because of their design of the sun and the moon embroidered on a red background. Saigo was the greatest of the Emperor's generals. It is difficult to find any evidence that Oyama performed with special distinction, but when the restoration came he held a succession of important posts and invented a mortar which was widely installed in the defense of Tokyo. His biographer credits him with having selected his favorite poem, a twelfth-century drinking song used to toast the host's health, as the national anthem. Though much sung, it was not formally accepted.

At the outbreak of the Franco-Prussian war in 1870, Oyama went to Europe as an observer. He was greatly impressed with the performance of the Prussian forces and contemptuous of the French, especially of the French officers, whom he had seen escorting women while in uniform and flirting with them in public. Such behavior, he predicted, was sure to lead to their defeat. He also visited the United States and England. Niagara Falls impressed him no less than England's shipyards. His return to Japan was only brief, and late in 1871 he set off for Switzerland, intending to spend ten years in military study. The growing unrest of part of the Satsuma clan brought him home.

Saigo had argued strongly after the restoration in favor of employing the many unemployed samurai by invading Korea. In bitter protest against the government's rejection of this he had retired to Satsuma. From a distance he viewed the government's reforms with increasing concern. The introduction of conscription, he believed, struck at the heart of the samurai system and denigrated the warrior class. In 1877, his followers rose in revolt, not against the Emperor but against Yamagata and other advisers who had led him astray.

The conscripts led by some of Saigo's closest friends proved their mettle. Oyama fought as a divisional commander against his old comrade-in-arms.

[45]

Kodama Gentaro was his chief of staff, and Yamagata his commander-in-chief.

All three participated in the final dramatic action of the civil war when Saigo's outnumbered forces were besieged at Castle Hill in Kagoshima. Oyama's guns, bought from Krupp in Germany, blasted the castle, annihilating Saigo's legions. Saigo took his brush and wrote a poem of farewell:

> Now with a broken sword,
> And my good steed fallen dead,
> 'Tis time for me also to go,
> And leave my weary bones
> To be bleached by the autumn breeze
> Upon my native hills.

The poem finished, Saigo rejoined the battle. A bullet struck him in the groin and he was unable to walk. One of his lieutenants carried him out of the fray. "This is enough," Saigo said, and while bowing in the direction of Tokyo he committed hara-kiri. His lieutenant finished the task Saigo had begun by decapitating him, and then fell on his own sword.

For his services in the battle Oyama was rewarded with the ministry of war, and in 1882 he married Yamakawa Sutematsu, one of the first foreign-educated Japanese women. Two years after the restoration the new government had chosen five girls to be sent abroad for their education. Sutematsu was one of them. She stayed in America for twelve years, graduating from Vassar in 1881. Her husband was far from handsome. Even larger than Saigo, he was slow and ponderous, with an oval pockmarked face like a sponge, and a formidable temper.

As for Saigo, he became a sort of lesser deity. He was canonized by Satsuma soldiers and sailors and officially forgiven by the Emperor, who later conferred the title of marquis on his son in recognition of his father's services before the Satsuma uprising. With funds contributed by Oyama and other Satsuma leaders, a statue of Saigo in bronze was cast by the great sculptor Okakura Kakuzo. This stands in Ueno Park in a Tokyo suburb, an enduring monument to the restoration and the militancy of the new Japan. It shows Saigo's massive girth dressed casually in his rabbit-hunting attire. His widow did not care for it. She preferred the statue at Kagoshima that showed Saigo in his military uniform, but it was a convenient symbol and conveniently placed for the ultranationalists, who used Saigo's name and legend to whip up the war fever that gripped Japan in the months before the Russo-Japanese War.

Three years after Saigo's death a group of samurai met in the Kyushu seaport town of Fukuoka to form the *Genyōsha*, or "Black Ocean Society."

Hiraoka Kotaro, a rich coal-mine owner, became its first president and provided the initial funds, but Toyama Mitsuru was its guiding spirit and greatest strength. It was called at first the "Turn to the Sun Society" and advocated the establishment of a national assembly and a people's rights program. Many of its members, however, were more concerned with the conquest of Korea than they were with people's rights, and a split took place, with the ultranationalists breaking away to form the *Genyōsha,* named after Genkainada, the gulf north of Fukuoka across which the armies of Kublai Khan came in the thirteenth century.

As early as 1882, Toyama had begun to organize a group of young Japanese students to gather intelligence about China. In 1891 the society set up a school in Shanghai to train Japanese agents. It began with an enrollment of 150 and subsequently expanded. Graduates went into Japanese business firms, the armed forces, consular offices, and other occupations where they could use their cover for espionage. The society's methods included both persuasion and political assassination.

In 1901 Toyama and Uchida Ryohei formed the *Kokuryūkai,** or "Black Dragon Society," for the specific purpose of preparing for war with Russia. Links between this quasi-secret, ultranationalistic society, the military, the government, and the great family industrial enterprises, or *zaibatsu,* grew close.

Among these was the Mitsui family enterprise, which was established in the seventeenth century through the untiring efforts of one of the first successful Japanese businesswomen. Women of noble birth were often given as wives or concubines to further their fathers' advancement. The peasant woman's place was in the kitchen, where she tied up her hair with straw and ate the leftovers. The rise of the merchant class also saw the beginning of the rise in the status of women, however, and by the seventeenth century they were occasionally called on to run the family business.

Mitsui Shuho was among them. Single-handed, she conducted her husband's saké shop and pawnshop in Matsuzaka in Ise province. Later, her son opened clothing shops and pawnshops, all of which were immediately successful. At the beginning of the Meiji period the family supported the forces opposing the shogunate and provided them with money. Thereafter, the family resources were placed at the disposal of the restoration government. Among its rich rewards for service were coal mines in Kyushu. One of Mitsui's directors, Yamamoto Jotaro, was an intimate friend of Toyama, patron of the Black Ocean and Black Dragon societies, who was also supported by the Yasuda family, another great commercial group. Masuda

*Named after the Amur, or Black Dragon River.

Takashi, the head of Mitsui Bussan ("Mitsui Products"), also had close relations with Inoue, Yamagata, and Ito. He built Yamagata a summer house on the lot next to his own at Odawara, a favorite holiday resort among Japanese political leaders. It was all in the family, as it were, since Yamagata's mistress had a sister who was Masuda's second mistress.

The Iwasaki family was no less adroit. Iwasaki Yataro, who provided the boats for the Satsuma troops during the restoration war, was rewarded about 1870 with thirty-one ships with which to start his own steamship company and to lay the foundations for the Nippon Yusan Kaisha line and a fortune for the parent Mitsubishi company, soon to be the biggest of all the private commercial empires in Japan. Mitsubishi took control of the Takashima coal mines, the Nagasaki shipyards, and the Tokyo Marine Insurance Company. Later, the railways in Kyushu were added to its lists. Kawada Koichiro, Mitsubishi's top executive, became governor of the Bank of Japan in 1889 and for seven years reigned over the country's finances. "If you want to talk to us, come over yourself," top executives used to say to Finance Minister Watanabe Kunitake.

Kawada was succeeded in 1896 by Iwasaki Yanosuke, who brought Mitsubishi and the Satsuma clan together. By marriage, the important Tosa clan also had links with the Satsuma.

Though the policy-makers were subject to outside influences and pressures, real authority was vested in the hands of just a few key men in the interrelated imperial advisory groups. The most important of these were the *genrō*, or elder statesmen, an extra-constitutional body consisting at the time of the Russo-Japanese War of Marquis Ito Hirobumi, Field-Marshal Yamagata Aritomo, Field-Marshal Oyama Iwao, Count Inoue Kaoru, and Count Matsukata Masayoshi. Inoue had taken part with Ito in the attack on the British legation in 1862, accompanied him to England, and unsuccessfully tried to prevent the Choshu clan from attacking the western naval squadron at Shimonoseki. He remained close to Ito thereafter and the two men had worked together to write the constitution. Count Matsukata, founder of the Bank of Japan and later prime minister, was a Satsuma and a financier of great skill.

At the inner circle of his advisers, therefore, the Emperor relied exclusively on the men from Choshu and Satsuma. The privy council, which was appointed by the Emperor, included three of the *genrō* (Ito, Yamagata, and Matsukata) and also insured that the combined vote of Choshu and Satsuma members outnumbered all others. Next in order of precedence came the cabinet, another extra-constitutional body, first set up in 1885. Again, the principal membership often tended to be interlocking with the *genrō*, or with the privy council. Ito, for instance, became Japan's first prime minister in 1885, and, in 1888, as president of the privy council he approved the constitution that he and Inoue had drafted. Yamagata was minister of home affairs in the first Ito cabinet, became prime minister in 1890, and in 1892 took over the presidency of the privy council. Matsukata had held numerous offices, in addition to the prime ministership and governorship of the Bank of Japan.

The constitution laid down that the Emperor had supreme authority in naval and military affairs and that he would exercise this power with the advice of the responsible ministers of state. Yamagata, the Choshu and architect of Japan's army, was in and out of office as prime minister and, as we have seen, was also a member of the privy council. Oyama rose to the position of chief of staff of the army, was for a brief period a member of the privy council, and was for a long time minister of the army. His successor in this post, General Terauchi Masatake, was a Choshu.

The navy was run by sailors from Satsuma. For ten years, between 1895 and 1905, the post of chief of the navy general staff was held by Viscount Admiral Ito Sukeyuki. He was born in 1843 and with Togo and Oyama had taken part in the battle between the Satsuma shore batteries and the bombarding British squadron. His chief, as minister of the navy, was Admiral Yamamoto Gonnohyoe, another Satsuma.

Katsura Taro, a Choshu and an army general who had long been identified with the work of Yamagata and Oyama, became prime minister in 1901. At the next level were a group of fast-rising men who had been too young to have played much part in the restoration war but were important enough to join the decision-makers in their own right. These included, most notably, Lieutenant-General Kodama Gentaro, who was only fifteen when the restoration took place. A tiny, brilliant man, with a reputation for ruthlessness during his governorship of Taiwan (which Japan had acquired), he, more than any other Japanese leader, knew when to make war and when to make peace.

At the next level were the career soldiers, many of them quite old, who had grown up with the restoration and demonstrated their loyalty in the campaign against Saigo. Among the most colorful, and eventually the most controversial, of these was another Choshu veteran, General Nogi Maresuke. Aged fifty-six in 1904, he was a tall, wiry man, with gray hair and beard and piercing black eyes which shrank to iron-colored points when he gave his orders in battle.

As a child, he had been given the name Nakito (literally, "Nonexistent Person") because his father, having lost two sons, imagined that a child without a name might have a chance of surviving. As a young man he wanted to become a farmer and a poet. His father had the last word, and he became a soldier. His courage was never in question, but during his early days in the army he was often suspended for insubordination and for drinking "green liquors under scarlet lanterns." He could also be brutal. During the Formosan campaign in 1874 he once "tried out his sword" on an unfortunate native who happened to be standing nearby. An eccentric, he never recovered from the effects of an incident during the campaign against Saigo's forces at Kumamoto Castle. Nogi, acting against orders, became separated with 240 of his men from the main government forces and came under attack from a much stronger Satsuma force. After taking many casualties, Nogi was forced to retreat. He also lost the regimental standard, presented personally by the Emperor, the loss of which meant dishonor not only to Nogi but also to the regiment.

Nogi had decided to commit *seppuku* in atonement when he was over-powered by his men. Weeping, he agreed to confess his guilt and ask for punishment. General Yamagata decided that Nogi should die for dishonoring the flag, but others pleaded on his behalf. The confession of guilt was sent to the Emperor and Nogi went back into action, bent on his own destruction. Enemy bullets failed to kill him, and once again he was restrained from killing himself. He carried the dishonor, and an intense death wish, with him always. Saigo had died with honor but Nogi lived on by order of the Emperor, "suffering beyond death."

There was nothing in the Japanese governmental structure that could be identified as a direct constitutional chain of command. The navy minister was appointed to cabinet from senior flag officers on the active list. He had direct access to the Emperor, but the chief of staff was independent of the navy minister and also had the right of direct approach to the throne. The same situation existed in the army. Only a general or a lieutenant-general could be appointed to the office of war (or army) minister, and his role, like that of his counterpart in the navy, was rather like that of business manager. The chief of staff was responsible for defense and for the movements of the army. In other words, the navy and the army appointed their ministers and continued to exercise real power, since no cabinet could be formed without their participation. The cabinet could also be brought down by their resignation.

When it came to matters of war or peace, the system brought into play all sorts of pressure groups and accounted for the importance of organizations like the Black Dragon Society. It encouraged clandestine activities by comparatively junior officers to bring pressure on their seniors. It explains why no decision could be made without a conference of the elder statesmen, together with the cabinet and the chiefs and vice chiefs of the navy and army, and it also helps to explain why Japan in 1894 plunged into war with China over Korea, in a full-scale dress rehearsal of the Russo-Japanese War.

Ito Hirobumi, who had earlier negotiated a standstill agreement with the

Chinese over Korea, was prime minister. Although he was always a man of peace rather than war, Ito was faced with a hostile Diet, strong public feeling in favor of action in Korea, his own misgivings about Chinese policy there, and insistent pressure from ultranationalists and militarists who wanted to go to war.

Few people outside Japan understood the quite extraordinary military progress that the country had made. The Japanese had no doubts about their own capacity or the weakness of the Chinese. At Yamagata's instigation and with encouragement from the Black Dragon Society, Japan pressed its plans vigorously. While professing to seek common accord with China so that together the two countries could bring much-needed financial, administrative, and military reforms in Korea, Japan was intent on war, and the Japanese minister in Seoul received instructions that he was to use any pretext to begin positive action.

This aggressive approach had not been lightly decided upon. Japan appreciated that other powers, notably England and Russia, had interests in Korea. It assumed that if England could be persuaded to adopt a neutral stance, Russia would probably do likewise. It was important, therefore, to discover whether England had any secret agreement with China that would involve it in the war. The Japanese minister in London was instructed to ascertain the views of Downing Street and learned that, so long as Japan confined itself to administrative reforms in Korea and had no intention of grabbing any of its territory, London would welcome any amelioration of conditions there.

The Chinese north coast fleet had visited Yokohama in July 1891, and thousands of Japanese flocked to see the flagship *Ting-Yuen* and other large Chinese ships, including the 7,220-ton battleship, *Chen Yuen*. These ships were much bigger than the Japanese cruisers, *Naniwa* and *Takachiho*, and their armament was far heavier. The Chinese invited Japanese naval officers aboard, wining and dining them in style. Only Commander Togo, the Satsuma, who believed that warships should be regarded as sacred, was unimpressed. He joined with the other Japanese officers in a succession of feasts, but he also absorbed the deficiencies of the Chinese ships, noticing piles of rubbish on the decks and washing hanging from guns. The Chinese fleet, he said, was like an over-fired sword, fashioned by an excellent swordsmith from the best of steel but no sharper than a rusty kitchen knife.

The war began when a Japanese squadron met two Chinese warships, the battleship *Chen Yuen* and the *Kwang-Yi*, off the coast of Korea. Both sides claimed that the other had opened fire first, but the evidence suggests that Togo on the *Naniwa* began the action.

The first minutes of the engagement set the pattern for things to come.

The *Kwang-Yi* was wrecked after taking repeated hits from the Japanese warships, and the *Chen Yuen,* which was set on fire after being hit more than four hundred times, fled under cover of smoke.

The battle, if such it can be called, had only just ended when the lookouts on the *Naniwa* sighted two other vessels heading toward them from the west. One was a sloop, the *Tsao-Kiang,* and the other the merchantman *Kowshing,* flying the English flag and carrying 1,200 Chinese soldiers, packed on the deck like ants in an anthill, according to Togo. The *Tsao-Kiang* fled in the direction of the disappearing *Chen Yuen* as Togo bore down on the *Kowshing.* Togo fired two rounds of blank ammunition as a warning to the Englishman and signaled it to drop anchor. The *Kowshing* obliged, and Togo prepared to leave in pursuit of the *Chen Yuen* and the *Tsao-Kiang.* He quickly changed his mind when the *Kowshing* ran up flags requesting permission to leave. The *Naniwa* changed course and circled the *Kowshing* several times before lowering a boat that went across to the now-anchored English ship. The English captain protested bitterly against the detention of his ship, unaware that hostilities had already begun. Under protest, he agreed to follow the *Naniwa.*

As soon as the Japanese boat had pulled away to return to the *Naniwa,* the Chinese seized control of the *Kowshing* and prevented the captain from carrying out Togo's orders. For three hours Togo tried to persuade the *Kowshing* to surrender. Lacking the means to send a boarding party against the armed Chinese troops, Togo signaled that he intended to open fire. At a distance of no more than two hundred to three hundred yards, *Naniwa* fired a torpedo at the *Kowshing* and followed this with a broadside from five guns, including three six-inch guns. The transport began to list heavily. As the Chinese troops swarmed over the decks, *Naniwa* followed the broadside with a hail of fire from every available weapon. The Chinese replied with rifle fire, an unequal contest that could have only one end. Before the *Kowshing* went down, the Chinese succeeded in lowering two lifeboats which, crowded with men, were then sunk by the *Naniwa*'s guns. The *Naniwa*'s boats then picked up all the Europeans in the water, leaving the Chinese to drown or shooting them as they tried to swim away.

A storm broke out in the western world as soon as the sinking of the *Kowshing* became known. Tokyo reacted with fear and consternation. "Stupid fools," Ito shouted when he received the report from the navy minister. "This is a time when we must do all that we can to have England on our side." Ito pounded the table and a glass flew off and shattered on the floor.

Two British authorities, in a joint letter to *The Times,* helped to soothe ruffled British opinion with their conclusion that Togo's action did not constitute a breach of international law. Though there were suggestions in Japan that Togo might commit suicide to atone for his action, it seems unlikely that the thought seriously entered his head, especially since the Emperor Meiji let it be known through one of his lords-in-waiting that he thought Togo had done well.

Japanese newspapers printed the declaration of war on crimson paper. Priests performed ceremonies in the courtyards of the temples, shaving the head of each soldier with a long razor to show his renunciation of life. Heroes performed miraculous deeds of valor. A bugler ordered to sound the charge to attack had blown but once when a bullet passed through his throat, throwing him to the ground. His comrades tried to take the bugle from him, but the courageous bugler seized it back, lifted it once more to his lips, and sounded the charge with his last breath before he fell back dead. This scene, re-enacted in a popular play, caused theater-goers to rise in honor of the dead man, with tears streaming down their cheeks. A book, *The Sound of the Bugle*, swept the country and became required reading for primary-school students.

Cheap colored prints stimulated the war fever and embellished the glory of victory. Japanese illustrated books, stretching concertina fashion for seven or eight feet, showed Japan forever winning over her enemy. Every Japanese soldier, sailor, or statesman appeared to be six feet tall, always smartly dressed, while the Chinese, with their queues, were depicted as squat and ugly and attired in traditional silk robes. In these books no Japanese soldier ever fell in action, no sailor perished on the seas. Japanese warriors pushed screaming Chinese over high cliffs and watched as they jumped from the rigging of the ships. The waters were red with Chinese blood, the battlefields piled with Chinese dead. For page after page the Japanese were handsome, tall, and European-looking, whether lopping off Chinese heads, fighting under the water with the aid of flashlights, or on horseback in the snows of Manchuria. Japanese officers pored over their battle maps aboard ships, sitting on round-backed dining-room chairs, their charts spread across tables covered in daintly embroidered cloths. Hero emulation in the name of the Emperor stirred the people as never before.

By revising its earlier treaty with Japan on the eve of the war, England relieved some of the more extreme feelings of race rancor and xenophobia that were inherent in the new Japanese nationalism. Beneath the surface, however, tensions remained. The English-language newspapers published in the treaty ports mostly continued to support China, casting doubt on the prowess of the Japanese military and belittling their victories.

Victories they most certainly were. The Japanese destroyed the Chinese fleet off the mouth of the Yalu River and finished it off at Wei-hai-wei on the Shantung Peninsula. The Chinese admiral took an overdose of opium and died. Victorious Japanese wept in appreciation at his death and cheered their own victory.

[53]

Japanese ground forces swept up the Korean peninsula, into Manchuria, and on to Port Arthur. Field-Marshal Oyama, who led the Japanese Second Army, had not put a military foot wrong. He earned a reputation as a martinet, driving his men on in the depths of winter. A popular song lamented the hardships of the troops serving under him. Tokyo banned it for fear that it would cause antiwar feelings, though it is still sung in Japan today. The Japanese lost fewer than 800 men in battle. Cholera killed 1,600 and returning Japanese brought the disease back home. Thirty thousand people died of cholera in the summer of 1895.

With Wei-hai-wei in Japanese hands, and the Chinese fleet destroyed, the road to Peking was now open. The plan was to send one Japanese army with its four divisions to march inland. This new threat produced quick action.

Li Hung-chang, administrator of the Peking home province of Chih-li, arrived at Shimonoseki on March 19, 1895, as peace envoy plenipotentiary, and he was received by Ito. A flurry of diplomatic activity in the western capitals had already anticipated some of the claims the Japanese might be tempted to make, and the German minister had warned the Japanese foreign office that a demand for cession of territory on the Asian mainland would be particularly calculated to provoke European intervention. Nevertheless, Ito had no scruples about forcing the Liaotung Peninsula and Port Arthur from the reluctant Li Hung-chang, who almost lost his life when a would-be assassin shot him in the face.

After Li's recovery, Ito set out the Japanese peace terms in greater detail, and these eventually became the basis for the treaty that was signed on April 17. China relinquished all claim to suzerainty in Korea. It ceded Formosa, the Pescadores (a small group of islands off the southwest coast of Formosa), and the Liaotung Peninsula to Japan and agreed to pay a huge indemnity. It also opened up four new ports to trade. Under a separate treaty of commerce, Japan got most-favored-nation treatment in China, and Japanese could travel freely about the interior to set up business and manufacturing industries.

But there was still that slip between cup and lip, between signing the treaty and exchanging the deeds of ratification. In Paris, Berlin, and St. Petersburg, things were moving. At Shimonoseki a Russian agent tipped off Li Hung-chang that China was not without friends, that all was not yet lost. Russian help, he said, was coming.

The Japanese stalled for time while they pressed anxious inquiries in London and St. Petersburg. Did the Russians really intend to fight? And what help might Japan expect from England? The replies were not reassuring. The Japanese minister in St. Petersburg called on Prince Lobanov-Rostovski, the foreign minister, with the request that the Russian government reconsider its stand. This the Japanese foreign office later concluded was a fatal step, for Russia refused to change her stand, and, in company with Germany and France, adopted such a warlike posture that the Japanese thought it was now too late to demand an assurance that these powers would not themselves annex the Liaotung Peninsula and Port Arthur in the future. England made it clear that nothing could be expected of her but benevolent neutrality.

The treaty had already been signed and the exchange of ratifications was to take place on May 10. Whatever the decision about the Liaotung Peninsula, it was obviously not in Japan's interests to invite Russian military intervention by delaying the ratification. Eventually, Ito accepted the inevitable and advised Emperor Meiji to accept, under threat of attack, the Russian, French, and German demands, increasing the indemnity China was obliged to pay now that Japan had abandoned its claim to the peninsula. On May 10 the treaty was published together with an imperial rescript, which attempted, not very successfully, to save face for the abandonment of the Liaotung Peninsula. He had decided, the Emperor said, to accept the advice of friendly powers.

The Japanese nation reacted with astonishment, hate, and venom. A group of young officers at Port Arthur even discussed plans for marching across country to Vladivostok to exact revenge or to perish in the attempt. The Emperor calmed the clamor by showing his confidence in Ito, who was rewarded with the title of marquis and the Grand Cordon of the Chrysanthemum. The war cost Japan an estimated 232.6 million yen. The indemnity totaled 4,700 million yen. In both St. Petersburg and Tokyo the pace began to quicken.

Dearest Nick [wrote the German Kaiser to Tsar Nicholas II], I was glad to be able to show how our interests were entwined in the Far East, that my ships had been ordered to second yours in case of need when things looked doubtful, that Europe had to be thankful to you that you so quickly had perceived the great future for Russia in the cultivation of Asia and in the Defense of the Cross and the old Christian European culture against the inroads of the Mongols and Buddhism, that it was natural that if Russia was engaged in this tremendous work you wished to have Europe quiet and your back free; and that it was natural and without doubt that this would be my task and that I would let nobody try to interfere with you and attack from behind in Europe during the time you were fulfilling the great mission which Heaven had shaped for you. This was as sure as Amen in Church.

Instead of building railroads in Korea and Manchuria as it had planned, Japan now used its indemnity to build battleships in England. The Japanese had tasted victory. Now they planned revenge.

[55]

CHAPTER *3*

ഊഊഊഊഊഊ

Russia, the Boiling Pot

Sᴛ. ᴘᴇᴛᴇʀꜱʙᴜʀɢ ɪɴ the winter of 1903–1904 was drab, gray, and shabby. An unseen sun provided no more than four or five hours of daylight. The streets and shops were dimly lit, as gloomy as the spirits of the Russian people, whose grinding poverty had been made worse by four years of depression. Poor peasants, living on rye bread and very little else, had fled to the city in search of employment. When it was available, they found themselves little better off, working for eleven and a half hours a day on low wages and living either in the deplorable barracks provided by the factories, or by the "bed and corner" system, occupying as tenants a corner of a room, or even the corner of a bed.

In summer, when the ugly and uncomfortable little droshkies jolted over the large and uneven cobblestones, the city at least had sound and life. Now the sledges had taken over, moving noiselessly over the snow-covered streets. So intense was the cold and so thick the ice on the River Neva that streetcars ran across it. In the vast and rambling Winter Palace, stretching for nearly two hundred yards along the Neva, Tsar Nicholas II customarily presided over the brilliant winter "season" with its banquets and ballets. Now he found himself at war with a nation that he despised and slighted —and was sure he would defeat. An absolute ruler, with full control over the legislative, executive, and judicial functions of government, he drifted rather than led. He had no prime minister and his subordinate ministers did not meet as a cabinet. One thought a small war smartly won would help to divert the people's attention away from their own domestic grievances and help to unify the nation. Others captured his imagination with dreams of national greatness to be won in the East. Those who warned him of the dangers were thrust aside.

If America's Perry and Russia's Putiatin were the catalysts that changed Japan from an inert, isolated feudal state into a dynamic, militant, and expansionist industrial power, Russia's great victories in 1812 and 1814 over Napoleon served as a catalyst of an entirely different sort. The victories brought Russia international honor and glory. They also fed the fires of discontent among the more than thirty million serfs and the intelligentsia. Both believed that the liberators of Europe would also be liberated. They were wrong. When Alexander I, who, like all the other tsars, ruled us an autocrat, returned to a postwar policy of repression, the seeds of insurrection began to take root. Russia, a visiting European found, had become a boiling pot. The Tsar's dilemma was not merely to withstand the enemies at the gate but to resist the internal demands of the many nationalities who wanted freedom. The problem was as big as Russia itself.

From the time of Ivan the Terrible in the fifteenth century, Russia had been reaching out, swallowing territories and peoples: the Finns, the Poles, the Estonians, the Latvians, the Lithuanians, the Armenians, the Georgians, the Mongols, and the Turko-Mongols. Never satisified, it sought to devour more. It had become more than a nation; it was a world, covering nearly a sixth of the earth's surface, with a population of 129 million and nearly two hundred races, tribes, and peoples, of whom fewer than half spoke the Russian tongue.

Nicholas I, who succeeded Alexander I in 1825, put down a Guards' rebellion on the first day of his reign by a show of force and trust in God. After making the sign of the cross, he went out to face the rebellious soldiers who were determined to kill him. "I did nothing extraordinary," he told a visitor. "I said to the soldiers, 'Return to your ranks.' And at the moment the regiment passed in review, I cried 'Kneel!' They all obeyed." He warred with Persia, with Turkey, and with Poland, and earned for himself the nickname "Gendarme of Europe."

By 1856, after the humiliating loss of the Crimean War when Britain and France defeated the Tsar's forces, Russia had been reduced from its proud position as the dominating military power in Europe to that of one among several equals. The shock persuaded Alexander II, the "Tsar-Liberator," that some reforms were necessary in the countryside. The decision was made to abolish serfdom, but the scheme was much less than generous and there were peasant riots in 1861, the year of the reforms. The peasants resented being asked to pay for land they regarded as theirs. They simmered with anger, feuded with the landlords, and helped to rob Alexander of much of his reforming zeal. To unrest among the peasants was added student

[57]

disorder in the smaller cities and even at the universities of St. Petersburg and Moscow. What might have been described a century later as a hippie cult developed. As a sign of dissent, male students started to wear long hair and beards and girls cut their hair short and indulged in free love. Together they took to the streets in political demonstrations. The Nihilists, as they were called, a phrase coined by the novelist Turgenev, showed scant respect for authority or autocracy. Nor were the girls made less revolutionary by the charter of 1863 that barred women from the universities.

Poland, which had been seized by Alexander I after an uprising in 1831, also erupted in revolt in 1863. This had few repercussions in Russia proper, though it added strength to the arguments of those who believed that the rule of the autocracy had to be maintained with the firmest of hands. This view gained further strength in 1866 with the creation of a revolutionary organization named Hell and the attempted assassination of the Tsar. The attempt failed and the would-be assassin was executed summarily. Police detained several hundred other students and ex-students and clamped down so hard that they put the lid on the revolutionary pot at home for several years.

Alexander II was a handsome, arrogant man, with a commanding manner. Frederic Hamilton, then a young British diplomat in Russia, remembered being received by him in Peter the Great's throne room seated on Peter's throne, where he addressed members of the diplomatic corps "with something in his voice and a look in his eye reminiscent of the Great Mogul addressing an earthworm." A second attempt on Alexander's life occurred in 1867 at the Paris Exhibition. This time a young Polish revolutionary fired point-blank at the Tsar as he watched a parade on the right of the Emperor Louis-Napoleon. Again, the shot missed.

"Things are moving," Karl Marx wrote in a note to Friedrich Engels. "And in the next revolution, which is perhaps nearer than it seems, we (i.e. you and I) have this powerful machinery in our hands."

Revolutionary activity began to stir among the students again in the 1870s, and hundreds went down to the countryside to impress on the peasants the need for revolt. Their evangelical efforts met with little success, but they moved the autocracy to repressive action. Revolution feeds on repression, and there now occurred one of those minor but dramatic incidents that so often help to change the course of history.

Nearly two hundred young revolutionaries were given a mass trial and the unique opportunity to spread the gospel of revolution. The day after the trial, Vera Zasulitch, daughter of a well-to-do family who had first been arrested when she was sixteen, shot but failed to kill the chief of police in St. Petersburg. Now twenty-seven, she was brought to trial and told the court that she had tried to kill the policeman because he had reintroduced

[58]

flogging, which had been abolished. The jury acquitted her and the crowd cheered as she made a dash for freedom. Before the authorities could rearrest her she had been spirited out of the country.

The shooting, the spectacular trial, the acquittal, and finally Vera Zasulitch's escape electrified the revolutionary movement, and a wave of assassination and violence spread across the land. The peasants began to show more interest in the Nihilists' psychological warfare. Industrial workers started to move, also. On April 2, 1879, the third attempt was made on the Tsar's life. A young revolutionary schoolteacher fired five shots at him outside the Winter Palace. Again, he escaped injury.

There were so many assassination attempts that the People's Will Committee, formed expressly to kill the Tsar, became alarmed after twenty-one of their members had been executed. "We are consuming our capital," lamented the chief of the assassination organization.

One would-be assassin, a workman from St. Petersburg, obtained employment in the Winter Palace and detonated a bomb in the white marble private dining room of the palace, timing it to go off soon after the Tsar sat down at the table. Alexander was kept working late on the night of the assassination attempt. Though many servants were killed, the Tsar escaped. A search of the Winter Palace revealed dozens of unauthorized tenants, relatives of the many servants, living on the top floors of the building. Ducks, pigs, and piles of hay were tucked away in upstairs rooms. In a top-floor bedroom a full-grown cow, smuggled into the palace, placidly chewed her cud. Fed on hay stolen from the stables, she provided fresh milk for the many servants' children. In the confusion, the assassin got away and was not arrested until the following year.

In another attempt on the Tsar's life, the revolutionaries bought a building in Moscow and tunneled beneath it to place a bomb on the railway line on which Alexander was to travel. He took a train going in a different direction, and once again escaped death.

Luck deserted Alexander, when, in broad daylight, in March 1881 he rode back from a military parade. The assassins waited in the snow, and as the heavy coach, pulled by four magnificent gray horses, lumbered along the Catherine Canal in St. Petersburg, a bomb, painted white to look like a snowball, came hurtling beneath its wheels. Several Cossacks in the Tsar's escort and some passersby were killed, but Alexander stepped unhurt from the wrecked carriage into the blood-spattered snow to commiserate with his injured coachman. "Thank God I am still alive," he was saying, when a second assassin stepped up close to him and threw another "snowball" between his legs. "It is too early to thank God," he shouted as the Tsar fell, his legs almost severed from his body, his face and stomach torn open. He was carried by sledge to the Winter Palace where he died an hour later on a couch in his study. The horrified royal family, including his second wife, whom he had married only nine months earlier, clustered around. Among those at the bedside were his grandson, thirteen-year-old Nicholas, dressed in a blue sailor's suit.

Five people were hanged in the center of the city for their part in the crime. They included a young and beautiful girl, Sophia Perovskaya, daughter of a general. Before she died she wrote a farewell letter to her mother, telling her not to grieve. "My darling, I have lived according to my convictions and it would have been impossible for me to do otherwise. So I wait here with tranquil conscience." The man who had thrown the fatal bomb was killed in the explosion, but Sophia Perovskaya's lover died with her, although he had been in prison at the time of the assassination.

Alexander III, who succeeded his father to the Throne at the age of thirty-six, declared that he would not now grant Russia a constitution for "anything on earth." The police got more power than ever, student organizations were prohibited, and restriction of the country's five million Jews, several of whom had been identified with the assassination plot, increased. "We must not forget that it was the Jews who crucified our Lord and spilled His precious blood," Alexander wrote. He took the advice of Constantine Petrovitch Pobedonostsev, his tutor, and Procurator of the Holy Synod, who advocated a policy that would "convert a third of the Jews to Christianity, destroy another third by starvation, and drive the last third into emigration."

Alexander II's efforts to give some form of liberty to the people had been met by a bomb, and his son never forgot the torn body in the Winter Palace. He recalled, too, that his ancestor Catherine the Great had acknowledged the danger in education for the masses and had advised the governor-general of Moscow not to trouble when parents failed to send their children to the schools she had reluctantly provided for them. Alexander followed her edict. Education for the masses, he said, would be limited to the three Rs, "beyond which all else is not only superfluous but dangerous." A ukase directed that the children of coachmen, servants, cooks, laundresses, small shopkeepers, and the like should be discouraged from rising above the sphere in which they had been born.

Alexander III nevertheless liked to think that he understood the peasant mind. Whenever possible he wore simple peasant costume and moved out into the countryside to mix with the working people. He was full of vigor and enormously strong. He washed in cold water each morning, made his own coffee in a glass percolator, and drank many cups before he settled to work in his study. This giant of a man, who, like his grandfather, Nicholas I, towered over his family and his people, held his country and the multitudinous Romanov clan in his powerful hands. With these strong hands he liked to bend horseshoes, pokers, and the royal silverware. With his equally strong personality he kept his relatives, including the grasping cousins, uncles and their wives, in some sort of order, so that there were no family scandals during his thirteen-year reign.

Alexander had violent ikes and dislikes. He adored, and was even a little afraid of, his tiny wife. There was no bending the table silver when she was present. "My mother would have been furious," remembered his daughter Olga. His wife had become engaged to Alexander's brother, Nicholas, heir to the throne. Just before Nicholas died of tuberculosis, he called his brother and his fiancée, the Princess Dagmar of Denmark (sister of Alexandra of England), to his bedside and taking their hands joined them on his breast, bequeathing to Alexander both his throne and his chosen wife. The following year the new Tsarevitch and the solaced Danish princess were married.

Dagmar, now called Marie, shone at the many court balls. At formal dinners she added beauty and wit to the conversation. Marie could dance all night and would have if Alexander, who hated pomp and "dressing-up," had not broken up festivities by turning off all the lights so that the guests, the orchestra, and the reluctant Tsaritsa took the hint. He was fortunate that electricity had recently been introduced to Russia. Before, the palace had been lighted with more than a hundred thousand wax candles.

The French dream of alliance with Russia came true in 1892 when the two age-old enemies forgot their differences in the excitement of the new bond between them. In France, during a visit by the Russian fleet, people were crushed to death in the struggle to see the Russian sailors. "Long live the Russian emperor!" they cried. "We love him and peace." Leo Tolstoy wrote with bitterness of this strange alliance:

> All the French suddenly became extraordinarily religious and carefully deposited in the rooms of the Russian mariners the very images which a short time previously they had as carefully removed from their schools as harmful tools of superstition, and they said prayers incessantly. . . . Besides the throwing of flowers and various little ribbons and the presenting of gifts and addresses, the Frenchwomen in the streets threw themselves into the arms of Russian sailors and kissed them.

For the time being, Alexander loved the French as passionately as they were loved by his people. His hatreds included the British, Queen Victoria in particular. Alexander II's daughter Marie married Queeen Victoria's son Alfred in the 1880s. Although Victoria was against the marriage, she realized that a union of this sort between Russia and England might relieve the dangerous tensions between the two countries which had grown out of their rivalry in Central Asia and British fears of Russian designs on India.

Reluctantly, she admitted that her new daughter-in-law had "nice eyes" and spoke very good English. Marie tolerated Victoria but occasionally wrote letters back to her brother in Russia, complaining of the weather and the dreadful food. Her mother-in-law, she confided, drank whisky, usually without water. Marie's brother, Alexander III, loathed Victoria and was especially irritated by British reaction when Russian officers kidnapped Prince Alexander of Battenberg, ruler of the new state of Bulgaria. He called her a pampered, interfering, nasty old woman; Victoria referred to him as barbaric and half-Asiatic. The loyal children of the Russian royal family decided that Victoria cared only for her German relatives, and to the Tsar of Russia Germans were as repulsive as the English.

Alexander despised William II of Germany, even when the Kaiser was a child. Whenever the arrogant young prince turned up in St. Petersburg, Alexander ignored him, turning his back and talking over his shoulder. Willy once suggested that Germany and Russia should divide Europe between them. Alexander looked at him with distaste, telling him not to behave like a "whirling dervish." "Look at yourself in the mirror," he said.

Alexander III had never liked the great, gloomy Winter Palace, with its 1,050 rooms, and now, with the ghost of his assassinated father haunting it, he moved his family to Gatchina Palace, thirty miles from St. Petersburg, where they shared the 600 rooms with hundreds of servants. Their bedrooms were stark in their simplicity, with hard campbeds, flat pillows, and very thin mattresses. There were no comfortable chairs or sofas, only straight-backed bentwood chairs with cane seats. Cold baths and plenty of fresh air were prescribed by the Tsar, and meals for the children were plain: English porridge, bread and butter with jam, mutton cutlets, and baked potatoes. They all disliked the undercooked beef, introduced by an English nanny, but they ate whatever they were given.

As the children grew older, they were occasionally allowed to eat with their parents in a private dining room, which Marie, their gay Danish mother, had improvised from a disused bathroom. The enormous white marble bathtub, flanked by four gold mirrors, was kept filled to the brim with pink and white azaleas. Where the wife of Nicholas I had once bathed, the family ate.

Though revolutionary activity was at a low level during the 1880s, the threat of assassination was never distant. In 1887 Alexander Ulyanov, a university zoology student, became official chemist for the People's Will. He had already won a gold medal for his research work on earthworms. He gave up this study to concentrate on dynamite and the construction of bombs; he and his friends pooled their savings to buy the chemicals. Their only attempt failed. The studious Alexander had not been chosen to take part in the actual attempt on the Tsar's life, but he was arrested with his companions. At the trial he tried to take all the blame for the plot that failed and astonished his mother and the court with his volubility. "There is no finer death than death for one's country," he cried. "Such a death holds no terror for sincere and honest men. I had one aim—to help the unfortunate Russian people."

Alexander, the zoology student, elder brother of Vladimir, a sixteen-year-old high school student, later to be known as Lenin, died on the gallows. Alexander, the Tsar, signed his death warrant and that of his four companions, but continued to believe that his people still thought of him affectionately as the "Tsar-Muzhik" ("Peasant Tsar"). He had great personal courage, but, after the attempts on his life, he reluctantly agreed to use the armor-plated carriages which had once belonged to Napoleon III. These carriages were so heavy that the horses pulling them soon died of overwork and were constantly being replaced. The authorities responsible for his safety insisted that he use the steel-plated carriages, drawn by a train which had also been bought from the effects of Napoleon III. There were nine handsomely fitted cars on the imperial train, and the timetables were changed so that they differed from the published times and routes.

Nicholas, the heir, continued to enjoy his role of playboy. At nineteen he was given command of a squadron of horse guards and fitted in well with the messroom frivolity, often getting "stewed," as he put it. About the same time he fell in love with a tiny ballerina, Mathilde Kschessinska, a gay and brilliant dancer, but this romance was no more acceptable to the Tsarevitch's parents than was his long-standing, long-distance love for golden-haired Princess Alix of Hesse-Darmstadt, granddaughter of Queen Victoria, whom he had met when they were children. Alix had been brought to St. Petersburg for inspection but had not been approved of by the Tsar or the Tsaritsa. A German daughter-in-law, reared by his enemy, England's Queen Victoria, was too much for Alexander.

In October 1890, an attempt was made to discourage Nicholas from either an unsuitable match or protracted dalliance with Mathilde Kschessinska. He and his younger brother, the Grand Duke George, who had contracted tuberculosis, were sent on a tour of Egypt, India, and the Far East aboard the battleship *Pamiat Azova*.* In Athens, they were joined by Prince George, a son of Empress Marie's brother, the King of Greece.

It was hoped that the sea cruise would improve George's health and that Nicholas would forget his two loves. But in India, the heat proved too severe for the ailing George and the abundance of red English uniforms too much

---

*Literally, *Remembrance of the Azova,* a special honor conferred by the Tsar after the battle of Navarino, when he ordered that one ship of the fleet should always be so named and carry on her ensign the Order of St. George.

for Nicholas. George returned to his convalescence, high up in the Caucasian mountains, where he was to die some years later, and Nicholas continued the tour with his cousin.

An incident in Japan nearly brought the journey to an untimely end and helped to color Nicholas's views. On their way back to Kyoto from Otsu, the procession of about fifty jinrickshas was proceeding at a trot along a lane about eight paces wide. On both sides the lane was lined with policemen, spaced about eight to ten yards apart. At the head of the line of jinrickshas was the chief of police, followed by the Japanese master of ceremonies. Forty paces behind came Nicholas in his jinricksha, with one man in the shafts and two pushing at the sides. Behind him was Prince George of Greece, who, in turn, was followed by Prince Arisugawa.*

> The criminal, Tsuda Sanzo, was among the watchers over the safety of the illustrious guest of Japan [wrote Prince Esper Ukhtomski, official historian for the journey, whose style of writing did not allow him to call a policeman a policeman]. He stood on the same spot in the morning, but allowed his prospective victim to pass without, as it appeared afterwards, showing the slightest of any criminal intention. He knew that the Cesarewitch was to return by the same road. Scarcely had His Imperial Highness' jinricksha passed him when he leaped from the ranks, and, drawing his sword, dealt from the right and somewhat from behind, between the jinricksha and the man of the right hand, a swinging two-handed blow on the head of the Cesarewitch, who, turning and seeing that the villain had raised his sword for a second blow, sprang out of the equipage to the left side of the street. At the same moment, Prince George jumped from his jinricksha and struck the man from behind with a bamboo cane.

The real hero of the affair was the coolie pulling Nicholas's jinricksha. Unarmed, he threw himself with a flying tackle at the policeman's feet and brought him to the ground.

Nicholas behaved with commendable calm. "It is nothing," he said, as he sat on a bench near the site of the attempted assassination. "If only the Japanese will not think that this incident can in any way change my feeling toward them and my thankfulness to them for their cordiality." Though the

---

*Translators in the past have not made it easy to distinguish between princes of the royal family and the top court rank of "prince" conferred by the Emperor on his subjects. Since the Japanese imperial family has no surname, imperial princes are called after their residence, or estate, as Prince Taruhito of the Imperial House of Arisugawa (a suburb of Kyoto). The title "prince," as in the case of Prince Ito, is perhaps better translated as "duke."

wound was not severe, he was to carry the scar on his forehead all his life, along with a bitter hatred for Japan and the Japanese.

Nicholas's affair with Mathilde Kschessinska continued after his return to St. Petersburg. He presented her with diamond bracelets and took her for long, starlit sledge rides. But the affair with Princess Alix was much more serious.

Nicknamed "Sunny" because of her bright, red-gold hair and warm smile, Princess Alix had been brought up by Queen Victoria and English nannies after her mother died. She was intensely religious and serious as a child, with solemn, gray eyes, and a smile that lit her whole face. The rare smile was her real beauty. "It was like the gift of a big silver coin," wrote an admirer. "It turned her mouth into a flower. It did something unforgettable to her beautiful eyes—years later, those who would see that smile—however rarely—felt as though the sun had broken across a sullen, wintry sky." Another characteristic of the princess, however, was her extreme shyness. When it overcame her the smile was gone. Her face changed completely, the lovely eyes became hooded, the pretty mouth tight and hard.

It was the smile that won Nicholas. He was determined to marry the German princess, despite his family's objections and the differences in their religions—strict Lutheran and Russian Orthodox. In his diary Nicholas recorded his misery, his hopes, the arguments, and the pleas. Though Alix declared her love for him alone, she was adamant that she could not change her religion. Nicholas did not give up hope, and his diary is full of love for her. The chatter of actresses and champagne parties, which had filled its pages for years, disappeared forever. On April 5, 1894, while in England, he wrote of her beauty, her sadness, and of her decision to adhere to her own religion. Three days later the diary announced "a heavenly, unforgettable day. My betrothal with dear beloved Alix—in a dream all day long." Alix had capitulated. They had tea with Queen Victoria, exchanged rings, and went for long walks, gathering flowers and holding hands.

Catechism lessons and tuition in the strange new religion began for Alix, and Nicholas reluctantly returned to Russia. "All was paradise," according to his diary. Even the sudden illness of his father, now fifty, could not rob him of his joy. Alexander III had developed dropsy and Nicholas found him too ill to lie comfortably in bed. The once-robust Tsar now spent his days sitting in a wheelchair at an open window, looking down at the oleanders that sloped toward the sea at Livadia in the Crimea, where the family had moved to escape the cold of St. Petersburg.

Princess Alix was summoned to Russia to be accepted at last by the dying Tsar. She hardly saw her fiancé and wrote in his diary that he must be firm:

"Show your mind and don't let them forget who you are. . . . Forgive, my love. . . ."

Alexander's confessor arrived and was at the Tsar's bedside when he died. They knelt around the bed—children, cousins, aunts, uncles, and priests. All kissed the dead Tsar on the forehead and the hand, and then they kissed his widow. There was no sobbing in the room. Moments passed, and then, as an afterthought, everyone turned to Nicholas and for the first time kissed his hand.

Nicholas, Tsar at twenty-six, was overcome with fear and sorrow. "What am I going to do?" he asked one of the uncles. "I have no idea of even how to talk to the ministers." Sobbing on his little sister's shoulder, he repeated over and over again that he did not know what would become of them all. He had never wanted to be Tsar. "It was all my father's fault," said his sister Olga. "I know how he disliked the mere idea of state matters encroaching on our family life—but, after all, Nicky was his heir."

The regime was beginning to totter long before Nicholas came to the throne. Gorki had warned of the stormy petrel that would appear "like black lightning," the forerunner of a great storm, and Chekhov's *The Three Sisters* spoke of the same forebodings. "The time has come, an enormous thing is moving down on us all, a mighty, wholesome storm is gathering; it is approaching, is already near, and soon will cleanse from our society its indolence, indifferences, prejudice against work, and foul ennui."

Like the city of St. Petersburg, built on shifting sands, the autocracy was slowly crumbling. Everywhere there were imposing structures, but the ministers within their walls were only the servants of the Tsar. And Nicholas, when his time came, had neither the physical nor the intellectual strength of his ancestors, including his father and his grandfather. His ambitions exceeded his capabilities. He could control the vast country no better than he could the crowd of grasping relatives surrounding him. "Poor, unhappy Emperor," wrote Serge Yulievitch Witte, Russia's ablest statesman of the times, "he was not born for the momentous historical role which fate has thrust upon him."

Amid the increasing rumbles of discontent, the frequent assassination of officials, and the consequent punishment by exile or imprisonment or by hanging on the public gallows, the Church of the Tsar dominated the lives of the people. The Church in its own way was as unenlightened as the state. But in the pageantry of the churches and cathedrals the mass of Russian people found their only luxury. Surrounded by jeweled ikons, golden crucifixes, lofty pillars of white Siberian marble and pink jasper, they could forget the miseries of earth in the glory of the church. Their money went to build the hundreds of magnificent churches where choirboys sang like angels in silvery tones without the aid of musical instruments, which were banned in the Russian Orthodox Church. One third of their children died before their first year, but the parents were comforted, like Maxim Gorki's beloved grandmother who lost all but three of her eighteen children. "The Lord took a liking to my blood," she told her grandson. "He took and took the kids for angels. And I'm sad, but happy, too."

With the soft blue haze of incense about their kerchiefed heads, the peasants, dressed in uncured sheepskin jackets turned inside out so that the wool warmed their bodies, stood with the rich, dressed in jewels and sables, to worship God. Rich and poor alike were hypnotized by the pealing of the bells, the singing of the little boys in their long blue gowns, and the chanting of the priests garbed in jeweled vestments.

In the cities of St. Petersburg and Moscow the rich lived in luxury. The poor in the cities and the peasants in the villages wrapped themselves in rags and eked out an existence in hovels and unpainted log cabins. "Russia is the dreariest land on earth," wrote a traveler from France. Looking at the Russian faces and thinking about what passed for existence "for these poor devils," he asked himself what man had done to God that so many of the human race should be condemned to live in Russia.

Nicholas II, convinced that he was in the hands of God and owed allegiance to Him alone, could see no reason for change in the autocracy. Pobedonostsev, his tutor, a wizened and cynical little man, had drummed into him the dangers of parliamentarianism. The grand dukes, his uncles and cousins, all clamoring greedily for money and power, had reminded him constantly from childhood that one day he would head the Russian nation. He stood in awe of the four uncles, brothers of his father, who towered above him physically and intellectually.

Nicholas and Alexandra—Princess Alix's Russianized name—were married ten days after Alexander's funeral. There was no wedding reception and no honeymoon, and for the first months of their marriage they lived with the Empress Dowager in a six-room suite of the Anitchkov Palace, Marie's home. They had no dining room of their own, and all meals were taken with Marie at the head of the table. Whenever the Tsar had official callers, his wife had to retire to their bedroom. "Petitions and audiences without end," wrote Nicholas in his diary a day or so after the wedding. "Saw Alix for an hour only."

Nicholas started on the "awful job I have never wanted," hemmed in by advisers, quite apart from his mother and his wife, but often the mistakes he made were his own. Soon after their marriage a deputation arrived at the palace, hoping to receive sympathetic response from the new Tsar on constitutional reforms. Replying to the loyal address, Nicholas horrified the members of the delegation with his references to their "problems," telling them to put all ideas of dreaming out of their minds: "Let everybody know that I hold to the principles of Autocracy as firmly as my father did," he said. The Tsaritsa, standing a little behind her husband, dressed all in black, cold-eyed and frightened, was blamed for the speech.

The coronation itself was marred by tragedy. Nicholas, pale with fright, stood for five hours, the great crown cutting into the scar inflicted by the Japanese saber. Behind him were the two empresses, Marie first, as always, then Alexandra in a pearl-studded white gown. Nicholas and his wife ate alone according to tradition during the coronation feast, still wearing their ermine-trimmed wraps and the heavy crowns. "They looked so lonely—eating alone—just like two birds in a golden cage," said the impressionable Olga. But they were happy. Alexandra pressed an electric button hidden in a bunch of roses and the whole of Moscow blazed with lights.

The next day belonged to the people. The Tsar and his wife were to attend the coronation feast for the people on the Khodynka Meadow, a rough military field outside the city and now the Moscow airport. The people came by the hundreds of thousands and gathered outside the railings of the paradeground, eager to receive souvenirs of the coronation—enameled mugs full of cheap candy. Just after dawn a rustle started in the great crowd when a rumor circulated that there might not be enough presents to go around. One or two people jumped the railings, racing across the rough, hole-pocked ground toward the center of the field. More followed, and soon people were streaming by the thousands toward the stalls where the presents lay piled.

The few hundred Cossack guards were helpless to stop the flow of humanity as it spilled across the field, and in minutes the stream had become a deluge. Some children were saved by being passed over the crowd. Others tripped on the rough ground and the crowd rushed over them, on and on toward the stalls. Nearly three thousand people were trampled to death or suffocated in the wild dash toward the stalls holding the little tins of candy.

In his *Memoirs,* Serge Witte remembered a conversation he had with Li Hung-chang. The Chinese leader had come to St. Petersburg for the coronation, and they talked of the death of thousands of people in the stampede.

"But His Majesty does not know, does he?" asked Li. Witte assured him that Nicholas knew everything. "Well," remarked Li, "I don't see the wisdom of that. I remember when I was governor-general ten million people died from the bubonic plague in the provinces confined to my charge, yet our Emperor knew nothing about it. Why disturb him uselessly?"

"I thought to myself," wrote Witte, "after all, we were ahead of the Chinese."

Though Nicholas gave hundreds of thousands of roubles from his private funds to assist the families of those killed, the tragedy of his coronation day added one more misfortune to the reign of the Tsar who had been born on Job's day.

Japan's victory over China and its determination to seize the Liaotung Peninsula provided Nicholas with his first major international crisis. According to Witte, Nicholas was "merely possessed of an unreasoned desire to seize Far Eastern lands." Witte wanted a stable but passive China. "It appeared obvious to me," he wrote, "that it was imperative not to allow Japan to penetrate into the very heart of China and secure a footing in the Liaotung Peninsula, which to a certain extent occupies a dominating position. Accordingly, I insisted on the necessity of thwarting the execution of the peace treaty between Japan and China." Russian hopes that England might be persuaded to assist in this plan were quickly dashed. England, though not yet ready to spring to Japan's defense, had grown disillusioned with China and was preparing to switch its support.

Prince Lobanov-Rostovski, who had taken over the foreign ministry, and, according to Witte, knew no more about the Far East than the average schoolboy, doubted whether Russia should resort to coercive methods if the Japanese refused to evacuate the Liaotung Peninsula. He suggested that it should be indicated to the Japanese government, "in the friendliest possible terms," that the seizure of Port Arthur would be a lasting impediment to the restoration of cordial relations with China and grounds for a breach of peace in the Orient.

Nicholas agreed initially about Port Arthur but thought it "would be well to consider the occupation by us of Port Lazarev or some other port in eastern Korea." As the days passed, Nicholas's view hardened. By April 5, 1895, he had concluded that "for Russia a year-round free and open port is absolutely indispensable. This port must be on the mainland [in the southeast of Korea] and must without fail be linked with our previous possessions by a strip of land."

Kaiser William indicated to St. Petersburg that he would "join in any step Russia might deem necessary to take in Tokyo to the end of impelling Japan to renounce not only her seizure of southern Manchuria and Port Arthur but the Pescadores Islands [off the southwest coast of Formosa] as well."

In his opening speech at a ministerial conference at St. Petersburg on April 12, 1895, Witte painted a gloomy picture of what might follow the collapse of China.

When they get their indemnity of six hundred million roubles from China, the Japanese will fortify themselves in the localities they have seized, win over the highly warlike Mongols and Manchus, and then start a new war. In such a state of affairs, the Mikado might, not inconceivably, in the course of a few years, become Emperor of China.

[69]

If we now admit the Japanese into Manchuria, then the guarding of our possessions and of the Siberian road will require hundreds of thousands of troops and a considerable increase in our navy, since sooner or later we shall inevitably come into conflict with the Japanese. This raises the question: which would be better—to reconcile ourselves to Japan's seizure of the southern part of Manchuria and recoup ourselves after the completion of the Siberian road, or to make up our minds here and now actively to prevent such a seizure. It would appear to be to our advantage to pass to the former procedure at once, and, without aspiring for the time being to the rectification of our Amur boundary, or, in general, to seizures of any sort, in order not to have China and Japan both against us at once and be correct where Europe is concerned, definitely declare that we cannot permit Japan's seizure of southern Manchuria, and that, in the event of our demand not being made, we shall be forced to take suitable measures.

Witte envisaged the bombardment of Japanese ports by the Russian fleet in the unlikely event that Japan refused to withdraw, and was not impressed by the strength of the Japanese army, which he put at no more than 70,000 men and scattered over Korea and Manchuria. General P. S. Vannovski, the liberal-minded war minister, who had been appointed as a sop to rebellious students, presented a far from encouraging report on the state of Russia's war readiness, but added that the "Japanese armies at the present time are harmless as far as we are concerned." They could not advance a single step, whereas in six months the Russian forces in the Far East could be raised to 50,000. If Japan failed to accept the ultimatum proposed by Witte, he supported the use of force. Witte spoke a second time to insist that if Japan refused to withdraw from Manchuria it would be to Russia's advantage to decide on war "for, if we do not, Russia will have much larger sacrifices to make in the future."

The Tsar now called his own inner council together to resolve the issue, and under his chairmanship, his uncle, Grand Duke Alexis, Witte, General Vannovski, and Prince Alexsei Borisovitch Lobanov-Rostovski met on April 17. Nicholas still hankered after his free port in Korea, but Witte finally prevailed and the council agreed:

(1) To seek to preserve the status quo ante bellum in northern China and in pursuance of this to advise Japan, at first amicably, to desist from the occupation of southern Manchuria, for such an occupation would injure our interests and would be a constant menace to the peace of the Far East; in case of Japan's refusal to follow our advice, to declare to the Japanese government that we reserve to ourselves freedom of action and that we shall act in accordance with our interests;

(2) To issue an official statement to the European powers and to

China to the effect that, while on our part we do not seek any seizures, we deem it necessary, for the protection of our interests, to insist on Japan's desisting from the occupation of Southern Manchuria.

France and Germany agreed to Russia's demand, and off went the ultimatum to Tokyo. Less than a week after the signatures were affixed to the Treaty of Shimonoseki, three similar warnings were presented by the ministers of Germany, France, and Russia to the Japanese foreign office. The Russian note read:

The government of His Majesty the Emperor of All the Russias, in examining the conditions of peace which Japan has imposed on China, finds that the possession of the peninsula of Liaotung, claimed by Japan, could be a constant menace to the capital of China, could at the same time render illusory the independence of Korea, and would henceforth be a perpetual obstacle to the permanent peace of the Far East. Consequently, the government of His Majesty the Emperor would give proof of their friendliness for the government of His Majesty the Emperor of Japan by advising them to renounce the definite possession of the peninsula of Liaotung.

The Japanese, as we have seen, backed down—and prepared for war. And Nicholas, flushed by this first success, increasingly saw the Far East as the means to satisfy his ambitions. In the past, the Russian Far Eastern fleet had been accustomed to spending the winter in Japan's ports, away from ice-bound Vladivostok. In the winter of 1895–1896 the usual Japanese hospitality was not forthcoming, and the Chinese, in unwise gratitude, offered anchorages at Kiao-chau on the Shantung Peninsula. The Russians found it unsatisfactory and began to look about for a suitable alternative.

A Russian joke about Nicholas was that, while Alexander had been his own prime minister, Nicholas had no prime minister at all. Nicholas was too weak to rule himself and too proud to let others rule for him. Blocked in the west by Austria and the growing power of Germany, he sought to build on the work of his predecessors and to expand in the east. No one had the power to stop him. The men who mattered fell into two categories, those whose advice he rejected and those whose advice he accepted. The former carried more weight but in the end were less important.

The man who stood head and shoulders above the rest was Witte, who, until the eve of the war when Nicholas dismissed him from office, held the post of finance minister, and for a long time virtually ran Russia's foreign affairs. Born in Tiflis in 1845, Witte sprang on his paternal side from Dutch ancestor–migrants who went to the Baltic provinces when these were under Swedish rule. His mother was a woman of noble Russian birth, and his father a senior official in the government of the Caucasus.

[71]

Witte held it as a grievance against his mother that she did not suckle him herself, and his early precocious recollections were of his family's eighty-four servants and of ugly scenes between his wet nurse and his nursery-maid and her drunken husband. He was tutored privately, first by a retired Caucasian veteran, who also drank heavily; by a retired officer in the French navy, who was deported by the authorities after a scandalous love affair; by a Swiss who became enamored of his governess; and, finally, by a German, who seems to have been addicted neither to the bottle nor the charms of the female retinue that attended young Witte's calls.

Witte's natural brilliance triumphed over the disorder of his early education, and he graduated with the highest honors from the University of Odessa, spurred on now by the death of his father and the total collapse of the family fortunes in the cast iron business.

His ambition was to become a professor of pure mathematics. Instead, he went into government service with the Odessa Railroad. For six months he sold passenger tickets, studied freight traffic, worked as assistant stationmaster, and acted as train inspector. At the end of that time he was promoted to the position of director of the traffic bureau, a post that he eventually abandoned to become the highly paid director of the Southwestern Railroad, a private company.

Soon Witte was offered, and accepted, the post of director of the department of railroad affairs, a branch of the finance ministry. The new post meant a considerable reduction in salary from the 50,000 roubles (£5,000 sterling) Witte was earning with the private railroad company. Alexander was so impressed by him that he doubled the salary from his own funds.

This was in 1889. In February 1892, Alexander made Witte minister of ways and communications and in August of the same year promoted him to the loftiest pinnacles of power by entrusting him with the ministry of finance. When Witte moved into this portfolio Russia had an annual revenue of 965 million roubles. Ten years later its revenue was 1,947 million, and Russia was on the gold standard with its credit firmly established abroad. Not that Witte received many thanks, either from the people or from Tsar Nicholas II, who detested what he regarded as Witte's rudeness and uncouthness and his contempt for court life.

Finance ministers are rarely popular at the best of times, and the masses disliked Witte because, among other things, he took over the sale of vodka as a state monopoly. This was accepted abroad as a great achievement on the part of a dedicated apostle of temperance. The Russians did not ascribe any such sentimental notions to Witte. They assumed that he arranged the monopoly as a highly profitable means of extracting money from a nation which was drinking itself to death.

His lack of grace, his discomfort in evening clothes, and his contempt for the small-talk of the salon made him out of place in the brilliant atmosphere of the court. "Stiff and formal in his deportment, cumbersome in gait, cold in manner, unpolished in address, hard, almost clumsy, angular, slow to speak, prompt to act, he is devoid alike of physical charm and of the art of pleasing," said *The New York Times* in a profile. President Theodore Roosevelt, who met him later, found him selfish, vulgar, and a braggart.

Though it was conceded that he had a keenness of insight that bordered on prophetic vision, the court loathed Witte. In part, its anti-Semitism helped to fashion its attitude toward him. About a year after the death of his first wife, Witte met Madame Matilda Ivanova Lisanevitch, a Jewess, an actress, and the mother of a small daughter. After helping to arrange her divorce, Witte married Madame Lisanevitch, who followed him to St. Petersburg. Though conventions counted for more than morals, the court rocked with gossip about her alleged affairs. It was not until 1905, when Witte returned from the United States after the peace treaty, that she was accepted at court and society came knocking at her door.

In any event, affection was not easily conferred upon a man whose power was second only to that of the Autocrat himself. A story circulating at the time reflected the general feeling of bitterness against Witte and his financial policies and the Tsar's weakness in failing to get rid of him. The Tsar, it was said, had a strange dream about three cows, one lean, one fat, and the last stupid. No one in the court would provide him with a satisfactory interpretation of the dream, and he therefore called in Father John of Kronstadt.

"The lean cow, Your Majesty, is the Russian people," said Father John. "The fat cow is the minister of finance."

Then the priest stopped. "Go on," said the Tsar. "Who is the foolish cow?"

"Your Majesty, I dare not speak, for I fear your wrath," said Father John.

"Fear not," said the Tsar.

Reassured, Father John went on. "The foolish cow is the Tsar, our Little Father," he said.

Firmly entrenched during the latter part of the reign of Alexander III, Witte could not easily be shaken loose by Nicholas, who was learning the responsibilities of office. For his part, Witte was constantly angered by Nicholas. "Emperor Alexander III," he remarked once, "was economical and did not throw money away, but Nicholas II does not know how to count."

Despite the obvious clash in personalities and Witte's subsequent disclaimers, the two men seemed to be riding well enough in tandem at the beginning of the reign. Witte saw the Far East as the area of least resistance

[73]

and of greatest growth potential. Prudent policy, he believed, called for neutrality to guard Russia's western flank and rapid expansion in the Far East. Nicholas had similar ideas but different goals. Witte accused him of having become engaged in the Far Eastern "adventure" because of his youth, because of his natural animosity toward Japan, and, finally, because of a hidden craving for a victorious war.

Race hatred also had something to do with court attitudes toward Witte and the world at large. Nicholas despised the Japanese. He was in the habit of referring to them even in official documents as *"macoes"* (monkeys). He had a similar antipathy for the English, whom he called Jews, an epithet of considerable virulence in the anti-Semitic court. "An Englishman," he liked to repeat, "is a *zhid* (Jew)."

Religion was yet another matter on which Witte differed sharply with the court. He regarded himself as a Christian, but essentially as a tolerant one. He had little patience with the consuming devotion of the court to the Russian Orthodox Church, with its mystic rites and superstitions. Nicholas seriously believed that he had been appointed by God. Witte, who stalked past holy ikons, even in the imperial palace, regarded the Tsar as a not overly bright, very ordinary human being who resorted to underhand methods to achieve his ambitions.

Though Witte professed to see in Nicholas's personal attitude toward him nothing more than a desire to free himself from the tutelage of the entrenched and powerful officials whom he had inherited from his father's rule, the conflict went deeper than that. The Tsaritsa loathed him. Nicholas detested his vulgarity and frankness and resented the power he exercised—not only in the finance ministry but in many other ministries, also. If the Trans-Siberian Railway stirred Nicholas's dreams of empire, it also fed Witte's own ambitions. He built Dalny and squandered vast sums on it. He treated the railway and the Russo-Chinese Bank as if they were his own. Witte found Nicholas's views and attitudes unacceptable, even contemptible. Despite his early posturings as a peacemaker, Nicholas was a militant expansionist. Witte was a realist and a commercial opportunist who, while ready enough for war in 1895, knew a decade later that Japan's strength had become immeasurably greater, and he therefore opposed the war.

Among the more notable of his ministerial colleagues was Viacheslav Constantine Plehve, a former secretary of state for Finland. Plehve was reactionary, violently anti-Semitic, and devious. He became minister of the interior in 1902 after the assassination of his predecessor. His promotion was welcomed by an organization known as the "Black Hundreds," which was sponsored by the court and by other avowed Jew-haters who surrounded the Tsar. It specialized in counter-terror. Plehve believed that the Socialist movement in Russia was largely Jewish in origin and that by attacking the Jews he also attacked Socialism and the forces of revolution. He saw it as his God-given duty to destroy all three, and his police turned a blind eye to anti-Semitic acts, including violence.

He came from a noble but impoverished and largely Polish family of Lettish-Jewish origin. A Polish nobleman adopted him. Later, when Plehve was made an imperial consul in Warsaw, he demonstrated his loyalty by hunting down all those suspected of treason, including members of the family that brought him up. His foster parents were sent to Siberia. No one questioned his capacity for work, or even his courage. And Nicholas, who shared many of his views, saw him as a vital prop for the autocracy.

Witte and Plehve agreed on nothing. Witte had not an ounce of anti-Semitism in his makeup, and he constantly reproached not only Plehve but also Nicholas when the Jews were detained or became the unprotected victims of Russian violence. Witte came to believe that war with Japan was criminal stupidity. Plehve insisted that it was a necessity for domestic as well as foreign political reasons and was convinced that the Russian forces were more than adequate to cope with the Japanese.

If the Crimean War had reduced Russia's status among the powers, it also had the effect of stimulating some drastic professional reforms in the army, which had lagged far behind those of Germany, Austria, and France in professional organization. Conscription was introduced in 1874 and the chain of command simplified. The military colleges were improved and an effective reserve was created. The peasants who filled the ranks, and whose conditions of service had been deplorable, even learned to read and write at army expense. The new army had been put to the test in a war with Turkey in 1877 and had performed creditably.

Two young and notable military leaders emerged in this period, one of them General Mikhail Dimitrievitch Skobolev, who crossed the Balkans in a severe snowstorm, attacked the Turkish army, and captured 36,000 men. His most renowned effort, if that is the proper description, took place in the barren lands east of the Caspian Sea. There, in the Black Sands desert, Skobolev in the winter of 1880–1881 fell on the clay walls of the Turkoman tribal fortress of Geok-Tepe, or Green Hill. He breached the walls of the fort with an explosive charge and killed twenty thousand Turkomans, sparing only the women and children. He also set free 25,000 Persian and Russian slaves. Thousands of other slaves who had refused to embrace Islam had been either buried alive or nailed by their ears to walls where they were left to starve.

By Skobolev's side was a rapidly rising young officer named Alexei Nicolaievitch Kuropatkin. Born on March 17, 1845, the son of a provincial official, Kuropatkin owed his advance in the Russian army to his courage and charm, and his association with Skobolev, rather than brilliance or birth. After graduating from the cadet corps at the Pavlovsk War School at the age of eighteen, he was posted as a lieutenant to the First Turkestan Rifle Battalion, where he so quickly distinguished himself in action in Central Asia that he was promoted to command a company when he was still only twenty. The staff college was the next step up the ladder, and later he broadened his experience on exchange with the French Foreign Legion in Algeria, where he learned to speak French without an accent. At the age of thirty-four he became a major-general.

Sven Hedin, the great Swedish explorer, who knew both Skobolev and Kuropatkin well, described Skobolev as a man who loved war for its own sake and "greeted the stirring trumpet signal to charge as the invitation to a feast, a man, who, on his white horse and with the breast of his white uniform glittering with brilliants and decorations, loved to gallop to the front with a sublime contempt for the showers of bullets falling all around him." Kuropatkin regarded war

> entirely from its serious side, as an unavoidable evil, an art that must be studied with industry and thoroughness, leaving nothing to chance, or to the enthusiasm of the moment. Whereas Skobolev by his mere presence possessed the power to electrify his men and kindle their enthusiasm, Kuropatkin inspires his troops with a feeling of unruffled calmness, confidence, and security.

With his long background in central Asia, Kuropatkin saw the pattern of Russian expansion. Russia had begun to strengthen its Far Eastern defenses immediately after the war between China and Japan. The war had shown up the extreme political and military weaknesses of China and the power and energy of Japan—conditions that he regarded as of immense significance for Russia. He believed, with good reason, that Japan had designs on Korea and that it was in Russia's interests to thwart her, but only with the utmost caution. "Though we feel no necessity to annex the country ourselves," he wrote, "we can under no circumstances consent to the establishment in it of an energetic Japan or any other power. . . . And so, in this case, just as in Persia and North China, we must work toward gradually acquiring absolute economic control of the country."

Kuropatkin believed that circumstances were likely to force Russia into a war with Japan early in the twentieth century. Aware of the deficiences of the Trans-Siberian Railway, he warned, therefore, against the dangers of being drawn into war at a disadvantage and with insufficient troops in the Far East. After the death of Skobolev at the age of thirty-nine in 1882, Kuropatkin's rise to the preeminent post of war minister was assured. His efforts were directed against those who failed to take the extreme care he had advocated so strongly in preparing for the war, but his fate, ironically, would be to lead the Russian armies before they were ready.

When he died in 1775, Peter the Great of Russia left behind the largest fleet in the Baltic, constructed with the aid of English shipbuilders. Only in the north did Russia have a coastline, however, and Peter had to get his seamen where he could. Often the men who manned his ships were soldiers, boatmen from inland rivers, or foreign mercenaries. After his victory over the Swedes in 1771, he organized a procession through the streets of Moscow, complete with warships carried on sleds. Though the Muscovites were suitably impressed by the Tsar's display, they were still not anxious to man these monsters and take them to sea.

The navy, like the army, had been reorganized, but in 1904 it was still a motley collection of ships. As president of the Admiralty, Grand Duke Alexis had under him Admiral Fyodr Karlovitch Avellan, the navy minister, and ten admirals, twenty-eight vice-admirals, thirty-seven rear-admirals, and thirty-five senior staff officers. Admiral Avellan had been a seagoing admiral, but he was no strategist. Rear-Admiral Zinovi Petrovitch Rozhdestvenski, chief of the naval general staff, who saw service first in the Russo-Turkish War in 1877–1878 and had helped subsequently to refurbish the Bulgarian navy, was the closest thing to an organizer. Until transition from sail to steam had brought a new class of officer into the ward rooms —the engineer, in the eyes of fellow officers, ranked no better than a train driver—the navy had been more of a social gathering than an armed force. Princes and counts predominated in high places, and with one notable exception—the Grand Duke Alexander Mikhailovitch, who had warned Nicholas strongly against risking war—were not notable for their seafaring knowledge.

By 1902 the special sections of the naval general staff charged with contingency planning for war had not even been organized, nor was there a naval operations section at the time. It was formed only in 1903 and concerned itself initially with the Baltic, not the Far East.

The situation was even worse below decks. Conscription applied to recruitment for both the army and the navy. At first the navy had taken its recruits only from the maritime provinces; now it took them from all parts of Russia, and peasants who had never seen a ship suddenly found themselves at sea. Pay was poor and conditions of service worse. The Baltic and Black Sea fleets were in commission for only six months in the year. Promotions were slow and the inadequate number of junior officers badly trained. Often midshipmen were left in charge of hundreds of sailors in the naval depots, with chaotic results.

The most distinguished Russian sailor was also one of the few who had risen from the ranks—Vice-Admiral Stephen Ossipovitch Makarov. The sea was in his blood. His grandfathers had been noncommissioned officers, both serving for twenty-five years, then the required period of military service. Young Makarov went to naval school in Siberia when he was ten and quickly showed promise. He was an impressive-looking man, with a bald head and a long, blond beard hanging to his chest. Known in the navy as "Little Grandfather" or "Beardy," and uninterested in politics, he was worshiped by the men but was unpopular with a number of fellow officers. "Those who have political ambitions can never hope to become good soldiers," he wrote. "Let men give up their swords first if they will ape statesmen. It is a regrettable thing for the country that men half-statesmen and half-soldiers should hold sway." Makarov rose on ability and courage. In the Russo-Turkish War in 1877–1878 he led four torpedo boats into the Bay of Batum on the Black Sea in an attack against the Turkish fleet. Since the torpedoes were attached underneath the boats and had to be released at close range, Makarov's feat won wide applause and he became a hero of the day. Naval historian F. T. Jane wrote:

> They [the Russians] had no fleet to start with, and they used an almost unknown weapon. We cannot judge Makarov's exploits by the light of present-day knowledge; he had to invent his tactics. . . . Nor, because their loss of life was small and insignificant, can this be held to detract from the individual bravery of the Russian torpedoists; on going into action there were absolutely no reasonable prospects of such an extraordinary survival.

Thereafter, Makarov made a study of the torpedo as an naval weapon. He also invented an armor-piercing shell and developed a cofferdam (or drydock) for repairing damaged ships. His book *Sea Warfare* was used everywhere by naval officers, including Vice-Admiral Togo, who had it translated into Japanese during his time as director of the naval college. Though Togo rarely mentioned the book to his officers, he had it beside his bunk during long spells at sea and read it frequently.

As tensions rose between Russia and Japan, Nicholas listened less and less to the advice given him by Witte and Kuropatkin and more and more to Plehve and others, including the three more senior of his uncles, Grand Duke Vladimir, commander of the Imperial Guard; Grand Duke Alexis, grand admiral and commander-in-chief of the Russian Navy, who knew more about boudoirs than battleships; and the bitterly reactionary Grand Duke Serge, governor-general of Moscow, who rode roughshod over the students, the men of commerce, and the Jews.

The quite rapid economic development in Russia during the last decade

[78]

of the nineteenth century had been accompanied by increasing industrial discontent among the three million factory workers during the depression of 1899–1903. Plehve in the interior ministry attempted to cope with this by a rapid expansion of the Okhrana, the secret police. Both the workers and the students had become more active. A nationwide students' strike in 1899 led to the conscription of striking students and this, in turn, to a renewed wave of violence and assassination.

Finland was also in an uproar. It had come under Russian domination in 1809, with the status of an independent grand duchy that enjoyed at first a considerable degree of autonomy. This state of affairs continued until the rule of Alexander III, who set out to qualify its independence with the ultimate goal of absorbing it within the Russian empire as a province. Nicholas continued where his father left off. His appointment of General Nikolai Ivanovitch Bobrikov as governor-general in 1898 provoked a storm of protest, in which his mother privately joined and which was soon to be repeated when Bobrikov began to take full power into his own hands.

"My dearest Nicky," Marie wrote from Denmark on October 1, 1902,

> It is a complete puzzle to me how you, my dear good Nicky, whose sense of fairness has always been so strong, now choose to be guided and deceived by a liar like Bobrikov! And my disappointment is all the stronger for the fact that when we discussed the subject last—it was in March in your study in the Winter Palace—you promised me to write to him yourself and to restrain his too great zeal: you must remember this—I even got up to thank you for that promise with a kiss. But since then he came to Petersburg himself and succeeded in changing your ideas completely. You have repeatedly made it clear that your firm intention was to change nothing in that country—and now just the opposite is happening! There, where things had always gone well, where the people were perfectly happy and contented, now everything is broken up, everything is changed, disorder and hatred sown—and all in the name of so-called Patriotism! What a perfect example of the meaning of that word! All that is being done in Finland is based on lies and deceit and leads straight to revolution. . . . Do believe me and dismiss Bobrikov, that evil genius. . . .

Nicholas insisted on putting his priorities in their proper order. He replied on October 20 that he had just suffered a heavy personal grief,

> the loss of dear old Iman [his dog]—it happened right at the beginning of October, almost on the same day as with poor Raven. He had been ailing ever since summer and on arriving here I had the veterinary to attend to him. He was isolated and living in the basement. The sores on his body were healing rapidly, but one day his strength began to fail

and he died in the night. I must confess the whole day after it happened
I never stopped crying—I still miss him dreadfully when I go for walks.
He was such an intelligent, kind, and loyal dog.

Bobrikov quickly killed whatever loyalty there might have been in Finland, first of all by ordering all Finns to submit to five years' military service
and then by introducing measures designed to reduce the status of the
country to that of a Russian province. Nicholas blindly ignored Marie's
advice, and the situation continued to deteriorate.

It grew worse at home, also. Most Russians, regardless of class, were
frustrated with the social injustice and the poverty that weighed so heavily
on the people. The intelligentsia resented the backwardness of the state and
its divorce from liberal developments in Europe. Many opposed the system,
and few, including those who worked within it, were ready to spring to its
defense. The climate was tailor-made for revolution.

By 1904, the revolutionary thrust came largely from the Russian Social
Democratic Labor party with its two wings, the Mensheviks, who were
reconciled to a long period of bourgeois democracy and were contemptuous
of the role the peasants might play, and the more revolutionary Bolsheviks,
who broke away under the leadership of Lenin at a conference in London
in 1903. Both were Marxist and both had their origins in the League of
Combat for the Liberation of the Working Class, of which Lenin had been
a leader since 1895.

A second party, the Socialist Revolutionary party, was the descendant of
the People's Will, which organized the assassination of Alexander II and
was firmly committed to achieve its ends by similarly violent means. Its
militant arm was the Battle Organization, led by Evno Azev, one of the
most unsavory double agents in history. The son of a poor tailor, Azev
financed himself through engineering school in Germany by reporting on
the political activities of his fellow Russian students to the Okhrana. A
founder member of the Socialist Revolutionary party, he was physically
repellent, with a fat, sweaty body, thick lips, and dark, brooding eyes.
Despite his appearance, he had an immense following among the students,
who regarded him as dedicated to the revolution. Azev, whose infiltration
into the ranks of the terrorists had been approved by Plehve himself, pleased
the police no less with his services. In more than fifteen years as a double
agent, he sent scores of his revolutionary colleagues to death, imprisonment,
or exile, at the same time conducting the affairs of his terrorist organization
with immense skill, daring, and profit, and, as events were to prove, with
considerable impact on Russia's future.

CHAPTER 4

眾眾眾眾眾眾

Korea, the Cockpit

GENERAL DOUGLAS MACARTHUR, his peaked cap shading his eyes, stands in bronze on a hilltop overlooking the Korean port of Inchon or, as it used to be called, Chemulpo. He is martial, grand, and many times larger than life. He ought to last there forever, the imperishable guardian over this little port that has seen so many historic invasions, including his own. Inchon is truly the proper place for the statue, for it was here that MacArthur's military genius fulfilled itself for the last time. And it was here, also, in two earlier conflicts—the Sino-Japanese War in 1894–1895 and the Russo-Japanese War in 1904–1905—that the last war he fought had its genesis.

The route from Seoul to Inchon passes along new highways and through old lanes. It begins among the tiny gray houses with tip-tilted eaves, clinging together, insanitary and stifling, and crawling up the stark hills with not a foot between them. It moves through new developmental areas, with their small but neat houses, red, blue, green, and yellow tiles gleaming, like toy cottages in a child's play set, and on into the traditional countryside, where peasants with A-frames on their backs bend, like their oxen and their miniature ponies, under impossible loads. The new and the old intermingle in the shadow of MacArthur's statue above the nearby waters of the harbor, where the Japanese landed their troops when they went to war with China and again when they fought the Russians. It was here that a Japanese squadron attacked two Russian ships in the first hours of the Russo-Japanese War. And just a few miles away Togo Heihachiro fired the first shot in the war against China.

There were many reasons why the Japanese went to war with the Russians, but Korea ranked highest on the list. To the Chinese, this grim peninsula was for centuries a vassal state. To the Russians, it represented the warm-water ports they coveted. For the Japanese, however, it was a dagger pointing at their underbelly. Let it fall into hostile hands, they believed, and their security would be gravely imperiled. Kublai Khan leaped from its southern shores in an attempt to invade Japan in the thirteenth century. It needed a divine wind to hurl him back. With the coming of the nineteenth century, the Japanese were no longer willing to rely on the wind but preferred the force of arms. For thirty years the struggle and the intrigue went on. It was marked by murder, violence, and duplicity that centered on the palace in Seoul and, in particular, around the person of Queen Min Chii-rok.

Like the Japanese, the Koreans bitterly resisted the efforts that were made to open their doors to trade. Lacking more effective weapons, they threw dust in the eyes of unwelcome Americans who tried to force their way in. Missionaries came by the score—and were summarily decapitated on the executioner's block. At first the Russians and the French were pushed away; the Japanese broke in. After them came the Russians again, and for the next thirty years Korea was a cockpit where the Chinese, the Japanese, and the Russians fought for advantage in the medieval court, a battle in caricature that was twice to erupt in full-scale war.

During its own long period of isolation, Korea had maintained a nodding acquaintance with the Tokugawa shogunate through the *daimyō* of Tsushima. Goods continued to be exchanged from the island of Tsushima through the Korean port of Fusan, now known as Pusan, and it had been customary for the court in Seoul to send an embassy to convey its goodwill and congratulations on the accession of a new shogun in Japan. The Treaty of Peking in 1860, under which the Chinese ceded large stretches of territory to St. Petersburg, brought the Russians to the Korean back door. This, the infuriating behavior of the Christians and their western backers, Japan's apparent spinelessness in acceding to foreign pressure and Korea's own seeming success in dealing with the French and the Americans in the face of their gunboat diplomacy, encouraged the Koreans to resist any further attempts by the barbarians to intrude into the "Hermit Kingdom."

Abandoning their historic diplomatic courtesy in 1868, the Koreans snubbed the restoration ceremonies in Tokyo. Instead of an ambassador bearing gifts, they sent a letter accusing Japan of trucking with the barbarians. The message, though a long-kept secret in Tokyo, was finally made public and served to increase the aggressiveness of the martial Satsuma clan, who were thirsting for war.

To find a means of occupying the Satsuma samurai, who were now penniless and unemployed, and to punish those responsible for eating Japanese castaways on the Ryukyu Islands, the Tokyo government in 1874 had sent a military expedition from Satsuma to Formosa. Fearing the intervention by European powers, China decided against meeting the Japanese expedition with force. As a consequence, this little martial expedition by Japan succeeded in exacting an indemnity of 500,000 of the then highly regarded Mexican dollars from Peking and tacit recognition of Japan's claims to the Ryukyus, the long chain of islands south of Japan, including Okinawa, which China also claimed as a tribute state, in exchange for the recognition of Formosa as part of the Middle Kingdom.

Pleased with the success of this expedition, some Japanese led by Saigo Takamori, the great Satsuma leader, now saw in the insulting communications from Seoul the prospect of a war with Korea and the chance of preserving the samurai as the backbone of Japan's new fighting force. They favored immediate military action. Others counseled restraint, arguing that it would be too dangerous to go to war before Japan had accustomed itself to the restoration. For the time being, the peace makers prevailed and continued their fruitless and frustrating attempts to expand the Tsushima trade and their base of operations in Fusan. The Koreans stalled. Every question had to be referred back to Seoul for decision. Answers took weeks and even months to arrive, and in the meantime Japanese living at Fusan were molested and abused.

Tokyo bided its time. In 1875, when the fort batteries at the mouth of the River Han near Seoul opened fire on a survey boat, the Japanese sent a landing party ashore, captured the forts and used the action as a pretext for opening negotiations with Seoul.

This time the Japanese were better briefed on the Perry techniques than an American mission that had preceded them. Their negotiators, including Count Inoue, had called for every available report on the Perry mission and were prepared not merely to follow his example but to back their words with substantial force. They anchored off Seoul with two men-of-war and three transports loaded with troops. In the Treaty of Kangwha, which was signed on February 26, 1876, Japan got trading concessions and extraterritorial rights for all Japanese living in Korea. No less important for the future was the Japanese interpretation of the Korean signature as a signal of Korean independence from China, though this remained an issue that continued to generate heat until the Sino-Japanese war in 1894–1895.

Japanese interest in Korea stimulated deeper Russian interest. Following their withdrawal from the island of Tsushima under English pressure in 1861, the Russians in 1866 had arrived at the port of Wonsan off the northeast coast in a gunboat with demands for commercial privileges and the threat of military action if these were not granted. As usual, the Koreans pleaded the excuse that Korea was only a tributary state of China and that this was therefore a matter for Peking to decide. The Russians withdrew.

They were back knocking at the door in 1880, and again in 1885, when they attempted to negotiate for Port Lazarev, near Wonsan. This time the British moved to deny the Russians their warm-water port, seizing Port Hamilton, a small island on the southern approaches to the Straits of Tsushima, where they would be in a position to interfere with ships going to Vladivostok. Unwilling to press for negotiations in the face of British opposition, the Russians withdrew, announcing their intention never to occupy Korean territory under any circumstances whatever.

Russia, not Japan, was China's greatest concern. Believing that Korea, by entering into treaty arrangements with all Western powers, would help to keep the Russians at bay, Li Hung-chang, the Viceroy, or governor-general, of Chih-li, the province surrounding Peking and Tientsin, advised King Yi Kojong to open his doors. The United States, with the good offices of Viceroy Li, signed a treaty of amity with Korea in 1882. England and Germany signed treaties in 1883, Italy and Russia in 1884, and France in 1886. At the same time, China used its resident minister in Seoul, Yuan Shih-k'ai, to reestablish Peking's predominant position in the affairs of the Korean government.

There now began a period of cloak-and-dagger conspiracy within the ancient walls of the stark and forbidding city of Seoul. One of the characters in a short story by the gifted modern Korean novelist, Hahn Moo-Sook, looks across the drab, gray roofs of Seoul and concludes that they are scabs formed over innumerable boils—take the scabs off and bloody pus will gush out! It was an illusion that many others must have shared eighty years ago. Open sewers ran through the city's maze of narrow lanes, producing some of Asia's most powerful smells. In summer, the city stifled with heat. In winter, lack of fuel kept most houses bitterly cold. On autumn nights, tigers prowled the streets. Law and order were maintained at night by segregating the sexes when they appeared on the streets. An immense bronze bell sounded the first curfew for all male inhabitants except blind men, officials, foreigners' servants, and persons carrying prescriptions to druggists. The massive gates in the city walls closed and only women, heavily veiled lest their faces be seen by any of the men legally permitted on the streets, were allowed abroad. At midnight, the bronze bell tolled again. The women returned to their homes and the men were allowed out. No one could enter or leave the city at night without royal decree. The penalty for scaling the walls was death by public decapitation, the standard punishment for many offenses. Slavery and torture were approved by law. To obtain confessions, prisoners were beaten with huge paddles, which were so heavy that their victims' bones were often broken, leaving them crippled for life.

To this capital in the mid-1880s, diplomats, advisers, traders, and missionaries made their way. Emaciated prisoners chained by the neck and lashed by their guards with the cat-o'-nine-tails were often seen on the streets. Missionaries' wives, armed with pins, took part in another form of assault, endeavoring with the highest moral rectitude (and scant success) to persuade the Korean women to cover up their breasts as they went about their way.

The law was no less harsh in its treatment of women than of men, except that instead of a humiliating and public death by the ax they were allowed to take poison in private. Since the poison was often made from the juice of boiled centipedes, a concoction that caused the most agonizing death, privacy was not without its penalties.

Korean folklore is rich in tales of young Korean girls who suffered death, and a fate worse than death, to kill Toyotomi Hideyoshi's Japanese invaders, whose barbarism inflamed such hatred among the Koreans that it was to be recalled in vivid detail three centuries later when the Japanese returned to complete their unfinished business.

Hideyoshi's ambition was to conquer China as well as Korea and to embrace the whole world in one family under one roof. "The earth," he said, "is the earth's earth." Japan was, of course, the earth. In 1592 he sent an armada of 3,000 to 4,000 boats and an army of 250,000 men to invade Korea, a country as sweet and lovely, he believed, as the face of a young virgin, dazzling bright with gold, silver, and fine colors and rich in every kind of treasure. The governor of Pusan, hunting in the early morning, looked out and saw hundreds of boats approaching. Hideyoshi had arrived to take Korea. "I shall do it," he boasted, "as easily as a man rolls up a mat and puts it under his arm."

The Japanese held Scoul for seven years. In one battle ten thousand Koreans, their bows and arrows unable to cope with the Japanese muskets, lost their lives. The Japanese cut off the ears of the dead, preserved them in saké, and sent them back to Japan. On land Hideyoshi was victorious, but on the sea the results were different. The inventor of an armored ship, possibly the world's first, Admiral Yi Sun Sin caused havoc among the Japanese ships and their lines of supply. His boat looked like a giant tortoise and was, in fact, called *kwi-sun,* or tortoise boat. Its curved deck of iron plates sheltered the bowmen and oarsmen beneath. Sharp metal spikes covered the back to discourage boarding parties. Since the deck was of iron, it was resistant to fire arrows, a much-used Japanese weapon. It had six cannon on each side, two in the tail and two in the mouth of the enormous, crested head. No men appeared on the decks, and all the guns and arrows were fired from below the armored superstructure. The "tortoise boat" also had the advantage, despite its weight, of being faster than the Japanese boats. Since it could be rowed to go either forwards or backwards, it could also be used very effectively to ram the Japanese boats. The Japanese lost more than seventy boats in one battle and with them the command of the sea and their vital supply line with Japan. Now, three centuries later, they were to make their next effort.

By insinuating themselves into the twisted threads of the declining Yi dynasty, the Japanese set out to destroy first of all the tributary links between China and Korea. The dynasty was founded in 1392 by General Yi Sungke, and, while paying tribute to China, exercised absolute power within Korea, unfettered by any equivalent of the *daimyō* in Japan. The ginseng crop, Korea's most important export, and the Orient's most treasured aphrodisiac, was worth its weight in gold in Peking and five times its weight in silver. Its sales filled the royal purse. In principle, the government was a benevolent autocracy, but the system was neither efficient nor just. The majority lived in grinding poverty. Treachery, murder, corruption, and intrigue were characteristic of the court where Yi Ha-eung, who had ruled as regent when his twelve-year-old son ascended the throne in 1863, with the title of Prince Taewongun, the "Lord of the Great Court," fought an interminable battle with his daughter-in-law, Queen Min.

History has few more remarkable characters than the Queen. Wedded at fourteen to King Yi Kojong, she died hideously at the age of forty-six after a lifetime filled with bloodshed. Attractive and gifted, she marshaled the power that stripped her father-in-law of his authority when the King was crowned in 1873. With cunning and with skill, she tried to steer her ill-fated country through the treacherous waters of nineteenth-century diplomacy.

Confident that his powers were more than a match for the young Queen if he could only free her from parental influence, Prince Taewongun sent a bomb handsomely wrapped in a lacquer box to the Queen's family. Her father and other members of the family were blown to bits. Thereafter, the war between the Queen and her father-in-law was to the death. Once, when he imprudently attempted to seize power again and had the temerity to claim the right to use the royal entrance into the palace, she showed her authority by festooning the gate with the heads of a score of his followers.

Men and women were both deeply attracted by her. Hundreds, perhaps thousands, died by her command. A biased observer of the scene quotes a member of the court who professed to be able to count 2,867 other deaths which were directly attributable to her orders.

She was ephemeral, elusive, conspiratorial, and quick to strike. Sometimes the Japanese or the Chinese thought she was theirs. They were wrong. Despite her cruelties, which were an accepted part of a court at which kings killed their own sons, and concubines knew that a cup of poison might be the reward for a poor performance in bed, the Queen fought to preserve what she thought to be Korea's national interests. And in pursuit of her goals, she used the Japanese, the Americans, the Chinese, and the British. Her bereaved husband later tried to use the Russians—but by then it was too late. Japan had won the day.

By the beginning of the 1880s the struggle for power in Korea was no longer simply a domestic issue within the court. It had taken on much broader political and international aspects, though it polarized around two groups: the conservatives led by the Taewongun, who were opposed to the opening up of Korea, and the progressives, with whom the Queen was identified, who favored establishing relations with other powers.

In the early spring of 1882 a Japanese military instructor arrived at Seoul and began to train Korean troops in modern techniques. His arrival also coincided with the appointment of P. G. von Moellendorf, a German citizen and an employee of the Chinese Maritime Customs, whose task was to integrate the Korean customs service with that of China and to act as principal adviser to the Korean foreign office, which had just been created. This renewed foreign intrusion, and the newly signed treaty with the United States served the Taewongun's ends. He used it to arouse feeling in Seoul against the foreigners, linking their reception by the court with the acute shortage of food caused by the drought and the shortage of pay for the Korean troops.

The Taewongun's family, which controlled a substantial section of the forces in Seoul, accused the Min family of stealing both rice and the army payroll. On July 23, 1882, the crisis broke. Troops, assisted by the hungry population, rioted and sacked the rice granaries. Next morning, urged on by the Taewongun, they also attacked the royal palace and the barracks, where the Japanese were training their selected force of Korean soldiers. They next turned their attention to the Japanese legation, which they reached just after six o'clock, and began to attack it with stones. Later, they set fire to the neighboring wooden houses. With the Japanese flag held high, the minister and his entourage flung open the front door of the legation. Guns blazing, they killed about twenty men and made their escape to Chemulpo. Here they were again attacked, and four policemen and several other members of the party were either killed or wounded in the melee.

Hanabusa Yoshimoto, the resident Japanese minister, had been one of the first Japanese to enter into serious negotiations with the Koreans on behalf of the Meiji government in Japan. Early in the 1870s he had even managed to have himself invited to stay at the palace and had remained there as a guest for several months. He knew the Queen well, entertaining her with a toy telephone and other western curiosities. On the afternoon of the riot he received a few minutes' warning of the impending attack. It said simply: "In great hurry, cannot write long. A band of riotous people with soldiers on their side seem to be intending attack upon your legation. Be prepared for defense, and, should they come to actual attack, will it not be better for you to get out of danger even by the use of arms?"

The arrival of Japanese officers and students living in Chemulpo saved the minister. They found him a small junk and in this he set out in the hope of attracting the attention of a friendly vessel. On the evening of the twenty-sixth he was picked up by an English survey ship, the *Flying Fish,* and taken to Nagasaki.

That night the palace guard, armed with spears and matchlocks and wearing coats of mail, were thrust aside by the mob. Before dawn four of the King's Council were dead, and the Queen had fled for her life. The mob thought that they had found her, nevertheless. Instead, one of the serving maids, dressed in the robes of the Queen, had taken a cup of poison and lay dead in the private apartments, while the Queen herself fled into hiding.

The triumphal return of the Taewongun ended the mob rule, but not before 300 liberals had been killed and their homes burned. The Queen's death was proclaimed, the court went into mourning, and the Taewongun assumed full powers. He did not hold them for long. Two members of the royal entourage were visiting China and appealed for assistance. Land and sea forces were quickly on their way. Six gunboats and two transports with picked troops under the command of Li Hung-chang arrived at Chemulpo and kidnaped the Taewongun, shipping him off to China. In the streets of Seoul placards appeared proclaiming that Korea was a tributary of China.

The Japanese minister arrived back in Seoul on August 16, accompanied by an armed escort of 800 men, with an additional 1,500 to follow. A Japanese landing party, including Lieutenant-Commander Togo Heiha-chiro, now captain of the cruiser *Amagi,* marched on Seoul to support Hanabusa when he presented his ultimatum: 500,000 yen to Japan, a new legation, the dispatch of an embassy to Japan to make formal apologies, the right to station troops in Korea to protect the legation, and the extension of Japanese rights in Korea to trade and travel.

Through the long hot summer and into the early winter, Togo and the *Amagi* remained in Korea. Here Togo met Yuan Shih-k'ai, finding him pompous and dogmatic as he lectured him for two hours about the need for Sino-Japanese cooperation.

"I don't understand you," said Togo when Yuan had finished his monologue. Yuan's impressions of Togo are not recorded.

With the kidnapping of the Taewongun, Queen Min emerged from hiding.

Back again in the palace, she now strongly opposed the Japanese. The Chinese built a fort close to the palace gates and two others outside the city walls to command the approaches along the Han River.

With Yuan Shih-k'ai's weight and influence added to that of the palace, the struggle between the conservatives and progressives changed form and in the process became sharper than ever. Promulgation of new regulations on trade between China and Korea gave the Chinese favored-nation advantages over other foreigners on the basis that Korea was a tributary state. Moellendorf even suggested inviting Russia to send instructors to train the Korean army and to grant it the ice-free port of Lazarev, which it had long coveted. Chinese arms came across the Yalu River for the Korean military forces, and Chinese traders flocked into Seoul. The influence of Yuan Shih-k'ai continued to grow.

Still, Li Hung-chang's hopes of building up a sufficient military force to resist the Japanese received a heavy setback, this time at the hands of the French, who were busy annexing Annam, which Peking regarded as a tribute state in Indochina. His fleet of steamships lay at anchor in Foochow. Alongside, fresh from flying their flags in honor of the Chinese Emperor's birthday, were eight French ships. At 2 P.M. on August 23 the French ships, without bothering to declare war and as a warning to the Chinese to stay out of Indo-China, opened fire and the entire Chinese fleet went to the bottom of the river. By treaty in the following year the French extended their influence to embrace all of Indochina and Chinese suzerainty over Annam (Central Vietnam) came to an end.

This demonstration of China's weakness stimulated the Japanese and their Korean friends to take new initiatives. At a dinner at the Japanese legation on November 3, at which most of the diplomatic community, including the British, American, and Chinese consuls were present, Japanese speakers denounced the Sino-Korean relationship and ridiculed the Chinese consul, who, since he knew no Japanese, listened politely and applauded with the rest. The following day the Korean government agreed to permit the Japanese to trade in Seoul on equal terms with the Chinese.

Chinese troops in Seoul were placed in a state of alert. The Japanese replied by conducting firing practice outside the walls of the palace. A new plot was in the making, and the Japanese were in the thick of it. Since all the leading members of the conservative party were high officials, the plotters decided to set fire to one of the detached palace buildings while their assassins went to work. The occasion selected was the opening of the post office, which was to be celebrated by a state banquet attended by the diplomatic corps and leading members of the conservative and pro-Chinese faction.

According to a Japanese version, both the King and Queen had been persuaded that there was no future in the relationship with China. One of the leading plotters claimed to have discussed the affair in detail with the King and Queen and to have received a secret order, written, signed, and

[89]

sealed by the King himself, to carry out the plot. In the light of subsequent events, the claim seems implausible. The plot nevertheless worked well—up to a point. The guests in their national costumes had just left their places at the dinner table when the fire broke out. The finance minister, ostensibly a member of the progressive and pro-Japanese faction, was assassinated in the first moments of the coup. Other members of the same faction immediately went to the palace. Here, the King, under duress, sought Japanese protection, and a mixed Japanese and Korean force took possession of the palace. One by one messengers were sent in the King's name to his ministers. While the Japanese troops held the palace against possible attack, the assassins killed each minister as he arrived.

The first and only mail received through the post office was delivered on December 6. The following day the post office was burnt down and no foreign mail was handled again in Korea for the next sixteen years.

The speed of the coup took the Chinese by surprise. By morning a new pro-Japanese government had been sworn in, and the King, in the presence of the Japanese minister, received Lucius H. Foote, the U.S. minister and the British consul-general in the baroque and galleried audience hall, with its golden dragons surrounded by clouds and flames. The King appeared relaxed and spoke of the need for *coups d'etat* in nations undertaking a thoroughgoing reform. Lucius Foote expressed his agreement. By nightfall Korea had declared its independence of China, abolished the court officers, and concentrated all financial affairs in the hands of the new finance minister, a Japanese nominee.

The heavy hand of the Japanese had been too openly revealed, however, and some of the progressives and pro-Japanese switched to the conservative and pro-Chinese camp. At 3 P.M. ON December 6 fighting broke out as a force of 5,000 Korean and Chinese soldiers under Yuan Shih-k'ai converged on the palace. The action began when Chinese troops broke through one of the palace gates. Though the Japanese detonated a mine which killed ninety Chinese soldiers, the palace guards defected, and the tide of battle quickly changed. The Japanese company of 140 Japanese soldiers and their minister fought their way to the Japanese legation and on to Chemulpo, accompanied by most of the newly appointed progressive officials. That night the Japanese legation was burned down, and the homes of several westerners were looted. The British, American, and German diplomatic representatives retired to Chemulpo, where they were joined by a large party of Japanese who had sought safety at the American legation.

Within forty-eight hours the city was again in the hands of the conservatives. They burned down the homes of the progressives and rounded up all remaining pro-Japanese groups, disposing of them either by poison, decapitation, or strangulation. According to Korean law, those summarily disposed of in this way included the wives and children of the conspirators. Many of the bodies were left in the streets for the dogs to eat.

A high level Japanese delegation led by Count Inoue and including senior army and navy officers, 2,500 troops, and several warships arrived at Chemulpo at the end of December 1885. Their arrival coincided with the arrival of 3,000 Chinese reinforcements and Yuan Shih-k'ai, who was immediately visited by the King. Neither side was ready for a showdown. Count Inoue's primary concern was to absolve the minister from any suggestion of guilt of the murder of the Korean ministers in the palace on the night of December 4. The Chinese, from their position of strength, were willing mediators —provided, of course, that their own special status was not jeopardized. Inoue settled for the usual mission of apology to Tokyo, an indemnity of 110,000 yen for the Japanese killed, another 20,000 yen to rebuild the Japanese legation, and a new barracks for Japanese soldiers. The two parties also agreed to the ceremonial execution of the Koreans responsible for the death of a Japanese officer who had been traveling in the interior. Negotiations in China between the representatives of the Chinese and Japanese governments also took some of the heat out of the situation. Ito Hirobumi met with Viceroy Li Hung-chang. Both sides agreed to withdraw their troops on the understanding that, provided they informed each other before sending them, they should have the right to station forces in Korea.

Ito felt Japan was not yet sufficiently modernized to risk war with China, and that any decision to embark on war would play into Russia's hands. He believed, also, that there was no cause for haste, since, in any event, Japan would become more quickly modernized than China. After six sittings, the negotiations ended with the signing of the Treaty of Tientsin on April 18, 1885. China had not renounced its suzerainty over Korea, but Japan, having obtained recognition that it was on the same footing as China, appeared to have made a substantial advance.

Any concessions that the Japanese had won through the treaty were quickly neutralized by Yuan Shih-k'ai, however. As Chinese pro-consul in Seoul he claimed the right to be carried in his palanquin to the audience hall and to be seated in the presence of the King. To their undisguised rage, other envoys were required to walk and stand. Yuan ran the government. He insisted on the dismissal of all advisers friendly to the Japanese and even threatened to depose the King unless he blocked Russian proposals to open inland trade with Korea, thus putting the final veto to Moellendorf's earlier proposition that Russian military instructors should be hired to train the Korean army and that Russia should be granted the ice-free port it sought at Port Lazarev.

Frictions continued between Seoul and Tokyo. There were disputes over Korea's decision to prohibit the sale of rice to Japan and over the linking of Seoul and Peking by telegraph in violation of a secret agreement that the Tokyo link would be Korea's sole means of international telegraphic communication for twenty years. Japan's willingness to grant asylum to members of the progressive Korean faction who had fled after the 1884 *coup d'etat* also led to angry exchanges. Japan rejected Korean demands for the exiles' extradition, and Korean assassins in the pay of the government in Seoul made their way to Japan, where their presence and plans, some of which were made public, exacerbated the tensions.

In pursuit of exploitable opportunities for the Korean intrigues, the Japanese were helped by one of those quasi-religious, quasi-shamanistic groups that so often sprang up in and on the peripheries of Chinese society —the Tong Hak party, or Society of Eastern Learning. Founded in the 1850s, the Tong Haks, who claimed to be able to cure all forms of sickness, practiced secret rites in the hills. They also addressed themselves to rural grievances, which were valid and manifold. Toyama's Black Ocean Society made contact with the Tong Haks, equipping them with funds, stimulating their xenophobia, and providing much of the intelligence on which the Japanese military based their operations when war finally broke out.*

The Tong Haks were both a vehicle and an excuse for intervention. Though they were receiving funds from the Black Ocean Society, much of their xenophobia appeared to be directed against the Americans, the Europeans, and the Japanese. The Americans and the Europeans were accused of stealing Korean children and boiling them for food, and their access to milk gave rise to a story that they cut off the breasts of Korean women to obtain their supplies of this delicacy. Only a royal proclamation that the milk came in condensed form prevented an uprising.

Later, there were threats to drive out the Japanese. Abusive placards appeared on American and Japanese homes, and plans were announced to march on Seoul. The crisis reached its peak in June 1894. On June 1 the Tong Haks routed the royal forces. Though the royal troops recovered the ground they had lost two days later, the King, on the advice of Yuan Shih-k'ai, had already turned to China for assistance. Chinese troops moved toward the Yalu River, and warships and transports arrived at Chemulpo. At the same time, Peking, in fulfillment of its agreement, advised Tokyo of its action.

Imprudently, it also referred to Korea as a tributary state, as a protectorate, and as a dependency. The Japanese government replied that it did not

---

*Some Japanese historians deny any connection between the Tong Haks and the Genyōsha, attributing the idea to propaganda of the Black Dragon Society.

recognize China's suzerainty over Korea, and, having already mobilized three divisions, immediately embarked a force to land at Chemulpo. Thus, while two thousand Chinese troops were marching on June 8 to Asan, forty miles south of Seoul, to put down the Tong Hak uprising, Japanese marines, with heavy reinforcements to follow, were about to take possession of Seoul and to launch the war with China.

Following the combat and routing of Chinese troops, the Japanese turned their full attention to Korea. They carried their reforms to all parts of the land, its customs, and its institutions, including the royal seraglio. With meticulous attention to detail and a prudery that won the approval of the missionaries' wives, they set out to correct the modes and morals of the land. After spending a month as Japanese prisoners, the King and Queen were released on condition that they grant the constitutional and other reforms demanded by their uninvited guests. The renunciation of Chinese suzerainty was at the head of the list. But no matter was too important, or too trivial, to escape the attentions of the "dwarfs."* The King lost his autocratic power. Queen Min's family was purged from all offices of state. Even the wearing of topknots was banned. Japanese troops armed with scissors at the city gates cut the locks of all male Koreans, causing an uproar since the topknot, a tight bunch of hair kept in place by string and surmounted by a tall gauze hat, was regarded as a symbol of manhood.

To complete his humiliation the Japanese insisted on the King proceeding to the Altar of Spirits of the Land, there to proclaim the country's independence from China and to swear before the spirits of his ancestors to make the required reforms. He resisted to the last. Seoul fasted and went into mourning before he finally bowed to Japanese pressure, abandoned his stately palanquin and its thirty-two bearers, and emerged from the gates of the palace carried in a plain wooden sedan chair. It was a sad procession. Scarlet- and blue-robed men in hats that looked like dunces' caps carried huge flags on trident-headed poles. Behind them came the King's personal servants clad in yellow, and the unhappy King escorted by all the Japanese functionaries on gayly caparisoned ponies.

With the King's surrender, the Japanese demanded concessions designed to give them a monopoly of trade and industry. Queen Min did not give in.

---

*The term "dwarf" or "midget" translates the Chinese word *"wa"* or *"wai,"* by which Japan was known in the fourth century. It had its origins in two Chinese myths about how Japan came to be populated. The first myth was that a boatload of children were wrecked on the unpopulated shores of Japan and founded the Japanese race, which remained small in stature, and the second that the wrecked ship contained a cargo of monkeys.

[93]

Soon after the withdrawal of Count Inoue as resident minister and his replacement by Lieutenant-General Miura Goro, she succeeded in dismissing some of the functionaries appointed by the Japanese.

General Miura was a soldier who believed in action, and he was ready to listen to the entreaties of Sugimura Fukashi, the first secretary, who had been plotting with the Taewongun to get rid of the Queen. He ordered the Japanese troops outside the palace gates to force an entry for ten Japanese dressed in uniforms taken from captured Seoul policemen. The Queen, code-named "Fox," was to be dealt with "as exigency might require." Since for all effective purposes, the palace was guarded on October 8, 1895, the date set for the coup, only by Japanese or by unarmed trusties, the operation went smoothly.

There was to be no escape this time for the Queen. The Crown Prince caught a glimpse of her running down a corridor followed by a Japanese soldier. The minister of the royal household tried to protect her by thrusting out his arms to keep her assailants at bay. They slashed off both his hands, and he died a few minutes later in a pool of blood at the King's feet. The Crown Prince heard his mother call his name three times before the Japanese cut her down. Doubt remained, however, whether the dying woman was really the Queen, and ladies-in-waiting were dragged in to identify her. Flailed by the assassins' swords, they cried that it was indeed the Queen before they, too, were hacked down.

No contingency had been overlooked. The Japanese plan called not merely for the murder of the Queen but for the destruction of the evidence. Nothing was to be left of this woman who so stubbornly refused to cooperate. They wrapped the body of the Queen in a blanket—according to some reports, she was still alive—and carried her to a pine grove not far from the household apartments. There they soaked her in cooking oil and lit a fire in the hearts of the Korean people that will never be fully extinguished. As the funeral pyre died down, the murderers kept on pouring on more oil. When dawn came all that remained of the Queen were a few smoldering bones.

A proclamation issued in the name of the King reduced the dead Queen to the rank of prostitute. "We knew the extreme of her wickedness," said the decree, "but we were helpless and full of fear of her party. We are convinced that she is not only unfitted and unworthy to be the Queen but also that her guilt is excessive and overflowing . . . so we hereby depose her from the rank of Queen and reduce her to the level of the lowest class."

When it became apparent in Tokyo that the Japanese representatives in Korea could not talk their way out of their guilt, Marquis Ito announced that the offenders would be placed on trial. The hearings at Hiroshima were farcical, for though they clearly established the guilt of General Miura and his fellow murderers, all were acquitted on the ground that there was insufficient evidence to prove that any of the accused "actually committed the crime originally meditated by them."

Guarded only by a venerable American who had arrived in Seoul in 1888 and was an instructor in the palace guard and American missionaries who assisted him in the watch, the King was under constant threat of assassination. Since he could not trust the food prepared for him in the palace, he had his meals cooked for him in the American or Russian legations and smuggled to him in locked and guarded boxes.

The Russians continued to build up the strength of their legation guard. British, French, and Russian warships appeared in Korean waters and dropped anchor at Chemulpo, and reinforcements of U.S. Marines turned up to guard the American legation. The King was more closely guarded, and more deeply fearful for his life, than ever before.

The ladies-in-waiting—and the Russians—whisked him out of the palace in sedan chairs usually reserved for women. The coup went flawlessly. Within the day the King had created a new cabinet, and members of the Taewongun's entourage fled for their lives when the royal command went out that the heads of the traitors were to be cut off and presented to the King at the Russian legation.

Once China had its hand on the Korean helm. Japan had taken over very briefly. Now it was the Russians' turn. They made the best—and the worst —of it.

All the cards had passed into Russian hands. The Russians now entered into negotiations both with the King of Korea within his sanctuary at the Russian legation and Field Marshal Yamagata, who had arrived in Russia for the coronation of Nicholas II. Anticipating history by half a century, Yamagata proposed the division of Korea along the 38th parallel, with the southern half, including Seoul, under Japanese influence and the northern part passing under that of Russia. But St. Petersburg's eyes were still fastened on the warm-water ports of the southern part of the peninsula, and other plans were in the making. Thus, while Prince Lobanov-Rostovski was duly negotiating an agreement with Yamagata, which ostensibly assured for Japan a condominium in Korea, he was also in the process of receiving the King's agreement for the dispatch of Russian military instructors to Korea, responsibility for the King's bodyguard, the appointment of military and financial advisers, and the conclusion of a loan to the Korean government. What the Japanese had hoped to achieve first by war with China and then by murdering the Queen, the Russians had accomplished for themselves by the simple expedient of providing the King with sanctuary.

While Yamagata no doubt thought that he was saving something from the wreck of Japanese aspirations in Korea, the Russians were also busy insuring, as they hoped, that Japanese interests, which tongue-in-cheek they professed to respect, were finished forever.

In August 1896, one of Witte's men in the Russo-Chinese Bank arrived in Seoul and immediately began to bombard St. Petersburg with messages. French appetite for financial investment in the region had been whetted by the loans Witte had arranged through Paris to finance China's indemnity after the Sino-Japanese War. The French were ready now to offer money to build railroads out of Seoul in all directions. The British were interested as well.

At his first meeting with the Russian banker, the King asked him for a loan of three million roubles to avoid burying the Queen, "murdered by the Japanese," with Japanese money. The Russian was more than anxious to oblige, especially as the Hong Kong and Shanghai Bank had arrived to explore the possibilities in extending credits. Already the activities of an Englishman, J. McLeavy Brown, who had taken over the post of chief commissioner of customs in 1893, had proved embarrassing to the Russians. Customs was the major source of revenue, and the Russians wanted to get their hands on the controls. Back in St. Petersburg, however, Witte continued to drag his feet and the loan fell through. A small Russian military advisory group arrived to train the royal guard and five battalions of infantry. Another of Witte's men had taken over the post of financial adviser and succeeded in ousting the Englishman, Brown, from customs. This arrangement did not last long. The British were jealous of their preserves, and on December 27 seven British warships dropped anchor in Chemulpo. The English *chargé d'affaires,* presented himself in Seoul with a Marine guard to demand Brown's reinstatement. Brown was reinstated.

With the Russian coup in Seoul, Japan found that more of the spoils of the Sino-Japanese War had been torn from her grasp. Russia had been instrumental in pushing Japan out of Port Arthur only to seize it herself. Now Japan had lost her protectorate in Korea. An agreement signed in Seoul on May 14, 1896, between the Russian and the Japanese representatives left Tokyo with only 200 gendarmes in Korea to guard a telegraph line it had built during the Sino-Japanese War and 800 soldiers to look after the interests of Japanese residents in the settlements at Pusan, Wonsan, and Seoul. All the rest of its troops had to be withdrawn, while the Russians were permitted to match the size of the Japanese garrisons.

The Russians failed to press this advantage at this time, however, and in 1897, when the King left the Russian mission to live in a newly built palace, they had let the opportunity to consolidate their position slip through their fingers.

Within three years, however, Russian activities in Manchuria and a timber concession on the Yalu River combined to create new fears in Tokyo.

When the King was still the guest of the Russian minister in Seoul, a Russian trader named Julius Ivanovitch Bryner,* who had built up a big import–export business in Vladivostok, with connections through Japan, Korea and along the China coast, acquired a timber concession along the Yalu River. It stretched along the northern frontier of Korea from the mouth of the Yalu River on the west to the mouth of the Tiumen River in the east and covered an area of 3,300 square miles. In May 1897, when Bryner put the concession up for sale, the Grand Duke Alexander Mikhailovitch and Captain Alexander Mikhailovitch Bezobrazov, the son of a wealthy marshal of the nobility in St. Petersburg, and others arranged its purchase by the cabinet of Nicholas II. The intention was to set up the East Asiatic Company, using the concession as a springboard for further development and exploitation. The company was to differ from ordinary commercial organizations and was given the character of a political institution to develop Russian interests in Korea. In March 1900 the project was launched with a capital of two million roubles and four hundred shares, each of five thousand roubles. Half of the shares were to be held by the cabinet and the rest to be divided among a group close to the court and others to be carefully chosen.

Since Russia was now on the brink of war with China, Witte, who understood how seriously the Japanese would view the activities of this "official" company, intervened to win a postponement of the company's activities until things became more settled. Bezobrazov reacted angrily. "We suffer not from China's big fist but from St. Petersburg's," he declared in a bitter attack on Witte. "Instead of bringing our own best power into play, we left the work to Jews and Poles whom [Witte] commissioned to be our color-bearers."

He continued his campaign against Witte with Nicholas, whom he saw frequently, sometimes twice a week and occasionally for hours on end. His efforts at this time proved fruitless, and in February 1902, when the time

---

*Actor Yul Brynner's grandfather. Yul added another "n" to the original Swiss family name of Bryner. The family left Harbin in 1945 when the Red Army invaded Manchuria. They were interned by the Soviets for six months near Vladivostok. Catherine Brynner, Yul's sister, who is employed by the publicity department of the Australian Broadcasting Commission, writes:

Their reason for holding us was father's business concern and his extensive property and the fact that mother had been one of the leading actresses of the Moscow Arts Theater and had escaped with father from Moscow, after being refused an exit visa. The Swiss government obtained our release as father was a Swiss consul and had diplomatic immunity which the Soviets had ignored. We were taken to Moscow and released there with an official apology from the Soviet government.

expired for the first deposit on the shares, Bezobrazov had collected nothing. Nicholas ordered the liquidation of the company.

All might still have been well, but Bezobrazov was not prepared to let the matter rest here. He became one of the principals in the campaign to drive Witte out of office. He had not abandoned his view that Russia should annex Manchuria in its entirety and create a barrier along the Yalu River, and he was convinced that the timber concession could still be used to immense advantage. Within a year he was up to his ears in dangerous intrigues that soon helped to land his country in war with Japan.

CHAPTER 5

శ్రీశ్రీశ్రీశ్రీశ్రీశ్రీ

Carving Up China

FOR TWO THOUSAND MILES the Yangtze River cuts through the heart of
China—a brown, swirling stream whose waters in this one valley mean life
and livelihood to nearly half as many people as there are in the United
States. Through centuries the pattern of life here had never changed. The
people lived on the river in junks, and by the river, human horses, harnessed
and bent as they struggled along the banks, towed the cargoes of rice that
others grew so carefully in the bordering paddy fields.

Away to the north, beyond the Great Plain, China's Sorrow—the mighty
and unpredictable Yellow River—brought its annual crops of fertility and
floods and famine to other countless millions of Chinese. For almost all,
poverty, hunger, distress, and overwork were day-to-day experiences accepted year after year as were the seasons of summer and winter, spring and
fall.

Ninety percent of the population in this vast peasant society of four
hundred million received little or no education and exercised even less
influence on government. This was the responsibility of the proud manda-
rins, the scholar–gentry class that traced its cultural traditions to the era
before the birth of Christ and watched with contempt as the westerners
approached with their opium and demands for trade.

Unlike the Japanese, who used the western intrusion to copy and to take
initiatives of their own, those who ruled China relied for too long on
cultural superiority. Why should Superior Man engage in altercation with
birds and beasts? the great philosopher Mencius had asked. But the birds
and beasts of the nineteenth century brought modern weapons, and in the
age of imperialism those who used the best guns prevailed.

[99]

"We have admitted you to the courtyard, now you wish to get to the rooms where we house our wives and small children," cried Li Hung-chang, the most notable of China's late-nineteenth-century administrators, when the Russians, who had pledged themselves by secret treaty to protect China against the depredations of others, tramped into Manchuria and demanded the right to build a railway south from Harbin to Port Arthur, which they had just seized. It was a *cri de coeur* wrung from Li by what he regarded as bitter betrayal. Though China's invitations were few, his remark might have been directed also against the British, the French, the Germans, and the Japanese whose jackboots also helped to crush the finery of China's traditional past and brought the ruling Ching dynasty to its knees and ultimate death.

Manchuria is one of the five great divisions of China, half as big again as Texas. From earliest times some Chinese lived in Manchuria but until the eighteenth century immigration by Han Chinese was not permitted by the Manchus in Peking, who since 1644 had enjoyed the Mandate of Heaven to rule China. It was not until 1900 that Manchuria was integrated with China proper and ceased to be the private preserve of the Manchu rulers of China and their Mongol allies. Now it was to become the battleground in the war between Russia and Japan.

For two centuries the Manchus had tried pathetically to hold the passes, first against the Russians, who came from far away across the steppes to the great rivers and sparsely populated lands to China's north, and then against the Europeans and the Japanese, who had designs on the coast. The Manchus' first line of defense was cajolery; it never worked, and when they fell back on military force their guns sometimes were loaded with sawdust instead of gunpowder.

In 1683 they used force to drive the encroaching Russians from the mighty Amur, the Black Dragon River, which runs for 2,700 miles across the top of China. They had cannon and matchlocks and won a fleeting success. In June 1689, a Chinese caravan of 4,000 camels and fifteen horses left Peking for Nerchinsk, an outpost on one of the tributaries of the Amur about 400 miles east of Lake Baikal, bearing a Chinese embassy of nine thousand, including camp followers and Jesuit interpreters. The Russians wanted the Amur as the boundary between the two countries. The Chinese demanded that the Russians should withdraw completely. Deadlocked, both sides prepared to resume hostilities, but the mediation of a French Jesuit attached to the Chinese embassy proved successful and the Russians agreed on August 27, 1689, to put their signature to the Treaty of Nerchinsk, which obliged them to retire from the valley of the Amur.

It was to be China's only victory in that vast arena. Though the treaty pushed the Russians out of the Amur Valley, it also served to stimulate their interest in the Far East. It led eventually to quasi-religious and quasi-diplomatic contacts with China, which later provided Russia with unique advantages over its English and French rivals. It established Russia's right to set up a caravanserai in Peking, it helped to promote interest in the fur trade, and for a time it diverted Russian exploration and exploitation to the northeast, where before long the first Russian explorers were to make contact with the Japanese.

In Kamchatka, the mountainous and volcanic peninsula that juts out from northeastern Siberia into the north Pacific Ocean, Cossack explorers found rivers that swarmed with salmon, forests filled with poplars, birches, and alders, with rhododendrons and wild roses, with woodcock, snipe, and grouse, and with the richest of the fur-bearing animals, the sable, the mink, the fox, the beaver, and the bear. They seized Kamchatka in 1707 and immediately violated the Treaty of Nerchinsk by running supply boats down the Amur to their new posts.

The land settlers, the exiles, the soldiers, and the tax collectors had already begun to colonize western Siberia, but it was not until the middle of the nineteenth century that the Russian Far East began to acquire peasant farmers. By this time, the fur traders of the Russian-American Company, chartered by Tsar Paul to compete with the British East India Company, had spread across the Bering Sea to Alaska (or Russian America,* as it was then known) and down the coast as far as San Francisco.

Ivan the Terrible, who sought the hand of England's Queen Elizabeth and slew his own heir, was the first tsar to encourage the eastward migration and the first, also, to discover the exploitable use of forced labor in the iron, silver, and salt mines of the Urals and Siberia. The Russian move to the east acquired new momentum between 1826 and 1847 when 150,000 political prisoners and common criminals, accompanied in many cases by their wives and children, trudged eastward from Moscow along the Vladimir Track, walking all the way, to populate, or to perish in, the virgin lands. They came in chains with their heads shaved.

The Far East was so remote, and the lands so inhospitable, that until famine struck western Russia few other than adventurers could be encouraged to go east of their own free will. Forced labor was the answer, and the prisoners provided a constant and ready source of supply. During the nineteenth century, the population of Siberia increased rapidly—from

---

*In the hope of embroiling Britain with the United States, the Russians sold it to America in 1868 for $7,200,000.

1,500,000 in 1811, to 2,681,000 in 1851, to 4,314,000 in 1885. Another sharp increase occurred with the building of the Trans-Siberian Railway, which began in 1891. By 1897 the population had grown to nearly six million.

Tomsk, midway between Moscow and Vladivostok, became a forward post on the convict route across Siberia. To the east new towns sprang up around the prison stockades, with their fifteen-foot walls and dull red roofs. A daily march of thirty versts (about twenty miles) was normal for prisoners making their way to the East. Women were rarely chained, and political prisoners, if they had any money, could ride on the bone-breaking, spring-less carts, their heavy wooden wheels rimmed with iron, and even wear their normal clothing.

As the years passed, Russia's motives in settling Siberia changed. Where once it was interested almost exclusively in the fur trade, its Far Eastern empire eventually became locked in the power struggle of the waning century. It hoisted the flag on the island of Sakhalin, thus laying claim to Japanese territory, and in further violation of the Treaty of Nerchinsk, founded the trading posts of Nicolaievsk and Mariinsk near the mouth of the Amur.

In 1858 it presented the governor of Heilungchiang province in Man-churia with an ultimatum and a draft treaty. Under threat, the Chinese signed and granted the Russians the left bank of the Amur and a common proprietary right over the vast territory lying between the Ussuri River, a major tributary of the Amur, and the sea—an area as large as France and Spain together. Both the great Manchurian branches of the Amur, the Sungari and the Ussuri, were to be open to Russian merchants and travelers.

With heavy reservations, Peking accepted the Treaty of Aigun, which resulted from negotiations on the Amur. It ordered the local governor to take defensive measures in strict secrecy and to do his best to control the "barbarians." Events were far beyond his control. By 1859, though the treaty had not yet been ratified, 20,000 Russians had moved into the Amur Valley. Alarmed at the inroads into its territory that now came from all directions, Peking stripped the governor of his rank and ordered him home for punishment.

From 1757 the Chinese had restricted all foreign trade to Canton, but western demands constantly increased. China had tea, silks, and ceramics that the western world wanted; the westerners, especially the British, had opium to sell in exchange. When Peking continued to resist, the British used force and in the first Opium War, which was concluded by the Treaty of Nanking in 1842, Canton, Foochow, Shanghai, Amoy, and Ningpo were all opened to foreign trade. The British also acquired Hong Kong.

Continued Chinese resistance to the foreigners led in 1856 to the seizure of a small vessel flying the British flag and carrying opium, and to the murder of a French missionary. The British and French took to the field and the Chinese forces were defeated. They signed the treaties of Tientsin and were making ready to meet the British, French, and American envoys to exchange the ratifications of the treaties.

Two days before the Anglo-French flotilla had reached the Taku forts that guard the river approaches to Tientsin on the Pei River, Major-General Count Nicholas Ignatiev, who had already crammed a lifetime of diplomatic activity into his twenty-seven years, arrived in Peking with a new Russian draft treaty. His timing was fortuitous. The British and French had ignored the Chinese requests that they should go overland and were intent on sailing up the river. Although there is evidence that the Chinese had prepared elaborate quarters in Peking for their arrival, the British and French were outraged when they found that the Pei had been blocked. These were not days for standing on ceremony, and Sir James Hope, commanding the British squadron, which was reinforced by a French frigate and gunboat, landed and launched the assault designed to remove the iron stakes and heavy chains that barred their approach along the river. The cost was three ships and ignominious defeat in which the British, in particular, imagined evidence of a giant conspiracy, with the Russians aiding and abetting the Chinese.

While the British and French retreated to Shanghai to gather reinforcements, the Americans, who were also interested in the treaty port revisions, adopted more placatory methods. John E. Ward, the American envoy, went overland to Peking. Ignorant of protocol, he elected to go by cart instead of sedan chair, the mode of travel used by high Chinese officials. With banners proclaiming that he was traveling as a tribute-bearer to the Manchu court, he made his humble entry into Peking. On arrival, he was informed that he would be required to kowtow to the Emperor. "Tell them," he said, "that I go on my knees only to God and woman," whereupon he was confined to his quarters, and, after five days, sent back by cart to Peit'ang where formal ratification of the Treaty of Tientsin took place on August 15, 1858.

With this successful handling of the American barbarian and the rebuff to the British and French, the Emperor was in no mood to accept Russian demands in the type of draft treaty now presented to him.

Back on the Amur, however, Count Muraviev "Amurski," the Russian Far Eastern governor-general, who had forbidden the Chinese to navigate the lower reaches of the river, received orders from St. Petersburg to occupy all the country between the Ussuri and the sea if the Chinese refused to sign the new treaty.

Early in 1860, Ignatiev, who had unsuccessfully continued negotiations in Peking, joined the new Anglo-French expedition now preparing in

Shanghai to march on Peking. His role theoretically was that of observer; his advice to the British and French, who were still in ignorance of the Russian territorial demands, was to press on vigorously with the attack on the Taku forts.

Sir Hope Grant, who had been named as commanding general, took the forts from the rear, reached Tientsin on August 25 and moved to Tungchow, the gateway to the capital, his troops looting as they went. Behind them in every town they passed through they left a trail of smashed ceramics and ripped-up books and scrolls. Indian troops serving with the allied forces dressed up in clothes torn from looted shops and houses. Chinese women tried to kill themselves with overdoses of opium to avoid being raped.

Harry Parkes, the British consul in Canton, who had joined the Anglo-French expedition as interpreter for the special British envoy Lord Elgin, met the Chinese and arranged for the Anglo-French advance to continue without resistance. Next day he and his party of thirty-eight were ambushed and taken prisoner. They were hauled before a Chinese officer who ordered Parkes to kowtow. When Parkes refused, the prisoners were placed in covered carts and taken to Peking. Here, Parkes was taken before the board of punishment and told to write a letter to Lord Elgin asking him to call off the advance on Peking. Parkes again refused. Members of his party were then bound with wetted ropes and thrown in an open courtyard, where they were beaten if they spoke or cried out and rewarded with mouthfuls of excrement if they called for food or water. Parkes himself was spared this torture, but half of the party died and were left to rot among the living.

What part Ignatiev played in blocking negotiations during this critical period is unclear, though he subsequently claimed some of the credit for having refused to act as a mediator when approached unofficially by the Chinese. In any event, the Hsien-feng Emperor, though a weakling, now seemed fully determined to resist, and had so announced in a scorched-earth edict:

Last year the Barbarians endeavored to force the entrance to the Pei River, but in a twinkling of an eye their ships were sunk and thousands of their bodies floated on the water for a distance of one league from the shore. . . . My anger is about to strike and exterminate them without mercy. I command all my subjects, Chinese and Tartars, to hunt them down like savage beasts. Let the villages be abandoned as these wretches draw near. Let all provisions be destroyed which they might secure. In this manner their accursed race will perish of hunger like fish in a dried-up pond.

The Emperor's efforts to halt the Anglo-French advance collapsed on the canal connecting Tungchow with Peking. Tartar cavalry supported by lines of infantry and backed by artillery met the oncoming forces, and a furious seven-hour battle ensued before the Chinese forces broke and fled, sadly let down by their artillery whose shells passed harmlessly over the heads of the British and French. Although the Anglo-French force was a sizable one— 25,000 men—never was the decay of Manchu China more eloquently expressed. Among the teeming millions of China a western regiment could move anywhere with impunity.

Ignatiev had now established communication with the Russian mission inside Peking. Since it was important for his own plans for negotiations to get there first, he counseled Elgin to halt outside the capital. His information was impressive. On October 5 he informed Elgin that the timid Emperor, whose edict had breathed such fire, had now flown and that his brother, Prince Kung, was in charge of the government.

The decision to flee was a panic-stricken, last-moment act of desperation, and the abrupt departure of the court to the mountain lodge at Jehol left the Summer Palace unguarded. The Anglo-French forces saw Chinese looters climbing over the walls and soon they joined them, officers and men alike filling their pockets with priceless treasures and destroying what they could not carry. Finally, in reprisal for the treatment accorded to Parkes—who was released by Prince Kung fifteen minutes before he received the official order from the Emperor to put him to death—Elgin ordered the palaces to be destroyed by fire.

"It covered an area of many miles," wrote Brevet Major Charles George Gordon, subsequently known as "Chinese" Gordon, whose military career in China began with the bonfire.

The Palace of Adrian at Tivoli might have been hidden in one of its courts. . . . All the artistic treasures, all the curiosities—archaeological and other—that Chinese wealth and Chinese taste, such as it was, could bring together, had been accumulated in this magnificent pleasaunce. . . . After pillaging it, [we] burned the whole place, destroying, in a vandal-like manner, most valuable property, which could not be replaced for four millions. It made one's heart sore to burn them; in fact, these palaces were so large, and we were so pressed for time, that we could not plunder them carefully. Quantities of gold ornaments were burned, considered as brass. It was wretchedly demoralising work for any Army. Everybody was wild for plunder.

Among the plunder were four trunks filled with Chinese diplomatic documents relating to Russia, which Ignatiev got back from an English interpreter who, presumably, had not bothered to glance through them. Still in the dark about Ignatiev's real mission, both Baron Gros, the plenipotentiary for France, and Elgin confided in him as they waited outside the walls of Peking with the smoke from the burning debris of the Summer Palace still heavy in the air. Elgin blamed Gros for not having prevented the looting, and Gros in turn was angry with Elgin for the burning. The Englishman even showed Ignatiev the ultimatum he had sent to the Chinese and speculated that it might serve the British ends if it were rejected, since they could then sack Peking, transfer the capital to Nanking, far from the Manchus' power center and headquarters for the Taiping rebels (who had been causing trouble since 1848). They could then put a pretender on the throne and "control China with four gunboats."

Elgin's loose talk was just what the Russian needed. The Anglo-French ultimatum was due to expire at 10 A.M. on October 20. The Chinese, in desperation, turned to the Russian as a mediator. Ignatiev, who had already persuaded Baron Gros that Elgin wanted to put the torch to Peking and to the dynasty as well, now communicated the same intelligence to the Chinese. He would mediate, he said, only on written request from Prince Kung, and if all the Russian demands were granted. On the night of October 19, Prince Kung, his personal safety guaranteed by Ignatiev, gave in.

The British signed the Treaty of Peking on October 24 and the French the next day. Elgin made a triumphal entry into the city on a palanquin carried by sixteen Chinese bearers robed in scarlet. English troops lined the streets and a military band played *God Save the Queen*. Lord Elgin spoke not one word to Prince Kung in the Tribunal of Rites where the treaty was signed. The proceedings were only slightly less formal when Baron Gros signed on behalf of France. The Baron apologized for his lack of ceremonial dress; he had lost the appropriate clothes in a shipwreck off the coast of Ceylon. Prince Kung, who had lost his wardrobe and other personal belongings in the Summer Palace, made a similar apology for his inadequate dress. "Your uniform was destroyed by water and mine by fire," he said.

With the treaties now signed—and Elgin and Gros placated by a huge indemnity (£24 million to England and France) and the acquisition of Kowloon by the British—Ignatiev and the Chinese got down to the serious business of the Russian treaty. The allied forces withdrew on November 6, and Ignatiev, still encountering some residual Chinese resistance, wrote to Prince Kung reminding him that it was not difficult to renew the war and threatening to recall the allied troops. The blackmail worked.

The Sino-Russian Treaty of Peking was signed on November 14, 1860. A week later Ignatiev left for home, borne in a manner worthy of Lord Elgin: he rode in triumph on a palanquin carried by sixteen richly robed bearers to present to the Tsar vast new lands—a river bigger than the Danube, both sides of the lower course of the Amur River, a thousand miles of navigable waterway, and the land stretching down the coast to the south as far as Korea.

The Russians prepared to move their Far Eastern naval headquarters—which had been transferred from Petropavlovsk in Kamchatka to Nicolaievsk at the mouth of the Amur only two years earlier—to Vladivostok, the "Conquest of the East," and they began to build a new port. Thirteen years of field work by Muraviev and brilliant diplomacy by Putiatin and Ignatiev had been richly rewarded, though immense problems, and dangers, lay ahead.

The site for Vladivostok was virgin forest land. The surveys were finished by the end of 1860, and two years later the first shanties were built for government officials and laborers. The oak and pine forests were filled with tigers which frequently made their appearance within the new settlement. Another ten years passed before the new base was ready to cope with the needs of the Russian Far Eastern fleet, and by 1878 the population was only fourteen hundred.

Growth after that was quite rapid. Korean laborers, Chinese merchants, and Japanese servants arrived to tend to the wants of the Russians—and to report on the forts, earthworks, docks, navy yards, houses, and impressive government offices that appeared along the Gulf of Peter the Great, rubbing shoulders with shanties knocked together out of rough planks. Springless Korean oxcarts, commissariat wagons, and troikas with three galloping horses shared the ungraded streets. Women were few in number, and the bars, the principal places of entertainment, were boozy, bawdy, and brawling. Spring was brief and bright, the summer hot and wet, the autumn cheerful—and then came the long chill winter that froze the Gulf from Christmas until the end of March, cutting off communication by sea. Toward the end of the century the Russians began to use ice-breakers to tow blocks of ice out to sea. By this time, also, the Trans-Siberian Railway provided a corridor to the West. Instead of satisfying Russian ambitions, however, the frustrations of the ice-bound port served only to whet St. Petersburg's appetite for a new port in the warm water to the south.

If this was not yet obvious, it was quite clear that the treaties with Russia, Britain, and France had shattering consequences in China. The invincible Manchus, the great Tartars, had been humbled by the barbarian invaders. Was not this a sign that the Mandate of Heaven had been withdrawn from their rule? Revolts kindled and flared. Two were quickly extinguished, but a third, the Taiping Rebellion, which between 1848 and 1865 cost some twenty million lives, got a new lease on life. If disease and famine were the biggest killers, China itself, unwilling to make the changes that the times demanded, was the principal victim.

One of the barriers to reform that might have led China to copy the Japanese model was a remarkable woman named Yehonola, the daughter of a Manchu officer, whose youthful beauty led her from bed to power. Her links with China's destiny began one night when a eunuch carried her wrapped in a red silk scarf and laid her naked at the foot of the bed of the Emperor Hsien-feng. Yehonola bore a son to the sickly Emperor, won the title Empress of the Western Palace, gained access to the state papers, and was thereafter known as Tzu-h'si, which means "maternal and auspicious." She prodded the Emperor into opposing the British and French forces when they marched on Peking in 1860. Plotting courtiers planned to kill her when the Emperor died, but Tzu-h'si, or one of her entourage, stole the state seal without which the dying Emperor's decree transferring authority to regents who detested her could not be validated. In a dramatic contest of wills, Tzu-h'si outwitted her opponents. One was decapitated, and two, as a special dispensation, were allowed to hang themselves.

Hsiao-ch'en was the dead Emperor's principal wife; she was appointed co-regent with Tzu-h'si until the latter's young son became of age. Since Hsiao-ch'en had no interest in affairs of state, the Empress of the Western Palace became the effective ruler of China. For a time Prince Kung, the dead Emperor's brother, arrogated to himself what Tzu-h'si considered excessive powers. He was duly humbled and subsequently permitted to return to his duties under Tzu-h'si's firm direction.

Corrupt, able, ambitious, and ruthless, Tzu-h'si, the Dowager Empress, watched over the growth of her son, Tung-chih, with increasing concern. When he came of age in November 1872 he decided that he could rule without his mother's aid. Forbidden now to see the state papers, the Dowager Empress relied for support on Li Lien-ying, the chief eunuch, crafty, corrupt, and, in effect, warden of the Forbidden City.

Three years after he had taken office, the Emperor Tung-chih, whose licentious way had become the scandal of Peking, contracted smallpox and died. Rumor said that Li Lien-ying, the chief eunuch, arranged the infection. The Emperor's death caused little sorrow for Tzu-h'si, who was now instrumental in breaking the dynastic laws to select as Emperor the four-year-old son of her sister. When he became of age and ruled as Emperor Kuang-hsu, she retired but maintained close links with the provincial governors-general, all of whom had been her personal appointees.

Foremost among these was Li Hung-chang, who was born in Anhwei province of a well-to-do family in 1823. Big, pock-marked, able, and corrupt, he was a scholar and a soldier. With "Chinese" Gordon, he crushed the Taiping rebels after the Anglo-French occupation of Peking. He was responsible for Chinese diplomacy in the latter part of the nineteenth century, and earned himself 500,000 taels from the Russians when he agreed to the Port Arthur leasehold. His own protégé was Yuan Shih-k'ai, for many years the Chinese representative in Korea, where he fought fruitlessly to check the growing power of the Japanese.

As Viceroy of Chih-li for many years, Li tried hard to improve China's armed forces. He employed German instructors to train the troops and set up China's first arsenal in Shanghai. In 1890 Gordon set out for him a detailed plan for arming China.

In the brief period of time before the war with Japan in 1894, he did his best. His German officers trained 50,000 troops, but his elites were officered from the same province, and there was no corps of trained officers available for replacements. Even among his best forces, the battalion commanders continued to pad their payrolls. Battalions with a theoretical order of battle of 500 men rarely had more than 200 to 300 men on strength.

The Emperor had been boldly advised by other officials to prepare for war. "If we do not prepare for war but leave matters in their present inactive condition," the board of censors advised, "Japan will continue making military and naval preparations while we shall be delaying. The power of Japan will be steadily progressing, while ours will remain stationary."

The recommendation went to the board of military affairs which recommended that Li Hung-chang should be ordered to prepare a plan for invading Japan. His advice was to hasten slowly, though he felt that Japan was laboring under financial difficulties and suffering from the burden of a terrible national debt. Several samurai revolts, culminating in the Satsuma Rebellion in 1877, had affected its power, and both the navy and the army were weak. In his memorial to the Emperor he wrote: "An ancient maxim says, 'Nothing is so dangerous as to expose one's plans before they are ripe.' It is for this reason that I recommended to Your Majesty that we maintain extreme caution, carefully concealing our object whilst all the time increasing our strength." He advocated an immediate increase in the size of the navy, along with the strengthening of other national defenses, and emphasized again that there was no hurry to attack Japan.

The result was twofold: Li formed the board of admiralty, created a naval college and ordered Yuan Shih-k'ai to strengthen China's hand in Korea. He argued that China could not intervene in Korea's domestic affairs and that Japan had no right to do so either. He ordered the Chinese troops in Korea to avoid provocative action that might bring them into hostilities with the Japanese. But the Japanese troops kept pouring into Korea and soon outnumbered the Chinese two to one. Yuan Shih-k'ai, who had escaped from Korea on an English vessel before the arrival of the Japanese in Seoul, had repeatedly assured him that England would intervene on China's side if the Japanese attacked. Li had his doubts.

On paper, everything seemed to favor China. Its armies were bigger. Its navy, also built up by Li Hung-chang, was superior in tonnage and numbers of men. Against the Japanese cruisers it boasted two battleships, each of more than 7,000 tons. Although its sixty-five large naval vessels and forty-three torpedo boats were divided among four fleets, its northern fleet alone was comparable to that of the Japanese, with fourteen warships. But the Chinese admiral was a cavalry officer who knew nothing about war at sea, and his German co-admiral was also a soldier, though a wise one. Repeatedly, he urged the Chinese to increase the production of ammunition and to buy more—but when they faced the Japanese fleet in full-scale battle order off the Yalu River there were only three rounds of quality ammunition for each gun in the main batteries and fourteen for the smaller guns. Some of the shells contained sawdust. The money earmarked for ammunition had been appropriated by the Dowager Empress and the chief eunuch, Li Lien-ying, to rebuild the Summer Palace at Peking. The new terraces and pavilions had all come from Li's military program. "What does it matter?" said one of the palace eunuchs when the war war over. "The Japanese would have beaten us all the same. As it is, at least we have the Summer Palace."

Li Hung-chang lost the three-eyed peacock's feather from his hat and, though the least deserving, got most of the blame. The captain of the *Chen Yuen*, who had fled during the first engagement at Asan when he met Togo in the *Naniwa*, was decapitated for cowardice. The admiral took an overdose of opium and died, and the Dowager Empress canceled the plans to celebrate her sixtieth birthday and talked to the manager of the Hong Kong and Shanghai Bank in Peking about sending off £8,250,000 in gold and silver bullion to London.

Like vultures, the European powers, which had been circling when Japan went to war, now clawed for their own cut of the carcass. Within six months the first installment of the Japanese indemnity had to be paid, and, lacking funds of its own,* Peking had to borrow abroad, if it could. Witte saw the opportunity and offered Russia's good offices in securing the money.

After the constant rapacious attacks of the western powers to which she had been subjected for more than half a century, China's credit was not good enough on the international markets. Seeing the door opening into China, Witte pledged Russia's resources as security for the loan. "Furthermore," he said, "I took practically complete charge of negotiating and arranging for the transaction on the French money market." Thus, the Russo-Chinese Bank was created, with French financiers as chief shareholders, and the right granted to trade, to transport commodities, to issue currency, to collect taxes on behalf of the Chinese treasury, to build railways *anywhere within the confines of China,* and to lay telegraph lines. By

---

*Between 1895 and 1900 the Chinese had to pay Japan 200 million taels of silver; the government's total revenue was only about 90 million taels in 1900.

insisting on a majority of Russians on the board of directors, Witte maintained control over the bank's operations.

The loss of the war had stunned China and divided the court. The Dowager Empress berated the Emperor Kuang-hsu for losing, and Kuang-hsu responded by drawing closer to those who called for domestic reform. The Dowager Empress stood obdurately against him. In a desperate effort to destroy her influence, the Emperor sought the cooperation of Yuan Shih-k'ai, now installed as a military commander in Chih-li province, to bring about her arrest. Yuan was an unfortunate choice. If he owed nothing to the Dowager Empress, he had close ties of affection with those upon whom she depended for protection, and he immediately gave word of the plot.

Tzu-h'si responded vigorously and with alacrity. With Li Lien-ying in the van, a group of eunuchs went to the Emperor's room and carried him off to imprisonment in the same isolated pavilion in Peking where the Empress Dowager was to have been held. Here, deprived of all comforts, including his favorite, the Pearl Concubine, he learned that fifty-three of his eunuchs had been beaten to death for their part in the plot against the Dowager Empress. The reformers fled into exile, and traditional China entered its terminal throes. The Germans, the Russians, the Japanese, the British, and the French all assisted in the rites.

In November 1897 two German Jesuit priests had been murdered in a village on the Shantung Peninsula. The murders took place on November 4 and the news reached Berlin on November 6. On the same day Kaiser William ordered his Far Eastern naval squadron to seize the Shantung port of Kiao-chau. The Chinese were quick to punish the offenders but not quick enough for the Germans, who produced an impressive list of demands to compensate for the loss of the priests, whose order was banned in Germany! These included the lease of Kiao-chau for ninety-nine years as a naval base, together with a large stretch of surrounding territory, including the port of Tsingtao; the right to construct a railway on the peninsula and to exploit the mineral resources; an indemnity to meet the costs of the German occupation; another indemnity to compensate the families of the murdered priests; and the erection of a monument in their memory.

As his ships were moving to Kiao-chau, the Kaiser, self-styled "Admiral of the Atlantic," asked Nicholas II, "The Admiral of the Pacific," for his approval. Nicholas replied: "I can neither approve nor disapprove your order to direct the German squadron to Kiao-chau, since I have just learned that the harbor was in our hands only temporarily in 1895–96." His message was neither an affirmation nor a denial, but it was sufficient for William, who had long been planning to seize a port in China.

Li Hung-chang, who had attended the coronation of Nicholas II, had received a substantial bribe from Witte and a secret treaty promising Russian assistance in the event of an attack on China by Japan in exchange for permission to allow the Trans-Siberian Railway to pass through Manchuria. Now, he believed, was the time to put Russian friendship to the test, and he immediately asked his friends in St. Petersburg to send a squadron to Kiao-chau. The orders were, in fact, given but quickly rescinded, though Nicholas, with a rare show of courage, went so far as to indicate to the Kaiser that he was "very much surprised" to find the telegram interpreted as sanctioning. William was very nice about it all: he invited the Russian fleet to spend the winter in his new port on the China coast.

The idea quickly gained ground in St. Petersburg that what Germany could do Russia could do, also. The Russian use of Port Arthur and Talienwan (soon to be renamed Dalny by the Russians and subsequently called Dairen) had already been envisaged in the event of war. Count N. C. Muraviev, son of Muraviev "Amurski," who had become foreign minister, drew up a memorandum that pointed out the favorable opportunity to seize Port Arthur provided by the German move. Nicholas himself presided over the meeting to consider the memorandum. Finance Minister Witte foresaw the long-term dangers in the situation and argued strongly against the proposal. It would be the "height of treachery and faithlessness," he said. He understood with his usual clarity the effect that the German occupation of Kiao-chau would have on Nicholas, and pleaded with the German minister to urge on William the abandonment of Kiao-chau. As an alternative, he recommended that the Germans ought to take a port in southern China; otherwise, he felt sure, Russia would seize Port Arthur or some other port, Japan would be encouraged to take similar action, and eventually Russia and Japan would go to war. So strongly did he feel that he even proposed sending the Russian squadron to Kiao-chau and having it stand by until the Germans packed up and left.

Witte believed that he had won the day. He reckoned without Muraviev, who, like his father before him, worried about British goals in the region. Behind Witte's back, Muraviev urged on Nicholas the necessity for moving quickly to circumvent the British. Nicholas listened to his advice and set his own forces in motion, thus falling into Germany's trap. For by involving Russia in the Far Eastern quagmire, William saw his own hand freed for action in Europe.

"You know, Serge Yulevitch," Nicholas told Witte when he saw him a few days later, "I have decided to occupy Port Arthur and Talienwan. Our ships with troops are already on their way there." Witte left gravely disturbed. Outside the Tsar's study he ran into the Grand Duke Alexander Mikhailovitch, Nicholas' cousin and inventor of a strategical naval war game widely used by Russian staff officers, who had already been briefed on the Russian plans. "Your Highness," said Witte, "Remember this day: this fatal step will have disastrous results."*

St. Petersburg advised Peking of its intentions, implying that the entry of the Russian ships into Port Arthur was purely a temporary arrangement "up to the conclusion of the Kiao-chau affair." Since Li Hung-chang had rushed to the Russian legation to seek assistance as soon as he learned that the Germans had landed on the Shantung peninsula, and had remained there until his appeal had been encoded and sent off to St. Petersburg, there was little that he could do but take the Russians' word at face value. Moreover, he desperately needed a new loan to meet China's obligations to Japan under the Treaty of Shimonoseki, and the Hong Kong and Shanghai Bank had refused to put up the money.

Witte, despite his overwhelming misgivings about the Tsar's action, was ready to exploit the economic advantages of the situation. He was willing to provide the finance China needed in exchange for railway and industrial monopolies in Manchuria and Mongolia; the grant of a concession to the Chinese Eastern Railway for a branch railway from the trunkline to "that harbor which shall be selected for this purpose by the management of the railroad on the coast of the Yellow Sea, east of the port of Yingkow; and authorization for Russia to construct at this harbor a port with right of entry for ships under the Russian flag."

Superficially, there does not appear to have been much difference between Witte's approach to the situation and the attitudes of Nicholas and Muraviev. But whereas Witte understood the correlation between industrial strength and political power, Nicholas believed simply in his God-given rights in the Far East. Muraviev tended to see it all as a game of chess, in which the pieces were valueless without the maneuver. To put England in check was his primary concern.

The Russian move into Port Arthur had entirely different consequences. With their squadron now concentrated at Port Hamilton in the Straits of Tsushima, the British began alternately to squeeze Peking and to offer large bribes to reject Witte's loan and to take a British loan instead. There were the usual threats of military force and hints by the British legation in Peking that, if the loan went to Russia, England would be obliged to "revive various old claims."

Having taken this great leap forward in Manchuria, Russia was willing at this time to take a small step backward in Korea. In March and April

---

*The Grand Duke was one of the few among Nicholas' closest associates who counseled against war with Japan. He warned Nicholas that the Japanese were not afraid of Russia.

1898, the Russian military instructors and financial advisers left the country and the Russo-Korean Bank closed its doors. By agreement with Japan on April 13, Russia sanctioned the dominating position of Japan there. "If we had faithfully adhered to the spirit of this agreement," Witte noted ruefully, "there is no doubt that more or less permanent peaceful relations would have been established between Japan and Russia. We would have quietly kept the Kwantung peninsula, while Japan would have completely dominated Korea, and this situation could have lasted indefinitely, without giving occasion to a clash."

But it was not to be. Nor was Witte as perceptive as usual. Not only Japanese interests were involved but German, British, and French. To prevent Russo-German domination of the Gulf of Korea, Liaotung, and Chih-li, England now moved to seize the strategically important port of Wei-hai-wei at the entrance to the Gulf of Chih-li, thus neutralizing the Russian and German moves. Old Far Eastern hands, like Dr. George Morrison of *The Times,* began to talk of war and to lobby for an Anglo–Japanese alliance.

On January 1, 1898, a new element was introduced into the Russian equation. General Kuropatkin became war minister. Far from wanting to withdraw from Port Arthur and Dalny, Kuropatkin, who had once so strongly opposed building the Trans-Siberian Railway through Manchuria, wanted the cession of both ports to Russia, a thirty-six-year lease of the Kwantung Peninsula, and the construction of a branch line linking the area with the Trans-Siberian Railway. Witte offered his resignation as finance minister, agreeing to stay on and help with the new policy only after he had been assured by Nicholas that it was too late to change the new policy. His function now was to force Chinese acceptance of the Russian demands with a bribe of 500,000 roubles to Li Hung-chang. The Chinese signed the treaty on March 15, 1898, and by the end of the year the Russians had moved twenty thousand troops into their two new warm-water ports. Cossack guards, the pennons flying both the Russian colors and the Chinese dragon, patrolled the railway line and protected the work of building the fortifications.

China now was in renewed ferment. The inroads of the Germans into the Shantung peninsula had caused great unrest, and Manchuria, in reaction to the Russian pressures, was explosive. It was in Shantung, however, that trouble began. Birthplace of both Confucius and Mencius, Shantung raised some of the sturdiest people in China, long accustomed to adversity. After centuries of overcropping and underfertilization, their soil had become exhausted. The peasants battled with the soil as the fishermen battled with the seas in the bitter northwestern gales that struck across the Sea of Japan. These were not the people to accept the indignities that the Japanese and the Germans had heaped upon them. Hard-headed but spiritually devout, they had always resented the presence of the missionaries. Yet the missionaries liked Shantung. The markets were held in the larger villages at intervals of five days and were so arranged that the salesmen could move from one to another without loss of time. This meant that the preachers, also, could cover a lot of ground quite easily, bringing the Word of God to the heathen as they bought and sold pigs and peaches in the market places.

The Word was not always appreciated. In Shantung, as elsewhere in China, as the missionaries probed inland from the coast, extraordinary stories were concocted—and widely accepted—about their activities. Their compounds were believed to be haunts of the devil, where fiendish activities were practiced. Some missionaries were even said to remove the eyes from children and boil them down to make their powerful medicines.

The Germans, who had virtually annexed most of Shantung after their landing at Kiao-chau, soon found that they needed troops to protect the missionaries as they went about their work. The principal opposition came from a secret organization, the Society of Righteously Harmonious Fists, or, simply, the Boxers, whose peasant members believed that the coming of the Germans and the work of the missionaries had angered the spirits, causing a succession of famines.

Mission compounds, missionaries, and converts all came under attack. Peking sent a new governor to Shantung to restore order, and he quickly became converted to the Boxers' cause, which now spread around the Gulf of Chih-li and to the hills surrounding Peking, where most of the foreign communities, advised by the complacent and venerable Sir Robert Hart, British director-general of the Chinese maritime customs, saw little danger —at least from within the foreign compounds.

A small detachment of American, French, English, Russian, and Japanese soldiers arrived in Peking at the beginning of June 1900 to provide some additional protection for the foreign legations. The Boxers' answer was to tear up the passengers' tickets on the Tientsin–Peking line. When this failed to stop the traffic, they tore up the lines and burned down the foreigners' grandstand at the racecourse just outside Peking.

On June 10 a force consisting of 915 Englishmen, 540 German, 312 Russians, 158 French, 112 Americans, 54 Japanese, 40 Italians, and 25 Austrians, and headed by Admiral Sir Edward Seymour of the Royal Navy, a Crimean War veteran, began to march to the relief of Peking. Two days later the legations sent welcoming committees to the station to meet them and to care for their baggage. The Europeans quickly became tired of waiting when the trains did not arrive and went home. Only a Japanese official remained. The Boxers caught the Japanese and beat out his brains with their rifle butts.

While Seymour's relief column was still far from Peking and heavily embattled—it did not arrive for two months—the Boxers entered Peking. On June 19 the Dowager Empress considered a colorful account of the victories she had enjoyed at the expense of the allied force, together with the intelligence that the invaders had demanded the surrender of the Taku forts. (The forts had, in fact, fallen two days earlier.) In the afternoon the eleven foreign ministers and Sir Robert Hart received large scarlet envelopes from the Tsungli Yamen, the Chinese equivalent of the foreign office. Since the allied fleets had threatened to attack the Taku forts, and this constituted a declaration of war, the ministers were advised to pack up and leave the capital within twenty-four hours, otherwise their protection could not be guaranteed. If they elected to leave, they would be given safe conduct to Tientsin.

Against the strongly voiced opposition of Baron Klemens von Ketteler, the German minister, who was sure that the ultimatum was a trap and that they would all be killed as soon as they left Peking, the ministers accepted the ultimatum but requested an audience with two of the Yamen princes. Next morning the Baron left his legation to keep his own long-standing appointment at the Tsungli Yamen. An imperial bannerman, so called because of the colored banners under which the bannermen fought, shot and killed him.

All thought of risking the journey to Tientsin was now abandoned and at 3:59 P.M. June 20, one minute before the expiration of the ultimatum, the siege of the legations began. Next day the Dowager Empress issued an edict declaring war on the world.

In what he called "an appeal from the lion's den," Reverend W. A. P. Martin, president of the Chinese Imperial University, cried for help:

> May this terrible sacrifice prove not to be in vain! We are the victims of pagan fanaticism. Let this pagan empire be partitioned among Christian powers, and may a new order of things open on China within a new century. . . . The perils of the siege have obliterated the lines of creed and nations, making a unity not merely of Christians but the Japanese into brotherhood with us. To them the siege is a step towards Christianity.

The Chinese at first allowed the foreign diplomats to send encoded messages to their governments, and, until the siege began in earnest, the westerners sent out impassioned requests for help. Nearest to hand were the Russians, who had now enlarged their garrison at Port Arthur to 20,000 men. Sir Claude MacDonald, the British minister in Peking, perhaps the last man in the world who would have wanted to turn to St. Petersburg for help, sent a message to Admiral Alexeiev, the Russian naval commander in the Far

East and governor of Kwantung, asking for a detachment of troops. Foreign minister Muraviev immediately recommended to Nicholas that 4,000 troops should be sent to avoid the risk that Japanese troops might become involved.

A dramatic message from Sir Robert Hart, "The situation is desperate, make haste," arrived in Tokyo and inspired Baroness d'Anethan, the wife of the Belgian minister and sister of the writer Rider Haggard, to write a poem for the *Japan Times.*

> Make haste! Make haste! Ah! list the frenzied cry
> We fling across the world. Will none reply?
> While powers pause, while armies vacillate,
> We vainly pray for help. Come not too late.

The poem caused almost as much stir in Tokyo as the plight of the foreign missions, and Sir Claude MacDonald later attributed the speedy dispatch of Japanese forces to it. "The Japanese sent their troops immediately after its publication," he told the authoress. "They had many women and children there, and your poem made a great impression on them."

Sir Claude exaggerated. Prime Minister Katsura and Army Chief of Staff Oyama had decided as early as June 23 to send two divisions of troops. The advance guard left Ujina on July 6 and was followed during the month by the balance of the force of 10,000 men.

To out-maneuver the Japanese without breaking with China was Russia's dilemma. China and Russia, bound by secret agreement, were, after all, allies; and first the mortally ill Muraviev, and later Count Nicholas Lamsdorf, who succeeded him as foreign minister, insisted that the Russian intervention should be small, low key, and confined to "safeguarding the security of the mission, defending the life and property" of Russian subjects, and "supporting legitimate authority in its struggle with revolution."

These lofty goals were soon abandoned, though at first it seemed that Witte and Lamsdorf would effectively apply the brakes. The Japanese with 10,000 men (they were willing to send 30,000, but the Kaiser, hoping to curry favor with Nicholas, objected) provided the bulk of the force that now gathered for the relief of the legations. The Russians contributed 4,000, the British 3,000 (including about 500 Australians), the Americans 2,000, the French 800, the Germans 200, the Austrians 58, and the Italians 53.

A series of exchanges between Li Hung-chang (banished to Canton but nevertheless still important) and Witte promised some slight hope for the preservation of Sino-Russian relations. Witte cabled Li promising that Russia would not declare war on China and offering full support in exchange for the preservation of the peace in Manchuria and the protection of Russian subjects in Peking. He also set in motion Russian financial aid for Manchuria, with promises of more to come if peace and order were maintained.

But such a task was clearly beyond the competence of the Chinese authorities. Yuan Shih-k'ai, who had now taken over the governorship of Shantung, put down the Boxers with a heavy hand in their home province, but Manchuria erupted in widespread violence. To General Kuropatkin, the situation provided Russia with a unique chance to move. He recommended that the Russian forces should advance for the purpose of "polishing off Peking" and "that the general leadership of the allied detachments be entrusted to Admiral Alexeiev."

In Berlin, the Kaiser fumed at the contradictions and double-dealing that he suspected in St. Petersburg. While Witte was doing his best to arrange the earliest possible contact with Li Hung-chang, the Kaiser was promising to arrest the Chinese leader on sight if he showed up anywhere he could be seized. Much of this ill-feeling also spilled over in Peking, where the other foreigners suspected that the Russians were working with the Boxers.

Kuropatkin was a great disappointment to Witte, who had seen in him a potential ally in the campaign for the peaceful acquisition of economic supremacy in Manchuria. At other times Kuropatkin was cautious and indecisive, but he now saw in the situation exploitable possibilities arising from what he regarded as the extreme political weakness of China and the great power and energy of Japan. He concluded that "we naturally cannot remain indifferent to this development." Since he thought war with Japan was a probability at the beginning of the twentieth century, it was therefore in Russia's essential interests to deny Japan any opportunity for consolidating itself in either Korea or Manchuria. The best means of denial was for Russia to "work toward gradually acquiring absolute economic control" of Manchuria.

Earlier Kuropatkin had advocated the utmost caution. With the whole world now united against China, however, there seemed scant risk in taking bold action—the sort of daring he had shown as chief of staff to the great Skobolev. He was reinforced in his conviction that the summer of 1900 was the right time for action, and that since the Trans-Siberian Railway, against his opposition, was crossing Manchuria, it should be properly defended. Witte and Lamsdorf were mere procrastinators.

Kaiser William was yelling for blood. "You must know, my men, that you are about to meet a crafty, well-armed, cruel foe," he told the departing detachment of German troops. "Meet him and beat him. Give no quarter. Take no prisoners. Kill when he falls into your hands. Even as a thousand years ago, the Huns under King Attila made such a name for themselves as still resounds in terror through legend and fable, so may the name of Germany resound through Chinese history a thousand years from now. . . ."

With some unhappiness on the part of the French, a German, Field-Marshal Count von Waldersee, was appointed commander-in-chief of the international relief force. No better man could have been chosen to execute the Kaiser's wishes. Before he got the chance, Witte hoped that negotiations with Li Hung-chang would avert the bloodshed that he so vividly saw ahead when the relief column reached Peking. Kuropatkin calmed his fears by telling him that the column would not get under way before September.

Kuropatkin no longer took either Witte or Lamsdorf into his confidence, rejecting their efforts to resolve the situation to Russia's advantage through Li Hung-chang as too slow. He continued his direct action, appointing Lieutenant-General Nicholas Petrovitch Linievitch, a sixty-two-year-old veteran of the Crimean War, and at the time Russian army commander in the Far East, to lead the Russian forces on the march to Peking.

The efficient and sizable Japanese force led the way. They threw back a Chinese counterattack soon after the force had left Tientsin. As the allied advance moved inexorably toward the capital, the Dowager Empress commanded repeatedly that Li Hung-chang should return from Canton with all haste. He took ship to Shanghai and then dispatched his answer:

> I myself am nearly eighty years of age, and my death cannot be far distant. I have received favors at the hands of four emperors. If now I hesitate to say the things that are in my mind, how shall I face the spirits of the sacred ancestors of this dynasty when we meet in the halls of Hades? . . . You should take steps immediately to appoint a high official who shall purge the land of this villainous rabble, and who shall see to it that the foreign ministers are safely escorted to the headquarters of the allied armies. . . . Your Majesties have not yet adopted a policy of reason, but are still in the hands of traitors, regarding these Boxers as your dutiful subjects. . . .

The Japanese stormed Tungchow and sent the Chinese fleeing in retreat on August 13. Early next morning the Sikhs and Rajputs of the British contingent entered Peking through the Water Gate* and reached the besieged legations. Tzu-h'si, the Dowager Empress, stayed for just one more day. Next morning, long before dawn, the concubines and the eunuchs and the hapless Emperor Kuang-hsu assembled to learn that the Son of Heaven was about to leave the capital, and that the concubines were to stay behind. The Pearl Concubine, whose favors had been withdrawn from the Emperor, pleaded to be allowed to go, too, and was seized by two eunuchs who wrapped her in a carpet and threw her down a well outside the palace.

---

*Also known as the Jade Canal; it was little more than an open sewer. In 1925 it was filled in and a garden laid out to replace it.

Dressed in homespun peasant costume and traveling by cart, Tzu-h'si and the rest of the imperial party set out for distant Sian in Shensi province, far from Peking, the coast and revengeful foreigners.

With a sense of propriety that did not inhibit him from collecting his own share of the loot, General Linievitch declared the Forbidden City off limits. The rest of the city was declared open. The allies made the most of it. The Summer Palace, rebuilt after it had been sacked by the British and French in 1860, was no exception. The Japanese went for the treasury and seized three million taels of pure silver and the government silk and rice stores. The British treated it all like an official auction sale, selling the goods that they had stolen and dividing the money among the officers and noncommissioned officers. The Germans sacked the imperial observatory and shared the plunder with the French. For weeks the looting and the destruction went on. The troops wanted silver and smashed priceless ceramics in their eagerness to probe into every possible place of concealment. Scarcely a building escaped the attention of the gallant soldiers. Rape was not an offense, but a pastime; murder of the Chinese, an entertainment.

Field Marshal von Waldersee turned up at the end of September to take over his command and to organize the punitive expeditions prescribed by the Kaiser. At the insistence of Witte and Lamsdorf, however, the Russian forces withdrew from Peking before the Germans spread themselves through the countryside to continue their plunder. On Kuropatkin's orders, they had no intention, however, of withdrawing from Manchuria, into which they had moved on July 9.

Five days later regular Chinese forces, working with the Boxers, and mounted guerrillas blew up a Russian ammunition dump and killed about thirty officers and men. They tried to blockade the Amur River, destroyed the Russian railway near Harbin, and blocked rail transport to Port Arthur.

These actions provided the Russians with the opportunity Kuropatkin wanted. The Russian commander in Blagoveshchensk ordered the immediate deportation of all 8,000 Chinese residents. At the point of a bayonet, they were driven into the Amur to make their way as best they could to Chinese territory on the other side of the river. A few got away and were shelled by Russian guns. Some 4,500 were either killed by shell fire or drowned. A large force of Russians now crossed the Amur and by October had occupied the entire three eastern provinces of Manchuria. St. Petersburg called this a "temporary" measure designed solely for the protection of the railways. As soon as conditions permitted, Russia planned to withdraw.

Some weeks later, the Russians held a thanksgiving service in the wreckage of the town of Sakhalin, across the Amur from Blagoveshchensk. The high priest of the Russian Orthodox Church who conducted the service said: "Now is the Cross raised on the bank of the Amur which yesterday was Chinese." At Newchwang, a Russian gunboat landed Cossacks and infantrymen who drove the Chinese population out of the town into the countryside, where the cavalry with long swords hacked men, women, and children to death by the hour.

Foreign Minister Lamsdorf saw the Tsar to protest against this sort of brutality. "His Majesty," Witte wrote to D. S. Sipyagin, the minister of the interior, "was gracious to the minister, but often interrupted him, saying that, after all, the Asiatics deserved the lesson which they had been taught."

During the following months, Russian policy in China had a curious ambivalence. In Manchuria, it was clear that the Russians had come to stay. Although both Witte and Lamsdorf continued to press for modifications to Kuropatkin's occupation plans, the agreement that Admiral Alexeiev, the Russian governor of Kwantung, pushed on the governor of Mukden was signed on November 26, 1900, and assured Russian control of Manchuria for as long as she wished, or as long as the governor's signature could be regarded as binding.

In Peking, however, the approach was entirely different. Witte's lines of communication with old Li Hung-chang remained open. Lamsdorf, who shared Witte's anxiety that the allied force should not become a punitive expedition, came out in a note dated August 25, 1900, which called for the withdrawal of allied forces from Peking. Since the other powers rejected the note, St. Petersburg achieved, though only temporarily, the diplomatic advantages that it had hoped for: to have itself regarded still as a friend and ally in Peking.

Field-Marshal von Waldersee had not even arrived to begin his pogrom when the Russian note was delivered, and, once again, the Kaiser was outraged. In the end, however, the Russian maneuvers served little purpose. It soon became obvious that St. Petersburg was running with the hare and hunting with the hounds.

By its virtual annexation of Manchuria, Russia threatened China with what it feared most: partition. In meeting this challenge, Peking found itself helped, if indirectly, by the United States. Though they had kept out of the land-grabbing that had gone on in China, their acquisition of the Philippines had helped to make the Americans very much part of the region. Unwilling to use the gunboat tactics of the European powers, but equally unwilling to see herself squeezed out of the profitable China trade by further European, Russian, and Japanese acquisitions, America took a lead from Britain, which, still commanding the greatest share of the China trade, had a vested interest in maintaining China's territorial sovereignty and the equality of economic opportunity there. In notes to England, Germany, Russia, France, and Japan in September 1899, John Hay, the secretary of state, spelled out the Open Door Policy.

Hay's initial note confined itself to matters of trade and customs, with the object of insuring that no single power should attempt to assume an authority that would exclude others. In particular, the United States was concerned to see that the European spheres of influence in China did not become colonial possessions. Britain was delighted and accepted the note, conditionally on the exclusion of Hong Kong and Kowloon. Germany, France, and Italy accepted, provided that the other powers also accepted. Russia, believing that the United States was concerned more with the protection of its own commercial interests than it was with China's rights, did not concur. It insisted that all its forces would be withdrawn as soon as the railway was secure in Manchuria.

On July 3, 1900, before the allied forces were ready to march on Peking, Hay carried the Open Door Policy a stage further and pledged the United States to protect China's territorial integrity. "The policy of the United States is to seek a solution which may bring about permanent safety and peace to China, preserve Chinese territorial integrity and administrative entity, protect all rights guaranteed to friendly powers by treaty and international law and safeguard trade with all parts of China," the note said.

The message was loud and clear for the allies: no partition. The Russians continued to protest that the forces would be withdrawn from Manchuria "as soon as peace was restored and the security of the railway assured." Yet all the time Russia continued to strengthen its hold, seizing most of the principal Manchurian cities. It took Liaoyang in September, Mukden and Tieh-ling early in October, Feng-huang-cheng and Antung in December. Mukden was the capital of Manchuria, and, as the seat of the ancestral tombs of the Manchus, of particular importance to the court in Peking. Feng-huang-cheng and Antung were close to the Korean border and therefore of concern to the Japanese. These acquisitions the Russians justified on the ground that the British had proposed the continued occupation of Chih-li province until China should submit to the demands of the powers.

For the Russians, who were determined to pursue separate negotiations with China, it was a race against time. They were helped by quarrels and disagreements among their allies, by their residual influence with Li Hung-chang, who had been nominated as one of the two principal negotiators with the allied powers, and by their refusal to associate themselves with the punitive demands of the other allies. Lamsdorf told the British ambassador in St. Petersburg that his government took no interest in missionaries and was not concerned with the punishment of their assassins.

After months of wrangling in St. Petersburg, Kuropatkin, Witte, and

Lamsdorf finally agreed in February 1901 on a draft treaty with China. It consisted of fourteen articles which ostensibly provided for China's continued sovereignty over Manchuria but in fact transferred to St. Petersburg the absolute control over the territory for an indefinite period of time. George Morrison, the Australian doctor of medicine turned newspaperman, telegraphed a clearly well-informed account of the Russian demands to *The Times* and quickly set off a sharp international reaction.

The Russians emphasized to the Chinese the need to complete the treaty before other powers protested, but they were not now alone in applying pressure. In January 1901, Komura Jutaro, the Japanese minister in Peking, urged Prince Ch'ing (who, with Li Hung-chang, was responsible for the negotiations with the allies) to press for the speediest withdrawal of the Russian troops from Manchuria. The Prince assured him that he would not concede anything to the Russians other than permission to maintain the forces needed to guard the railways. At the same time, the Japanese minister in St. Petersburg pressed Lamsdorf for an explanation of Russian activities in Manchuria. He got a curt reply. "The Manchurian question is a matter which concerns only Russia and China," Lamsdorf told him. "I have no need to answer questions from the Japanese government. However, in fact, Russia will, in accordance with her repeated declarations, return the administration of Manchuria to Chinese authorities and withdraw troops from the area."

Speaking to Li Hung-chang, Komura reverted to threats. "If China allows Russia to have territorial and other privileges," he told the Chinese official, "the other powers will also bring out similar demands in their spheres of influence." This prediction does not seem to have had much effect. Li Hung-chang, clearly hoping still to have Russia's backing in the peace negotiations, considered that the treaty would not impair the sovereignty of China in Manchuria.

Tokyo, on Komura's advice, now turned to Chang Chih-tung, the governor-general of Hupei and Hunan provinces, and Liu K'un-i, the governor-general of Kiangsu, Anhwei, and Kiangsi provinces, both of whom were semiautomonous lords of their domains. Odagiri, the Japanese consul-general in Shanghai, set out on January 29, 1901, on an urgent mission to pursuade the two men that China faced the gravest dangers in submitting to the Russian demands. Liu K'un-i was soon persuaded to work together "earnestly opposing Russia's conspiracy." Japan, the United States, Germany, and England also combined to issue a warning to China.

Faced with the nonrecognition of the Port Arthur agreement, Russia submitted a new draft treaty, the contents of which quickly became known to Komura. On February 27, he again conferred with Li Hung-chang, and pretending that he knew nothing of the contents of the new draft agreement,

[123]

warned him of the danger involved in acceding to Russia's demands in disregard of the allied warnings. Li was adamant. "If we don't accede to Russia's demand," he said, "Russia may withdraw the proposal for the return of Manchuria. Therefore we have to accept."

After hurried consultation by telegram to the world capitals, Komura and the British, German, and American ministers reissued their warnings to Li Hung-chang, who, under renewed pressure from the Russians, had been given two weeks in which to sign. March 26 was the deadline. The date passed without any further action, and the following day the Empress Dowager from her retreat at remote Sian appealed to the Tsar to amend the treaty draft. As the allied protests poured into St. Petersburg, the Russians replied blandly that there had been no draft treaty prepared along the lines suggested by Morrison, or confirmed by Komura and Sir Ernest Satow, the British minister in Peking. Lamsdorf's explanation was that a program had been under consideration, but at no time had he the powers necessary to sign any agreement entrusted to him. To the Japanese he said he "could give an official assurance" that "neither the sovereignty and the integrity of China in Manchuria nor the treaty rights of any other power were affected by the proposed agreement; that it was of a provisional nature, and a necessary preliminary to the Russian troops evacuating the province."

The Japanese government was dissatisfied with the explanation, and on April 5, 1901, it lodged a second protest with St. Petersburg. On the same day the *Official Messenger,* the organ of the Russian government, blamed the foreign press for publishing false reports about alleged treaties and noting that, as a result, negotiations for the gradual evacuation of Manchuria had been dropped.

Well aware of the sharply rising political temperature in Japan, Lamsdorf reported to the Tsar that the war party was gaining in strength and influence in Tokyo and "conflict with Japan might easily arise on the most insignificant pretext," even could Japan not also rely on the effective cooperation of England and the other powers. "Japan's attitude," he predicted, "may become more accentuated at the end of the Peking conferences, and also at the close of the current year [1901], when the re-equipment of her army shall have been completed."

The British and the Germans had come out jointly in favor of the preservation of the Open Door Policy, and in January 1901 there were discussions in London between Lord Lansdowne, the foreign secretary, and the German minister about the possibility of taking action jointly with Japan to force Russia to end its independent and aggressive policy in Manchuria. The Germans professed their neutrality, though they helped things along by informing the Japanese that they had no engagements that would oblige them, in the event of a Russo-Japanese or other clash, to side with the enemies of Japan.

Against this background of international intrigue, the allies squabbled among themselves about the terms of the settlement that they would impose on China. Not until September 7, 1901, did they agree on a final draft. Because of America's stand on the Open Door Policy, there was no land-grabbing this time, though it was agreed that each country might renegotiate its commercial treaty with China. The protocol imposed a huge indemnity of 450 million taels ($336 million), which was distributed among the powers according to their proportions of the 231 civilian lives lost in the Boxers' rampage and the property destroyed. Officials guilty of helping the Boxers were to be punished by the Chinese government, and many were either beheaded, banished, or presented with the silken cord to end their lives.

The Empress Dowager denounced the Boxers and returned to Peking after an absence of two years to institute the reforms she had so resolutely opposed. But China now was beyond imperial repair. The Boxer revolt had been the final gasp of despair. The Old Buddha, as the Empress Dowager was now called, had responded to the genuine feelings of the Chinese people against the foreign humiliations, but she had also gravely misunderstood the weakness of the Manchu administrative system and the need for revolutionary change if China were to throw off the retarding influence of the old-fashioned bureaucracy, with its disdain for anything smacking of industry and commerce, and take its place in the world.

Not long after the Sino-Japanese War, Ito Hirobumi told Li Hung-chang about his experience as a young man in England. "When I returned home, the Prince of Choshu asked me what needed changing in Japan," he said. "I replied, 'Everything.' "

Everything needed changing in China, also, but Li Hung-chang, who understood the need, died in November. His passing posed new problems for China—and for Russia. Into his place as Viceroy of Chih-li slid his old protégé from Korea, Yuan Shih-k'ai, who, when the Russians proved remorseless in their Manchurian demands, was to prove as helpful to Japan in the years immediately ahead as Li Hung-chang had been when he had tried to help Russia in the past.

CHAPTER 6

❦❦❦❦❦❦

The Wedding of the Moon
and the Mud Turtle

B<small>Y THE BEGINNING</small> OF 1902 Britain had become the most unpopular country in Europe. The Boer War was still dragging on, and the European press was about as complimentary to Britain's efforts in South Africa as it would be to the Americans in Vietnam seventy years later. For forty years Britain had watched the southward advance of Russia through Central Asia with fear and apprehension for the proudest of her imperial jewels, the Indian subcontinent. Russia's railroad imperialism had upset the British as early as 1885 when she started to build a line south to the Afghanistan border. All along the Persian and Afghan frontiers the British saw their interests threatened by Russian expansionism. Not all the threats were imaginary. In the reign of Alexander II, Grand Duke Michael Nicolaievitch had drawn up plans for the invasion of India, a scheme ardently supported now by Prince Ukhtomski, leading St. Petersburg newspaper publisher, friend of the Tsar's and for a long time one of Witte's subordinates. To a lesser but important extent, Russia's activities in Manchuria threatened Britain's predominant commercial position in China.

Nothing brings nations together so quickly as common enemies; and thus when Japan, equally friendless in the Far East and seeing her own position even more seriously threatened by Russia, turned to Britain for comfort, she found a receptive audience. Britain had been angered by the Russian seizure of Port Arthur, and the government had been heavily censured for making no more than a diplomatic protest. It was natural, therefore, that Japanese inquiries about a treaty should meet with a favorable response, especially since the Russians in Port Arthur were seen to threaten Peking.

Old China hands used to call the Russo-Japanese War "Morrison's war" after *The Times'* Peking correspondent. It was Count Hayashi Tadasu's war, too. In the summer of 1895, Hayashi, who had close connections with Fukuzawa Yukichi,* publisher, managing editor and founder of the newspapers *Jiji Shimpo* in Tokyo, set out in the columns of *Jiji* a program for the rapid militarization of Japan. "What Japan has to do is to keep perfectly quiet," he wrote, "to lull the suspicions that have arisen against her, and to wait, meanwhile strengthening the foundations of her national power, watching and waiting for the opportunity which one day surely must come to the Orient."

Soon after publishing this article, Hayashi was appointed Japanese minister to China. Just after he had left for Peking, the *Jiji Shimpo* published a second article in which Hayashi emphasized the need for Japan to conclude some sort of treaty arrangement with England to safeguard their interests against the predatory European powers that had so threatened Japan at the end of the Sino-Japanese war.

In March of 1900, Morrison was returning to Peking from a long vacation when he met Hayashi in the Kojunsha Club in Tokyo. The club, which, like the *Jiji Shimpo*, had been founded by Fukuzawa Yukichi, shared the same building with the newspaper. Two years earlier Morrison had been the center of a diplomatic storm in Peking when he broke the news of the Russian demands for Port Arthur. At their meeting now, Hayashi and Morrison found that their views coincided. For the Japanese, victors in the Sino-Japanese War, the intervening years had been marked by a contraction of their interests in Asia, while Russia, racing ahead with the construction of the Trans-Siberian railway complex, had not only seized what Japan had won on the Kwantung Peninsula, but was busy taking advantage of the Boxer Rebellion to occupy Manchuria, and to renew activity on the Korean border. Japan had embarked on a program of rapid military expansion, but the country had not reached the stage where it could meet the Russian threat without the backing of another power. Britain, Morrison and Hayashi agreed, was Japan's obvious choice as an ally.

Hayashi's appointment as minister to Britain provided the opportunity to translate their thoughts into action. He arrived in London at a time when England, still enmeshed in the Boer War, found herself lacking friends on the Continent, disturbed by the growth of German naval power, and suspicious of Russian intrigues in the Far East. Many people in England, with patronizing generosity, believed that even Christians could not have re-

---

*Also the founder of Keio University, the oldest private Japanese university, Fukuzawa was a renowned educator and pre-Meiji enthusiast for western culture. He was the author of an all-time best seller that described conditions in western countries.

sponded better than the Japanese to the Boxer challenge in Peking. Hayashi, looking over the scene, concluded that "pro-Japanese sentiment in England extended from the highest to the lowest and humblest citizen." Such was the warmth of his reception that he became the first Japanese Freemason.

Circumstances, however, did not yet fully favor Hayashi's scheme. Ito, who, for the fourth and last time, succeeded Field-Marshal Yamagata as prime minister on September 15, 1900, had not abandoned hope of settling Japan's problems with Russia peacefully. Alexander Izvolski, the Russian minister in Tokyo, had similar hopes, and in secret talks with Ito and other leaders proposed the neutralization of Korea under the joint protection of Russia and Japan.

This did not deter Hayashi, as early as April 1901, from raising the possibility of an Anglo-Japanese alliance with Lord Lansdowne. He also sounded out Baron Hermann von Eckardstein, the German chargé d'affaires in London. Hayashi told him that Japan was ready, provided she was assured of the neutrality of England and Germany, "to go to the limit" if Russia attempted to establish herself in Korea. Von Eckardstein told him, in exchange, that contrary to the idea prevalent in Tokyo, there was no secret understanding between Russia and Germany on Korea, where the diplomatic (and undiplomatic) struggle for supremacy between Japan and Russia continued.

Because of the need to maintain sea as well as land communications, their acquisition of the naval base at Port Arthur had increased, rather than lessened, the Russians' ambitions for a base on the south coast of Korea, and they made two attempts, both of which the Japanese thwarted, to obtain title hold to sizeable tracts of land on the foreshore at Masan on the south coast. Without a port in southern Korea, the Russians feared that the Japanese might be able to close the straits of Tsushima to their vessels travelling between Vladivostok and Port Arthur.

In his discussions in London with Hayashi, Lord Lansdowne wanted to know why Japan had not responded to Russia's initiative on neutralization. Hayashi told him: "It is quite useless to attempt to hold a neutral position. The Koreans are totally incapable of governing themselves and we can never tell when civil war will break out. In the event of civil war, who will hold the reins of government? It is after all very natural that the international interests in Korea should be conflicting."

To this stage, Hayashi had been negotiating only within the framework of an instructional telegram to the effect that the Japanese government was unable to express any view, "but there is no reason why inquiries should not be made among British government circles provided such inquiries are done as a matter of personal opinion which does not bind the imperial government." Events were now moving rapidly in the direction that Hayashi had hoped, however. The Ito cabinet fell and into the prime ministership stepped General Katsura Taro, first Japanese governor-general of Formosa, a protégé of Field-Marshal Yamagata, a Choshu and a Russophobe. With Yamagata, the country's most powerful military man, in support, and with Komura Jutaro, a sturdy Anglophile, soon to take over in the foreign ministry, the way was clear, or almost clear, for Hayashi in London.

He continued to report optimistically. On June 15, 1901, he advised the government that Sir Claude MacDonald, British minister in Tokyo, had been granted an audience with the King during his leave in England. "The King spoke throughout the interview of the need for permanent co-operation between Britain and Japan," he reported. Lord Salisbury, the prime minister, went even further, according to Hayashi. He advocated an actual military alliance, urging on Hayashi the need to ensure that Japan did not come to an agreement with Russia, which the British continued to regard as a serious threat to their interests in India.

Hayashi's messages created a sensation in official circles in Tokyo. "England plans friendship with us for her own profit," said Katsura's diary entry. "Her principal policy is to oppose Russia's invasion of the Far East by using us. . . . It is advantageous to accede to Britain's demands."

Ito and Katsura together drafted a message to Hayashi with instructions to protect Japan's interests in the treaty by demands that matched the British demands. "If Britain accedes to our demands, we should sign an agreement. If she rejects our demands, we will not have lost anything. Rejection would not be against our interests."

Ito and Katsura parted on good terms, but their views thereafter of what took place at Long Cloud Mansion, Katsura's seaside villa, where the message was drafted, were heavily at variance. On the assumption that he had Ito's full approval, Katsura returned to Tokyo and invited Marshal Yamagata, now president of the privy council, and the other elder statesmen to his official residence. He showed them Hayashi's report and asked for their support. Only Count Inoue demurred. Yamagata was strongly in support.

On August 8 Hayashi received the telegram he had been hoping for. The Japanese government agreed in principle to the British government's proposal for an alliance and expressed its determination to prevent further Russian encroachments in Manchuria or Korea.

During the summer, Komura returned from Peking and took over the foreign ministry. One of his first acts was to send Hayashi the plenipotentiary powers that he sought, along with a message of firm support. "The Japanese government has carefully considered the question of the proposed alliance with Great Britain and has formed a definite policy supporting the same and approving the course taken by you. . . ."

On October 16 Hayashi called on Lansdowne at the foreign office and the two men quickly got down to discuss a draft treaty. Hayashi spoke of Japan's interest in Korea and her determination to keep it out of Russian hands.

"What, then, is your policy in China?" Lansdowne asked.

"As I have stated, we entirely agree with the British policy in the country," Hayashi answered. "We wish to maintain the territorial integrity of China and the principle of equal opportunity."

In less than a month, Lord Lansdowne presented Hayashi with a draft treaty that met most of Japan's needs. Britain was ready to come to Japan's aid if Russia should find an ally to help it with a war fought over China and Korea.

The treaty was not quite signed, sealed and delivered, however. Though he had lost the premiership, Ito, the most distinguished of all the Japanese leaders in the post-restoration period, remained a formidable force.

Day-by-day management of affairs had passed from his hands, but his opinions as the principal elder statesman weighed heavily with the Emperor. On the advice of Count Inoue, Ito decided to visit St. Petersburg, when he could have private talks with Witte, Lamsdorf and others to pave the way for an effective treaty between the two countries. Because of the delicacy of the negotiations with Britain, the last thing in the world that Katsura wanted at this stage was to have Ito talking in St. Petersburg, but it was inconceivable in the nature of Japanese political society that he should say so. With the utmost reluctance, he therefore approved of the Ito trip and held a farewell party at his private residence.

As Ito made his way to the United States and on to France, the Anglo-Japanese Alliance was rapidly beginning to take shape. Ito and Hayashi met in Paris on November 14. Ito was astonished to learn that negotiations with England had gone so far, and Hayashi was at a loss to know what to do when he learned of Ito's mission, since the British had already made clear that the two treaties were mutually exclusive.

By this time, London had become suspicious. Hayashi returned from Paris on November 19 and on the following morning saw Lord Lansdowne who immediately asked him for the Japanese government's reply to the draft treaty. To his own embarrassment, Hayashi was obliged to reply that he had not yet received it. Lansdowne answered that there was grave danger in delay, since the news of the proposed treaty might leak out and cause complications. Britain was concerned both with its interests in India and its trade with China, both of which the treaty was designed to protect. Premature disclosure of the discussions might have aroused the suspicions of the Germans, the French and the Russians.

"The Marquis then asked me about Marquis Ito's visit to Russia and expressed a wish that he should come to England," Hayashi wrote later. "He appeared to be rather annoyed that he had not done so. He said that if it was the intention of the Japanese government to negotiate a convention or agreement with Russia whilst the negotiations with Britain were in progress the British government would be very angry."

Hayashi, who understood Britain's fears of Russian designs on India, ventured a feeble explanation: Ito's visit to Russia had no meaning at all, and, unfortunately, he would not be able to visit London in November because the London weather was at its worst, fogs were general and would be damaging to his health, which was not good.

Lord Lansdowne was not impressed. If Ito was traveling for his health, he asked, why did he go to St. Petersburg in winter?

The British now began to apply strong pressure, warning Hayashi that though the Russians might sign a treaty with Japan which appeared to be more advantageous, they were not to be trusted. Their warnings had the desired effect in Tokyo. And though Ito found the Russians receptive to his ideas, he was unable to convey a sense of urgency to his hosts in St. Petersburg without disclosing that Japan and England were about to sign a treaty. Instead, he cabled a final protest to Tokyo against the Anglo-Japanese Alliance. "I should most sincerely urge upon the imperial government to strive for friendly harmony," he wrote. "This, however, would become impossible after the conclusion of an alliance with Great Britain." The enmity Britain felt for Russia was fully reciprocated.

With their minds already made up, the Japanese cabinet met on December 9 to consider Ito's telegram. To a man, they rejected his advice. Katsura and Komura then went to the palace to report that all cabinet members disagreed with Ito. As usual, the Emperor sought the counsel of the elder statesmen. The next day Katsura informed Ito that, since a satisfactory formation of a Japan–Russian agreement was not yet to be expected, unnecessary delays might cause Britain to withdraw her proposal, thus causing the antagonism of both Britain and Russia. The Emperor commanded the elder statesmen to reexamine the matter, and upon receiving advice that they had not changed their view, sanctioned the amended plan. Ito's mission had failed. The way was clear for the Anglo-Japanese Alliance, which would protect Japan while it prepared for war.

The treaty was signed on January 30, 1902, and published ten days later. Katsura was made a count and Hayashi a viscount. Komura was made a baron and all other members of the cabinet were either given a rank or elevated to higher ranks in the peerage. "Your honor is a proper reward for your effort," an acquaintance said to Komura, "but for all the cabinet to be given these honors seems to be a case of all-round tips."

Komura laughed. "They kept the negotiations completely secret," he said. "That alone was worth a peerage."

"The alliance was really an epoch-making event," Hayashi wrote later. "It stands out in the history of the world. The glorious victories of our army and navy in the Russo-Japanese War, and the great fight in the Straits of Tsushima, were in themselves almost unprecedented in the history of warfare, but they could never have taken place without the Anglo-Japanese Alliance."

People who had regarded the Katsura cabinet as third-rate now began to take it more seriously. Ito's prestige declined. "It was like a marriage between the moon and the mud turtle," Ubutaka Toshio, a famous essayist and humorist, wrote of the alliance. "Naturally, for the mud turtle this was a happy occasion."

Since 1895, when the Japanese government spent its China indemnity on battleships in Britain, the Japanese people had regarded war with Russia as inevitable. The Russian occupation of Port Arthur and now the delaying tactics adopted by St. Petersburg in Manchuria had simply confirmed the view. With the support of Britain, there was now no cause, they believed, for delay. When nearly 300 troops died of frostbite while marching on Mount Hakkoda, in northern Japan, it was assumed that the army was preparing for a Siberian campaign.

The meaning of the alliance was not lost, of course, on St. Petersburg, which immediately proposed a joint Franco–German–Russian response. The Germans were not interested. They emphasized that their interests were purely commercial. They were concerned about their sealanes and feared that the sort of joint response advocated by Russia would have the effect of encouraging the United States to identify itself with the alliance. In the event of war between Russia and Japan, Germany would be neutral. At the same time, William was very glad that St. Petersburg had taken the news so seriously. He promised that he would keep his hands free "to cover the Tsar's rear flank in Europe and secure him from threat of attack in Europe either by sea or by land."

Though he was not prepared to make a common declaration of intent with Russia, the Kaiser commended Nicholas for his determination to prevent other powers consolidating and thus to avoid the danger of war. By September 2, 1902, he was entreating Nicholas to look upon the German and Russian navies as "one great organization belonging to one great Continent whose interests it must guard on its shores and in distant seas. . . . This means practically the Peace of the World." William detected "certain symptoms in the East." These seemed to show that "Japan is becoming a rather restless customer and that the situation necessitates all coolness and decision of the Peace Powers." He was alarmed to learn that the Japanese military attaché in Peking was taking in hand the reorganization of the Chinese army—

> i.e., for the unavowed object of driving every other foreigner out of China. . . . Twenty to thirty million of trained Chinese helped by half a dozen Japanese divisions and led by fine undaunted Christian-hating Japanese officers is a future to be contemplated not without anxiety; and not impossible. In fact, it is the coming into reality of the Yellow Peril, which I depicted some years ago, and for which engraving I was laughed at by the greater mass of the people.

The Kaiser remained "your most devoted friend and Cousing (*sic*), Willy, Ad. of Atlantic."

Privately, William was convinced that Nicholas was fit only to live in the country and grow turnips, but his letters to the Tsar, written in English, were typically Germanic in style and full of endearments. "Dearest Nicky," they began, ending with such salutations as "ta, ta, best love to Alix" to whom he referred as "that adorable, charming and accomplished angel who is your wife." Alix loathed him. Even William's mother, a daughter of Queen Victoria, found her son always impertinent to her, disagreeable and rude. There was no love lost between the families. "My dear, darling Mama," Nicholas wrote after an exhausting visit from William and his wife. "Thank God the German visit is over and one may definitely say without boasting that it went off successfully . . . on the whole Wilhelm was very cheerful, calm and courteous, while she [his wife] tried to be charming and looked very ugly in rich clothes chosen without taste; the hats she wore in the evenings were particularly impossible."

"My advice to you," William would say, tapping Nicholas on the shoulder in a patronizing way, "is more speeches and more parades, more speeches, more parades." William loved parades and uniforms, which he collected the way that some people save stamps. Nicholas tried to break the news gently in a letter to his mother that he had to give William the rank of admiral in the Russian navy. "However disagreeable it may be, we are obliged to let him wear our naval uniform and, what's much worse, I'll have to greet him as such at Kronstadt [naval base]. It makes me vomit."

Born with a withered arm, William from his earliest years reacted strongly to this deformity.

"He was as rude, as disagreeable to me as possible," his mother wrote to Queen Victoria, her own mother.

Witte, who detested William, believed that William's malign influence with Nicholas pushed him into the Far Eastern swamp. "It is certain," he wrote, "that by the seizure of Kiao-chau William furnished the initial impetus to our policy. The German diplomats and the Kaiser were clearly making every effort in those days to drag us into Far Eastern adventures. . . . William is the author of the war." He persuaded Nicholas that it was clearly the great task for the future of Russia to cultivate the Asian continent and to defend Europe from the inroads of the great yellow race.

William, forty-five years old in 1904, was infatuated with power. Like the British, the Russians, and the Japanese, he was profoundly impressed with Captain Mahan's *The Influence of Sea Power upon History.* Von Moltke also contributed to William's dreams of naval grandeur. In the early 1870s, long before Germany's naval build-up had begun, he told him that he saw no great risk in attacking England if the attack could be made swiftly and by surprise. William needed little encouragement. "Our future lies on the water," he said. "That trident ought to be in our hands."

His early insistence on German naval expansion was rebuffed, but in 1898 and 1900 two naval bills passed the Reichstag. The object was to give Germany a fleet of such strength that, even for the mightiest naval power, a war with Germany would "involve such risks as to jeopardize her supremacy."

Berlin refrained from telling the Russians that Britain had raised the question of a defensive agreement between Germany and Britain and that Berlin had responded with an invitation to both England and Japan to join the Triple Alliance—Germany, Austria and Italy. The Japanese response was to ask Germany to enter into an agreement with Japan and Britain to maintain the Open Door Policy in China. Since Germany had refused to join England against France in Morocco in May 1901, Britain's interest in a treaty relationship with Germany now cooled, though both Britain and Japan had been assured in advance of Germany's intention to maintain its neutrality in the event of war between Russia and Japan.

Germany was torn between the consolidation of its power in Europe and William's desire for a colonial empire and a powerful fleet to defend it. Its iron and steel industry in the Ruhr had made it Europe's greatest industrial power. Time would soon make it Europe's greatest military power, also. It would have welcomed a war between Britain and Russia, but, just as it had refused to ally itself with Britain and Japan, it was equally unwilling to become involved on Russia's side. That Britain through the alliance could fight a war by proxy with Russia in the Far East was in itself undesirable, since it did not commit England to pay in blood and treasure. It was a compensating factor, however, that the alliance would cause Russia to strengthen its eastern defenses, thereby easing any strain from that quarter on Germany and providing it with much more room for maneuver in

Europe, and the opportunity to keep a more watchful eye on France, which, until the closing years of the nineteenth century, had sharp differences with Britain.

The French alliance with Russia in 1892 had been followed by French participation with Russia and Germany in the ultimatum to Japan to get out of Port Arthur in 1895. French loans had also made possible much of Russia's expansion in the Far East, and French anger when Britain got financial control in Egypt almost led to war in 1898.

Still smarting under its defeat by Germany in the Franco-Prussian War of 1870, however, France clearly understood that the principal threat still came from its highly industrialized German neighbor. The alliance with Russia was insufficient protection. With the death of Queen Victoria in 1901, Edward VII succeeded to the British throne. He was fond of Paris and Paris was fond of him, and, with the end to the Boer War, relations between the two countries quickly began to improve, and were soon to lead to the *Entente Cordiale*.

Allied to Russia but disapproving of its role in Manchuria, France tried to act as intermediary as Japan and Russia moved toward war. Théophile Delcassé, the French foreign minister, worked on London and Washington to persuade Tokyo to reduce the Japanese demands. There was no inclination in either capital, however, to tell the Japanese what they ought to do, and, though the British government was divided on what action it should take in the event of a Japanese defeat, it took no step to restrain Japan from going to war. "A war in which we were not actively concerned, and in which Japan did not suffer serious defeat, would not be an unmixed curse," Arthur Balfour, the prime minister, advised King Edward VII. Britain, like France, Germany, and China, intended to stay "neutral." The term was to have many meanings.

Neutral was the stance adopted by the United States also. After arousing Japan from its two centuries of slumber in 1853, it had clung passively to Britain's Far Eastern coattails until 1898 when it annexed the Hawaiian islands. This momentous first step across the Pacific caused serious concern in Japan, which had no wish to see another great power approaching by water as Russia had approached by land. The following year the United States launched deeper into the paths of imperialism when, as part of the spoils of the war with Spain, she took possession of the Philippines.

Trade with China was the motivating force. The Russians in Port Arthur; the Germans in Kiao-chau; the British in Hong Kong, Wei-hai-wei, and the Yangtze valley; and the French in Indochina and with a sphere of influence in Hainan and the three southern provinces of Yunnan, Kwangsi, and Kwantung—all these established themselves in commanding positions to carve up the China trade. The Philippines would serve America's interest in precisely the same way and add authority to its voice when it demanded the Open Door and an end to all dreams of partitioning China.

Since Russia was now demonstrably intent on partition in Manchuria, and Japan, with Britain, was opposed to it, the Americans with their Open Door Policy calmed the immediate Japanese fears and, indeed, strengthened their hand. Secretary of State Hay made repeated protests against Russian activities in Manchuria. On February 1, 1902, he demanded absolute equality of treatment of all nations in trade navigation and commerce in China. A year later he protested the terms of the treaty the Russians were trying to persuade the Chinese to sign and which would have prohibited treaty ports and foreign consuls in Manchuria. On the eve of the war he made what the Russians regarded as common cause with Japan when the United States, on October 8, 1903, signed a trade treaty with China that opened Mukden and Antung to international residence and trade.

The inclusion of Antung stung in St. Petersburg, for it was close to the Yalu River and therefore at the center of the quarrel between Russia and Japan. Whether this was by accident or design is unclear. What was not in doubt, however, was President Theodore Roosevelt's sympathies for the Japanese.

He, too, believed in maintaining a neutral posture in the war—"benevolent neutrality," he called it. The benevolence extended to warning Germany and France "in the most polite and discreet" fashion as soon as war broke out that if they repeated their tactics at the end of the Sino-Japanese War and combined with Russia against Japan he would "promptly side with Japan and proceed to whatever length was necessary on her behalf."

And so the great powers defined their positions and stood by to await developments, most of them professing the utmost surprise when the conflict that in their own interests they had helped to encourage and make possible burst upon the world.

CHAPTER 7

ଌଌଌଌଌଌ

The End of
the Mangy Triumvirate

THE BLIZZARDS THAT HOWLED out of the Arctic Circle across Lake Baikal in the winter of 1903–1904 tore at the tenuous Russian lines of communication with the Far East, now so ominously threatened by war. The lake is nearly 400 miles long and varies from fifteen to forty-five miles wide. It is 1,500 feet above sea level and walled by mountains that rise steeply to a height of 8,500 feet. Russian engineers had been working desperately all summer and fall to blast their tunnels through the mountains, but when winter descended in its frozen fury they were still far short of their goal. Lake Baikal was still the unbridgeable gap in the line.

By the end of December ice had already begun to form on the surface of the lake. By the end of January, the *Baikal,* which had been ferrying five troop trains a day, and a smaller ferry, the *Angara,* which was not equipped to take troop trains, could no longer break through, and Russian troops heading for the East were obliged to march across the ice, halting at four-mile intervals in heated shelters to recover from exposure.

Storms were frequent and the ice often cracked, leaving immense fissures into which the unwary troops often fell. With a growing sense of urgency as the war clouds added their threat to the winter storms, the Russians had mobilized 3,000 horses to draw sledges loaded with supplies across the lake. Since supplies were often lost in mountainous quantities, engineers experimented with a line laid across the ice. Though the ice would not stand the weight of a locomotive, it was found that horses could be used to draw loaded trucks. In the first two weeks that the new system was in use, however, only twenty trucks reached the eastern side of the lake.

To those who had contemplated the war with Japan with equanimity, the weaknesses of the Trans-Siberian Railway, especially here at Lake Baikal, came as a grim shock. Things had not been nearly so difficult when it came to moving troops from European Russia in the Boxer Rebellion: but the Boxer Rebellion, as the Russians were soon to learn, also, was not to be compared with the struggle that lay ahead, nor were its demands of the same order as the insatiable call for manpower and material that was to come from Port Arthur and the battlefields of Manchuria.

When the line was built, it seemed one of the wonders of the world, a rainbow joining West and East, with treasure untold waiting at its end. As soon as the Treaty of Peking had been signed in 1860, Count Muraiev "Amurski," the Russian governor-general in East Siberia, had begun to bombard St. Petersburg with the idea for the great new railroad leading from the Urals into the new Russian territories of the Far East. Before 1875 the scheme attracted little official attention, and it was not until 1880 that it was agreed to make a start in European Russia.

Two years later, Alexander III decided that the line should be extended to Siberia. Despite this imperial interest, planning did not get off the drawing boards. Annotating a progress report from the governor-general of East Siberia in 1886, Alexander observed: "So far as I have read, I am grieved to observe that the government up till now has done practically nothing to meet the requirements of this rich but neglected country, and it is time—indeed time—that something should be done."

Another five years were to pass before this royal impatience translated itself into action. Witte was the driving force behind the railroad, and Nicholas became its patron when he traveled for 1,500 miles by boat up the Amur River from Vladivostok after he had been attacked in Japan, and was convinced of the need. After leaving Japan he had gone on to Vladivostok, where he laid the foundations of a dry dock and wheeled the first barrow load of dirt for the foundations of the new line, which, with record-breaking speed and often lamentable workmanship,* now began to cross the wastelands of Siberia. Spanning the widest rivers, the Irtish, the Ob, and the Yenesei, it was manned by an army of 36,000 laborers, 13,000 carters, 5,850 surfacemen, 4,300 carpenters, 4,000 stonemasons, 2,000 riveters, and thousands of technicians.

The difficulties were horrendous. From December until July the ground in central Siberia was frozen to a depth of six feet. Every wooden block on which the rail lay had to be hand cut. At the Vladivostok end prisoners from Sakhalin were put to work on the Ussuri section but without success. Later,

---

*One corrupt contractor laid the rails on packed ice and snow. When the thaw came, the line of course collapsed.

in the bleak mid-Siberian section, the Russians, who used Siberia as a place of exile for political prisoners and felons, tried an incentive system to advantage. Eight months' labor on this stretch of the line counted for a full year's imprisonment with hard labor. For those who more than two years previously had been transported for life, the waiting period for a dwelling place was reduced by half. And for those compelled to live in far Siberia, the period of deportation was shortened by a year or two. Successful efforts were also made to induce settlers into the region. Around Tobolsk and Tomsk male settlers were encouraged by grants of up to forty-two acres of suitable land, with sometimes extra grants of forest land.Between 1892 and 1895 the line progressed at an average rate of 387 miles a year. Spurred on by the Japanese successes in the war against China, Witte pushed through the construction of 836 miles in 1895.

The line, of necessity, was crudely built. To save money, it was single track. Bridges were made of wood instead of steel. To avoid expensive circuitous routes in mountainous areas the gradients were excessively steep, and trains, at first using wood for fuel, labored their way. Eighteen miles an hour was a high average speed, and in some sectors seven miles an hour was the limit. Even at this speed, accidents were numerous.

For strategic reasons, the Russians had elected to build their railways on an extremely broad gauge—five feet, one inch, compared with the standard European gauge of four feet, eight and one-half inches. By this stratagem, it was hoped that invading forces would not be able to make use of the Russian railway system, but, when it happened, the hope proved false. When the opportunity was theirs, the Japanese simply lifted one rail and relaid it to their own gauge of three feet, six inches, and then cut off the end of the "sleepers," or wooden supports on which the line was laid, thus prohibiting their re-use by the Russians.

At places in the mountains beyond Lake Baikal water was scarce and often salty, and conduits were difficult to build because of the intense cold. Even in western Siberia the line could handle only three trains a day in each direction when it was first built, and the Lake Baikal bottleneck caused many delays.

"When the road for sledges is not yet, or is no longer, firm enough, traffic across the lake stopped altogether [in the winter of 1900–1901 for forty-seven days]," Witte complained.

Navigation is also much disturbed by gales and fogs, and this again reacts unfavorably on the regularity of railway traffic east and west. The work performed by the two steamboats themselves is, after all, very poor. Each of the two steamers makes on the average only one and a half trips in twenty-four hours. Each boat carries twenty-seven trucks, and thus brings forty of them over in twenty-four hours—that is to say, eighty-eight goods vans less than could be dispatched even last year on the most difficult stretches of the Siberian railway. . . .

Apart from the immense technical difficulties in building the railway through the cliffs at the southern end of Lake Baikal, there were further problems in the course followed by the Amur River, which sweeps to the northeast, thereby necessitating a similar prolongation of the railway if the line was to be laid entirely in Russian territory. Witte therefore proposed that the railway should be built across Chinese territory in Manchuria to Vladivostok, thus saving 340 miles in construction, and a substantial sum of money. Since both the French and the Germans had already demanded new concessions from much-weakened China, the Chinese were chary. The Russian minister to Peking telegraphed to St. Petersburg on December 28, 1895, that "the feeling of gratitude cherished toward us by China is beginning to weaken and to give place to a certain vague feeling of apprehension and distrust, evoked by a premonition that before long we are going to make extraordinary demands, the significance and proportions of which are still being kept from her." Fear of Russian intentions was matched, however, by China's worries about where the money was coming from to finance the next installment of the Japanese indemnity, since the first contribution of £10 million sterling from the Russo-French groups met only a small proportion of the demands.

At the same time, there was opposition within Russia itself to the idea of building a railway across Manchuria. "In vain," General Kuropatkin wrote later, "did the commander in the Pri-Amur district protest and point out the risks of such a course. He argued that if the railway passed through Chinese territory not only would it be of advantage to the Chinese instead of to the Russian settler population but it would be insecure. His view did not find acceptance, and this great artery of communication, of incalculable importance to us, was laid through a foreign country."

The director of the Asiatic department of the ministry of foreign affairs was another who argued against it. He did not oppose the shortcut but wanted the line to aim for Blagoveshchensk instead of Vladivostok. He insisted that the security of the line would be impossible without military occupation and talked of the "enormous risk" involved in Witte's plan.

At the other extreme, there were men like Peter Alexandrovitch Badmaev, the court physician, who wanted to push the line through Kyakhta, southeast of Lake Baikal on the Russo–China border, and on to Peking. He dreamed of another line to Lanchow in China's Kansu province and the promotion of a rebellion there to provide the excuse for Russian conquest. Before Witte's disapproval put an end to this venture, he had been given a grant of two million roubles to take preliminary steps in the railroad project.

Witte saw immense commercial advantages in a line running through northern Manchuria to Vladivostok and envisaged branch lines eventually taking off in all directions, with Russia profiting immeasurably from the trade. He dismissed the arguments of Kuropatkin and others as alarmist and those of Badmaev as too adventurous—"a railroad to Peking would arouse the whole of Europe against us."

The visit to St. Petersburg of Li Hung-chang for the coronation of Nicholas II was the means by which Witte effected his coup. To make sure that Li did not fall prey to the bribery of the European powers first, Witte sent Prince Ukhtomski aboard the *Rossiya* to meet him at Port Said in Egypt before he could get in touch with the European powers and to bear him in state to Odessa. There he was given an honor guard in keeping with his rank and seniority. Pushing aside Prince Lobanov-Rostovski, the foreign minister, "who was entirely ignorant of our Far Eastern policy," Witte took over the negotiations.

Persuading Li Hung-chang to agree to the construction of the Trans-Siberian Railway through Manchuria posed many problems. Witte knew that patience and ceremony were two of the keys to success. When Li called on him in his official capacity as finance minister, Witte greeted him dressed in the full regalia of office. Witte bent his huge frame in a deep bow to Li, who returned the courtesy. Tea was served in a second reception room. There Witte and Li sat and sipped their cups. "When we had taken our tea, I inquired of Li Hung-chang whether he did not want to smoke," Witte recalled. "He emitted a sound not unlike the neighing of a horse. Immediately two Chinamen came running from the adjacent room, one carrying a narghile [hookah] and the other tobacco."

Witte believed the Trans-Siberian would be Russia's answer to the Suez Canal and the Canadian Pacific Railway. England now controlled two-thirds of the exports leaving Chinese ports, and Russia's only means of winning this trade away from her was to push on with the railway as rapidly as possible.

"I dwelt on the services which we had recently done his country," Witte wrote of his negotiations with Li Hung-chang.

I assured him that, having proclaimed the principle of China's territorial integrity, we intended to adhere to it in the future; but, to be able to uphold this principle, I argued, we must be in a position, in case of emergency, to render China armed assistance. Such aid we would not be able to render her until both European Russia and Vladivostok were connected with China by rail, our armed forces being concentrated in European Russia.

All of this was preliminary to the final argument that "to uphold the territorial integrity of the Chinese empire, it was necessary for us to have a railroad running along the shortest possible route to Vladivostok, across the northern part of Mongolia and Manchuria."

Li Hung-chang held out adamantly against the construction of a Russian government railway across Chinese territory, but finally agreed that the railway should be built by a private corporation. This, as Witte pointed out, was merely a face-saving device since the Chinese Eastern Railway Company "was, of course, completely in the hands of the government." China agreed to cede a strip of land sufficient for the construction and operation of the railway and to the presence of Russian railway police "to exercise full and untrammeled authority." The quid pro quo was the Russian obligation to defend China against attacks by Japan. Japan was specifically designated, but in the drafting of the text of the treaty the word was omitted. When the two parties were about to sign, Witte noticed the omission and was aghast. A defensive alliance with China against all the powers was a very different kettle of fish from a defensive alliance with China against Japan.

Witte approached Prince Lobanov-Rostovski, who, as foreign minister, was preparing to sign on behalf of Russia. "My God," said the prince, "I forgot to tell my secretary to insert that paragraph in its original wording." Looking at his watch and seeing that it was fifteen minutes before noon, the Prince clapped his hands for servants and announced that lunch would be served. When the delegates gathered again in the afternoon, new drafts including the word "Japan" had been prepared and were duly signed.

Little word of this secret treaty leaked out at the time. All that was known was that China had agreed to grant the Russo-Chinese Bank a concession for the construction of the Chinese Eastern Railway, a continuation of the Trans-Siberian. But this was sufficient to raise the cry that the Russians had bribed Li Hung-chang. Witte denied it in his *Memoirs,* but his denial by no means resolves the question. St. Petersburg knew that it was impossible even to dream of approaching a settlement without recourse to bribery. Li was notoriously corrupt and was believed by some contemporary observers to have been the richest man in the world. "For his signature to the treaty as such, the old man [Li Hung-chang] received no cash in hand," wrote B. A. Romanov.

> Payment was promised at different and rather remote dates: the first million [roubles] upon receipt of the imperial order for granting the concession to the Russo-Chinese Bank and the document ratifying the main principles of the concession; and the second upon the final signing of the concession and the confirmation of the exact direction of the line; and the third when the construction was entirely completed.

Despite the speed with which surveys were undertaken, it was not until the spring of 1898 that the building of the line across Manchuria got underway, and by that time circumstances had changed. Russia had seized Port Arthur and not only needed a line through Manchuria to Vladivostok but a branch line to its new warm-water port.

To the village of Harbin in Central Manchuria in the hot, wet summer of 1898 came platoons of Russian railway construction workers and Witte's armed escorts, or "Matilda's guards," as they were called after Witte's wife. Harbin was no more than a cluster of huts when the Russians first arrived, but soon the Russo-Chinese Bank appeared—solid, brick, and a symbol of the new presence. A telegraph office maintained communications with St. Petersburg and along the railroad. A shabby hotel, soon the haunt of prostitutes who followed the railway, and a collection of Chinese squatters' huts made up the remainder. The town grew rapidly and abominably.

Manchuria's principal exports at the time were soya beans and soya products. The beans were collected during the winter by carts which traveled across the frozen Liao River and were then shipped by junk in the spring to Newchwang on the Gulf of Chih-li.

As the railroad pushed on toward Port Arthur and Dalny, the Russians hoped to capture the bean trade, but the transport charges on the railroad were too high. Nor was there any enthusiasm among the Chinese merchants to use the railroad for other commercial traffic—the transport of silks, furs, tobacco, and ginseng.

The freight sections of the railroad were, nevertheless, busy. When Witte imposed new excise duties on vodka, the merchants rushed their supplies east to Manchuria. Freight car after freight car contained nothing but vodka. The Russian expatriates at all the little stations along the great railroad saw it as a patriotic duty to attempt to reduce the size of the vodka stores. When the line reached Port Arthur and the first trains came through, the vodka cases rose like Everest and became one of the principal sights of the town. Not to be outdone, Harbin built its own grand pile and later Mukden had the most celebrated and massive dump of all. At ten cents a bottle, the meanest functionary could afford to drink himself into insensibility night after night. And did. The railroad to the East was paved with Nicholas's dreams of empire and the discarded empties of his subjects.

On April 8, 1902, almost two months to the day after the public announcement of the Anglo–Japanese Alliance, the Russians signed a convention with China under which they agreed to a three-phased withdrawal of their forces from Manchuria. The withdrawal was to be completed within eighteen months. That Russia agreed to such a proposition was due largely to the Japanese, the British, and the Americans, who, as each new Russian demand leaked out, applied the firmest pressure on China to stand firm.

[143]

Diplomacy and public clamor went together. On February 12, 1902, Komura cabled Uchida, the Japanese minister in Peking, instructing him to warn Prince Ch'ing that if China were to disregard her obligations to the powers which she had agreed to under the Boxer Protocol of September 7, 1901, the "Japanese government, in order to correct the serious inequality of interests arising from the agreement, would have to consider what demands it should make on the Chinese government." The British issued a similar warning.

In the tangle of international relations that had now begun to develop, the United States leaned more and more toward the Anglo–Japanese position. China, through Yuan Shih-k'ai, was busy reestablishing amicable relations with Japan. France and Russia had ties through the Franco–Russian Alliance of 1892. Paris was St. Petersburg's principal source of finance, and Nicholas needed all the money that he could lay his hands on to rush through the building of the Trans-Siberian and Chinese Eastern railways. A Franco–Russian declaration reaffirmed the determination of both powers to maintain the independence of China and Korea and said that if aggressive action by third powers threatened their own interests the two governments would consider means to safeguard them.

Witte visited the Far East during the summer of 1902 to study the Chinese Eastern Railway. He returned with advice Nicholas did not want to hear: that Russia must regard Manchuria as "unconditionally and forever lost." He called for the evacuation of Manchuria and "the securing of our influence in the Far East by peaceful means exclusively." "The report failed to impress His Majesty," Witte noted. "Had he followed my advice, we would have avoided the unhappy war with all its disastrous consequences."

Witte ran headlong into Nicholas's own concept of his destiny, his contempt for, and ignorance of, the Japanese, the military appreciation that northern Manchuria should be held at all costs, the encouragement given to the Tsar by Kaiser William of Germany, and the activities of a band of adventurers who were rapidly gaining influence at the court. The Trans-Siberian Railway had been extended through Manchuria against military advice. But, having seen it built, the military now argued sensibly that it had to be protected. Kuropatkin even set out an ingenious if outrageous plan to sell China all of southern Manchuria, which was, of course, its own territory, in exchange for China's concession of all northern Manchuria to Russia.

Kuropatkin approved of the first two phases of the evacuation, which called for the withdrawal from the rest of the province of Mukden, including Mukden itself and Newchwang. On his instructions, barracks were hastily built between Khabarovsk and Vladivostok to accommodate the troops. Everything was going well when Admiral Alexeiev, the Kwantung governor, suddenly canceled the order without explanation, but at a time when he was entertaining Captain Bezobrazov. Bezobrazov, who had succeeded in interesting the Tsar in the Yalu River timber concession, was visiting the Far East with two million roubles in state funds drawn by order of Nicholas himself; he had an indomitable belief in the wealth that could be generated in the region by the exercise of military power. With this large sum to his credit, Bezobrazov dispensed his patronage where he saw fit— 40,000 roubles to the Russian hospital in Mukden and 35,000 to the newspaper *Novoye Krai* in Port Arthur to start an English language newspaper to counter the anti-Russian propaganda of the English-owned papers along the China coast and in Japan. Much more importantly, with the money that Witte had reluctantly deposited to his account in the Russo-Chinese bank in Port Arthur, Bezobrazov could now proceed with the plan, long dear to his heart, to develop the timber concessions on the Yalu River.

The generosity of his gifts and the splendor of his mode of transportation left no doubt that he traveled with the full authority conferred on him by the Tsar. By the time he had finished his tour even Alexeiev had become something of a convert, though he opposed Bezobrazov when he wanted to recruit a force of ex-soldiers to serve on the Yalu concession.

Bezobrazov was a fluent speaker with an easy presence. He first came to Nicholas's notice early in the reign when he served in a senior post in the imperial household. Later, he went to the Far East for a year's tour of duty at Russian headquarters and had returned to St. Petersburg to expound on the political and economic value of the Korean concession. He soon became the leading figure in a clique that became, though briefly, more than a shadow government, pursuing its own independent course in opposition to that advocated by Witte, Lamsdorf, and Kuropatkin.

While Witte continued to enjoy the support of Interior Minister Sipyagin, however, there was little that Bezobrazov could do to diminish the powerful authority of the finance minister. An assassin's bullet was soon to serve as his ally. Sipyagin was killed in April 1902 by a student member of the Battle Organization, leaving Witte's flanks dangerously exposed and the way open for Bezobrazov.

Conflict between Witte and the new minister of the interior, Viecheslav Constantine Plehve, was open and immediate. Inevitably, Plehve arrayed himself on the side of the Bezobrazov group and against Witte when the adventurers' plans were the subject of ministerial debate. "In all the discussions I figured as the implacable enemy of the Korean adventures," Witte reported. "I did not try to spare anyone's sensibilities, and I used the harshest and most scathing terms in denouncing Bezobrazov."

By the time Witte returned from his Far Eastern tour in 1902 his position was already heavily eroded. Only Kuropatkin and Lamsdorf wanted to listen to his unacceptable views, and Kuropatkin did not fully accept them. Under the Tsar's sponsorship, the tentacles of the Bezobrazov group had become far-reaching. Admiral A. M. Abaza, Bezobrazov's cousin, and members of Kuropatkin's staff were included among their recruits. Bezobrazov, Abaza, and Abaza's wife even transmitted messages in code to keep their activities secret from Witte, Lamsdorf, and Kuropatkin, "the mangy triumvirate" who opposed their activities on the Yalu. Witte was "nostril," Kuropatkin "grouse," and Lamsdorf "tadpole."

While Kuropatkin was busy sending telegrams to discover the reason for the halt in the evacuation of Newchwang, Lieutenant-Colonel A. S. Madridov, a member of the Russian general staff, was equally busy with counter-telegrams to Admiral Abaza. Madridov, who had mapped the frontier regions of Manchuria and Korea, had also acquired by dubious means a concession on the north bank of the Yalu River which Bezobrazov hoped to incorporate in the Bryner concession.

Anticipating Alexeiev's action and the reaction of the "mangy triumvirate," Bezobrazov had cut short his Far Eastern tour and was racing home with the intention of persuading Nicholas to order the suspension of the evacuation of Mukden province on the grounds that it would result in the liquidation of the affairs of the timber company. On April 8, 1902, the day on which the evacuation of Mukden should have been completed, he wired one of his officers in Port Arthur: "There will be an understanding attitude toward the affair after I make my report. I am only afraid of being too late, as I shall not get there until April 16 and the Chief leaves for Moscow on April 17."

By the time Bezobrazov's train reached St. Petersburg, two international scandals, both of them highly damaging to Russia's prestige and its relations with foreign powers, including the United States, were about to burst. On the Easter Sunday and Monday the Christian inhabitants of the largely Jewish town of Kishinev, the capital of Bessarabia, and near to the Black Sea port of Odessa, responded to the urgings of P. A. Krushevan, a local newspaper publisher and friend of Plehve's, and fell on the Jews. Krushevan had accused the Jews of ritual murders in which the blood of Christian children was drunk, and, for two days, while the police stood by, the Christians pillaged and destroyed all the Jewish houses, shops, and establishments, killing and wounding many, including a large number of women. One woman had her abdomen cut open in the form of a cross. A carpenter had his hands cut off with his own saw. A child had its tongue torn out. Of the ten men subsequently charged with murder, six were acquitted, and four who were found guilty were sentenced to four years' imprisonment.

Reports were stll coming out about Kishinev when the details of new secret demands by the Russians on the Chinese leaked out, together with reports that the second phase of the evacuation of Manchuria, which was due to be completed by October 8, had been halted. St. Petersburg now wanted to prohibit treaty ports and to exclude foreign consuls (other than Russians) from Manchuria and to prevent all other foreigners from accepting administrative posts there. Lamsdorf issued the usual denials, but they made little impression, since Secretary of State Hay was now able to tell Count Cassini, who had moved from Peking to Washington, that Cassini's successor in Peking was the source of the information.

Bezobrazov wrote his report as the train lurched its way west. At the urgent request of Witte, Lamsdorf, and Kuropatkin, a special council meeting presided over by Nicholas met on April 8. Supported by the Grand Duke Alexis, a mighty man and Grand Admiral of the Russian navy, the three ministers argued that Bezobrazov's scheme was calculated to lead to trouble with the other powers and to war with Japan. They wanted to restrict activities on the Yalu to the legitimate exploitation of the forest reserves there and to invite the participation of foreign capital. Lamsdorf argued vigorously against Bezobrazov's proposal to stop the withdrawal of troops from Manchuria. The three ministers left the meeting under the impression that all was well, especially since Nicholas expressed the opinion that war with Japan was "extremely undesirable" and that Russia "must endeavor to restore in Manchuria a state of tranquillity."

They were quickly disillusioned, and on May 15, Nicholas, without consulting his ministers, ordered Alexeiev to prepare to put a new course into effect under his immediate direction. The penetration of foreign influence into Manchuria was not to be permitted, and Russia's fighting power in the Far East was to be increased as quickly as possible without regard to expense. "One incredible scheme of Bezobrazov's followed another," wrote Kuropatkin.

> His idea was to utilize the timber company as a sort of screen or barrier against possible attack upon us by the Japanese, and during 1902 and 1903 his activity, and that of his adherents, assumed a very alarming character. Admiral Alexeiev refused some requests, but unfortunately consented to send 150 mounted rifles to Sha-ho-tzu [close to the Manchuria–Korea border] and to move a Cossack regiment with guns to the latter place. This action was particularly harmful to us, as it was taken just at the time when we were under obligation to evacuate the province of Mukden altogether. Instead of withdrawing, we advanced toward Korea.

Nicholas promoted Bezobrazov to the rank of state secretary and asked him to act as the coordinator of another strategy conference. By the time the new conference met in May, Kuropatkin, unaware of the new developments and firmly convinced that the Tsar did not want war, had left on an inspection tour of the Far East. Witte, Lamsdorf, Plehve, and General V. V. Sakharov, representing the absent Kuropatkin, were present, and also Bezobrazov, Abaza, and another member of their group, Major-General Vogak.

Nicholas was in a jovial mood. He offered Witte a cigar, lit the match for him, and sat back to listen to his minister's comments on the report written by Bezobrazov and distributed before the conference that reiterated his view for a firm forward policy in defense of Russian interests in Manchuria. Witte made his final bid for a policy of moderation. Lamsdorf argued that diplomatic affairs in the Far East should be left to diplomats and that solemn treaties should be honored. Plehve replied that bayonets, not diplomats, had made Russia and that Far Eastern problems would have to be solved by bayonets and not diplomatic pens.

Bezobrazov and Plehve must have been articulate advocates. Even Witte conceded that "upon the whole, the conference viewed rather favorably Bezobrazov's plans," and Kuropatkin, though his report was only second-hand, said of Witte's behavior at the meeting: "After having had an explanation from State Counselor Bezobrazov, he, the minister, was in no disagreement so far as the essence of the matter was concerned."

The meeting resulted in the announcement of the formation of the Russian Lumber Company of the Far East, a private, non–joint stock company in which shares would be apportioned by private agreement. Though Abaza and Bezobrazov were named by Nicholas to draw up the administrative plans, the task ultimately fell to Plehve. The Tsar, Grand Duke Alexander Mikhailovitch and Count Alexei Ignatiev were among those who contributed to the company from their private means. The news of the creation of this highly unusual "official" company, and its subsequent activities, rang new alarm bells in Tokyo.

Bezobrazov, without consulting Kuropatkin, obtained the Tsar's permission to send two additional brigades of troops to the Far East. And very soon groups of armed Chinese recruited by Bezobrazov's agents arrived on the Yalu—"Chinese robber bands," Witte called them—accompanied by Russian troops wearing civilian clothes to deceive Japanese and Chinese spies.

The other ominous development of the May conference was Nicholas's decision that Far Eastern matters requiring joint discussion among the various ministries would henceforth be considered by a separate Far Eastern committee. He named Abaza as the convenor. Even on matters affecting their own ministries, the "mangy triumvirate" were now circumvented.

Kuropatkin had begun his journey to Japan and Siberia in good cheer, especially since Nicholas had asked him to cover the tracks of Bezobrazov's activity in the Yalu. He had prepared for the trip by talking with Kurino Shin'ichiro, the Japanese minister in St. Petersburg, to whom he proposed that he take the opportunity while he was in the Far East of going on to Tokyo. Both Kuropatkin and Kurino appreciated the urgency of the situation, though the Russian could have had little conception of the deep links between the Japanese military leadership and the idealism and romanticism of the ultranationalists, who were to endow the forthcoming war with the fervor of a crusade.

On April 8, 1903, while the details of Kuropatkin's visit were still being arranged, the Anti-Russian League, a Black Dragon Society creation, held a mass meeting at Saigo's statue in Ueno Park to protest the Russian failure to withdraw from Manchuria and to demand a firmer line toward Russia generally. A delegation called on Foreign Minister Komura with these demands.

April 8 was of course the critical date, for this was the day that the second withdrawal from Manchuria was due to begin. A Japanese intelligence report from China claimed that the Russians were not withdrawing but had increased in number. From Cheefoo, another officer reported that Russia was buying coal and manufacturing army bread. At the beginning of May there were further reports that the Russians had begun to establish a settlement at Yongampo on the Yalu River.

General Tamura Iyozo, the vice-chief of the general staff, circularized the reports from the military attachés and agents in Korea and Manchuria and called a meeting at the Army Club on May 9. Major-General Iguchi Shogo, chief of the general affairs division of the general staff, presided over the meeting, which was also attended by a representative of the chief of the naval general staff.

"I cannot make a definite statement about the views of the general staff," General Iguchi told the meeting, "but my private view is that the selfishness and high-handedness of Russia is such that it is impossible to restrain it with words of mouth. It is inevitable that the empire must come to a resolute decision." The navy spokesman's observation was similar: he said a day's delay in making a decision would be a day's loss for the empire.

May 10, 1903, was a Sunday and therefore a holiday, but the departmental heads of the general staff met urgently. Colonel Matsukawa Toshitane, assisted by two experts in Russian affairs, submitted a draft statement urging a decision to meet Russian encroachments by force. Both Oyama, then chief of the general staff, and Tamura were much more cautious. Oyama was indecisive and remarked that "Russia is a big country, so those in positions of responsibility must deal with her with great care." Tamura, who was responsible for much of the early contingency planning for the war, did not commit himself. Oyama repeated as he left the meeting that "Russia is a big country, you know," but several days later he told Prime Minister Katsura that Japan would have to take a stand.

Disturbed by the hesitancy of their senior officers, relatively junior army and navy officers, and foreign office officials, all of whom strongly advocated war, now sponsored a secret and historic meeting at the Kogetsu (literally "Moon on the Lake"), a high-class house of assignation just behind the Shinbashi station in Tokyo, on May 29.* For security, the meeting was not held in one of the banquet rooms but in the store room.

Among those present at the meeting were Major-General Iguchi Shogo, chief of the general affairs division of the Imperial General Headquarters; Colonel Matsukawa Toshitane, chief of the first division of Imperial General Headquarters; Major Tanaka Giichi (later prime minister), a member of the faculty of the war college and chief of the Russian section of the Imperial General Headquarters; Major Fukuda Masataro, Oyama's adjutant; Rear-Admiral Tomioka Sadayasu, chief of the first division of the navy general staff; Captain Yashiro Rokuro (later full admiral and minister of the navy), who was then captain of the cruiser *Asama;* Lieutenant-Commander Akiyama Masayuki, a member of the faculty of the navy war college and later Togo's most brilliant staff officer; Yamaza Enjiro, chief of the political affairs bureau of the foreign office; and Honda Kumataro, Komura's private secretary and subsequently ambassador to China and author of a number of books.

The meeting heard lively demands for war from General Iguchi and Colonel Matsukawa, who were strongly supported by foreign office and navy speakers. The result was a strong and unanimous resolution: "If the empire does not make a great decision and does not restrain Russia's arrogance, even at the cost of war, the future of the empire will be fraught with danger. If today's opportunity were to be lost, there would never be an opportunity to recover the fortunes of the nation." The group now set out to work on the Japanese political and military leaders.

Against this background, the Japanese government was not without concern for Kuropatkin during his visit. Recalling the attempt made on the life of Nicholas more than a decade earlier, when relations between Japan and Russia were more or less cordial, it took elaborate precautions to insure his safety. Kuropatkin, who had left St. Petersburg on April 28, was treated with great ceremony as a state guest, lodged at the Shiba Detached Palace,

---

*Authorities differ slightly about the date. According to the historical source material for the *Biography of Emperor Meiji,* edited by the army ministry (May 1927) and written by Oyama's adjutant, the meeting took place on May 17.

and assigned an escort which was led by General Terauchi Masatake, the army minister, and included Major Tanaka Giichi, one of the war party who had recently returned from St. Petersburg.

The Japanese government's invitation was for a private visit, and Kuropatkin had no authority to speak officially for St. Petersburg. But the Japanese nevertheless attached considerable importance to his presence, especially since he was known to be one of the leaders of the antiwar group in St. Petersburg.

He saw the Japanese educational system at work and realized the depths of the martial indoctrination of the schoolchildren, the exuberant patriotism, the anger that persisted over the loss of Port Arthur after the Sino-Japanese War (and Russia's subsequent seizure of it), and the samurai spirit that dominated the lives of the Japanese military.

"The system of education I have witnessed in military schools was of spartan nature, the physical exercise for the future officers being like nothing I have ever seen in Europe," he wrote. "It was really fighting of the fiercest kind." His conclusion, unbelievable in St. Petersburg, was that the Japanese army was fully equal to any European army.

Terauchi acted as his guide to military establishments and armament plants, hoping to convince him that Japan was not preparing for war. The effect was not what he had anticipated, though the results were as he had hoped. Kuropatkin was impressed with the state of Japan's military forces and became more convinced than ever that war should be avoided.

Katsura met him twice, and on each occasion the meeting lasted for several hours. But the Japanese prime minister had no intention of going into details, leaving this to Komura.

Ito and Yamagata were consulted about Russian activities on the Yalu at a secret meeting in Kyoto on May 12. Surprisingly, since Ito continued to oppose war, they agreed that no risk was too great to take to prevent further Russian encroachments into Korea, which they regarded as vital for Japan's defense. Komura and Katsura were even more emphatic. They agreed completely that, unless the Russians moved out of Korea, Japan would have to go to war. As prime minister and foreign minister, they did not have the power alone to make the decision for war. The elder statesmen, the army and navy ministers, and the army and navy chiefs of staff also needed to be persuaded. Nevertheless, their decision was crucial, especially in the light of the attitudes already expressed by senior army and navy officers.

By order of the Tsar, Kuropatkin spent five days fishing at Nagasaki because Nicholas did not want him to arrive in Port Arthur before Bezobrazov, whose style of travel was in marked contrast to Kuropatkin's. To decorate the tables at a banquet he planned to hold in Port Arthur he sent a cruiser to Japan to buy flowers.

The mood of the Japanese leaders did not escape Kuropatkin's attention.

I do not dare conceal from Your Imperial Majesty my apprehensions that now that our enterprise in the Yalu region has become known to the whole world and that the high interests of the Autocrat of Russia in the undertaking has also become a matter of common knowledge, both at home and abroad, it is no longer possible to present this enterprise as a purely commercial venture, and in the future it will inevitably preserve a great and alarming political importance [he reported to the Tsar].

On the basis that Korea could be resigned to the Japanese, Nicholas was still willing to begin negotiations with Japan as soon as two brigades of reinforcements asked for by Bezobrazov had passed Lake Baikal. Whether this was apparent to Alexeiev, Kuropatkin, Bezobrazov, and the other Russian Far Eastern authorities who met at Port Arthur from July 1 to July 10 is unclear. Kuropatkin's version of the conference was that its purpose was to find, if possible, some means of settling the Manchurian question without lowering the dignity of Russia. On the other hand, Bezobrazov has also been accused of having withheld a vital telegram setting out the Tsar's willingness to permit Japan to occupy Korea. The issue is clearly important. To have withheld such information to further his own ends would not have troubled Bezobrazov's conscience, and the fact that he cabled the Tsar at the end of the conference that it had had no "practical significance" suggests that he was disappointed with the conclusions.*

Alexeiev was against him, insisting that the Yalu enterprise should have a purely commercial character and that Russia ought to evacuate all of Manchuria, including the north. The meeting concluded that military–political activity in connection with the Yalu project should come to an end, and Kuropatkin ordered Colonel A. S. Madridov on the general staff to resign if he wished to continue his connection with the timber company.† Kuropatkin was later perplexed to discover that Alexeiev did not withdraw the Russian forces from Feng-huang-cheng and the mounted rifles from the Yalu. But then he had not fully guessed Bezobrazov's new status as Nicholas's special adviser on the Far East and state secretary, nor was he aware of the official downgrading of the "mangy triumvirate."

---

*Japanese intelligence subsequently attached credence to a similar story involving Admiral Abaza, secretary of the Far East Committee, who, it was said, had failed to transmit the Tsar's willingness to accept Japan's rejection of a neutral zone at the 39th parallel in Korea.

†Madridov later mapped the area of Manchuria along the Korean border.

Kuropatkin left for St. Petersburg on July 13, Bezobrazov the next day. Kuropatkin was anxious to make this report on the need for peace with Japan, Bezobrazov to list his grievances against the triumvirate for its attempt to undermine the "new course" and to mislead Alexeiev. He told Nicholas that Witte, Lamsdorf, and Kuropatkin had adapted the truth to suit their own purpose—to force the abandonment of south Manchuria in the event of war and, in proposing to concede Korea to Japan, to permit Japan to turn the peninsula into a secure base for operation against Russia on the continent.

Witte was the principal villain, and Witte had to go. In the case of Lamsdorf and Kuropatkin, it was enough to remove all power and authority from their hands by elevating Alexeiev's position in the Far East to that of Viceroy, responsible through the newly established committee on Far Eastern Affairs only to the Autocrat himself and charged with full authority for diplomatic and military activities in the Far East.

On August 12 the Tsar announced the creation of the Far Eastern Viceroyalty, a decision most of his ministers, including Lamsdorf, learned of only when they read it in the newspapers. Two days later Kuropatkin submitted his resignation as war minister. After what he described as great maneuvers about his future, he was granted long leave, expecting that his place would soon be filled. On August 29, the Tsar dismissed Witte from the finance ministry, replacing him with Eduard Dmitrievitch Pleske, the assistant minister of finance and director of the State Bank. "Now, I rule," Nicholas confided to his diary when he "promoted" Witte to the figurehead post of chairman of the committee of ministers.

Ruling without Witte and Kuropatkin proved to be no easier than it had been before. Pleske was in the dark about the activities of the Bezobrazov group and found himself to his dismay bombarded with a request for six million roubles for the lumber company. Seeing himself as destined to be a drab successor to Witte, he did not respond as Bezobrazov had expected. When the request came in for six million roubles, he simply turned off the tap. By the end of the fall of 1903, when the Yalu froze, the lumber company had run out of funds and had 700,000 roubles' worth of timber of unwanted lengths in its yards.

Bezobrazov's fortunes had fallen with those of the company. "I know we must throw him out," Nicholas told Kuropatkin early in September. Since it was Nicholas's habit to tell his ministers what they wanted to hear, it is difficult to say how much importance should be attached to this, but two months later Bezobrazov left for Switzerland in ill health and the lumber company was bankrupt. Nicholas authorized another 200,000 roubles in December to keep it afloat, but this was scarcely enough to pay the wages. Immediately ahead was the prospect of war.

CHAPTER 8

𝕊𝕊𝕊𝕊𝕊𝕊

And So to War

Aɴʏ ᴅᴏᴜʙᴛs ᴛʜᴀᴛ the Japanese military would press vigorously for war came to an end on October 12, 1903, when Baron Kodama Gentaro left the home and education ministries, and his concurrent post as governor of Formosa, and became vice-chief of the general staff. Kodama was fifty-two and being groomed for the prime ministership when he accepted the appointment. He demanded, and was granted, great authority.

Kodama had a pointed head, penetrating eyes, a keen sense of humor, and a capacity to charm those with whom he came in contact. Oyama was too indecisive to be more than a figurehead. Kodama, tough, keen, calculating, and cool, was a leader through and through. A Choshu, born near Iwakuni in Yamaguchi prefecture; uniquely among the top eight men who were to lead the Japanese army and navy into the field against the Russians, he had no links with the Satsuma clan. Though there were reports at times of violent disagreements between him and Oyama, the arrangement worked well. Oyama was the father figure, Kodama the brilliant tactician. He was more than that. As governor of Formosa, he had not only been ruthless but proud of his ruthlessness. A raconteur with a keen sense of humor, he was singularly free from any breath of scandal. With the bearing of a man who enjoyed power, he walked with the swing of an actor, relaxed over a glass of champagne or a cigar, and planned the campaigns ahead with scientific and mathematical skill. He was "clear-headed, energetic, vivacious, indefatigable, and resolute," the German official account of the Russo-Japanese War eulogized.

Like Tamura and Kawakami, Kodama had studied under von Moltke. He began his military career in 1868 at the age of sixteen as a squad leader with the shogun's army. The Japanese called him "the Rivet," or "the Rivet in the Fan," meaning that without him the military machine would have fallen to bits.

His association with Oyama was long standing. In 1885, when Oyama became war minister in succession to Yamagata, he decided to make radical changes in the Japanese forces, abandoning the French military instructors and replacing them with Germans, who found that the Japanese military system, though it looked very good on paper, was totally unsuited for effective military operations. "So to speak," one German commented, "there was not a single packhorse that could be mobilized." Though divisional formations had been organized by the French instructors, officers had no idea of how a division should be fought. Divisional orders did not exist. The Germans and Kodama, then a major, set to work to introduce Prussian efficiency and to teach Prussian tactics at the war college.

The Japanese arsenals were increased in number and in performance. What they could not make, Oyama set out to buy. In 1886 he ordered two 14-centimeter cannon from France. The plans were to send them back by two Japanese naval craft, but the ships lacked the deck space to accommodate what were described as the biggest guns in the world. For a fee of £780 sterling, Mitsui was commissioned to transport the cannon to the naval base at Yokosuka.

Oyama had no illusions that his big guns could do much to defend Japan against an invader. By their very size, however, they were a symbol of the militarized state, self-dependent in weapons and munitions, that he hoped to build. To what extent he had succeeded when the crisis began to unfold in 1903, the hesitant Oyama was still unsure. To go to war with China was very different from tackling imperial Russia.

Many agreed with him. Pushed by his subordinates, however, Oyama was persuaded at least to demand greater efforts to prepare the nation for war. On the eve of the Kuropatkin visit, he and Foreign Minister Komura exchanged notes on the Russian situation. Oyama followed this correspondence with an "opinion" which he submitted to the Katsura cabinet. He referred to the greater vigor being shown by the Russians in Manchuria, to their dangerous plans to seize the three eastern provinces, and the threat they posed to Korea. The cabinet discussed Oyama's appreciation and sent it on to the Emperor, without whose approval no serious plans for war could be made.

By June 23, 1903, the opinions of the extremists had made considerable headway. A meeting on that day, attended by the Emperor, the elder statesmen, Prime Minister Katsura, Army Minister Terauchi, Navy Minister Yamamoto and Foreign Minister Komura, considered what Katsura now regarded as a dangerous and deteriorating situation. Komura made a long statement, which was debated for several hours, and ended in resolute opposition to the cession of one inch of Korean territory to the Russians. The meeting also recognized that there would be grave difficulties in obtaining Russian acceptance of this, short of war. In effect, therefore, the meeting agreed that Japan was willing to fight if negotiations left it no alternative.

Ito, the peacemaker and Russophile, was now defeated and effectively removed as a barrier to war. Katsura demanded "for the good of the state" that he should either resign from his position in the *genrō* or abandon his leadership of the Seiyukai party, which he had formed to strengthen his position in his political fight with Yamagata, and which now controlled the senate. Ito replied that it was impossible for him simply to give up being an elder statesman, of which Katsura was well aware. The result was an imperial "intervention" inviting Ito, a firm believer in constitutional government (as opposed to Yamagata's absolutism), to return to his former office among the bureaucrats as president of the privy council.

Ito relinquished his presidency of the party to Prince Saionji and took up his privy council appointment. He thus not only bowed to the inevitable, he also withdrew his opposition to the stronger line that Japan was now to pursue when Toyama and three of his closest associates in the Black Dragon Society called on him with the intention of killing him if he was afraid of war with Russia. "After first killing him, I intended to fight Russia," Toyama declared. Scarcely bothering to conceal his threat, Toyama demanded Ito's support as, next to the Emperor, the greatest living Japanese. If the Emperor had not already agreed to war, if circumstances so dictated, at the June 23 meeting, it is likely that Ito would have continued to hold out against the policy that he so strongly disapproved. But to oppose the Emperor was to oppose everything in the New Japan that he had worked to create.

War fever mounted quickly in Tokyo. The *Asahi* led the newspaper outcry, with ultranationalists and leading intellectuals adding their weight to the call to arms. At the same time, there was strong public resistance to war in intellectual and Socialist circles. Leading newspapers, including the *Mainichi,* the *Nichinichi* and the *Yorozu Choho,* opposed the war, as did Socialist Kotoku Shusui, Christian leader Uchimura Kanzo, poetess Yosano Akiko (famous for her antiwar poems), and Socialist and trade union leader Katayama Sen, who publicly shook hands with G. V. Plekhanov, the Russian Social Democrat, at a congress of the Second International in August 1904 after the war had started.

On July 28, 1903, the Japanese government sounded out Russia on the subject of negotiations. It declared that the seven new demands which Russia had made on China were designed to consolidate Russia's hold on Manchuria, compelling the belief that she had abandoned her intention of retiring from the country, while her increased activity on the Korean frontier raised doubts regarding the limits to her ambitions. The permanent occupation of Manchuria, she believed, would create conditions prejudicial to the security and interests of Japan. From Manchuria, she argued, Russia would be a constant menace to the separate existence of the kingdom of Korea, where Japan possessed paramount political, commercial and industrial interests, which for the sake of her own security she was not prepared to surrender or to share with any other power.

Before a reply had been received, the Tsar had announced Alexeiev's appointment as Viceroy for the Far East, reinforcing the views of people everywhere who now believed that war was inevitable. "The question of peace and war in the Far East is already trembling in the balance," the British Minister at St. Petersburg reported to London. Nevertheless Kurino's discussion with Lamsdorf about Japan's anxieties over Manchuria and Korea began auspiciously, and, when he presented a Japanese draft treaty on August 12, Lamsdorf told him that "an understanding between the two countries was not only desirable but was the best policy."

Examination of the text of the Japanese draft treaty, however, convinced the Russians, including those who advocated a firm forward policy and those who wanted to avoid provocations, that the Japanese did not regard Manchuria as lost to her. The Russian reply when it eventually turned up nearly two months later invited the Japanese to recognize that Manchuria was in all respects outside her sphere of influence.

On August 23 the Russians asked that the negotiations should be held in Tokyo, instead of St. Petersburg, which the Japanese had requested, on the grounds that Foreign Minister Lamsdorf was to accompany Nicholas on an extended visit to Europe. To the Katsura government this seemed deliberate procrastination. It sensed interminable delays while the foreign office in St. Petersburg sought clarification of matters of detail from Alexeiev.

Weeks passed without progress. The Tsar went to Germany in September and by-passed Lamsdorf and the foreign ministry, conferring directly with Alexeiev, who, lacking in experience in international negotiations, believed that to show any willingness to compromise was to reveal weakness. Alexeiev advised Nicholas that should the Japanese land even one brigade in the Korean Gulf the Japanese government should be notified that further landings "would entail our taking military measures as well." The measures he had in mind were a naval blockade to prevent further landings by sea and then the immediate mobilization of Russian troops on the Kwantung Peninsula and in Manchuria.

The Tsar appeared undisturbed. He told William that there would be no war because he did not wish it. As usual, the Kaiser contributed inflammatory intelligence, warning Nicholas of Japanese attempts to build up the Chinese "behind your and my backs and against us." He said that the Japanese had concluded a secret engagement with China to provide the army with 20,000 new rifles and ammunition, forty-eight field guns, and twelve mountain (rapid-firing) guns.

> The Chinese troops are drilling day and night. . . . Commanded by Jap instruction officers, whose numbers are steadily increasing! Nice business. I believe the Chinese might not be allowed to have Japs in their Army! They are sure to rouse Chinese hopes and inflame their hatred against the White Race in general and constitute a grave danger to your rear in case you would have to face a Jap adventure on the Sea-shore. Begging your pardong [sic] for my liberty I have taken, I hope the Admiral of the Pacific will not be angry with the Admiral of the Atlantic's signals, who is always on the look out! Ta, ta, best love to Alix from
>
> Your devoted friend and cousin toujours en vedette!
> Willy

Alarmed by developments, Kuropatkin cut his long leave short, and instead of his expected retirement, returned to duty, warning the Tsar of the dangers that he saw ahead. His concern went unheeded. Nicholas's comments, annotated on Kuropatkin's report on October 23, 1903, read: "The alarm in the Far East is apparently beginning to subside."

Twice, in October and later in December, Kuropatkin recommended the abandonment of southern Manchuria as urgently necessary to prevent war. "The economic interests of Russia in the Far East are negligible," he wrote in his December report. "The success or failure of a few coal or timber enterprises in Manchuria is not a matter of sufficient importance to justify the risk of war." Copies of his report went to Lamsdorf, who had no power; to Plehve, who wanted a small war anyway; and to Alexeiev.

"I thought that a rupture with Japan would be a national calamity and did everything in my power to prevent it," Kuropatkin claimed later. Still worried by the inadequacy of the Trans-Siberian Railway and the lack of proper military preparations, he continued to argue in favor of compromise until the difficult link south of Lake Baikal had been completed—or at least until May 1904, when he believed that the required number of reinforcements would have had time to reach the Far East. But the ministers, lacking real authority, were now powerless to prevent the drift to war, and Nicholas was too irresolute, and too ill-informed. The adventurers prevailed.

Almost without exception those with the most immediate access to the Tsar were monumentally ignorant. To most Russians, Japan was a fairy-book sort of place, filled with fascinating little people who lived in paper houses, indulged themselves with geishas, and wasted hours on flower arrangement and tea ceremonies. "We knew the Japanese were skillful and patient artisans," Kuropatkin wrote.

We were fond of their productions, of which the delicate workmanship and brilliant color enchanted us. Our services spoke with appreciation of the country and its inhabitants and was full of pleasant reminiscences of their visits, especially of Nagasaki, where they appeared to be popular with the inhabitants. As a military factor Japan did not exist. Our sailors, travelers, and diplomats have entirely overlooked the awakening of an energetic, independent people.

This was less than fair to the highly perceptive, if unrecognized, reporting by Baron Roman Romanovitch Rosen, the Russian minister in Tokyo. But the Russians, it is true, were deplorably served by their staff at general headquarters and many of their attachés. A handbook, updated each year, gave all available details about the Japanese armed forces, but often reports from Japan by military attachés and others were pigeonholed when they arrived at headquarters.

Two major reports in 1903, including one dealing with the formation of Japanese reserves, were both extremely well-informed and important. When the reports reached the Russian general staff, senior officers dismissed them as alarmist and unreliable.

As a result, on the eve of the war, the Russians had no information that they regarded as reliable, or credible, about Japanese reserves. The number of fighting men Japan could put into the field was therefore greatly underestimated. Worse, it was generally accepted that one Russian soldier was the equal of three Japanese. Even at the time Kuropatkin was in Japan, the Russian military attaché assured him that Japan could put into the field only ten of its thirteen divisions. Of the country's 400,000 reserves and troops assigned to work of a sedentary nature in the army's various depots, he knew nothing. A single officer on the Russian general staff was alone detailed to Japanese intelligence. "And unfortunately," Kuropatkin noted, "our selection was bad."

Russian military observers at a Japanese naval review at Kobe in April 1903 reported that the officers and crews were ill-trained and would not pass an operational test. The military opinions picked up by Bezobrazov from men like Major-General Vogak and passed on to the Tsar were even more irresponsible. Vogak, who was concurrently senior military attaché in Peking and Tokyo, was openly contemptuous of the Japanese army, and, in the closing days of 1903, brought his uninformed opinions to bear on Alexeiev, who emerges from the scene pathetically—opposed to war but encouraged and misled by others who deceived him as they deceived the Tsar.

From the beginning of the negotiations, the principal difference between Japan and Russia was that, while the Russians wanted to restrict discussions to the Korean problem, the Japanese put more emphasis on China's independence and the security of Manchuria. On December 1 the Russians attempted to break the deadlock and proposed that the area north of the 39th parallel in Korea (along the Pyongyang–Wonsan line) should be made a neutral zone. Japan, in turn, asked that in exchange for abandoning plans to discuss Manchuria, the superiority of Japan in Korea should also be recognized. In Alexeiev's view that was tantamount to granting a protectorate over Korea, and he so informed the Tsar in a telegram dated December 26, 1903.

Much of the blame for the final Russian steps toward war rested with Admiral Abaza, Bezobrazov's cousin and secretary of the Far Eastern committee, who deliberately distorted the Tsar's own views in messages to Alexeiev. Anxious to curry favor with Nicholas, Alexeiev responded by recommending a stronger line, and, thus armed, Abaza himself ignored protocol and official channels and, without even bothering to inform Lamsdorf, tried to put pressure on Kurino. On another occasion, Nicholas sent a long message to Alexeiev advocating the cession to Japan of all Korean territory adjacent to the areas of Russian interest and ordered that copies should be sent to the Russian ministers in Tokyo, Peking, and Seoul. Alexeiev ignored the instructions, and Lamsdorf remained unaware of the matter until after the war had broken out.

On December 29, Admiral Abaza reported to the Tsar that even if war with Japan was avoided, the troop strength in the Far East should be increased urgently. "To maintain peace among the people of the Far East, the presence of troops is necessary, even if the troops are not used," he said. "The Japanese proverb, 'The strong does not unsheath his sword,' which your humble subject remembers, is especially appropriate."

In contrast with the lamentable Russian intelligence, Colonel Akashi Motojiro, the thirty-six-year-old Japanese military attaché in St. Petersburg, had begun to spread his net over a wide and fruitful field of inquiry. The movement of the Russian reinforcements to the Far East, as recommended by Bezobrazov and other members of his group, was soon reported back to Tokyo. Akashi told with amusement of the penetration even of the Russian war ministry. He was busy one day in his small apartment with a Russian staff officer when to his dismay a Russian general rang his doorbell and dropped by for a chat. The apartment was very small, and, before answering the doorbell, Akashi pushed the officer, clutching a map of Siberia in his arms, into the lavatory. Akashi and the general had been talking for a few minutes when Akashi saw to his further embarrassment that a Russian military document marked SECRET lay on top of his desk.

The general was unobservant, finished his talk, and went on his way. The alarmed young staff officer emerged from the lavatory and continued his treacherous briefing.

The Japanese worked confidently and successfully on the assumption that the Russians could not tell the difference between Chinese and Japanese. A Japanese colonel, disguised first as the assistant to a Buddhist monk and later as a Chinese merchant, provided the first authoritative reports of the presence of Russian troops on the Yalu River. With great perception, he tipped off the Japanese Imperial General Headquarters that the quantity of military equipment being stored in the old walled city of Liaoyang, 200 miles north of Port Arthur, indicated that, in the event of war, this would become the Russians' main military concentration point. He and a fellow officer recruited Chinese spies and taught them to report on such matters as the color of the caps worn by Russian troops, and the number, kind, luggage, and epaulettes of the troops.

As a result of the activities of Akashi and the Manchurian agents, many of them members of the Black Ocean and Black Dragon societies, a steady flow of intelligence reached Tokyo late in 1903 to reinforce the arguments of the war party. Major-General Iguchi wrote in his diary:

> The situation has developed where Koreans, toadying to the powerful [i.e., the Russians], insult our nationals. Though it may be too late, if the cabinet does not take the great decision to send troops into Korea, there may not be an opportunity to restrain, for the sake of our nation and of the peace of the Orient, Russia's high-handedness . . . diplomatic negotiations are liable to result to our disadvantage. I demanded of [Major-General] Fukushima [who had been made acting vice-chief of staff following the death of General Tamura and pending Kodama's appointment] to urge Yamagata and Katsura to come to a decision. Yet, I fear that Katsura's decision will not be firm, that his shilly-shallying will finally mislead the nation in its critical hour. Further, Field-Marshal Yamagata is dispirited; there is none of the vigor that one used to see in him in the past. Ah! General Kawakami died four years ago and Major-General Tamura followed him into the grave. Oyama lacks fighting spirit. There is no harmony between the army and the navy. The army and navy ministers, especially Yamamoto [the navy minister], know only their commands and not the nation. They are blind to opportunities. They have no resolution to fight a decisive battle. The great crisis for the empire is about to pass. How extreme is Heaven's favor for Russia!

Iguchi noted that he was about to believe that Heaven showed signs of destroying the great Japanese empire when Kodama's appointment was announced as vice-chief of the general staff. "I now know that Heaven has not yet abandoned our empire," Iguchi exclaimed. "What joy! What pleasure!"

His judgment did not err. In his new post Kodama soon fulfilled himself in the eyes of the war party. In one period of thirty days, while he was working on battle plans, he did not leave his office. Wrapped in a red blanket and with an hibachi under his table for warmth, he worked late into the night on plans that envisaged every contingency.

Instead of pulling out of Manchuria on October 8, Alexeiev had staged a military review at Port Arthur and raised emotions among the ultranationalists in Japan to a fever pitch. "Japan and Russia are on the eve of war," Baroness d'Anethan, the wife of the Belgian minister in Tokyo, noted in her diary on the following day.

> It is difficult to see how it can be averted. It does not look as though Russia, in spite of her promises, seems inclined to give up the occupation of Manchuria. . . . The Japanese are most bellicose and equally indignant. Russia thinks the latter are playing a game of bluff, but they are mistaken, and there is not the slightest doubt that the Japanese are in deadly earnest.

Kodama was for war. Ito confided in him some of his continuing misgivings, and Kodama rebuked him. "I told him that if we lack certain things, I suppose that the opponent lacks some other things," Kodama said. "We cannot say with certainty that with our present military power we cannot win against Russia. I told him this and urged that he make up his mind."

Kodama gave similar advice to the division chiefs of the chief of staff's office when he addressed them on October 30. Of Oyama, he said that he was suffering from the ambivalence of his dual position, that of chief of staff and elder statesman. "There is no sense in his being one yet two persons," he told the meeting.

> He submitted a statement of view to the cabinet on June 23, and this statement was at the same time shown to the throne. In this he stated that the present opportunity must not be allowed to escape to settle the Korean question. He should express the same view at the elder statesmen's conference, and he should adhere to his decision.

Blunt, frank, and direct, Kodama forced the pace of the general staff, contributing greatly not only to planning but to the authorship of the first strategic paper on the war. This was ready on October 23—on the very day that Nicholas in St. Petersburg concluded that the danger was passing.

The Japanese had completed their naval expansion program in 1902. Aware that the balance of naval power in the Far East had moved against them, the Russians, in the late summer of 1902, had begun to reinforce. The first-class protected cruiser *Askold* and the third-class protected cruiser *Novik,* the latter to prove the bravest of them all, were the first to arrive, but many others followed in their wake. By February 1904, the position so far as Russia was concerned was much more favorable. The Far Eastern fleet consisted of seven battleships, four of them armored, five first-class and two third-class cruisers, twenty-five destroyers, seventeen torpedo boats and ten sloops and gunboats.

For the time being, the Japanese still had quantitative and qualitative superiority. Their six first-class battleships and eight first-class armored cruisers were mostly British-built, modern, and faster than the Russian ships. Sister battleships *Fuji* and *Yashima,* launched in England in 1896, were the fastest and most heavily armored battleships in the world when they were built. They could fire an 850-pound shell every eighty seconds. In 1901 they were refitted and equipped with additional guns, including sixteen rapid-firing twelve-pounders. Two years later, the battleships *Asahi* and *Shikishima* were launched in England with four twelve-inch guns, fourteen six-inch guns and twenty twelve-pounders, which could fire twenty shells a minute. Both ships had wide steel belts, extending five feet below the waterline, and thick armored decking. Both carried five torpedo tubes and were fitted with six twenty-four-inch searchlights.

The torpedo, used with such effect at Port Arthur on the night of February 8, was one of the more interesting refinements of the weapons system. The Whitehead torpedo, named after an English engineer, Richard Whitehead, who had worked on his invention since 1864, was powered by a compressed air engine driven by a single propeller. It represented a considerable advance over the ramming spars and man-manned torpedoes that were used in the Russo-Turkish War in 1877. Since it had a maximum range of about 700 yards and a speed of only about seven knots, its effectiveness on the high seas was slight, but against a fleet at anchor, as Togo was about to demonstrate, it was devastating. Earlier, in addition to the ramming spars, fitted with explosives set at the end of long poles, torpedoes had been carried in small boats to the target. At the last moment, the crew abandoned the boat and set it on its course. If they missed their mark, they climbed on board, reaimed and jumped overboard again. "Yellow cigar," the Japanese called the Whitehead torpedo. It was used first by the British against a Peruvian ship in 1877 and by Admiral Makarov, then a lieutenant, in a daring attack against the Turkish ships in the Russo-Turkish war.

The Japanese flagship *Mikasa* (named after a sacred mountain in Japan) was launched in England in 1900. Four hundred feet long and seventy-six feet wide, she was the biggest and most powerful of the world's battleships. The rate of fire from her four twelve-inch and fourteen six-inch guns was three shells every two minutes, and she carried a complement of 830 officers

THE TIDE AT SUNRISE

and men. Her top speed was eighteen knots, and she was more heavily protected than any of the other Japanese ships. The Japanese were also more adequately equipped with second- and third-class cruisers, destroyers, and torpedo boats than the Russians. Of Japan's nineteen destroyers, fifteen had been built in Britain and were capable of thirty-one knots.

Russia's real weakness was the uneven quality of her vessels and the poor gunnery of her officers. Some of her battleships mounted the same heavy guns as the Japanese, but these were fired inaccurately, if at all. The ships varied greatly in speed, armament, and protection and thus were extremely difficult to operate together tactically at sea.

Against this, the Japanese fleet would have the onerous task of protecting convoys transporting troops and supplies. Japan, moreover, was still entirely dependent on foreign shipyards for her armored vessels. Her shipyards were not capable of replacing losses among ships of the line. Despite the great increase in Japanese merchant shipping, only 300,000 to 400,000 tons were available for use of the armed services, and these could not be concentrated in one port. It was clear, also, that the needs of the expeditionary forces in Korea and Manchuria would place an immense strain on the Japanese railway system. If the war dragged on, there were even more formidable problems of manpower to be faced.

Russia had its difficulties with the Trans-Siberian Railway and also problems involving the national character. Dostoevsky believed that all of Russia was drinking itself to death. "The people are drunk," he wrote. "The mothers are drunk, the children are drunk, and in the courts of justice you hear nothing but the words: 'Condemned to two hundred lashes.' Let the generations grow up! What a pity that we cannot wait! They would all be drunk!"

The ordinary Russian seaman had little access to the vast quantities of vodka that poured across the Trans-Siberian Railway. He drank his meager ration and stole from the officers' stores when he needed more.

Under good leadership, the Russian seaman responded and worked well. When the officers were bullying or lax, the men became slack and disrespectful. "Ivan is a big, strong, burly fellow," wrote F. T. Jane. "He is sluggish, good-tempered—rather like a New Foundland dog. He is simple and childish. Ivan's idea is that he exists to be shot at: our Jack Tar, that he exists to shoot others." The British bluejacket, he added, would have nothing to do with the Russian seaman. "'E arn't clean enough," was the general verdict.

The Japanese crews were much better disciplined and much better trained. Japan could draw her seamen from thousands of miles of coastline. Many had served in pirate craft, deep-sea fishing boats and with whaling fleets. The patriotism of the crews was almost a religion, and the officers were confident that, should the need ever arise, they could beat the German, the American, and the French navies and even fare well against the British, who had taught them. There were only four rules for Japanese crewmen, a Japanese officer told a British instructor: "Feed them well; treat them with politeness and consideration; do not encourage them to read the newspapers, least of all the gutter journals of Tokyo and Osaka; and drill into them the fact that the navy has nothing to do with politics but exists for the glory of Japan."

Catherine the Great used an English naval commander in her wars against the Turks and the Greeks. He had trouble with the Russian officers and men who found unexpected happiness in foreign ports with good wine and willing women. Hundreds died at sea and those who survived fought badly. Catherine was furious. "Our fleet is rusty, but this expedition will get rid of the rust," she said.

Peter the Great saw the need for a navy and understood the difficulties in obtaining suitable recruits. "He who has only land troops fights only with one hand," he wrote. "He who has a fleet as well fights with two." But "thinking" officers much later than Peter the Great's day were regarded as revolutionaries and sent to the mines or to the cells beneath the massive Peter-and-Paul fortress in St. Petersburg. Even in 1904 Russian seamen had little knowledge of the sea or ships. Their officers used either too little or too much discipline. On board ship the officers lived the life of luxury they had known in St. Petersburg and relied heavily on holy images to save them from disaster or to reward them with victory. Their peasant sailors were homesick as well as seasick when they were transplanted to the ocean.

At the beginning of February 1904, the active Russian army consisted of 1,100,000 men, compared with Japan's 180,000. The Russian active reserve totalled 2,400,000: unknown to the Russians, Japan had 200,000 men in the first reserve* and another 200,000 in the second. By scraping the bottom of the barrel and putting every man who had ever had any military training into the field, the Japanese could muster 850,000 men. This was six times the Russians' estimate.

Still, if even the best-laid Japanese military plans went wrong, they could clearly go very wrong indeed. Small wonder, then, that the western diplomats in Tokyo were betting on a Russian victory, or that the Japanese

---

*All Japanese males between the ages of seventeen and forty were liable to military service. After three years on the active list, the soldier moved into the first reserve for a period of four years and four months, after which he passed into the second reserve for an additional five years.

military appreciated so clearly that the beginning of February, when the Trans-Siberian Railway would face the most serious of bottlenecks at Lake Baikal, was the best time to attack.

Kodama worked on the assumption that Japan's immediate superiority in arms in the theater of war would soon be challenged and then reversed as the Russians drew on their large European reserves to reinforce the Far East.

While St. Petersburg's attitude toward Japan was one of indifference, almost that of the buffalo to the gnat, Tokyo had become wholly absorbed in Russian activities in Manchuria and Korea. The Russia of Nicholas II was interested in the profits to be won by the Manchurian adventure: its concern with Japan was peripheral. In a very real sense, therefore, Russia underestimated Japan and Japan grossly overestimated both Russian intentions and Russian interest in Japan.

Kodama was correct, however, in assessing Russia's strategic interest in Korea. "Though we feel no necessity to annex the country ourselves," Kuropatkin noted,

we can under no circumstances consent to the establishment in it of an energetic Japan or any other power. . . . And so, in this case, just as in Persia and North China, we must work toward gradually acquiring absolute economic control of the country. The occupation of the Kwantung Peninsula and the permanent fortification of our position there, and the completion of the roads running through Manchuria, are steps in advance, and important ones, on the problems of the future.

In pursuit of this policy, Russia increased its troop strength in the Far East during 1903 and at the same time raised an additional thirty-two battalions in European Russia. Given time, the Japanese believed, the Russians would build on their eight East Siberian Rifle brigades (seven were composed of four regiments of two battalions and the remaining brigade of four three-battalion regiments) and turn them into eight divisions, each of twelve battalions. Their assessment was correct. Kuropatkin planned to reinforce the Far East but, if possible, without causing alarm in Japan. Unfortunately for St. Petersburg, his two objectives were mutually exclusive. Every additional battalion was quickly noted by Japanese intelligence and the alarm by the end of 1903 had almost reached the point of hysteria. If Japan saw no alternative to war, it could not afford to wait.

The principal land forces immediately available to the Russian command in the Far East were the eight brigades of East Siberian Rifles, six battalions of reserve infantry, two under-strength European brigades which had arrived during 1903, one regular regiment of cavalry, and about five-and-a-half regiments of Cossacks. The East Siberian Rifles were far from an elite force. Many of the troops were reservists who had already performed their military service. They included both migrants from western Russia and Asian tribesmen.

The cavalry had been trained to fight both mounted and dismounted, but most were Cossacks whose reputation had been exaggerated. They were badly led and badly trained. The infantry were little better. The Russian soldier always carried his rifle with bayonet fixed. The steel, he was taught, was more important than the bullet. The Maxim machinegun, named after Sir Hiram Stevens Maxim, its inventor, an American who lived in England, had been distributed to only a few of the Russian units. By a curious coincidence, his brother Hudson also invented a smokeless powder that, when used in the Maxim machinegun (since it was built by Vickers, a modified version became better known in World War I as the Vickers machinegun), was soon to make it a powerful weapon, both in defense and in covering advancing troops with concentrated fire.

As part of the buildup in the Far East, the Russians were in the process of changing over their artillery to what was known at the time as "quick firers." In earlier artillery pieces the gun and its mount recoiled for long distances after each round had been fired and had to be manhandled by its crew back to its firing place. The new gun had its tube suspended on a cradle. As the gun fired, heavy springs took the recoil, and the gun carriage did not move. Few of the Russian officers and men understood the new gun, and it seems that many of the guns fired their first shots in action against the Japanese.

Thirty-six field artillery pieces supported each Japanese division. These were the old-fashioned variety and were generally inferior to the Russian guns. They fired a smaller projectile and their range was shorter. At the army level, however, the Japanese were soon to produce some surprises for the Russians, and in their first major land action the use of a much heavier howitzer over ranges of 3,500 to 4,000 yards proved highly effective.

Since Kodama was planning to become mobile, the Maxim machinegun, with its heavy tripod and casing, was thought to be of limited use to his troops early in the war, though by the end of 1904 it was being used more and more extensively in offense and defense by both sides, with murderous results. The Japanese captured eight in their first major action and also a number of the "quick-firing" field guns, which they soon organized in batteries and put to use against the Russians.

The real Japanese strength lay in the infantry. With the invention earlier in the nineteenth century of breech-loading rifles using metallic cartridges, muskets and muzzle-loaders had been cast aside, but the Russians had not yet appreciated the true value of the new weapon. In training, they spent most of their ammunition rations on unobserved fire. The Japanese trained on the range. The Russian soldiers shot badly, the Japanese excellently. The Russians fired in volleys. The Japanese learned to aim and to shoot to kill. They were trained in close-quarters fighting, but they carried the bayonet in a scabbard and fixed it only to "stack" rifles, or when about to go into hand-to-hand combat, led by officers carrying short two-handed slightly curved and very sharp swords. Though the samurai class had been buried by conscription, swordmanship remained the mark of the Japanese officer and gentleman.

Kodama, who had been so actively involved in the creation of the new generation of Japanese soldier, had no doubt that man-to-man he was better than his Russian counterpart. His problem was to set the Japanese military machine in motion quickly but not rashly. On the assumption that the Russian fleet would concentrate on Port Arthur and, in the early stages of the war, seek to avoid an encounter with the Japanese fleet, he planned to move two armies into the field as quickly as possible. Early command of the sea was vital. If this could not be obtained, one of the three divisions to be committed in the early stages of the war would be required to occupy Seoul to insure that the Russians did not initiate any move there, and the Japanese might lose the initiative. Since the navy declined to commit itself to any definite assurance that Japanese troops could land in safety anywhere except on the south coast of Korea, a heavy responsibility rested on Togo. The main Russian squadron at Port Arthur had to be contained. Japan had no reserve of armored vessels on which she could fall back and no shipping yards in which they could be built. Togo was therefore required not merely to prevent the Port Arthur squadron from harassing Japanese military transports but also to be cautious. Port Arthur might have been his for the taking on the night of February 8, but not by desperate gambles like this could a militarily inferior power make war with a giant like Russia.

As Kodama was well aware, the Trans-Siberian Railway was Russia's Achilles heel, and his plans included guerrilla actions along the railway and in the rear of the Russian lines. Preparations for this sort of activity had long been in the making.

In 1899, Ishimitsu Makiyo, who later became a captain in the Japanese Army and an intelligence agent in Manchuria, was sent to Russia as a student. He arrived in Vladivostok with Colonel Tamura Iyozo, later army assistant chief of staff. During their stay in Vladivostok, Ishimitsu and Tamura visited a Japanese Buddhist temple in the town, where Major Hanada, a Japanese intelligence officer masquerading as a priest, was in charge.

"How are things going?" Tamura asked him. "I came over because we're not getting much information."

Major Hanada made no reply but went to the kitchen, returning with a pot of tea.

"Are things going well?" the colonel asked again.

Hanada bowed deeply, touching the torn tatami with his forehead, and replied: "Thank you very much, sir. I have become friendly with the Japanese residents here and every month a large congregation listens when I preach."

"I mean work, Hanada," said the exasperated Tamura. "You haven't been sending reports for a long time."

Hanada insisted on talking about his religious activities and remarked that he was happy in his life as a monk. Tamura ordered him to return to Japan. Instead, Hanada resigned his commission and stayed on in Vladivostok until the eve of the war, when on Kodama's instruction he formed a mounted intelligence and guerrilla organization which called itself the Army of Justice and operated behind the Russian lines in Manchuria. Ishimitsu was there, too, working as a photographer in Harbin.

From these and other sources of intelligence, Kodama knew that more than 20,000 Russian frontier guards protected the railway. A large Japanese force had no chance of infiltrating into Manchuria without detection, and small forces, though they might create temporary difficulties for the Russians, would be highly vulnerable. This was not a war to be won by commando raids.

Port Arthur's strategic importance rested simply in the presence of the Russian naval squadron. If Togo succeeded there and quickly seized control of the sea off the west coast of Korea, then the port of Chemulpo (Inchon) could be used as it had been used in 1894 in the war against China for the speedy disembarkation of Japanese ground forces. If Togo failed, Chemulpo, less than 250 miles from Port Arthur, would be too hazardous a landing place. The alternative was to land at Fusan (Pusan) on the southeastern coast, another four hundred miles distant from Port Arthur and much closer to Japan. The Japanese had linked it by railway with Seoul after the Sino-Japanese War. This was an advantage, but any operation through Fusan promised to be time consuming, and Kodama's plans called for the speediest possible movement of his forces to the Yalu River—and beyond.

Japan had no right, of course, to dictate to Korea as to which power to cooperate with nor was it within her rights to protest against any incursion into Korea. These difficulties she intended to overcome by a treaty forced on Seoul at gunpoint.

No decision was taken at this time on the occupation of Port Arthur or Sakhalin. These were details that could await developments. Kodama's immediate intention was to launch his armies so that they would pose an early threat to the center of the Russians' main line of communications, the railway linking Harbin with Port Arthur and the Kwantung Peninsula.

The plan was brilliantly devised to exploit success. It was no less brilliant in the attention paid to contingencies. If Togo held the Russia fleet at bay, the army would land at Chemulpo. If he failed, the landing would go on at Fusan. If the First Army achieved its mission on the Yalu and succeeded in driving into Manchuria, the Second Army would be ready to land between Port Arthur and the Yalu, thereby threatening the Russian main line of communications from the south as well as from the east. If the First Army ran into difficulties, the Second could be quickly disembarked to help it out.

Since a road linked the old Manchurian city of Liaoyang on the Port Arthur–Harbin railway with the Yalu River, and Kodama had already been informed of the buildup of supplies there, he saw with clarity that Liaoyang would be the key to the land war. It was 120 miles as the crow flies from the Yalu to Liaoyang. The task facing Kodama was to move his forces there in sufficient strength before the Russian armies in the field could be reinforced heavily from Europe over the Trans-Siberian Railway.

Spurred on by Kodama and the Black Dragon Society, the military were in a hurry. Without success, they urged the unification of political and military strategies: the government, alarmed by Britain's refusal of a loan on January 1, continued its efforts to negotiate until as late as January 13, 1904, when Japanese intelligence reported that the Russian chief of the general staff and the Russian war minister had already completed plans to attack Japan and that these plans, having been approved by Tsar Nicholas, had been transmitted to Alexeiev.

With four Russian cruisers and eighteen torpedo boats in Vladivostok reported by agents to be ready to sail to reinforce Port Arthur, and with two new Japanese cruisers, *Nisshin* and *Kasuga,* in the Indian Ocean on their way to Japan, Marshal Oyama at last came out strongly in favor of war. The sooner the Japanese seized the initiative, the better, he advised in a "Judgment on the Situation" to the throne.

Kodama was aware, like almost everyone else, of the immense risks that Japan was taking. But he was confident that in the early phases, provided that Japan used overwhelming trength to win initial victories, the war could be conducted with reasonably favorable results; in this he now carried the hesitant Oyama with him.

France had made an attempt to mediate on January 6, 1904, but Alexeiev was busy reinforcing the Russian positions on the Yalu, and the French effort produced no response. Russia was ready to meet Japan halfway in Korea but continued to insist that in all respects Manchuria was outside Japan's sphere of interest.

The British government had neither encouraged nor discouraged its Japanese ally. Some of its officials abroad were less restrained. Asked by a member of the Japanese mission in Peking in December 1903 whether, in his private view, Japan ought to fight, Sir Ernest Satow pondered and then said, "Yes." When the Chinese asked him why England, America, and France did not persuade Japan to pursue a more moderate course so as to avoid war, Satow answered, "as befitted such nonsense," that the British government considered Japan to be entirely in the right. He viewed Alexeiev's appointment as Viceroy as "most serious, and pregnant with the seeds of fresh complications and dangers to the peace of the Far East."

The Americans were still concerned about their commercial interests in Manchuria. Their agreement with Peking in August, whereby two additional Manchurian ports were to be opened up to foreign trade, had the effect of increasing the isolation—and the anger—of Russia, especially since the agreement was announced on October 8, 1903, just as Alexeiev's white-coated troops were putting on a display of strength in Port Arthur.

An improbable, but important, figure in Japanese preparations for war was Yuan Shih-k'ai. When the ceasefire brought hostilities between Japan and China to an end in 1895, the Japanese sent emissaries to contact the Chinese forces in the field. Carrying a white flag and attended by a bugler and some Chinese notables, the emissaries, under the leadership of a young staff officer named Aoki, came under Chinese fire. Several of the Chinese with the group were killed and Aoki was forced to retire. As soon as the news reached Tokyo, the Japanese complained angrily to Li Hung-chang, who had arrived at Nagasaki for the peace talks. He responded by ordering his protege, Yuan, to the front with instructions to bring about an immediate ceasefire. This was the first meeting between Aoki, who four years later became Japanese military attaché in Peking, and Yuan. It marked the beginning of an important and, so far as Japan was concerned, highly profitable relationship. At Yuan's invitation, Aoki left his post in the Japanese legation in Peking in 1898 and became head of a secret Japanese military advisory group with the Chinese army, with headquarters at Tientsin. Later, when Yuan was appointed governor of Shantung Province, Aoki accompanied him there and helped him with his early campaign of suppression against the Boxers.

Aoki's background was well known to the war party, and in November 1903 Kodama called on him at his home in the Ichigaya district of Tokyo. "Russo-Japanese relations have now entered a critical stage," he told him.

It will not be long before hostilities begin. I am sure you would want to take your regiment into battle, but there is a task to be performed which is many times more important than combat duty. It must be undertaken by someone closely associated with the Chinese northern leaders, and I know from Major-General Fukushima Yasumasa that there is no one closer to Yuan Shih-k'ai than you.

Aoki returned to China with a threefold appointment: to organize in cooperation with Yuan Shih-k'ai an intelligence agency specifically directed at Manchuria, to plan attacks against the Russian lines of communication, and to coordinate the efforts of armed bands as a means of threatening the Russians' rear and flank. He left Tokyo immediately to take up his appointment and met Yuan Shih-k'ai in Tientsin. Yuan had moved even faster than Kodama. "I have already sent scores of investigators to Port Arthur and to every part of Manchuria," he told him, "and their reports will be shown to Japan without fail in future."

As reports from the border areas flowed in, they were immediately translated by a Japanese captain and sent to the Japanese garrison commander at Tientsin, who transmitted them to Tokyo. Not love of the Japanese but fear of Russia motivated Yuan, who was convinced that the war would be a determining factor in shaping the future of East Asia. Should Japan lose, the Chinese empire could no longer exist, he said, and he was therefore prepared to spend any amount of money to assist in anything that he thought might be to Japan's advantage, regardless of how small or large the matter might be.

Toward the end of 1903, Kodama increased the staff of China experts and instructed Aoki to raise a force of volunteers for suicide tasks mostly against the Trans-Siberian Railway. To a man, the Japanese community in Peking responded. Only fifty men and women were needed at first, however, and some who were turned down committed suicide because they were not taken. By the middle of January Japanese agents, including women, were deployed at key points through Manchuria. At the same time, the Japanese decision-makers concluded that, despite Yuan's collaborations, the fiction of Chinese neutrality should also be observed. The "yellow peril" had been raised by Kaiser William and by Nicholas II. An alliance between Japan and China might give credence to these views and lead to a general war which Tokyo was anxious to avoid.

Pressure mounted from the military for an early initiative and public opinion rose to fever heat. The Japanese government, having decided that negotiations were hopeless, made its fourth and final appeal to Russia to reconsider the situation on January 13, 1904. Foreign Minister Komura's message to Kurino, which he was required to deliver verbally to Lamsdorf, went about as far as the Japanese government could reasonably have been expected to go in accepting the Russian position in Manchuria. It provided that Russia be obliged to respect the territorial integrity of China there and not to obstruct Chinese treaties with other powers, including Japan.

On no less than four occasions Kurino pressed Lamsdorf for an early reply. Meeting Witte at a party at the Winter Palace, he sought the former finance minister's cooperation in impressing Lamsdorf with the need for haste. He spoke with exceptional frankness. Japan was at the end of her patience, he said, and if within a few days no reply was given hostilities would break out. Witte passed on Kurino's message to Lamsdorf. "I can do nothing," the foreign minister replied. "I take no part in the negotiations."

Oyama reviewed the situation again—and again reached the conclusion that any further delay in going to war would favor the Russians. Already in the Far East the Russians had a total force of a hundred infantry battalions, supported by seventy-five cavalry companies and thirty batteries of artillery. Against this force, Japan could put into the field 156 infantry battalions, 54 cavalry companies, and 106 field and mountain artillery batteries. That this superiority could not be indefinitely maintained when the Russian reinforcements began to arrive from Europe was obvious. If need be, there were a further 400,000 reserve infantry troops, but, if the negotiations dragged out any further and the Russians continued to reinforce, Japan's position would deteriorate steadily.

Toward the end of January the Russians moved three battalions of the East Siberian Rifle Regiment to Feng-huang-cheng, close to the Yalu River. Early in February these were reinforced by two additional battalions. Japanese intelligence reports from agents in the field continued to confirm Russian warlike preparations both on the Yalu River and in European Russia. Russian forces in Siberia were being mobilized, and the Tenth and Seventeenth Army Corps, including four infantry divisions and four artillery brigades, had been alerted to move to the Far East. Forces were also being sent eastward from western Siberia. In addition, one battleship, seven cruisers and four torpedo boats had left the Red Sea and were expected to reach Port Arthur in six or seven weeks, giving the Russians a greater tonnage of warships than the Japanese.

Oyama's appeal for an early war reached the Emperor on February 1, 1904. Two days later it received urgent backing with a report that the Russian squadron in Port Arthur had left, decked for action, and that its whereabouts was unknown. This new intelligence was weighed together with Kurino's assessment that he did not think that Russia wanted war in the Far East but "seems to be laboring under a tremendous conceit which leads to the opinion that an agreement regarding Manchuria would be looked upon as a great humiliation."

[173]

There is no evidence that the Japanese general staff actually had possession of Kuropatkin's own evaluation of how the Russian campaign should be conducted. It was not, in fact, circulated as a classified document until the war had been in progress for a week. But Oyama and Kodama perceived clearly what it would contain:

1. The struggle between the fleets for the command of the sea.
2. Japanese landings, and operations to prevent them.
3. Defensive operations, accompanied by delaying and guerrilla actions, up to the moment when sufficient forces had been concentrated.
4. The assumption of the offensive:
   (a) Expulsion of the Japanese from Manchuria;
   (b) Expulsion of the Japanese from Korea.
5. The invasion of Japan; defeat of the Japanese territorial troops; operations against a popular rising.

Initial Russian tactical plans called for the concentration of three independent detachments to delay the expected Japanese advance. The first section under the command of Lieutenant-General Linievitch was to be based on Liaoyang and to have as its striking force—60 infantry battalions, 160 field pieces, and 64 *sotnia* (literally, "hundred") of cavalry. The second, in the Maritime Province, was much smaller and consisted of only eight infantry battalions and six *sotnia* of cavalry, in addition to supporting artillery. The third, based in Harbin, and ready to reinforce either the Liaoyang or the Maritime theaters, was to be based on forces arriving from Siberia and European Russia.

The task of the Liaoyang detachment was to divert the Japanese forces, to prevent them from making a full-scale attack on Port Arthur, to hinder their advance to the Chinese Eastern Railway from across the Yalu River, and to allow time for the arrival of reinforcements. The second independent unit was to protect the Maritime Province, including Vladivostok. If the Japanese were to try to advance from this region against Harbin, the detachment here would work along their flank and behind them in cooperatuon with the main Russian force.

A series of three vital meetings took place in Tokyo on February 3, 4, and 5, the last in the presence of the Emperor. At dawn on February 4 the Emperor summoned Ito to the palace and greeted him in his night attire. The Emperor learned that Ito had now fully withdrawn his opposition to the war, and, when page boys carried the important documents from the meetings of the cabinet, the *genrō*, and the general staff to the Emperor's study later in the day, they were given imperial sanction.

[174]

No final decision could be made, however, without a conference before the Throne. The Emperor sat on his throne flanked on either side by the elder statesmen. Immediately in front of the Emperor, but some distance from him, was a large map desk. On the Emperor's right along the side of the desk sat the army leaders; on the left were the navy. Behind the desk and facing the Throne were the senior cabinet ministers.

By tradition, the Emperor asked no questions when the ministers and officers made their reports. He simply said "good" as each report ended. To have asked a question would have required a formal reply, "which His Majesty was considerate enough not to force upon the participants."

It was a singularly defeatist gathering. Though Kodama's war planning met general approval, there was no underestimation of Russia's capacity if the war dragged on. Even at this stage, before a shot had been fired, it was decided to ask the United States at the appropriate moment to act as mediator, and Baron Kaneko Kentaro, a Harvard graduate, was briefed by Ito to leave immediately for Washington, there to establish the closest possible relations with President Theodore Roosevelt and to win the American people to the Japanese side.

On the evening of February 4, after the meeting before the Throne, Ito prayed for victory and spoke in the gloomiest terms of the prospects to Baron Kaneko. But along with everyone else, he was now fully convinced that "if Russia is left alone, she will go on to take complete possession of Manchuria, and after that, would invade Korea, and eventually threaten Japan. In these circumstances, there is no alternative. We are bound to fight, even at the price of our very national existence. I say frankly that I expect no success." The Emperor spoke in similar terms to the Empress and others. "Finally, we are going to fight Russia," he said. "It is not my wish. But it couldn't be helped. . . . If we should fail, how could I face the people?"

Tokyo's foreign community shared Ito's views. Most diplomats thought the Japanese were bluffing* and that, having decided on war, they would lose. From St. Petersburg to Port Arthur, most Russians concurred. The court was contemptuous of the Japanese "upstarts." If war came, they would be defeated with little trouble, simply by throwing their caps at them, or by sticking pins into them, like butterflies. Japan was a joke.

In Mukden, Russian reinforcements looked forward to the war with contempt. "Well," said one, "at least there will be no war worth mentioning. Peace will be signed in Tokyo within three weeks of the first shot." "It

---

*On February 4, while the imperial council was making its decision for war, Sir Claude MacDonald assured a correspondent of *The Times* of London that it would never occur.

is suicidal folly for Japan to defy us," said another, "for now we shall wipe her off the map."

General Kuropatkin was one of the few who did not share these views. On February 8, when Togo's Combined Fleet was already on its way to Port Arthur, he expressed some of his fears at a conference presided over by Nicholas himself. When the conference adjourned, Nicholas cabled Alexeiev to be ready to resist any Japanese landing on the west coast of Korea.

What the Russian optimists failed to understand was that their government was about to go to war not with just another government but with an entire people. Torn by internal dissent, restless, and rebellious, the Russians accepted the war as just one more fardel added to their already unbearable load of misery. "When crawling locusts cross rivers it happens that the lower layers are drowned until from the bodies of the drowned is formed a bridge over which the upper ranks can pass," wrote Leo Tolstoy. "In the same way the Russian people are being disposed of." They had no stomach for a war they did not understand against a people they did not know. Manchuria was as remote as Mars and the Yalu only another river far across the steppes. In Russia the cradle and the tomb were both coffins: in Japan a man died to save his spirit. The serf demanded food in his belly: the samurai would forego all for the Emperor. The Tsar of All the Russias sought Russian hegemony over Manchuria and far beyond: the Emperor Meiji believed he was fighting for his country's life. Japan was not without territorial ambitions of its own, but the need to keep Korea free of Russian influence seemed of paramount importance to its own security. Not just the soldiers and the sailors were going to war but the entire society with all its institutions.

Britain feared for India and dispatched Sir Francis Younghusband to Tibet to sign the Anglo–Tibetan treaty to keep the Russians off the Roof of the World. She was only slightly less concerned about losing her commercial preeminence in China.

Convinced that the future history of the United States would be more determined by its position on the Pacific facing China than by its position on the Atlantic facing Europe, President Theodore Roosevelt did not bother to conceal his support for Japan. From its new bases in the Philippines, the United States was intent on securing its share of what it regarded as the fabulous trade of the Orient. A Japanese victory, it seemed, would hold open the door into China.

Germany, in the middle of her great naval expansion, had helped to push the Russians into the war, to tie them down in an evangelical role against the "Yellow Peril" while Kaiser William prepared his own plans for European hegemony.

Humiliated and betrayed so often by the European powers, deceived—

and worse—by Russia, China saw its only hope of avoiding partition in a Japanese victory. A successful Russia, it had no doubt, would run footloose not only over Manchuria but over all of China. It proclaimed its neutrality in all territory west of the Liao River in Manchuria and went to work quietly for the Japanese, and what Yuan Shih-k'ai in his innocence hoped would be the dawn of a new era in a land that had already suffered more than its share from foreign rapaciousness, ignorance and brutality.

Sir Robert Hart, Inspector-General of the Chinese Maritime Customs, saw more clearly perhaps than anyone else the opportunities the war presented for China. He called for the imposition of a land tax as the means to finance a China powerful enough to make its voice heard when the time came to settle the war. *The Times* reacted in horror. His proposals, it said, "will doubtless be read with a shudder by all alarmed at the threatened development of the yellow peril."

III

THE
EARLY
STAGE

❦❦❦❦❦

CHAPTER 9

One Hundred Victories in One Hundred Battles

MIDNIGHT HAD PASSED and it was early morning on February 6, 1904, when the cutters carrying the rear-admirals and captains of the Japanese Combined Fleet began to converge on the flagship, the English-built 15,140-ton battleship *Mikasa*, as she lay at her moorings in Sasebo naval base. They had been summoned urgently from their bunks by Vice-Admiral Togo Heihachiro, commander-in-chief of the Combined Fleet.

Togo stood solemnly, eyes downcast, in the center of *Mikasa*'s large staff cabin. Before him was a table covered with a white cloth on which lay his long and short swords and an array of champagne glasses. Behind him on the paneled wall was the Emperor's photograph draped in a purple curtain. Flanking the commander-in-chief were his somewhat eccentric staff officer, Commander Akiyama Masayuki, and Vice-Admiral Kamimura Hikonojo, commander of the Second Fleet, another member of the Satsuma clan. Lined up in front of them the forty other commanders and captains stood stiffly to attention in four tightly packed rows.

"This day intelligence was received from the Naval General Staff that the diplomatic relations with Russia had been finally severed and our nation would now assume a free hand," Togo said, in the slow, deep-toned voice his officers knew so well. "The Imperial Command has been handed down and with reverence I will now convey this to you, gentlemen."

The officers had been waiting ten years for this moment, but they listened to their Commander-in-Chief's message with mixed emotions.

At that moment I felt as if something had hit me hard in the head [wrote Staff Officer Moriyama Keizaburo of the Second Fleet]. I looked

[181]

down and felt tears streaming down my cheeks. That moment the feeling that went through my entire body was for our great Japanese empire, which had continued for more than 2,500 years. Would it perish forever because of this war? I had been wondering until then why we had not started fighting, why we had been dilly-dallying. So when I heard that the Imperial Command had been issued, I cried instead of jumping up in joy . . . when a man is strongly moved he apparently cries before he rejoices.

There was a tense atmosphere in the big cabin as Togo read the Emperor's rescript. When the long, all-night conference had finished, all the officers bowed to the Emperor's photograph, and Togo led three *banzais* for the Emperor and another three for the Combined Fleet. "We must now plan and establish strategies to achieve one hundred victories in one hundred battles," he said. Champagne toasts were drunk and reverently the commander-in-chief replaced the deep purple cloth over the Imperial portrait.

Ten destroyers, with heavy armored ships in support, were to attack the Russian First Pacific Squadron at Port Arthur. A cruiser force with torpedo boats was to go to the Korean port of Chemulpo (Inchon), 240 miles from Port Arthur, to attack two Russian warships in the harbor and to escort transports which would disembark troops to be sent to Seoul. A third division of destroyers was to search for Russian forces at Dalny (Dairen), forty miles from Port Arthur by train but only twenty-five miles by sea.*

Togo's initial appointment to command the Standing Squadron in October, 1903, had dismayed most of his contemporaries. If Togo was surprised, he was also delighted beyond all expectations. For the last two years he had been supervising the construction of a new naval base in the Japan Sea. Now he commanded the greatest fleet in Japan's history. A Japanese newspaper reported that when he emerged from the navy ministry late in the afternoon there was a sparkle in his eye and an unusual sprightliness in his step. A mild attack of rheumatism that had put him in bed for several weeks was forgotten, and he kept the appointment with Admiral Yamamoto Gonnohyoe, the navy minister, despite his wife's protests. "I shall be well the moment I set foot on deck and drink in the salt-laden air," he told her. He had married when he was thirty-three and his bride seventeen. Till then he had always been too busy to take much interest in women. He was also

---

*The Japanese were mistaken. There were no Russian ships at Dalny. The only ship in the bay was the *Foochow*, crammed with Japanese refugees. The ship was lucky not to be attacked by the Japanese destroyers, which took her for a Russian minelaying ship. On closer investigation, they found *Foochow* full of their own countrymen and, without an enemy to attack, returned to Round Island, thirty miles south of Port Arthur.

described by the proprietor of a Yokosuka restaurant as a "gentle" drinker, though occasionally he and his friends stayed at the inn for days on end. The chambermaids regarded him as a nuisance, because he took so long to finish off a bottle of saké.

During Togo's training period in England, Saigo Takamori, the Satsuma leader, was in trouble at home, and Togo deliberated for a long time before deciding to remain in England rather than return to Japan. It was a difficult decision for him to make. Saigo, now a rebel leader, had been his hero. "He spoke to me affectionately whenever he saw me. If I asked him a question, he would give me a full answer," he told Vice-Admiral Viscount Ogasawara Nagayo, his biographer. "He never tried to teach me when I was not ready. He was always smiling. I felt somehow very close to him, this I cannot forget."*

All the other Satsuma men training in England were anxious to return to Japan to assist Saigo. Togo decided to stay. "I am here under government orders to study," he said. "I am here to study naval technology from the great naval power, Britain, so that I can take an active part in building up a navy of our own. This is my main task. No matter what may happen at home, I am not going home until I have learned all that I came here to learn." Later, while still in England, he heard of the battle between the Satsumas and the government forces at Castle Hill. His whole family fought on Saigo's side against the government. One of his brothers was killed, another wounded and taken prisoner. In an anguished voice, Togo told his fellow-students that the least he could so was to finish the job he had been set.

Togo did not have a particularly impressive bearing. His broad, slightly stooped shoulders made him appear even shorter than his five-feet-three-inches. The large flat face, with grizzled hair hanging over a wide forehead, enormous ears, and bristling short beard and mustache showed little emotion. Observers were struck by his modest manner—the demeanor, as *The Times* correspondent described it, of a blushing young girl. The keen black eyes which "pierced men even to the bottom of their hearts" were the outstanding features of his sleepy, almost dull outward appearance. He could also be stern and demanding. The commander of one of the destroyers to attack Port Arthur wrote in his diary before the war that, though he acknowledged Togo's ability, he was very glad to have command of a destroyer and to be at a certain distance from him. "He is an unpleasant neighbor for his inferiors."

---

*Both Togo and Saigo were born in Kajiya-Machi near Kagoshima. "Togo" means "east village" and "Saigo," "west village."

Togo inspired his officers and men by his own long hours without rest. During the war with China he never went to bed in his nightgown, and in both wars he wore full-dress uniform to all meals. His tiny night cabin, with a high wooden bunk, desk, and washbasin and an adjoining Japanese-style bathroom was sufficient for his needs when he was not in his staff cabin or on the bridge of the flagship.

Captain (later Admiral) William Christopher Pakenham of the Royal Navy, who was with Togo's fleet throughout the war as an observer, became firm friends with the Japanese admiral. It was said that Togo often consulted Pakenham and another British naval attaché, Captain Thomas Jackson. Pakenham referred to the rumors as "rubbish." On board the battleship *Asahi* ("Morning Sun"), Pakenham also insisted on being faultlessly dressed in correct uniform, with a high, stiffly starched collar, and monocle in his eye. During the Russo-Japanese War, he stayed on board ship for fourteen months, not daring to set foot on shore for fear of being left behind.

Winston Churchill wrote glowingly of Pakenham's service with the Royal Navy during World War I when he spent fifty-two months of constant service with the British battle-cruisers: "Since Nelson himself no British naval officer has been so long at sea in time of war . . . he never on any occasion at sea lay down to rest otherwise than fully-dressed, collared and booted, ready at any moment of night or day."

Togo and Pakenham were alike in many ways. They had both started their naval careers as young boys. They were both taciturn, with a quiet sense of humor, and dedicated to their profession. The Englishman admired the Japanese commander for his efficiency and for his dogged devotion to duty. "Never, at any time, have his limits appeared to be in sight," he wrote. "He is, indeed, a noble man."

Ever since the conference at Imperial Headquarters in May 1903, the navy minister, Yamamoto, had favored action. By August he had already recalled the fleet from routine exercises in Japanese and Korean waters to refit and refurbish at the naval base of Sasebo on the southern island of Kyushu. The first week of October brought in a flock of disquieting reports —the Russian rejection of Japan's demands on the territorial integrity and independence of China and, more seriously, the arrival of Russian reinforcements in the Far East. The day after Togo's appointment to command the Standing Squadron the general staff began to draw up its plans for an offensive war. The time had come to translate the blueprints into action.

On December 28, 1903, the Standing Squadron was dissolved. The First and Second fleets became the Combined Fleet. Togo was commander-in-chief of the Combined Fleet and also commander of the First Fleet, while Vice-Admiral Kamimura Hikonojo led the Second Fleet.

At the beginning of the new year, Sasebo harbor, the biggest naval port in the East, bristled with the masts and funnels of more than a hundred warships and other vessels loading supplies of food and fuel. Everyone knew that war was near, but Japanese newspapers were prohibited from reporting military matters. Officers and men were restricted to the town of Sasebo. Foreign correspondents—or, as Captain Pakenham called them, "paid disseminators of news"—were not permitted into the area.

The navy wanted to anticipate the Russian fleet's movements, "and to take the initiative . . . by delivering a heavy blow which would decide the preponderance at the very beginning of the war." As early as December 15, Admiral Yamamoto had sent Togo a private letter setting out the anticipated Russian moves:

1. They will collect the whole fleet at Port Arthur and will attract us thither; they will choose a position favorable to themselves, forcing us to spend our strength in running about. Since the point they must consider is the expenditure of coal and stores, they will not come further than the south coast of Korea.
2. They will make Vladivostok into a base for four cruisers and six destroyers, and take advantage of their high speeds to harass the neighborhood of Otaru and Hakodate [coastal towns on the northern Island of Honshu] and to divide our fleet.
3. If they have a chance, the Port Arthur and Vladivostok squadrons will make arrangements to come out together and engage our fleet.

On January 10, Togo ordered all ships to be painted with a mixture of one part black to three parts white. He also laid a deep sea cable to facilitate military communications between Sasebo and the islands of Hakko-ho, off the southwest coast of Korea, which were to be his first fleet base. On January 20 came the orders to fill up with the highly regarded Welsh coal and to place the fleet in such a state of alert that every ship could be ready to sail in less than twelve hours. Final preparations were made for operating in the intense cold off the Manchurian coast. The Emperor's aide arrived with the Imperial Message and inspected the fleet, stirring up warlike enthusiasm. The navy, the whole country, was itching to fight.

I really loathe that country [a destroyer captain noted in his diary]. That which the Russians call "fear of death" is unknown here, but I know something about it having read of it in their books, and my Uncle Kato has told me about it. It seems to me to be simply a folly, caused by their stupid religion. Fortunately, our politicians have not introduced it among us, and their half-imbecile missionaries will not succeed in making lunatics of us.

To fight to the death was simple. The military wanted to make absolutely sure that the Russians would be taken by surprise. Vice-Admiral Ijuin

Goro, vice-chief of the naval general staff, in a telegram to Togo on February 2, made it clear that a formal declaration of war would come only after the first decisive blow had been struck. "The time of the opening attack on the Russian Fleet has a very close connection with the final diplomatic negotiations," he wired.

On February 4, he telegraphed Togo: "It has been decided to give sailing orders to the fleet at the same time as we break off diplomatic relations." Togo now decided to send ten destroyers direct to Port Arthur and to wait in the background with the Combined Fleet until they had launched their surprise torpedo attack against the Russian ships. Admiral Uryu Sotokichi would go to Chemulpo to attack the Russian ships there and to protect an initial landing of troops of the Twelfth Division. If the Russian ships in Chemulpo harbor prevented this landing, the troops would be forced to land at Fusan.* An armored cruiser, *Chiyoda,* was at Chemulpo and would report on the suitability of the port for a landing. Meanwhile, if the Russian ships at Port Arthur or Chemulpo were put to sea again and appeared near Sasebo, Togo was instructed to consider that as a hostile act and to attack at once.

It was imperative to strike the first blow. The foe was formidable. The main Russian squadron, including seven battleships and six cruisers, was back at Port Arthur after a brief period at sea. At Vladivostok, the Russians had the first-class cruisers *Rossiya, Rurik, Gromoboi, Bogatuir,* and seventeen torpedo boats. At Chemulpo, they had the first-class cruiser *Varyag* and a gunboat, *Koreetz.*

As soon as he received his appointment as Standing Squadron commander, Togo had taken the Fleet to Sylvia Basin, a secluded harbor near Masan on the south coast of Korea. Here he had practiced amphibious landings and other exercises, including torpedo firing, long-range firing at high speeds, experiments with wireless telegraphy, and maneuvering. A series of confidential communications passed between Vice-Admiral Ito Sukeyuki, chief of the Japanese naval general staff, and Togo, in which they exchanged ideas for taking the initiative against the Russians before a declaration of war.

Togo's Combined Fleet now consisted of two main fleets and a supply "train" of two divisions, including gunboats, merchant cruisers, and auxiliaries. The First Fleet consisted of the battleships *Mikasa, Asahi, Fuji, Yashima, Shikishima,* and *Hatsuse,* forming the First Division; the Third Division, of cruisers *(Chitose, Takasago, Kasagi,* and *Yoshino),* three destroyer flotillas, three torpedo boat flotillas, and a dispatch vessel. Vice-

---

*Fusan, Japanese reading; Pusan, Korean reading.

Admiral Kamimura Hikonojo had the Second Fleet, with its six armored cruisers, *Izumo, Azuma, Asama, Yagumo, Tokiwa,* and *Iwate,* forming the Second Division, and four cruisers, *Naniwa, Akashi, Takachiho,* and *Niitaka* making up the Fourth Division. Two destroyer flotillas, two torpedo boat flotillas, and a dispatch boat made up the rest of his fleet.

After the conference of February 6 on *Mikasa* the Combined Fleet sailed out of Sasebo and thousands of women and children, carrying lanterns, came in rowboats to bid farewell. The Sasebo administration naval band on board a steamboat cruised in and out between the departing vessels playing *The Warship March.** Crowds lined the shores to shout parting *banzais.* "It was a scene of tragic beauty," wrote a Japanese historian.

While Togo with the main fleet was heading for Port Arthur, Vice-Admiral Uryu Sotokichi, a forty-six-year-old Annapolis graduate and one of the youngest and most capable of Japan's senior officers, left Sasebo early in the afternoon of February 6, with four cruisers from Vice-Admiral Kamimura's Second Fleet. These were the *Naniwa,* a second-class protected cruiser, which had been Togo's ship in the war with China, the *Takachiho*† and the *Niitaka,* second-class cruisers, and the *Asama,* a first-class cruiser built in England in 1899. Heavily armored with steel beltings and carrying four eight-inch and fourteen six-inch quick-firing guns, all operated electrically, the *Asama* and her sister ship, *Tokiwa,* were the world's first "battle cruisers."

Outside the harbor Vice-Admiral Uryu was joined by three transports loaded with troops, horses, and equipment for a landing at or near Chemulpo on the west coast of Korea. On the following day he met the *Akashi,* a protected cruiser, and two flotillas of torpedo boats.

When Vice-Admiral Uryu's ships were passing Ninepin Rock, on the way to Chemulpo, at ten o'clock on February 7, a message came in from *Mikasa* that a merchantman, the *Rossiya,* had been captured. The Japanese sailors, eager for battle, shouted like schoolboys, "Russia is taken!" and "Russia has been captured!" They took it as another good omen when the cruiser *Takachiho* collided with a large whale. The whale was badly hurt, and the sailors watched with glee as the water beneath them turned to crimson.

The armored cruiser *Chiyoda,* which had been keeping an eye on the Russian ships in Chemulpo harbor for many months, signaled Admiral Uryu that the Russian first-class protected cruiser *Varyag* (6,500 tons), the gunboat *Koreetz* (1,200 tons), and *Sungari,* a transport, were still lying in

---

**The Warship March,* which had been composed four years earlier, was also played daily by Japanese radio stations during World War II.

†Named after the mountain near Kagoshima, where, according to Japanese mythology, the grandson of Amaterasu established the dynasty.

the harbor. With them were several foreign warships: *Talbot* (English), *Pascal* (French), *Elba* (Italian), and *Vicksburg* (an American dispatch boat).

Chiyoda had been on duty at Chemulpo since April 1903, fulfilling the dual purpose of protecting the 10,000 Japanese nationals in Korea and acting as a watchdog on the Russians. Her commander, Captain Murakami Kakuichi, had dutifully reported the arrival of several small batches of Russian soldiers en route to Seoul, and during January and the first week of February kept the navy minister in constant touch with developments at the port. His request to take the ship to sea to practice torpedo-firing was refused. He was to remain in Chemulpo with his eyes wide open.

Captain Murakami had become friendly with the captains of the two Russian warships that lay on either side of the *Chiyoda* in the harbor at Chemulpo. On social visits to the two ships he took the opportunity to visit their wardrooms and always sent officers to investigate any new ships that arrived in the harbor.

As the days passed, the diligent Captain Murakami, though lacking official information, sensed that the crisis was near. He secretly prepared to make his ship ready for war, taking pains that the Russian and other foreign ships in the harbor did not realize his intentions. On January 3, *Koreetz*, which was anchored to the north of *Chiyoda*, changed berth so that she lay closer to *Varyag*. Murakami realized that the two ships could now see his preparations and were also in closer communication with each other. He became worried.

On February 3 he became even more worried when he received a message that the Russian Pacific Squadron had left Port Arthur, destination unknown. He hurriedly changed his moorings to the east of the English ship *Talbot*, farther away from *Koreetz* and nearer the exit from the harbor. *Talbot* now hid him from *Varyag*. In some ways this was a good move, he thought, since the Russian ship could not keep a watch on his preparations; but it also meant that *he* could not see the Russians. He therefore sent out boats at night to keep watch. In the event of Russian ships entering the harbor to land troops, Captain Murakami planned to sail into the port in front of the British consulate and a Russian-owned railway office, and to wait for his own fleet to turn up. At the same time, he would fire at the Russian ships until he ran out of ammunition, in a desperate attempt to hold them at bay. Guessing correctly that diplomatic relations were about to be severed, he sent off a message, suggesting that perhaps it would be a good idea for him to take *Chiyoda* out of the port on reconnaissance. He was instructed to meet Admiral Uryu and to advise him that, since foreign men-of-war were at anchor in Chemulpo, it would be contrary to international law to take action against the Russians inside the harbor.

As soon as it became dark, Murakami issued instructions that no lights were to be shown and complete silence maintained. Coolies who had been working on the ship and tradesmen who had brought in supplies were paid off and sworn to secrecy about the movements of the ship. At 11:30 P.M. on February 7 the *Chiyoda* crept silently past *Talbot,* all lights extinguished and with sound kept to a minimum. Not a soul stirred in the harbor, and there were no lights at the entrance. Half an hour after midnight *Chiyoda* steamed for the open sea and her rendezvous with Admiral Uryu's ships.

Early that morning, after *Chiyoda* had joined his detachment, Admiral Uryu called all commanding officers to the flagship to discuss plans. Captain Murakami reported that there was little to fear from the Russian ships at Chemulpo, and it was decided to land the troops there.

Russian ships met outside the port were to be attacked and sunk, but unless the Russians inside the harbor began warlike operations, there was to be no attack by the Japanese ships. *Chiyoda* was to enter the harbor first with *Takachiho* and *Asama* heading the torpedo flotillas and transports. They were all to proceed quietly, without frightening the enemy and maintaining a peaceful demeanor. Two torpedo boats would anchor in a position where they could not be seen by the Russian ships, and another two, also showing no warlike intention, would anchor where they would be able to deal "instant destruction on the enemy," one taking on *Varyag,* the other *Koreetz.* If the enemy opened fire, they were to retaliate. The presence of foreign ships in the harbor was to be disregarded under these circumstances.

On board the Japanese ships the men hid themselves by their guns. From all outward sign the ships were on a peacetime mission. As they approached Eight-tail Island and the entrance to Chemulpo harbor about 2:15 P.M. on February 8, the Russian gunboat *Koreetz* was putting to sea. She was carrying dispatches and mail to Port Arthur from the Russian minister at Seoul. To the Japanese on *Asama* she seemed completely unprepared for battle. As the ships passed, only a hundred yards from each other, the Japanese could see her guard lined up on the forecastle, saluting. Realizing that the Japanese presence could have only one meaning, however, *Koreetz*'s commanding officer turned about and started to run back to harbor. His ship was an eighteen-year-old gunboat with little fighting value. She had no armor and only one long-range gun. Her top speed was thirteen knots.

There are differences in the accounts of these first moments of the war. *The Official History of the Russo-Japanese War (Naval and Military),* published in London for the Historical Section of the Committee of Imperial Defence, reported that *Koreetz* fired the first shot. The order was immediately countermanded, "but through a misunderstanding two shots, the first of the war, were fired by a light gun." *The Japanese Official Naval History* said that, as the Japanese ships closed in on *Koreetz,* the torpedo boat *Kari* discharged a fourteen-inch Whitehead torpedo at 300 meters range. *Koreetz* altered course, and the torpedo missed her. Two other torpedo boats pressed closer, and *Koreetz* opened fire on them. Two more torpedos were fired by the Japanese but also missed.

The captain of the *Koreetz* claimed that before he gave the order to fire the Japanese had already fired three torpedoes at her. Sailors in the foreign ships in the bay heard no firing. Other Japanese reports claimed that, rather than having started the war without a declaration, their ships had been fired on by the old Russian gunboat first and therefore Russia had forced *them* into war. In fact, the Japanese had already captured a Russian merchant ship in Fusan harbor, so the war had already begun, though the Russians at Chemulpo did not know it.

Whether she fired the first shot or not, the *Koreetz* now returned as quickly as possible to the comparative safety of the anchorage, alongside the bigger Russian ship, *Varyag*. Built at Cramps's shipyard in Philadelphia a few years earlier, *Varyag* had armament that included twelve six-inch guns, but she was only partly armored. Her hull was completely unprotected, and only thin metal shielded her guns, which were all on the upper deck of the ship. She had a nominal speed of twenty-three knots, but during tests in 1903 she made only fourteen knots.

With the *Asama* and two torpedo boats keeping watch over the Russian ships, the transports anchored. The cruisers *Naniwa, Niitaka* and *Akashi* steamed around the harbor to show their war strength, and then the first two came to anchor with the torpedo boats outside the entrance, while *Akashi, Chiyoda, Takachiho,* and the torpedo boats anchored near the transports to protect them while the troops were landed.

Soon after six in the evening the troops and horses started to go ashore on the beaches of Chemulpo from flat-bottomed sampans that had been carried on board the transports. Each transport ship had five large sampans carrying forty men and six horses as well as fifty-foot boards for the construction of landing piers. Carrying eight days' provisions, tents, and blankets, the men streamed ashore in their new gray uniforms, white puttees, and sheepskin neck mufflers. Major-General Yasutsuna Kogishi, who commanded this advance guard of 3,000 men, was an impressive figure as he directed proceedings, dressed in a scarlet-lined overcoat, dark blue uniform decorated by a large silver star, and high thigh boots.

On board the Russian ships sailors crowded at the rails, shoulder to shoulder, to watch the landing of Japanese troops. *Varyag* had no smoke coming from her funnels, and neither of the Russian ships was prepared for battle.

The streets of the town were covered in snow, and ice was floating on the harbor. Japanese flags appeared over doorways of shops and houses, and

Japanese civilians mingled with the white-clad Koreans as coolies with numbered paper lanterns took up positions along the shore to show the troops where to land.

About nine o'clock a light flared up at the entrance to the harbor, followed by another and another until it seemed that thousands of huge fireflies were settling on the water. The myriad flickering lights were huge torches which the Japanese soldiers carried as they came ashore in launches. All along the shore large bonfires burned and huge iron tripods were erected to carry pots of burning charcoal. The blaze from the torches and fires revealed the long lines of landing boats, full of troops, and columns of soldiers standing at attention on the banks. Foreign war correspondents had been in the town for several days, waiting for the invasion, and the magnesium flares of *Collier's* correspondent-photographer Robert L. Dunn added to the brilliance of the scene.

The Russians "behaved with the utmost unconcern," wrote a Japanese torpedo-boat captain. "Their washing was hanging out to dry and their swinging booms [were] out as if they were wholly indifferent to the great drama about to be enacted."

Disembarkation went on until about three in the morning of February 9. The three thousand soldiers marched off in an orderly manner and were billeted in Japanese houses in the town or started the march to Seoul, the capital of Korea, twenty-four miles away.

At 9 A.M. on February 9, all the Japanese transports and warships left the harbor, except for *Chiyoda,* which was ordered to deliver letters from Admiral Uryu to the Russian and foreign ships in harbor. *Varyag, Koreetz,* and the transport *Sungari* received an ultimatum: to leave by noon that day or be attacked in harbor at 4 P.M. Letters to the captains of the foreign ships and the Russians and other foreign consuls at Chemulpo announced that hostilities had begun between Japan and Russia and told them of the ultimatum to the Russian ships. Admiral Uryu urged the neutral ships to leave the scene in order to avoid danger, adding that the attack would not take place before 4 P.M. Any ship remaining at that time would do so at her own risk.

The captains of *Varyag, Pascal,* and *Elba* met on board the *Talbot.* As a result of the conference, the commander of the *Talbot,* Captain (later Admiral) Lewis Bayly, visited Admiral Uryu's ship, the *Naniwa,* with a protest from all the captains on behalf of their respective governments against the Japanese proposed attack inside the three-mile limit and the violation of Korean neutrality.*

---

*To reach the three-mile limit it would have been necessary to steam more than

"I come as senior captain of the ships of the nations here to visit you, the senior Japanese captain," he said. "If you respect Chemulpo as a port of a neutral country, I believe that you will not fire guns or perform any other action likely to injure foreign men-of-war. What do you think about it?" He was assured that, so long as the Russians inflicted no damage on them, the Japanese would not damage foreign men-of-war.

The two Russian ships, having hastily prepared for battle by throwing overboard all unnecessary materials, including tables and spare ventilators, began to leave the harbor, flying their battle flags.

The English sailors forgot their meals and their jobs and rushed to the sides of the ship and up into the rigging to see what was going to happen. "We did not expect to see them get away, nor did we think they would ever come back again," reported Captain Bayly, who had already received a bag of letters from the Russian ships addressed to wives and sweethearts in Russia.

The captain of the *Koreetz* called his crew together and told them that they were going out to face the Japanese. "We must fight to sustain the honor of the Russian flag," he said. "Remember, brothers, we must fight to the last. There will be no surrender. May God help us! Let us cross ourselves and go boldly into this fight for our Faith, our Tsar, and for Holy Russia!" Cheers went out for the Tsar, for the captain and for the ship. The band struck up the Russian national anthem and the sailors harmonized like a well-rehearsed church choir, their voices "making stange music over the bay."

As they passed the foreign ships, *Koreetz* and *Varyag* played the *Marseillaise, Hail, Columbia,* and *God Save the King.* "Hurrahs" and "Vivas" came over the water and the Russian sailors saw that all along the sides of the English, French, and Italian ships men were cheering them, waving their caps and wishing them luck. On *Talbot,* the English sailors on the decks and the rigging cheered the two ships on their way to death. "Three cheers for the *Talbot,*" shouted the Russian sailors. "They gave us three and we returned them three very good ones," wrote Captain Bayly in the log.

Here were 694 Russian officers and men going to almost certain death —for no one expected them, or at any rate very many of them, to survive the most unequal conflict—and yet they had their bands playing and were cheering, and their cheers being heartily returned by about four hundred British officers and men, who felt very sorry for them, and admired their pluck in giving battle.

---

eighty miles from Chemulpo because of the many islands along the coast.

At 11 A.M. Admiral Uryu ordered his whole squadron to prepare for action and be ready to sink the ships in the mouth of the harbor. It was a clear, bright day and the sea was calm. *Varyag* came first, her battle flag fluttering at her masthead, followed by the old, slow *Koreetz*. At 11:45 A.M. *Asama* opened fire with her eight-inch guns at a range of 7,500 yards, and *Varyag* replied.

It was a dramatic, tragic, and almost completely one-sided battle, which lasted for just over an hour. The faster *Varyag* might have stood a chance alone, but encumbered by the lumbering *Koreetz* she had no hope of escaping. Five shells hit *Varyag* in quick succession, one from *Asama* shattering her upper bridge, causing a fire in the charthouse, and bringing down the fore-rigging. A junior navigator who was taking range was killed, and all the range-takers at No. 1 station were either killed or wounded. After ten minutes *Varyag* was seen to be in difficulties, her steering engine was out of order and fires had broken out in many places. Homer Bezaleel Hulbert, editor and owner of the magazine, *Korea Review*, who saw the battle, reported that most of the work at this time was done by *Asama* and *Chiyoda*. All the fire was directed at *Varyag*—"the roar that went up from those terrible machines of destruction tore the quiet of the windless bay to tatters and made the houses of the town tremble where they stood."

The commander of the *Varyag*, Captain Rudnev, standing between the conning tower and its entrance, with a bugler and a drummer on either side of him, was wounded in the face by shell splinters. The bugler boy and the drummer were both killed. *Varyag* zigzagged as the eight Japanese ships formed a semicircle around her. Another eight-inch shell from *Asama* struck her on the port side, below the waterline, and water flooded the stokeholds, causing the ship to list heavily to port. Men wept at their guns, firing wildly into the ring of Japanese ships. "They stood by their guns as if petrified and dumbfounded, serving them and firing like automatons. Utterly without protection, they were exposed to the enemy's shot and shell, which horribly mangled and tore into shreds a large number of men," wrote an officer on *Varyag*.

Varyag was listing now. Both bridges were destroyed, and more fires had broken out on her quarterdeck and in the captain's cabin. Her four tall yellow funnels were perforated and two had collapsed on the deck.

The Japanese closed in, led by *Asama*, until the crippled *Varyag*, her masts down, her steering rods shot through and ventilators and boats riddled, crawled back toward the entrance to the harbor, firing the few six-inch guns still serviceable. *Chiyoda* fell behind. She had not been supplied with the good Welsh coal which the other Japanese ships carried, and after her long spell in Chemulpo harbor her bottom was covered with barnacles. The old Russian gunboat, *Koreetz*, which had been unable to get within range of the Japanese ships with her two light guns, became *Chiyoda*'s target. Exactly twice the weight of the Russian ship and armed with ten 4.7-inch guns and twenty other guns of various sizes, *Chiyoda* gave chase. Only one hit was scored on *Koreetz*, but she was set on fire and ran back to harbor on the heels of the blazing *Varyag*.

Admiral Uryu realized that if he chased the beaten ships inside the harbor there might be damage done to the foreign ships. "This would stir up trouble in the harbor itself and also leave behind a very difficult diplomatic question to be settled." He stopped the action and turned back.

"It was a sort of suicidal duel, for they might as well have fired in the air as aimed at the enemy, so completely did they fail to injure the Japanese," reported the *Times* correspondent. "They incommoded nobody but the fish," a Japanese officer wrote in his diary that night. The Russians were using high-explosive shells, most of which failed to explode. In their shells the Japanese used a type of powder known as "Shimose" after a naval chemical engineer, who invented it in 1885. It generated more heat and much greater blast power than other powders of the time.

The two Russian ships returned to their old anchorages and during the afternoon officers and men were taken aboard the other European ships, which during the short fight had prepared for action. The American ship, *Vicksburg*, did not take survivors, but picked up some and took them to the other foreign ships. While Admiral Uryu was reconsidering going into the harbor to deal with the *Varyag* and *Koreetz*, the Russian captains decided to destroy their ships—a decision that provided another dramatic spectacle for the crews of foreign vessels and for the townspeople in Chemulpo, many of whom lined the shores around the harbor or rowed out to a small island from which they could obtain a good view.

The transport, *Sungari*, which had stayed inside the harbor, was set on fire and burned till the next day, when she went to the bottom. Homer Hulbert, who was watching from the shore, described the destruction of the *Koreetz*. "It was thirty-seven minutes past three when the waiting multitude saw two blinding flashes of light," he wrote.

A terrific report followed, which dwarfed the roar of cannon to a whisper and shook every house in the town as if it had been struck by a solid rock. The window-fastenings of one house at least were torn off, so great was the concussion. An enormous cloud of smoke and debris shot toward the sky and at the same time enveloped the spot where the vessel had lain. A moment later there began a veritable shower of splintered wood, torn and twisted railing, books, clothes, rope, utensils and a hundred other belongings of the ship. The cloud of smoke expanded in the upper air and blotted out the sun like an eclipse.. The startled gulls flew hither and thither, as if dazed by this unheard-of phenomenon, and men instinctively raised their hands to protect themselves from the falling debris, pieces of which were drifted by the upper currents of air for a distance of three miles landward, where they fell by the hundreds in people's yards.

Varyag went quietly. Shells had torn huge holes in her sides, above and below water. All the men in the fighting tops were killed. Entire gun-crews were killed or wounded. She rolled on every wave of the incoming tide and as the Russian sailors were transferred to the foreign ships, they slipped in the wreckage and blood on the decks. The crew opened the seacocks and laid charges to destroy the torpedoes that went off one after the other.

Varyag slipped gently into the mud, taking with her forty-one dead men whose bodies had been left in a large cabin. Russian and foreign sailors in rescue boats and aboard ships in the harbor sprang to their feet to cheer. Again, the Russian bands, which had sought sanctuary on other ships, played the national anthem. Sailors cheered and waved their caps, and thousands lining the shores applauded. Admiral Uryu hoisted the signal, "*Banzai* for His Imperial Majesty," and the crews of all the Japanese ships turned toward the east and bowed.

The Japanese claimed to have escaped without injury, apart from the grounding of one torpedo boat at the beginning of the action. *Varyag* fired a total of 1,105 rounds during the battle from her six-inch twelve-pounder and three-pounder guns. Russian reports said that she scored a number of hits on the Japanese ships. Togo reported that the Princes of the Blood on board the ships were safe: "We were not once hit, no one was killed or wounded, and we did not suffer the slightest damage.... Our men in general fought with presence of mind throughout the battle, acting as if they were at ordinary maneuvers." Some neutral reports mentioned that *Asama* had been so badly damaged by *Varyag* that she had to return to Japan for repairs. In this action, as in others that followed, little reliance could be placed on statements made by the Russians of injuries inflicted on Japanese vessels. The Japanese, too, proved themselves masters of prevarication and exaggeration.

CHAPTER *10*

@@@@@@

"A Place of Honor in the Naval Annals"

VICEROY ALEXEIEV REFUSED at first to believe the disaster of the night attack outside Port Arthur. "Impossible," he retorted when he was told that three ships, including two battleships, had been put out of action. Later he issued an order to the fortress, concluding: "You must all keep calm, in order to be able to perform your duty in the most efficient manner possible, trusting to the help of God that every man will do his work, remembering that neither prayers to God nor service for the Tsar are in vain."

Many prayers and much service to their Tsar were needed that morning to put the fortress in order.

Port Arthur awoke early. The military personnel, reported E. K. Nojine, the accredited Russian correspondent in the fortress, were in chaos.

> The disorganization of the fortress staff particularly was almost ludicrous; officers hurried hither and thither, contradictory and impossible orders were being issued, and countermanded, and above and through all this confusion resounded the ceaseless chattering of the telephone bells. It was not a sight to inspire confidence. It seemed as if the staff momentarily anticipated some fatal and sudden blow but did not know what to do to ward it off.

Among the civilian population, a few people who were aroused from sleep, or from a party, had been up all night, and by dawn the whole town was on the streets. The wounded came ashore and were taken to the navy hospital, and a big crowd gathered outside Saratov's restaurant. Two young naval officers who had missed their ship stood near the dock at Quail Hill, looking ashamed and dejected. Rumors flew wildly around the town. A new

[196]

issue of *Novoye Krai*, in which Nojine's reports appeared, was eagerly bought up, but there was nothing in it about the Japanese attack.

At 10:30 A.M. members of the Viceroy's cabinet and the generals, mounted on horseback and in full uniform, paraded through the streets to give confidence to the garrison and the civilian population. Their appearance did nothing to calm fears, and rumors only increased when General Stoessel, commander of the fortress, issued orders that stories about the garrison's lack of preparedness must cease immediately and that rumormongers would be severely punished.

The three Russian ships were badly damaged, but all remained afloat long enough to reach shallow water. *Pallada* grounded close to the lighthouse on the west side of the entrance to the harbor. The two battleships, *Retvizan* and *Tsarevitch*, attempted to make their way through the narrow channel leading to the dockyards. They both went aground and there remained, in all their non-glory, leaving only a narrow passage on either side.

"Arthur" blazed with anger against the fleet. Madame Stark's "party" was the source of one of the wildest rumors. Some said that there had been a dance following the party and that many officers did not get to their ships at all. And so the rumor spread and became the reality.

Andrew Petrovitch Steer, an officer aboard the unprotected cruiser *Novik*, which alone among the Russian ships had set off to pursue the departing Japanese destroyers, and was to distinguish herself again during the day, was bitter and angry. "I still feel the sting, the indescribable ill-will of which our squadron was the subject and still hear the echo of the libelous legend to the effect that the Japanese were able to carry their torpedo attack so easily because our officers were feasting and dancing on shore at the house of Admiral Stark," he wrote after the war. "The admiral never dreamt for a moment of inviting anyone to dance at his house." He admitted that there had been foolish confidence at Port Arthur, that they had been assured there would be no war and that everyone could sleep soundly in their beds.

Since the cable between Port Arthur and Korea had been cut by the Japanese on the morning of February 7, no one in Port Arthur knew of the attack at Chemulpo that had taken place early in the afternoon of the eighth. Admiral Stark, who had tried in vain to have the *Varyag* brought from Chemulpo to join his fleet, denied that he had been entertaining guests during the attack on his ships. It was rumored that in his pocket he had a note signed by Alexeiev, and written in his well-known green pencil, which showed that it was the Viceroy who had denied permission for the fleet to be ready to repel a Japanese attack, and which would clear his own name of what some called treason, or at the least, criminal carelessness.

Early in the morning of February 9 Admiral Stark visited the Viceroy to

[197]

put his case and to make sure that Port Arthur would be prepared, should the Japanese return. He had no doubt now that they would return.

In the outer harbor the fleet, with steam up and decks cleared for action, waited orders to put to sea. Among the civilians ashore the early excitement gave way to fear, and many people who had taken their children to see the grounded ships returned hurriedly to their houses and closed the doors. Others, more adventurous, boarded up their shops and returned to vantage points around the harbor.

Out to sea, a faint smudge appeared on the horizon. This time Admiral Togo had sent Rear-Admiral Dewa Shigeto with four cruisers to reconnoiter after the night torpedo attack. Eighteen miles off the entrance to Port Arthur he came across the shipload of Japanese refugees from Dalny under the care of Midzuno Kokichi, the Japanese consul from Cheefoo, who had visited Port Arthur with his "valet" the previous day. As the cruisers passed the English steamer *Foochow,* the Japanese civilians rushed to the ship's rails, waving their hands and handkerchiefs to cheer the fleet to victory. *"Banzai, Nippon, banzai!"* from hundreds of loyal subjects reached Dewa and his sailors across the early morning mists. It was an encouraging start.

Outside Port Arthur, Admiral Dewa counted about twelve Russian ships, "all mixed together in no sort of order." They were huddled under the protection of the forts, in obedience to Viceroy Alexeiev's orders. Admiral Dewa could see that two, at least, appeared to be damaged. No shots were fired at him, and he immediately signaled Admiral Togo that in his opinion the Russian Fleet looked depressed in spirit. "I consider it would be extremely advantageous for the First and Second divisions to come quickly and bombard the enemy outside port." Now was the time to follow up the night's work. Since the Russians appeared disorganized and unprepared, Togo decided that he would take the risk of exposing himself to the fire from the forts. "We are now on our way to attack the enemy's main force," he signaled the fleet. "Go to dinner."

Togo sat with his staff in *Mikasa* at 11:45 A.M. and was about to drink a final champagne toast when he received the report, "Enemy ships seen." Togo raised his glass in a toast to the Emperor and the fleet, and the naval flag was hoisted to the mainmast of the *Mikasa* with the signal: "Victory or defeat will be decided by this one act. Let every man do his utmost." An officer on *Mikasa* wrote later that he felt someone had suddenly pickled his soul in red pepper.

"The sky that day was perfectly clear; mist girdled the shore; the sea was smooth and quiet; and a slight breeze blew gently from the south," read the poetic official Japanese naval report. Half an hour later, the clear blue of the sky had turned black with smoke and the still waters of the harbor were disturbed by shell-fire.

[198]

Admiral Stark, who had been in consultation with the Viceroy, arrived just in time to board the flagship before the battle began. The first shell fell among the Russian torpedo boats at the entrance to the harbor. The next came hurtling and turning horizontally toward the town, so that its shape could be clearly seen, and buried itself in one of the terraced pathways of the New Town. A third shell fell on the Russo-Chinese Bank and another on the mills of the Yalu Timber Company in which the Tsar had a personal financial interest. "The Japanese shells must have eyes," said a Russian cynic. People from the town had congregated in little groups on Signal Hill and the terraced roadway outside the mayor's house to get a better view of proceedings, and in the nearby church a young officer and a girl from the town were being married in the long-drawn-out ceremony of the Russian Orthodox Church. The wedding continued throughout the bombardment, but, as the shells began to fall in the streets, sightseers on the surrounding lookouts grabbed their children and ran in panic for the safety of the hills or their homes. Hundreds of Chinese coolies at work in the basin dropped their tools and fled in terror around the harbor, streaming across the ice toward the hills away from the town. Many were too frightened ever to return to their homes, and long afterwards their frozen bodies were found near the Tiger's Tail and White Wolf Hills.

Correspondent William Greener of *The Times* who reported that he was personally elated by the bombardment—"I grew bigger and bigger, and walked on air"—said that among the foreigners the English alone behaved calmly. "The Americans were less phlegmatic; some were just bundles of nerves, others as ready to go off as a handful of fireworks." People dashed for shelter in cellars and ditches. One man ran blindly into the distance and turned up, hatless and breathless, many hours later, at a sentry box miles from the waterfront.

The Japanese ships came in three divisions. Togo led with the flagship *Mikasa,* five other battleships, *Asahi, Fuji, Yashima, Shikishima,* and *Hatsuse,* and a torpedo gunboat, *Tatsuta.* The Second Division of five armored cruisers, under Vice-Admiral Kamimura, came next, followed by Admiral Dewa's Third Division of four protected cruisers, *Chitose, Kasagi, Takasago,* and *Yoshino.*

As each Japanese ship, steaming in single line, got within range of the Russian ships, she opened fire, the battleships first, then the cruisers. The Russian ships, still within the shelter of the forts, but moving to avoid becoming stationary targets, answered the fire. *Mikasa* opened up with her twelve-inch guns just after mid-day at a range of 8,000 meters and a few minutes later, under heavy attack, was hit by several shells. One cut through the ropes of the mainmast and the battle flag and part of the bridge fell into the sea. Another flag was run up, but it, too, was shot through. Thick black smoke rose over the Japanese fleet and there were so many shells it was impossible to count them. The battleships *Fuji* and *Hatsuse* were both hit by shells from the Russian ships and the shore batteries.

Only *Novik* of all the Russian ships dashed out to intercept. An eight-inch shell from the cruiser *Yagumo* burst amidships, but, before retreating, the small Russian unprotected cruiser sent a torpedo among the Japanese ships.

From the forts ringing the hills around the town the Russian batteries leaped into action, revealing at the same time the inadequacies of the defenses. The guns lacked range and ammunition. Some continued to fire blanks. Others, unable even to contribute to the noise, maintained a dignified silence. Some scored very well, however, and few of Togo's ships escaped damage.

Novik retired but she attempted what the rest of the Russian fleet did not dare. Steer spoke for all Russians at Port Arthur of a lost opportunity.

> The entire Japanese fleet steamed past us in one well-kept line ahead, the cruisers bringing up the rear, always following in the wake of their battleships, then very quietly steamed away, complete in numbers, after they had traversed the arc of fire of our guns ashore and afloat. Any sea officer with the slightest notion of what war meant, or simply possessing some energy, would not have hesitated to fall upon this tail of the line, so as to cut it off from the main body, which would then have been obliged to turn back. Everyone was expecting this maneuver when the signal came in, "Destroyers to attack the enemy." This was sheer folly, seeing that it was absolutely impossible for the small flotilla we possessed to get unharmed within torpedo range in broad daylight. This signal which was negatived after some moments of hesitation, before even our destroyers could get under way, had only served to furnish the proof that our leaders had on that day lost all judgment. To the present day I remain convinced that if instead of obstinately sticking to a passive defense we had shown the slightest spurt of enterprise, things might in the end have perfectly well turned out to our advantage.

After Togo's First Division had made its run, he withdrew it from the line and the cruisers took their turn, firing only for five or six minutes before they also retired. The Third Division now steamed past the front of Port Arthur, but the fire from the shore batteries had become intense, shells falling like rain around Dewa's ships. Reluctantly, Admiral Dewa obeyed Togo's orders to withdraw. At 12:45 P.M. all the Japanese ships had hauled down their battle flags, after just one run which had taken about an hour, leaving the Russian ships going slowly around in circles like a disturbed hornets' nest.

Admiral Kamimura, whose Second Division had suffered little damage, suggested another attack early the next morning, but Togo, not anxious to push his luck, replied that he did not believe the Russians would still be outside the harbor. He ordered the fleet to meet him at Asan Bay, south of Chemulpo, where they would consider further action.

The Japanese suffered 132 men killed and wounded, and the Russians 150 in the two attacks. *Novik, Askold, Diana,* and *Bayan* were damaged, but all eventually returned to the fleet, along with the three ships hit in the torpedo attack. Admiral Togo reported that "the fighting strength of the squadron is absolutely unimpared," but considerable damage had, in fact, been caused to *Mikasa, Shikishima, Fuji, Iwate,* and *Hatsuse,* among others.

About thirty twelve-inch shells had fallen in the town, and a heavy cloud of black smoke lay over the streets. A large crowd swept up Pushkin Hill, in the direction of the racecourse. There were broken glass windows all along the waterfront. Walls were down, and merchandise from shops littered the streets. The wedding ceremony continued long after the bombardment had ended, and the bridegroom left Port Arthur that night to join his regiment on the Yalu. On the Bund one shell had made a hole "large enough to hold an omnibus and team," said Greener. By late afternoon stretcher-bearers began to carry wounded civilians, mostly cut by flying glass, to the hospital. The railway station at Quail Hill was crowded, and the trains departed so laden with refugees that some passengers had to travel in the luggage racks. Soon the crowds disappeared in the streets, which by late afternoon were quiet and deserted.

Gallant *Novik,* which had braved the enemy, came into harbor under her own steam, in the early afternoon, with a hole on her waterline. When she had left Germany, where she was built, the captain and officers of the ship, at their own expense, had started a band. During the attack even the bandmaster, a civilian, had dropped his baton to man a gun. Now, as *Novik* came in with her band playing the national anthem, soldiers on the shore batteries and sailors in other ships cheered lustily.

Tsarevitch, the biggest ship in the Russian Far Eastern squadron, which had been pulled out of the shallows by tugs, came in about the same time. Her masts and funnels tilted about fifteen degrees, listing heavily, she looked a broken hulk. But her band was playing, as it had on the previous evening, and again the Russian national anthem wafted over the waters of Port Arthur. "That stirring hymn was sung many times afterwards inside the walls of Port Arthur and on the decks of the ships imprisoned in the harbor," wrote Brindle, the *Daily Mail* correspondent, "but never again with such fervor as on that day."

After the shock of the two surprise attacks had worn off, the residents of Port Arthur realized how close they could have been to complete disaster. "If, simultaneously with the attack on the Fleet, the Japanese had landed ten thousand men on the peninsula, there is little doubt that they could have taken the whole place by surprise," wrote one correspondent. Some of Togo's own men regarded his action as unnecessarily timid. "What could have stopped him?" a destroyer captain asked.

No Russian ship could have offered serious resistance. They would all have been taken by surprise, unprepared for the conflict, and inca-pable of maneuvering. Naturally, we should not have taken Port Ar-thur, for we were not carrying men whom we could have landed, and we could not use the crews of the ships. But it is probable that we should have been able to destroy the battleships and cruisers which were in the roadstead. What a glorious victory! . . . It is to be hoped that the inactivity of the Admiral that night will not be repeated. All naval history goes to prove, and the English in some measure also teach us, that only an attack delivered with energy and determination can be successful. I do not think that Nelson with his squadron would have remained inactive before Port Arthur as Togo did.

Togo had left everything to his destroyers in the night attack, not daring to risk his battleships without first assessing the Russian strength. The two attacks on the fortress, according to Captain Pakenham, were simply scout-ing expeditions. Nevertheless, Togo had wasted precious hours early in the morning of February 9 and by the time he arrived at Port Arthur, the Russians had recovered from the worst of their confusion and were able to hit back. If his nighttime attack seemed timid, wrote Pakenham, "this was the reason, it was incomprehensible that he would find everything in such a state of unpreparedness."

In the harbor basin at Port Arthur the Russian ships were closely packed together when Russian reinforcements for the navy arrived by train from the Baltic the following morning. Among them was a young officer, Vladi-mir Semenov, who had hoped to arrive in time for the opening of the war. As the train got closer to Port Arthur, the troops heard of the surprise attacks on the ships and cursed that they had not been there. "Oh, gentle-men," sobbed a civilian who had fled the town, "I saw where they had been. . . . just below the lighthouse—the Russian squadron, and there is not a single dock. How is such a thing possible? Now, of course, they will build docks, money being no object, but it is too late for our squadron." The voice of a young officer came to them from along the carriage: "We shall know how to die." An old captain sitting at the same table replied sadly, "That is our specialty, but it is a pity to do it without any object."

The picture that Japan now sought to present to the world was that of a gallant little nation forced into war. It succeeded very well. Tokyo excelled in psychological warfare and secrecy. A murderer in Tokyo, awaiting execution, gave his life savings to the war funds. Empress Haruko prepared bandages which, it was said, had miraculous healing powers. They were first used by the officers, then disinfected and used by the ordinary soldiers. The Empress also helped to make special handkerchiefs, embroidered with crisscross stitches, which the soldiers and sailors took with them into battle. These mementos from the Empress became a sacred link with home, and sailors and soldiers took great care that they were not lost.

Not until victories were assured were the Japanese people encouraged to communicate with the troops at the front. Victories made headlines. Defeats, whenever possible, were ignored. Togo's wife did not know where he was until she read his name in the papers after the bombardment of Port Arthur.

The premature attack on Port Arthur, so similar to the one to be unleashed on Pearl Harbor thirty-seven years later, caused no qualms of conscience in Tokyo. Negotiations had already broken down, diplomatic relations had ended—and, anyway, that first shot at Chemulpo, it was widely asserted, had been fired by a Russian ship. Japan held herself blameless. Her troops had already marched on Seoul and forced the Korean Emperor to agree to the landing of Japanese troops. Precedents for war without declaration filled the Japanese newspapers, including ten cases involving Russia when it had gone to battle before announcing its intentions. "Regarding the alleged sudden attack upon two Russian men-of-war in the port of Chemulpo," announced the Japanese government, "it is only necessary to say that a state of war then existed, and that, Korea having consented to the landing of Japanese troops at Chemulpo, that harbor had already ceased to be a neutral port, at least as between the belligerents." The landing was, in fact, illegal. It was not until February 25 that the Koreans, under duress, signed a pact allowing Japanese occupation and the right to use Korea as the road to Manchuria.

Both of the surprise attacks were widely praised in other parts of the world. The Russians, it was said, had been tricked by a backward little country fighting for its life. One or two countries thought that it was not "cricket" to go to war without a formal declaration. Cricket-loving England, whose team was playing a match in Melbourne against Australians, did not agree. *The Times* reported cheerfully on both the cricket match in Australia and their ally's battle against Russia: "There was a sensational finish here today [in Melbourne], the Englishmen getting out Victoria for

15, the smallest score on record in a first-class match in Australia, and winning by eight wickets."

For *The Times* the war news was even better: "Our ally put her navy in motion with a promptness and courage that exorted the admiration of the world and her action in doing so before war had been formally declared, so far from being an international solecism, is in accordance with the prevailing practice of most wars in modern times." *The Times*'s military correspondent congratulated the Japanese for their act of daring, "destined to take a place of honor in naval annals." The Russian squadron, he said, was inviting attack by standing in the outer roadstead. "This invitation had been accepted with a promptness and a punctuality that do high honor to the navy of our gallant allies and establish the Japanese at a single stroke upon a footing of equality with the best navy afloat, which might have equalled but would not have surpassed this dashing and courageous exploit."

The New York Times protested weakly that Japan had been in too much of a hurry. The U.S. State Department disclosed that the Japanese government, when it informed the American minister in Tokyo on February 6 that it was about to break off diplomatic relations with Russia, had assured him that hostilities would not begin until after a formal declaration had been made.

American reaction to the war, and the Japanese means of starting it, had been the cause of serious concern to those participating in the conference before the Throne on February 4. On the evening of February 4 Viscount Kaneko Kentaro, a member of the House of Peers, a privy councilor, and a classmate of President Theodore Roosevelt, received a phone call from Marquis Ito Hirobumi, the senior elder statesman, asking him to see him immediately.

Ito's plan was to send Kaneko to the United States to do what he could to enlist American sympathy. "I am asking you," he said, "because we have no one better for the task."

Kaneko was far from enthusiastic. He recalled Russian help to the northern forces in the Civil War and that a Russian fleet had come to New York harbor to forestall the entry of hostile British naval forces, that wealthy Americans were related to Russian aristocrats, and that business circles in New York, Philadelphia, and Chicago had close relations with Russia, which they regarded as an important customer. "No matter how eloquently I may speak in America," he said, "I could not possibly draw it away from Russia."

Fearful of failure and praying that American mediation would aid them if the war went badly, the Japanese leaders attached such importance to Kaneko's mission that the Empress herself called at his home to wish him well on his journey. Officials from the imperial household ministry descended on the Kaneko residence, bringing with them a chair and a desk to serve as a throne. "We ask Kaneko to do all he can for our country," said the Empress.

"I will fulfil my task for the country at the risk of my own life," he replied.

He sailed for America on February 24, feeling, as he said, that he was going to a "Land of Darkness." His target was the man in the White House. The Kishinev massacre had already shocked Roosevelt, who was in a receptive mood when Kaneko arrived and addressed a letter to him, reminding him of their previous acquaintance. Roosevelt read widely about Japan. He became fascinated by *bushido** and *jujitsu*, and both Kaneko and Takahira Togoro, the Japanese minister in Washington, were only too happy to provide him with an instructor.

Privately, Roosevelt insisted that, though he admired the Russian people, he loathed the Russian government. In the early stages of the war, he showed more and more admiration for Japan. "I have done all that I could, consistent with international law, to advance her interests," he said. "I thoroughly admire and believe in the Japanese." As Japan's successes on land and sea grew, he became more cautious. Some Americans predicted that Japan might become puffed up with pride, "which will lead her to think that she can conquer the world." Roosevelt became worried, also, that Japan might turn her eyes toward the Philippines, and he was determined to keep the army and navy ready. But, while the war lasted, his sympathies were all with the Japanese.

"No human beings, black, yellow, or white could be quite as untruthful, as insincere, as arrogant—in short, as untrustworthy in every way—as the Russians under the present system," he was to write in early 1905. Misquoting Kipling, he referred to "the bear who only walks like a man." The analogy came from his considerable experience with bear-hunting (he sometimes shot two in a day). The Russians were not ignorant about Roosevelt's attitude, and a rumor, attributed to Lamsdorf, spread in St. Petersburg—and naturally reached Roosevelt's ears—that his family name was Rosenfeld—Jews from South Germany.†

---

* *Bushido* is a comparatively modern term. "The way of the samurai," or "the way of the warrior," merely characterized traditional ideals of conduct that controlled all Japanese society. It included justice, courage, sincerity, loyalty, and obligation not only to the emperor, but to parents, country, ancestors, and family. Death in battle was not sought. The warrior knew when to die, and if dishonorable capture or defeat occurred he resorted to the sword, the soul of the samurai. In this war *bushido* became the privilege not only of officers but of the ordinary conscript.

†The Nazis used the same story to vilify President Franklin D. Roosevelt.

With the ground so well prepared at the top, Kaneko found the American climate of opinion much more favorable than he had expected. In his lectures and articles, he worked shrewdly on the assumption that influential Americans were interested in business opportunities, and he warned that they would fail if they disregarded "the importance of Japan in Chinese affairs."

In London, Alfred Stead worked equally well in the Japanese cause. Long an admirer, he felt that most books on Japan were superficial and frivolous, whereas he believed that in a few years it would be one of the great nations of the world. Early in the war he edited a book titled *Japan by the Japanese,* a collection of articles written by leading Japanese—teachers, bankers, merchants, soldiers, statesmen, and lawyers. It was received as a book of immense value—essential reading for anyone who wanted to learn about the real Japan, "which cast off the shackles of feudalism thirty-seven years ago, and has never once looked back," as the *Morning Post* put it.

Japan was on the way to becoming the great nation envisaged by Stead. She had proved to skeptics at home and abroad that her action against Russia had been worthwhile. The people had been worked up to a pitch of fevered excitement. Now that the first successes were announced, the country went wild with joy. A popular poet, Ishikawa Takuboku, who had long urged war with Russia and her "devil's army" in the Far East, composed a song for the people who wished to sing but had no song. "I don't know why, but my blood boils and my eyes burn," he wrote. "What joy! What joy!"

On February 10, 1904, nearly two days after the first attack on Port Arthur, Japan officially declared war. The Emperor's five-hundred-word message called on the army and navy to defeat the enemy and stressed Japan's wish for a quick peace: "It is entirely against our expectations that we have unhappily come to open hostilities against Russia." He sent a message of congratulations to Togo, but the celebrations in the streets were for Admiral Uryu, who had sunk the Russian ships at Chemulpo. "The whole silent city opened its doors and awoke," wrote *Collier's* correspondent. "The populace rushed hither and thither shouting, '*Banzai Dai Nippon, Banzai!*' (Long Live Great Japan!)."

Russia waited eight days before declaring war. The Tsar had received a telegram from Admiral Alexeiev, informing him of the first Japanese attack as he was returning with the Tsaritsa from a theater in St. Petersburg. A little later a second message came in from the Viceroy, reporting the daylight bombardment. "Our fleet is going out to meet them supported by fire from the fortress," it concluded. That night, Nicholas wrote in his diary the first entry of the war: "This without a declaration of war. May God come to our aid."

God went into battle with the Russian soldiers and sailors, and successes were attributed to holy ikons accompanying the long-haired priests on board ships of the navy and in the troop-carriers. The army made way for the church. "Its shrines and banners were planted on the positions. Its holy emblems were carried to the firing line. The line opened to receive them," reported Associated Press correspondent Frederick McCormick.

> The sacred relics of the mother churches of Moscow and other ancient cities in Russia were assembled to carry God into the battlefield and to carry His vengeance to the enemy. The militant priesthood mounted horses and escorted the Cossacks to their raids. . . . In every camp were its altars. On every grave its emblems. At dawn could be heard the morning Mass . . . at dusk the evening hymn, which, heard from every direction of the battleground, was like a chorus from some great invisible choir.

The Tsar's aunt, Grand Duchess Elizabeth Fedorovna, sent off elaborately decorated "churches on wheels" across the Trans-Siberian Railway to Manchuria. Prayers were said morning and evening as the trains carried fresh troops to the front, the soldiers singing and the priests giving the benediction. Portable altars were carried into the battle lines, and hymns of praise drifted across the sea from sinking ships. As the war dragged on, Nicholas and Alexandra handed out to departing soldiers tin images of the newly created St. Seraphim of Serov, a hermit monk and healer of the eighteenth century. "They attack us with artillery and we pay them back with 'Te Deums'; they blow us up with mines and we defend ourselves with holy images," cried General Mikhail Ivanovitch Dragomirov, Russia's leading strategist, whose books on military matters had even been translated into Japanese. At seventy-four he was too old for active service, though the suggestion was considered, but he continued to denounce the conduct of the war.

Alexandra had made the pilgrimage to Serov Abbey, in Tambov province, to pray for a son after the birth of her four daughters and had great faith that her prayers would be answered. Seraphim had only just been canonized by the Holy Synod, and the unfamiliar features of a new saint did not inspire the troops. They would have preferred reliable old St. Nicholas, who had supported the Russian empire through many centuries.

After a service to pray for victory in the chapel of the Winter Palace, Nicholas appeared at a window of the great White Hall to acknowledge the thousands of cheering, banner-waving people who had gathered below to sing hymns. For one brief moment it seemed that the people were united.

A newspaper started a subscription list to replace the sunken Russian vessels with wooden ships. Members of the nobility donated substantially, and the Tsar announced that he would rebuild *Varyag* and *Koreetz* at his own expense. He considered the war losses as his own private business, and, as things became worse, he smiled his gentle smile and behaved as though nothing of importance had happened. Nicholas, well aware now of what he had let his country into, merely preferred to keep his grief to himself.

When the survivors of the *Varyag* and *Koreetz* returned to Russia, they were treated like conquering heroes. The streets of Odessa, St. Petersburg, Sebastopol, and Moscow were decorated with banners and triumphal arches, and salvo after salvo of guns greeted their arrival in each city. Each man received a gift of silver from the Tsar and money. Jewels and clothing were showered on them by members of the public. Wherever they appeared, crowds followed them, breaking through the police lines to kiss them or to touch the hands of the sailors who had fought bravely against great odds.

Nicholas granted the officers and men of the sunken ships an audience at the Winter Palace and personally presented each man with one of the four classes of the Order of St. George. But he appeared unconcerned at the course the war was taking. This brought him more enemies, while alone with his diary at night, he poured out his heart—putting down within its covers all that he was afraid to show to his people. He wrote of his sorrow at the death of Russian soldiers and sailors, his private fears and the horror of the poor opinion people would have of his country.

He desperately needed someone to confide in, as he could to his diary. He had thought that the Japanese would not fight, that there would be no war unless he declared it, and now he was afraid of the consequences. His sister, Grand Duchess Olga Alexandrovina, who died in 1960, was convinced that Nicholas did not want war and that he had been pushed into it by generals and politicians who were sure of quick victory. She saw her brother as a kind and generous husband, father and brother. "I never saw him trying to push himself forward, or getting angry when he lost at some game or other. And, there was always his faith in God," she said. She was writing many years after the Russo-Japanese War of a brother whom she had loved and admired when she was a young girl, but even Serge Witte, who had been dismissed by Nicholas from the office of minister of finance for what the Tsar called "tiresome interference," had once said of Nicholas that "he carried in himself the seeds of the best that the human mind and heart possesses." (In his *Memoirs*, Witte later contradicted this sympathetic statement as he blamed Nicholas for the war with Japan—"if, indeed, it is possible to condemn a man who is responsible for his deeds to none but God.")

When Russia at last issued its declaration of war, it called the attack on
Port Arthur

a violation of all customary laws governing the mutual declarations of
civilized nations. Without previously notifying us that the rupture
. . . implied the beginning of warlike action, the Japanese government
ordered its torpedo boats to make a sudden attack on our squadron in
the outer roadstead of the fortress of Port Arthur. After receiving the
report of our Viceroy on the subject, we at once commanded Japan's
challenge to be replied to by arms.

A week later Viceroy Alexeiev issued a much stronger proclamation to
the people of Manchuria. "Let the military, merchants, gentry, and people
of the three provinces of Manchuria all tremble and obey. . . . I, the Viceroy,
fully expect that you the people will sympathize with the Russian troops.
Should the Chinese officials and people regard with hatred the Russian
forces, the Russian Government will certainly exterminate such people
without the slightest mercy and will not fail to take suitable measures for
the protection of her national interests."

He continued to live in Port Arthur in the vice-regal palace from the
windows of which he could look down on the narrows of the harbor, still
waiting to be dredged, and the stranded and broken ships of the fleet.
General Stoessel stayed on as commander of the fortress, awaiting the
arrival of Lieutenant-General Constantine Nikolaevitch Smirnov, one of
Russia's best tacticians, who was on his way from Warsaw to replace him.
Stoessel would then be free to work as military governor of all the Kwantung Peninsula and to deal with the tactical situation there.

Though the Russian ships were eventually repaired, the country's naval
strength had been drained. Japan had command of the sea. A message from
the Emperor, probably drawn up by the Grand Council of War after receiving Admiral Togo's report, declared: "We have heard that the Combined
Fleet has completely carried out the duty of landing the troops in Korea;
has swept the west coast clear; has attacked the enemy's ships at Port
Arthur and destroyed several of them, thereby vindicating Our prestige. We
are greatly pleased. Officers and men—fight with increasing vigor."

The message from the Empress and the Crown Prince mentioned only
the damage to the enemy ships and the glorious victories at Port Arthur
and Chemulpo. The Emperor's thanks were first for the landing of the
troops which had been made possible by the naval actions. Togo's role was
to protect the overseas lines of communication, to hold the Russian fleet in
check, and, if it accepted battle, to destroy it.

CHAPTER *11*

᪥᪥᪥᪥᪥᪥

Practical Joke

Nobody there had expected the events of February 9, but now that it was over, an attempt was made to prepare Port Arthur for war. The forts were strengthened and an inner wall was built to encircle the Old Town. Working parties cleaned up the wreckage in and around the harbor and ships, and men labored day and night to tow *Retvizan* from her mud bank at the entrance.

Fresh from Russia, Vladimir Semenov, who had arrived to become second-in-command of the destroyer *Boyarin*, felt the excitement in the air as tugs and steamers crossed busily over the harbor, blowing their sirens and carrying stores to the warships. Huge cranes lifted crates and machinery high over the waters of the harbor, and the air was filled with cries of men struggling under heavy loads. Bands played, and the sound of hammering was everywhere. Despite the turmoil, things were moving. Semenov was glad to be at the war and eager to take part in it.

He walked through the town, jumping frozen puddles in the rough roads. Ahead loomed Golden Hill, on the high cliffs rising from the sea. The blue, white and red Russian flag flew over the batteries and ramparts and the four square ribs of the wireless station. *Novik* was in the dry dock and behind the gray roofs of the workshops *Retvizan*'s masts and funnels were silhouetted against the Tiger's Tail peninsula where she had grounded. The Tiger's Tail forts bristled with big guns, searchlights, and strong concrete facings.

Most of the twenty coastal forts had heavy guns, but the outer fortifications, which ran in a semi-circle from east to west for twenty miles, were armed only with small cannon and machineguns. Six permanent fortifications to the north of the town were still not completed. Fortunately for the

Russians, there were still some old Chinese forts directly above the town that, with some improvement, could be used as provisional defenses. The most prominent feature of the eastern defenses was a covered way that had been built earlier by the Chinese. It was still called the Chinese Wall, but the Russians now were beginning to strengthen it. The mud and brick wall, ten feet high, ran through the grim, gray hillsides and was well sheltered against direct fire. Similar covered roads joined up with other battery positions, and behind them a good roadway linked the town and the forts so that heavy guns and provisions could be carried to the forts.

The town itself was in utter confusion after the attacks. Food prices soared as traders tried to make quick profits before leaving. At the Russo-Chinese Bank, where a shell had landed, the clerks disappeared with large sums of money. Droshky drivers put up their prices, and many people trying to get out of town had to walk to the railway station, carrying their possessions through deep snowdrifts.

The trains were still operating to Dalny and Harbin, though most were requisitioned for military use. The Chinese, forbidden to travel by train, converged in thousands on the foreign ships remaining in the harbor. Sampan owners made fortunes ferrying passengers from shore to the ships, which were all British-owned and desperately seeking permission to leave, with or without passengers. No one in authority seemed to know how to handle the situation. Britain and Japan, after all, were allies.

One ship, the *Colombia*, escaped during the daylight attack and disappeared in a cloud of smoke with her passengers. Neither the Japanese nor the Russians saw her leave, and she sailed off unchallenged to safety. Several of the remaining ships were fired on by Russian guard vessels when they tried to leave. Another, the *Pleiades*, was allowed to sail, taking with her thousands of sacks of flour, sold to a trader who had already fled.

With the departure of the panic-stricken Chinese servants and laborers went any efficiency that had existed in Port Arthur. Though the streets were piled with coal, there was now no one to carry it to houses, hotels or the public bathhouse. Laundries closed down, and sanitary arrangements collapsed. "Never in so short a time did the social organisation of a civilised community go so completely to pieces," wrote correspondent William Greener, the *Times* correspondent who had found himself a deserted Chinese house behind the Bund, within easy reach of a gravel quarry where he could find shelter if there were more bombardments.

Casualties during the two attacks were much higher than had first been thought, and twenty bodies at a time went off to the trenches for burial. Port Arthur tried to return to her old gaiety, but now after dark the streets were unlit. Many of the circus artists and entertainers had left town. Order 64 issued by Stoessel provided for music on the boulevards for two hours every afternoon, but it was a poor substitute for the music halls and restaurants.

The droshkies were put to military work. Often the drivers who collected the wounded were women. The time came when Baratovski's performing horses found themselves confiscated by the cavalry. The circus itself became a Red Cross hospital. Girls from the restaurants were conscripted as nurses. "Away were the dashing officers, away, alas, those with the soft eyes," wrote Ernest Brindle. "It was hard to recognise, in the demure, soberly dressed damsels with the Red Cross badges round their arms the bright butterflies of a year ago. The whole gay throng had disappeared."

Since the new fortress commander, General Smirnov, had not yet arrived, General Stoessel was still in charge of Port Arthur and its defenses. He had always wanted to fight, and his frustration at being cooped up in Port Arthur produced renewed punishments for drunkenness, suspected spying, and general disobedience. It soon became dangerous to appear on the streets for fear of arrest. There was little justice in Port Arthur, and to be arrested was to run the risk of being flogged.

Discontent and gossip proliferated, and General Stoessel reacted: "It has come to my knowledge that in the garrison club officers busy themselves over matters which do not concern them, criticize the course of the military operations, and repeat various stupid stories, picked from God knows where," he wrote in a special order. "An officer's duty is to think how best to carry out his orders, and not to judge the actions of his seniors. Those who cavil do much harm, and I, of course, will punish them to the utmost of my power."

Before the war was a week old the Russians had suffered further losses. On February 11 two destroyers were damaged in a collision. The same day a new mine-layer, *Yeneisei*, was sent to drop mines near Dalny. Her commander, who had designed the mine-layer, had already laid 400 submerged mines when he received a report that one had come to the surface. A strong gale had risen and he was not able to re-moor the mine in the heavy seas and blinding snow. Unwilling to leave the mine exposed to the Japanese, he decided to explode it by gunfire. Before he had time to do so, the *Yeneisei* struck another mine. Boats were lowered to rescue the crew, but the commander, seriously wounded in the head and body, refused to leave his ship. *Yeneisei* sank in twenty minutes, taking with her the captain, four other officers, and eighty-nine men.

Back at Port Arthur, it was thought that the mine-layer might have been destroyed by Japanese ships, and the cruiser *Boyarin* was sent out to look for her. Not knowing the exact location of the mines, *Boyarin* kept well out to sea and was about to anchor when she also struck a mine. Boats were quickly lowered, and the ship abandoned.

On the same day, four Russian cruisers from the Vladivostok squadron came out of harbor with the help of ice-breakers and sank two unarmed Japanese merchantmen, carrying a few passengers and a cargo of flour and rice in the Tsugaru Straits. For this sort of news the Japanese press broke its silence. This time Japan and the world learned of the "unfair" tactics of the enemy. It was called "an attack of fiendish savagery and depravity, enough to make even the most cold-blooded person grind his teeth. . . . an ineffaceable blot upon the history of the Russian navy."

Japanese newspapers said that Japan would never have behaved with such brutality to ships that had already hauled down their flags. "Regretfully," the Japanese government felt compelled to hand over to the prize court (set up to determine the distribution of spoils of war) two Russian merchantmen that had been held at Sasebo. The face Japan wanted to show to the world was one of firmness, mixed with the love of humanity, but in fact orders had already been issued to sink all naval vessels and transports wanting to surrender in order to avoid the trouble of capturing them.

The day following the attack on the Japanese ships, Japan showed how well it could behave to its enemy when the Russian minister to Korea, Paul Pavlov, and his wife left Seoul, which had been occupied by Japanese troops on February 9.

Pavlov had been in Korea for many years, departing only for vacations and on one unfortunate occasion when he and his family had gone to Japan for treatment after a painful and dangerous encounter with a mad dog. The dog scratched Pavlov and bit several members of his household. He was a popular and powerful figure in Seoul, where, with his beautiful young wife, he entertained lavishly in a house overlooking the city walls. "Nothing there was too great for him, and his friends already saw him the real ruler of the state, with the emperor a puppet in his hands," wrote Frederick McKenzie of the *Daily Mail*, who was at the railway station to see him off. As the Russians were evicted from Korea, McKenzie and the other correspondents commented on the impeccable behavior of the Japanese dignitaries who arrived in richly decorated sedan chairs, carried by Koreans in gay costumes. "The large Japanese colony did not come to proclaim over a fallen enemy," he wrote. "The Japanese stayed away. There was not a shout or sign of rejoicing. The soldiers and statesmen did their work as quietly and as inoffensively as possible. The Japanese minister, in plain morning clothes, stood, hat in hand, among the other ministers to bid good-bye. A well-known Japanese general was deputed to escort the Russian minister to the sea, and did not seem to enjoy his task." The Russians departed proudly, with kisses, handshakes and "au revoirs." "We will return," they said to the foreign friends who had come to wish them farewell, but as the train pulled out people on the platform could see tears in the eyes of the Russian minister's "girl-wife."

[213]

The behavior of the Japanese in the railway station at Seoul when Pavlov and his wife departed was world news, as was the courageous attempt a day or so later when the Japanese destroyer *Asagiri* appeared at the narrows of Port Arthur in a blinding snowstorm to attack the Russian ships. Two other destroyers accompanying her could not cope with the huge waves that broke over their decks. They returned to Asan Bay to join their flotilla, but *Asagiri* battled with the waves and kept on for Port Arthur at twelve knots. Just south of Old Iron Mountain she turned toward the fortress and saw three Russian destroyers steaming around on guard outside the harbor and two other ships close to shore. She fired a long-range torpedo at one of the ships hugging the shore, turned to leave, and met up with the guard ships. As she was firing on them, the shore batteries opened up. She ran back to the rendezvous, in imminent danger of capsizing in the high seas. Though she did not succeed in damaging any Russian ships, the story of her gallant single-handed attack made headlines in the Japanese press. The Emperor sent a message of congratulations to *Asagiri* and the two other Japanese destroyers, which had attempted to engage the enemy in such wild weather conditions, disregarding danger. If most of the American and British newspapers were not quite so fulsome as the Japanese press, the theme was usually the same: the Russians were cowardly and uncouth; the Japanese, full of valor and chivalry. In London, Bishop Montgomery, father of Field Marshal Viscount Montgomery of Alamein, wrote with satisfaction that the Japanese government had given instructions that all interpreters to English and foreign correspondents with their armies must be Christians. It was a sign, he said, that the Japanese government desired to procure the most trustworthy men for the foreign visitors.

The first weeks of war brought hardship and loss to the people of Port Arthur. What they needed was just one piece of good news, one victory.

Just before dawn on February 24 the crew of the stranded *Retvizan* and soldiers on the surrounding forts saw a fleet of ships approaching the harbor entrance. So calmly were they heading for the harbor that some people thought they were long-awaited supply ships. Since the ships were steaming in single line abreast straight for the entrance to the inner harbor, however, *Retvizan* became suspicious. Although she was still stuck on the rocks, she was able to use some of her big guns. As the boats approached, she opened fire and was immediately joined by the forts.

In the wardroom on *Angara* to which Semenov had been transferred after the loss of *Boyarin*, there was much debate. Some thought that *Retvizan* was firing at Russian supply ships.

Perhaps, someone said, they were Russian ships being chased by Japanese torpedo boats—that was the reason for their dogged behavior. The night was frosty and the sea smooth. In the intervals of firing there was an oppressive silence. Voices rolled out across the sea from *Retvizan:* "Quick, quick, the turret, quick, quick." In *Angara*, they heard the high penetrating voice and from the fort on Tiger's Tail hill, another voice in reply: "Are you asleep at No. 3? Don't take your eye off the sights, you peasant from Irkutsk." The officers on *Angara's* bridge tittered. One man remarked, "Probably a Siberian—they are all like that."

In fact, no one knew what was going on. In the glare of her guns *Retvizan* looked like a volcano. Perhaps the Japanese were trying to land in open attack? Across the sea came the bugle sounding for action. It was repeated on board all the ships.

The battle lasted for over an hour. Searchlights from Tiger's Tail and Golden Hill lit up the approaching ships and terrific fire came from the shore batteries on all sides. Flames and smoke rose beyond the lighthouse on Old Iron Mountain. It seemed that the coastline was on fire. One of the ships making for the harbor came straight at the grounded *Retvizan* and the big Russian battleship caught it in her searchlights and fired all the guns on her seaward side. The joy of the Russians on ships and along the cliffs of the fortress was unbounded.

When daylight came, the five strange-looking Japanese ships were piled up on rocks, blown to pieces or sunk with their funnels sticking out of the sea. Fires were still burning on some of the wrecked ships. Alexeiev cabled the good news, with special mention made of the brave action of the injured *Retvizan*.

It was a short-lived victory. The five destroyed Japanese ships in the harbor were old merchantmen. Loaded with coal dust and stones and fitted with explosives, they had been sent to block the mouth of Port Arthur's harbor—an idea suggested at the end of 1903 to Imperial General Headquarters by Lieutenant-Commander Arima Ryokitsu.

Ten days after the first attack Togo reluctantly decided that it was time to gather volunteers for the strategic task. A *kesshitai*, or band of men prepared to die for the country, was selected. Two thousand men volunteered, some sending in applications written in their own blood. "It is a pity that, in carrying out this plan, capable officers and men must be sent to certain death, but that there are those who have volunteered to carry this out is a fact worthy of admiration," Togo wrote. The sailors, preparing to die, called it a "practical joke."

Like the samurai of old the crews of the blockships were prepared to give their lives for the Emperor, but *bushido* ("the way of the warrior") did not insist on death without reason. "To rush into the thick of battle and to be slain in it is easy enough," the warrior code taught. "It is true courage to live when it is right to live, and to die only when it is right to die."

Seventy-seven men were chosen from the long list of volunteers, and ceremonies were held aboard ship to bid them farewell. On the battleship *Asama*, Captain Yashiro spoke to the volunteers and warned them that they had one chance in thousands of returning alive. "I feel as if I were sending my beloved sons," he said. "But if I had one hundred sons, I would send them all on such a bold adventure as this, and had I only one son I should wish to do the same with him." From a silver cup presented to him by the Crown Prince before he left Japan, the captain, in *bushido* fashion, drank their health in water as part of the farewell ceremony. Russian reports later insisted that the drinks passed around to the volunteers were not water but saké, and that the courageous Japanese went into battle dead drunk.

Still, the story that went out to the waiting Japanese public, and to the world, was one of courage and selflessness. The sailors, whether primed with water or with rice wine, had the words of their commander in their ears as they took their blocking ships toward Port Arthur harbor. "In performing your duty," Captain Yashiro ordered, "if you happen to lose both hands, work with both feet; if you lose both feet, work with your head, and faithfully carry out the orders of your commanders."

Escorted by destroyers and torpedo boats, the five old ships approached the harbor. The night was calm and fine, and they crept steadily on without lights. Suddenly, the Russian searchlights found them. One by one they were picked out by fire from ships and the surrounding forts. Two of the ships were blown up before they got to the harbor entrance, and another sank when her captain opened the seacocks. Crews of the three ships were taken aboard the accompanying destroyers. The success of the blocking expedition now rested on two ships, *Jinsen Maru* ("Inchon") and *Hokoku Maru* ("Patriotism"). A shell from the *Retvizan* wrecked *Hokoku Maru's* steering gear just as she was running in to ram the Russian battleship. She was set on fire and went aground just outside the harbor entrance. Her captain, Lieutenant-Commander Hirose Takeo, tried to blow up the ship, but the wires had been cut by the Russian shells and no explosion took place. One man was killed, but the rest took to the boats. *Jinsen Maru* headed for the searchlight on Golden Hill, but just as she was making her run for the narrow entrance she struck a mine and blew up.

A Japanese officer aboard an escorting destroyer commented on the failed effort to block the harbor: "Everyone was in a bad temper. It is enough to drive one crazy! I feel like turning into a Christian from sheer rage."

Next day, when the smoke had cleared away, the jubilation of the Russians vanished. The Tsar was informed that it was not, after all, a glorious victory.

Novik was sent out to Pigeon Bay to ascertain the fate of the Japanese steamers and to pick up survivors, if possible. She found four of the old ships still on fire and the sea covered with the wreckage of broken lifeboats and empty lifebuoys. When the crew of *Novik* tried to take the few survivors away in their boats, many of the Japanese attempted to commit suicide. One officer jumped overboard and swam ashore where he stood on the rocks and fired his revolver at the Russians until his last bullet had gone. He then tried to strangle himself with his belt, but he and one or two others were overpowered and taken back to Port Arthur. "These were our first prisoners of war at Port Arthur," said an officer from *Novik*. "It must be confessed, alas, that we did not take many more."

The next morning a group of Japanese cruisers came in on a scouting expedition. The Russians had christened them "the greyhounds" and everyone knew when they appeared that the main Japanese fleet would not be far behind.

Togo stood a long way out to sea with his First and Second divisions and attacked the few Russian ships that could be seen and the fortress. For several hours there was a running fight between the six Japanese battleships and six cruisers and *Novik, Askold,* and *Bayan.* The fire from the forts was fierce, however, and under this protection the Russian ships managed to return to port. All three were damaged and casualties came to twenty-two men killed and forty-one injured. Another twenty-one were killed and wounded on shore.

Two destroyers were sent to seek out the Japanese. On the following morning they were headed for home, close to the shore, when Admiral Dewa with his cruisers found them. The two Russian destroyers, *Bezstrashni* and *Vnushitelni,* fired at a range of 10,000 meters and started to run for home. *Bezstrashni* made a dash and reached the harbor, but the second Russian destroyer decided to make for Pigeon Bay. The Japanese admiral searched the seas for the Russian ship, skirting around Old Iron Mountain and looking in all the small bays. He was about to give up when a shot fell among his ships from the Russian destroyer. The Japanese cruisers steamed in the direction of the shot and found the ship close to the shore of a small bay. They poured fire into her as they advanced, "just as at target practice." The captain of *Vnushitelni* set fire to his ship and the crew took to the boats. *Yoshino* was ordered to finish off the Russian with her six-inch guns, and, as the Russian sailors tried to escape, three shells hit their ship and others landed close to the boats. "They were altogether overwhelmed with consternation," reported *Yoshino's* captain. He was anxious to smash her to pieces but there were mines in the area and shells from the forts were coming perilously close. *Yoshino* rejoined her consorts and reported to *Mikasa* that the Russian destroyer must have gone aground because she had not sunk. She had completely lost her fighting power. After the Japanese cruiser had left, *Vnushitelni's* captain sank his ship and with his crew walked back to Port Arthur, arriving there on the following day.

A "risk nothing" policy was soon instituted in Port Arthur, and ships remained within shelter of the shore batteries whenever they ventured out to sea. Many of them had given up their guns to the batteries on the slopes of Golden Hill and Lighthouse Hill, and, even if the Japanese had appeared, few ships would have been able to go out to meet them. Commander Semenov's ship *Angara*, which before the war had been the Viceroy's private yacht, was ordered to disarm. He and his men were anxious to get into a fighting ship. "The dear, keen youths," Semenov reflected. The spirit of the navy was still high. The heroism of the crews of *Varyag* and *Koreetz*, destroyed at Chemulpo, was made much of in Port Arthur. If higher headquarters regarded the loss of these ships and the damage to the Port Arthur squadron as a "flea bite," the fleet itself was eager to get even with the enemy. But for ten days after February 26 no Japanese ships appeared in front of the fortress. Nobody tried to find out what they were doing, and the squadron sank into despondency in the inner harbor.

In the town things went from bad to worse. Admiral Alexeiev, under instruction of the Tsar, was soon to leave for Harbin, which was the most convenient center for administering the scattered Russian interests in the Far East. In a dramatic telegram to a friend, General Stoessel, anxiously awaiting the arrival of General Smirnov to take his place, proclaimed, "Farewell forever, Port Arthur will be my tomb." He issued orders that confused the garrison and the public. He was sure that Chinese civilians were signaling from the hills to the Japanese and ordered everyone to catch the culprits. On February 26 his order read: "Although twenty men were caught yesterday in the act of making some kind of signals, about 3 A.M. this morning someone was seen signaling with a lantern between my house and the commissariat depot. It was impossible to catch him, as he ran off to the New Chinese Town. Pickets detailed for this work will in future fire on any men seen signaling, if they run."

"Chinese were shot like partridges," wrote one observer. Many left the town. Many took to looting, but this was not confined to the Chinese alone. Shops deserted by well-to-do Japanese were robbed as townspeople and soldiers "souvenired" what had been left behind.

The Chinese were treated atrociously by the military police. "I have seen men cruelly kicked because they could not lift heavy loads no man could carry," wrote Greener, an Englishman who stayed in Port Arthur for the entire siege. "I have seen them beaten and mauled for no other offence, that I could discover, than that they were Chinamen. I have seen ears torn, and queues lugged until the scalp was ripped—preliminary punishment by the street police when conveying unresisting coolies to prison, there to answer a charge."

Soldiers, shocked by the Japanese surprise attacks and disheartened and without confidence in their leaders, also came in for much ill-treatment. Floggings for drunkenness continued to take place daily.

General Stoessel's order of February 27 insisted that there could be no retreat from the fortress. Yet he drew freely on his supplies to support the garrisons elsewhere on the Kwantung Peninsula. Instead of being a fortress preparing itself for siege, Port Arthur resembled a general market, providing stores for the main army. Although Stoessel allowed only three restaurants to remain open and closed the gambling dens, men continued to drink and gamble and spend their money on perfume, fancy garters, and sweets for their girlfriends. "Never in my life have I witnessed such orgies as I saw that February in Arthur," correspondent Nojine reported.

The attitude toward the Japanese was casual. General Fock, commanding the Fourth Siberian Rifle Division, assured everyone that the Japanese were fools. Sitting astride his horse before his regiments, he explained carefully that they were fools because in their field regulations it was laid down that in an attack the firing line should extend at wide intervals. Then, "Front rank, tell me why the Japanese are fools," he ordered. The soldiers would all shout together, "Because, when attacking, their firing line extends widely." Drill sergeants kicked their men for making mistakes on the paradeground where they behaved like automatons: "Long live the Tsar, hooray! Long live the Tsar, hooray!" they cried. But there was no heart in either their parade drill or in their forced cheering for Nicholas, the Tsar who had sent them to this God-forsaken place.

In spite of Stoessel's orders, drunkenness continued. Order No. 62 was clear enough for anyone to understand. "This day I saw in the street two or three drunken men, and all of them our people. Notice is therefore given that from the nineteenth every drunken person found on the street will be arrested and taken to the lock up, and set to hard labor on the fortress. It is impossible for anything to be done now with drunkenness allowed."

Despite the chaos inside the fortress, Port Arthur's defenses were much stronger than the Japanese had expected or were prepared for. Their agents had been busy at Port Arthur, as elsewhere, but most of the secret military reports came from infantry officers who lacked the engineering skills needed to determine the strength of the new fortifications, which were, of course, restricted areas. Their view was that, apart from the addition of trenchworks for infantry, the fortifications had not been improved since the Sino-

Japanese War and that the Russians had no intention of building permanent defenses. The second section of the Japanese Imperial General Headquarters prepared its estimates with maps on a scale of 1 : 20,000, and these were completely inadequate, especially since the extensive Russian building program had changed the topography of the fortified positions.

The most useful piece of intelligence came from Lieutenant-General Nagaoka Gaishi, who was to replace Kodama as vice-chief of the general staff as soon as he left for Manchuria with Oyama. In 1902, Nagaoka passed through Port Arthur on his way back to Japan from Europe. He stayed with the head of the Mitsui branch office, who had tried to get inside the fortress but failed. Still, he had learned that the Russians had used 200,000 barrels of cement to build the new defenses. "If they've used as much as that, it really must be impregnable," Nagaoka said. "Even if it's not quite as impregnable as all that, the topography itself—with its precipitous hills and cliffs—would make a frontal attack difficult and protracted. It would be best to have a small number of troops in the front area, just enough to keep the enemy troops from coming out to attack, and have the main force shift westward for surprise attacks. In this area the defenses are probably not as strong as at the front."

Major Morita, a Japanese intelligence officer at Cheefoo, discovered that the tops of the hills at Port Arthur had been cut off. This, together with General Nagaoka's intelligence, should have sounded a note of warning, but it was not heeded when the plans for the assault on Port Arthur were drawn up. Major Morita was blamed for his lack of strategic thinking.

Major Tanaka Giichi, a member of the war party and one of those present at the meeting of the Kogetsu in May 1903, took charge of Port Arthur planning. Although he favored the creation of the Third Army for the specific task of attacking Port Arthur, he got little encouragement from his seniors, including Kodama, who were less worried about its impregnability than other tactical considerations. Kodama realized that numerical superiority, increasingly, would be with the Russian forces in Manchuria and he had little inclination to risk defeat in detail by dividing his own forces. Port Arthur could be left to wither on the vine, with its ships held in check by Togo and the fleet. Kodama thought that it would be enough to build bamboo fences behind Port Arthur and merely to keep a watch on the fortress. The green and yellow of the bamboo "wall" would act as camouflage. He even ordered his staff to estimate the quantities of bamboo and ropes required for such a purpose.

With faulty intelligence, indifference, and even disagreement at the highest level of Imperial General Headquarters, the Japanese engineers and ordnance sections were ill-prepared for their tasks. There were no plans to deal with moats, underground passages, or the use of high explosives, and the siege guns were inadequate.

Several types of guns had been inspected at the Krupp works in Germany as early as 1899, but for various reasons, including Japan's desire to make its own, few were bought. There were even disputes about the numbers of rounds for each gun that the attacking forces would need. The original plan called for each siege gun to be provided with eight hundred shells, but, apart from the fifteen-inch mortars, which were amply provided for, there were no stocks for the other guns. When the attack eventually began, some of the guns had been lost at sea and others were limited to one round a day.

This was a type of warfare for which the Japanese were untrained and with which they were unfamiliar. They had used siege guns as field artillery with outstanding success in the Sino-Japanese War and thought that these tactics would be adequate now. The fifth section of the Imperial General Headquarters had drawn up a manual for fortress operations based on the German manual, but the army ministry was not interested enough even to bother printing it. It thought that Port Arthur would fall the moment the land assault began, and even arranged for Shimoda Jisaku, a lawyer, to be on hand to prepare for the Russian surrender before a shot had been fired on the ground.

With his eyes riveted on Liaoyang and the planned envelopment of the Russian armies there—a tactic borrowed straight from his German military experience—Kodama had a blind spot where Port Arthur was concerned. Intelligence inside Port Arthur admittedly had been faulty, and the fortress had been a pushover in the war with China, but this was little excuse for the arrogance of Kodama and his assistants now.

CHAPTER *12*

࿇࿇࿇࿇࿇࿇

"Little Grandfather" Arrives . . .

VICE-ADMIRAL S. OSSIPOVITCH MAKAROV, one of Russia's most respected naval officers, was appointed by St. Petersburg to replace Vice-
Admiral Stark under whom the Pacific Squadron had suffered the early
disasters of the war. Makarov had an international reputation as a naval
strategist. His inventions were numerous and successful, and he was regarded as a hero for his bravery in the war against the Turks in 1877,* in
which he used the old ramming spar, towed torpedoes, and the newly
invented "fish" torpedo, employed with such effect by the Japanese in the
surprise attack on Port Arthur. He had also invented the world's first
ice-breaker, and, although his ambition to take it to the North Pole for
experiments was not realized, it had helped to open up the frozen waters
of Siberia.

At the beginning of the war Makarov commanded the naval station at
Kronstadt, an island fortress on the Gulf of Finland, which guarded St.
Petersburg. He believed that politics and military matters did not mix—a
view not calculated to find favor with the Viceroy, Admiral Alexeiev, who
had used politics in his own climb to power. Alexeiev had no understanding
of the needs of the common sailor, and even now he did not care to hear
anything except that all was going well. He was all-powerful, and every
requisition had to be signed by him. Few in the fleet thought of ordering

---

*One of his officers, Lieutenant Zinovi Petrovitch Rozhdestvenski (later Admiral)
was to play a tragic part in the war against Japan.

[222]

even necessities without his signature. It was a safeguard. "If you possess something in black and white, you stand there as pure as snow. In the other case, it will go hard with you, as with the Swedes at Poltava," the second-in-command of a ship damaged in the first Japanese attack was told when he tried to get necessary equipment to carry out repairs.

Whoever was to blame for the squadron's misfortunes in early February, no one in the garrison was willing yet to make direct accusations. The same attitude affected the civilians, most of them government employees. No one wanted to take sides. "At Port Arthur one saw only fear, pale-faced fear of the almighty, irresponsible government," wrote Semenov, who had worked with Admiral Makarov at Kronstadt before the war.

Semenov was overjoyed to find that he was to serve again with Makarov, who had given him fatherly advice as he set off for Port Arthur. "Don't push yourself forward needlessly," Makarov had told him. "One's fate, no doubt, overtakes one, anyway, and when volunteers are called for, of course, one must respond. Simply do your duty, that is all. Don't push forward. There is nothing hard about death, but it is stupid to get killed to no purpose."

Semenov, though anxious to get into battle, kept his Admiral's advice in mind. He knew, as the rest of the squadron knew, that Makarov would ask nothing of his men and officers that he would not attempt himself. He admitted that it was not easy to serve under Makarov.

Often there was no time for either eating or sleeping; but for all that it was a splendid life. What was especially characteristic in Makarov was his horror of all routine and his hatred of the old office custom of devolving everything on others, of avoiding any and every responsibility, and therefore of never coming to an independent decision, but of passing on every paper to someone else "to be dealt with."

Scraps of paper signed in green pencil by Alexeiev would not be allowed to hold up the work of the squadron when Makarov arrived. The "risk nothing" policy growing out of the fleet's unpreparedness early in February would not be tolerated by "Beardy." The news of Makarov's impending arrival at Port Arthur put new life into the Russian squadron and officers and men often worked for twenty-four hours on end putting their ships in shape. The "Master" was coming and would decide for himself what was wrong.

The seven years of laxity since the Russian annexation of the peninsula, the disgrace of the first two Japanese attacks on February 8 and 9, and the landing of enemy troops at Chemulpo had left their mark. On the last day of February General Stoessel issued an ironic proclamation that set the tone for the whole garrison:

> The troops know well, and I now make known to the civilians, that there will be no retirement; in the first place, the fortress must fight to the last, and I, its commandant, will never give the order to retreat; in the second, there is no place to which to retreat.

Makarov arrived on March 7, and, since Admiral Stark, looking tired and old, continued for the time being to fly his flag in *Petropavlovsk*, Makarov hoisted his own flag on the cruiser *Askold*, which, with the "toy" *Novik* and *Bayan*, had seen action in the past month. When the Admiral's flag appeared, sailors and civilians took off their caps and crossed themselves. They all believed in Makarov, their "little grandfather." Now things would be different.

On the day he arrived, the *Retvizan* was refloated and moved inside the harbor for repairs. The coincidence was regarded as a good omen. As soon as Makarov had arrived things started to move. He was not a man to tolerate nonsense.

The Russian fleet had only two drydocks at Port Arthur, and neither of these was ready for the first casualties. One was still under construction and the other could hold neither a cruiser or a battleship. Admiral Alexeiev had asked St. Petersburg many times for money to complete the docks, but the reply always was that the ships at Port Arthur were practically new and would not require such luxuries as dry docks. "It may be a galley yarn," said an officer of a damaged ship, "but we have been told that if anything were to happen to one of the battleships she would be sent to Japan, which is amply supplied with docks and basins of all dimensions."

Trained engineers and workmen arrived from Russia at the same time as Makarov, however, and it was these who had put the final touches to *Retvizan*'s release from the rocks. The dockyard hands preferred to put it down to Makarov's magic. They had complained before his arrival that they worked day and night on ships which never took to sea. Now they looked forward to some results for their hard work. Both *Retvizan* and *Tsarevitch* were pumped out, repaired, and refloated.

Makarov had been in Port Arthur for only three days when he ordered two destroyer flotillas to sea to hunt the Japanese destroyers and torpedo boats that crept along the coast, slipping from headland to headland, to lay mines outside the harbor. Some of these Japanese ships were second-class torpedo boats, fitted up with bamboo and canvas structures which, from a distance, changed their silhouettes so that they appeared to the Russians to be much larger first-class destroyers. H. C. Seppings Wright, a correspondent–artist, served aboard one of the smaller of the second-class torpedo boats. It was just under ninety tons and living conditions aboard were rather cramped, he wrote. A canvas bath for the use of officers and men was stretched between the gangway on the port side, and dozens of small Japanese towels were usually wrapped around the funnels for drying. Running between the funnels was a clothesline. Packing cases, boxes, and crates of chickens filled the deck. Most of the ships had mascots which accompanied them to sea on mining and raiding expeditions. One of the torpedo boats had a duck which flew around the Russian harbor during the day, almost always returning to its ship at dusk.

The Japanese did not anticipate finding any Russian ships outside the harbor, but Togo had sent off his First and Second destroyer flotillas to attack any enemy destroyers that could be found as a prelude to a general bombardment on the following day.

Four ships of the Japanese First Destroyer Flotilla—*Shirakumo, Asashio, Kasumi,* and *Akatsuki*—patrolled outside the harbor all night on March 8–9 and early next morning ran into four of Makarov's destroyers returning from their fruitless search. The Japanese were unprepared for what happened. "Experience up to the present had shown that the enemy, as soon as they saw us, bolted as fast as they could, and never dared to stand up to us," reported the *Japanese Official Naval History.* This time Makarov's new, aggressive policy made it a vigorous, though disorganized, fight. At one stage a broadside to broadside battle between individual ships took place at ranges as close as fifty yards, and at least one torpedo was fired by a Russian destroyer before she fled in flames toward Port Arthur. In the darkness both sides overestimated the numbers of ships taking part. Collisions were avoided by feet, and considerable damage was inflicted on all ships on both sides. But, as the Russians turned back to Port Arthur, they felt that they had fought a far better fight than they had put up before.

The Japanese Third Destroyer Flotilla spent the night of March 9–10 outside the entrance to the harbor under orders to come close to the entrance and to attack any Russian ship that they could see or, if none was visible, to steam about outside and drop dummy mines to deceive the enemy and make them waste their ammunition. According to the commander of one of the four Japanese destroyers, the *Sazanami,* the mines were real. In his diary he admitted that the job had been amateurish. "I should certainly not like to assure Admiral Togo on my word of honor that I had placed the mines at the correct depth, and that the anchors had taken hold. It is more probable that one or two of them, as often happens, are floating at liberty over the waves, and have become as dangerous customers for us as for the Russians."

After dropping their mines, whether real or make-believe, the four Japanese destroyers paraded outside the port until sunrise, encouraging the Russian forts to open fire on them, even trying, without success, to bring fire on themselves by flashing their lights. They then "slid out to sea like eels," according to the commander of *Sazanami,* and ran straight into two Russian destroyers, *Ryeshitelni* and *Steregushchi,* which had become separated from the rest of their flotilla. The four Japanese ships maneuvered to cut the Russians off from their base. When the enemy destroyers were about three hundred yards away, the Japanese opened fire in a vigorous bombardment, each pair of Japanese vessels taking on one of the Russians. It was a bitter and closely fought battle, and, though the outnumbered Russians had no hope of victory, they badly damaged three of the Japanese destroyers.

Ryeshitelni escaped because of the bravery of a young midshipman, who, when the ship's steering gear broke down, took the wheel and managed to turn her away from the Japanese and run her into harbor. *Steregushchi* was not so fortunate. Her engine was shot away just as she was coming within range of the forts. The four Japanese destroyers surrounded her and poured in a heavy fire. "We were sweating all over in spite of the intense cold, and it was lucky that we were so near the enemy, for otherwise—I ought not to say this, although it is true—my gunners would never have hit their target," wrote the captain of *Sazanami.*

> I will not say that my crew would have behaved like the Chinese in the war of '94 who, instead of resting their guns against their shoulders, rested them against their stomachs, shut their eyes, and fired; certainly it did not get to this pitch, but they did not aim with precision, and I seem to have seen a man cursing a 4.7-cm. gun as though it were to blame for not having hit the mark.

In his anonymous diary, published after the war, the officer described the scene as his destroyer approached the Russian ship: "I saw a great column of thick steam escaping and some men trying to get away. These we were killing and wounding with deadly aim. It was indeed a sight which is seldom seen at sea, and from which one derives peculiar gratification—fighting against men full of vitality instead of inert steel." While two other Japanese destroyers stood guard, *Sazanami*'s captain was ordered by the commander of the destroyer flotilla to board the Russian ship and take her in tow. As the boarding party set out in a boat in the direction of the burning *Steregushchi,* Russian sailors swam toward the guardships, begging to be picked up. The two nearest were rescued but the Japanese could not reach the others and they disappeared in the heavy seas.

As soon as the Japanese boarding party had reached the Russian ship, she lowered her flag as a sign of surrender. The boarding party bounded along like "wild beasts." "There was nothing to stop us," wrote the officer in charge. "On the deck lay stretched thirty or forty dead or seriously wounded, many of them horribly mutilated, and lying about the place were arms, feet, a head, a heap of entrails . . . but nothing could upset us, and my crew turned the corpses over and over to convince themselves that death was real and not feigned." Twenty dead and wounded men were piled up aft of the bridge, and iron girders pinned down wounded men on the decks. The Japanese flag was hoisted, and *Sazanami* was ordered to tow the Russian ship, which was beginning to settle down. The rope parted and the leader of the boarding party had time only to go through the commander's cupboard in search of secret documents and money before the destroyer began to founder. The Japanese officer, with the ship's flag clutched in his hand, led his joyful crew in a burst of cheering as *Steregushchi* went down. "We wanted to save the still living remainder of the enemy, but the fort's fire became increasingly intense, and they were therefore abandoned," *The Japanese Official Naval History* reported.

Though the battle brought little victory to the Russians, the squadron and the garrison were encouraged. Admiral Makarov, his flag flying on *Novik,* the pet of the fleet, ran to the rescue of *Steregushchi.* Arriving to find that she had already sunk, he set off in pursuit of the Japanese destroyers, only to run into the whole Japanese squadron heading for Port Arthur. He turned back, pursued by battleships, destroyers, and the greyhound scouts, but *Novik* returned safely. As she came through the narrow entrance of the harbor, thousands of men stood on the decks of their ships and lined the forts and clifftops to cheer. For the Admiral of the Fleet to go to the rescue of a ship in trouble was unheard of in Port Arthur. The "risk nothing" era had ended. The Admiral had shown the way. "He had conquered all hearts at one stroke and could henceforth be justified in speaking of 'my' squadron. Everyone was his, body and soul," wrote Commander Semenov.

Though reinforced in spirit, the Russian fleet and Port Arthur had worse to come that day. The Japanese squadron came back and for four hours the six battleships standing more than six miles out to sea bombarded the town, the ships, and the forts, by indirect firing over Old Iron Mountain. The Japanese battleships fired about 150 rounds into the harbor where the whole Russian fleet was lying, damaging *Retvizan* again and putting one of *Askold*'s guns out of action. The fortress batteries were unable to reach the Japanese, and the Russian ships could not leave port until high water late in the afternoon after the Japanese had withdrawn. Shells killed soldiers on the forts, sailors on board ship, and civilians in the streets of the town. The naval store on the waterfront was badly damaged, and guns on Golden Hill Fort destroyed. But considering the great number of shells dropped on Port Arthur, comparatively little damage was caused there. Yet Japan's main object was achieved. The Guard Division landed unopposed at Pyongyang, midway between Seoul and the Yalu River on the west coast of Korea.

After the bombardment Makarov started a system of indirect firing so that the guns of ships in harbor could be controlled by telephone operators and signal posts on the surrounding hills. He also put the fleet through a vigorous training program to learn how to enter and leave the harbor. Navigating the narrow and shallow entrance to the inner harbor had hitherto taxed the seamanship of the Russians. Before Makarov arrived it used to take twenty-four hours for the entire fleet to enter or leave the inner harbor as only one ship passed through at a time. To the efficient Makarov, this was intolerable, and he set to work to improve the navigational skills of his officers. After long days of practice, the entire fleet could move through the entrance in two-and-a-half hours.

Soon after the bombardment of the town and harbor Makarov took all his ships out to sea. One after the other they made their way to the outer roadstead where they anchored while gunboats swept the sea for mines. Only dummy mines were found, and cruisers which had been stationed as lookouts reported that no Japanese ships were in sight. Makarov steamed with the fleet five miles out to sea and put his ships through the first exercises they had had in months.

Apart from necessary exercises in fleet maneuvers, Makarov took other steps to make the harbor more secure against torpedo boats and blockships. He stationed gunboats at the neck of the entrance and kept destroyers sweeping the channels for mines. He also sank two old merchantmen off the western shore, with a boom between them, and erected observation posts so that his ships could defend themselves from indirect fire when the next Japanese attack came.

The Japanese noticed the change for the better in the Russian squadron. *Steregushchi*'s battle against great odds, and Makarov's flight to save her, had made an impression. "In comparison with their usual behavior of bolting like rats whenever they saw our destroyers, this was a distinct advance toward recovering 'face,'" the *Japanese Official Naval History* conceded. "We saw that the enemy still had a fleet which could not be despised."

Things were beginning to sharpen up in the Port Arthur squadron, and with the arrival in mid-March of Lieutenant-General Smirnov* to take over the defenses of the fortress, spirits rose again. On the same day General Stoessel, who had been given command of the Third Siberian Army Corps

---

*For his courage and daring in the war against Turkey he had received the nickname of "Seven Devils."

but still remained in Port Arthur, issued an order which declared: "Arthur is now an impregnable stronghold." But after the bombardment of March 10, everyone knew that the defense would be difficult. The newly formed Council for the Defense of Port Arthur hired 5,000 laborers to strengthen the defenses in the rear and on the seafront. Great naked rocks stood where gun emplacements should have been erected. Many of the guns had not yet been mounted and some had been so badly mounted that they had to be reinforced. Though wages were fairly high, the Chinese laborers drifted away in droves. The Japanese had issued leaflets warning that Port Arthur was about to be cut off and then captured. "No Chinaman who has in any way assisted the Russians to defend the place will be given quarter," they announced.

To reinforce their dwindling labor force, Smirnov, helped ably by Major-General Roman Isodorovitch Kondratenko, set the Eighth East Siberian Rifle Divison troops to work toiling ceaselessly on the rocky hills in an effort to transform Port Arthur into the stronghold it should already have been. They set up mine defenses, installed new telephone lines, and borrowed guns from the navy for the coast batteries. Now that *Retvizan* had been removed from the gullet of the harbor, the guns that she had used so effectively had to be replaced. Guns from smaller ships such as *Angara* were placed on the hills at the entrance to the harbor. Commander von Essen, the courageous commander of the cruiser *Novik,* that "regular retriever which was always into everything," was made captain of the battleship *Sevastopol,* a most unusual appointment for a commander. Another appointment during Makarov's reshuffle of the fleet sent a twenty-nine-year-old officer, Alexander Kolchak, to command a destroyer attached to the admiral's flagship.* Appointments such as these were not appreciated by Alexeiev, but Makarov was determined to make the utmost use of the best material in the fleet.

The new admiral ordered his battleships to leave harbor as often as possible, and the Japanese stood well out to sea trying to entice the Russians closer. The Russians were not often in action against the Japanese, but the efficiency of the fleet was improved and Admiral Makarov's personality and drive inspired everyone under his command.

The Japanese made another torpedo attack at the harbor entrance on March 22 and the following day started to bombard the town and the ships. The Combined Fleet's Confidential Order No. 246 ended with the words: "We must put our firm trust in the gods, and I pray that we may return

---

*Both von Essen and Kolchak were to become distinguished admirals in World War I. The latter was sentenced to death by the Irkutsk revolutionary tribunal and executed by firing squad in 1920.

with many prizes." But Makarov had ordered indirect fire over Old Iron Mountain where two Japanese battleships, *Fuji* and *Yashima*, were bombarding the harbor and the town from seven miles out to sea. None of the Russian ships was hit. A shell damaged the barracks on Tiger's Tail, killing and wounding fourteen men. This time the Russian fleet, led by Admiral Makarov in *Askold*, came out to meet the Japanese. As soon as the Russian ships were seen leaving harbor, Admiral Kamimura's Second Division closed in to lend support to the battleships *Fuji* and *Yashima*. They stood out of reach of the shore batteries, but the Russian ships managed to damage the *Fuji*. Togo, who came on board after *Fuji* was hit, was not pleased. His chief-of-staff admitted grudgingly to the crew of the battleship, then on its way to Sasebo for repairs, that the Russian fire had been marvelous. Makarov was to blame, wrote a Japanese officer that night. "I hope and trust that a Japanese shell will very soon prevent him confirming his reputation for intelligence and initiative at our expense."

After the attack Makarov took his ships back into the harbor rather than leave them exposed to torpedo attack outside during the night. By 3 P.M. the ships had all returned to harbor. For the first time the Russian fleet had gone to sea, attacked the enemy, and come back again on a single tide.

Japanese Imperial General Headquarters realized that the Russians remained a danger to their lines of communications. Their ships were still able to enter and leave harbor, in spite of the qualified success of the blocking attempt in February. Togo was instructed to make another effort to seal up the Russian ships in port. He obtained four twenty-year-old merchant ships and ordered them to be fitted with explosives and loaded with a mixture of cement and stones so that they would stay down for at least a year. This time the name "Special Service Transports" was changed to "Transports for Use at the Advanced Base." Togo was optimistic. He summoned the captains of the blockships and the torpedo boats and destroyers that were to accompany them for the final rundown. The Port Arthur harbor was to be turned into a lake, he told them. His detailed orders ended on a note of good cheer: "If one acts with determination, even devils and gods give way. Courage is the greatest protection. From the blockships to the sections told off for guard and rescue, all, with a firm heart and trusting in Providence, will do their utmost to fulfil their several duties. This must lead to a great success."

At 7 P.M. on March 26, the First and Third divisions of the Japanese fleet formed a guard of honor through which the blockships sailed on their hazardous mission. Men lined the sides of the escorting ships and stood aloft on masts to cheer the suicide crews on their way. "They seemed calm and collected, as if they were going on a fishing expedition," wrote an officer on board an escort ship.

[230]

At 2:20 A.M. the four blockships left the escorting destroyers and torpedo boats and advanced toward the entrance to the harbor. It was a calm, misty morning, with smooth seas and little moonlight. Nothing could be seen but the long fingers of the Russian searchlights flicking through the darkness. The four ships waited until a cloud went over the pale moon and rushed ahead as fast as their old engines would take them. About two miles from the entrance a searchlight picked up *Chiyo Maru*, commanded by Commander Arima Ryokitsu, the originator of the blocking expeditions. Shore batteries on either side of the entrance opened fire, and *Chiyo Maru* blew herself up in the entrance to the channel close to Golden Hill. Another ship anchored and exploded in the opening of the channel nearby. Blinded by the searchlights, the third ship blew herself up in the same area.

Only one of the four ships remained, *Fukui Maru*, commanded by Lieutenant-Commander Hirose Takeo. Remembering the failure of some ships to explode in the earlier expedition, Hirose had given great attention to the explosive equipment of his ship and had arranged the mechanism so that if wires were cut the explosives would still be set off. His chief warrant officer stood on the deck waiting for the command to switch on the explosives. Commander Hirose came quietly up behind the nervous warrant officer. "Beautiful view," he said and proceeded to recount the advice of a famous Japanese swordsman and judo expert. "He knew what fighting meant," said Hirose. "You get so excited that you don't realize the state of mind you are in. . . . A good way to find out is to put your hand in your groin and feel your testicles. If you are excited, then they will be found to be shrunken and stuck to the top. If you are calm, they are stretched and dangle. If they dangle, you will win. If you find them shrunken, you'd better run."

The warrant officer braced himself to set the explosives, while Hirose, wearing an old civilian overcoat over his uniform, sat at the stern of *Fukui Maru*, repeating over and over, "Did you feel your testicles?"

The ship was about to anchor in the channel when she was hit by a torpedo and blew up. Hirose, finding his warrant officer missing, searched the sinking ship as fire from the Russian guardships and from machineguns on shore raked the rescue boats. Reluctantly Hirose stepped into a lifeboat. He was immediately hit by a shell and his body went overboard, only a lump of flesh, "about the size of a two-sen coin," remaining in the bottom of the boat.

Hirose was posthumously made commander and awarded the Distinguished Service Order (Third Class), an exceptional honor. He had spent many years in St. Petersburg before the war as a member of the naval attaché's office, working in intelligence. Among his effects was found a letter which spoke of his admiration for Russia and the Russians. "I regard Russia

[231]

as my second home," he wrote. "I want to pay my debt to her. When the blockade is successful I want to get permission to leave the ship for a time, get a Chinese junk and go to Lushun [Port Arthur] to see Alexeiev and explain to him the situation and recommend that he surrender. . . . If this were to work, it would be to the advantage of Japan and Russia. I want to do this, even if it costs me my life."

Hirose's bid for peace failed, but this time the blocking expedition had been almost complete—just one more ship in the entrance and the Russian fleet would have been sealed in the harbor "lake." Togo reported that he regretted there was still a gap of more than 200 feet through which the Russian ships could pass, though large ships would find the passage difficult.

The scrap of Hirose's flesh was taken by transport to Japan to be buried. As the ship passed by the *Asahi*, on which Hirose had served, the engines stopped and she lay motionless alongside the battleship. The Hirose legend had begun. "It was as though the brave Hirose even in death refused to be separated from the ship in which he had held command," observed a Japanese newspaper.

Hirose's flesh was buried after a ceremonial procession through the streets of Tokyo, with the petals of the cherry trees thick in its path and Chopin's funeral march, played by a naval band, mingling oddly with the ear-splitting blasts of the Shinto flutes. "As half-saint, half-hero, the memory of Commander Hirose now ranks in Japan near to that of the Forty-seven Ronins," wrote war correspondent Richard Harding Davis.

A bronze statue of Hirose and his warrant officer was erected in Kanda in the center of Tokyo and the commander was made the first "war-god" of the Russo-Japanese War.* It was removed at the instruction of General MacArthur's headquarters in November, 1946.

---

*Newspapers called him "gunshin" (war-god, or divine soldier). In the Second World War, Lieutenant Matsuo, one of the midget submarine commanders who sank the Manly ferry in Sydney Harbor, was also made a "war-god."

CHAPTER *13*

೫೫೫೫೫

. . . *And Fights*

BELLS TOLLED IN RUSSIA as churches and cathedrals filled with rejoicing people to celebrate the great Easter festival. After the religious services came parades, and, at Court, days of eating rich food and the exchange of eggs and other gifts. Fabergé, Court jeweler to the Tsar, created two exquisite jeweled Easter eggs for Nicholas to present to Alexandra and Marie, while the children of members of the royal family handed out decorated cakes to visiting schoolchildren and members of the imperial guard.

In Port Arthur, Easter passed almost unnoticed. Work stopped for only a day. Admiral Makarov was too busy to change his clothes and slept in his uniform. He spent Easter night in a guardboat, on patrol with his ships. There was no Easter parade. Just a few days earlier the garrison had celebrated the seventh anniversary of Russian occupation with religious services and military processions, but Port Arthur was wearied of parades. This Easter the town was blacked out and after the church services people found their way home in the dark. Although Admiral Alexeiev had left to visit Mukden, the only house lights shining in the town were in his two-storied lodge overlooking the dockyard. The lights were left burning to give confidence to the garrison, and nobody seemed to realize that they might also be of assistance to the watching, waiting Japanese, out at sea.

Several restaurants remained open, and, since the railway was still in operation, fresh caviar and other foodstuffs were readily available. One or two *cafés chantants* kept busy, although few of the girls were left to entertain the patrons. Those who had not been accepted into the Red Cross had gone farther afield to similar establishments in Liaoyang. Spies were thought to be everywhere, and all new arrivals were closely examined by the police, who could usually be paid off with a small bribe. One foreigner, arrested on suspicion, was released when he announced that he was a resident of the "Amerikanski Dom," one of the brothels. The police chief explained that the madam of the house was a good friend of his.

General Smirnov and his men toiled on the rocky hills surrounding Port Arthur, fortifying the batteries, dragging guns to emplacements around Old Iron Mountain, and fortifying outlying defense posts. Admiral Makarov continued to strengthen the sea defenses by sinking old ships near the entrance to prevent attempts by the Japanese to enter the harbor. He had a cruiser moored outside the gullet in front of the sunken Japanese block-ships, and day and night he kept his destroyers outside in search of the enemy. Both Smirnov and Makarov were determined that the fortress would not be taken by surprise again.

Despite the long, hard days of work Makarov found that his officers and men were so badly trained that excursions outside the harbor often ended in disaster, as ships collided at exercises. With difficulty he kept his temper. "It is too late now to start on systematic training," he told his crews.

Every captain, every specialist, in fact every officer who has charge of any department or part of the ship, no matter how trivial in itself, must hunt out with the utmost keenness any and every defect and work seriously at its removal. Let superiors and subordinates assist one another in this. Don't be afraid of making mistakes. Even a piece of work which starts on wrong lines and has to be given up bears fruit. . . . Remember that we do not know what time we have for our preparations. It may be months, it may be hours, nay, minutes, which still separate us from the final issue. . . . Everyone—understand me well —everyone must be penetrated with the importance of his particular task.

General Kondratenko continued to work with Chinese coolies in an attempt to strengthen the rear defenses. The guns from *Tsarevitch* and *Retvizan,* both undergoing repairs, were borrowed for land forts, and rein-forcements for the garrison continued to arrive almost every day. At the end of March, Makarov issued the following proclamation:

"Every vessel of war or of commerce which shall be discovered in the Sphere of the Theater of War having no lights by night or flags by day and which does not hoist them after having been warned to do so by a cannon shot will be considered as belonging to the enemy and will be sunk."

April came, and with it heavy rains, thick fogs, and temperatures even lower than they had been in mid-winter. The Japanese fleet was hidden in the mists that hung low down over the ships in harbor at Port Arthur.

Though the Russians could not see them, the Japanese were far from inactive.

On April 11 Togo took his First Division to sea. Behind it came two boats fitted up as mining launches and covered with tarpaulins. They steamed toward Port Arthur early in the morning, accompanied by the light cruisers, which had instructions to come in close to the entrance as decoys so that the Russians, seeking a weak force of enemy ships, might be lured out to sea. The six armored cruisers were close at hand, though out of sight, ready to pounce if the Russian ships came out.

At the same time, Togo dispatched Kamimura, with the Second, Third, and Fourth divisions, to keep a watch between Shantung and the Sir James Hall group of islands off the Korean coast immediately south of Pyongyang Inlet, in case the Russians tried to run for Vladivostok. On a similar mission, Vice-Admiral Kataoka Shichiro went with destroyers and torpedo boats to guard the Tsushima Straits.

The Grand Council of War had decided that it was unlikely the Russian ships would try to join up with the Vladivostok squadron, "being so completely obsessed by the policy of protracted inactivity," and arranged for the army and navy to get together to discuss the landing of the Second Army, midway between Pi-tzu-wo and Dalny, after a third attempt to block the harbor entrance had been made. Whether the blocking was successful or not the landing of the army would take place soon after the attempt had been made. The landing here had the twofold purpose of cutting the Russians' main line of communications with Port Arthur and posing a second threat to their concentrations at Liaoyang.

At 5:40 A.M. on April 12 the mining party broke away from the battle squadron and set out for Port Arthur amid the usual cheers from the battleships and cruisers. Instructions to the remainder of the fleet were clear: "Should the enemy have the courage to come ten miles outside the port, the fleet will immediately attack them . . . furthermore, the destroyers and torpedo boats will be ordered to rush up and attack them even in broad daylight should an opportunity occur; and must accordingly have their minds made up to be prepared if the enemy's destroyers follow to attack the main fleet when it withdraws. They will be repelled by our destroyers and torpedo boats after they have been enticed sufficiently far out." Destroyers and torpedo-boats were to fly a "very plain" naval flag at their mastheads, and at the starboard yardarm the two flags, "Name of Officer," "Name of Merchantship," for identification.

The two fast armored cruisers, *Kasuga* and *Nisshin*, making their first public appearance, were to display themselves to the enemy, "as a sign of our power," but the armored cruisers, *Tokiwa* and *Asama,* were to keep out of sight until required.

While Togo was organizing his fleet, Makarov, on the night of April 12, sent all his destroyers around the Elliot Islands, north of Dalny, and about seventy miles from Port Arthur, where the Japanese were believed to have set up a base. A cruiser was to go out before daybreak to lead the destroyers back if they had not returned. Because of her distinctive appearance—she was the only ship in the Far East with five funnels—*Askold* was detailed for this duty. *Diana* would have been faster but Makarov knew that she might be mistaken for the Japanese cruiser *Iwate* and he had promised a cruiser unlike any Japanese ship. *Askold* could be recognised without signals, even in the dark. They went out full of new-found confidence, anxious to find the enemy. Makarov had given them all the time he could afford, but he was nervous and mildly bad-tempered as he waited on the cruiser *Diana* for them to return. At 10:30 P.M. the destroyers had not come back. Watching through the drizzle, a lookout man alongside the Admiral thought that he saw "something" in the beams of a searchlight. "Shall I open fire?" he asked Makarov.

The Admiral, worried about his raw destroyer crews, answered rather crossly, undecided what to do. "Oh, who can tell what it is? They are probably our own destroyers. They know nothing of night work. Some of them probably got separated from the rest and are now pottering about in front of Port Arthur. They can't find the others, and dare not return into harbor from fear of being taken for Japanese. Bad luck to it!" He made a note to have the spot carefully searched the next morning in case "something unpleasant" had been dropped outside the entrance to the harbor.

Makarov was right on both counts. What he had seen just outside the harbor was the Japanese mine-laying expedition. *Koryu Maru* and the launches were busy in the drizzling rain. The sea was calm but through the inky darkness the Russian searchlights from shore and ships lit up their activities. "They seemed to be keeping a stricter lookout even than usual," reported the commander in charge of the Japanese flotilla. It was a good night for mine-laying. In spite of five or six Russian searchlights, forty-eight mines were laid in the mouth of the harbor. Before retiring, the escorting Japanese destroyers amused themselves by firing at the Russian searchlights, which, though they frequently lit up the Japanese ships, failed to pinpoint them.

Makarov's guess that his unskilled destroyers may have become lost was also correct. *Strashni,* one of the destroyers, became separated from the other ships at night and at about two in the morning made toward some lights, only to find when daylight came that she was in the middle of four

Japanese destroyers of the Second Destroyer Flotilla, which had been acting as escort for the mining party. All four ships opened fire on her.

Her captain and most of the crew were killed after a fight that even Admiral Makarov would have been proud to see. A young officer took over from the commander of *Strashni* and managed to fire a torpedo from the stern tube, which narrowly missed its target, going between two of the Japanese destroyers. A second torpedo was about to be fired when a shell hit it and it burst. Every man nearby was killed. The four Japanese ships closed in, firing from eighty yards. "The Japanese clung to their victim like hounds in a chase," reported an observer with the Russian batteries. The dying Russian officer ordered his crew to perish rather than surrender, and crawling to one of the few remaining guns scored a shot that destroyed the bridge of one of the enemy destroyers and the funnel of another before he collapsed at the gun. *Strashni*, loaded with dead and dying men, and on fire from stem to stern, began to sink.

Bayan, Askold, Diana, and *Novik* all rushed to the rescue, miraculously missing the mines, and Makarov, his flag now on *Petropavlovsk*, also got safely through the entrance with the battleship *Poltava*. In his anxiety to save his flock, Makarov failed to check for mines, though before he left for the rescue of the lost destroyer, he gave orders for the area to be swept. In the excitement, his orders were not carried out.

Bayan, speeding to the scene like a "rampant wild boar," arrived first and fought off the Japanese destroyers and two armored cruisers, *Asama* and *Tokiwa,* from Admiral Dewa's division. Behind them came Dewa with his flag in the *Chitose,* followed by the *Takasago, Kasagi,* and *Yoshino,* all cruisers. In spite of heavy fire from the ten Japanese ships, *Bayan*'s captain opened up with light and heavy guns "The bursting shells bowled over man after man until the decks were slippery with blood," reported the *Novoye Krai.* "Amid the crash of the guns, the hiss of the flying projectiles, and the thunder of their explosions, the smashing of splinters, and the din of the working engines, the surgeons labored quietly among the wounded on the hospital tables."

By the time *Novik, Askold,* and *Diana* arrived, survivors from the sunken destroyer had all disappeared. Admiral Dewa picked up wounded from the Japanese destroyer *Ikazuchi,* which had been damaged by *Strashni*'s last shots, and withdrew. His orders were to reappear when the main Russian force emerged from the harbor.

At eight o'clock *Petropavlovsk* and *Poltava* joined the Russian cruisers, and Admiral Dewa reemerged, according to instructions, drawing the Russians out, in full chase away from the protection of the forts.

"Relying on their strength, the enemy chased us very closely," said the official Japanese report. Dewa was doing his best to entice the Russians farther out into the open sea. When he saw the Russian battleship, *Sevastopol,* in front of the entrance with *Peresvyet* and *Pobyeda,* he telegraphed Togo that the Russian main force was approaching. Togo's First Division was about thirty miles from the entrance but they could hear the guns, even though they could not see anything of the battle. He sent the two fast armored cruisers, *Nisshin* and *Kasuga,* to the rear of his division and steamed in single line ahead toward the thunder of the guns.

The two admirals, "the yellow and the white," as the European newspapers referred to them, were about to meet at sea for the first time. Each had fought bravely in other wars for their countries, but Makarov's name was familiar to the navies of all nations.

Togo's childhood fight against the British was forgotten. Apart from sinking the British transport *Kowshing* in the Sino-Japanese War, he had been unknown outside Japan before the war against Russia began. He had not been idle in the period between the two wars, however. He made careful studies of the south coast of Korea where the Japanese had fought wars with Korea for centuries, and in all his travels he kept Makarov's book on naval tactics beside his bunk, until he almost knew it by heart.

Now, on the other Russian ships, men saw their commander standing on the bridge of *Petropavlovsk,* wearing an old overcoat with a fur collar, the wind blowing in his long fair beard. "Single line ahead on the *Bayan. Bayan* to lead the squadron back to the scene of the disaster. Everyone to keep a good lookout for wreckage," he signaled. He was waving his cap and smiling. "Your health, my lads!" he called in his mighty voice. "God grant a happy issue!" Crews on the nearest ships lined the rails as he passed. "We wish Your Excellency good health!" they called. Officers and men flourished their caps and climbed on each other's shoulders to see their "Little Grandfather."

"The Yellow Admiral's" ruse had worked. Makarov's fleet of five battleships, four cruisers, and nine destroyers had been lured more than fifteen miles out to sea by Dewa's decoys. A long-range battle started, with the Japanese ships slowly retreating farther and farther away. The first step in the carefully planned action was about to take place.

Lionel James, the thirty-two-year-old correspondent of *The Times,* aboard the chartered steamship *Haimun** and with his own telegraphic

---

*The story of James and the *Haimun* is one of the most remarkable in the history of war correspondence. James persuaded *The Times* to charter the *Haimun,* a 311-ton steamship, at a cost of nearly £3,000 a month. She was equipped with the new de Forrest wireless which communicated with his own receiving station at Wei-hai-wei on the Shantung coast. His crew included a Japanese intelligence officer transmitter, was nearing Port Arthur when he saw Admiral Togo coming in with his flag in *Mikasa,* followed by the five other battleships, *Asahi, Fuji, Yashima, Hatsuse,* and *Shikishima.* Behind them came the six first-class cruisers, with *Nisshin* and *Kasuga* bringing up the rear. This was the sight Admiral Makarov also saw when the mists lifted. He realized that the smaller Japanese force had been used to entice him away from the protection of the forts. Just as Dewa's ships had withdrawn when the larger Russian force had appeared, he now ran helter-skelter back toward the harbor.

By 9:30 A.M. Togo's ships were about twelve miles from the entrance to Port Arthur and rapidly overhauling Makarov and the remainder of the Russian ships that had gone to *Strashni*'s assistance. *Novik,* with her superior speed, darted past the slow *Diana,* which brought up the rear. *Diana* was steaming as fast as she could precisely over the spot where the ships had been the night before. Her captain was waiting for the *Petropavlovsk* to order firing, but no signal came. The Japanese were also quiet. Semenov on the *Diana* ordered his gunlayers to stay at their posts, but, when his gunnery officer suggested that they should go for a smoke, he agreed.

They came down from the bridge and walked across to where a small oil light, the "slow match," was burning to light their cigarettes. "Nothing of any importance is likely to happen now," said Semenov. "For today we have got everything behind us. We'll start washing decks. They haven't been touched since the hands were called." He was about to give orders for the decks to be washed when suddenly there was an explosion, as if a twelve-inch gun had gone off close by, and then another, even more powerful.

Cries of horror arose. "The *Petropavlovsk!*" "The *Petropavlovsk!*" Dreading the worst, Semenov rushed to the side of his ship.

I saw a huge cloud of brown smoke . . . in this cloud I saw the ship's foremast. It was slanting. It was slanting, helpless, not as if it was falling, but as if it were suspended in the air. To the left of this cloud I saw the battleship's stern. It looked as always, as if the awful happen-

---

who, when the boat was stopped by a Russian cruiser, disguised himself as a Malay steward. Dogged by constant misfortune and accused of being an agent by the Russians, James also incurred the wrath of Captain Pakenham and the doubts of the Japanese. In order not to interfere with the radio transmissions of the belligerents, James, under Japanese instruction, kept radio silence until Togo's ships were actually engaged with the Port Arthur batteries. On one occasion, however, when the Japanese guns had opened fire, James broke his silence and sent a brief report from within seven miles of Port Arthur, thus furnishing, as he proudly claimed, the first record of a telegraphic message reporting a naval engagement being sent direct from the scene of operations to the office of the journal which was to give it to the public—the first and almost certainly the last.

ings in the forepart were none of its concern. A third explosion! White steam now began to mix with brown cloud. The boilers had burst! Suddenly the stern of the battleship rose straight in the air. This happened so rapidly that it did not look as if the bow had gone *down,* but as if the ship had broken in half amidships. . . . For a moment I saw the screws whirling round in the air. . . . It appeared to me as if the afterpart of the *Petropavlovsk* [all that was visible of her] suddenly opened out and belched forth fire and flames, like a volcano. It seemed even as if flames came out of the sea, long after it had closed over the wreck. Never, even at times when the most important orders were being given, had such silence reigned on board our ship, as at this gruesome spectacle.

He looked at his watch, and then wrote in his notebook:
"9:43—Explosion on board *Petropavlovsk.*"
"9:44—All over."

On board *Novik* they saw the big ship heel slowly over and begin to go down, bow foremost, her propellers still revolving. Her bright green bottom rose high in the water and great sheets of flame ran along the length of the ship.

The deputy fleet commander, Rear-Admiral Prince Pavel Petrovitch Ukhtomski, with his flag in *Peresvyet,* hoisted the signal for the fleet: "Follow me in single line ahead." The dejected fleet started once again for the safety of the harbor. Half an hour later there was another explosion and *Pobyeda* began to heel over very slowly. There was no Japanese ship in sight.

Panic seized the Russian ships. Soon they were firing in all directions. Guns went off everywhere. "Ships were struck by shell, projectiles whistled over our heads, and splinters struck irregular fire. I was standing on the upper bridge with the gunnery lieutenant. At first we looked at one another, dazed, as if neither of us would believe his own senses and wanted to have his observation corroborated by the other," wrote Semenov.

"What are you firing at?" shouted the commander.

The crew of *Diana* wrenched the hammocks out of their nettings, tore lifebelts from the racks, and prepared to jump overboard. The gunnery lieutenant seized the bugler by the collar of his coat and dragged him to the bridge. "Sound the ceasefire," he ordered.

"What's the matter with you? Have you got something sticking in your throat? Sound again! Again! Don't stop. They don't hear it!" No one paid any attention to the wavering notes of the bugler. A shell struck the lifeboats from their davits. Men had to be pulled from their guns by brute force. No one knew why the firing had started. On *Diana* it was quickly over, but other ships were still blazing away and threatened to ram each other.

While the explosions were still resounding from *Petropavlovsk* a rumor spread through the ships that they were being attacked by submarines. Every ship in the fleet opened fire on pieces of wood and empty fruit cans floating in the water in the belief that they might be periscopes.

At about 10:30 *Peresvyet* signaled again: "Proceed into port, battleships leading." The ships, including the damaged *Pobyeda*, staggered back home, "crowding one upon the other like a lot of sheep."

As the fleet steamed into harbor everyone on shore and on the anchored ships looked for Makarov's flag. But the Admiral and 635 officers and men had gone down with the ship.

His heart breaking, the commander of *Diana* tried to encourage his crew. "Don't go about like a drowned rat," he said to his boatswain. "A battleship has gone down and the squadron has been weakened. We shall receive reinforcements. A fresh squadron is coming out. None of your hang-dog looks and idleness."

"Yes, yes, your honor," replied the boatswain. "We can't do without losses. It is not that at all, your honor. What is a battleship? They are welcome to sink another one, and even a couple of cruisers. That's not it; but we have lost our head. Oh, why had it to be him and not any of the others?"

He echoed the feelings of the entire Russian First Pacific Squadron.

Also dead on *Petropavlovsk* was the great Russian war artist, Vesli Verestchagin, a member of the British Royal Academy and the French Academy. Verestchagin's famous picture of a battlefield in the Russo-Turkish War showed dead and dying men lying bleeding in the distance. In the foreground of the painting was the Russian headquarters, strewn with empty champagne bottles and the rags of harlots. A great friend of Admiral Makarov, Verestchagin had been commissioned by the Tsar to paint pictures of sea and land battles in this new war. In Russia his loss was felt as deeply as that of the Admiral. "He had spent his whole life trying to teach the human race peace, and had come in his old age to this boiling-hot crater, so that he might catch perhaps a final horror with which to convince mankind," wrote a mourner.

Grand Duke Cyril, Nicholas's cousin, was in the water for twenty minutes before he was picked up, badly injured and burned on the legs. His brother, Boris, watching from the battery on Golden Hill, burst into tears and fainted while other spectators on land removed their caps and knelt in prayer.

Togo stood motionless, like a statue, on the bridge of *Mikasa*, watching through his glasses. Many of the men on the flagship took off their caps. Some cheered, and then, as the Russian ships were under the protection of the fort batteries, the fleet sailed away.

The Japanese press made much of the Russian loss, and the world heard that in Nagoya and Tokyo two nights after the sinking of the *Petropavlovsk* processions took place with thousands of white funeral lanterns carried by people who sorrowed for Makarov. The Russian Admiral was compared with the old samurai of Japan. An official Japanese history of the war said that Togo, ever the practicing samurai, sent a wireless message into Port Arthur a few hours before the attack, advising Makarov to surrender. All of this was believed in Japan. Much of the propaganda was also printed in other parts of the world and added to Japan's growing reputation for chivalry against a ruthless foe.

On the deck of the battleship *Shikishima,* the entire crew watched as the Russian ship went down in flames. "We were astonished but at the same time unconsciously shouted '*banzai,*' so happy we were," wrote the captain. "When the smoke somewhat dispersed, we saw nothing at all on the sea. One would have thought that a mast would show, but there was nothing. . . ."

From the battleship *Asahi,* Pakenham reported: "The silence of the Japanese fleet was broken by an involuntary burst of cheering and hand-clapping, which was, in its turn, succeeded by sympathetic murmurs as the awful probable significance of such an event as that just witnessed, was realised. All agreed that one of the recently laid mines must have been the cause of the explosion."*

A Japanese reconnaissance cruiser reported that seven or eight Russian ships outside the port were firing into the water, possibly in an attempt to destroy mines that had come to the surface. But it was the rumor that the Japanese were using submarines that had started the panic aboard the Russian ships after *Petropavlovsk* went down. According to Lieutenant Steer of *Novik,* who commanded submarines at Vladivostok long after the war with Japan, it was widely believed that Japanese submarines would emerge in the dockyard at Port Arthur, fire their torpedoes, and leave. An obstruction made up of nets had been invented to catch submarines in the same way as a poacher catches quail. Often logs of wood or seals playing in the water were mistaken for submarines.

So unfamiliar was the Russian navy with the new underwater vessels that Lieutenant Steer was once sent off in *Novik*'s steamcutter to chase a submarine outside Port Arthur with instructions reading:

---

* "*Gochin,* " the naval term for sinking by explosion, was coined by Togo after the sinking of *Petropavlovsk,* and it came into the Japanese language as meaning passing out after heavy drinking, or a man being raped by a woman.

Seize the submarine by its periscope, then smash it by blows with a mallet, so as to blind its crew; better still, wrap a flag or a piece of canvas around it; or lastly—and this is probably the best way of all—tow the said submarine by its periscope into the inner harbor.

In the months to come Russia and Japan accused each other of using submarines, but though the Russians had one at Port Arthur it was not used and was still in sections at the end of the war.* The Japanese had realized the value of underwater ships long before the war, and in 1902 a Japanese naval mission had visited America, England, and France to study their construction. Five submarines were laid down at Quincy near Boston in early 1904. Japanese naval officers who stayed in America to supervise the construction of the remarkable new boats accompanied them when they were loaded in numbered sections to be taken by rail to Seattle and thence by ship to Yokohama where four of them arrived in November 1904.

Smaller submarines were also built in Kobe from the design of American ships in 1904. While attending the launching of gunboats built for the Chinese at the Kawasaki dockyard, a British consul stationed in Kobe discovered two half-built submarines in a covered shed. All the men employed by the contractors were sworn to secrecy, but the consul learned from the American designer who had come to Japan to assist in the construction of these Holland-type submarines that they were expected to be completed by March 1905.

For some unknown reason neither the American-built ships nor those constructed in Japan were used in the war against Russia. The utmost secrecy surrounded the building of Japan's submarines, but as Captain Pakenham reported to the Admiralty, the Japanese had a great capacity for silence. Though he sent no reports of submarine additions to the Japanese fleet, he pleaded with the Admiralty to treat with absolute secrecy such information as he sent regarding the very long-range firing of the Japanese ships as well as their invention of dummy mines. "You will have understood the limitations that the wishes of my kind and generous host impose on the scope of my reports," he wrote.

Pakenham did not regard the loss to Russia of *Petropavlovsk* as of enormous importance. Even with this battleship, Russia was no match for the Japanese on the sea. He strenuously defended Togo for losing a golden opportunity during the first attacks in February. "The shades of Nelson and

---

*Late in the war the Russians experimented with a tiny submarine, the *Petr Kochka,* at Port Arthur. Originally operated by four bicycle pedals, it now had an automobile engine installed, but the invention proved unsuccessful.

other immortals were invoked to add authority to a theory that seemed already to have much in its favor," he wrote. "But today we are in the presence of a new phase of naval warfare." Makarov's fleet had been lured into the minefield trap, but Togo had not been looking for glory or for concentrated attack on his own ships by the Russian shore batteries. "Instead of subjecting themselves to a massacre and loss only inferior to that of their enemy, they lost not a man nor so much as a copper-punt."

For days after the loss of the flagship, the officers and men of the Russian fleet sought in vain to control their gloom. The fleet had lost its head and believed its situation to be as hopeless now as it had been before Makarov had arrived to take command.

In St. Petersburg a funeral service was held for Makarov and all who had perished with him. "Russia today is a grief-stricken nation," wrote the *Collier's* correspondent. Snow fell heavily in the streets but inside the church the darkness was lit by thousands of candles as priests chanted the Mass. Nicholas, Alexandra, and Empress Marie were all in tears as prayers were said. "Within that vast temple the marine minister, the heads of the staff, admirals and captains, the whole diplomatic corps, and the bowed figure of Madame Makarov are gathered together amid lugubrious surroundings to offer the last tribute of respect to the heroic dead who perished thousands of miles away," wrote the London *Daily Telegraph* correspondent.

Count Tolstoy, who had already decried the actions of both the Russians and the Japanese in the war, now furiously attacked the regime for sending innocent sailors to their death.

I am not alluding to Makarov and other officers—all of these men knew what they were doing, and wherefore, and they voluntarily, for personal advantage, for ambition did as they did by disguising themselves in pretended patriotism, a pretense not condemned merely because it was universal. . . . I allude rather to those unfortunate men drawn from all parts of Russia, who by the help of religious fraud, and under fear of punishment have been torn from an honest, reasonable, useful, and laborious family life, driven to the other end of the world, placed on a cruel senseless machine for slaughter, and torn to bits, drowned along with this senseless machine in a distant sea, without any need or possibility of advantage from all their privations, efforts, and sufferings, or from the death which overtook them.

Tolstoy had been the young Tsaritsa's favorite author when she was learning to be a good Russian. She had read his *Childhood* and *Sevastopol Sketches* and found in *War and Peace* all the devotion to the Tsar that she felt Nicholas deserved. Why could Tolstoy not write another *Anna Karenina?* Why did he have to concern himself with politics?

Nicholas's diary referred to "the sad and unspeakably mournful news," interspersed with snippets of information unconnected with the tragedy. Although he wrote that he could think of nothing else, he could not bear to dwell solely upon such news. He mentioned Alexandra's heavy cold and noted that snow had fallen during the night and that the ice on the Neva had given way. "May God's will be done in everything," he concluded the day's entry, "but we ought, poor sinners that we are, to ask Him for His mercy."

🌀🌀🌀🌀🌀🌀

CHAPTER 14

On to the Yalu

Mᴜᴄʜ ᴄʟᴏsᴇʀ ᴛᴏ ʜᴏᴍᴇ than Nicholas could have imagined, other events had now been set in train that were to have far-reaching effects on the war and on the fate of the autocracy. Before hostilities broke out, Colonel Akashi Motojiro, the Japanese military attaché in St. Petersburg, made arrangements to pay his agents 500 yen a month and set off for Berlin under instruction to take over the post of military attaché in Vienna as a cover for his work as chief European coordinator of Japanese military intelligence.

A hunch led him instead to Sweden. In Berlin Akashi had written to a Finnish exile in Stockholm and when no reply came he decided that it was important enough to go personally. When his ship threaded its way through the thick fringe of islands to the "Venice of the North," with its narrow, winding streets and gabled houses, Akashi still had no idea whether he had embarked on a futile journey. He booked into a hotel and wrote again, this time sending the message by hand instead of through the post. The letter came back unopened, dashing Akashi's hopes. But that evening a man with a long white beard and a tall hat called on Akashi and presented him with a sealed envelope containing a note acknowledging his messages and arranging a rendezvous for the following day. "Tomorrow morning, at 11 o'clock, stand in front of the hotel," said the letter. "At that time I will be in a carriage which will stop in front, come at once and join me. It has been snowing daily, the curtains will be down on the carriage, and we will be able to reach our meeting place unobserved by anyone." It was signed by Konni Zilliacus, a Finnish lawyer, journalist and adventurer, whose partnership with Akashi sealed a remarkable career in the cause of Finnish independence and Russian revolution.

Born in 1855, Zilliacus studied law but for a time after leaving university became a gentleman farmer. Farming proved unsuccessful and high living costly. He left Finland in the 1880s and spent many adventurous years abroad, working for a time as a journalist in Chicago and once running a railway camp in Costa Rica. He returned to Finland in 1898 and hurled himself into opposition to Tsar Nicholas' plans for russifying the country. When the newspaper he worked for was banned in 1900, he moved to Stockholm, where he published an underground paper, *Fria Ord* ("Free Words"), which he shipped clandestinely to Finland by a twenty-meter yacht built specifically for the purpose. At the Diet of Stockholm in 1903 Zilliacus demanded violence against the Russians. When the majority was against him, he set out on his own course. The Russian secret police knew all about Zilliacus, but time after time his boat gave them the slip among the thousands of islands between Sweden and Finland. He loved excitement and adventure and Akashi not only promised both but the chance to advance the cause of a free Finland.

At the appointed hour, he picked up Akashi and took him to the house of one of his Finnish associates. In the entrance hall were the document of his exile signed by the Tsar and a framed photograph of the Emperor Meiji; on another wall hung an autographed photograph of the Danish Crown Prince, brother of the Russian Dowager Empress, Marie Fedorovna.

Askashi wasted no time. At this first meeting he asked Zilliacus for information about the internal situation in Russia. "If it is a matter of politics, I will be glad to tell you what I know," Zilliacus replied cautiously. "But we cannot readily agree to your proposal about espionage, since this would be detrimental to our reputation."

Fortunately for Akashi, others had fewer qualms, and out of this meeting came not only the vital association with Zilliacus but the establishment of a contact in Swedish army headquarters, where a staff captain named Asinov served as a post office, transmitting Akashi's secret letters and funds to Japanese agents in Russia.

Early in March, Finnish dissidents in Stockholm held a mass meeting to protest against the Finnish Senate's message of loyalty to the Tsar. Afterward, the committee called on the Japanese legation in Stockholm to say that the organization was deeply sympathetic to the Japanese and wanted to help.

The Poles also began to move. In a proclamation in February, the Polish Socialist party concluded that the war would weaken Russia and that Poland would benefit from a Japanese victory. After first establishing contact with Count Makino, the Japanese minister in Vienna, Dr. Witold Narkiewicz Jodko, a member of the central committee of the Polish Socialist party, went to London to propose to Hayashi that a Polish volunteer force to fight for the Japanese should be organized among Poles living in exile, and that a major campaign should be launched in Manchuria to persuade Polish soldiers to desert to the Japanese side.

Hayashi telegraphed Tokyo, and the Japanese foreign office gave qualified support to the proposals in a report sent to Imperial General Headquarters. It instructed that the Polish plan to use volunteers should not be dismissed out of hand. The Poles were to be given discreet encouragement. Hayashi subsequently discussed the possibility of extensive sabotage on the Russian railway system with Jodko, holding out the hope of Japanese financial assistance as soon as results were achieved.

Through Hayashi, Jodko arranged to send to Tokyo James Douglas, an Englishman born in Poland, ostensibly to act as a newspaper correspondent but in fact to represent the Polish Socialist party. Douglas left immediately and arrived in Tokyo on June 7, where Hirota Koki, a future prime minister and at that time a law student at the Imperial University, was briefed to help him. His arrival was preceded by that of Roman Dmowski, leader of Polish National Democratic party, who, unlike Douglas and other members of the Polish Socialist party, saw great dangers in "any attempt being made to exploit the Poles in exciting anti-Russian diversionary activities in the West."

Two other Polish travelers, both of them from the Polish Socialist party, Josef Pilsudski and Tytus Filipowicz, who was traveling under the alias "Karski," arrived in Tokyo about this time. Formerly editor of the radical underground newspaper *Robotnik* in Lodz, Pilsudski had been arrested in 1901 and kept in a dungeon in the Warsaw citadel for twelve months. After feigning insanity, he was transferred to a hospital in St. Petersburg, where he was rescued by friends and smuggled out of the country.

Pilsudski wanted guns, and Hayashi lent his support to his mission. In a telegram to Komura he said: "Although it may not be probable that the party can accomplish a great achievement, namely crippling the power of Russia, the apprehension of its increased activity and of a rising at any moment will necessarily divert Russian attention and impede to a certain extent greater freedom of action."

Under the influence of the British government, Japan still hesitated to give material assistance to Polish and other revolutionary movements. Douglas performed useful tasks among Polish prisoners, but Pilsudski, the president-to-be, and Filipowicz, who later became Polish ambassador to the United States, left disappointed with the results of their visit.

The sinking of the Russian ships at Chemulpo and the actions at Port Arthur had given Japan what it needed most at the outset of hostilities: freedom to use the western approaches to Korea. Instead of having to rely on Fusan as a beachhead, with all the delays this would have entailed in moving forces toward the Yalu, Tokyo decided to land the Twelfth Division at Chemulpo, to consolidate its control in Seoul, and, having pushed north, to land the Imperial Guards Division and the Second Division, both encamped at Hiroshima, as soon as the ice melted in the coastal ports of northwestern Korea.

The navy had declined to commit itself to definite assurances that Japanese troops could land in safety anywhere except on the south coast of Korea. This reluctance had necessitated the drawing up of no less than four contingency plans by the Imperial General Headquarters. On February 9, however, the navy had advised that the landing at Chemulpo could proceed safely—news received with great jubilation by the army. A debate ensued whether to put one or two divisions ashore at Chemulpo. Those who knew Korea well—and the shortages of food that the Japanese might expect to find there in the closing months of winter—vigorously opposed the suggestion that two divisions (the Twelfth and the Guards) should march up the peninsula from Seoul. Other, more senior members, anxious to waste no time before engaging the Russians on the ground, were insistent that the Guards should follow the Twelfth Division as soon as the Twelfth had reached Seoul. The more aggressive strategists sought to commit the maximum number of troops in the shortest possible time.

After tempers flared, Kodama took matters into his own hands, and the Twelfth Division was ordered to advance to Pyongyang after occupying Seoul, while the Guards would remain at Hiroshima to await developments.

Chemulpo was accustomed to invasions, both Japanese and Chinese, but it had never seen an expeditionary force like the Twelfth Division, which disembarked there on February 16. The troops landed in the snow, wearing long brown blanket coats with sheepskin collars, and carrying blue cloaks, red blankets, knapsacks, haversacks, water bottles, baskets for cooked rice, cooking pots, rifles, pouches, bayonets, and special boxes of "Russian invasion pills" containing creosote to cure intestinal troubles. "The cavalry horses are overloaded in proportion," commented a British military observer for *The Times.*

Overloaded the troops may have been, but the landing in a port where there is a twenty-foot difference between high and low tides was a model of military efficiency. To facilitate the operation, the division came equipped with four landing stages, each about 150 yards long, and a plank roadway ten feet wide, supported by sampans that rested on the mud at low tide and floated at high tide. Steam launches towed groups of sampans to the stages.

Troops, light two-wheeled baggage carts, horses, and equipment came ashore quickly and without incident.

The Japanese military presence in Seoul quickly brought about the first diplomatic victory of the war. On February 25 Japan established a protectorate over the peninsula. Korea agreed to accept Japanese "advice" in administrative matters in exchange for Japanese guarantees of independence and territorial integrity.

While Imperial General Headquarters in Japan was waiting for the thaw to facilitate the landing of substantial reinforcements along the coast, sixty-year-old General Kuroki Tametomo, of the Satsuma clan, was appointed to take command of the First Army. Westerners who knew him well described him as a charming-looking man, with a gentle and sympathetic smile and an addiction to cigars. The Japanese were franker. "Rude and simple," was one description. During the Sino-Japanese War he commanded the élite Sixth Division, which was recruited from Kagoshima and other parts of southern Kyushu—the Saigo country. An historian, he was regarded as bookish and not likely to take risks.

As Togo led his fleet to its second and third attacks at Port Arthur, and the Twelfth Division held the country against the remote threat of a Russian attack from the north, the Guards Division disembarked at Chenampo, about twenty miles up the Pyongyang inlet, between March 14 and March 18. Kuroki arrived with his staff on March 21, and on the same day steam launches began to land supplies just below Pyongyang. As the supply columns began their march north to the Yalu, the first breath of spring began to stir the poplars along the narrow track. Its ungraveled surface turned into a bog and melted the ice on the unbridged streams.

Pontoon trains came on the backs of Japanese ponies. Every river and stream had been measured by Japanese intelligence. Nothing was left to chance. All three divisions of the First Army—the Second, the Twelfth, and the Guards—were now ashore and plentifully supplied with uniformed, but unarmed, coolies to act as porters. Working three to a cart, one in the shafts and two pushing, they slipped and grunted and sweated their way to the war. Torrential rain in the first part of April greatly hampered their task, as floods destroyed one bridge built by Japanese engineers over the Tatong River and threatened another.

For the artillery the going was always heavy. Six ponies dragged each gun, but the Japanese were poor horsemen and casualties were numerous. The troops flogged the horses when the guns bogged or overturned. Locally recruited Korean porters were the toughest and most useful of all. With bundles weighing fifty to sixty pounds attached to their A-frames, they marched in platoons, the leader with a flag stuck in his pack setting the pace, which often averaged, despite the conditions, nearly three miles an hour.

A small force of cavalry imaginatively used could have delayed the Japanese at Pyongyang or even upset the landing at Chenampo, but the Russians made only two weak and ineffective attempts.

Although the war was little more than a month old, and the action so far had been confined almost exclusively to the Port Arthur blockade and the landing in Korea, Tokyo had already reached important conclusions. Bombardment alone was not enough to reduce Port Arthur: it would have to be blockaded by sea and contained by land. Kuroki had to press on as rapidly as possible to the Yalu River and attack the Russian forces there, while the Second Army under General Oku landed in the vicinity of Dalny and cut off land communications with Port Arthur.

From Tokyo disgruntled correspondents and military observers criticized Kuroki's progress north as far too slow. It was, on the contrary, accomplished with quite astonishing speed. Both the troops and their hand-drawn transports sometimes covered twenty-five miles in a day.

Again, Japan derived full benefit from its intelligence services in Manchuria. Basing its calculations on the problems of supply, Japanese Imperial General Headquarters estimated that the Russians would need one handcart to maintain ten men in the field on the Yalu, 120 miles across the mountains from Liaoyang, and that nothing like a sufficient supply establishment had been assembled. Kuroki, headquarters concluded, would meet the Russians in his first engagement with the inestimable advantage of heavy numerical superiority.

Few military observers believed that Kuroki's advance would tempt General Kuropatkin, who had been appointed commander of the Russian forces, into committing a large force so far away from his own main base at Liaoyang so early in the war, especially since Dalny and Port Arthur were clearly vulnerable. With this assessment, Kuropatkin himself was in full agreement. On a salary of 100,000 roubles a month, a forage allowance for twelve riding and eighteen carriage horses, and with the gift of a warhorse from the city of Moscow, he traveled east by train to take up his command. At all stops he expressed public confidence in early victory—a position that his own attempt to prevent the war, and his private views, so clearly belied. For the early months of the war, he was convinced that the only possible course was retreat. He sensed that the great wave of popularity with which he was accompanied to the war would not last very long. "I am carried in people's arms, I am given warhorses, I am offered all sorts of presents, I have to listen to speeches of welcome, I am considered almost the savior of the country," he said to Count Kokovtsov, who had taken over the finance ministry after the death of Pleske.

And so it will continue until I reach the troops; my star will go higher and higher. Then, when I reach my destination, issue orders to retreat to the north and withdraw my troops pending the arrival of reinforcements from Russia, the same papers which are now singing my praises will wonder why I am not busy beating the "macques." My star will fall lower and lower, and when I suffer small but inevitable defeats, it will continue to descend until it reaches the horizon. Here is where I want you to assist me, for here it is that I shall begin an offensive in which I shall mercilessly beat the Japanese.

Kuropatkin had reckoned without Viceroy Alexeiev, who, swayed by the highly optimistic reports of General Vogak and others, sought immediate victory, not strategic retreat. Where Kuropatkin was emphatic that no operations should be undertaken without an assured numerical majority and that nothing, certainly, should take place before August, when he hoped that sufficient reinforcements and supplies would be available, Alexeiev wanted decisive action at the beachheads or, next best, at the gateway to Manchuria, the magnificient Yalu River, which, in its lower reaches, flows between banks more than three miles apart to empty into the Yellow Sea.

Kuropatkin reached Liaoyang on March 28 and established his headquarters there in a train. Any doubts about the difficulties that he had foreseen in organizing his command were now reinforced a thousandfold. The officers being sent to join him were second-raters, the troops untrained. Liaoyang, which was to become the concentration center for his forces, was 200 miles north of Port Arthur and 120 miles from the Yalu, from which it was separated by a massive mountain range. Vladivostok was another 470 miles away to the northeast. His sixty-eight battalions of field troops, 120 guns, twelve horse artillery guns, sixteen mountain guns, and thirty-five squadrons of Cossacks were scattered from Port Arthur northward. The command was equally diffuse. Kuropatkin himself had charge of the Manchurian Army. General Stoessel in Port Arthur reported both to Alexeiev and to Kuropatkin. General Linievitch directed the Ussuri Corps on China's eastern border under a separate command.

Immediate disagreement broke out between Kuropatkin, on the one hand, and Alexeiev and Stoessel, on the other, over the priorities in men and matériel that ought to go to Port Arthur. Kuropatkin believed that four divisions were more than enough until August when he hoped to have worthwhile reinforcements from Europe. Alexeiev and Stoessel thought otherwise. Not quite facetiously, Witte had advised Kuropatkin to arrest Alexeiev as soon as he arrived in the Far East and to send him back to St. Petersburg. The advice sounded frivolous, but, as Kuropatkin now began to appreciate, it was wise, if obviously impracticable.

Essentially, the task now confronting Kuropatkin was similar to the one that was to confront the United States' General Walton Walker when he fought to defend the Naktong River line against North Korean attacks in the summer of 1950 while General Douglas MacArthur prepared to launch his thrust against the enemy's main line of communications with an amphibious landing at Inchon. Kuropatkin had to fight for time while reinforcements were coming. Unlike Walker, however, Kuropatkin lacked both mobility (except along the railway) and subordinates responsive to his orders. No doubt Walker had his difficulties with MacArthur, but the latter was a great soldier: Alexeiev was a mediocrity. Nor was Kuropatkin a Walker. Now fifty-six, the Russian had not commanded forces in the field since Plevna.

The tactics for a delaying action on and beyond the Yalu were nevertheless self-evident. The Yalu itself was a formidable barrier. In its upper reaches, it flowed swiftly and darkly through deep gorges and dense rain forest. It seemed impossible for Kuroki to force a crossing here. The lower reaches of the river were easier, but the current was strong and the river wide. There were no bridges.

When war broke out the Russian forces in the general region of the Yalu consisted of two infantry battalions, three squadrons of Cossacks, and twenty-two guns. These were immediately reinforced by the understrength Third Siberian Rifle Brigade of eight battalions and twenty-four guns. By the time Kuroki's advance guard was approaching the river, the Russian force had grown to twenty-one battalions of infantry, ten batteries of artillery, and sixteen squadrons of Cossacks. Since there were possible crossing places over a distance of twenty-five miles, the Russian Eastern Detachment, as the Yalu force was now known, was spread thinly. It was nonetheless adequate enough for the sort of delaying operation Kuropatkin had in mind.

Kuropatkin telegraphed Major-General Kashtalinski, who led the Eastern Detachment, on April 18 and gave details of the Japanese force advancing on the town of Wiju on the southern bank of the Yalu. His orders called for avoidance of any decisive engagement against superior forces. Across the miles of mountain passes and defiles separating the Yalu from Liaoyang there were months' worth of ambush sites where a company of men could hold up a regiment—and a regiment, an army. This was the role Kuropatkin contemplated for the Eastern Detachment.

Kuroki's plans had been drawn up in Tokyo and now the Imperial General Headquarters urged him not to tarry. The naval situation had moved substantially to Japan's advantage. The Russian forces in Vladivostok put to sea occasionally but quickly returned to base when they sighted a Japanese force. The command of the Yellow Sea had passed to Togo, who was planning to attack the Russians in Port Arthur in the last week of March or the first week in April, at the latest, thus making it impossible for the Russians to continue operations beyond the harbor.

Japanese intelligence reports suggested that the Russians were worried about the possibility of a landing in the Kaiping–Newchwang area. This was strategically tempting but much too hazardous for the Japanese to contemplate. The two towns were at the head of the Gulf of Chih-li. Kaiping was on the railway, about 125 miles north of Port Arthur, and a landing here could have isolated the Russian garrison at one stroke. To reach the landing zone, however, meant traversing the strait between the Shantung and Kwantung peninsulas and exposing the transports to the possibility of Russian naval attack. The news that the Russians feared an attack here had exploitable value, however, and the navy was ordered to bombard the coast and make a feint landing while the Second Army came ashore near Dalny. It was clearly important that Kuroki should move across the Yalu. Unless the Second Army were to be exposed to undue hazard from the Russian forces at Liaoyang, Kuroki's attack had to be of such weight as to command the most urgent attention of Kuropatkin and his staff. Kodama insisted that there should be no half-measures, and his slogan of "absolutely winning the initial battles of the war" was drilled into every commander.

The risks were carefully weighed. If the intelligence reports were correct, the Russians now had the equivalent of nearly five divisions in the plains around Liaoyang. To move these forces into action against the Japanese landing at Dalny would take a minimum of thirteen days. If everything went according to plan and the Second Army disembarked within the scheduled eight days, it would have five days in which to prepare for action against a force potentially bigger than itself.

Weather was an unpredictable factor that might easily play into Kuropatkin's hands, and rain, in particular, could upset Kuroki's plans. More than ever, therefore, it was necessary for Kuroki to advance with all speed, defeat the Russians on the Yalu, move into Manchuria, and push on in the direction of Feng-huang-cheng, a road junction forty miles beyond the river. A threat here would at least make Kuropatkin think twice before taking action against the Second Army when it was landing at Dalny.

On April 15, Imperial General Headquarters asked Kuroki when he expected to cross the river. He replied on the following day that it was probable that the crossing could be made by May 2. Next day he was instructed to speed up his plans and to cross the Yalu on April 30.

The Second Army was now at sea. General Oku Yasukata, its commander, and Major-General Iguchi of Imperial General Headquarters, who was accompanying him, met Togo on April 25 to coordinate their plans and came to the conclusion that because of landing problems, they could not meet the deadline for a landing on May 1 or May 2, and that the transports should not sail for the landing before May 3.

An eleventh-hour message to Kuroki to delay his own attack across the river until dawn on May 3 drew the answer that since all preparations had been made it was now too late to change the date of the attack. The Russians were strengthening their defenses, the weather was fine, and any delay would be to Kuroki's disadvantage.

Both to the Tsar and to the forces under his command, Kuropatkin continued to emphasize the need for fighting a defensive war in the early stages. In a report to the Throne acknowledging his appointment, he had written:

> In the first phase of the campaign, our main object should be to prevent the destruction of our forces in detail. The apparent importance of any single locality or position, fortresses excepted, should not lead us into the great error of holding it in insufficient force which will bring about the very result we are so anxious to prevent. While gradually growing in numbers and preparing to take the offensive, we should only move when sufficiently strong and when supplied with everything necessary for an uninterrupted advance lasting over a fairly long period.

On April 15 he issued a memorandum to the army that set out similar views, and on April 25 he warned Lieutenant General M. I. Zasulitch, who had arrived from Warsaw to take command of the Eastern Detatchment, that he was to avoid an unequal combat with superior numbers, retiring slowly and keeping in touch with the enemy. On the same day Lieutenant-General Vladimir V. Sakharov, Kuropatkin's chief of staff, repeated the warning: Zasulitch was "to determine the Japanese form, dispositions, and line of march and to retreat as slowly as possible before retreating again."

The orders were precise enough. But Zasulitch, younger brother of Vera Zasulitch, who was soon to be in touch with Colonel Akashi's spy ring in Europe, scoffed at Kuropatkin's suggestion that the Japanese were to be regarded as the equals of European troops. He had come direct from Warsaw, filled with prejudice and contempt for his enemies.

Chances had been lost before he took command. General Mishchenko's Cossacks had made a couple of harassing raids against the northward march of the First Army at Pakchon, midway between Pyongyang and the Yalu, on March 8. Twenty days later, with a larger body of cavalry, the Cossacks attacked again but were driven off with minor losses. The forces committed were inadequate for the task and bound to fail. Nevertheless, the psychological effect on the Russians was serious. They were now much too anxious to put the Yalu between themselves and the understrength Japanese advance guard. They abandoned the town of Wiju on the south bank of the Yalu, destroyed all their installations there, and withdrew from Korean soil, concentrating their forces on the right bank of the Yalu with the intention of making use of the natural obstacle caused by the river to bar further Japanese advance.

Much reduced in size by transport difficulties and the state of the roads, the Japanese advance guard, which had started out as a full brigade, began to dribble into Wiju on April 8. Five vital days passed without serious incident before it had concentrated there. It posed no threat to the Russians and was itself highly vulnerable. But the Russians were not disposed to move.

Weather favored the Japanese. The ice on the Yalu broke just before their advance guard reached Wiju. Though the Russians had plenty of boats, there was no bridge across the river, so that only an amphibious assault could have dislodged the Japanese on the south shore. Kashtalinski preferred to err on the side of caution rather than take even minor risks against Kuroki's understrength and unsupported advance guard.

Lacking any supporting force, Major-General Asada's advance guard would have been easily destroyed. Its loss would have set back the carefully prepared Tokyo plans by weeks, not only so far as the First Army was concerned, but also the landing of the Second Army. Kuropatkin would have even bought some of the time he so urgently needed. "Fortune was in a mood to be wooed," wrote Sir Ian Hamilton. "It was not to be."

The Japanese were helped now and later by the general contempt in which the Russians held their enemies, by the quality of the Russian forces in the field, and by the judgment of one of the German military attachés at Mukden that Kuroki's forces would halt at the Yalu. Alexeiev and his staff were much impressed by this argument. Among them the war was simply not being taken very seriously. Major J. M. Home, a British army observer with the Russian forces, reported from Liaoyang that the general feeling even among foreign military observers there was that the war would be a mere "promenade" for the Russians. The railway was working very slowly, but there was no feeling of urgency about moving up new units and no ammunition columns had arrived at Liaoyang.

When General Zasulitch arrived to take command, the Eastern Detachment numbered about 26,000 effectives. These he deployed on April 26. In what he considered to be the critical area between Antung and Chiu-lien-cheng, a distance of about six miles, he had two forces. One consisted of three battalions, two artillery batteries, a machinegun company, and mounted scouts—in all, 2,580 riflemen, 400 scouts, sixteen field guns, and eight machineguns. The second force was larger but it lacked machineguns. It had 5,200 riflemen, 240 scouts, and sixteen field pieces. Zasulitch's reserve was at Tien-tzu, about four miles from Antung on the Feng-huang-cheng road, deep in the Manchurian mountains. It consisted of 5,000 rifle-men and sixteen guns.

To prevent Kuroki from attempting to outflank him on the left, Zasulitch posted two regiments, with a mountain battery of twelve guns, forty miles up river. Watching the coast from the mouth of the Yalu to Ta-ku-shan was General Mishchenko's Cossack Brigade, reinforced by an East Siberian Rifle Regiment, supported by eight field and six horse artillery guns. The front covered 172 miles and, with the forces available, could not have been expected to hold out at any point against the concentrated attack of the three Japanese divisions. To Kuropatkin this was the essential fact. Alex-eiev, who was also on the end of the telegraph line to Zasulitch, saw the situation differently. He believed the line could be held, and Zasulitch himself was not a man to cut and run before these "macaoes."

From the gently rounded hills overlooking the Yalu there was little to show that the Japanese were preparing for an early attack. Their prepara-tions were conducted with the strictest of military discipline and remarkable ingenuity. No Japanese soldier ever appeared on the skyline. Nothing was attempted by daylight that could be more secretly performed by night. To cover the mile and a quarter of road leading from Wiju to the Yalu, Kuroki planted an avenue of full-sized fir trees. Single trees and even clumps of trees were moved backward or forward as the situation demanded and screens of millet were built to cover the movement of all troops and supplies. The puzzled Russians peering across the river with their binoculars were never quite sure whether what they saw today had been there yesterday.

Unlike the Japanese, the Russians made no attempt to conceal their presence or their activities. Troops wandered about on the skyline, their white coats visible for miles. Even without their spies and the activities of their reconnaissance patrols across the river, the Japanese would have had little difficulty in assessing the approximate strength of the Russians or the whereabouts of their positions.

A road of sorts linked Antung, about eight miles down river from Wiju on the opposite bank, with Chiu-lien-cheng, which was directly opposite. Any movement of troops here was within full view of the Japanese observa-tion posts on the southern bank. The roads leading back from Antung and Chiu-lien-cheng toward Feng-huang-cheng converged at a point about five miles from Antung. Within this triangle there were only tracks. With most of the cavalry committed to the flanks and with the heaviest concentration of forces deployed in fixed positions or held in reserve with the intention of reinforcing Antung, Zasulitch had deprived himself of any real means of maneuver.

Chiu-lien-cheng and Wiju were three-and-a-half miles apart across the

Yalu and the Ai rivers. Apart from flash flooding during storms—Kuroki's abiding fear—the Korean rivers usually fill only with the early summer rains. Since the rains were still to fall, the river bed was now an immense sandy plain broken into islands by the numerous branches of the two rivers. On three of these islands, Kyuri, Oseki, and Kintei,* all of which were several miles long, the Russians held outposts. Also in their hands was a magnificent rocky feature known as Tiger Hill, near the confluence of the two rivers and a mile or two above Chiu-lien-cheng and Wiju. From its summit the Russian observers had an uninterrupted view for thousands of yards along the river front. They should have seen everything; in fact, they saw almost nothing.

Japanese reconnaissance units disguised as Korean fishermen cruised along the left bank of the Yalu, noting Russian outposts on the islands, taking the depths, and occasionally selling fish to the Russian troops. Their task was hazardous but highly necessary. "We thought at first that the reconnaissance would have been easy, as we had crossed the river at the same place in 1894," a Japanese staff officer told military observers. "But the changes had been too great. Our carefully prepared map was useless. Channels had changed. Spots where fords had existed required bridging, and points out of range of the right bank were now within range of it, so our labor and money had been wasted."

This threw into disarray some of the best laid Japanese engineering plans, and a bitter argument took place among Kuroki's staff officers about the feasibility of crossing the river. Kuroki's force did not have enough bridging material for the task ahead. In their hurry to evacuate Yong-em-po, however, the Russian timber company workers had left behind a number of anvils and forges. Japanese armorers and blacksmiths went to work and by April 25 the shortages had been overcome. There still remained the problem of reconnoitering the right bank of the Yalu, a task that necessitated occupation of the islands of Kyuri, Oseki, and Kintei, the stepping-stones that Kuroki intended to use on May 1 for his march into Manchuria.

The first real land fighting of the war occurred on the night of April 25–26. The Japanese Guard Division seized Kyuri Island about two miles east of Tiger Hill, and the Second Division took Kintei Island, which stretched for eight miles from near Tiger Hill almost to Antung. With the loss of the two islands, the Russian outpost also fell back from Tiger Hill.

Japanese reconnaissance units disguised as Korean fishermen continued

---

*These are Japanese names. For convenience in checking with English and American sources, English and Japanese names have been used often instead of Korean and Chinese names.

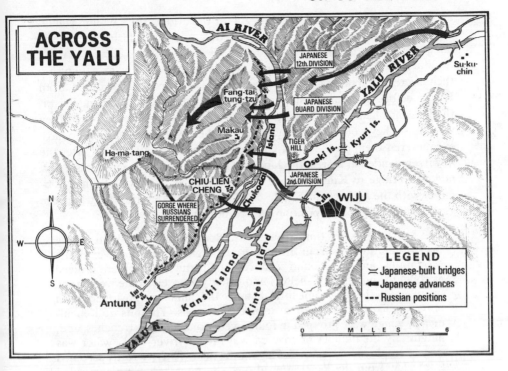

ACROSS THE YALU

AI RIVER

JAPANESE 12th DIVISION

YALU RIVER

Su-ku-chin

Fang-tai-tung-tzu

JAPANESE GUARD DIVISION

Makau

Kyuri Is.

TIGER HILL

Oseki Is.

Ha-ma-tang

CHIU-LIEN CHENG

JAPANESE 2nd DIVISION

WIJU

GORGE WHERE RUSSIANS SURRENDERED

Chukodai

Antung

Kanshi Island

Kintei Island

YALU R.

LEGEND

Japanese-built bridges
Japanese advances
Russian positions

0   MILES   6

their operations. Other Japanese patrols stripped off their clothes and swam through the icy water to the far bank, returning with valuable information about the extent and disposition of the Russian forces. So well did they do their work that they overestimated the Russian numbers by only a thousand and underestimated their guns by two.

The Japanese capacity for camouflage, concealment, and deception reached remarkable peaks during the next few days. In full view of the Russian observers on the hills bordering the right bank of the Yalu, they now began to build a long trestle bridge across the stream. From two positions the Russian artillery opened fire on the bridge. They were to maintain this fire for four days until their guns were knocked out. While the Russians were thus engaged, the Japanese built nine other smaller bridges ready to be rushed into position at the last moment across narrower parts of the streams. Not a man, not a round of ammunition, crossed the main bridge, nor was there any intention that it should be used for the main assault. At a time when surprise in tactical maneuver was still considered unmilitary, or at least unsporting, Kuroki threw his old-fashioned enemy across the river into utter confusion. As for the bridge, the Russians squandered their ammunition on it, and succeeded only in disclosing the whereabouts of the batteries.

While the Russians were blazing away, the Japanese were hauling up their secret weapons—4.7-inch howitzers. These had been bought from Krupp before the war and shipped in the utmost secrecy to Japan. Even if the Russians had been aware that they were in Japanese hands—and they were not—they would not have expected in their wildest nightmares to have encountered them on the Yalu. On the night of April 29, a week after the howitzers landed in Korea, the Japanese gunners moved them across a new pontoon bridge to Kintei Island. Captain Vincent, a British military observer with the Japanese forces, described the elaborate care with which the guns were brought into position and camouflaged:

> The heavy baulks of timber which are floated down the Yalu during the summer months from the wild forest regions near the Ever White Mountains, and were found scattered about the islands, were utilized as roofs for bombproof shelters and other purposes. Some were stuck up on end in the sand some little distance in front of the howitzers, with branches fixed between them to act as screens. The pits and epaulments, which were grouped in fours, were connected by trenches, and, judging by the number of covered ways to the river bank, water was largely employed as a means of laying the dust. Thus perfectly screened from view from the Russian positions, the howitzers were connected by telephone with two observation stations on the high ground, some three or four thousand yards in rear . . .

The Japanese artillery was fretting to go into action. Everywhere along the front the Russians provided them with tempting targets. Troops bunched together on the crest of the hills on the far side of the river, apparently absorbed by what might lie behind the changing landscape on the Korean bank. The Cossacks watered their horses at the banks of the Yalu in full view, as if they had no care in the world. In the evening the Russian bands played and the sounds of martial music drifted across the river.

Unlike some of his now observant and seriously alarmed subordinates, General Zasulitch was puzzled but complacent. To coincide with the capture of the islands, Kuroki on April 25 had sought the assistance of the navy to create a further diversion in the lower reaches of the river. A small naval force entered the Yalu and engaged scattered bands of Cossacks on the right bank. Next day the gunboats were followed by a large number of junks loaded with timber. At Liaoyang, the feeling persisted that Kuroki's next move would be delayed until the Second Army had landed at Newchwang, or between the mouth of the Yalu and Ta-ku-shan. General Zasulitch shared this opinion but was now more than ever convinced that Kuroki would seek to cross the river at Antung.

Kuroki had altogether different plans. Zasulitch was strong around Antung and weak beyond Tiger Hill. The opportunity clearly existed for a flanking movement around the Russian left. Eight miles up stream from Tiger Hill the river was found to be suitable for a combined bridge–ford operation. A bridge here offered much better tactical opportunities than the bridge near Wiju. Since it could be built on the left bank out of effective range of rifle fire from the right bank, one division could be used for a flanking movement here if only the country on the far side of the river proved somewhat less formidable than the maps suggested. Kuroki had wrestled with this problem all the way from Tokyo. There was only one way to resolve it—by reconnaissance.

On April 26 while the navy was active at Antung, a detachment of the Twelfth Division crossed the river from Su-ku-chin, occupied Anping on the far bank, and immediately sent patrols into the hills. Seeing his lines of communication with Zasulitch's main force threatened, the commander of the Russian cavalry detachment upstream advised Kuropatkin that he could not both bar the alternative road to Liaoyang and maintain contact with the Eastern Detachment. Kuropatkin, who had repeated his orders to General Zasulitch not to stand and fight but merely to delay, replied that the preservation of the lines of communication had the highest priority.

The alarm bells were beginning to ring along the Russian positions on the Yalu, though not for General Zasulitch. General Trusov, holding the left flank of the main Russian position, could see how events were moving. At 11 P.M. on April 26 he reported to General Zasulitch: "The enemy is about to force the passage in superior strength by means of an enveloping movement against my front and left flank. I desire either reinforcements or permission to retire at the proper time."

"His Majesty has made me a member of the Order of St. George," General Zasulitch replied, "and I do not retreat." Nor was he prepared to draw on his reserves.

At dawn the next morning there was the usual mist. It cleared early. At 3 A.M. the Japanese Twelfth Division, equipped only with mountain guns, had crossed the Yalu at Su-ku-chin to cover the passage of the main force on the following night. The outnumbered Russian forces on the opposite side of the river fell back with its infantry and artillery on the main Russian line of defenses along the Ai, while the cavalry went off to the extreme left flank. By noon the Twelfth Division, following tracks pointed out by Chinese farmers and identified by previous reconnaissance, was advancing in three columns through the rugged hills between the Yalu and the Ai, threatening the Russian positions to the rear of Tiger Hill. Still convinced that the movement of the Twelfth Division was a feint, General Zasulitch sent only one additional battalion and four guns to reinforce the Russian positions here.

At 4 A.M. the Guards' divisional artillery reported that it was in position south of a bridge leading to Kyuri Island and on a hill north of Wiju. Six batteries of the Second Division artillery were also in position among the trees on Kintei Island, west of newly erected bridges, while on their right and to the rear were the five treasured batteries of howitzers. Hamilton recognized "the very trees that had been shifted about as unconcernedly as a gardener transplants a rose bush" and confessed that he was "fairly surprised."

The Russians invited destruction. David Fraser of *The Times* reported that no precautions of any kind were taken to conceal the Russian guns, "the spokes of their wheels, the gunners and their every movement being plainly discernable with glasses from the Korean bank."

Around 10 A.M. the Russians opened fire on two boatloads of Japanese engineers in the main stream of the Yalu opposite Chukodai Island. Instantly seventy-two guns and twenty howitzers were at them. Authorities on military science at this time were generally agreed that an artillery preparation before an infantry attack was ineffective. Until the advent of the quick-firing, breech-loading gun, they believed too much time was wasted in relaying the gun so that it could be brought to bear on its target quickly and accurately.

The well-trained Japanese gunners quickly dispelled some of these notions. They were invisible to the Russians on the opposite bank, while the Russians were not only everywhere conspicuous but vulnerable, also. Within thirty minutes their guns had been silenced.

An hour after the Japanese bombardment had begun, the Russians brought a fresh battery into action on a knoll east of Makau. Within two or three minutes the Guards' artillery on Kyuri Island had knocked it out. "Thus," wrote Ian Hamilton, "in an easy triumph ended the anxiously anticipated artillery duel." He thought it was probably the last of its sort that would ever take place!

The Russians had doubted the Japanese capacity even to move field guns across the Korean roads in the spring thaw. When the howitzers opened up, the Russians simply could not believe at first what they were seeing. They had no idea where the fire was coming from. The trees and the carefully watered sand gave no hint of the whereabouts of the guns. The Russian commanding officer reported that the fire was "unbearable," and told General Kashtalinski that he "could not guarantee the quiet withdrawal of his men from the trenches if fire was specifically directed upon them the following day."

No less serious than the effectiveness of the Japanese artillery was the activity of the three columns of the Twelfth Division. After the easy pre-dawn crossing of the Yalu at Su-ku-chin, the division's left hook had taken it into a region of high hills and deep ravines. Only the Fourth Regiment, which followed the downstream course of the river toward Tiger Hill, had easy going, but all advanced with considerable speed. To their astonishment, the Japanese found that no one tried to bar their way. The Russians had pulled out.

That evening Kashtalinski put the situation in blunt terms for General Zasulitch.

It is to be presumed that their batteries will advance into the islands tonight and that they will then be able to deliver an effective fire on our trenches tomorrow. In agreement with one of the commanders of sections in the line of defense, I think we ought to occupy this evening, while there is yet time, the hills behind Chiu-lien-cheng, leaving on the present line of defense our outposts, which should retire at daybreak. I abstain from any comments on the strategical situation, which is better known to Your Excellency than to me. The 2/6 East Siberian Artillery has had heavy losses. . . . It was silenced in sixteen minutes.

During the evening, Zasulitch's chief staff officer, who had come under the bombardment in the morning, returned to headquarters to support Kashtalinski's argument. Not only Kashtalinski but every senior officer on the ground believed that the time had come to pull back to the second line of defenses. Zasulitch was in no mood to listen. The temporary withdrawal of two Guards battalions and a battery of artillery from Tiger Hill on April 29 had prompted him to send a message, which had been relayed to the Tsar in St. Petersburg, that the Japanese had been driven back in disorder. He looked for victory, not withdrawal.

"The general commanding the detachment forbids the troops to abandon their positions on any pretext whatsoever," he replied to Kashtalinski. The only doubts he had were about the morale of his officers and troops.

It was as well for Zasulitch's peace of mind that he could not see, nor was he given any hint of, the scene that began to unfold on the Yalu as dusk closed in. "The whole army was moving forward along the little roadways and paths from village to village, across the islands, wading the smallest streams and getting up to the middle in mud, crossing the largest streams by boat or bridges hastily pushed together after dark," wrote *Daily Chronicle* war correspondent Thomas Cowen. Before midnight the Japanese army was over the river and moving silently into position for a dawn attack.

This was a classic approach march. Kuroki, fearing that the Russians would use searchlights on likely crossing points and would there concentrate massive fire, did not want to be caught in midstream at midnight. But there were no searchlights and no outposts to give the alarm. He was helped by the mist that covered the river, but he remained deeply concerned about the rain clouds hiding the moon. A flash flood would have spelled disaster for his plans. But nothing went wrong. Kuroki put his army across the Yalu on this critical night with the loss of only a single man.

Though a report came in around 3 A.M. that outposts had heard the sound of wheels on the islands and of guns crossing bridges, Zasulitch still refused to believe that the Japanese attack was imminent. Apart from a machinegun company that he added to General Kashtalinski's detachment, he made no move to shift forces from Antung, or Tien-tzu, where he was holding his reserves.

Kashtalinski's men peered uneasily into the fog as daylight came, their fears fed by the muffled sounds that had come to them during the night. With them, on the top of the highest hill overlooking the Yalu, was General Zasulitch himself. As dawn approached, he could detect the shape of the mist-enshrouded islands and the rugged outline of Tiger Hill. No sign of life seemed to exist.

The fog lifted about 5 A.M. The Russians rubbed their eyes and found that from opposite Chiu-lien-cheng to above San-lan-kou, a semicircle covering a distance of about six miles, they were confronted by the infantry of the entire First Army. All that separated them from the Japanese now were the shallow and fordable waters of the last remaining channel of the River Ai. The rainclouds had vanished.

On the river line the Japanese got their baptism of fire. "About 5 A.M. the sky was beginning to whiten," wrote Lieutenant Tamon Jiro, a Japanese platoon commander:

> The morning had come. From our front, three or four troops, in white singlets and underdrawers, came returning with a dead comrade on their shoulders. From his shoulders to his chest he was covered in blood and his pale face was hanging limply in front. He was our first casualty. The troops stared at the courageous and proud-looking faces of the scouts. Inwardly, I felt the horror of death as I saw the blood on the dead officer. When I told the troops, "We're all going to be like this," they smiled grimly.

The lifting of the fog was the signal for the Japanese howitzers to begin their work. Their target once again was the Russian artillery positions beyond the Ai. The Japanese gunners pounded the Russian positions, but from the Russian guns, under orders from Kashtalinski not to reveal themselves, there was no reply. "When the enemy fires very heavily, it is unpleasant," said a Japanese staff officer to Hamilton, who was watching the battle from Kuroki's headquarters on a hill about a mile north of Wiju. "When he does not fire at all, it is terrible."

Many at Kuroki's headquarters were afraid that the Russians had taken note of the bombardment on the previous day and had withdrawn their artillery beyond range of the howitzers. The silence, Hamilton noted, was very trying. "Then at last six guns of the Russian battery near Makau fired a few rounds. At this the whole of the attacking force breathed more freely and stepped forward with gay alacrity. The artillery of the Guards was upon the battery like a cat springing upon a mouse and in two or three minutes had reduced it to silence."

No man stepped more gaily than Lance-Corporal Ohashi Keikichi, of the Seventh Company, Third Regiment of the Guards, who was ordered to strip off and wade across the Ai to test its depth. He left his uniform with the rest of his platoon, waded across the river without difficulty, and was immediately followed by the rest of the regiment. In the excitement, Ohashi's clothes were left behind, and he spent the day naked, performing, according to the folk stories of the time, all sorts of legendary feats in the battle that followed.

Kuroki had planned to continue his encircling movement with the Twelfth Division, pushing it across the Ai at a point where little opposition was expected, before throwing the Second Division and the Guards into action. With the Russian artillery so easily and so quickly silenced, however, he decided now to throw all three divisions into a simultaneous assault.

About an hour had passed since the bombardment began. Now the white sands of the Ai changed color as thousands of blue-clad Japanese infantry headed for the river. The fords available for the Twelfth Division were few in number and instead of approaching together in extended line, the troops advanced in column, one after the other, so as to present the smallest possible target. Still, no shot came from the Russian trenches until the Japanese reached the Ai.

Trained, as much as they were trained at all, to fire in volleys, the Russian infantrymen opened fire from the trenches as the first Japanese troops entered the water. It was waist high, and in some places even higher. Opposition to the Twelfth Division was light, but the Second, which was to play a major part in the capture of Chiu-lien-cheng, came under heavy fire and was for a time disorganized.

If the Russian artillery had been left with any breath in its body, Kuroki might have been thwarted even then. But the Russian guns were silent, and the infantry made the far shore and the safety of the dead angle of the bank.

They drove the Russians from their trenches, exposing them to heavy artillery fire when they attempted to withdraw to the second line of defenses in the hills.

With blind courage the Sixth Company of the Twelfth East Siberian Rifle Regiment fixed bayonets nearly half a mile from the Japanese and began a counterattack that was cut to pieces. This attempt to cover the withdrawal served merely to open up new exploitable opportunities for the Second Division. Colonel Tsibulski, who had made his concern known the previous evening, now saw his predictions coming true. He was in immediate danger of being surrounded. As early as 8:30 A.M. General Kashtalinski ordered him to withdraw. On Kashtalinski's left the position was even more critical. Lacking orders and any sort of understanding of what General Zasulitch had in mind, Colonel Gromov, with the Second East Siberian Regiment, found himself overextended and trying to hold a crumbling wall against an avalanche of troops. Troops on the right flank of the Japanese Twelfth Division had found the waters of the Ai deep and difficult after their hard forced march from Anping, and it was a bedraggled force that climbed the hills at Fang-tai-tung-tzu well behind the rest of the assault force. Its appearance was enough, however, to spread panic in the Russian ranks, two miles away to the northwest on a wide curve of the Ai. About the same time, Colonel Gromov also decided that further resistance was out of the question for the two battalions of the Twenty-second Regiment, which also began to pull out.

Of these developments General Kashtalinski was unaware. The reverses on the right were painfully obvious, but while his left flank remained firm, the prospect of withdrawing his main force behind a small river, the Han-tu-ho-tzu, which crossed the line of his withdrawal about three miles along the road to Ha-ma-tang and there to continue the delaying action on the second line of defenses, seemed reasonably bright. But the abrupt withdrawal of the Twenty-second Regiment opened up the valley of the Ai to easy Japanese advance, which threatened to cut off the ultimate line of retreat along the road to Feng-huang-cheng. Not only Colonel Gromov and General Kashtalinski were now in danger but also the forces that General Zasulitch had posted at Antung and his reserves at Tien-tzu.

Still confident that Colonel Gromov was holding his own to the north, Kashtalinski made his stand on the Han-tu-ho-tzu and was pleased that the situation was as well in hand as might be expected. Then came the dismal news that Colonel Gromov had been routed and that the Japanese Twelfth Division was marching west.

Kashtalinski went by horseback to see for himself and found disaster. He immediately ordered the withdrawal of the force on the Han-tu-ho-tzu and sent one fleeing company of Colonel Gromov's Twenty-second Regiment to take up a new position on the hills to the north of Ha-ma-tang. He detached two battalions of the Eleventh East Siberian Rifle Regiment, which General Zasulitch had sent him from the reserve, and deployed them on Hill 570, a mile to the east of the village, the highest feature near Ha-ma-tang.

This meant dispensing with the artillery batteries that had been sent forward with the infantry. Eight supply wagons got away, but the Japanese fire halted the gun carriages. The riflemen picked off several horses, forcing the Russians to unlimber the guns under fire and to attempt to join the action in support of the two infantry battalions in the hills.

With the Japanese forces beginning, if belatedly, to converge on the gorge through which General Kashtalinski had to withdraw, it was clear now to the participants that this was where the climactic battle for the Yalu would be fought. A single Japanese company, the Fifth Company of the Twenty-fourth Regiment, which had marched rapidly across the hills, played the key role in the battle. Though it suffered fearful casualties, losing half of its strength in killed and wounded, it continued to stand fast, thwarting not only the artillery at its feet in the valley but also the much more mobile Russian infantry in their efforts to get away. It closed the pass while the Guards and the Twelfth Division were moving in for the kill.

Some of the Russians got away. A priest of the Russian Orthodox Church, who had been shot in the lung and wounded in two other places, told war correspondent Douglas Story from his hospital bed in Mukden that he was with the detachment that fought its way out. "There was but one thing to do and that was to cut a way through," recounted Story. "The priest, long-haired and bearded and in full canonicals, wearing the high-peaked mitre of his priestly rank, raised the Holy Cross and marched down the avenue of death. Behind him came the assistants and the sub-priests and then a long line of the 11th Siberian Rifles, chanting 'Godspodi Pomilui,' ('Lord Have Mercy')." They were among the last to get through. With the Twenty-fourth Regiment now ahead of the remnants of the Russian rear-guard, the Thirtieth Regiment in their rear and the Third and Fourth Guards coming over the hills between the two, the several hundred surviving Russians "huddled together at the bottom of the valley under a murderous fire from the heights surrounding them."

At its widest point the valley was only about half a mile across. It was jammed with guns and wagons and troops all in utter confusion and, as one observer described it, all "commanded by the Japanese as people in the stalls of a theater are commanded by the people in the gallery." It was suicidal to continue to fight, but the Russians, with their artillery pieces pointing in all directions, kept up their fire until the Tenth Company of the Fourth Guards charged with fixed bayonets. Up went the white flag.

It was 5:30 P.M. on Sunday, May 1, 1904, and the world has not been the same place since.

It was not a very great battle in terms either of numbers involved or casualties inflicted. The day cost the Japanese 1,036 killed and wounded of their force of 42,500 men. Some 2,700 Russians were killed, wounded, or captured. But this was not a day, or a battle, to be measured in terms of body counts. Japan had now established itself in the eyes of the world as a significant military power. It was no longer a collection of tiny islands inhabited by curious little people but a new and serious factor in international affairs.

There were other, more immediate effects. Kuroki had established Japan's credit rating. The financial backing to continue the war would now be available. No one could now deny funds to this gallant nation that had whipped the Russian bear. As recently as January 1904, the Japanese had failed to get British approval for a loan. With the Yalu victory to their credit, the Japanese loans in May were oversubscribed in both London and New York.

Korea was no longer a dagger pointing at Japan's heart but a springboard for the great adventures that now lay ahead in Manchuria—and were to continue to lie ahead for the next forty years. Bezobrazov's timber concession on the Yalu no longer existed, and all the circumstances that Kuropatkin envisaged and feared had come to pass.

One may sympathize with Zasulitch for the conflicting orders that came to him from Alexeiev at Port Arthur and Kuropatkin in Liaoyang. In the end, he obeyed Alexeiev and his instincts—and both were wrong. One may sympathize, also, with the unhappy Gromov, who was asked to do the impossible but did not really try. Unlike Zasulitch, who had too many orders, he did not get enough. He was later court-martialed for his part in the debacle and blew his brains out.

At Liaoyang, Kuropatkin's response was much as the Japanese Imperial General Headquarters had hoped. He immediately dispatched three battalions of troops to reinforce the local garrison and General Zasulitch's now thoroughly disorganized force. Both flanks of the Russian position had caved in. General Mishchenko had abandoned his coastal watch and the cavalry on the left flank had also fallen back on Feng-huang-cheng. Kuroki was in no position to threaten Liaoyang, but it was enough to facilitate the initial task of the Second Army at Dalny that Kuropatkin should think there was such a threat and so dispose his forces to meet it. Kuroki had unfolded the first page of Kodama's plan without putting a foot wrong. Less than forty-eight hours after Kuroki had signaled Tokyo of his victory, Togo, less honestly but with the independence that was to characterize his operations, reported from outside Port Arthur that "the harbor entrance appears to have been completely blocked to the passage of cruisers and larger vessels." To Baron Oku's Second Army, waiting aboard seventy transports in the Pyongyang Inlet, went the word to be ready for immediate departure.

Oku, a fifty-seven-year-old veteran of the Formosan expedition in 1874 and of the Saigo uprising in 1877, knew the ground. As the commander of the Fifth Division, he had fought over it in the Sino-Japanese War. Imperial General Headquarters in Japan began to breathe more easily. There were difficulties ahead, but the first phase of the land war had begun gloriously.

CHAPTER 15

𝕰𝕰𝕰𝕰𝕰𝕰

Russia's Day

Two MONTHS AFTER the beginning of the war there was still sufficient food for the townspeople, the garrison, and the Russian navy at Port Arthur. But food prices had soared. Troops were put on short rations, though supplies of vodka and caviar continued to arrive while the railway remained open.

"Though the rail had not been used as it might have been to bring in food," wrote Nojine, "that mountain of packing-cases near the station showed that it had not been idle. This mound, which served as a landmark —a sort of triumphal arch by the entrance to the Old Town—was composed entirely of vodka! We might lack food in Arthur, but never drink. Can a more hopeless state of things be imagined? For of all places in the world where drink can do harm, a fortress full of half-nourished men is the worst."

Prince Boris, brother of Prince Cyril, who had been badly burned in the sinking of the *Petropavlovsk,* was in trouble for walking the streets of Port Arthur wearing a nurse's uniform and singing loudly.

Admiral Makarov, while he lived, and General Smirnov had worked together to prevent a Japanese landing on the peninsula. But now, with Makarov gone, Smirnov had to work under the inefficient Stoessel, who countermanded his every order. Prince Boris and his fellow officers had reason, perhaps, for their drunken outbursts.

Port Arthur felt that it had been deserted, not only by the Tsar but by his representatives on the spot. The day after the death of Makarov the Japanese returned with a force of battleships, cruisers, and destroyers and for two hours bombarded the inner harbor and the town. No ships were hit, but a shell killed seven people in the town and caused considerable damage to houses.

The first criticism of the Japanese for shelling the town appeared in the world press when the news was published of the new attack. Captain Pakenham, British naval observer aboard the Japanese battleship *Asahi*, leapt to Togo's defense in a dispatch to the Admiralty. Implicit obedience was often bad service, he wrote. Togo was merely following instructions. The bombardment of the town that followed the sinking of the Russian flagship was a supplement to the mining and had been planned long before. "They [the Japanese] have bought at a great price knowledge now part of the stock in trade of every naval scribbler," Pakenham wrote. Togo should not be blamed for actions that were beyond his control.

The fortress at Port Arthur now became a haven for a fleet that dared not move out to attack. The "risk nothing" policy revived. Viceroy Alexeiev returned and took temporary command of the fleet until Vice-Admiral Nikolai Illarionvitch Skruidlov arrived from the Baltic to take over after Admiral Makarov. Alexeiev's orders were specific. No operations without permission. No ship was to look for trouble. Everyone knew that the fortress would soon be cut off and that the Japanese were preparing to make a landing on the Liaotung Peninsula. Men and food had to be sent out of the fortress to secure the approaches.

As for the navy, all of Admiral Makarov's plans collapsed. "The squadron went back to slumber in the basins of the inner harbor," wrote Semenov bitterly. *The Times* commented: "The siren harbor of refuge, as its custom is, and always will be, kept whispering of the soft solace of that fatal shelter." *The Times* military correspondent had kept up a running argument with the Russian newspaper, *Viestnik*, in Kronstadt, on the gulf of Finland, which insisted that, once the Russian fleet left harbor to seek out the Japanese, it would abandon the coastline to the mercy of the Japanese. He pointed out the vast differences between the Russian and British concepts of naval strategy. "Let those who vaunt fortresses build them to their heart's content; but let them emblazon the hedgehog in an attitude of defense upon their escutcheon, count themselves helots, and abandon for ever the dream of Imperial rule."

In spite of the Russian fleet's inactivity, however, Port Arthur was proving more difficult to overcome than the Japanese had anticipated. Since the Russian ships would not come out, and he could not confine them absolutely in the harbor, Togo could not give the army an unqualified assurance that it could go ahead safely and land troops on the Liaotung Peninsula. He decided on one more attempt to turn the harbor into an inland lake from which the Russian ships would have no exit to the sea. Togo telegraphed

[271]

imperial headquarters for twelve ships so that he could block up the entrance to Port Arthur.

While he waited for a reply from Tokyo, Togo ordered Vice-Admiral Kamimura, commander of the Second Fleet, to lay mines outside Vladivostok so that the Russian ships at that port would not be able to join up with the Port Arthur squadron. Kamimura left Gensan (Wonsan) in northeastern Korea on April 22 and sailed for Vladivostok, 340 miles to the north, taking with him ten cruisers and four destroyers.

The Russian fleet at Vladivostok moved at the same time. Now that the ice was breaking up around the Golden Horn—the peninsula that protects the northern slopes of the harbor on which the city is built—Rear-Admiral von Essen* ventured out to sea to attack Japanese transports and merchantmen. The Russian and Japanese fleets braving the thick fogs and drifting ice covering the Sea of Japan passed without sighting each other.

On the morning of April 26 the Russian admiral with his four fast cruisers, *Rurik*, *Rossiya*, *Gromoboi*, and *Bogatuir*, and two torpedo boats, came across a Japanese transport, *Kinshu Maru*, with troops of the Thirty-seventh Infantry Regiment aboard. The Russians ordered her to stop and surrender within the hour, otherwise she would be sunk. Some of the crew took to boats, but the soldiers remained aboard, refusing to surrender. They tore the shoulder straps from their uniforms to conceal their regiment and opened fire with rifles from the decks. When the hour was up, the Russians torpedoed the ship, and she began to sink. Many officers committed suicide in their cabins and soldiers bayoneted each other on the decks. Fifteen men left on the sinking ship jumped into the water and were rescued by the boats. Only sailors and laborers were taken aboard the *Rossiya*—not a single soldier surrendered. Admiral Kamimura, lost in the dense fog with his Second Division, was powerless to help. He returned to base after laying seventy-five mines outside Vladivostok. The Russian Vladivostok fleet was still free to attack Japanese coastal and overseas communications.

There was a great outcry in the Japanese and foreign press after the *Kinshu Maru* went down, but Admiral Togo had set the precedent long before when he sank the steamer *Kowshing* in 1894 and started the war with China. "The operation is a perfectly legitimate one," wrote Admiral Sir Cyprian Bridge of the Royal Navy, who disagreed with the protesters. ". . . No officer would shrink from sinking a transport that persistently refused to surrender."

The Japanese fleet's task now was to insure the success of the landing on

---

*Not to be confused with Commander von Essen, who later became captain of the battleship *Sevastopol* at Port Arthur.

the Liaotung Peninsula. From his new base in the Elliot Islands, Togo enforced a rigorous blockade, swept the sea meticulously for Russian mines, and began preparations for the third blocking attempt at the entrance to the inner harbor at Port Arthur.

Volunteers to join the suicide squads were plentiful, but the reply from Tokyo was not encouraging. Japan was running out of ships. Almost all the merchant fleet had been taken over as transports for the Second Army, and jealousy between the army and navy was bitter. The army had been irritated by the navy's success at Chemulpo and felt that the landing of troops was more important than another attempt to block the harbor. "Should you use up the twelve ships you require for this blockade without completely or effectually achieving success, you will probably want several more ships for blocking purposes," Tokyo replied. Togo agreed to take whatever ships could be spared to him, explaining that the blocking of the Port Arthur harbor was more important than ever. Twelve old ships were found—four military and eight naval transports—and were fitted up in Japan, loaded with concrete and stone, and prepared with explosive charges. Several of the ships also carried mines.

The new suicide group of 224 officers and men maintained complete secrecy during loading operations. No members of the crews were permitted to send letters or to have other communication with the shore. On May 1 the twelve ships, led by *Shibata Maru*, sailed for Port Arthur, escorted by the Combined Fleet. As they left Hai-ju anchorage the weather was fine and the sea calm. By the night of the second day thick fog had appeared, the seas became mountainous, and visibility practically nil. Weather forecasts predicted calm seas at Port Arthur, however, and it was decided to carry on with the operation.

Shibata Maru suffered steering trouble and frequently had to withdraw from the line to make repairs. Another ship sprang a leak in her boilers and had to retire. Soon the line of old ships became ragged and communications between them and the escorts broke down. Still, ten of the ships eventually were assembled in formation and passed close by the *Mikasa* to be cheered by the crew.

Now they were on their own. The waves became rougher and ominous-looking, and heavy clouds hid the moon, making the sea pitch black. After several attempts to rejoin the line, *Shibata Maru*'s commander decided that the night was too stormy for a successful attempt and tried to recall the other ships. Two got the message and followed *Shibata Maru* back to base. The others made their way, one by one, toward Port Arthur, while the destroyers and torpedo boats, which were to attract enemy fire from the blocking ships and were unaware of the change in plans, waited for the suicide squad to make its dash.

[273]

One after the other, with only the lights of the Russian harbor to guide them, the little ships, tossed like corks on the enormous waves, faced the searchlights and fire from ships and forts. *Totomi,* caught in the Russian searchlights and fired at from all sides, began to fall apart. Projectiles of all sizes burst on the water. The ship's sides were pierced and her masts were broken off. Mines exploded all round the ship. *Totomi*'s two machineguns were smashed to pieces before there was a chance to fire them. A shell hit the main steampipe, the foremast broke off, and the compass was in pieces. Her commander, believing that he had taken his ship far enough into the entrance, gave the order to blow her up. She sank at once. Only one lifeboat was now intact and *Totomi*'s commander, hacking with his sword through the ropes which tied it to the blockship, managed to get the surviving men away from her before she went down.

By this time seven of the blockships had blown themselves up, and the whole of the enemy fire from the fortress was concentrated on the only remaining ship, *Asagao Maru* ("Morning Glory"). She was held in the crossbeams of the Russian searchlights and the crossfire of all the fortress guns. Her steering went, and she ran ashore just below Golden Hill fort, where the crew blew her up. Of her crew and that of three other ships, not a soul was saved.

Russian scouting parties found survivors from other ships clinging naked and half-frozen to the masts and rigging of sunken ships. They were crying for help, but when the Russians reached them, they attempted suicide rather than be taken prisoner. Some who reached the shore threw themselves on the Russians and had to be tied up with ropes.* Another Russian rescue party found a Japanese boat washed up on shore on the Huwei Peninsula. When they attempted to capture the men, the Russians saw to their horror that the Japanese were beheading one another with their swords.†

Russian reports also stated that many of the volunteers were drunk, even after their swim ashore in the icy waters. Large numbers of half-empty liquor bottles were found on board several of the wrecked fireships. "This discovery was all the more extraordinary as the Japanese are a most sober

---

*After the war the Russian cemetery on the slope of Pei-yue-shan was dug up, and the bones of Japanese who had taken part in this blocking expedition were found, including the commander, two officers, and eleven men from *Asagao Maru,* as well as twenty-five officers and men from other ships. Some had traces of shot wounds and others had ropes lashed around their waists.

†This was part of the *seppuku* ceremony (an apology to the emperor). Accomplices followed the same ritual when Mishima Yukio, the gifted Japanese writer, committed suicide in 1971.

people," wrote an officer. "Their national beverage, saké, is not stronger than our ordinary beer, and it is drunk out of tiny cups. This shows that not even Japanese nerves could face the truly hellish situation the fireships found themselves in when making for their goal. The Japanese were inebriated with patriotism and the joy of victory, but this had evidently to be supplemented with alcohol."

Stories of drunken Japanese sailors spread through the ranks of Russian seamen, most of whom considered it as much a sin to drink hard spirits on the eve of battle as before Communion. "That's not the way of doing things," a petty officer was heard to say. "You should face God pure as a candle burning before a shrine."*

Despite much evidence to the contrary, Admiral Togo decided that the third blocking attempt had been a success. "As five out of the eight blocking vessels entered the harbor mouth successfully and sank, the harbor entrance appears to have been completely blocked to the passage of cruisers and larger vessels," he reported. He said that all but one ship, which went ashore, managed to block the entrance to some extent. *The Japanese Official Naval History* later reported that none of the ships was closer than 1,800 feet to the entrance and not one had gone right into the channel. On the basis of Togo's report, however, the landing of the Japanese Second Army only sixty miles from Port Arthur took place on schedule. It was a dangerous risk. The entrance to Port Arthur had not been blocked, and of this Togo, despite his message, must have been aware. By a deliberate falsehood, he risked not only his own reputation but the lives of the men of the Second Army.

Again the British observer, Captain Pakenham, defended Togo's rash action. The Japanese admiral had to decide whether to announce the blocking attempt as a success or a dismal failure. If he reported the truth of the matter the army would not go ahead with the scheduled landing. "Togo had only to express an adverse view in order to make himself quite safe," he wrote. "Only military strategy would have been embarrassed thereby." From this time Togo felt free to make his own decisions without obtaining permission from higher authority.

Togo's message to Imperial General Headquarters that the Port Arthur harbor had been blocked was the signal for the great movement by sea to the shores of the Liaotung Peninsula. On him fell the heavy responsibility of protecting an amphibious landing within five hours' sailing time of the

---

*In this war, as in World War II, Japanese often went into battle intoxicated. At the time of the Russo-Japanese War, however, brandy was imported from France and would have been far too expensive for use in war. What was probably used was *shochu*, distilled but not completely refined spirits made from grain.

still intact Russian fleet at Port Arthur. Since he had failed to seal off the harbor, the blockade had to succeed if the Second Army and the almost equally important merchant fleet of seventy ships, which had been mobilized to transport the troops, were not to run the grave risk of destruction.

At the Korean port of Chenampo on the Pyongyang Inlet, where the transports had assembled to await the result of the battle of the Yalu, the Japanese had clamped down martial law. No one was allowed to enter or leave the town. Aboard the transports moored over an area of about eighteen miles, the First, Third, and Fourth divisions and the First Artillery Brigade were squeezed in, as a Reuters report put it, like rats. There were 3,800 men aboard one ship. Every deck was so packed that it was impossible for the men to take any exercise, and most could not get fresh air.

There was wild excitement among the troops when they were told on May 2 of Kuroki's victory on the Yalu and quiet confidence among the commanders when Togo's message the following day announced the blockading of Port Arthur. By the time this message was received the first flotilla of sixteen transports was already on its way to the landing place about thirty miles north of Dalny. High seas precluded any chance of a landing on May 4. For twenty-three hours the flotilla hove to under the shelter of the Elliot Islands, waiting for the seas to subside. There were further delays when two auxiliary cruisers with a naval landing party found the original landing site unsuitable and had to move some miles farther down the coast than had been anticipated.

In order to preserve the utmost secrecy, the Japanese had eschewed the advantage of detailed reconnaissance. This was another gamble, but again it paid off, and there was no opposition when the landing party of six officers and about a thousand men began to wade ashore at 5:30 A.M. on May 5. In selecting a landing place only sixty miles from Port Arthur, the Japanese recognized that they were committing what was termed by a naval officer on the staff of the Japanese minister of the navy an "impertinence" and by a high military staff officer as *"un coup audacieux."* The Japanese Imperial General Headquarters hoped that the harbor was sufficiently blocked to prevent large vessels passing out but, despite Togo's reports, were not fully reassured. They thought it was possible for destroyers to pass and assumed that a torpedo attack on the transports was a certainty. Accepting that, they took steps to minimize the danger as far as possible. All available Japanese destroyer and torpedo boats, about sixty in all, were stationed either off Port Arthur or between Port Arthur and the Elliot Islands. They protected the anchorage with booms and nets, laid dummy mines, arranged a system of patrol boats and anchored protecting ships in suitable positions for covering the transports. It was hoped that about three-quarters of the attacking force would be destroyed before getting within torpedo distance of the transports, but it was accepted that, if the attack was properly carried out, some destroyers would get within striking distance. This was a risk that had to be taken, but to meet the danger every transport was moved into shallow water so that, if she were sunk, the upperworks would remain above water, and there would be a chance that the troops and stores would not be lost.

At Port Arthur, however, the Russian fleet declined to take risks. As soon as the Japanese began to place booms and mines across the passages in and near the Elliot Islands, the general landing area became clear enough.

Alexeiev immediately asked the Tsar "most humbly and respectfully" what he, personally, was to do. Nicholas authorized his departure, and Alexeiev left Port Arthur by train at 11 A.M. on May 5. His train passed safely through Pu-lan-tien, but later that day a second train, which had left Port Arthur with refugees and sick, was fired on by a strong Japanese reconnaissance party that had reached the railway line with orders to break rail and telegraphic communications between Port Arthur and Liaoyang. The train halted and hoisted the Red Cross. As soon as the Japanese gunners ceased fire, it started again and dashed through Pu-lan-tien at full speed.

After their first move forward to the railway, the Japanese pulled back, feeling that the force there was too exposed. One ammunition train ran the gauntlet to Port Arthur on May 10 and two trains of immense length crawled out of Port Arthur and picked up some of the hundreds of refugees, most of them women and children, who had been waiting for hours, and even days, at the Nan-kwan-ling junction. Several of Port Arthur's merchants and the manager of the Russo-Chinese Bank got away on this day.

Before he left Port Arthur, Alexeiev, who had suddenly abandoned the "no risks" policy, had strongly recommended fleet action against the Japanese transports. But Rear-Admiral Vilgelm Karlovitch Vitgeft, who took over the command of the fleet on Alexeiev's departure, was not a man of action. He said quite frankly that he was not going to undertake operations outside the harbor. He would concentrate his efforts on the defense of the fortress. "For the remainder of the war the squadron will observe the strictest of neutrality," said a Russian navy wit.

Vitgeft's appointment was accidental. After Alexeiev left Port Arthur, Vice-Admiral Skruidlov, an officer with long and distinguished experience, was appointed to take command, but, with the closing of land communications, he became stranded in Vladivostok and soon thereafter was appointed to command and combine the First and Second Pacific squadrons. The Second, under command of Admiral Rozhdestvenski, was now assembling in the Baltic. Vice-Admiral Petr Alexeievitch Bezobrazov, sent out to take command of the First Pacific Squadron, was unable to reach Port Arthur and became the third fleet commander at Vladivostok. Vitgeft simply happened to be the most senior officer available in Port Arthur. At his first meeting with the flag officers he confessed his ignorance of the sea. "Gentlemen," he said, "I expect you to assist me with words and deeds. I am no leader of a fleet." The officers thought it would have been better if he had held his tongue.

There had been bad feeling between the navy and the army since the first attack on February 8. The army said that the squadron had been caught unprepared, and the navy accused the army of having neglected the fortress defenses. Now that some of the ships had been stripped of their guns to reinforce the land defenses, the feeling became intense. Some navy officers threatened to go to sea, and, if the fortress tried to stop them, to fire at the forts. The soldiers on the forts ridiculed the navy for giving up its guns. "The irritation against us became so great that in all seriousness the proposal was made for the fortress artillery to fire on the squadron to force it to put to sea and fight," wrote Semenov. Anonymous typewritten leaflets had appeared, expressing the animosity between the two services.

The Far Eastern Squadron was again turning into a floating barracks. Everyone expected that the Japanese could land on the coast whenever they wished, and yet nothing was ready to repel them. The "beautiful plan" for turning Port Arthur into a stronghold was far from being fulfilled. Men from *Novik* were taken from their ship to build platforms for guns along the coast. Every day signals came for the men from *Novik* and other ships to drag guns up the steep slopes around the Eagle's Nest. It was work they were unaccustomed to, and nobody was really surprised when the military engineer came to inspect the work of the sailors and found that one gun could not use its whole arc of fire because it had been badly mounted.

"I feel wretched," Semenov wrote in his diary.

I don't feel inclined to write any more. We are giving up the fleet. . . . Kuropatkin is to drive the Japanese into the water; that sounds fine . . . we ought to go out and fight, not sit here in idleness . . . we are sacrificing the squadron and trying to save Port Arthur. It looks like self-sacrifice on our part. In reality, we thus have greater chances of saving our lives: one can't be drowned on shore. The *Diana* surrenders two six-inch and four twelve-pounder guns, but that is nothing, much worse is in store . . . we are suffering from hydrophobia. . . .

Even when Alexeiev telegraphed his plan of attack on May 6, Vitgeft continued to vacillate. He was not encouraged by most of his subordinates, who thought it hardly likely that the Japanese would work round-the-clock to disembark the Second Army, and that there was little chance, therefore, of a successful night attack. Twelve destroyers were available, but the feeling among the top men ashore was that they should not be sent out alone, and that to escort them with cruisers or battleships was much too dangerous. The consensus was that it was better to take no action than to take risks. This was not the consensus in the fleet. On the contrary, according to Semenov, suppressed indignation prevailed there. In addition to the twelve destroyers, there were still three undamaged battleships, and the *Sevastopol*'s damage had not prevented her from getting out on March 18 and April 10, when Makarov was there to inspire an offensive spirit. But Makarov was dead, and Alexeiev had flown. And so, while the Japanese Second Army moved ashore, established its beachhead, and began to find its way through the now freshly cultivated fields of maize and into the hills beyond, the Russian Pacific Squadron simply watched and procrastinated.

Though he had failed to block the harbor entrance, Togo redoubled his efforts to prevent the Russians from coming out to upset the reinforcement of the Second Army. With his battle squadron by day and destroyers by night he watched and waited at the door to Port Arthur, ready to pounce. Torpedo boat flotillas took up positions as near to Port Arthur as possible, so that they would look larger, and destroyers and other ships patrolled farther out to sea so as to look smaller.

Flying his flag in the 15,000-ton battleship *Hatsuse* and with two other battleships, *Shikishima* and *Yashima,* several cruisers and a destroyer flotilla, Rear-Admiral Nashiba Tokioki joined the standing patrol. *Yashima* had been under construction in England for action with China but was still not completed when the war finished. She displaced nearly 13,000 tons and carried four twelve-inch, ten six-inch, and sixteen twelve-pounder guns. *Shikishima,* built two years later, displaced over 15,000 tons and had much heavier armament. *Hatsuse,* also built in England, in 1899, was practically a sister ship of *Shikishima.* Her big twelve-inch guns weighed forty-nine tons with magazines holding 240 shells, while nearly 3,000 shells were available for the six-inch guns.

A thick, low-lying fog hung over the Elliot Islands on May 15 as Rear-Admiral Nashiba left on his way to Port Arthur. Blowing his siren and using his searchlights to cut through the gloom, he ordered the ships under his command to keep an eye out for submarines. Old Iron Mountain showed out of the darkness and the fog at 8:15 P.M. and the Japanese admiral sent off two destroyers to report on the state of the Russian ships. When they returned to report that there were no enemy ships outside the port, he moved on warily at a slow six knots until at 10:50 P.M. he could just see the top of Golden Hill.

The Japanese ships patrolled the entrance, picking up bodies and personal effects, including caps, swords, and binoculars, still attached to the wreckage of the blockships, and laying mechanical mines. That morning

Togo had reported the loss of a small ship, *Miyako*—the first Japanese warship to be sunk in the war—while engaged in minesweeping operations. Otherwise, all was going according to plan. "All the ships of my command in this quarter are busily engaged [in blockade work]. There has been no rest since May 1, when this work was begun, but the morale of the men is continually excellent, and they show no signs of fatigue; there is no relaxation of the vigilance of our watch over the enemy on the sea."

From the ships and forts in Port Arthur the Russians watched the Japanese with little concern. They were used to destroyers and torpedo boats. Battleships were harder to resist, however, and when Admiral Nashiba appeared with his three battleships in single line, there was a sudden flurry of excitement. The fog had now cleared and the day was bright and sunny.

Some weeks earlier, Admiral Makarov had begun laying mines outside Port Arthur and Vitgeft reluctantly planted more, about seven miles to the southeast. But, as everyone knew, the Japanese always stayed at least ten miles out to sea, taking no risks from the shore batteries and hoping to lure the Russians out. Vitgeft had given strict orders that the ships were not to be tempted, and, since this applied to the mine-layer also, there was little chance that any of Togo's ships might strike the Russian mines.

One evening, however, in a thick fog, Captain Fedor Nikolaevitch Ivanov of the *Amur*, the squadron's only mine-layer, had decided to risk providence and the Admiral's wrath by laying his mines beyond the limits determined by Vitgeft. Vitgeft was furious and threatened to remove Captain Ivanov from his command. Such foolhardy action was just the thing he had warned against. But the mines were down and there was little to be done now that this "mad prank" had been perpetrated.

What caused the excitement now was not just the appearance of the battleships but the fact that they appeared to be heading straight for the newly laid Russian mines. Soon the Russian ships were crowded with men, all hoping and praying that something would happen. Along the clifftops facing the sea soldiers from the forts and people from the town waited in anticipation.

Hatsuse was directly in front of the entrance to the harbor when Admiral Nashiba felt a huge explosion under her stern. He ordered the other battleships to alter course and signalled: "A mine has struck our bottom astern and smashed the steering engine. Send boats." Men were set to work the pumps, to launch the boats and to make rafts from spars and mess tables, while the ship prepared to be taken in tow by *Kasagi,* one of the accompanying cruisers. *Yashima* ran to the rescue and was just about to lower her boats when she also struck a mine and became enveloped in smoke and flames. At the same time a second explosion rocked *Hatsuse,* snapping off her mast and sending her funnels crashing to the decks.

In a little over a minute *Hatsuse* had disappeared in a backward dive beneath the waves. The other Japanese ships rushed to rescue the crew but the battleship went so fast that the men between decks had little hope. Only 300 of her crew of 800 were saved, including Admiral Nashiba, who clung to the rails of the ship, determined to go down with her, and was picked up unconscious by the gunboat *Tatsuta.*

Yashima was in great distress, and her captain, realizing that he could not save her, ordered about 180 of the crew to abandon ship. He then steamed slowly to the north, towing his boats, in an effort to get away from the Russian destroyers approaching from the fortress.

On shore and in the Russian ships the reaction was instantaneous. "There burst forth a kind of ferocious joy, a joy of savages without restraint, with caps thrown into the air and with cheers, and the people all but rushed into one another's arms," wrote Lieutenant Steer, of *Novik,* which ran out to chase the Japanese ships. He remembered how the world press had reported the overwhelming sadness of the Japanese people at the loss of the *Petropavlovsk.* "I was always somewhat skeptical on that point," he wrote. "If we Russians, with an essentially easy-going and peace-loving nature, gave way to such demonstrations of savage joy at seeing hundreds of our enemies go down, I feel not the slightest doubt that the jubilation of the Japanese, who are after all cruel and vindictive Malays, must have passed all bounds."

Now was the time for the Russian ships to go in to attack. But Admiral Vitgeft was no Makarov, and, anyway, it was a Russian holiday. Few of the ships were ready for action, and many of the men were on shore. Vitgeft belatedly sent off sixteen destroyers and *Novik,* "to worry . . . but not to attack." According to Japanese reports, some of these destroyers concentrated their fire on survivors in lifeboats and launches being towed by rescue ships. The Russian destroyers retreated on the approach of Japanese torpedo boats and one or two old cruisers.

Limping slowly around Encounter Rock, *Yashima* was out of sight by four o'clock. At five she came to a stop, and her captain signaled that he could not avoid sinking. Having saved confidential papers and the wardroom portrait of the Emperor, Captain Sakamoto assembled the surviving members of his crew on the quarter deck. They had all changed into clean uniforms and now stood in line on the deck and sang *Kimi-ga-yo* ("The Reign of the Lord"). The flag was slowly lowered with a royal salute, three *banzais* were given, and signal flags lashed to the rails so that they would not float off. At 6 P.M. the crew took to the boats. *Yashima* was taken in tow by *Kasagi* and was still afloat at eight that night, but sank soon afterward, well out of sight of the Port Arthur hills.

Even the foreign naval observers on board the Russian cruiser *Diana* had become excited when they saw *Hatsuse* go down. The German clapped his hands. The Frenchman waved his cap, shouting *"Finis les japonais! Rien ne va plus!"* However these neutral foreigners on the spot may have reacted to the Japanese disaster, the Anglo-Saxon world said that the Russians had behaved disgracefully by placing mines in a seaway used by commercial shipping. The Japanese would never have behaved in such a fashion. The world had swiftly forgotten the *Petropavlovsk.* The Japanese were gentlemen and could do no wrong.

Pakenham reported to the Admiralty in his usual descriptive style, but this time with much more bitterness about the Russians, whom he seemed to regard not only as Japan's enemies but also as his own. "It is a pity," he said, "that a bold and clever device, crowned with success that may properly be described as appalling, should have contained in its execution an element so deserving of public reprobation." A "generous enemy" would have given due warning before using such a weapon.

Togo was in difficulties now. The Russian mines had destroyed one third of his capital ships. Nor was this the total of his misfortunes. Seven hours before the battleships struck the mines, the cruisers *Yoshino* and *Kasuga,* had collided in the fog outside Port Arthur. *Yoshino*'s captain together with thirty officers and 287 men, went down with the ship. On the same day, two gunboats, the *Oshima* and the *Akagi,* also collided in the fog. The *Oshima* sank immediately. The *Miyako,* a communications ship, and torpedo boat No. 48 sank on the fourteenth, and on the seventeenth, the destroyer *Akatsuki* struck a mine and went down with forty-three officers and men. The *Tatsuta,* to which Admiral Nashiba had transferred his command after the loss of *Hatsuse,* went aground a short time after he boarded her, and was not refloated for a month.

The Japanese reacted typically by deciding to suppress the news of the disasters. Under no circumstances were the Russians to be given a chance to recover their morale.

Pakenham visited Togo on board *Mikasa* to offer condolences and encouragement. Merely nodding his thanks, "like a man receiving gifts," he sat "calm, Buddha-like and unmoved, irradiating renewed confidence that all would yet be well, and thus hoping to influence those who looked to him for guidance. His attitude was worthy of the mortally great." Togo expected to be relieved of his command. He had used battleships for a task that could have been performed by torpedo boats. But at a meeting before the Throne on May 18 he was exonerated and enjoined to keep the losses secret.

The Russians, including the hundreds of sightseers on the surrounding cliffs and in the riggings of ships, had seen *Hatsuse* go down. Intercepted Russian telegrams made this clear to the commander-in-chief of the Japanese fleet. They had *not* seen *Yashima* disappear, however. The Russians thought a second battleship had also been injured, if not altogether destroyed, but knew nothing about the cruiser *Yoshino*. It seemed wise to the Japanese to admit to the loss of the smaller ship and to say nothing of the *Yashima*.

Imperial General Headquarters reluctantly decided to make public the loss of the two ships. This dire news was issued to Japanese and foreign newspapers on May 19, and two days later Togo received a message from the chief of staff: "The people at large express deep sympathy for the dead and realize the grave difficulty in which the authorities are placed. The foreign correspondent of *The Times* in his telegram can be said to voice the general opinion. He says, 'The loss of the *Yoshino* and *Hatsuse* have not affected the spirit of the nation. The people place still firmer trust in Admiral Togo. All the foreign correspondents severely blame Russia's lawless action in placing mines in the public channels.' "

Rumors drifted around Tokyo that there had been even greater losses, but the navy and the newspapers said nothing. The loss of the second battleship, *Yashima*, remained a secret for more than a year. Even Captain Pakenham was amazed that such a loss could be concealed. He explained to the Admiralty how it happened and how disclosure of the losses affected the Japanese people who had been spared the knowledge that not one but two battleships had gone down on the same day.

Dreading in another world neither an eternity of happiness nor of pain, and above all, with a press that has not reduced to a fine art the cultivation of sensationalism and the substitution of a selfish and introspective sentimentality for principle, the Japanese are still permitted to take a manly view, not only of the insignificance of the individual life when compared with the welfare of the State, but of the unimportance of the death of tens, hundreds, or even thousands of their fellows to all outside the little circle in which each unit has had its being. If a few lives shall be lost, organs of public opinion do not confront their readers with the apparently authoritative assertion that a great catastrophe has overtaken their country, nor is their attention kept concentrated for many days on embroidered details of the search for the bodies, with an assiduous elaboration of every incident that can give death its sting and ensure for the grave a victory. . . . It is this chivalrous conception of the insignificance of the unit that has enabled Japan to bear without a murmur, almost without a word, a blow that would have shaken any other country to its foundations and that would have caused the western press to exhaust itself in hysterical superlatives.

Togo reported that the battleships had struck mines, but this did not end the spate of speculation in the fleet that the Russians were using submarines. Two ships reported "round objects like the conning towers of submarines." *Shikishima,* the only battleship involved to survive the catastrophe outside Port Arthur on May 15, repeatedly reported firing on suspicious objects in the surrounding seas. When the Russians saw ships firing into the water they often sent out signals to bluff the Japanese into thinking they were using submarines, such as: "The First Submarine Flotilla is to come back," and "Second Submarine Flotilla, stop where you are!"*

The momentous days in May had brought longed-for victory to the Russians. Japan lost seven ships, totaling 34,325 tons, 1,000 men, and 160 cannon. She could better spare 20,000 men than two first-class battleships. In Port Arthur, however, there was little appreciation of victory. The two services continued to bicker. "It was a case of the kettle and the pot," wrote Semenov. There were loud and drunken brawls in the drinking houses of the town between the sailors in the squadron and the soldiers in the garrison forces.

Vladivostok was still full of fight, however. The Russian squadron continued to carry out raids on dozens of Japanese transports and German and British ships carrying supplies of food, railway supplies, and guns for the Japanese. Three big cruisers, all well over 10,000 tons—*Rurik, Rossiya,* and *Gromoboi*—accompanied by an armed merchantman and a flotilla of torpedo boats cruised the Sea of Japan, through eighteen-mile-wide Tsugaru Strait, between Hokkaido and Honshu, and along the east coast of Japan in search of transports. They also kept a lookout for a steamer from San Francisco reported to be carrying £2,000,000 worth of gold for the Japanese government. She escaped them, but the appearance of Russian ships close to the Japanese shore put fear into the hearts of the Japanese public and the naval and military authorities.

Gromoboi sank a 3,000-ton merchant ship carrying sick and wounded from Dalny to Japan on June 15. The Russian cruiser took more than a hundred men aboard, but three boatloads of Japanese escaped to the shore and a few who refused to leave the ship went down with her. On the same day a 6,000-ton transport, *Hitachi Maru,* suffered a similar fate, going down close to the Japanese mainland near Shimonoseki, with 2,000 men. Some survivors, troops of the Imperial Guard rear reserve, were picked up by fishermen or washed ashore on a nearby island. The first shells from the *Gromoboi* missed their target but she soon had the range of the Japanese

---

*The Russians had one unassembled submarine at Port Arthur. Japanese intelligence had not confirmed whether it was operational.

transport. "The heads of men flew across the room," reported one survivor. "Their bodies were scarlet with blood. Their limbs were lumps of flesh. The room was a veritable sea of blood. If there is truly a hell on earth, this was it . . . the enemy shells flew against the ship just like hailstones . . . there was nothing we could do except wait for the ship to sink." He went on deck to ask for orders and returned below to report that each man was to save himself. "I had cigarettes called 'Chrysanthemum World' which I gave to forty or fifty men, saying, 'This is the end. Let us have a farewell smoke.' Before we finished smoking the room turned yellow with a shell hitting the ship and we could no longer see anything." Only one boatload of survivors reached the Russian cruiser.

The loss of arms, locomotives, and Krupp siege guns intended for the bombardment of the Port Arthur fortress was a serious blow for the Japanese. The guns had been kept for the defense of Japan itself, in the event of Russian invasion, and they had been spared most reluctantly for the more immediate task of bombarding Port Arthur. Three batteries of these guns, the heaviest ever used by an offensive army, would have hastened the fall of Port Arthur by many months.

Admiral Kamimura, sent to guard the transports, was bitterly criticized in Japan, especially in Tokyo, where many of the troops had been enlisted. Kamimura, a brave if somewhat short-tempered and impetuous man, chased the Russian ships through the storms and fogs of the seas without success. In Tokyo, not only stones but a short sword were thrown at Kamimura's house, with the advice that he should commit hara-kiri. Angry deputations waited on the navy minister, Admiral Yamamoto. Oku Izuzo, a member of the House of Representatives, further inflamed public opinion when he criticized the navy, inverting the word *nomu,* which means "dense fog" and making it read *muno* ("inability"). The play on words upset the men of the Second Division so much that they were said to have wept as they continued the ineffectual chase through the fogs.

Apart from the loss of the two Japanese battleships in May—and the Japanese public had been told that only one had been lost—the most serious setback was the sinking of transports that had all been lost with troops and arms aboard. Kamimura had also been unable to catch the Russian ships when they came to the mouth of Tokyo Bay. Kamimura had four armored cruisers, five protected cruisers, and two flotillas of torpedo boats, but he had two tasks, and possibly two masters. In Japan, Imperial General Headquarters, pushed by public opinion, wanted the eastern coast of the country protected, especially around the capital. They also agreed with Togo that the main Russian fleet might try to burst through the blockading fleet and make for Vladivostok, now that Nogi's Third Army was closing in on the fortress. Admiral Kamimura had to attempt to remain in telegraphic communication with Togo in case he was required on the east coast of Japan and also to watch out for the Russian Vladivostok squadron as it moved up and down the eastern shore.

To take his mind off his overwhelming troubles, Kamimura occasionally went fishing in a small boat. Worried about the morale of his men, he also took them on mountain-climbing expeditions on the rare occasions when they put into port, and encouraged them to engage in sumo wrestling.

One of his officers followed him on a mountain climb and found the Admiral struggling up a steep hill in front of his men. "It must be difficult for you, sir," said the officer.

"What, to climb mountains?" asked Kamimura.

"No, sir, but from your appearance you look to be in pain," said the officer.

"Do I look like that?" asked Kamimura. The officer saw tears in his eyes.

"I can feel for you, sir," he said, "but I will pretend not to have noticed anything."

CHAPTER *16*

୬୬୬୬୬୬

Nanshan

COLONEL NIKOLAI ALEXANDROVITCH TRETYAKOV, the commanding officer of the Fifth East Siberian Rifle Regiment, rubbed his eyes when he was awakened at his headquarters at Nanshan, forty miles northeast of Port Arthur, on the night of February 8–9, 1904, and read a telegram from Major-General Yakov Grigorievitch Jilinski in Port Arthur "The Japanese fleet is making for Port Arthur," said the message from Alexeiev's chief of staff. "Be on the alert."

Tretyakov had been entrusted with one of the most critical tasks in Manchuria: the defense of the approaches to the Kwantung Peninsula and Port Arthur.

During the Boxer Rebellion, Tretyakov had helped to fortify the position at Nanshan. From Hand Bay on the east coast of the peninsula to Chinchou Bay on the west was a distance of less than three miles. The water on either side was shallow for a distance of about a mile even at high tide and much more when the tide was out. Through this narrow neck ran the road and railway line to Port Arthur. To lose Nanshan, therefore, was to lose the vital overland link with the fortress.

Early in the morning after he had received the message from Port Arthur, Colonel Tretyakov inspected the remains of the defenses he had helped to build four years earlier. All had been neglected and were in ruins. Conscious now that there was no time to lose, he detailed parties to begin work on the fortifications. The ground was frozen, and the earth, when it could be prized loose by picks and crowbars, was as hard as rock. Five thousand Chinese coolies reinforced the Russian soldiers on the job. Among them in disguise were Colonel Doi of the Japanese army, a Chinese assistant whom he had recruited at Newchwang, and other Japanese who had arrived to help him spy.

Tretyakov disapproved of the defensive position and wanted to move farther south where he could have met the Japanese on a broad front while they were confined in the isthmus. With only a single regiment to hold the line, and vulnerable to Japanese naval action in support of ground operations, he thought his position was not only difficult but dangerous, despite the reserves available in Port Arthur.

The Fifth Regiment alone was inadequate for the task, and Tretyakov's superiors at Port Arthur gave him little hope that he might expect adequate reinforcements. When he told General Fock, commander of the Fourth East Siberian Rifle Division, that it would be difficult to defend the position with one understrength regiment, the General replied: "Do you know, if I were in your place, I should say to my commanding officer, 'Leave me only two companies and I shall know better how to die with them than with the whole regiment.'"

The position consisted of a series of hills, circular in shape, stretching almost from sea to sea, and about a mile in diameter. The northern face was penetrated by three salients, each of which was separated from its neighbors by deep and precipitous ravines, which made communications extremely difficult. Colonel A. L. Haldane, a British military observer, who had been imprisoned with Winston Churchill during the Boer War, was nevertheless highly impressed with the position. He thought that "nature and art had made this position well nigh impregnable, for its slopes are bare and glacis like, the field of fire is extensive and, on the day of battle, a network of barbed wire fronted the assailant as he rushed to the attack."

The eastern approaches were much better defended than the western. Two fences of barbed wire enclosed a minefield covered by fire, while on the western flank Colonel Tretyakov relied heavily on the muddy foreshore to deter a flanking movement by the Japanese forces.

Terrain, he felt, was not his problem, but the men with which to defend it. General Stoessel, under whose command from Port Arthur the Fifth Regiment was to operate, was himself overstretched. Of his force of about 30,000 men, the headquarters of the Seventh East Siberian Rifle Division and the Fifteenth East Siberian Rifle Regiment were in Port Arthur, but detachments were spread thin along the coast. There was danger not only at Nanshan but everywhere, and this Kuropatkin clearly recognized in a letter addressed to General Stoessel on the eve of Kuroki's attack across the Yalu.

Stoessel added his own memoranda to the letter before passing it on to General Fock. "Personally," he said, "I think the best course would be for you to order the Fifth East Siberian Rifle Regiment to hold the position and to assume the offensive as soon as the main army approaches, otherwise the strongly fortified position will be lost."

With two battalions of the Fifth Regiment and a battery of artillery, Colonel Tretyakov made a reconnaissance in force under Fock's general direction to assess the significance of the Japanese landing. Maps were scarce and the roads numerous, confusing, and bad. The chief of staff, who had the detachment's only map, could not control his horse, which often dashed far ahead, leaving no guides to say where he had gone. The troops straggled over the hills, showing themselves on the skyline, devoting their principal efforts to keeping in touch and almost no effort at all toward finding the enemy. "It was lucky," said Colonel Tretyakov, "that we were the defenders and not the attackers." After wandering about aimlessly in this manner, sometimes with the artillery in front of the infantry, without making contact, the detachment turned back toward its base at Nanshan. The business of the day over, the men marched home singing loudly.

As if the threat of Japanese attack was not serious enough, the troops also came under fire from Chunchuses,* or armed bandits, often Japanese-led, who were to plague them for the rest of the war. A succession of senior officers arrived from Port Arthur to inspect the defenses at Nanshan and in the nearby town of Chin-chou, which Tretyakov planned to use as an outpost. General Fock came constantly and had little patience with Tretyakov's complaint that he had too few troops. "You know that less heroism is required to defend this position than to retreat from it," he told the Colonel. But Tretyakov had only eleven companies with which to hold the isthmus, and the troops, he knew, would be spread far too thin to provide anything but the weakest lines of defense even if he kept the irreducible minimum of one company in reserve.

To add to his worries, General Fock told him that no other forces could be held in reserve for the regiment. Yet no one spared him advice about the type of resistance he had to provide. General Kondratenko, the idolized commander of the Seventh East Siberian Rifle Division, told him bluntly that the Fifth Regiment should be prepared to defend the position to its last drop of blood.

---

*Bazoku, or "mounted bandit," would be a better term. The word "Chunchuse" is probably a German transliteration of the Chinese word hung-hu-tze. Since it had wide currency at the time of the war, it is used here. The bazoku were bands of rebellious peasants who organized defense against the Ch'in Dynasty officials, big landlords, and invading Tartars and Mongols in Manchuria. They were given special training in guerrilla warfare. Before the Russo-Japanese War, they were contacted by Japanese intelligence, who used them for espionage and sabotage. If the Japanese spies or soldiers committed acts which were inconvenient for the authorities, it was always the bazoku who were blamed for them.

By May 14, Oku felt confident enough to move across the peninsula in some force, but he was not yet ready to exploit his position. The ammunition trains and hospitals, and the Fifth Division, which was to be added temporarily to his force, were still at sea. He contented himself, therefore, with strong patrol actions against Tretyakov's outposts, which ran from the sea to the walls of the city of Chin-chou, and then southeast to Nanshan station and Hand Bay. Even this pressure was expressed with force and determination.

Dismayed at the inadequacy of the force under his command—he was being asked to hold with a regiment what should have required at least a division—Colonel Tretyakov appealed for two infantry scout detachments from the reserves. With these additional forces, he strengthened his outposts. On his immediate front he was not unduly worried. The thick, high walls of Chin-chou were an extremely difficult initial hurdle for the Japanese. His reinforced company there had filled sixty sandbags with explosives which they planned to detonate under the advancing Japanese troops.

Yet the strain was beginning to tell. "We hardly had a moment's peace," Tretyakov wrote. "I never once undressed, or took off my boots. Messages kept coming in and hardly gave me a chance of closing my eyes. Such was the strain, and we were quite worn out."

The strains and stresses were not all on one side. On May 19 the Japanese public learned of the sinking of the *Hatsuse* and *Yoshino*. Oku's orders now were to take no risks. Imperial General Headquarters had no illusions about the nature of the task they had set him. The Fifth Division and the First Cavalry Brigade had begun disembarking on May 15, and, until they were ready to lend a hand, Oku was to wait. At the same time, Kuropatkin added to the encouragement in Port Arthur following the loss of the Japanese ships by promising to assume the offensive as soon as he was strong enough. His letter, written on May 17, reached Port Arthur by blockade runner on May 19. "I envy the simple and glorious task which will fall to the lot of the splendid army of the Kwantung Peninsula should it be called upon to bear the heaviest of the fighting," his letter said. "If it were not the question of supply, I should feel perfectly at ease, no matter how great were the forces directed against you."

With bitter recollection of the Yalu reverse and General Zasulitch's foolhardy defense, Kuropatkin also emphasized the folly of delaying a withdrawal from Nanshan for too long. "It appears highly desirable that General Fock's troops and the guns on the Nanshan position should be withdrawn in good time," he added. "Otherwise it will be a case of more trophies, perhaps forty guns, falling into the hands of the enemy, a calamity which would have a most depressing effect on the troops."

Oku had now moved his three divisions, the First, the Third, and the

Fourth, in a half-circle around the Nanshan position and the town of Chin-chou. The Fourth was immediately north of Chin-chou on the coast. The First held the high ground due east of the town and the Nanshan position, and the Third had moved out of the high ground into the highly cultivated plain east of the railway and north of Hand Bay. Weather permitting, all was ready to go.

Colonel Tretyakov was far from ready. On the evening of May 22 he received a six-inch naval gun which he decided to install in the center of his redoubt so that it would command the bays on both flanks. But the gun had still not been mounted when the Japanese artillery bombardment finally began. It was to fall unused, and undamaged, into the enemy's hands before it had fired a shot.

The Russian artillery commander repeatedly asked without success for more ammunition. The batteries had an average of only one hundred fifty rounds each. Four old Chinese guns, which commanded the right flank, had no traverses, and no bulletproof shelter for the gunners or ammunition, nor were they connected by phone with the commandant. Within their limits, however, Colonel Tretyakov's men had worked like beavers to prepare the orthodox infantry defense. In front of his position the barbed wire entanglements now stretched across the isthmus. Behind the wire and the minefields the trenches had been carefully roofed and covered with fresh earth, leaving only slits through which the infantry would fire.

As the final elements of the Fifth Division came ashore, the weather turned sour, and many landing craft carrying troops, horses, and supplies overturned and were lost. The bad weather also forced Togo's supporting gunboats to seek shelter. Both sides suffered from the storm. Colonel Tretyakov, still disturbed by the inadequacy of his force and worried that his six-inch gun was not yet mounted, looked out of his shelter on the morning of May 25 to see that the earth covering the minefields in front of his position had been washed away by the rain. There was no time now to repair the damage.

Oku jumped off soon after daylight that morning. Russian searchlights had played over the Japanese positions during the night, and now, at the height of the bombardment, a Russian balloon rose above the lines, causing much astonishment and attracting much Japanese fire. As a diversion, it had some effect, though Colonel Tretyakov was at a loss to understand why it had been brought to the position, since his own vantage spot on Nanshan provided all the observation he needed.

During the morning, Russian outposts fell back into Chin-chou but half-hearted attacks on the town itself by the Fourth Division were repelled by the defenders. At 3 P.M. the naval support that Togo had promised had still failed to appear, and Oku called off the attack for the day.

Barking dogs disclosed the Japanese movements soon after midnight on the night of May 25–26, and Russian searchlights picked up the troops moving across the open fields through heavy rain. Again, Chin-chou was the first objective. Despite the weather, the searchlights and the lightning enabled Tretyakov to see that the Japanese were beginning to encircle Chin-chou.

Midnight was the time Oku had set for the capture of Chin-chou, and its continued occupation by the Russians promised to interfere seriously with the plans for the attack on Tretyakov's main position on the hill line south of Chin-chou. Four engineers from the First Division now volunteered to make an attempt against the eastern gates of the town. They stripped down to their underwear to avoid becoming caught in the barbed wire and succeeded in making their way to the gate, where, though they were all seriously wounded, they detonated a mine.

Through his binoculars, Colonel Tretyakov could now see the Japanese enveloping movement unfolding. Oku's artillery batteries had moved in an unbroken semicircle from Chin-chou Bay to Hand Bay, and were being brought to bear in maximum strength on the entire Nanshan position, where, with his ten companies of the Fifth East Siberian Rifle Regiment, he was to hold the pass. At daybreak four of Togo's gunboats appeared in Chin-chou Bay, adding three 10-inch and four 4.7-inch naval guns to the weight of the bombardment.

The advancing infantry of the Third Division were the first to feel the weight of the Russian infantry fire from Nanshan, and soon Tretyakov could see the Japanese infantry, wearing khaki for the first time, beginning to form, like the artillery, a semicircle around the northern and eastern part of his position. He felt pleased with the marksmanship of the infantry, for the advancing Japanese, he saw, left many men behind them on the ground. He was also cheered by the arrival in Hand Bay of a gunboat whose three big guns added useful artillery capacity, though after about two hours the ebbing tide forced her to return to Dalny.

Since the Japanese, apart from their naval support, had 198 guns and Colonel Tretyakov only fifty, it was not long before the disparity began to show. Only sixteen of Tretyakov's fifty guns could be brought to bear on Chin-chou Bay. His other guns were no match for Togo's gunboats. As early as 8 A.M. Russian ammunition began to run short. An hour later one battery ceased fire and by 11 A.M. only two guns were still in action. By noon there was not a round of ammunition left among the lot. In the last battery to stop firing, one man remained alive. He continued to fire each gun in rotation until a direct hit from a Japanese field piece ended his life.

From early morning Colonel Tretyakov had watched his right flank, where the Third Division was attempting to push its way up the hill and

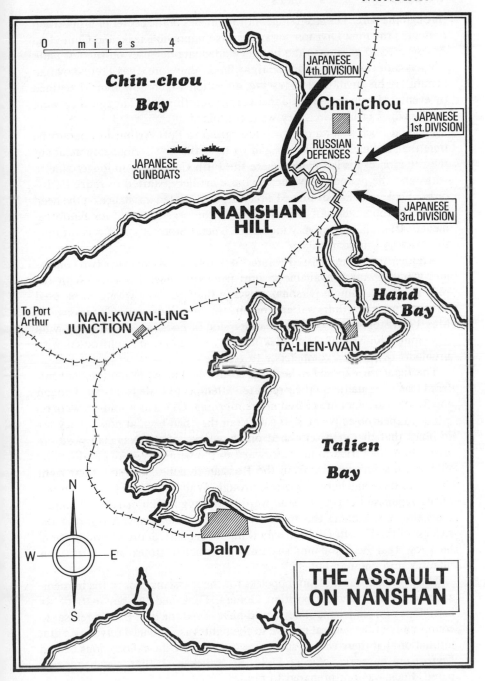

0   miles   4

Chin-chou Bay

JAPANESE
4th. DIVISION

Chin-chou

JAPANESE
1st. DIVISION

RUSSIAN
DEFENSES

JAPANESE
GUNBOATS

JAPANESE
3rd. DIVISION

NANSHAN HILL

Hand Bay

To Port
Arthur

NAN-KWAN-LING
JUNCTION

TA-LIEN-WAN

Talien Bay

N

W   E

S

Dalny

**THE ASSAULT
ON NANSHAN**

through the wire. The steep slopes of the ravines in the center of his position presented the First Division with an almost impossible task, and Chin-chou Bay seemed to guarantee the not very adequate defenses on the left flank from assault there. It was to the right flank, therefore, that Tretyakov had committed his small tactical reserve, an action which now seemed justified by events. Nowhere had the Japanese broken through. Though they were on the edges of his wire, they were contained.

General Fock sent an optimistic telegram to Port Arthur just about the time that Colonel Tretyakov began to have the first serious doubts about the situation of his left flank, where the Fifth Company, no longer able to withstand the pounding by the Japanese artillery, started to retire in disorder. Fock, who had dismissed Tretyakov's repeated insistence on the need for more troops, did not respond now to the urgent appeal for reinforcements. After all, at that very moment General Stoessel's staff was toasting the "victory" in champagne.

Another four hours passed before Fock told Tretyakov that two companies would be made available to him from the general reserve. With the reinforcements came a personal message that the troops were to be used only to cover a withdrawal and not in the line. Kuropatkin's message of May 17 to Stoessel lay behind the indecision of Fock, a police general, who now found himself in a complex military situation and confronted with problems beyond his competence to resolve.

The Japanese, exposed to heavy, well-directed machinegun fire, had suffered fearful casualties in their repeated attempts to scale Nanshan. Though the Russian artillery fire ceased in the morning, Oku's foot soldiers were no closer to their objective at 3:30 P.M. than they had been at noon. They lay in holes that they had scratched on the slopes of the Nanshan position. Every time they tried to move forward to the wire they were cut down by rifle and machinegun fire from the Russian trenches. Only on their right flank was there any hope of a breakthrough. Waist deep in water, the troops of the Japanese Fourth Division were ready to go. Oku decided to launch a general attack along the entire front as the best means of insuring the success of the Fourth Division's flanking movement. Short of ammunition, he knew that he could not sustain a protracted attack and turned his infantry into "human bullets."

The situation was far from hopeless for the Russians. For to the immediate rear of the Nanshan position General Fock had the best part of six battalions of fresh troops. They could have saved the day. Fock's refusal to commit any of the general reserve to the fight was Colonel Tretyakov's first intimation that there was no substance to the do-or-die exhortations he had heard from his senior officers while the Nanshan position was being prepared. Fock was not prepared to fight.

[294]

Tretyakov wanted only a single battalion to throw into the line. Though he was denied it, his troops continued to hold against the renewed Japanese artillery and infantry attack. Disregarding all losses, the Third Division attacked repeatedly on the right flank. Again at fearful cost, it succeeded in breaking into the Russian minefield but was pinned down and partly surrounded by the Russian infantry. The First Division fared no better. In two companies of the Third Regiment all the officers and more than half of the men were killed or wounded.

During this assault, Tretyakov remained without even the limited reinforcements that Fock had promised. It was not until 6 P.M. that the two companies turned up. Tretyakov decided to ignore at least part of Fock's order and sent half of one company to the center of his position.

Not in the center, or on the right, but in the inadequately defended left was where real trouble lay. The Fourth Division was not highly regarded in the Japanese army. It came from Osaka and was ridiculed as soft and spoiled by city life. Yet on this May afternoon its troops waded for a mile along the coast, floundering in mud holes and buffeted by the waves before it turned toward the shore and action. Soon after six o'clock, when bullets began to whistle over the heads of the Russian defenders in the center of the Nanshan position, Colonel Tretyakov saw the "yellow coats* streaming up and shrapnel bursting."

Tretyakov threw his remaining reserves into the action with orders to attack. At the same time, General Fock, who had taken over personal command of the operation at noon, sent the order to retire. To add to Tretyakov's grave troubles, Fock's order failed to reach him, but was delivered to the troops holding the left flank.

Oku's forces made the most of the confusion. A renewed artillery onslaught against the crumbling defenses ended the day. The Fourth Division pushed into the ravines and over the Russian position, and on the right flank the First and Third Divisions also broke through. Nanshan was theirs.

Even now Tretyakov refused to concede defeat. In anticipation of the possibility of an attack from the south as well as from the east and the west, he had built the second line of defenses on which to fall back. Or so he thought. But Fock, having decided to abandon the immediate Nanshan position, had also decided to abandon all. His staff ordered the destruction of reserve ammunition dumps, without taking the precaution to warn either Tretyakov or his troops who had fought so well and for so long.

Just after dark, and after redeploying his forces in the southern position,

---

*The Second Army had discarded the conspicuous blue uniforms and switched to khaki.

[295]

Tretyakov started a tour of inspection of his new line. Noticing that the small railway station of Ta-fang-shen was on fire, he went to investigate. "Suddenly there was a terrific explosion and I was covered with fragments of burning planks and hot bricks," he wrote. He had the narrowest escape from death: a major and twenty other men were killed. Later, when he discovered not only that the station had been blown up by orders of Fock's staff but that what he described as the entire Fourth East Siberian Rifle Division* was camped in a wide valley at Nan-kwan-ling within easy marching distance of the front lines, he was understandably bitter.

Because Fock's order to retreat failed to pass through the proper chain of command and was distributed to only some of the companies, many small groups of Russians held on and died at their posts. Tretyakov told the story:

> Lieutenant Krageoski refused to retreat and bade each of his men farewell as they passed him. Captain Makoveiev, commanding the Eighth Company, declared that he would never retreat and was true to his word. He remained in the trenches and was killed only when he had expended all the cartridges in his revolver. Major Sokolov, commanding the Ninth Company, also refused to retreat and sabered several Japanese before being bayoneted to death.

Until the last moments of the battle, Tretyakov's casualties had been relatively light. He lost only 450 men during the day: in the retreat another 650 fell.

Like most retreats conducted in such circumstances, it quickly became a rout. A baggage wagon careened down the road to Port Arthur followed by a field battery that paid no heed to anyone who got in its way. Tretyakov watched in dismay as a mass of wagons, mounted men, riderless horses, and unarmed men joined the stampede. Someone shouted, "Japanese cavalry, Japanese cavalry," to add to the panic and confusion. "From bivouacs behind us shots and volleys were heard," wrote Tretyakov. "Together with the other officers near me, I rushed to the rest of the column to restore order." He found the regimental band and ordered it to play and to lead the march to Nan-kwan-ling, eight miles along the road toward Port Arthur.

The Japanese losses were light during the breakthrough and very heavy during the day. In all, 739 men were killed and 5,459 wounded. But in this

---

*Colonel Tretyakov was probably mistaken. Only the Fifteenth Regiment appears to have been at Nan-kwan-ling, though the point was well taken: there were ample reserves in the immediate vicinity to have halted Oku's exhausted and badly mauled forces.

one action the troops expended more ammunition than all the Japanese armies had fired during the Sino-Japanese War. The news shocked Imperial General Headquarters.

They kept their apprehensions to themselves, however, and the world saw the battle as one more example of Japanese military skill and determination. "The magnificent qualities of pluck and endurance displayed by the Japanese in the battle, and the incomparably more favorable conditions in which the attack upon Port Arthur can now take place, must cause home-staying Russians to tremble for the safety of their fortress and their fleet," *The Times*'s military correspondent concluded.

Not only the home-staying Russians were trembling. All day long the noise of battle had rolled over Talien Bay into Dalny. Many civilians had already evacuated the town, but Stoessel, in an attempt to keep up morale, had encouraged business as usual and promised that word would be sent in plenty of time if there was any need to leave. If proof were needed of Russian confidence, there was a regiment of East Siberian troops, supported by an artillery brigade, in its comfortable Dalny barracks. Nothing the Japanese could do would be a threat to such a force.

It was a disturbed Dalny that prepared to go to bed that night. At 11 P.M. the panic began. A train pulled in from Nan-kwan-ling bringing the news of the fall of Nanshan. At the same time, Stoessel sent a telegram to the mayor authorizing the civil evacuation of Dalny, but not by train.

The retreat of Tretyakov's gallant troops needed no embroidery to warn Dalny's unhappy inhabitants of the dangers that confronted them. The town was less than eight miles from the Nan-kwan-ling junction. The two roads from Dalny to Port Arthur put a greater distance between the Japanese forces and the fleeing civilians, but there were almost no horses available to move them and the journey by junk was hazardous. People feared a massacre by the Japanese or Chunchuses, and many wandered helplessly about the town, not knowing what to do.

The Russian population met in Upravlensk Square, where the mayor ordered the immediate evacuation of the town. Three hours later a bedraggled collection of men, women, and children, some on horseback, some in jinrickshas, and some on foot, were headed for Hsiao-ping-tao, about twelve miles to the south. In all, 470 Russian men, ninety-two women, and fifty-seven children left during the night.

As they made their slow way along the road to Hsiao-ping-tao, keeping some sort of order and with their speed dictated by the progress of the slowest, the military began to blow up Dalny's installations behind them. They were not very successful. Though they destroyed the railway bridges, hundreds of loaded wagons and godowns filled with food and other supplies fell into Japanese hands. The Japanese also took over intact a first-class port through which men and materials would soon flow for the assault south on Port Arthur and the advance north on Liaoyang.

Few of the refugees carried enough food or water for the journey. Children became sick and exhausted. Tretyakov's column was not in much better shape. General Fock had ordered the regiment's rear echelon back to Port Arthur, and it had left taking with it the mobile kitchens and all the food. Tretyakov fed his men on bread obtained from the Fourth Division. This, and some salt to add flavor, was their only food available on the night after the battle.

They marched toward Port Arthur on the following day and slept that night without food of any sort. The next day, May 29, they found the way blocked by the exhausted refugees from Dalny. Finally, in the evening they caught up with their rear echelon and for the first time since the battle for Nanshan went to sleep on full stomachs.

No heroes' welcome awaited Tretyakov's men. "You are a wretched, undisciplined corps of traitors, cowards and blackguards," Stoessel said when he addressed them on May 30. "I will try the lot of you by court-martial. How did you dare leave Chin-chou? Don't dare to show yourselves in Arthur, lest by your presence you infect the whole garrison with your cowardice." Stoessel had nevertheless been commanded by the Tsar to distribute the Cross of St. George to all wounded who had remained in the ranks. More than 300 stepped out, a number far in excess of his supply of crosses. Stoessel thereupon ordered the doctors to separate the seriously wounded from those with only light wounds, and sixty were decorated. "These were the sole recipients of rewards for the Nanshan battle," Tretyakov wrote bitterly, "those slightly wounded receiving nothing for their bravery and the number of such was great."*

---

*He was not quite correct. Later, Stoessel awarded Fock the Third Class Order of St. George for his role in the battle. For this he was subsequently charged by court-martial with having, intentionally and improperly, made false statements about the battle. Fock also was charged for his failure to give adequate support to Colonel Tretyakov's regiment and for other failures in command.

❧❧❧❧❧❧

CHAPTER 17

The Siege Begins

"Fortresses are useful, in offensive as well as defensive warfare," Napoleon Bonaparte once wrote. "True, they will not in themselves arrest an army, but they are an excellent means by which to retard, weaken, and annoy an enemy." Port Arthur proved Napoleon prescient.

With single-minded determination, Kodama sought to bring about the envelopment of the Russian armies at Liaoyang, and it was there that he had always planned to fight, and to win, the first great battle of the war. Nothing should be allowed to stand in its way. The navy's task had been to make that battle possible. Though Togo had lost two of his battleships in the containment of the Russian fleet at Port Arthur, it was enough that the Japanese transports carrying men and materials for the battlefront in Manchuria had been able to move in safety. Victory at Nanshan was full confirmation of the wisdom of the Japanese strategy to this point of the war.

But now there was Port Arthur to retard, weaken, and annoy. Kodama wanted to forget about it. Japan lacked sufficient forces on the ground to attempt an assault on Port Arthur and at the same time to proceed with the great envelopment movement toward Liaoyang. But, if Kodama was willing to turn his back on Port Arthur, Imperial General Headquarters could not. The Russian ships in Port Arthur had been repaired. Under command of a Makarov, they would assuredly have been tempted to wrest the command of the sea from Togo, with disastrous possibilities for the armies that had now been transported to Korea and Manchuria. To employ only a small force against Port Arthur invited both a rebuff and a weakening of the effort at Liaoyang, with even more fatal long-term consequences for victory in the war. Yet every day troop trains crawling along the Trans-

Siberian Railway added their weight to Kuropatkin's growing military machine. If an attack against Liaoyang were delayed too long, Kuropatkin would have sufficient men to launch his own offensive.

Faced with this dilemma, the Japanese made the same cardinal error that had already been forced on Kuropatkin. They divided their forces. Before the year was out, four Japanese divisions were to be required for the assault on Port Arthur. Two only were earmarked for the task. To command this force, now known as the Third Japanese Army, Imperial General Headquarters appointed General Nogi Maresuke, who had taken Port Arthur with a single regiment in 1894. Escorted by armored cruisers, destroyers, and twenty torpedo boats, Nogi landed at Dalny, taking command on June 6, 1904, on the same day that Togo was promoted to full admiral.

Nogi's attempt to kill himself after he had lost the regimental flag in 1877 when fighting against the Satsuma rebels had been thwarted by command of the Emperor. His war injuries healed, but the disgrace of the lost flag remained with him always.

Death by disembowelment would have been easy. "I will open the seat of my soul and show you how it fares with it," the laws of *bushido* taught. "See for yourself whether it is polluted or clean." Nogi was denied the right, and without a war in which to die he returned to "drinking under the scarlet lanterns." His marriage to the nineteen-year-old daughter of a Satsuma official began badly. He spent the wedding night in drinking and debauchery. On many occasions during their married life Nogi and his wife lived apart, he with his dominant and overpowering mother, his wife with the two sons of the marriage.

In 1886 he was sent to Germany to study warfare, and after eighteen months returned to Japan convinced that the Kaiser's army was far too frivolous. He became stricter than ever in his relations with his wife and family. Harsh discipline toward them and his troops now took the place of his former heavy drinking and intemperate ways.

Always the dishonor of losing the flag remained with him, tainting his life and his relations with others. "He appears to be considerate of others' feelings, yet he often ignores others' favors or feelings," wrote one Japanese biographer. "He is full of love and affection, yet he does not show them, or shows them in the opposite manner. He must have thought of his home and family, yet he is often cold toward them."

Yamagata, who had ordered Nogi to commit suicide in order to clear the name of his regiment in 1877, now chose him to command the Third Army. The appointment surprised many other members of the imperial general staff. But senior generals were few in number, and Port Arthur seemed unlikely to present a serious challenge. Nogi had fought bravely in the war against China and after serving in Formosa as governor was given the rank of baron. He had been living a quiet and lonely life in semi-retirement in Nasu-No, close to the Emperor's detached palace, writing poetry, farming, and spending his meager allowance on books extolling the emperor system. Feudalism had taught him that money was "dirty," and Nogi believed soldiers did not require it. He also thought it was depraved for a man to be drawn toward a woman for love. Retired and retiring, almost a recluse, and with little knowledge of, or interest in, modern military techniques, he had been thrust into what was to prove the most difficult of all the Japanese field commands. With no real confidence in his own ability, and after two years and nine months in retirement, he was content to leave the decision-making in the hands of his chief of staff, Major-General Ijichi, a Satsuma, who was related to Oyama and reflected in full the clan's aggressive spirit.

The day he left for the war, Nogi told his wife that she would not hear from him until the war was won. His two sons, Katsusuke and Yasusuke, were also in the army and their mother prepared a special dinner the night before her husband and sons left home. "Please show a smiling face at least for once," she pleaded with her husband. Nogi looked sternly at her. "This is not a smiling matter," he said, as he sipped a farewell glass of wine. "A father and two sons are going to the war," he told her. "None of us knows who will be killed first. There should be no funeral until all three are returned in coffins."

All three male members of the family were to die for their Emperor, to avenge the wrongs of the father.

Nogi arrived at Dalny to learn of the death of his eldest son Katsusuke at Nanshan. Before the son died, he presented to a fellow officer the sword that his father had given him. "I give it to you," he said as he passed it over to his brother officer, "and you shall enter the city of Port Arthur instead of myself. My soul is in the sword."

"I am glad he died so splendidly," said Nogi. "It was the highest honor he could have."

Nogi was a fanatic, and the men under his command had been worked up to the same pitch of fanaticism. Love of the Emperor and revenge for what the Japanese lost in the war with China had been instilled into them. They marched toward Port Arthur singing battle hymns addressed to the spirits of men killed in the war of 1894.

One of Nogi's men was Lieutenant Sakurai Tadayoshi, an infantry officer who had worked as an intelligence agent in Russia while Japan was preparing for war. After the war he wrote a bestseller titled *Human Bullets* about the siege of Port Arthur. It sold more than a million copies in Japan and was translated into English and many other languages. He and his fellow soldiers were all samurai at heart, if not by birth. Waking to the thunder of the guns at Nanshan, Lieutenant Sakurai's men literally ran toward the battle: "March, tear on! We spread our legs as wide as possible. We kicked and spurned village after village, field after field." Canteens empty, panting and perspiring, they sped past Japanese hospital tents, filled to overflowing with wounded, past the mounds of dead and dying men and the cremation fires of a thousand Japanese soldiers, an honor infrequently conferred as the war progressed since wood for the funeral pyres was almost unobtainable on this desolate peninsula and was reserved only for the cremation of high-ranking officers.

The Third Army came upon Russian casualties, crosses around their necks, ikons clutched in dead hands, dead horses, and jumbled masses of dead and dying Japanese and Russian soldiers, piled together. "Only one more hill in front of us! Beyond that were blood-streams and corpse-hills. When we reached this spot the deafening cannon-roar suddenly ceased— the mountains and valleys recovered their ancient silence. . . ." They had missed the battle of Nanshan. But there were many bloodier battles to come. The eager soldiers of the Emperor had been told that the taking of Port Arthur in 1894 had been "not quite so easy as to twist a baby's arm." This time many thousands of "human bullets" would be required to bring the fortress once more under the flag of the Rising Sun.

Nogi visited the Nanshan battlefield and was shown the grave of his son, marked by a plain wooden plaque with Katsusuke's name written on it in india ink. He took two bottles of beer from his adjutant and placed them before the grave. Soon afterwards Nogi, the frustrated poet, still courting death, wrote one of his first poems of the war, in classical Chinese, the preferred medium for many Asian scholars:

> Mountains, rivers, grass, and trees: Utter desolation.
> For ten miles the wind smells of blood from this new battlefield.
> The steed advances not, men speak not.
> I stand outside the town of Chin-chou in the light of the
> setting sun . . .

Though Nogi was to become, along with Togo, the greatest Japanese "hero" of the war and honors were to be showered on him, he was essentially a product of the Japanese psychological warfare system, with its need always to win and to create heroes, even if none existed. Despite the evidence of his own eyes at Nanshan, he approached his task at Port Arthur overconfident and underprepared. He still remembered, in common with many other veteran officers, the ease with which Port Arthur had been reduced in the war with China. "The Sino-Japanese War was only a rabbit hunt compared with this war," wrote Shiki Moriharu, a platoon commander with Nogi during the 1894 war, and now a battalion commander in the Third Army's Eleventh Division. He had been shocked by the Nan-

shan casualties and the inadequate hospital facilities. But of the difficulties
ahead most officers were still blissfully unaware. As the Eleventh Division
was making its way toward the forward Russian defense lines, a staff officer
from Third Army headquarters tapped Major Shiki on the shoulder. "Say,
Shiki," he said. "We survived the Sino-Japanese War in good health. We
won't have to waste our lives this time either, will we?" Shiki did not know
how to reply. Staff officers led sheltered lives, he thought. He had no doubt
that the task ahead was likely to be much more formidable than anything
that he had encountered when he fought the Chinese.

The problems of command, however, were not all confined to one side.
With Nanshan, Chin-chou, and Dalny lost in a night and a day, General
Stoessel continued to wrangle with his commandant, General Smirnov.
"You will remain commandant," he declared, "but I shall run the fortress.
Whether legal or not, it is my affair. I will answer for that."

There were now many more mouths to feed. The refugees from Dalny
streamed in tired, hungry, and exhausted. Though neutral ships were still
running the Japanese blockade, General Stoessel refused demands by General Smirnov for preserved meat, vegetables, and medical supplies. Only
after much persuasion would he agree to take desperately needed supplies
of tinned milk offered by a French merchantman whose captain was ordered
not to come in again. Many officers and men at Port Arthur felt that
General Stoessel should be examined by the chief medical officer, declared
insane, and placed in the hospital. But Stoessel was backed by the Tsar and
was, with Alexeiev, the center of a bitter controversy with Kuropatkin over
Port Arthur's defense.

The St. Petersburg correspondent of the *Echo de Paris* interviewed an
officer of the Russian general staff who insisted that Kuropatkin would not
move on orders from the Tsar, though Nicholas wanted desperately to
relieve Port Arthur. "The Emperor confined himself to inquiring of General
Kuropatkin if the situation admitted of his advancing on Port Arthur,
adding that he was merely expressing a wish, and left to the general commander-in-chief the task of examining the possibility of complying with it
and of forming an entirely independent judgment." General Kuropatkin
replied that it was impossible. He would not leave Liaoyang. The *Echo de
Paris* correspondent said that the commander-in-chief would sooner have
resigned his position than have executed an order, even from the Tsar,
whom he respected, if it had appeared to him disastrous for future operations. "I do not say that he will not move at all," he wrote. "I do not even
say that he is not at present on the march, but you may state that he is acting
on his own initiative, unhampered by the current authorities. He has not
yet defeated the Japanese but he has defeated Admiral Alexeiev."

[303]

The Kaiser, always eager to see Russia overextended, wrote to Tsar Nicholas on June 6, beginning his letter "Dearest Nicky" and sending his love to Alix and Mama:

I feel the more proud as I may infer from this fact that you count upon me as your *real friend* as you rightly express it. So it is! And I can assure you that nobody follows all the phases of the war with greater interest and assiduity than I do. Your remark about Kuropatkin was a perfect revelation to me!—I am astonished of his shortsightedness in not implicitly obeying your commands. He ought all the more to have followed your counsels—as you had been to Japan yourself, and therefore were a much more competent judge of the Japs than him. Your warnings were quite right and have been fully borne out by the facts. I only hope to goodness the General won't jeopardize the final success of your forces by rashly exposing them to an "echee" before the whole of his reserves have joined him, which are as I believe still partly on the way. The old proverb of Napoleon I still holds good—*la victoire est avec les gros Bataillons;* one can never be too strong for the battle; especially respecting the artillery; an absolute superiority must undoubtedly be established to insure victory.

The Russians at Port Arthur did not realize that the Japanese were equally anxious to avoid a sea battle. As in the case of the battleship *Yashima,* they concealed the loss or damage to ships whenever possible. And the Russian intelligence service in Port Arthur was inefficient. Its only source of information was the local Chinese, who, working both for the Russians and the Japanese, favored those who paid the most. The Japanese rates were high: the Russians paid a "starvation wage." General Nogi and the other Japanese generals knew much that happened inside the fortress, including Stoessel's quarrels with General Smirnov.

About the middle of June Nicholas and the Higher Naval Board in St. Petersburg decided to send the Baltic Fleet, under Rear-Admiral Zinovi Petrovitch Rozhdestvenski to the assistance of the Port Arthur and Vladivostok squadrons.

Togo apparently knew of the formation of the new Russian squadron before the final decision had been made in Russia. As early as May 30, he telegraphed his need for a thousand more mines to be laid to blockade the enemy's ships at Port Arthur and Vladivostok and to bar the way of the Baltic Squadron.

Timid Admiral Vitgeft had failed to go out to attack the crippled Japanese fleet on May 15 when *Hatsuse* and *Yashima* were sunk. True, he did not know that not one but two battleships had been destroyed, and getting in and out of Port Arthur had become a difficult and lengthy business. The mines outside the harbor were a great deterrent. There was always a long delay while minesweepers cleared the exit for the Fleet to emerge—and another on the return journey. By now the Japanese had given up the idea of blocking the harbor and concentrated on laying mines. Almost every day Japanese ships were at the entrance to the harbor, either dropping mines or pretending to drop them.

Togo learned in the middle of June that the Tsar had ordered Port Arthur to be held, but if it should capitulate Stoessel was to destroy all the forts and buildings. The ships were to try to get to Vladivostok "as best they could, blowing themselves up if they could not attain that object." On June 18 Togo's orders to his fleet commanders were specific and concluded: "The above orders explain what is intended to be done in case the enemy come out; but as the object of our strategy is to prevent them from escaping, our blockading squadrons are always to bear this in mind, and frighten the enemy by letting them see our ships. . . . The destroyers and torpedo boat flotillas are to lay mines and cause the enemy to hesitate before attempting to get out."

Togo's efforts to frighten the Russians could not have been more effective. Vitgeft was afraid to move. Under pressure from Alexeiev and, ultimately, from the Tsar himself, he made timid sallies out with the faint-hearted hope of reaching Vladivostok. On June 5, under heavy pressure, he decided that a sortie should be made on June 13, when all the damaged ships would be repaired. Two days later he canceled the order, though *Novik* and the destroyers went out occasionally to harass the Japanese ships bombarding the forts. On one of these sorties the minelayer *Amur*, which had so successfully prepared the trap for the two Japanese battleships in May, struck a sunken Japanese blockship and had to be abandoned.

On June 13 Vitgeft again ordered the fleet to put to sea. By June 20 it was ready, with steam up. The Admiral addressed the fleet: "With the help of God and the Holy St. Nicholas, the wonder worker, who is the protector of mariners, we will endeavor to fulfill our duty loyally and conscientiously and to defeat the enemy. . . . May God be with us."

With astonishing disregard for security, the news of the fleet's impending departure was published in a special edition of *Novoye Krai,* the official newspaper in Port Arthur. The news swiftly reached the Japanese, and at 10 A.M. on June 20 Vitgeft called the officers of the fleet to the flagship *Tsarevitch,* which had been successfully repaired, and told them to let their fires die out. Copies of the special edition of the *Novoye Krai* were recalled. "Quite useless," remarked a torpedo boat officer. "The Japanese have already read the order—probably they have a proof sheet."

Day after day the sailing orders were issued and repealed. In his diary, Semenov wrote: "We are waiting for the Japanese to inform us that they are aware of our intentions; why, we are simply provoking them. At 9 P.M.

on June 21 we get a circular to the effect that ships are to be ready to sail at 2:30 A.M. on the twenty-second; toward midnight, the signal—'Sailing postponed.' "

On June 23, at four in the morning, the fleet once again started to move out of harbor, *Diana* leading, with *Novik* close behind, followed by the other cruisers and the battleships. Ten or eleven mines were destroyed in the first hour. "God has helped us," said the sailors crossing themselves.

By noon the Russian ships were all moving again. Everyone cheered up, the younger officers on *Diana* calling for champagne to celebrate the occasion. At 1:40 P.M. a *Te Deum* was celebrated. The ship's chaplain, dressed in a bright green and gold embroidered cassock, walked the decks with the Cross and the Holy Water. The choir sang, "O Lord, Save Thy Servants," and heads were bared to receive the blessings and to kiss the Cross.

At half-past four, Admiral Vitgeft dismissed the sweeping party and led his fleet out to sea. The line was headed by the *Tsarevitch,* followed by *Retvizan, Pobyeda, Peresvyet, Sevastopol, Poltava, Bayan, Pallada, Diana,* and *Askold. Novik,* to starboard, escorted seven destroyers.

It was almost 6 P.M. when, twenty miles out of Port Arthur, they saw the Japanese fleet. *Mikasa* led the battle line, followed by the battleships *Asahi, Fuji,* and *Shikishima.* Then came the cruisers *Nisshin, Kasuga, Izumi, Akashi, Akitsushima,* and *Suma,* together with more than thirty destroyers and torpedo boats. Seven other cruisers were on the starboard side of the battle line and nearer the shore was another division, consisting of the three old cruisers, *Hashidate, Itsukushima,* and *Matsushima,* and the veteran ex-Chinese battleship, *Chen Yuen,* now renamed *Chin Yen.*

The appearance of the *Tsarevitch* and *Sevastopol,* which had been repaired, came as a shock to Togo, who had not expected these two Russian battleships. Togo had sent Admiral Kamimura, with four armored cruisers and four protected cruisers to the Sea of Japan to look for the Russian raiders that had sunk the transports, and he was still many miles off when the two fleets met. The Japanese had only four battleships against Russia's six but in total her fleet was made up of about fifty-three ships against the enemy's eighteen. If Admiral Togo was surprised to see not four but six battleships with the Russian fleet, Vitgeft was horrified when the huge Japanese armada appeared.

Both sides prepared for decisive battle. At 6:45 P.M. the two fleets were steering on parallel courses about eight miles apart when *Mikasa* altered course to close in on the Russian line. For five minutes it seemed that action was imminent. Though the sky was beginning to darken, there was a long twilight ahead and the promise of moonlight. But the prospect of a night battle against the strong force that Togo had been able to gather deterred Vitgeft. At 7 P.M. he turned *Tsarevitch* to starboard and led the fleet back in the direction of Port Arthur. Ahead of him was a journey equally as dangerous as the one to Vladivostok that he had abandoned. He had twenty-three miles to go before reaching the safety of Arthur's forts, and no hope of getting back inside the harbor itself until the next morning when the tide would be high.

If Vitgeft had lost his nerve, Togo, also, was cautious. For a time it appeared that he was going to give chase with his main fleet. He turned his ships eight points to starboard together, as if to follow, but a few moments later resumed his original course and sent only his destroyers and torpedo boats in pursuit.

Novik was sent on ahead with the destroyers, and the cruisers came up on the starboard side of the battleships. Just as the last rays of the sun disappeared, the Japanese destroyers and torpedo boats opened fire on the end of the Russian line. They came in all directions but their torpedoes could not find their mark. Unscathed in the fading light, the Russian ships approached the roadstead. In their haste to get away from the Japanese torpedoes they could not spare time to look for the channels which had been swept, but miraculously only the battleship *Sevastopol* struck a mine. With water pouring through her sides her captain managed to get the ship to White Wolf Bay, where he anchored close to shore in six fathoms of water. The rest of the Russian Fleet anchored along the western shore, set up their torpedo nets, and waited. "We all anchored in the roads at Port Arthur without signal, without any orders whatever, as if by inspiration, but we somehow did it well," wrote Semenov in his diary.

From 8:45 P.M. until dawn the next day the Japanese destroyers kept up a long-range torpedo bombardment of the Russian fleet, anchored in two lines outside their harbor, stretching from Golden Hill to White Wolf Hill. Searchlights from the fortress swept the scene while all the Russian ships opened up on the Japanese. "When we were firing with the guns of one side only during these torpedo attacks, the guns' crews at the disengaged side lay round their guns and snored," wrote Semenov on *Diana*. None of the Japanese destroyers came in closer than three miles under the blinding beams of the searchlights and the continual fire from ship and shore. Next morning the Russian fleet was ordered to return to port, against the wishes of almost everyone but the Admiral. "The shadow of death seemed to lie on our ship," wrote Semenov.

No Russian ship was hit by torpedo or gunfire in the action, and only one Japanese destroyer and four torpedo boats were slightly damaged by fire from the forts. After the long and wearying action neither side had gained an inch, but the effect on the two fleets was entirely different. The officers and men of the Russian ships were in the depths of depression. They felt their last chance of escaping annihilation by the Japanese had gone. "Yesterday morning God helped us—last night we remained unharmed by the grace of God," wrote an officer. There was little hope that the fleet would be given another chance to fight or to escape from Port Arthur.

Though the Japanese fleet had missed a great opportunity to damage the luckless Russian squadron, Togo and his men were elated. When the Russian fleet had appeared, Togo and his officers had been shocked to find that the superiority in battleships lay with their opponents. Togo had not wanted a general engagement and had avoided one, and yet his object had been attained. The Russian fleet had retired back into its haven, leaving the sea to the Japanese. "Can it be denied that this was victory?" asked Pakenham.

The view offered is that this was not only one of the most remarkable victories in history, but that it should have redounded more to the personal honor of Togo than any won by a military chief since the fate of battles was decided by single combat. Here were Togo and a Russian admiral face to face. The man Vitgeft quailed and retired before the man Togo. Is it possible to conceive triumph of armed and numerous force more personal to an individual?

On July 2 Togo issued new orders to his torpedo flotilla captains calling for attacks, even in broad daylight.

Moonlight nights should be even more favorable to us. There should be no useless waiting for the moon to set, and so letting slip a good chance for attack. I shall in future order torpedo attacks to be made even in the daytime; all flotillas must therefore be fully prepared for this. In such cases the method to be followed is for two flotillas to go up together, turn to port and starboard respectively, and make a simultaneous attack.

On several occasions in July these tactics were employed against Russian ships, but the destroyers and torpedo boats of the Japanese fleet had no success. The Russian ships stayed inside the harbor, and Admiral Ijuin, vice-chief of the Naval General Staff, advised Togo that, according to "reliable sources," the Russians were never going to give up their ships. "If the situation becomes desperate, they will destroy the ships before we can get at them." Count Makino, the Japanese minister in Vienna who had supplied this report, had information that the Russians were running out of coal at Port Arthur and might still try to get to Vladivostok, where supplies were plentiful.

Togo's task was to continue the watch for the Russian fleet, to keep an even stricter blockade, and to cooperate with the army. Nogi's Third Army was due to move in to attack Port Arthur on July 26.

Viceroy Alexeiev ordered Admiral Vitgeft to give all possible assistance

1. Russia entered the war with supreme confidence.
Contemptuous of Japan, ill-informed about its navy and
army, she expected an early and decisive victory. Many
agreed. In Japan, public opinion clamored for war, but the
government and the military were far from optimistic.
Though they had planned the war for a long time, they were
reluctant to challenge this European military giant. Fears of
Russian ambitions in Manchuria and Korea and the
psychological support of the British alliance led them on.
This cartoon from the immediate pre-war period was typical
of St. Petersburg's view of how the Russians would deal with
the Japanese if they proved foolish enough to go to war.

2. There would be no war because he did not want war, Tsar Nicholas II had said. Now there was not only war but disaster. The cobblestones in the courtyard of the Winter Palace in St. Petersburg rang with the sound of horses' hooves as Nicholas left to inspect troops leaving for the front.

3. Serge Yulevitch Witte, the Tsar's uncouth, ungainly, unloved but able, and far-sighted counsellor. He built the great Trans-Siberian Railway and thus provided the means for Russia to go to war. But he strongly opposed the Court intriguers whose Far Eastern ambitions led to war. This cost him the key post of finance minister on the eve of the war.

4. The Tsar was the "little father," head of the state, the army and the church, who believed that he was appointed by God. On their knees, his troops receive his blessing.

5. Admiral Eugene Ivanovitch Alexeiev, whose appointment as Russian Viceroy in the Far East spurred on the Japanese to rush their plans for war. No strategist, he intervened disastrously in military affairs in the early days of the war.

6. Gifted, much-loved Vice-Admiral Stephen Ossipovitch Makarov, who brought hope to the Russian Pacific Squadron and the fortress at Port Arthur.

7. Vice-Admiral Oscar Victorovitch Stark, weak and overruled. His career ended when Japanese torpedoes exploded among his ships, which were riding at anchor in the roadstead at Port Arthur, on February 8, 1904.

8. Admiral Zinovi Petrovitch Rozhdestvenski, leader of the unseaworthy Baltic Fleet on its epic voyage from Reval to the Straits of Tsushima, where Admiral Togo Heihachiro waited in ambush.

10. General Alexei Nicolaievitch Kuropatkin, the soldiers' soldier, whose leadership of the Russian forces in Manchuria until after the Battle of Mukden was bedevilled by incompetent officers like Grippenberg.

9. General Oscar Casimorovitch Grippenberg, 66-year-old veteran of the Crimean War, deaf, without formal military education, and an epileptic, who was appointed to lead the Second Russian Army in Manchuria.

11. Major-General Roman Isodorovitch Kondratenko, Port Arthur's hero.

12. Lieutenant-General Nicholas Petrovitch Linievitch, the "Siberian wolf," who assumed the leadership of the Russian forces in the field at the age of 67.

14. Prince Ito Hirobumi, the tiny dynamo of the Meiji era. He loved wine and women and was the most significant force behind the throne. Until the last moment, he opposed war with Russia.

15. General Kodama Gentaro, "the rivet in the fan," the war's most brilliant tactician. Better than anyone else, he knew when to make war and when to seek peace.

13. Mutsuhito, the Emperor Meiji, "heaven-descended, divine and sacred" ruler of Japan. Born in 1852, he succeeded to the throne at the age of fifteen. Tsar Nicholas ruled by the will of God, but the Emperor was god incarnate. In his name, the clans who had restored his authority led Japan from feudalism and isolation into the twentieth century and war with Russia.

16. *Above:* Field-Marshal Yamagata Arimoto, father of the Japanese army.

17. *Above right:* Field-Marshal Ōyama Iwao gave General Kodama a free hand when he commanded the Japanese armies in Manchuria.

18. *Right:* General Nogi Maresuke, the war's most tragic figure, won Port Arthur at a terrible cost. He lived and died for the Emperor.

19. *Below:* Colonel Akashi Motojiro, secret agent extraordinary, nourished the seeds of Russian revolution.

20. *Below right:* Captain William Christopher Pakenham, British military observer with Togo's fleet, wartime symbol of Anglo-Japanese accord, and gifted chronicler of the naval battles.

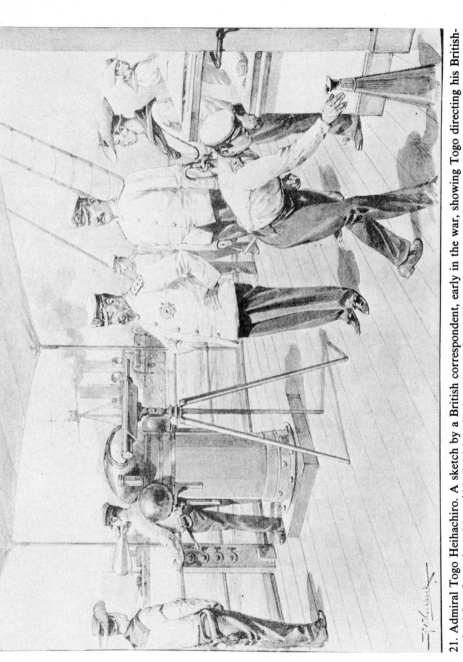

21. Admiral Togo Heihachiro. A sketch by a British correspondent, early in the war, showing Togo directing his British-trained fleet from the bridge of his British-built flagship, *Mikasa*. The artist described him as a modest, retiring little man. He was also stolid, efficient, ruthless and indefatigable. Togo's turn in the Battle of Tsushima—when he brought his battle fleet across the line of approaching Russians, thereby crossing the "T"—is regarded as one of the most remarkable feats in naval history.

22. The young Togo in England in his early twenties (circa 1871). As a naval cadet, he was remembered as diligent and plodding, but with all the instincts of the *samurai*.

23. Togo, grizzled, gray and slow to speak. He had just received the Grand Cordon of the Chrysanthemum, the highest order in Japan. Only one man had ever received it before (circa 1926).

24. Togo with his wife (left) and daughter (right) and other members of the family before rejoining the fleet on the eve of the Battle of Tsushima.

25. The last days of Port Arthur. Looking down shell-torn Pushkin Street toward the inner basin, with its wrecked Russian warships. The office of the newspaper *Novoye Krai* is halfway down on the right.

26. "The railroad to the East was paved with Nicholas' dreams of empire and the discarded empties of his subjects." Stacks of vodka at the railway station in Port Arthur.

27. Three times Togo tried to close the narrow Port Arthur entrance by sinking block ships. It was a costly and unsuccessful effort.

28. The unprotected, American-built Russian cruiser *Varyag*, at anchor in the neutral Korean port of Chemulpo on the afternoon of February 8, 1904. She was 6,500 tons and carried twelve 6-in. guns . . .

29. . . . but they were not nearly enough. Though war had not been declared, a Japanese force, led by six cruisers, ordered the *Varyag* and a smaller Russian ship to leave port or be sunk at anchor. Both chose to fight. With battle flags flying, the Russian ships steamed out of harbor and into hopeless battle. For an hour they fought without protection. Then, battered and on fire, and with many of their crews dead and wounded, they limped back into harbor, opened their seacocks, and blew up their torpedoes. The war had begun.

30. All that remained the next day were the topmasts of the *Varyag*.

31. Within hours of the sinking of the Russian ships at Chemulpo, the Japanese troops began to go ashore. After the ice melted in the rivers and harbors of northern Korea, they were joined by reinforcement divisions. They landed in heavy, blunt-nosed sampans, lashed together in groups of three or four, and sculled from the stern with huge sweeps. Laden down like beasts of burden, they began the march north to the Yalu and the first land battle of the war.

32. Drawings on this page by contemporary artists. Here, impressed coolies carry Japanese supplies in Manchuria. Insets show other forms of transport—the jinricksha and the sampan. In a world without television or movies, the "magic lantern slide projector," for which these pictures were painted, brought the war to the world.

33. Japanese soldiers fanning themselves during a break in the Manchurian summer campaign of 1904.

34. In the mountains that lay between the Yalu and Liaoyang, a company of troops might have delayed an army, but to the surprise of General Kuroki Tametomo, Motienling, the Heaven-Reaching Pass, fell into his hands with scarcely a shot fired. On July 17, 1904, the Russians launched a desperate counterattack against the Japanese forces holding the pass. Fierce hand-to-hand fighting occurred before they were driven off. Bookish, brilliant Kuroki (left) watched the battle from a nearby hill.

35. Much was expected of the gaudy, flamboyant Cossacks, but they proved surprisingly ineffective in the war.

36. The Russian infantry were brave but badly trained and badly led. Bunched together and inadequately protected, they suffered heavily from Japanese fire. Here, in a characteristic Manchurian position, they await the Japanese approach.

37. With inadequate boots and clothing, the Russians suffered bitterly during the Manchurian winter of 1904–5.

38. The fall of Nanshan on May 26, 1904, opened the way to Port Arthur. With a little more cooperation from higher headquarters, Colonel Nikolai Tretyakov's men might have held the position they defended so bravely and changed the immediate course of the war. Here, the Japanese take over the position.

39. On their long march north from Chemulpo to the Yalu River, the Japanese columns approach Pyongyang. Japanese intelligence had fully assessed the army's needs, and pontoon bridges were ready for every river. Despite the heavy going, the troops sometimes marched twenty-five miles in a day.

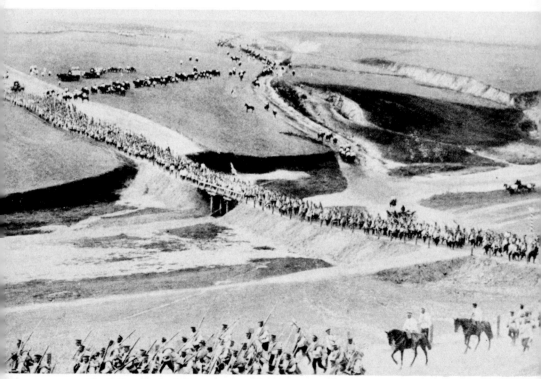

40. A Russian column crossing a stream in southeast Manchuria.

41. Liaoyang was a generals' battle, a test of wills and tactics, fought in blistering heat in fields of tall millet. Victory slipped from the Russians' grasp, and the Japanese, with nearly six thousand dead and their ammunition expended, could not seize it. Here, among the millet, the Japanese pause in the battle on August 26, 1904, to build a funeral pyre preparatory to burning their dead.

42. Mukden was the greatest battle of the war, and the biggest that man had ever fought, but it was not the decisive victory the Japanese, with their manpower spent, so desperately needed. On March 11, 1905, they marched into the city through its massive gates as the Russians fell back in disarray to the mountains in the north.

43. Wantai, the "Watcher's Terrace." In the center of the Chinese wall at Port Arthur, it dominated the surrounding country. Once taken, the advance on the fortress would be comparatively simple. With a 6-in. naval gun, hauled painfully up the hill from a stricken ship in the harbor, Russian sailors went to war on land.

44. After the disastrous Japanese frontal assault in August, 1904, Nogi reluctantly agreed that it was impossible to take Port Arthur by sheer weight of men. The troops would have to burrow their way into the fortress. Thirteen miles of trenches zigzagged through the hills outside Port Arthur, honeycombing the countryside.

45. On the bleak, bare and battered hills outside Port Arthur, tired Russian troops make their way to the front.

46. To match the Russian 6-in. naval guns the Japanese brought in 11-in. Krupp siege guns. The first of the huge five-hundred-pound shells came hurtling into Port Arthur at the beginning of October, 1904. By November, more than three hundred and fifty shells a day were dropped on the town, the defenses and the ships in the harbor. Here, one of the shells begins its deadly flight into the fortress.

49. Colonel Nikolai Tretyakov, the most able of the Russian junior leaders in Port Arthur. He fought bravely at Nanshan, but there, as in Port Arthur, he suffered from the inefficiency of his immediate superiors.

47. Lieutenant-General Constantine Nikolaievitch Smirnov, commander of the Port Arthur fortress. Nicknamed "Seven Devils" by the troops, he was a courageous and much-respected leader, who had constant trouble with . . .

48. . . . Lieutenant-General Baron Anatole Mikailovitch Stoessel, who refused to hand over the command of the fortress to Smirnov. He planned to make Port Arthur his grave but surrendered the fortress instead. Unlike Smirnov, Stoessel was hated by the troops.

50. Nogi's compliments to Stoessel: huge Japanese shells from the 11-in. siege guns waiting to be hurled at the Russian forts and ships at Port Arthur.

51. When the big shells burst on Port Arthur, some of the townspeople built their own bomb shelters, and for months spent their days below ground. Others made use of the rubble from wrecked buildings, sheltering behind it when the shells came in.

52. Two hundred Japanese buried by Russians inside a fort at
Port Arthur. Every man entering was killed by the Russians'
favorite weapon, the bayonet.

53. The shattered remains of Russian soldiers killed in the battle for 203 Meter Hill at Port Arthur, key to the security of the fortress. The Japanese ignored this tumbling, twin-peaked position for months, and the Russians neglected its defense until it was too late.

54. The end of the siege at Port Arthur. Japanese sentries take over from the Russians.

55. The morning after the siege. A hill of used cartridge cases at
Port Arthur.

56. *Mikasa*, Togo's flagship, victor of the Battle of Tsushima. . . .

57. And *Aurora*, which limped into Manila after the battle—one of the few Russian ships to escape.

58. The peacemakers: President Roosevelt on board the *Mayflower* at Portsmouth, New Hampshire, flanked by Serge Witte (extreme left). Witte negotiated the peace and gave to Russia its only victory; Baron Rosen (on Roosevelt's left), Baron Komura (on his right), and Ambassador Takahira Kogoro.

IN THIS BUILDING,
AT THE INVITATION OF
THEODORE ROOSEVELT,
PRESIDENT OF THE UNITED STATES
WAS HELD THE
PEACE CONFERENCE
BETWEEN THE
ENVOYS OF RUSSIA AND JAPAN,
AND
SEPTEMBER 5, 1905, AT 3.47 P.M.
WAS SIGNED
THE TREATY OF PORTSMOUTH,
WHICH ENDED THE WAR BETWEEN THE TWO EMPIRES.

to the defense of the fortress, and then to put to sea and make for Vladivostok, using his best endeavors to avoid action. Kuropatkin again ordered Stoessel to hand over the command of the fortress to Smirnov.

Stoessel pleaded that it was impossible for him to leave. Admiral Vitgeft called a conference of flag and commanding officers to consider his orders. The majority agreed with the decision to stay in Port Arthur until the arrival of the Baltic Fleet, which was expected in October. They would defend Port Arthur or perish with the fortress. Admiral Vitgeft reported to the Viceroy on the decision reached and on his behavior on June 23. "I did not go out for display, but in accordance with orders," he telegraphed.

> Change of circumstances required my return in order to avoid useless loss. After the departure of the squadron to Vladivostok, the enemy would clear a channel and capture Port Arthur with his fleet and troops in very short time; moreover, he would not permit our squadron, weakened by nightly attacks and with its ships damaged, to proceed forward or backward without an action. For the squadron there are only two decisions. Either it is necessary for it to defend Port Arthur in conjunction with the troops until reinforced, or to perish; the moment for a sortie to Vladivostok can only arise when death faces us simultaneously in front and rear.

Fuming, Alexeiev telegraphed urgently to Vitgeft to obey orders. Vitgeft in turn called another council on July 28, again affirming that the fleet should stay to defend Port Arthur. Alexeiev received the message on July 30 and appealed to the Tsar, who replied: "I fully share your opinion concerning the importance of the squadron making a speedy sortie from Port Arthur and breaking through to Vladivostok."

The Tsar's message was sent to Port Arthur, but the imperial message crossed one addressed to Viceroy Alexeiev in which Vitgeft defied all demands that he should desert the fortress.

> The squadron cannot go out; the roadstead has been sown nightly, during fogs, by numerous torpedo craft and mine layers with mines and especially drifting ones. . . . After praying and considering the situation we have decided finally that the squadron must withstand the siege or perish in defense of Port Arthur. The enemy has drawn near and our forces have retired to the forts. There are continual fogs. I have begun indirect firing on the Japanese troops.

Small arms were served out to all ship's crews, including stokers, who drilled each day. Only skeleton crews were left on the ships in the harbor, while soldiers and sailors together manned the forts. The Japanese were closing in.

On August 7, while the Russians in Port Arthur were holding a church service to pray for victory, Viceroy Alexeiev sent another urgent message to the commander of the Pacific Squadron.

I again reiterate my inflexible determination that you are to take the squadron out of Port Arthur. I must recall to you and all serious officers the exploit of the *Varyag*. The failure of the squadron to proceed to sea regardless of the Imperial will and of my command, and its extinction in the harbor in the event of the fall of the fortress will, in addition to the heavy legal responsibility, leave an indelible spot on the flag of St. Andrew and on the honor of the fleet. You are to make known this telegram to all admirals and commanding officers and are to report its receipt.

Inside the church, the women of the town wore their gayest dresses, the men their smartest uniforms, as they listened to words of encouragement issued by General Stoessel. The first sounds of gunfire were heard as they knelt in prayer. The congregation rose to its feet and knelt again as the priest hurriedly concluded services. The first shells fell in the main street of the Old Town, close to the hospital, and on the commercial quays. By the time church service had ended the town and the harbor were being bombarded by the Japanese land forces. And from that bright sunny day onward for many months to come, the sound of shot and shell resounded through the once gay and carefree town of Port Arthur.

❦❦❦❦❦

CHAPTER 18

Te-li-ssu and
the Motien Pass

WHILE COLONEL TRETYAKOV'S men were limping their way from Nan-shan toward Port Arthur on May 27, Kuropatkin was headed north to Mukden for a conference with Alexeiev, who had now established his headquarters in an unused train, roofed over and surrounded by newly planted flowers. Four days earlier Alexeiev's chief of staff had arrived at Liaoyang with a letter from Alexeiev advising him that the time had come for the Manchurian army to advance either toward the Yalu or Port Arthur.

Kuropatkin, who was now more than ever opposed to a premature offensive, was anxious to convince the Viceroy of the folly of moving until sufficient reinforcements had reached Manchuria. These continued to arrive only very slowly, though Prince Khilkov, the minister of ways and communication, had worked desperately to break the bottleneck at Lake Baikal.

By the end of March the thaw had begun, and movement across the lake continued by sleighs. By the end of April the ice had started to break and the ferries were able to operate again. Better, the link running for 162 miles through the high and desolate mountains south of the lake was sufficiently well advanced to enable the first trains to make their slow way through the thirty-nine tunnels and thirteen galleries that protected the track from landslides. The line at this point climbed three thousand feet above the lake before descending to treacherous marshlands. The difficulties were very great. Derailments were frequent, as were landslides. Trains were often delayed for days, and the average speed for military trains, including rest days and days lost, was only 5.94 miles an hour. Until this situation had improved, and adequate reinforcements were available, Kuropatkin was determined that he would not embark on an offensive.

Kuropatkin's train reached Mukden at 5 P.M. on May 27, and immediately he went to Alexeiev's headquarters with his staff. There now ensued a violent discussion between the two leaders. Alexeiev insisted that Port Arthur should be held at all costs and that a force be mounted immediately to attack Oku's victorious Second Army. He was adamant on the need for holding Port Arthur as the main base for the fleet, and in order to avoid the loss of prestige and morale that would result from its fall.

Kuropatkin came briefed with the news of fresh Japanese landings along the coast from Ta-ku-shan. He appreciated that the Japanese Imperial General Headquarters planned an enveloping movement with its armies against Liaoyang and was equally adamant that to weaken the position there either by attempting to drive Kuroki back into Korea or by attacking Oku as a means of reopening land communications with Port Arthur was fraught with both tactical and strategical dangers.

The conference ended with the Viceroy and the commander-in-chief still in total disagreement. That night the wires to St. Petersburg carried both arguments to the Tsar, who called a council of war to decide the issue. General Viktor Viktorovitch Sakharov, the minister of war, Admiral Avellan, the minister of the navy, and Plehve, the minister of the interior, attended.

Moved by the argument of Admiral Avellan that Port Arthur must be maintained as a base "all the more necessary, as the Baltic Fleet would not know where to go were Port Arthur to fall," the council instructed Kuropatkin to move against Oku "in spite," as he wrote, "of my opinions as to our unreadiness for any forward movement; in spite of the fact that out of twelve divisions of reinforcements only one had arrived; in spite of the inefficiency of the railway."

In St. Petersburg rumor spread that Kuropatkin had never given his heart to the Manchurian policy of the government and therefore he did not appreciate the political exigencies of the situation. News of the impending offensive became common gossip, and Akashi's office in Stockholm reported to Tokyo at the beginning of June that fifty-three-year-old Lieutenant-General Baron G. K. Stackelberg with the First Siberian Army Corps was preparing to attack. So many hopes rode with Stackelberg, a court favorite in St. Petersburg, that all thought of security was forgotten.

Unconscious of the new disaster that he had helped to shape, Nicholas embarked with the beautiful and pregnant Alexandra on a tour of inspection of the units headed for Manchuria. They distributed ikons to the troops and tin images of Seraphim of Serov, the new saint, whose canonization was now widely held to be responsible for Alexandra's desirable state.

Though the Imperial General Headquarters in Japan was still far from happy with the shipping available to reinforce Manchuria, the battle of

Nanshan coincided with, and was followed by, a vast movement of men and materials from the home islands. From Oku's Second Army, the First Division had been detached to join with the Ninth and Eleventh divisions in Nogi's Third Army. The Tenth Division, which had landed at Ta-ku-shan on May 19, later joined forces with the Fifth Division and, under the command of sixty-three-year-old General Nozu Michitsura, yet another member of the Satsuma clan, became the Fourth Army. Nozu, a notable connoisseur of French wines, had the reputation of being a highly talented soldier with a very difficult personality. His chief of staff was his son-in-law, Major-General Uehara Yusaku, another Satsuma, who had been his houseboy before marrying his daughter. According to popular belief, not nepotism but Nozu's nature was responsible for Uehara's appointment—no one else would work with him. "Nozu is a better soldier than I am," Oyama told Navy Minister Yamamoto when the appointment of a commander-in-chief in Manchuria was being considered, "but he couldn't possibly work amicably with the other generals."

The first move was to establish contact with Kuroki's First Army squatting at Feng-huang-cheng. With Port Arthur isolated, the way would then be clear for a general movement toward Liaoyang, a hundred miles away, and a set-piece battle with Kuropatkin's Manchurian Army.

Kuropatkin left his meeting with Alexeiev on May 27 still hopeful that reason would prevail in St. Petersburg, but reluctantly willing to meet Alexeiev's demands that initial steps should be taken to prepare for a countermove against General Oku. On May 28, therefore, he headed south to Hai-cheng, a railway town about forty miles south of Liaoyang, where Lieutenant-General G. K. Stackelberg, together with his wife, his sister, and a cow that provided them with a daily supply of fresh milk, had established his headquarters in another train. The weather was beginning to warm up, and Stackelberg employed a detachment of Cossacks to spray water on the roof of his train carriage.

Although he had a cavalry background, Stackelberg's notion of an offensive thrust was to advance through a series of defensive positions. He now chose his ground for the initial effort at Te-li-ssu, about three miles south of Wang-fang-kou, about eighty miles north of Port Arthur and about a 130 miles from Liaoyang. The position had good defensive possibilities, with the railway available to run supplies to the troops who occupied the hills commanding the narrow valley through which the line ran. There, under the cover of a cavalry screen, Stackelberg went to work with impressed Chinese labor to dig trenches and gun positions and to stock supplies. In his gleaming white uniform, he arrived at Te-li-ssu on June 13. Some of his complacency evaporated when he was told by officers on the ground of the extent of the Japanese activity on his front. Though he simply did not believe the report that Oku was marching north with 20,000 men, he immediately asked Kuropatkin to reinforce Te-li-ssu.

The Russian position extended about three-and-a-half miles, which gave Stackelberg a little over 5,000 men to the mile. His right flank was on some small hills with a narrow valley in front. The center was in a flat plain through which the railway embankment runs to Port Arthur, and the left was on some steeper but not high hills.

From this position of apparent strength, the defensive-minded Stackelberg planned to move south, creating new defensive positions from which to launch his offensives until one day Port Arthur was relieved. It was all chimera, since Oku's columns were now marching north in a broad front. His main force, consisting of the Third and Fifth divisions, followed the line of the railway embankment from Port Adams toward Te-li-ssu. The cavalry, on the right, came through the hills. The Fourth Division on the left

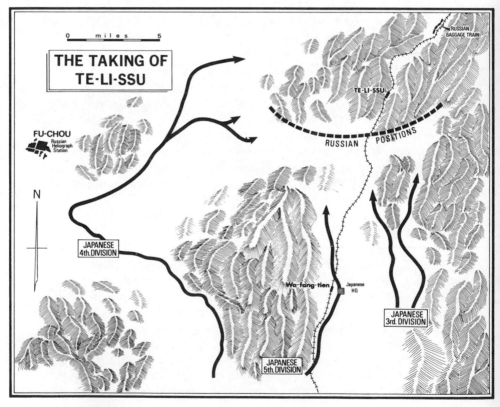

followed along three rough tracks with their axis of advance varying between five and ten miles to the west of the railway embankment.

By 8:30 A.M. on June 14 the Russian artillery was in action against Japanese advanced units. Though fighting was not heavy during the day, it was heavy enough to persuade Stackelberg that Oku was in earnest. Almost all the Russian artillery had joined in the action, and by nightfall the Japanese had plotted with considerable accuracy the position of the enemy batteries.

The main fighting occurred to the east of the railway, where General Stackelberg was a conspicuous figure in his white uniform. Having held the Japanese attack in the east, he intended to follow this blunting movement with a counterattack in which he proposed to commit a striking force of fourteen battalions. All that was wrong with this plan was the major flanking thrust that, unknown to Stackelberg, Oku was about to make to the west of the railway. Here the hills gave way to gentle, undulating country, heavily cultivated and with numerous farmhouses. About twenty miles from Te-li-ssu was the town of Fu-chou, where one squadron of the Fifth Siberian Cossack Regiment had an outpost, equipped with a heliograph station, which could flash signals by using the rays of the sun.

When the advanced elements of the Japanese forces appeared on June 14, the Russian cavalry squadron, fearing that it would be outnumbered, withdrew to the northwest and away from the main position at Te-li-ssu. Because of fog, the heliograph did not function, and the information about this movement of the Japanese Fourth Division around Stackelberg's right flank was therefore sent by courier. Whether the courier ever delivered the message is unclear. In any event, Stackelberg did not receive any warning that trouble was coming from the west until nearly noon on June 15.

If there was surprise in the west, there was also confusion in the east. Stackelberg had hoped his counterattack might jump off as early as 1 or 2 A.M. or at least before daylight, but the details were left to Major-General Alexander Alexeievitch Gerngross, who commanded the First East Siberian Rifle Division. Gerngross was supposed to make contact with Major-General Florian Francevitch Glasko, whose troops were to operate under his command. But the two generals were unable to meet during the night, and when dawn came both were still vague about their orders. They knew only that they were required to attack.

Unable to find Gerngross, Glasko sought fresh orders from Stackelberg and was told to send out scout detachments to locate and disturb the enemy positions. Since he had already taken this precaution, he was standing fast when dawn broke. General Gerngross, having advised Stackelberg that he would move at daybreak, was reluctant to take action without confirmation, which he failed to receive. When daylight came, he, too, was standing fast. Their indecision proved fatal, and before the Russian attacks could begin, the Japanese had preempted the offensive.

The Japanese Third Division swept along the line, established an artillery position in what had once been the center of the Russian defenses, and inflicted heavy losses on the Russian regiments as they tried to pull out. Some of the Russian troops were driven far into the hills to the east and continued to fall into Japanese hands days after the battle had ended.

A blinding rainstorm at about 3 P.M. provided the retreating Russians with some cover as they abandoned much of their equipment and fled north. It also served to slow down the Japanese advance, and the bulk of Stackelberg's corps got away. The Russians lost 477 men killed, 2,240 wounded and 754 missing. Oku reported 217 killed and 946 wounded. Sixteen field guns were among the booty.

Far from helping to relieve the pressure on Port Arthur, this hopeless expedition added to the demoralization of the Russian forces in the field. It put an unbearable strain on Kuropatkin's still inadequate forces, causing him to pull back from several excellent defensive positions in the east, exacerbated the already tense situation on the Russian home front, and further relieved anxiety in Japan. Having essayed this futile and premature effort to regain the initiative against his own strongly expressed opposition, Kuropatkin found his strategic plan dangerously compromised, while Japan was more encouraged than ever to press on as rapidly as possible with its plans to attack his main battle corps at Liaoyang.

St. Petersburg had not yet digested this latest disaster when an event much closer to home warned of even graver happenings to come. At 11 A.M. on June 16, as he was about to enter the senate in Helsinki, General N. I. Bobrikov, governor-general of Finland, was shot in the stomach and neck by Eugen Schaumann, the son of a former senator. Bobrikov, a former *aide-de-camp* to the Tsar and a member of the Military Advisory Board, died on the following day. His assassin committed suicide. In his pocket was a letter addressed to the Tsar which accused Bobrikov and Plehve of trampling on the rights and liberties of the Finnish people. "Knowing the good heart and noble intentions of Your Majesty," the letter concluded, "I implore you solely to seek information regarding the real situation in the whole empire, including Finland, Poland, and the Baltic provinces."

As *The Times* said in its editorial on June 17, the real importance of the crime lay in the revelation it appeared to give of the temper of the Finnish people. Not just the Finnish people, but the whole Russian empire was beginning to burn.

As early as May 1904 the war had begun to have a serious impact upon the economic life of Russia. The cessation of all normal trade with Siberia and the suspension of much domestic trade because the military had taken over the railways caused hardships everywhere. As one way to curb the revolutionary tendencies, Plehve embarked on a program to weed out Jewish liberals and to send them off to the front. Of the 180 doctors who left St. Petersburg in March, no fewer than 110 were Jews. As a mark of discrimination, they received only 900 roubles for traveling expenses compared with 1,250 roubles paid to their fellow practitioners who observed the rites of the Orthodox Church.

The discontent was not confined, however, to the national minorities, to the Jews, to the educated classes, or to the professional agitators. The 1904 wheat crop in Bessarabia was almost a complete failure, and the harvest elsewhere was poor. The grinding poverty of the peasants was felt more heavily than ever.

Inevitably, in the face of continuing reverses in the East, the widespread grievances began to polarize around the unpopular war. Late in March the Social Democrats published a manifesto that blamed the "selfish interests of the bourgeoisie and the capitalists, who in their profit hunting would sell and ruin their country, have provoked war, bringing numberless evils to the working people." To this outcry against the war, Leo Tolstoy added his influential voice. Revolution became a matter of public debate. The police in St. Petersburg discovered what they described as a widespread conspiracy designed to take the life of Plehve, and the Copenhagen correspondent of the *Daily Telegraph* reported that a large body of conspirators both in Russia and in Finland were determined to exterminate all the leading Russian statesmen and the officials responsible for the present system of government in Russia. On July 8 *The Times* and *The New York Times* carried a report under a Vienna dateline that the governor of Warsaw had applied to the Tsar for authorization to proclaim a state of siege throughout Russian Poland as the only means by which a revolutionary outbreak could be prevented. On June 29 about a thousand Socialists marched in procession through the streets of Warsaw carrying red flags bearing the inscription "War Against War" on one side and "Down with Tsarism" on the other. "The policemen and door porters not only made no attempt to stop the procession but they moved out of its way," the two newspapers reported. "Some even took off their caps."

To the rampant feeling of discontent was now added almost total disbelief in the official news of the war in the East. Even the official dispatches from Kuropatkin and Alexeiev's quartermaster general had ceased to be taken seriously by top officials, and the feeling among the public was that Kuropatkin's telegrams were modified, pruned, and amended during their process of filtration through various official sieves in a way that was too apparent not to be noticed.

Despite their victories, the Japanese remained cautious. But with the continuous threat of Russian fleet action still very much in the minds of Oyama and his staff, General Kawamura's Tenth Division was instructed to call off its advance toward Liaoyang and to build up supplies. "Recent reports lead us to suppose that the Russian Fleet is now in a condition to come out of Port Arthur," Kawamura was told. "This will make our oversea communications very unsafe and may have the effect of making it extremely difficult to collect the stores of all kinds that will be needed for the armies in Manchuria when they reach Liaoyang."

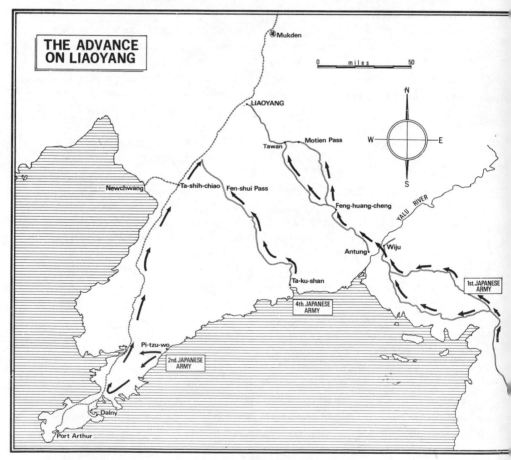

THE ADVANCE
ON LIAOYANG

Though the Japanese captured large quantities of rolling stock at Dalny, the Russians had had the foresight to remove or to destroy their locomotives. Japanese locomotives were made from a different gauge and could not be changed to the needs of the Russian tracks. With great foresight, the Japanese had bought several locomotives in America built for use on the Harbin–Port Arthur line. These were at sea in two freighters on June 15 when the Russian cruiser squadron from Vladivostok sank them in the Straits of Tsushima.

Like the Second Army, the First, with headquarters at Feng-huang-cheng, was also beset with supply problems. The Mandarin Road from Seoul to Peking could not cope with the army's needs. While Kuroki's men waited, engineers began to build a tramway linking the port of Antung with Feng-huang-cheng. Toward the end of June it opened for the first traffic, with coolies pushing loaded trucks. This relieved some of Kuroki's serious supply worries during the wet season.

The day after the tramway opened, Kuroki's army at Feng-huang-cheng marched into the mountains with the Twelfth Division on the right, the Second Division in the center, and the Guards on the left; the last were in touch with General Nozu's force from Ta-ku-shan. General Nishi's Second Division followed the course of the Mandarin Road and the parallel stream that wound its way through the green and terraced hills to the Motien Pass, the Thermopylae of Manchuria. But Kuropatkin had no Leonidas, and the pass fell into Kuroki's hands by default.

Kuroki had expected formidable opposition here in the mountains. There were many places where a handful of troops could have delayed his army's advance, and he could scarcely believe his good fortune when he found that General Kuropatkin had abandoned the eastern defenses of Liaoyang by sending so much of his force south to Te-li-ssu.

He took the Motien Pass in his stride and rested while the other armies converging on Liaoyang synchronized their movements. A single Japanese battalion held the pass, with a second battalion immediately behind in reserve. The Russians offered a feeble night counterattack. By daylight they were in headlong retreat along the Mandarin Road with the Japanese in hot pursuit.

All the dangers that Kuropatkin had envisaged in January if he failed to concentrate his forces were now fully revealed. By responding to Alexeiev's pressures, he had scattered his forces over a wide area and been defeated in a succession of actions. He had always been sure that it would take at least six months to build up an adequate force around Liaoyang. He found now that even this estimate was overoptimistic and that the bottlenecks on the Trans-Siberian Railway prevented him from reinforcing his forces as quickly as he had hoped. The situation left him at this time without a real plan of campaign. Another month was to pass before one was formulated.

The need to try to hold Port Arthur had proved fatal to Russian strategy. Though this was not yet evident, the need to take it was also to prove more than an embarrassment for the Japanese. But now their three armies converging from the east and south were poised for major action while Kuropatkin was fighting desperately for time. Kuroki was only three days' march from the railway line. In the south, Oku was pushing up the railway line and was knocking at the gates of Kaiping, only fifteen miles from Ta-shih-chiao, where the branch line of the railway ran off to the port of Newch-wang. Hai-cheng, twenty miles to the north, was threatened by Nozu making his way through the mountains from Fen-shui Pass.

While the three Japanese armies were acting independently, Oyama and Kodama had remained in Japan. Now, with the prospect of their joining hands for the offensive against Liaoyang, it was important to create a proper field command. Its creation posed problems.

The rivalry between the Satsuma and Choshu clans remained very strong, but the Satsumas had the weight of numbers in the upper echelons. Oyama, Kuroki, Nozu, and Kawamura were all from Satsuma. Oku was from a nearby part of Kyushu Island. Nogi had a Satsuma wife, and his chief of staff came from Satsuma.

In principle, Yamagata, the leading figure in the Japanese army, should have been chosen to lead the Japanese forces in the field, but he was from the Choshu clan and was regarded by the Satsuma generals as too precise and needling. Also, he was not in the best of health. Oyama was five years younger and, like Togo, reliable rather than brilliant, but a Satsuma. Kodama had all the brilliance that Oyama lacked. Of this Oyama was well aware, and, with the understanding that Kodama should have a free hand, Oyama was appointed commander-in-chief of the Japanese forces in Manchuria, with Kodama as his chief of staff. Yamagata replaced Oyama as chief of staff at Imperial General Headquarters, with Major-General Nagaoka as his deputy. The effect of these shifts in command was to move the coordination and execution of the strategic and tactical plans to Oyama and Kodama, and especially to the latter.

Tokyo was decked with flags, and cheering crowds lined the streets on July 6 to celebrate the departure of Oyama and Kodama for the front. To the roars of *"banzai"* they left Tokyo station for Ujina, sailing aboard the *Oki Maru* for Dalny. Every station was lined with cheering men and women. Where the men and women at their daily tasks in the rice fields had no flags to wave at the train, they were seen standing with their feet spread wide apart, their arms outstretched above their shoulders, their heads tilted back, and their eyes raised to heaven, as if to invoke the blessings of the gods upon the departing Japanese leaders.

On July 22 Oyama established his headquarters with Oku's Second Army. During his brief period away from the direction of the war, the situation had again changed in the Japanese favor. Having been overruled once when he submitted to the arbitration of the Tsar and his council of war, Kuropatkin had agreed reluctantly that Count Fedor Keller, who had succeeded Zasulitch in command of the Eastern Detachment, should attempt to dislodge Kuroki from the Motien Pass. Keller, an internationalist, had connections with leading Prussian and French families, including the de Beauvoirs, whose most notable member before the advent of Simone, the writer, was Roger de Beauvoir, an elegant man-about-Paris in the early nineteenth century and a writer of some note. Keller was also a close friend of Kuropatkin's.

On July 17, with six regiments of infantry from the Third and Sixth East Siberian divisions and the Ninth European Division, a battery of artillery, and a small force of cavalry, Keller attacked the Second Japanese Division at the pass. This was the first time that the much more highly regarded troops from European Russia had been committed against the Japanese. At Liaoyang, there was confidence that this time things would be different.

The usual thick, early-morning mist helped Keller's troops in the initial phase. Dawn was at 4 A.M. Two hours later, with enough light to see what they were doing and yet hidden from the Japanese at the pass, the Russian infantry forced their way past the Japanese outposts, climbed the ridges, and began to entrench.

When the fog lifted, there the Russians were, hard at work, on the forward slopes of the hill. Behind them in their thousands along two roads in the valley were their reserves, bunched together. "Destruction was as simple as bursting a bomb in a room full of men," wrote Frederick Palmer. "Shrapnel rained until the very road was crowded with dead and wounded. No Russian guns spoke in reassuring terms above the confusion." Without packhorses and with no artillery that could be moved off the roads, the Russians were massacred.

The weakest of the Japanese columns now converging on Liaoyang was the reinforced Tenth Division, which had entered the gateway to the Liao valley with the capture of Fen-shui Pass. The country through which the Japanese troops were passing consisted of symmetrical hills rising from about 500 to 1,000 feet above the valley and covered with thick, green, and almost impenetrable scrub. They reminded Sir Ian Hamilton of sugarloaves of all sizes covered in green velvet. When it was not raining, the weather was unbearably hot, with the thermometer climbing above 100 degrees. The troops wilted, but the crops of millet, beans, and peas grew almost visibly in the valleys and on the terraced lower slopes of the hills.

Oku's opinion was that Kuropatkin, having been forced to abandon the

Motien Pass because of Stackelberg's ill-fated action at Te-li-ssu, would make a serious attempt to engage the Tenth Division. He therefore decided to preempt any Russian move with an attack against the First and Fourth Siberian Army Corps, which, under Lieutenant-General N. P. Zarubaiev, had taken defensive positions at Ta-shih-chiao, sixty-five miles north of Te-li-ssu. Since a branch line of the railway ran off at this point to Newchwang, he calculated that the Russians would be obliged to make a stand here and abandon any thought of halting the Tenth Division on its approach to Hai-cheng.

Oyama had only just established his headquarters with the Second Army when Oku marched north. As at Te-li-ssu, he planned to make a frontal attack, using one division to turn the Russian flank. The action raged fiercely, but indecisively, on July 24. Oku was ready to renew the action on the following day, but Kuropatkin, concerned now about the hostile intentions of the Japanese on his left flank, ordered the Russian forces to withdraw during the night.

The Russians fell back through Hai-cheng, about twenty miles to the north, in considerable confusion and great discomfort. They were ill-equipped for the heat of the Manchurian summer. Their kit was too heavy, their boots were too flimsy, and their forage caps gave no protection from the sun. Lord Brooke, of Reuters, who rode with the withdrawal, saw wounded men dragging themselves along the road and many cases of sunstroke.

All of Kuropatkin's delaying actions had now failed. General Zasulitch had been driven from the hills to the east. The southern front was folding up. And the cavalry, of which so much had been expected, had proved a great disappointment. Mounted on wretched-looking ponies, the Cossacks were simply untrained yeomanry who spent most of their time foraging for food. They provided little information and, led by inexperienced young officers from St. Petersburg, did not seem to appreciate the tactical value of harassing flank attacks.

The Russians had begun the war in the confident assumption that the Chinese would be on their side. They relied heavily on Chinese agents for information and were unaware for months that many of the Chinese they employed were actually in the employment of the Japanese or, if not employed, were sympathetic to the Japanese.

Nor did they ever understand the activities of the Chunchuses. They continued to regard them simply as "mounted bandits." They had no idea that they had been organized by the Japanese to burn Russian ammunition dumps and provision stores. As they fell back now toward Liaoyang, the

Russians attributed the heavily increased activities of the Chunchuses along their lines of communication to the lawlessness of the country, and were blissfully ignorant that the raids from which they began to suffer so dearly were a well-organized part of the war.

CHAPTER *19*

ಣಣಣಣಣ

The Yellow Sea

THE RUSSIAN PORT ARTHUR squadron now found itself fighting on land, and its crews had to drag their own guns to positions in the forts. Some of the posts were so steep that the men had to crawl on their hands and knees, clinging to bushes and tussocks of grass as they dragged the guns behind them. This was not the work of seamen, and discontent spread throughout the fleet. There was now none of the enthusiasm that had come with Makarov's leadership. The spirit of revenge that had gripped the squadron for a time after the Admiral's death had vanished, and the sharp thrill of victory following the sinking of the Japanese battleship *Hatsuse* dwindled and died.

Since the fall of Nanshan and the Japanese forward movement on Port Arthur, Japanese naval guns had been firing on the inner harbor and the town, often causing fires. The Japanese Third Army had been reinforced by the arrival of the Ninth Division brigade, a rear reserve, and a large quantity of artillery. By the end of July the Russians had fallen back to their last line of defense outside their permanent fortifications. This line ran along the heights from Louisa Bay east to Feng-huang-shan ("Wolf Hills"), and south to Ta-ku-shan ("Big Orphan Hill"), 645 feet high, and Hsiao-ku-shan ("Little Orphan Hill"), 430 feet high. The whole Russian line had been weakly fortified, and the uncut millet allowed the Japanese to advance unseen to within a few yards of the Russian defenses.

It took the Japanese with heavy artillery only three hours to march on the Russian post at Wolf Hills, and they captured the position and the hills to the east of it without loss. The whole Russian line was evacuated, with the exception of Ta-ku-shan and Hsiao-shan, both about 1,500 yards from the first line of Russian fortifications.

It soon seemed clear that the Russian ships would be destroyed inside the harbor by the guns of the Japanese Third Army. Shells fell into the harbor repeatedly, and the anchorage was no longer safe for the squadron. The ships, including *Retvizan,* fired at the Japanese gun positions in the Lun-ho Valley, south of Wolf Hills, by indirect fire, but the big shells fired at long range and at high elevation were easily seen and the Japanese merely flung themselves into the hastily prepared bomb shelters when they saw them coming.

Admiral Vitgeft, the gloomiest of all the despondent Russian naval officers, had received direct orders from the Tsar to leave for Vladivostok. When he left, he said stubbornly, he would take with him the whole fleet, and not merely the strongest and fastest ships. "My orders are to go to Vladivostok with the whole squadron, and this I shall do," he said.

On August 10 he was ready. Guns that could be spared from the shore batteries were hastily returned to their places on board the ships, though the squadron was still without one twelve-inch, ten six-inch, and twelve twelve-pounder guns. One of *Sevastopol's* guns had been badly damaged, but, since there was no time to repair it, it had been replaced with a wooden facsimile. Some ships were short of men who had been left behind to man guns on the forts, and several of the captains took command of ships for the first time.

Daily the Japanese bombarded the fortress, the ships and the town, starting promptly at 7 A.M. and finishing as the sun went down, so that the Russians could not pinpoint their gun positions. "In the whole of Port Arthur there was not a spot as big as a handkerchief which could not have been searched by their shell," wrote an observer. With no way of firing back effectively at the Japanese, all that the ships crews in the inner harbor could do was sit and listen to the crash of the shells, drinking each other's health in brandy and vodka.

Several shells hit *Peresvyet,* and *Retvizan* was hit seven times, once below the waterline. She was still shipping hundreds of tons of water when Admiral Vitgeft reluctantly took the squadron to sea. The Admiral had been wounded by a shell splinter during one of the attacks and was in poor physical and mental shape for the dangerous journey ahead. Indeed, he confessed to a presentiment that he was going to be killed.

The ships left port with little hope. To those who came to bid farewell to the squadron, Vitgeft waved his hand in a gesture dismissing their words of encouragement: "Gentlemen, we shall meet in the next world." At dawn on August 10, as General Nogi and his Third Army moved up to attack, the Russian squadron steamed out of harbor. *Bayan,* struck by a mine on June 27, was left behind, but otherwise all the ships that had sallied out on June 23, when hopes of reaching Vladivostok had been so much higher, were there.

Admiral Vitgeft's flag flew in the *Tsarevitch.* She was followed by the five other battleships, then the three cruisers. *Novik* escorted the fourteen torpedo boats and destroyers, eight of which were to accompany the fleet to Vladivostok, while the rest were to return to Port Arthur after guiding the main fleet through the minefields.

Six minesweepers of the squadron led the way safely over its own electric mines, and by 10:30 A.M. the ships were also clear of Japanese mines. The cruiser *Ryeshitelni,* bearing dispatches from Admiral Vitgeft concerning the fleet's movements, came out of harbor at the same time and stopped in the entrance. When the fleet had gone, she ran for Cheefoo on the Shantung Peninsula, only three hours from Port Arthur by fast ship. The Russians maintained a consulate there and occasional blockade runners made the journey in safety.

The last ship to leave Port Arthur at 8 A.M., was the hospital ship *Mongolia.* She caught up with the fleet at 8:30 A.M., her shining white paint and red cross contrasting with the dirty yellow-brown of the warships. That she accompanied the fleet reflected Admiral Vitgeft's determination this time not to return to Port Arthur.

General Smirnov stood on Electric Cliff with a big crowd of sailors, soldiers, and cheering townspeople to watch the departure of the fleet, begrudging every shell, gun, and man it took with it. "May God grant it luck," he said, "but evil will be the day if it is defeated and does not return."

The Japanese squadron had been expecting the departure of the Russians for weeks, but Togo would have preferred to keep the entire Russian fleet inside the harbor at Port Arthur where it could be destroyed by the army, saving his own Combined Fleet for the coming battle with the Russian Baltic Fleet. He could afford to lose no more ships.

Since the beginning of August, he had been waiting at Round Island, south of Port Arthur, his ships loaded with coal and water and ammunition for the battle that he hoped not to fight. Each day between 7 A.M. and 7 P.M., the fleet lay off the island with engines stopped. Each night it moved to the northeast at a slow speed, returning at 1 A.M. to retrace its course. The minimum of coal was used in these exercises, and the fleet was always within forty miles of Port Arthur at times when the Russian fleet might attempt to escape.

On the routine run on August 10 the Japanese battleline consisted of *Mikasa, Asahi, Fuji, Shikishima, Kasuga, Nisshin,* and a dispatch boat. To the east and west of Port Arthur and close to the shore were the Third,

Fifth, and Sixth divisions, made up of three armored cruisers and eight protected cruisers.

In smaller ships Togo had a great numerical advantage—seventeen destroyers and twenty-nine torpedo boats to the eight Russian destroyers that were to accompany the Russian squadron on its run for Vladivostok. The Japanese torpedo craft would not come into their own until after dark when they would take over from the main Japanese force. The two main fleets were therefore well matched. The Russians had six battleships and three protected cruisers against the four Japanese battleships, three fully armored cruisers, and eight cruisers with protective belts of armor plating.

The weather was fine but hazy, with a calm sea, as the Russian ships emerged from the minefield. The last time that they had ventured out, the squadron had taken many hours to clear the minefields. This time they were much faster, despite the troubles that began almost immediately. *Tsarevitch* could steam only at about eight knots at first. When she corrected this, her steering gear broke down, and the fleet had to stop while she made repairs.

At 11 A.M., after several other delays caused by long lack of use in port, the rusty Russian ships were making good progress. Half an hour later the low-lying mists lifted temporarily and the two fleets came in sight of each other at a distance of about twelve miles. Vitgeft saw only the main force of the Japanese fleet, but for some unaccountable reason he assumed that *Yashima,* the Japanese battleship sunk on May 15, was among the enemy ships. This was a hallucination, though *Yashima's* former flag commander, Rear-Admiral Nashiba, was present, with his flag in *Shikishima.*

Togo held course until he had made out the Russian formation and at 1:33 P.M. turned sixteen points to starboard. He planned to cross the T and to cross the bows of the Russian ships. When his ships were directly ahead of the enemy he turned eight points to port and brought his fleet into line abreast, with the Russians astern. He then turned another eight points to port to bring his ships again into line ahead, in reverse order, with *Nisshin* in the lead. *Tsarevitch* and *Retvizan* opened fire on the Japanese flagship, and the Japanese replied. Firing was not yet general, however, as the distance between the two fleets was still over 8,000 yards.

Togo intended to lure the Russians farther to sea and then to bar their way to Vladivostok. Now there was a danger that they might escape. The sight of the entire Russian fleet steaming in strong formation shocked Togo into action that he had hoped to avoid. He had expected that some of the Russian ships would have remained in Port Arthur, damaged by his recent heavy bombardment. Whatever the risk, Togo had to fight.

At 12:30 P.M. Togo altered his course to bring his fleet directly in front of the Russian ships, but as he did so *Tsarevitch* turned sharply to starboard, with the rest of the fleet following. Vitgeft had just caught sight of the

[327]

myriad Japanese destroyers and torpedo boats and felt sure that they were dropping mines in his path.* This was the reason for his sudden change of course. As each ship passed, he warned it to look out for mines and then to steam south across the stern of the Japanese fleet, opening fire on the *Asahi* and *Mikasa* as they came into line again.

Several times Vitgeft turned to avoid suspected mines, and each time Togo himself turned until by 1 P.M. the two fleets were steaming past each other on nearly opposite courses and firing had become general. The turns had increased the distance between the two, but just after 1:30 P.M. the Japanese ships turned sixteen points together, returned to single line ahead in their original order, and steamed southwest, concentrating fire on the Russian flagship. But the range was more than 10,000 yards, and Vitgeft was steaming south at fourteen knots. If he could maintain his lead until dark, he had a fair chance of getting away.

Togo had to make a quick decision. He realized that the Russian force was much better than he had anticipated. He now had little hope of completely destroying it without great damage to his own ships. Conceivably, he could sink or capture the rearmost Russian ships, but this would be of little advantage to him, and the cost to his fleet might be considerable. He preferred to chase the whole fleet, either damaged or without so much as a scratch, back to Port Arthur rather than to destroy the lesser ships and allow the rest to escape. Kamimura with his six armored cruisers had his hands full guarding the Russian Vladivostok squadron. Even if he could attack the Russian fleet on its way into the Siberian port, he would be overpowered by the much stronger enemy ships.

By drawing out of range, Togo gave the Russian squadron the opportunity to return to its home base, where it would have less chance of eventually meeting up with either the Vladivostok cruisers or the Baltic Fleet when it arrived. His own ships would then be preserved for battle with the Baltic Fleet. He increased his speed to fifteen knots, praying that his weaker ships could keep up, and altered his course to starboard. The distance between the two fleets gradually increased.

The sky was clear and there was a light breeze blowing. *The Japanese Official Naval History* reported that it was "perfect weather for a fight." Ships on both sides had been damaged, but none had dropped out of line.

From *Asahi*, Pakenham noted the accuracy of the early Russian firing. The twelve-inch shells came without sound but the six-inch, though less effective, whined like express trains passing through a railway station. The

---

* *The Japanese Official Naval History* later reported that what Vitgeft took for mines were empty coal baskets thrown overboard by the Japanese ships.

Russian shells fell so close on either side of the leaders of the Japanese fleet, he wrote, that those falling to leeward might have almost been "dropped out of the lee boats." *Askold* and *Novik,* both unarmored cruisers, came in with their six-inch guns, which Pakenham described as ineffective peashooters. *Askold* was hit early but continued firing. Though neither she nor *Novik* appeared to have much effect on the Japanese battleships, even Pakenham was impressed. "They commanded the respect of a generous foe," he wrote.

As the range increased, the noise of the battle stopped. Now the stokers in both fleets were working below in temperatures up to 130 degrees, urging their ships along. Everything depended on speed. The Japanese gun crews fell exhausted at their posts and rested from the fighting, leaving the battle to others. Even on deck the heat was intense. Both fleets depended on canned and salted foods, and, especially on the Japanese ships, water supplies were dwindling. By the end of the first phase of the battle, half their water tanks were empty, and the stokers were getting drinking water from the test cocks on boilers.

The tension in the Russian ships died down for those abovedecks, and the gun crews went to lunch, faring better than the Japanese who had to be content with lumps of cold rice, washed down with cups of the precious water.

About 3:25 P.M., the Japanese ships changed course, still keeping the enemy in sight. Thirty-five minutes later, the distance between the two was again reduced to about five miles. Men went back to their guns and the rival ships resumed the action.

Hits on the Russian ships, whether battleships or destroyers, brought cries of joy on the Japanese ships, where brass bands and calls of *"banzai"* encouraged the crews. "Such things as the breakage of an enemy's mast, an outburst of steam, or a list of ship which, easily appealing to the eye, show the effect of our fire, have the greatest influence in stirring up the warlike spirit," reported the captain of *Kasuga.*

For the first half-hour of the renewed action, the Japanese casualties were so heavy that the first aid teams had trouble coping with the dead and injured. *Mikasa* was struck at the water level, belowdecks, and on the after-funnel by twelve-inch shells from *Poltava.* The dead were taken to an improvised mortuary in the stokers' bathroom, while the wounded found their own way to dressing stations. On *Nisshin* casualties were also heavy. One shell killed nearly all the men on the forebridge. The bodies of four were found but the others were blown to pieces.

As always, luck was with Togo. The first disastrous shots might easily have disabled *Mikasa.* She recovered but one shell hit just slightly forward of the conning tower where Togo was standing, piercing the deck and going through the engine-room casing. It burst on the mainmast, which was kept

[329]

up only by a beam of the engine-room casing. The huge mast was hurriedly bound up with 6½-inch wire and attached to the after-conning tower to save it from falling over.

Once there was near-panic on the flagship and the captain, to encourage his men, quoted with feeling from the imperial rescript to all Japanese forces. "This one battle might hold the key to victory or defeat," he told them. "You must break the enemy though you crush your own body and bones."

At 5 P.M. the Russian ship *Peresvyet* lost her main topmast and fore topmast, so that she had no way of making signals. *Poltava,* at the rear of the Russian line, bore a great deal of the Japanese fire. While *Mikasa* and *Asahi* fired at the Russian flagship and *Retvizan,* almost all other guns of the Japanese ships were directed at *Poltava,* but both she and *Sevastopol,* according to Captain Pakenham on board the *Asahi,* "were carrying themselves nobly."

Mikasa, badly hit, had her after-turret silenced for the rest of the afternoon. Hits on two other battleships, *Asahi* and *Shikishima,* reduced the Japanese primary armament from sixteen to eleven guns.

Both Vitgeft and Togo led their fleets and both were in constant danger, Togo and his staff were crowded on the pilot-house and forebridge of *Mikasa* when a shell struck the semaphore, killing four officers and smothering the commander-in-chief in blood. A shell splinter penetrated the fleshy part of his nose and blood streaked through his beard and splashed on the shoulders of his dark blue uniform. His steward, who had kept close to the Admiral, bringing him cigarettes, milk, and soda water, was wounded and taken below. From the sick-bay the steward sent a message imploring Togo to take shelter, but the Admiral refused, as he had refused so many times before when asked by his staff not to expose himself so openly to fire.

Time was running out with the sun. Another half hour, and Vitgeft would have won the race.

At 5:45 P.M. prospects changed dramatically. Two twelve-inch shells struck the *Tsarevitch* at the same time, bringing down her foremast and destroying her conning tower. A further succession of twelve-inch shells followed, honeycombing the ship. Every man on the bridge and conning tower was killed or injured. Captain Nikolai Alexandrovitch Matusevitch was severely wounded. Of Admiral Vitgeft only a bloody piece of one leg was found. Bodies of the dead were hurled against the steering wheel, jamming it, so that the big ship swung in a complete circle, cutting though her own line between *Sevastopol* and *Peresvyet.* As the flagship turned, there were cries of terror from the other Russian ships. It seemed from *Diana* that *Tsarevitch* was about to share the fate of *Petropavlovsk.* Semenov took notes:

"Our battleships are rushing at the enemy in single line abreast." This was scratched out. "No, it looks as if they intended to resume the old course and the old formation." This was also struck out, and across the top of his pad was written: "An error. No formation whatsoever. They are steaming without any orders."

The Russian fleet was in complete confusion. *Retvizan's* captain, thinking that he was conforming to the movements of his commander, followed *Tsarevitch,* and *Peresvyet* and *Sevastopol,* missed narrowly by the flagship, had to change course to avoid impact. *Peresvyet,* flying the flag of Prince Ukhtomski, commander of the battleship division, displayed his signal, "Follow Me." Both masts had gone from *Peresvyet,* however, and the signal flags were hoisted on the bridge rails where even the nearest ships could not see them.

After minutes of utter disorder Ukhtomski got the main part of the fleet under some sort of control and headed back toward Port Arthur. *Tsarevitch* turned toward the north, and, continuing to circle, disappeared from sight. *Diana's* captain decided also to break through the rabble of battleships. She was attacked by six cruisers, including *Nisshin* and *Kasuga* and four torpedo boats.

Novik, the swiftest ship in the Russian fleet, watched as Prince Ukhtomski in *Peresvyet* led the remnants of the fleet back to Port Arthur and decided not to follow.

> Possibly another commander, more brave or better prepared, would have attempted to continue on his road in face of all risks, but Prince Ukhtomski had always been considered a second-rate man, [wrote Commander Steer]. It is quite clear that he ought never to have been made a flag officer, but having been made one, one was bound to take him as he was. . . . One cannot *order* anyone to be a hero, at most one can express the wish that he be one.

Steer watched as *Askold* flew the signal to her ships, "Follow Me," and started off astern of her. The Japanese destroyers closed in like birds of prey.

In his book, *The Influence of the Sea on the Political History of Japan,* Admiral G. A. Ballard called the lucky double hit on *Tsarevitch* "the most critical minute of the war." Togo certainly took instant advantage of the two strikes that had turned the Russian line into disorder. All guns were now turned on *Retvizan,* the only Russian ship still fighting. *Retvizan* was covered in a mountain of smoke and flames but managed to fire with her heavy guns on a 640-ton Japanese gunboat, which came in under the cover of smoke to fire torpedoes. The smaller Japanese marauder went up in flames and nearly one third of her crew was killed. "If on board all the ships of our squadron the results of the battle are as serious as on board mine, the number of dead and wounded must be very great," wrote an officer on the crippled Japanese ship.

The attack on *Retvizan,* which had started out from Port Arthur shipping hundreds of gallons of water, though not the most important, was the most dramatic event of a most dramatic day. The battered Russian battleship was in the center of an arc of Japanese ships and every gun was trained on her. Even the twelve-pounders joined in. Some of the shells from the big twelve-inch and eight-inch guns threw up huge pillars of water twice as high as the Russian battleship's masts. *Retvizan* was almost completely enveloped in towering clouds of smoke, flame, and spray.

Retvizan was saved by the arrival of three Japanese ships which had been fueling at their base when the Japanese fleet took to sea in the morning. As the newly arrived Japanese ships ran toward the sound of firing, three Russian cruisers, *Askold, Diana, and Pallada,* turned back to assist the *Retvizan.* The Japanese latecomers all set out in pursuit of the Russian cruisers, driving them from the scene. *Retvizan* took advantage of the diversion and as the sun went down, she reformed her line and under cover of smoke led the remainder of the fleet back to Port Arthur.

The Russian destroyers, which had taken little part in the fighting, appeared ahead of Togo's main fleet. Now was the time for the seventeen Japanese destroyers to take over. But they were miles astern, and Togo realized that his battleships ran the risk of being torpedoed. If there had been one more hour of daylight, the Russian fleet might have been destroyed, but as the sun went down Togo turned his own battleships away. The chance to deliver a decisive blow to the Port Arthur squadron had gone.

But Admiral Togo could not have risked the possibility of more damage to his ships. Out of six battleships with which he had started the war, only four remained, and he was unwilling to risk another big ship chasing the battered Russian fleet back to Port Arthur.* When he faced the new Russian fleet en route from the Baltic, he would require every ship, every man, and every gun he could muster. Also, the Russian force had fought much better than anticipated, and its firing and marksmanship had been superior to that of the Japanese. Togo himself had been lucky to survive the fight.

No Russian ship had been destroyed or captured. Five battleships, one cruiser, and three destroyers succeeded in returning to Port Arthur. *Tsarevitch, Diana, Novik,* and *Askold* and four destroyers had run the gauntlet

---

*Togo had so successfully concealed the loss of *Yashima* that, in his report to the Tsar, Viceroy Alexeiev included her in the list of Japanese battleships engaged during the battle of August 10.

of the Japanese main force and were well ahead of the pursuing enemy destroyers and torpedo boats.

Of the Russian ships that fled northward in the general direction of Vladivostok, *Diana* and *Novik* were determined to keep on fighting. Their captains knew that if they returned to Port Arthur their guns would eventually be turned over to the batteries and their ships handed to the Japanese.

For fear of capsizing, the badly damaged *Diana* could not use her guns even when fired on by the Japanese torpedo boats giving chase. One torpedo came straight for her. Her crew watched from the deck as it flew from its tube and heard the sound of it, "like the snort of some big animal." The torpedo missed, and *Diana* set out for the German port of Kiao-chou at Shantung when her coal began to dwindle. Here she took on coal but could not wait to make repairs and continued, half-sinking, for Saigon. Almost immediately she was chased by a ship and recognized her as *Novik*. "There was not another little ship the least like her in the whole Pacific," wrote Semenov in *Diana*. But *Novik* took her for a Japanese and steamed away. *Diana* reached Saigon where she was disarmed on September 10, a month to the day after the battle in the Yellow Sea. Her colors were hauled down and her crew were forced to sign declarations that they would not take part in further action, though several officers, including Semenov, escaped to Russia and returned with the Baltic Fleet.

The hobbled *Tsarevitch*, hit by at least fifteen twelve-inch shells, ran to Kiao-chou, where she was interned with three Russian destroyers, and remained there until the end of the war.

Askold, running like a hare, eluded the Japanese for many days and eventually reached Shanghai, where she tried to make repairs, despite the laws applying to belligerent ships in a neutral harbor. She was accompanied by a destroyer, *Grosovoi*, which had also been battered. Japanese notes to the Chinese authorities insisted that only emergency repairs should be made. Ships of the Japanese squadron were immediately sent to Shanghai, and, though care was taken not to "wantonly" break the "neutrality" of China and captains of the ships were warned to show a peaceful demeanor, the threat was real. On September 1 the two Russian ships hauled down their flags and disarmed.

Novik steamed on until her boilers burst. "We went round the ship like souls in purgatory resigned to our fate," wrote Lieutenant Steer. In Russia she was later criticized for attempting to escape. She should have gone to a neutral port to disarm, said the Russian newspapers. No one in *Novik* wanted this. "It would have appeared to us an act of cowardice thus to hide from the enemy, like chickens who crawl under the protecting wings of the hen at the sight of a hawk," Steer commented. Two fast Japanese cruisers,

Tsushima and *Chitose*, among others, were detailed to chase and capture her. At dawn on August 31 they found her outside the town of Korsakov in Sakhalin and more than twenty shells were fired on her at close range.

Novik fought to the last. Many of the crew were swept overboard and Lieutenant Steer was badly wounded. After inflicting heavy damage on the *Tsushima,* she was scuttled in shallow water by her own crew. "Alas, she died in pain," wrote Steer. "Uninterrupted work had done for her in the end and reduced her to a state of immobility . . . the pitcher goes once too often to the well and is broken at last."

Novik's survivors were ordered by telegraph from Admiral Skruidlov to proceed to Vladivostok. They marched for hundreds of miles through forests and wild country inhabited by bandits, murderers, escaped convicts, and Ainus (aboriginal inhabitants of Hokkaido, Sakhalin, and the Aleutian Islands). Without losing a single straggler, they arrived on October 23, after forty-five days on the march. The men of *Novik* were gallant to the end.

The dispatch boat *Ryeshitelni,* which left harbor for Cheefoo on August 10, just behind the fleet, with urgent messages to be delivered to St. Petersburg, was discovered by the Japanese the day after the battle. The Chinese authorities in Chefoo were anxious to preserve the appearance of neutrality, but a Japanese task force arrived with orders to capture or sink *Ryeshitelni.* She was told to leave the port in two hours or surrender.

A determined effort was made by the Russian captain, Lieutenant Michael Sergyeevitch Rostchakvoski, to save his ship. He showed the Japanese the guns without breechblocks and the torpedo tubes without doors. But, despite protests from the American, British, and German consuls, the Japanese officer had orders to disregard these formalities and the Russian oath not to serve during the remainder of the war.

One Japanese officer with thirty armed men asked permission of Lieutenant Rostchakvoski to come aboard. His reply was that it was too early in the morning for social visits, especially from the enemies of his country, but the Japanese officer insisted. Lieutenant Rostchakvoski hit him in the face. "He grabbed at me and we grappled, and a moment afterward we went overboard together. At the same time I shouted to my men to throw overboard anyone who might get on board. Immediately the Japanese in the boats began firing and many of them climbed aboard, while the firing continued, together with hand-to-hand encounters."

While they were trying to drown each other the Russian commander pushed his fingers into the mouth of the Japanese officer. These were promptly bitten to the bone by the Japanese, who clambered back on board *Ryeshitelni.* The defeated Russian captain, with crushed and bleeding fingers and a bullet in his thigh, swam to a British merchant ship, where he was taken aboard. The triumphant Japanese began to hoist his flag on *Ryeshitelni* just as an explosion went off. One Japanese and several Russians were killed, and the lieutenant who had boarded the ship and ten other Japanese were wounded. Despite Chinese protests, the Japanese took *Ryeshitelni* in tow. She finished on the Japanese register, renamed *Akatsuki,* to replace the Japanese destroyer of that name that had been sunk on the night of May 17.

News of the battle in the Yellow Sea did not reach the Russian Vladivostok fleet until late in the afternoon of the following day. It was not until August 13 that *Rossiya, Gromoboi,* and *Rurik* set out to the assistance of the Port Arthur squadron. Rear-Admiral von Essen pushed the ships along as fast as they were able to go and early in the morning of August 14 met four Japanese cruisers under Admiral Kamimura, who had already received news of the battle between the two fleets.

The Russian ships, hoping to avoid action with the larger Japanese force, changed course and made again for the north, with Kamimura in full chase. He caught up with them when the rising sun was behind his gun crews while the glare was full in the eyes of the Russians. Three of *Rossiya's* six-inch guns were soon put out of operation, and fires broke out on *Gromoboi. Rurik* suffered most from the Japanese fire. Her steering gear was disabled and she had to steer with the engines, while the concentrated fire from the Japanese cruisers was on her. Von Essen in *Rossiya* tried desperately to take all the fire from *Rurik* as she steered in circles, but eventually he had to retire. Most of her own guns were out of action, and a large fire raged in her forecastle. All firing from *Rossiya* stopped while every man aboard tried to extinguish the flames. Von Essen then came close up to the *Rurik* and ordered her by megaphone to make for Vladivostok. Though she was sinking, *Rurik* kept up a heavy fire from the two guns still operating.

Admiral Kamimura continued to fire on *Rossiya* and *Gromoboi* for more than an hour until he began to run out of ammunition. He used his last rounds to sink *Rurik,* fighting to the end. Her last gun collapsed at 9:45 A.M. All of her senior officers were either dead or wounded, and a junior gunnery officer was in command. After he had fired his last torpedo, which missed its target, he ordered the valves to be opened so that the ship would not fall into enemy hands. One hundred seventy officers and men were killed, and the Japanese picked up 625 others. *Rossiya* and *Gromoboi,* with many officers and men killed or wounded, made for Vladivostok and reached port two days later.

Admiral Kamimura was once more back in favor. His destruction of the hated *Rurik,* which had wrought such havoc among Japanese transports, and his chivalry in picking up Russian survivors brought praise from the

Japanese press and public. A song commemorating his deeds was included in schoolbooks in Tokyo, and the Emperor praised his bravery in a special message.

Soon after daylight on August 11, crowds lined the cliffs at Port Arthur to welcome back the Russian Pacific fleet: "It did return; but heavens! in what a plight!," wrote Nojine. "Weakened by the loss of one of our best battleships and three of our fastest cruisers, the role of the fleet might be said to have come to an end, for the sea was held by an enemy powerful in numbers as well as quality, and until the coming of the Baltic Fleet our squadron would not be able to engage them in battle. All it could now do was to give us men, guns, and ammunition for the land defenses."

IV

❧❧❧❧❧❧

ELUSIVE
VICTORY

CHAPTER *20*

𐒻𐒻𐒻𐒻𐒻𐒻

The Disastrous
Frontal Assault

"In TRUTH, BARREN RESULTS have as often followed upon headlong, close encounters as upon the most timid tactical training," wrote Captain Alfred Thayer Mahan, the great American naval tactician in 1892. Mahan's sage advice was widely read. Admiral Togo had studied both Makarov's and Mahan's books. He knew when to fight and when to retreat. His apparent timidity at the battle of the Yellow Sea sprang from the need to preserve his fleet for the conflict that he knew must come when the Russian Baltic Fleet arrived.

The Japanese Combined Fleet returned to its base in the Elliot Islands where repairs were made to ships damaged on August 10. A few badly hit smaller ships returned to Sasebo and the acclamation of the public. But the watch on Port Arthur did not relax, and the blockade became more stringent than ever. Togo ordered that all Russian males, other than children, who broke the blockade were to be detained until they proved to be harmless. He gave instructions for mechanical mines to be laid outside Port Arthur harbor, in case the damaged Russian ships tried to escape and sent Admiral Kataoka with the Fifth Division to assist General Nogi in his advance on the fortress. Kataoka took the cruisers *Nisshin* and *Kasuga* to Pigeon Bay and cruised within eight miles of Old Iron Mountain, occasionally firing at Russian forts with his ten-inch guns.

The reappearance of the fleet outside Port Arthur was a blow to the Russians. Some of the Russian ships could be repaired, but the Japanese blockade and the mines made it difficult for merchant ships to bring in food and supplies to the fortress. The Baltic Fleet, so long in preparing on the other side of the world, had not yet begun its journey to the rescue, and all

[339]

thoughts of the Port Arthur squadron making another dash for freedom were forgotten. Captain Robert Nicolaievitch Viren of the *Bayan* was promoted to the rank of rear-admiral and took command of the squadron after the death of Vitgeft. The small Russian force at Vladivostok now had three admirals, von Essen, Bezobrazov, and Skruidlov, but none was able to reach Port Arthur. Viren's appointment superseded that of Rear-Admiral Prince Ukhtomski, the second in command of the Port Arthur squadron under Admiral Vitgeft. It was hoped that Viren would decide to take the fleet to sea, but he stubbornly turned down Viceroy Alexeiev's smuggled orders from Harbin to attempt another dash for Vladivostok. If he took his fleet out again, he said, it would surely be sunk. He preferred to preserve it for the fight that had to come when the Baltic fleet arrived. Meanwhile, he sent two companies of seamen and 284 guns to the defense of the forts.

At long last the Russian navy and army began to fight the common enemy together, though General Stoessel, ill with dysentery, continued to cause friction between the services. Life was too busy now for drunken brawls in town, but the army officers still had access to such great quantities of vodka that many of them in the advanced positions were drunk day and night.

Stoessel tried to curb drunkenness, but his daily orders to the troops confused the orders given by the commander of the fortress, General Smirnov, and his efficient, hard-working assistant, General Kondratenko, who realized that the forts were still not sufficiently strong to resist pending Japanese attacks. Though Stoessel had been ordered by General Kuropatkin to take over as commander of the Third Siberian Corps and to leave the defense of the fortified area to Smirnov, he refused to move. Since he was the senior officer in the garrison, he took command of the fortress over Smirnov's head.

There were other confusing divisions of authority at Port Arthur. So long as the artillery of the Fourth and Seventh East Siberian divisions remained in the field it was under the chief of artillery of the Third Siberian Corps, but when it was inside the defenses it came under the chief of artillery of the fortress. Though Kondratenko was in command of the land defenses, the senior artillery officers were responsible not to him but to General Smirnov.

Despite the cumbersome system of command, General Kondratenko and General Smirnov were respected by the troops of the various arms. The health of the men was still good, but by the beginning of August food supplies were dwindling. Merchant ships attempting to run the blockade were under constant attack, and since so few supplies were available it became necessary to issue horse flesh to the garrison in Port Arthur to supplement other meat for the 45,000 troops.

In the first ten months of the war the Japanese intercepted at least twenty-five ships, mostly Russian, carrying supplies to Port Arthur. Some of these were whaling or sealing ships, carrying food, ammunition, fuel, and military stores. Most were confiscated, renamed, and taken over by the Japanese government.

Nevertheless, Captain Hutchison, the British naval observer, complained to the Admiralty of the slackness of the Japanese blockade. "It is not surprising that the fortress is still holding out," he wrote. "The amount of stores that have been run into the fortress . . . must have been considerable and of immense value to the Russians." Junks were easy prey, and *Asama* captured thirteen in one morning, carrying provisions for Port Arthur. The bigger ships were more difficult to capture, and Captain Hutchison sympathized with the Japanese who had to watch for Russian ships coming in and out of harbor as well as dealing with the blockade runners. "It has been almost heart-breaking for the Japanese fleet," he reported.

The Russians were now fighting with their backs to the wall. On the hills overlooking the fortress there were still only a few six-inch guns, and communication lines had yet to be established. "We had no balloons in the fortress, nor had we pigeons or wireless telegraphy," Nojine complained. Caves had still to be built into many of the hills and the wire entanglements in front of the defenses were not as strong as they might have been. Only wooden posts were available, and these were difficult to imbed in the hard ground. Wire was also limited, and the entanglements were often made of telegraph wire. Running against time, Kondratenko worked ceaselessly to strengthen the forts, desperately trying to reinforce the inadequate defenses by installing landmines, thicker concrete walls around the forts, and electric fences and booby-traps in the siege trenches. One of these, a contraption made of planks of wood with five-inch nails sticking out, an early version of the "naily board" used sixty years later in Vietnam by the Viet Cong, were to prove effective as the Japanese in their assaults often wore straw sandals over cotton *tabi*.

Although many of the forts were incomplete and their construction weak, the Japanese in their suicidal rushes against the Russian defenses were unable to reach even the base of the forts without heavy losses. When they scaled the parapets, the Russian defenders were able to bring heavy fire on them from the cover of the gorges and from the bomb shelters in the forts themselves.

Big Orphan Hill, gloomy and desolate, rose with rocky, precipitous slopes high over the Suishien valley. Before Nogi could make his attack on the fortress, this hill and Little Orphan, slightly to the south, had to be taken. From the summit of the taller mountain the whole chain of hills outside Port Arthur was clearly visible. To the north it dominated a large part of the country toward Feng-huang-shan, which was now in Japanese hands, and from its top a complete view could be had of the plain stretching away to Louisa Bay in the west, over which the Japanese must bring their soldiers, guns, and supplies on their way to the front. The north, eastern, and western slopes of the mountain were almost impossible to climb. The southern side, though without cover, was gently sloping and with fewer outcrops of rocks. With the easier southern slope closed to him, Nogi decided to take Big Orphan and Little Orphan from the northwestern and northeastern sides, avoiding the area close to the sea from which Russian ships could assist the defenders on the two hills.

"They are like the meat between the ribs of a chicken, which is hard to get and yet we are reluctant to throw away," said the commander of Lieutenant Sakurai's division, which had been set the task of scaling the rugged sides of the two hills, four miles northeast of Port Arthur. Fighting in heavy rain, with shells falling all around it, the regiment came to the Ta-Ho, which the Russians had dammed. A kamikaze detachment of Japanese engineers leapt into the flooded river and managed to break the dam. The men waded across with heavy losses before they reached the foot of Big Orphan Hill.

"Above us the steep mountain stood high, kissing the heavens—even monkeys could hardly climb it," wrote an officer. The regiment was divided into two and ordered to storm the hill, while the Russian guns pounded them and the defenders at the top of the hill rolled down huge stones. The Japanese who got to the top disposed of the few Russians in hand-to-hand fighting and hoisted the Rising Sun with cries of *"banzai"* as the surrounding forts sent in heavy shells on to the newly taken position. The Japanese losses were over 3,000, but they retained Big Orphan and on August 9 went on to take the smaller hill.

After a fierce fight, the Russians fell back to their outer line of defenses, and the Japanese firmly entrenched on the two hills could now look down on the eastern section of Port Arthur's fortifications. While these preliminary operations were taking place, General Nogi worked on his plans for the general attack. Before leaving Tokyo he had favored a frontal assault, and, incredibly, he saw nothing on the ground to change his mind.

From the top of a high peak on Feng-huang-shan ("Wolf Hills"), five miles to the north of Port Arthur, he looked down on to the Russian lines of defense. To the southwest lay the strong Itze-shan Fort surrounded by walls where years before he had led his regiment through what was then one of the most powerful Chinese positions. On all sides were other hills he remembered—Erh-lung-shan ("Two Dragon Mountain"), Golden Hill, and Tiger's Tail—but many new forts had appeared since he took Port Arthur ten years earlier.

Below stretched the foothills and beyond them a wide valley through which the Chinese Eastern Railway ran to Port Arthur. In another valley stretching between Louisa Bay on the west and Ta-ku-shan in the east the land undulated, providing shelter for troops. On all sides there were erosions, some of them fifty feet deep. Nogi visualized these as ready-made approaches for his attack force as it worked its way toward the Russian defenses.

To the west of this valley were hundreds of rugged hills, broken by narrow gullies. From the highest of these peaks, Wantai Hill, or the Watcher's Terrace, ran a series of spurs, ten in all, some with permanent forts and others less heavily defended. Though Nogi did not know it, all these forts were connected by a covered way along the whole semicircular defense perimeter and sheltered from direct fire. The old Chinese Wall lay immediately in front of this arc of forts, providing protection for a roadway that carried provisions and ammunition to all points.

Along the western edge of the plateau was another range of hills, including 174 Meter Hill, 180 Meter Hill and 203 Meter Hill, named according to their height above sea level. The main fortifications were the two old Chinese forts that Nogi remembered from the war with China—Antze-shan and Itze-shan—with their almost sheer sides forming natural defenses. Much farther south were the inner row of forts around the harbor and town, and beyond the town itself the Tiger's Tail peninsula, where swivel-mounted guns could fire either out to sea or inland. Opposite the tail of the peninsula was Golden Hill, rising straight out of the sea with its tall, steep sides heavily fortified and guarding the narrow entrance to the harbor.

Port Arthur and its inner harbor were at the bottom of the basin formed by the ring of hills and mountains that sheltered it from all sides and obscured Nogi's vision. He could see only a blue speck of water, a minute part of the harbor. The hill defenses, he remembered, were interlocking.

Though there was ample cover to protect an approach march through the numerous gullies and the *kaoliang,* a type of millet sprouting in the valleys, nature had worked to the Russians' advantage. A direct attack against an adequately defended Port Arthur might be suicidal, though the Russians had built their strongest line too close to the town and the harbor, leaving the outer forts, including 203 Meter Hill, with hurriedly constructed and only semipermanent fortifications. Nevertheless, Nogi should have been impressed with the strength of the walls of the Russian forts, built of gray or red stone and what he took to be the long black muzzles of guns placed conspicuously on the highest points of the breastworks. This was no place to launch a frontal assault.

Both Kodama and Colonel Matsukata, chief of the first division of the general staff, had opposed any sort of attack, feeling that it was undesirable to divide their forces and that Port Arthur could be left until later. But the coming of the rainy season and the fleet's urgent need for repairs, which would probably take two or three months, caused the Imperial General Headquarters to reconsider its plans. Marshal Yamagata, who had taken over from Oyama, as chief of staff and Admiral Ito, the chief of the naval staff, met to discuss the situation, and on June 24 Nogi received the order to attack and occupy Port Arthur as soon as possible. Ten thousand casualties were regarded as an acceptable loss.

On July 3 a meeting of the combined army and navy staffs in Tokyo went a long step farther. It decided that even if much heavier sacrifices were required, and Nogi's preparations for frontal assault proved to be in vain, Port Arthur had to be taken without delay. If Port Arthur did not fall, Ying-kou, the port for Newchwang on the Gulf of Liaotung and with an invaluable rail link, could not be used safely to supply the Japanese armies and this would greatly hamper Oyama's offensive plans. If the Russian Baltic Fleet arrived before the Japanese ships had returned from dockyards in Japan, the Russians might recover the command of the sea, even if Port Arthur had fallen. If Port Arthur could be taken immediately, Togo's Combined Fleet could assist Kamimura in preventing further attacks by the Russian Vladivostok squadron.

On July 29 Nogi decided to proceed with his plans for the frontal assault: "All attacks which are time-consuming should be avoided. There is no time to consider whether or not the fortifications are strong or weak. We must realize that almost all of our cannon and the quantity of ammunition we hold are relatively limited."

The plan of attack was to capture Wantai, the Watcher's Terrace, in the center of the northeastern semicircle of forts, and from there to drive a wedge between the eastern fortifications and seize Erh-lung and Sung-shu ("Pine Tree Hill") forts, using the captured ground as the jumping-off base against the town itself, carrying by storm the secondary line of eastern defenses and overwhelming the garrison forces.

On the morning of August 16 Nogi sent an officer into Port Arthur, bearing a flag of truce and an offer of surrender. Nogi had discussed this with Togo, who agreed, requesting only that the enemy ships be surrendered to him. If the Russians refused to surrender, the general land attack would begin immediately.

The appeal to surrender asked the Russians to give up before more lives were lost. "Although the Russians have given signal proof of their gallantry, Port Arthur must inevitably fall," the appeal stated. "Therefore, in order to prevent useless sacrifice of life, and to avoid the danger of unnecessary damage by Japanese troops who may have to fight their way into the town, His Imperial Majesty the Emperor of Japan suggests the opening of negotiations for the surrender of the fortress."* A second message was sent personally by the Emperor.

His Majesty the Emperor of Japan, out of pure benevolence and goodness, sincerely desires that the noncombatants at Port Arthur may be kept, so far as is possible, free from the disastrous effects of fire and sword. In pursuance of this Imperial wish, you are ordered to escort to Dalny and to hand over to the commander of that port such women, children, priests, diplomats of neutral countries, and foreign military attachés at Port Arthur as may desire to leave the fortress. Those noncombatants who do not belong to the above category, but whose departure from the fortress will not jeopardize our strategical interests, may be similarly dealt with."

It was the offer of a foe looking for a quick end to hostilities, a cheap victory. It was also an opportunity to present a picture of chivalry and goodwill to the world.

The surrender offer made headlines, together with the curt Russian refusal to both Japanese requests. General Stoessel declared that no answer should be given. He stamped angrily up and down the room at the Council of War. When General Smirnov insisted that rules of military etiquette required an answer, he suggested sending a blank piece of paper. Eventually Smirnov drafted a reply which Stoessel grudgingly signed: "The honor and dignity of Russia do not allow of overtures of any sort being made for a surrender." The evacuation of women and children and other noncombatants was also spurned. Their going would undoubtedly reduce the strain on the food supplies, but the Japanese would get useful information from their captives. No one was to leave the fortress.

After the loss of the heavy siege guns aboard the *Hitachi Maru*, the Third Japanese Army launched its assault desperately short of heavy artillery and blissfully unaware of its need. Nogi fancied that siege guns were unnecessary for the task, and that the fire support available from the fleet would be adequate. Although reconnaissance had shown that the defenses were more formidable than the original estimates, he still appeared unconcerned. "The condition of the fortress, and the troops guarding it, are, to our present knowledge, such that storming attacks need not be unsuccessful," he said complacently.

---

*The Russian correspondent, E. K. Nojine, who accompanied the Russian truce party, gives a slightly different version of the note: ". . . therefore, to avoid useless loss of life and any possible violence, murder or looting by Japanese troops fighting their way into the town, which it will be difficult at once to prevent, His Majesty the Emperor of Japan suggests a discussion of negotiations for the surrender of the Fortress."

[345]

At Imperial General Headquarters several senior officers were much less sanguine. Major-General Iguchi shared General Nagaoka's view that Port Arthur might, in fact, be impregnable, and he was sorely concerned that Nogi intended to launch a frontal assault. He wanted to keep only a small number of troops on the frontal area and to move the main Japanese force to the westward for surprise attacks.

Nogi would not hear of it. When Iguchi, on his way to join Oyama, handed over a message from Yamagata setting out these fears, Major-General Ijichi Kosuke, Nogi's chief of staff, read it through and sniggered, as if to say, "What nonsense." Ijichi's views on the situation were so diametrically opposed to those of General Iguchi, not merely on the tactics to be adopted but on the need to hasten the attack, that the two generals almost reached the point of physical combat.

At dawn on August 19, General Nogi started his general attack with a bombardment, followed by the infantry assault. Only a mile separated the two forces. Before this space was crossed by the Japanese four-and-a-half months later, the two sides were to lose more than 100,000 men killed, wounded, or stricken by disease.

As soon as the attack began, all the weaknesses in Nogi's tactics and in intelligence quickly showed up. Even with the best telescopes available at Port Arthur the Japanese had not been able to assess the strength of the fortifications, and they were to receive some rude shocks. From the top of Ta-ku-shan, the Eleventh Division's observers reported that they could see a western-style, two-story house on the crest of Erh-lung, the second fort on the north of the semicircular Russian fortifications, inside the Chinese Wall. But the house was merely a shell built by the Russians immediately before the war. It covered a permanent fort with well-entrenched dugouts, its "windows" made not of glass but of solid concrete. Since the Japanese military had not anticipated a major assault here, their intelligence, weak as usual in Port Arthur, had failed to give details of the "house." It was to cost the Japanese military 16,000 casualties to find out.

The First Division attacked 174 Meter Hill, three miles north-northwest of New Town and commanding the approaches to 203 Meter Hill, which was only two-and-a-half miles from the port. Once again Colonel Tretyakov and the Fifth East Siberian Rifle Regiment were in the thick of the fighting, together with the Thirteenth East Siberian Rifle Regiment and two companies of seamen. Although the hill had been held only by scouting detachments until August 11, when the Russian fleet returned, Tretyakov had worked with his usual diligence to prepare the defenses, and the hill was now surrounded on three sides by rows of trenches. To the intense satisfaction of Tretyakov and his men, the much-admired General Kondratenko was in overall command.

The Japanese First Division attacked on August 19 and by daylight on August 20 they had destroyed the wire on the front of the hill and had a foothold in the main defenses on the northern slope. By mid-morning they carried the first line of trenches. Two hours later the second line went, but the third line, at the top of an incline, held on. During the afternoon the opposing forces clung to the opposite sides of the hilltop, with only fifty feet of ground between them and hidden from each other by outcrops of rocks.

Half of the men holding the hill had been killed or wounded, and the rest were too weary to repair damage done to the gun mountings and overhead parapets. Kondratenko brought up two more companies and sent another two to repair trenches that had caved in under the heavy fire. Few of the original defenders were uninjured, and all company commanders had been killed or wounded.

General Fock arrived from headquarters to say that 174 Meter Hill must be held at all costs. "This was quite obvious to all of us," Colonel Tretyakov remarked. "It is a very nasty thing to retreat by day under the fire of an enemy who is only a few paces off." Yet when the troops on the hill asked for reinforcements, General Fock refused to send them, despite the protests of Kondratenko and Tretyakov.

"What does this mean?" Fock asked. "You want to hold on until nightfall, and yet you send up your last reserve?"

"It is absolutely necessary," answered Tretyakov.

"It is not at all necessary," replied Fock, as he made his way back to headquarters.

"I saw that General Fock's assurance had overruled General Kondratenko's judgment," Tretyakov was to write later, "and I had not the moral courage myself to contradict him and insist on the dispatch of the last company, the more so, as Colonel Irman, my immediate superior, did not give me any support."

One or two men straggled down from the hill and launched the deluge. Men poured down the slopes, some without their rifles. An entire company left positions on the hill. A group of only fifty men from Tretyakov's own Fifth Regiment ran to the upper gun battery and stood on the breastworks to fire down on the enemy. Every other Russian had fled, and the fifty stalwarts were cut down as the Japanese fired over the heads of their own men.

General Kondratenko, Tretyakov, and Colonel Irman tried to stop the retreat, but their efforts were too late. The Japanese had taken Hill 174 with the loss of 1,700 officers and men. The Russian losses were 1,100 killed and wounded. Tretyakov pulled back, abandoning eight guns, and posted his regiment at the rear of Namako Yama and Division Hill, to the east of his old position.

Three miles to the east of 174 Meter Hill, a much bloodier action unfolded when Nogi's Ninth and Eleventh divisions, after a preliminary bombardment by artillery and naval guns, began to make their way through the watercourses and *kaoliang* to the Waterworks Redoubt, less than two miles north of the Old Town. Without too much difficulty, the Japanese seized an advance trench about 200 yards from the main defenses. From there they jumped off over open ground. All but thirty of the first attacking force of 180 were killed or wounded, but reinforcements continued to press on over the bodies of the dead and dying.

Under cover of the *kaoliang* the troops crawled to the entanglements surrounding the hill. The wires were electrified, and the Japanese scouts used special cutters with handles bound with old bicycle tires or strips of bamboo. Many were killed by electric shock; many others were cut down by the Russian guns. At night the Russian searchlights blazed over the scene as the Japanese tried to break through the wire. "I feel like a young bride!" cried Lieutenant Sakurai Tadayoshi, one of the attackers. "Exposed to such a full glare of light, I am awfully shy and bashful."

On the hills ringing the Waterworks Redoubt the ground was covered with the dead and dying. Trenches were taken and retaken, and corpses filled them to overflowing: "We lived in the stink of rotting flesh and crumbling bones, our own flesh wasted and even our bones seemed thinner. We were like a group of spirits with sharp, eager passions in miserable bodies, but still we were offshoots of the genuine cherry trees of Yamato," wrote Lieutenant Sakurai of the attack.

Next morning the trench was still in Japanese hands, and another party of 200 men had a foothold on the parapet of the fort and in the ditch encircling it. Between them and the new strong point lay 300 yards of bare, open ground. The Japanese who had been there overnight withdrew from the trench and fell back on their lines. The few who had reached the walls were picked off one by one by Russian machinegun fire, their bodies lying where they had fallen.

At West and East Pan-lung forts ("Mountain of the Dragon Ready to Attack"), just above the strategic Wantai fort, the attacks were even more furious as the Japanese moved along the watercourses toward the two positions. Here there were deep ravines that offered protection, but many men were cut off from their companies and got lost in the driving rain. They followed over the same trenches, each time finding them filled with more dead and dying men. Chaos took charge as each commander sought only to keep his own company together. Thousands of men trampled over the cadavers until the ravines filled with mangled bodies, over which the soldiers climbed. "We hardly found space to walk without stepping on them," wrote Sakurai. "It was an infernal tunnel of the dead and the dying. We groped to the right not to step on a dead comrade, only to kick a wounded one on the left. Where we stepped thinking that it was on mother earth, we found ourselves walking over the khaki-colored dead."

Lieutenant Sakurai kicked off his boots and wore Japanese *tabi* on his feet, "like a dancer at the rural festival in summer." On an improvised *obi* made from a small Japanese towel, he carried his sword, his water-bottle, and three hard biscuits, and a tiny coffin which would take his ashes. "Don't step on the corpses," he shouted to his men, as they picked their way forward. Several times he led his men back through the passageways filled with dead, now more horrible than before because the gun carriages of the artillery had also mangled them. The wounded now were dead, and the earlier bodies cut to pieces.

Nogi drove into the hard core of the Russian defenses. Regiment after regiment went in. Regiment after regiment went down. Bodies lay eight deep in the narrow crevices and ravines. Many companies, like Sakurai's, lost their way so completely that they finished in the ditches surrounding Fort Chi-kuan nearly two miles south of Pan-lung.

General Gorbatovski, the Russian eastern division commander, called for reinforcements. One after another all his officers were either killed or wounded and without help the attack could not be repulsed. General Smirnov assured him that the relief would be forthcoming and that by night they would have forced back the Japanese.

Since all the Russian troops knew that without reinforcements the hill could not be held, men began to pour down the reverse slope, some without their rifles, in the same headlong flight that had occurred at 174 Meter Hill two days before. General Smirnov, the fortress commander, furiously ordered Fock to send reinforcements. Fock's reply was that Gorbatovski was a traitor. "He is uselessly wasting the reserves—inviting a slaughter by putting them into the trenches," he told the agitated Stoessel. "If he does this, we'll have to surrender. He is a traitor, sir!"

General Smirnov, with the hill in imminent danger, calmed his colleagues. Quietly, he informed Stoessel that Gorbatovski was a hero, not a traitor. "For three days and nights he has been constantly under fire, directing the defense, and by his gallantry encouraging the men. I will see to the repulse of the attack; the reserve must be used when necessary."

Turning to Fock, still talking quietly, he said: "And you, sir, it appears, do not intend to obey my orders? Today, instead of at once carrying them out, you employed your time writing replies. . . . I never give an order twice. Bear that in mind." Thereafter, General Fock took no part in operations and spent his time writing long notes and giving his advice to the equally inefficient Stoessel.

The few Japanese survivors of the horrors of the ravines reached the parapets of East Pan-lung, where bitter hand-to-hand fighting took place. Almost all the Russians inside the fort had been killed, and the remainder began to leave in twos and threes. West Pan-lung was overlooked in the battle for the Eastern fort, and by 6 P.M. on August 22 two Japanese flags were flying from its crest.

Smirnov made a desperate attempt to recapture the two forts in a night attack, but companies of the Thirteenth East Siberian Rifle Regiment lost their way when they tried to take the Western fort from the rear. East Pan-lung was retaken briefly, but when daylight came the few Russians who had reached the fort found little protection from the broken parapets. Out of 637 men dispatched on the mission, more than 400 were killed.

There came a time when even the Japanese could fight no longer. The remnants of one regiment refused to leave its trenches when ordered into attack. A major dragged them out and led the assault. He was killed immediately. When the survivors fell back, they were sent to the rear and put on fatigue duty. A Shinto shrine to the spirit of the dead major was erected close to the camps, and every day the survivors of the Osaka-based regiment were paraded before it to atone for their disgrace.

Four naval companies were added to the Russian garrison but, one after the other, all the officers were killed or wounded, including the commander.

East Pan-lung eventually fell to the Japanese, but out of the 1,800 men of the Seventh Regiment only 200 remained alive. The end of the general assault came on the night of August 23 when the exhausted Ninth and Eleventh divisions, who had fought for almost sixty hours, hurled themselves against the Wantai Heights, starting out from the two captured Pan-lung forts. They reached the Chinese Wall, clambered over it and forced their way up the steep slopes of Wantai. The Russians used searchlights and magnesium rockets, blinding the men and turning them into easy targets as they attempted to force their way up the slopes. With the assistance of more than a thousand sailors from the fleet, the Russian defenders threw grenades and rocks and flaming bags down on their enemy. When dawn came the Ninth and Eleventh Japanese divisions had fallen back, leaving about a hundred men clinging to the almost vertical face of the Watcher's Terrace and the ground in front piled with dead and dying.

For months, thousands of bodies covered the ground between the Pan-lung forts and Wantai. Wounded on both sides crawled about for days on the slopes of the hill. Any movement brought down immediate fire. Bands of Japanese rescue teams crept out at night, hiding as well they could behind rocks and tussocks of grass, to the wounded men, taking hold of them by legs or arms or the collars of their uniforms and dragging them over the ground, back to the comparative safety of their lines. It was often a mixed blessing. After hours lying in the boiling sun, covered with flies and maggots, the cool of the night brought temporary relief. Being jerked over stony ground was a final torture. Many were killed, along with their rescuers, by Russian snipers who were gathering their own wounded. They had been tricked before by Japanese feigning death who suddenly came to life and rushed toward the entanglements to cut the wire surrounding the forts. The Russians tried to combat the hideous stench of the corpses by soaking strips of cloth in carbolic acid or camphor and hanging them over the trenches, but nothing could relieve the horror on the hills above Port Arthur.

"To take Port Arthur seems impossible," wrote a correspondent. "It takes men drunk with victory and strong in ancient might to dare the task . . . only madmen would attempt it." The Japanese fought like madmen, clinging to the hillsides and running across open ground to be mowed down by the Russian fire.

Nogi's assault on the fortress was insane in its conception. He could not forget the ease with which Port Arthur had been taken in the war with China. Inadequate intelligence was also to blame. The strength of the Russian fortifications was determined only at great cost during the first assaults. Nogi's staff showed little enthusiasm for personal investigation. "They are so far away that shells would not reach them," reported General Nagaoka.

> Reports of Nogi and his chief of staff state that "the enemy fortress batteries are stronger than we had imagined and walls are well-equipped.". . . It should not be necessary to kill 10,000 or more troops to discover this. . . . If the public knew this, what would be their reaction? Can the command headquarters be said to have carried out their task and responsibility? I therefore omitted this part when we had reports printed for the Emperor to see. . . .

After Ta-ku-shan fell no senior staff officer climbed the mountain, apart from one regimental adjutant who found to his amazement that he was looking down on the Russian forts and batteries to the east of Port Arthur. Visits from Nogi's staff to the front were extremely rare, and they had no idea of the conditions at the front line. All the staff did was to drive the troops forward again and again.

Military police were attached to each unit during the first assault to prevent looting and violence when the forces reached Port Arthur. Overconfidence, underestimation, and sheer military inadequacy at the highest level of the field command cost the Japanese dearly.

In Japan it had been thought that Port Arthur would fall as it had in the

[351]

war against China. All that was required was the spirit of *bushido*. Nogi, Imperial General Headquarters, and the general public all expected the town's early downfall. On August 19, when the attack began, reporters camped in the grounds of the war ministry in Tokyo all night, sleeping in tents and waiting for news from the front. Some newspapers had already printed "extras," without a date, saying "Official cablegram just arrived announcing the fall of Port Arthur." Many months and thousands of lives later the presses were still waiting for the news to come.

CHAPTER 21

Liaoyang

THE HATED PLEHVE fell to an assassin's bomb in St. Petersburg while driving in his carriage to take a train to the palace at Peterhof for his weekly report to the Tsar. The Associated Press correspondent was at the scene within five minutes of the assassination. Plehve's body, or what remained of it, lay in the middle of the road partly covered with a policeman's overcoat. The roadway was strewn for a hundred yards with the wreckage of the carriage and the red lining of Plehve's overcoat.

Plehve died on the orders of his own trusted agent, Evno Azev, whose tips to the police about plots to murder the minister had previously led to several arrests. As a Jew, he hated Plehve, but it was also important for his own future that credit for the assassination should go to the Battle Organization, whose funds he controlled.

The assassination set off further protests in Russia against the war. At Peterhof, a soldier on his way to the East broke from the ranks and threw himself under the wheels of a passing train. In the war zone, Kuropatkin decided to fall back on a line running through the villages of An-shan-chan, Lang-tsu-shan, and Anping in a semicircle stretching from the southwest to the east of Liaoyang. In a report to the Tsar on August 4 he listed his reasons, all of them highly flattering to the Japanese: 1) The Japanese superiority in numbers; 2) the fact that the Japanese were accustomed to hills and hot weather; 3) that the Japanese were younger, carried lighter loads, and had numerous mountain artillery and pack transport; 4) the Japanese energetic and intelligent leadership; 5) the extraordinary patriotism and military spirit of Japanese troops; and 6) the lack of such a spirit on the Russian side (caused by general ignorance of what they were fighting for).

No one had bothered to explain the war to the Russian people. They were fighting for Nicholas's imperial dreams, and these were not easy to translate into patriotic terms.

Confidence did not increase with time and the news from Port Arthur. Stoessel was now deeply pessimistic about Port Arthur's prospects of holding out and upset Alexeiev, who began to call again for some sort of offensive action. The rains, which had come late but bountifully, aggravated the gloom in Russia's Manchurian headquarters. The roads were washed out or became bogholes into which men sank up to their waists and guns disappeared.

Fearful heat followed the rain. The *kaoliang,* which had been only a foot or so high at the beginning of the month, shot up to a height of more than ten feet so that battalions could easily be hidden or lost in the fields. The millet was both a cover for the Japanese advance and a forest in which the badly trained Russian officers could lose their way.

The hopes of the Russian defenders wilted. Baron A. A. Bilderling, Seventeenth Corps commander, who had taken over the Eastern Front on July 31, wanted to withdraw to Liaoyang and abandon its outer line of defenses. The Tenth Corps commander favored concentrating the Manchurian Army between Liaoyang and Mukden. Alexeiev, with his eyes set on Port Arthur, continued to press for some action to relieve the siege.

Torn between these opposing views, Kuropatkin, under Alexeiev's pressure, elected to give battle in front of Liaoyang. By contemporary standards, he had now assembled a vast army, consisting of two European army corps and five Siberian army corps, fourteen divisions in all. Against him Oyama mustered the three divisions of the First Army, three divisions of the Second Army (the Third, the Fourth and the Sixth), the two divisions (the Fifth and the Tenth) of the Fourth Army, and a number of regiments and battalions from the second reserve. In terms of men and guns, Oyama had one hundred fifteen battalions of infantry, thirty-three squadrons of cavalry, and 170 guns—in all 125,000 men, of whom 110,000 were infantry. Available for the immediate firing line, Kuropatkin had 191 battalions of infantry, 148 squadrons of cavalry, and 609 guns—or 158,000 men, of whom 128,000 were infantry.

Though the numbers of Japanese involved were considerably lower than the estimate given to Kuropatkin by his intelligence staff, the combined forces facing each other totaled nearly 300,000 men. Of all battles fought in recorded history, only at Sedan, when the Germans overwhelmed the French between August 29 and September 1, 1870, were there more men involved.

Many of Kuropatkin's forebodings were based on his assumption that he was outnumbered. "We did not have enough men to retain the necessary superiority over any of the hostile groups without laying ourselves open to defeat by the other two," he wrote. "In the second instance, the rains had so seriously damaged the roads as to prevent the rapid movement—we had heavy guns and baggage—necessary for successful action even on interior lines."

During the last week in May, Lieutenant-Colonel Hashiguchi Isauma, leader of one of Colonel Aoki's task forces that had been recruited in Peking in January, had begun to assemble an armed guerilla force in the mountains. Early in June he moved his force toward Liaoyang and here, in cooperation with Yuan Shih-k'ai's agents in the town, began to gather intelligence for General Fukushima (Oyama's quartermaster-general whose responsibilities included intelligence) and to attack isolated groups of Russians.

Oyama therefore took the field not in the supposition that he was outnumbered but in the absolute certainty. He could not be wholly sure, moreover, that the First Russian Corps, which was known to be on the way to the East, would not add its weight to the battle at the critical moment.* The Japanese Second Army had the lines of rolling stock but not the locomotives to make full use of the railway, while the First and Fourth armies were dependent on carts to move supplies from Feng-huang-cheng and Ta-ku-shan.

As both commanders were well aware, the outcome of the forthcoming battle was certain to affect the course of the war. Kuropatkin's delaying actions at the Yalu, Nanshan, and the Motien Pass had all been fought to win time. In St. Petersburg's view, time had been won and now was the time for action. For Oyama, there was no alternative: he could not concentrate forces against Port Arthur until Kuropatkin had been fought and defeated. There were reports that fourteen pairs of trains (i.e., fourteen trains each way) were now running on the railway, and Kuropatkin's supply and reinforcement situation was improving all the time. Still, there was hesitation only at Kuropatkin's headquarters, not at Oyama's, and the decision was made to ignore the wet season and to push on with the attack at Liaoyang without waiting for the fall of Port Arthur.

Next to Mukden, Liaoyang was the largest town in Manchuria, of great antiquity and notable for its brick walls, nearly forty feet high and twenty feet thick, which enclosed a citadel three quarters of a mile long and more than half a mile wide. The Tai-tzu River, which rose in the mountains far

---

*In fact, two battalions of the Twenty-second Infantry Division arrived at the height of the battle and were committed on September 1.

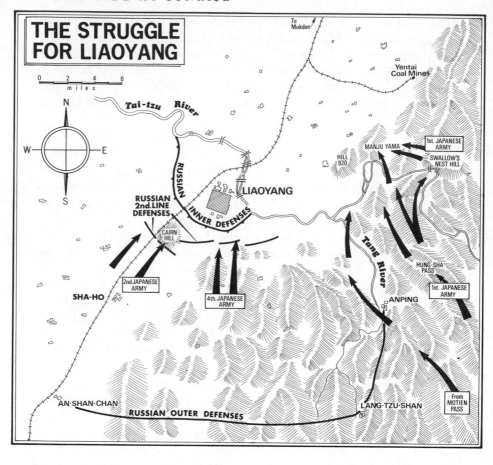

THE STRUGGLE FOR LIAOYANG

to the east of the town, passed by the city's northern walls. Its tributary, the Tang, flowed from south to north to the confluence about ten miles east of Liaoyang. Near the town the Tai-tzu was about 100 yards wide. Elsewhere, its width varied considerably. In places it was no more than seventy yards wide and at others it was more than 600 yards from bank to bank. During the dry season it was fordable in many places. On August 17, at the height of the wet season, it was a torrent, surging fourteen feet above its dry season level and nowhere fordable. Though the level receded each day thereafter, there were few places that could be forded when Oyama's armies began their thrust—a matter of considerable anxiety for Bilderling, who disliked the prospect of attempting a retreat with his back to a river that was so susceptible to floods.

[356]

The outer line of Russian defenses had been built during the early months of the war, specifically to block the Japanese advance along the lines of communication. To bar Oku's northern march one army group under General N. P. Zarubaiev sat astride the road and railway line from Port Arthur, with its center in the hills at An-shan-chan. Between Zarubaiev's forces and the eastern group under General Bilderling (part of which was north of the Tai-tzu), there was a gap of about twelve miles. Bilderling's forces were deployed to block the Japanese approaches along the roads leading from the passes in the mountains. On the flanks there were small detachments to guard against any surprise move by Oyama, while, under his own command, Kuropatkin had strong reserves which stretched back along the railway line toward Mukden.

The railway passed to the west of the walled town, and, with troops arriving at the rate of more than a thousand a day, the station had become the center of a busy Russian community. Its restaurant, with its own electric generator, was usually crowded with staff officers, Sisters of Mercy, and women of the town.

Facing the railway station was a large square containing the houses used by Kuropatkin and, briefly, by the Grand Duke Boris, who had left Port Arthur under a drunken cloud, which hung even more heavily over his head in Liaoyang. Rebuked by Kuropatkin for his behavior, Boris was said to have aimed a blow at Kuropatkin with his sword. Whether the report was correct or not, he was quickly on his way home. The headquarters train was covered by a flag-bedecked pavilion, which helped to keep it cool and to provide additional office space for the staff, who lived in smaller cottages around the station square.

As in Port Arthur, Dalny and Harbin, the vast Russian presence overshadowed the Chinese population. By the beginning of the summer in 1904, the Russians had commandeered most of the town's better buildings and had turned them into barracks and shops, while the engineers, with a large force of impressed Chinese coolies, worked feverishly to turn the town into a great entrenched camp.

Camp followers who had fled from Arthur and Dalny were joined by large numbers of others who had moved east. Seven Russian bordellos did thriving business, and there were girls to spare for music halls and bars. A Greek-owned restaurant for officers only had been built in the gardens of the great pagoda, and each night when weather permitted a Russian band played there while the officers dallied with other young ladies whose patriotic impulses had brought them to the war zone.

After the beginning of July, most of the dalliance and the drinking went on indoors. The rain cascaded down, turning the streets into liquid, dammed up along the sides with drier earth. Chinese coolies transported

[357]

pedestrians on their backs, dodging the horses and wagons that crowded the streets. There was mud everywhere—in the shops, in the hotels, in the lodging houses. "It might have been believed to be the cause of the Russian dissipation, for it was sufficient to drive the civil as well as the military to drink," wrote Frederick McCormick.

Kuropatkin himself was abstemious and highly moral, but the winds of scandal blew hotly around his staff. General Sakharov,* the chief of staff, an ornamental diplomatist who took no share in the hard work, all of which was done by Kuropatkin, even flouted military regulations by taking his paramour to war with him. During a lull in the battle, he found time to marry her and enjoyed a honeymoon while Liaoyang was falling.

His subordinates also found ample time for dalliance. The best hotel in town was the flea-bitten International, and here a profusion of staff officers wallowed in champagne, vodka, and beer. Champagne for breakfast was much in demand.

Resident Christian morality was embodied by Dr. A. Macdonald Westwater of the Presbyterian Church, who, as early as 1890, had broken down Chinese conservative opposition and won approval for his plan to establish a mission at Liaoyang. Most of the missionaries were murdered during the Boxer revolt. Dr. Westwater, who had escaped, accompanied the incoming Russian army during the Boxer Rebellion as a Red Cross surgeon. He managed to persuade the Chinese authorities not to resist the Russians, thus saving the town from destruction. Having survived these tests of faith, Dr. Westwater was not the man to flinch when Liaoyang and his mission became enveloped in war.

On August 12 an event occurred that brought a brief moment of cheer in St. Petersburg and at the front. The heir to the Russian throne was born, and with the boom of the first gun the traffic halted in the streets of St. Petersburg while people began to count the number of guns. Alexandra had produced four girls but no boy. If the child was again a girl, thirty-one guns would be fired; if it was a boy, the salute would go on until 101 rounds had been fired. "When the thirty-second boomed and the people were aware that at last an heir to the throne was born, there were scenes of rejoicing everywhere. Before the salute was finished the whole city had blossomed out in flags and bunting," *The New York Times* reported. The shipping in the harbor was dressed and the bells of the churches began to ring wildly.

Nicholas was overwhelmed with joy. "I am happier at the birth of a son and heir than at a victory of my troops," he said. "Now I face the future

---

*Vladimir Viktorovitch Sakharov, not to be confused with General Viktor Viktorovitch Sakharov, the war minister.

calmly and without alarm, knowing by this sign that the war will be brought to a happy conclusion."

In the sodden fields of millet at An-shan-chan, Kuropatkin took the salute at a parade to celebrate the birth of the Tsarevitch. Officers dressed in ceremonial uniforms put on a brave show. As one observer commented, the troops wading through the millet produced a spectacle that was scarcely equal to the polish of the annual British Aldershot review, but many of the troops regarded the birth as a sign from Heaven, a proof that their efforts had divine sanction. They awaited the Japanese armies with renewed confidence.

They did not have long to wait. Nogi's first attack on Port Arthur had begun on August 19. Two days later Oyama moved his headquarters to Hai-cheng, about forty miles south of Liaoyang, and gave his orders for the offensive. Outmanned, outgunned, and opposed by an enemy that had used the time available to him to create impressive forward and rear defensive positions, Oyama faced a formidable test. Messages reaching Hai-cheng from Port Arthur were not reassuring. The fortress, it was already clear, would not fall so easily as it had to the Japanese forces in the Sino-Japanese War. With the momentum generated by early successes, however, there could be no pause now. Though Oyama's forces had converged on Liaoyang without serious reverse, the two wings of his army—the Fourth and the Second in the south and the First in the east—were still twenty-five miles apart. Nor did they have any well-fortified positions in which to defend themselves if Kuropatkin siezed the initiative.

Compared with the challenge that now faced Oyama's armies, the previous battles had been skirmishes in which the advantages were usually on their side. The possibility for maneuver, so cleverly exploited by Kuroki and Oku at the Yalu and Nanshan, were not tactically feasible here. Against a force of this size, to attempt to outflank either of the main wings of the Russian army would be too dangerous, since the Japanese could easily be cut off. To strike through the gap was to invite Kuropatkin to execute a fatal pincer movement. Oyama therefore chose the only form of attack open to him: a frontal assault on the two Russian wings.

"Immense excitement," Sir Ian Hamilton noted in his diary on August 23. "The march against Kuropatkin's communications is about to begin. What a splendid thing to be alive and to be here taking part in the great final trek of the Manchurian war." This conviction that the war might be won or lost in the battle was not confined to the immediate observers. "It is the view of the authors of this book that the importance of the battle can hardly be exaggerated," pronounced the *British Official History of the Russo-Japanese War*. So long after the event, this conclusion still seems valid. This was, indeed, the critical test of arms and of wills.

[359]

Again, early honors went to Kuroki's First Army on the Japanese right flank. Hamilton found the grizzled Satsuma general on August 26 sitting in a deck chair on the top of the highest hill overlooking the tangled mass of mountains that separated the First Army from the plains of Liaoyang. About ten miles to the north and about two miles northeast of the village of Anping was the Hung-sha Pass, dominated by a peak that the Japanese called Kosarei. It rose sheer to a height of 1,900 feet and commanded the approaches to the Tang River. Immediately on the front was the broken mass of precipitous ravines that lay between the Lan and the Tang rivers. It was through this fearful country that Kuroki, ever on the lookout for surprise, had launched his strongest effort. He hoped to divert the Russian attention to the center of his front, while a smaller force tried to steal the Kosarei peak and control the Hung-sha Pass.

Though the countryside here had been carefully reconnoitered by Japanese patrols, Kuroki's staff had doubts whether troops could even climb the Kosarei peak. At 8 A.M., however, an adjutant informed Kuroki that his troops had driven the Russians from the most difficult part of the peak, though opposition continued to be heavy. This move was followed by a second message only twenty minutes later to the effect that the Russians had been driven off the northern part of the hill.

For many hours, a bloody battle continued over the possession of a narrow saddle that connected the bluff with the highest part of the hill. It was no more than forty yards long and a few yards wide, but the Japanese were slaughtered as they tried to cross it. Lieutenant-General Sluchevski, a sixty-one-year-old engineer who had never before led a division, commanded the Tenth Corps. He understood that it was critically important to hold the pass and asked repeatedly for reserves. Until the last moment General Bilderling, who commanded the Russian Eastern Group, remained convinced that the real threat lay elsewhere, on the right flank of the Third Siberian Corps, which held a seven-mile section of the front in the center of his positions. It was not until dusk that he could be persuaded to the contrary. North of the Tai-tzu River, and wholly uninvolved in the events of the day, were the Fifty-second Dragoon Regiment, eight battalions of the Third Infantry Division and forty-four guns of the Third Artillery Brigade under Major-General Yanzhul. They had taken no part in the action, nor was there any threat from this direction. Late in the afternoon the force was brought south across a bridge over the river. General Sluchevski pleaded for this force to be sent across the Tang to the aid of the hard-pressed defenders of the Hung-sha Pass.

Looking at the broader picture, Kuropatkin was concerned at this move, since it deprived him of all infantry immediately north of Tai-tzu, and of this he immediately made Bilderling aware. Bilderling himself, who had always been opposed to fighting with his back to a river subject to flash floods, was no less concerned, if for different reasons. Fighting had come to a temporary halt after 4 P.M. because of a torrential storm that quickly muddied and soon added to the flow in the still swollen rivers—a development renewing all his old fears. He nevertheless took the decision to commit the reserves two hours too late. Though the news did not reach Bilderling's headquarters until after dark, the Russian regiment had been driven from the Pass with 358 of its 2,400 men killed or wounded during the day. Kuropatkin learned of the loss of the position at 10 P.M. and ordered an immediate counterattack by the forces which had crossed the Tang and were now less than five miles from the pass. At midnight he canceled the order and issued instructions for a general withdrawal to the inner defenses of Liaoyang, thus handing to Kuroki and Oyama the most unexpected of victories.

So ended the first phase of the battle of Liaoyang. Kuropatkin made light of his reverse. "By delaying and inflicting heavy loss on the enemy on the Lang-tzu-shan and Anping positions, all the Corps were able to fall back on the positions at Liaoyang, where the Army was concentrated on August 29th," he reported.

Kuropatkin was lucky. Though an effective strike might have driven the exhausted Japanese back from the heights overlooking the Tang, it was fortuitous the following morning that the foul weather continued and a mist covered the narrow defile through which his supply trains had to pass. Unaware of the Russian withdrawal, the Japanese missed the chance to deliver a crushing blow. The mud was so thick that the men could not walk with their heavy boots—they took them off and went barefoot. Carts loaded with stores and ammunition had to be unloaded and the stores distributed among the men and horses. For the rearguard, things were much worse. A battery of artillery sank in the mud, and, though teams of horses were brought up to try to recover the guns, they sank deeper in the mire. "Soon the Japanese from behind began firing at the battery," Lord Brooke reported. "Every minute men and horses fell dead or wounded." Among those killed were the general commanding the rear-guard and a colonel in the Imperial Guards.

But for the thick mist that hid the early part of the evacuation, the Russians would have fared much worse. It gave them several hours' start. The Japanese Second Army was ready to launch a major attack against An-shan-chan and was surprised to find the position deserted.

Plodding through the mud, alternately soaked with rain and drooping in the humid heat, the Russians fell back slowly and painfully toward their prepared positions at Liaoyang. On occasions the roads were blocked for miles by the bogged transports, and both the infantry and artillery had to adjust their pace accordingly. The Japanese were on their heels and repeatedly columns had narrow escapes from disaster.

Oyama continued to urge his commanders into the attack. At noon on August 28 he instructed Kuroki to push on to the south bank of the Tai-tzu and cross the river. To the Second and Fourth armies went orders urging similar haste.

To Oyama, it was unclear whether Kuropatkin intended to stand and fight at Liaoyang or was intent on retreating beyond the town toward Mukden. Speed was essential. Though Oyama succeeded by his pressure in bringing the three armies closer together as they converged on Liaoyang, they were not able, under the appalling conditions of the roads, to produce the extra effort that might have caught Kuropatkin short of his prepared positions.

Months of effort had gone into the construction of the Russian inner line of defenses. Extending in a semicircle around the town with both flanks anchored on the Tai-tzu were seven heavily protected strongpoints. Between the strongpoints there were acres of barbed wire and minefields, all of them covered by fields of interlocking fire. In front of this inner ring of steel were the outer fortifications, which swept in a crescent for fifteen miles from the railway line east and north to the Tai-tzu. Between the inner and the outer defense lines there was a sea of millet that ended with the line of hills rising precipitously from the plain and now scarred with Russian trenches. Since work on these fortifications had not begun in some places until the second half of August, they obviously lacked the strength of the inner ring. Nor were the troops who were to occupy the line as familiar with them as they would have been if Kuropatkin had accepted Bilderling's advice and fallen back before the first action on August 26.

Despite the impact on morale caused by this first retirement, the situation should have favored Kuropatkin. The improving train service now added each day to the numbers of men he could put into the field, increasing the superiority in numbers that he already enjoyed. But of this he was still unaware. Rather, he was only too conscious that most of his units were understrength and that his infantry companies numbered only 140 to 150 men.

General Stackelberg's First Siberian Rifle Corps was on the right of the Russian line, with its right flank on a heavily entrenched and fortified hill, Cairn Hill,* which rose to 693 feet on the eastern edge of the railway line and about seven miles from the Liaoyang railway station. The corps' two divisions, the First on the right and the Ninth on the left, occupied a series

_____

*Known to the Japanese as Shou-shan.

[362]

of hills that diminished in size and eventually petered out among the fields of *kaoliang*. On Stackelberg's left, but separated from his corps by a wide gap and a stream known as Tai-tzu Brook, was Lieutenant-General Nikolai Yudievitch Ivanov's Third Siberian Rifle Corps. The Tenth European Corps was on the left of the Third Siberian Corps, and on its left, across the Tai-tzu, was General Bilderling's Seventeenth Corps. Spread over a distance of about twenty-five miles, Kuropatkin therefore deployed eight infantry divisions. Beyond these forces and on either flank was the cavalry, mostly Cossacks, whose performance had proved so disappointing, though the conditions should have favored their use. Tanks and armored cars were soon to replace the horse in warfare, but not before the Australian light horse units had fought with considerable effect in the Middle East in World War I.

A major Russian weakness was the lack of adequate maps. Kuropatkin's staff had prepared a good map of Liaoyang and the country to the south on a scale of 1.3 miles to the inch, but so few copies were available that they were not distributed to units that needed them most. Until just before the battle there were no maps of the country to the north of Liaoyang, where General Bilderling was now to operate. One was hastily prepared with a scale of 2.66 miles to the inch. It omitted the contours and was useless for military purposes. A revised and much improved edition was prepared on the eve of the second phase of the battle. Containing numerous errors, it was also far from adequate in detail and consequently led the Russians into trouble when fighting began.

The cairn on Cairn Hill was a principal target for the Japanese. "Against the stone tower where the telephone was, the shrapnel rained like hail," Lord Brooke reported. One soldier lying close to him had his rifle broken in two by a shell fragment. The single telephone line could not cope with the traffic to the guns at the rear of the hill and communication was established by a chain of men lying flat on their stomachs who passed written notes from hand to hand.

At 4:25 P.M., after nearly twelve hours in the field, Oku received a message from Oyama that the Russians had taken the initiative in front of the Tenth Division of the Fourth Army, which was on his right, and that he was therefore to launch an immediate attack against Cairn Hill, and, having taken it, go to the help of Nozu's men. At the same time, General Stackelberg was busy composing a message for Kuropatkin. The First Siberian Army Corps had not lost a foot of ground and he was proud of it.

This was a moment of crisis for both the Russians and the Japanese. The Russians' pressure against the Tenth Division threatened not only the flank of the Fourth Army but the entire Second Army, also. A breakthrough to

[363]

Sha-ho, where Oku had his headquarters, would have cut off the entire Second Army and led to its almost inevitable destruction. Even Oyama, who had established his own headquarters in a house at Sha-ho village, seemed to be in danger. Again, the Japanese attack failed. The Twelfth East Siberian Infantry Regiment, accompanied by twelve guns, was moving south along the railway line. It took the Japanese flank and stopped the attack dead.

At Oku's headquarters the staff was in despair. "When the reports of regimental commander Sakiya and battalion commander Tachibana and others reached headquarters, I felt as if I had been hit with a heavy object in the head, and sank into a nearby chair," Ishimitsu Makiyo, then the adjutant to the Second Army, recalled.

> I could not remain standing. General Oku closed his eyes, placed his hands on his knees and listened quietly. "Thank you," he said, when the reports had been read. That night the General's office was quiet, though it was lit. He called no one. The roar of cannon reverberating from the skies over the battlefront, and the sound of raindrops, were louder than the night before. Again this night many young heroes would breathe their last in a foreign land bathed in mud.

Three Japanese major-generals, including Tojo Hidenori, father of Japan's World War II leader, Tojo Hideki, were demoted for their "table top" strategy and unnecessary loss of lives.

Torrential rain had brought the daylight action to a close and obliterated any improbable thought that the Russians may have entertained about attempting to break through toward Sha-ho village. So heavy was the rain, and so inadequately drained were the Russian trenches, that the infantry got no rest during the night but had to stand deep in liquid mud, with many of their weapons temporarily unserviceable. They had, nevertheless, fought well. Japanese assaults west and east of Tai-tzu Brook had failed.

For Oyama's armies this was one of the bleakest days of the war. Along the entire front their attacks had been repulsed with heavy losses, and the Russians, for the first time, though bloodied, were unbowed and unbeaten. Kuropatkin had committed his reserves heavily, but he still had more in hand than Oyama. Nothing suggested that he was about to retreat, or that any repetition of the onslaught next day by the heavily mauled Japanese infantry would force a breakthrough.

At dawn, though, Oku's forces captured the hills immediately south of Cairn Hill and less than half a mile from it. They drove two Russian companies from the first line of trenches along the hill top. There, they came under heavy fire and by 8 A.M. the 300 men from seven companies that had taken the hill fell back to the cover of its foot, where they remained until nightfall. The First Battalion alone lost 272 killed and 314 wounded. "When we viewed the position, Russians and Japanese were lying intermingled waist-deep in the ditch, while from parapet to entanglement, perhaps 150 yards, the thick trail of prostrate khaki told a tale that no pen can describe," wrote *The Times*'s correspondent.

Trenches were taken, lost, and retaken. Lord Brooke saw a Russian soldier run to a trench that had been taken by the Japanese and thereafter remained mysteriously silent. "My comrades," the soldier shouted, "they have no more ammunition." The Russians fell over themselves in their haste to get to the trench. "In five minutes," wrote Brooke, "not a Japanese was left alive. In the trench the bayonet had done its work."

Oyama now committed the last of his reserves, the Fourth Division. Nothing that he could throw against the Russian line promised to crack it. Cairn Hill was being bombarded hotly from the plain, but the Russian trenches here were deep and the casualties relatively few.

The Russians thought the end was close, but none of their mounting apprehension was yet apparent to the Japanese who had gained nothing more after thirty-six hours of fighting than a precarious foothold in the Russian line at a cost of 7,000 casualties, most of them killed.

Colonel W. H.-H. Waters, a British military observer on Cairn Hill, saw things in a different light.

> It was now evident that the situation of the First Siberian Corps was becoming very critical indeed. General Stackelberg went down Cairn Hill at 12:35 P.M. in order to go to his reserve. . . . But, on arriving at the place where it was to have been, no reserve was there. Also at 12:35 P.M. Stackelberg had received an urgent note for reinforcements from Major-General Kondratovitch, who commanded his Ninth Division. Stackelberg, without the least sign of flurry, replied that he had no reinforcements to send, and that Kondratovitch and his men must die, if necessary, at their posts.

The First Siberian Army Corps was spent. Stackelberg had been slightly wounded and was ill. His troops were exhausted. Under no circumstances could the corps have launched a counteroffensive, but in comparison with the Japanese attackers the rest of Kuropatkin's army was relatively fresh and not badly scarred by battle. This was a time for imagination and enterprise. But these were characteristics that Kuropatkin, lacking in confidence in his officers and men, did not possess.

On both days he had toured the battlefront on his horse. Often the scene just behind the front is more alarming than the front itself. And so Kuropatkin appeared to find it. Many of the troops were suffering from heat exhaustion or sunstroke, and some had even become temporarily insane. Kuropatkin was impressed, as he had been before, with the ability of the Japanese troops to adjust to the climate. He was still under the impression that the Japanese forces outnumbered his own—a view strengthened by the numbers of Japanese riflemen who were at the front. But, above all, he was immensely disturbed by the movement still not yet established as a significant threat, but potentially most serious, that he now detected on his extreme left flank, where the major part of Kuroki's forces had been suspiciously quiet.

A variety of circumstances, in which luck and daring had their part, now led to an abrupt change in the whole character of the battle. From the hills to the east of Liaoyang, Kuroki's First Army looked over the fields of millet and the Tai-tzu River to the railway running north from the station in Liaoyang. According to his original instructions, Kuroki had been planning to break contact with the Russian forces on his front and, under orders from Oyama, to cross the river when the opportunity presented itself. At noon on August 30 the Japanese Guards Division from their vantage points saw considerably increased activity on the railway line. In fact, the Russians were merely evacuating their wounded, but the Guards thought that they were abandoning Liaoyang. The next day they noticed a series of fires in Liaoyang that again seemed to indicate the Russians were evacuating. At the same time, the observation balloon, which had floated over the town since the beginning of the battle, was pulled down.

Kuroki had responded immediately to the first communication from the Guards, and at 1 P.M. on August 30 he ordered a night crossing of the Tai-tzu. He was aware, of course, of the rebuff that the Japanese had suffered on the western front, but of Oyama's deep concern at Sha-ho village he knew nothing: the telephone line linking the First Army with Oyama's headquarters had been cut by shellfire. Though he was the initiator of the move, Oyama was thus in ignorance of it.

Kuropatkin guessed that Kuroki might have some such scheme in mind, and in the early morning of August 31 he issued Disposition No. 3, which set out the action to be taken in the event of strong hostile forces crossing the right bank of the Tai-tzu with the object of turning his left flank and cutting the railway line. Nevertheless, the move took most of the Russians completely by surprise. "Now it is a very remarkable fact that, with scarcely an exception, nobody had believed the Japanese would dare to attempt such a stroke," Colonel Waters commented.

The argument employed, and employed, too, by some of the foreign strategists present with the Russian army, was that, in order to parry such a blow, all Kuropatkin would have to do would be to cut the communications of the Japanese in his turn. They failed to appreciate the other fact that Kuropatkin, if he found his sole line of supply and retreat cut off, would be unable in practice, with an army by no means mobile, to do more than endeavor to get away if he could. It was interesting to hear the arguments of those who derided the idea of Kuroki venturing to assail the Russian communications, for they omitted one essential point: they based their reasoning on the false assumption that the Russian army could at any time be moved without difficulty in any direction.

Though they represented less than half of the First Army, Kuroki's men crossed the Tai-tzu as if they had no care in the world. The usual strict march discipline was not enforced, and the men smoked, talked, and even sang as, unopposed, they waded the swiftly flowing river some fifteen miles to the east of Liaoyang. Hamilton described the cigar-smoking Kuroki as radiant when he climbed the steep slope of the Swallow's Nest Hill to examine the battlefield. About seven miles to the west, or halfway between Kuroki's headquarters and Liaoyang, was Hill 920. On its eastern flank, and worthy of attention only because it clearly would have to be taken before any major assault could be launched against Hill 920, was a hill rising about the sea of ripening *kaoliang* and partly covered by it, known to the Japanese as Manju Yama. It was seventy-five feet high, no more than a few yards wide at the top and less than a quarter of a mile long, but, as critical high ground, it had to be taken before Kuroki could break through and fix himself astride the railway north of Liaoyang.

Seven miles to the north beyond some low, undulating hills, which were also covered with *kaoliang*, were the Yentai coal mines. To the northwest nothing was visible but the tops of the mud walls of several Manchurian villages, almost submerged in the *kaoliang*, and beyond, high on its embankment, the railway line—Kuropatkin's lifeline.

September 1, Kuroki's staff recalled, was the anniversary of Sedan, and another Sedan seemed in the offing in the first cheerful hours of the morning. Communications had been restored with Oyama's headquarters, and Kodama himself had assured Kuroki that the Russians were now falling back in front of the Fourth Army. Through their glasses the Japanese could see every truck, every wheel, even the firemen at their engines in the Russian trains puffing up and down the line. The final victory was at hand. "The bulk of the Russian army is retreating on Mukden," Kuroki told his men. "The First Army will pursue the enemy."

At 1:50 P.M. the Japanese mood changed abruptly. Through the fields of millet that separated the Japanese and their precarious toehold on the right bank of the unpredictable Tai-tzu from the enemy at Yentai came a Russian column two miles long.

It had no intention of risking an attack, however. Russian intelligence reports had doubled the size of the force that Kuroki had put across the river. Kuroki could have been slaughtered by an all-out assault by General Bilderling on the afternoon of September 1, but no attack came. Old, and cautious, Bilderling preferred to wait until the big regroupment of forces envisaged by Kuropatkin in Disposition No. 3 had been completed.

At 8 P.M. on August 31 Stackelberg's tired force began to redeploy to meet this new threat to the Russian left flank. The Thirty-fourth East Siberian Rifle Regiment had lost 1,700 killed and wounded in the two days' fighting. One battalion had been 600 strong on the thirtieth. As it began the night march across the Tai-tzu, it was down to eighty men.

Early on the morning of September 1, Kuropatkin began to feel the weight of the Japanese artillery on Liaoyang itself. With enormous effort the Japanese had hauled with them the Russian six-inch guns captured at Nanshan. Together with their field pieces now installed in the abandoned Russian gun pits on Cairn Hill, they began to pound Liaoyang station, which was still the main medical evacuation center. One shell fell on the platform among the wounded. A correspondent of *Le Temps* was at the station when three more shells landed. "In the mad hubbub everyone ran away without his baggage," he reported. "The Chinese coolies pillaged everything, while the Cossacks fell upon the champagne."

Lord Brooke saw "shells burst over the post office, the Red Cross tents, the station garden, the hospital, and also in the park under the ancient pagoda, where a crowd of people who had been refreshing themselves at a restaurant there, headed by the restaurant keepers, fled helter-skelter."

There was no *coup de grâce*. Oku's infantry had run out of steam. The artillery thundered on Liaoyang, but, though the Japanese infantry probed and pried, it could not break through.

Across the Tai-tzu, the heavily outnumbered Kuroki now decided to spurn the threat of Russian attack and to launch his own general offensive. The Fifteenth Brigade, supported by the combined artillery of the Second and Twelfth Divisions, prepared for a night attack against Manju Yama. As ever, the gods smiled on Kuroki. By 10:30 P.M. his troops were on the northern part of Manju Yama. The first shots by the Japanese had thrown the Russian defenders into a panic. The colonel commanding the four Russian battalions fled without waiting to be attacked, opening up a gap that enabled the Japanese to assault the hill from the rear. Another Russian regiment, after a shaky start, fought valiantly on the hill itself, but, having been outflanked, it had no option but to withdraw.

Soon after midnight on September 2, therefore, the Kuroki camp was full of good cheer. Once again an offensive posture had reaped its rewards. Kuroki used the chalk boldly on his map as he planned the operations for the coming day. With Manju Yama tucked away, the much more formidable Hill 920 now appeared in his sights. The march to the Yentai coal mines would push on.

Kuropatkin in his train parked near the railway bridge over the Tai-tzu was neither less busy nor less bold. At 1:15 A.M. on September 2 he issued Disposition No. 4 with its fresh orders to meet Kuroki's thrust by taking the offensive. He planned to hold the inner Liaoyang position, while advancing against Kuroki. But Russian communications, bad by day and worse by night, had let him down again. Kuropatkin did not know that Manju Yama, the pivot of his plan to mass the First Siberian Corps, the Tenth Corps, and Major-General V. N. Orlov's thirteen battalions at the Yentai mine against Kuroki's intrusion, was now a Japanese redoubt.

Worse confusion was to follow in the field. General Orlov failed to receive his copy of Kuropatkin's Disposition No. 4, and a multitude of other orders left him uncertain of what he was expected to do. He queried General Bilderling, but his runner lost himself in the *kaoliang.*

From the position Orlov had taken south of the Yentai mines he could see that General Bilderling was in action, and he heard that Manju Yama had fallen. With commendable spirit, but not much discretion, he decided to go to the relief of Manju Yama. Leaving half his force about a mile south of the mines, he set off into the sea of millet. He had gone less than a mile when one of his battalions encountered the advance guard of a Japanese brigade and fled in disorder.

Toward mid-morning, Orlov realized that he had little hope of reaching Manju Yama, and at 1 P.M., while still no more than two miles from his starting line, he ran into the main force of Japanese, supported by artillery: Orlov had lost his in the millet. Hoping to compensate for the lack of fire power by adding manpower, Orlov called in all his reserves with the exception of one battalion and quickly ran into more serious trouble. He then decided to pull back to Yentai station. Though heavily outnumbered, the Japanese gave him no quarter, and Orlov's men again fled into the millet where they fired at each other in panic. In a matter of minutes twelve battalions ceased to exist as an organized force.

Soon after daylight on September 2 Stackelberg's First Corps had begun a march toward its new battlefront, where Orlov's then fresh forces had been lent to them for the day.

Before they left in the morning Stackelberg addressed the troops. No men, he said, were to leave the ranks to help the wounded, who were to help themselves as best they could.

It was midafternoon when Stackelberg's men ran into some of Orlov's rabble. They were themselves too tired to inspire any spirit in the fleeing men, much less to turn them around and into action in support of General Bilderling's Seventeenth Corps. To give Orlov his due, he made every effort to do so himself. He still had one battalion in hand and wanted to use this as the nucleus around which to rebuild his force. Stackelberg, who was outraged by the performance of Orlov's troops, told him not to bother about trying to find the remnants of the battalions that were lost or skulking in the millet, but to renew the offensive with his last remaining battalion.

After a heated scene, Orlov, mounted on horseback, put himself at the head of the battalion and moved into the attack through the millet. The Japanese held their fire until Orlov was only a few yards from them and then opened up. Orlov was wounded several times but survived. His deputy commander was wounded and subsequently died. The rest of the battalion evaporated.

Wild scenes took place later in the day at Post No. 8, a siding midway between the Yentai mines and the main railway line, when someone shouted "Japanese." Orlov's survivors grabbed their guns and in panic shot each other and Stackelberg's rear echelon, adding substantially to the self-inflicted casualties of the day and providing part of the Eighty-sixth Wilmanstrand Regiment of the First Corps, which had just arrived from Europe, with a singularly unhappy introduction to the war.

Without maps and the assistance that he had expected from Orlov's detachment, with forces so weary that they could scarcely stand, Stackelberg tried to press on with his attack. To this end, he sought the cooperation of General Mishchenko, who had under his command the Independent Trans-Baikal Cossack Brigade and the Ural Cossack Brigade, with a total of twenty-one squadrons and twelve horse artillery guns. Though Mishchenko had been within a mile of General Orlov when he ran into trouble, he had made no effort to assist. This time, Mishchenko pleaded contrary orders and retired. His losses for the day were one man wounded.

So instead of attacking by moonlight, as he had planned, Stackelberg abandoned the Yentai mines, only eight miles from the main trunk line, and fell back himself.

Until early in the afternoon Kuropatkin had no knowledge of Orlov's reverse. The fall of Manju Yama had been a serious blow, but plans were now in hand for its recapture, with General Bilderling under instruction to take personal command. On the main position at Liaoyang, a heavy Japanese attack had been repulsed.

Then, at 2 P.M., came the news of the Orlov disaster. Kuropatkin's response was to go immediately to Yentai station, where he personally led an infantry company into action, and to redouble his efforts to recover Manju Yama.

By five o'clock no fewer than 152 Russian artillery pieces had been assembled to fire on Manju Yama, where troops of a Japanese regiment crouched in their holes on the reverse slope. In a semicircle spread out through the millet were twenty-five Russian infantry battalions. Like Orlov's unhappy force, however, they had difficulty in finding their way through the millet, and, as darkness fell, the infantry battalions became hopelessly mixed up.

Not that the defenders on Manju Yama were in the best of shape. No supplies had reached them during the blistering heat of the day. They were desperately short of water, hungry, and not well armed to meet the sort of assault force that had been assembled against them.

Scarcely an hour after dark they were driven out of their trenches. Fierce and utterly confused fighting continued. In the darkness it was impossible to tell friend from foe. Hoping to sort things out, the Japanese commander had his bugler sound the ceasefire. His guns had scarcely stopped firing when the Russian bugler sounded the same call and followed it with the call to assemble.

To chaos was now added Russian disaster. Blundering their way to the rear, three Russian regiments became involved in a fight among themselves and then fled from the battlefield. Their comrades were, in fact, still entrenched on Manju Yama, and during the next two or three hours they regained the summit; but the word had gone back with the fleeing troops that the Japanese had control. To the confusion among the troops was now added confusion in tactical command, and about 2 A.M. the Russians holding the top of the hill were ordered to pull out, leaving the battered and bloody pimple—to the surprise of the Japanese and the later dismay of Kuropatkin.

Two hours earlier, now confident that Manju Yama was his once again, Kuropatkin had announced his plans for the renewed offensive. This was again based on the assumption that Manju Yama could be used as the pivot from which Kuroki could be swept back over the river. "I shall not retire from Liaoyang," Kuropatkin told Bilderling.

It was with no sense of impending disaster that his staff went to work to draw up the detailed order. The Japanese Guards Division had been unable to make the river crossing. The main position was holding firm, and, despite the loss of the Yentai mines, man for man and gun for gun Kuroki was heavily outnumbered on the left bank of the river. The battle for Liaoyang was still within Kuropatkin's grasp. At all costs, however, he had to keep the Japanese off the high ground at Manju Yama. If they could take possession of the hill and reinforce, then the line of retreat of his armies would be directly imperiled. There was, therefore, a direct relationship between the Kuroki intrusion and the safety of the city.

At 3 A.M. Lieutenant-General N. P. Zarubaiev reported from the inner defenses of Liaoyang that his ammunition was running short. Kuropatkin had just absorbed this disquieting news when Zarubaiev reported for a second time. His reserves had dwindled to three battalions and he needed more. A messenger appeared from General Stackelberg's new headquarters at the village of Liu-lin-kou, several miles to the west of the Yentai coal mines: the First Siberian Corps had succumbed to casualties and fatigue; it was in no shape either to attack or to defend. Another messenger appeared, this time far from the immediate field of battle, with the most ominous tidings: the officer holding the eastern approaches to Mukden had retired to the Tunghuafen Pass, only sixteen miles from the city.

Mukden, the capital of Manchuria, was about forty miles north of Liaoyang. If it had not been for the pressure from Alexeiev, and from St. Petersburg, to make an effort to relieve Port Arthur, Kuropatkin would have preferred to have consolidated his armies beyond Mukden, at Harbin, another 300 miles to the north. At this stage, however, any threat to Mukden, remote though it might be, had the gravest strategic possibilities. If the Japanese were to break through at Mukden, all was lost.

The news was enough to conjure up the wildest thoughts of flanking movements. Daylight came with Kuropatkin still wrestling with these problems when yet another messenger arrived with the news that Manju Yama was in Japanese hands.

"Most unfortunate," Kuropatkin scribbled on his message pad. At that moment Liaoyang was lost. Deeply concerned with the implied threat to his lines of communication at Mukden, he now saw the tactical advantage at Liaoyang had passed into the Japanese hands. At any moment, Kuroki might launch his forces from Manju Yama and cut the railway. Lacking in faith—with considerable justification—in his subordinates, in his troops, in his communications, and in the intelligence he received, Kuropatkin believed in personal command, not merely to inspire but also to direct. But the battle was too vast for a man on horseback. To be won, it needed to be directed by a man like Kodama, in the middle of an effective communications network.

Kuropatkin sat now at his desk and brooded over the consequences. Curiously, he did not equate retreat with defeat. To advance was a tactic. To withdraw was a tactic also. "The abandonment of Liaoyang could not fail both to depress the troops who had so gallantly defended it and to encourage the enemy, but, on the other hand we should be extricated by such a retirement from a situation in which we were threatened in front and flank," he wrote later. At 6 A.M. he issued orders for the general retreat.

A thick mist descended in the early hours of September 4 to help the Russians disengage. Over Liaoyang the fog blended with the smoke. The Russian settlement was on fire, and, though the damage to the town proper was relatively slight, a Siberian rifle regiment sacked the Russian shops and the homes of wealthy Chinese before taking off.

It was not until 11 A.M. that Kuroki became aware that his enemy had fled. By this time his army had begun to share the exhaustion that had assailed Stackelberg's forces on the previous day. They could not follow up quickly enough to fall on their fleeing foe. And, like the rest of Oyama's armies, they were out of ammunition.

With extraordinary patience, the Russians endured the agonizing withdrawal. Artillery pieces, telegraph and pontoon wagons, and supply carts jammed the road north. Torrential rainstorms on the previous day had turned the road into a bog into which the wagons sank. Infantrymen and cavalrymen, in units or in small groups, tried to push their way through but only added to the confusion.

Hamilton went to Manju Yama. "When I stepped forward and viewed the western declivity my heart for a moment stood still with horror," he wrote.

> Never have I seen such a scene—a mad jumble of arms and accouterments mingled with the bodies of those who so lately bore them, arrested, cut short in the fury of their assault, and now with all their terrible menacing attitudes so very quiet. How silent, how ghastly, how lonely seemed this charnel house where I, a solitary European, beheld rank upon rank of brave Russians mown down by the embattled ranks of Asia.

The Japanese lost 5,537 men killed during the battle and 18,063 wounded. The Russian losses were 3,611 killed and missing and 14,301 wounded. Kuropatkin claimed victory. He had lived to fight another day, but the one great Russian opportunity of the war had been lost. Kuroki had gambled on the night of August 31. It was a bluff that Bilderling should have called. On the morning of September 1 not only Kuroki but the entire Japanese army was in the gravest danger. If there was ever a moment in the war when victory was within Russia's competence, this was it. General Nogi had been heavily repulsed at Port Arthur. A defeat for Oyama here would have been a fearful reverse for Japan, not only on the battlefield but in the financial markets of the world on which it was so dependent.

❦❦❦❦❦❦

CHAPTER 22

Nogi Fails Again

Gᴇɴᴇʀᴀʟ Nᴏɢɪ's ꜰʀᴏɴᴛᴀʟ ᴀssᴀᴜʟᴛ on Port Arthur had cost the Japanese over 18,000 men, far more than Imperial General Headquarters had reckoned on for the capture of the fortress. Some regiments had been wiped out in the wild assaults; others were far below fighting strength. Of the three regiments of the Eleventh Division's attack force only two battalions could be mustered. On the night of August 23, the Ninth Division ran out of ammunition and could continue to fight only by collecting cartridges from the dead. Yet the army and the division kept ordering assault at all costs.

Avalanches of Japanese rolled toward the Russian forts, falling, rising again, and running until they fell for the last time. Wave after wave of men followed, leaping trenches and the bodies of their dead comrades to reach the forts on the Chinese Wall, where savage hand-to-hand fighting inevitably took place. At 3 ᴀ.ᴍ., in the closing hours of the agony, a third and final wave came in. "[A] fresh wave of living flesh and blood rolled forward," wrote the Russian correspondent Nojine. "This time it was the attack—the spring—of a maddened, wounded, blood-drunk herd of tigers—not men. Our truly awful fire was of no avail; the mass rolled forward with the strength of a tidal wave."

By the end of August, the Russians had built strong semipermanent fortifications along the twenty miles of defenses stretching across the peninsula, including the northeast end of Namako Yama ("Sea Slug Hill"), to which Tretyakov had withdrawn after the fall of 174 Meter Hill. On dozens of bare, craggy peaks surrounding the garrison and the town, concrete supporting walls had been built and miles of intricate tunnels honeycombed the rocks, so that at long last Port Arthur began truly to be a fortress.

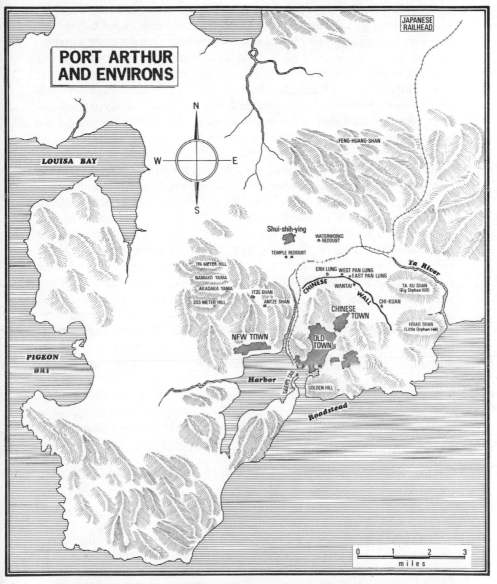

The Chinese Wall had been repaired and reinforced by six two-gun batteries, and many six-inch guns from the ships were used to strengthen the land forts. The two Pan-lung forts were firmly in Japanese hands, but the Russians had started to drive tunnels under the Chinese Wall to reach beneath both these positions where they hoped to install mines.

The Russians lacked material in their attempts to prepare the forts, but

[375]

the hard-working engineers, assisted by sailors and gangs of Chinese coolies, gradually brought improvements. The need for reconnaissance balloons to give a more precise picture of the Japanese positions became more apparent in early September, when Nogi reluctantly turned from human wave tactics to the slow, tedious trench-digging that would bring his forces closer to the forts. The eleven-inch Krupp howitzers replacing those lost in the *Hitachi Maru* months before had arrived from Japan, and day after day thousands of Japanese troops toiled up the steep slopes, dragging the guns toward the positions already captured. The guns had been part of Japan's coastal defenses, but it was now clear that the danger of invasion had passed, and Imperial General Headquarters released them for the siege.

At the beginning of September, the Japanese Third Army held a conference of division staff chiefs and artillery and engineer commanders to discuss the new form of attack against the fortress. On the following day assault manuals were issued to the units. So far, the Third Army had not appreciated the value of 203 Meter Hill. From September it was included in the positions to be attacked, together with an elaborate plan to advance trenches toward Wantai, Chi-kuan, the Waterworks Redoubt, and the Temple Redoubt. At last Nogi realized the need for heavy howitzers to demolish the Russian permanent forts. His engineers began to chisel through sheer rock and limestone in zigzag lines to avoid fire from the surrounding forts. Sixteen thousand infantry reinforcements joined the Third Army. Many more men were called in to dig trenches and underground tunnels, and several batteries of quick-firing guns and naval guns arrived to assist the besiegers. Admiral Togo, offering his sympathy to Nogi, sent four twelve-centimeter guns and a supply of ammunition, asking only that he would be glad if Nogi would, from time to time, fire on the Russian ships in the harbor.

Nogi ordered that the sapping should be completed in the shortest possible time, but many senior staff officers continued to urge an advance before the work was finished. Only those who advanced with their men and lived to see the results realized that, without adequate protection, attacks against the forts were a waste of time, men, and ammunition.

September brought more hardships to the garrison and its civilian population. Both the old and new towns suffered. General Smirnov was desperately ill with dysentery. General Stoessel refused to give up his command. He sent a telegram to General Kuropatkin, a friend since their schooldays, angrily insisting that he was well able to cope with the situation. "Everyone here knows me, Chinese as well as Russians, and they trust me, knowing that the Japanese will never get into the place over my dead body." General Smirnov, he said, was unknown to the officers and men and referred to them as cowards. "He may well be all right in his way, but he is a professor and not a fighting general. If you are determined that I should come to Liaoyang, I will do so on receipt of fresh instruction to that effect from you."

Kuropatkin had problems enough of his own, and, in any event, had no means of enforcing his orders. So Stoessel and Fock stayed on, though they were blamed bitterly for the defeat at Nanshan and their unpopularity increased week by week.

Smirnov had dismissed Fock in the middle of August for disobeying orders, but Stoessel overruled the decision. There were, in effect, two commandants and two staffs in Port Arthur now. Stoessel communicated directly with the Tsar by telegram and early in September was overjoyed to receive the order of St. George from his Emperor, who instructed him that as a reward for their fighting all ranks in the army and navy should count each month's service as one full year. It was small compensation for the hard-pressed Russian garrison, digging trenches, reinforcing the fortifications, pulling guns up the hills and slipping out each night on patrol to harass the Japanese sappers, digging like moles along the lines of Russian defenses.

As soon as he had recovered from his illness, General Smirnov, accompanied by Nojine, inspected the new line of defenses. Returning, they ran into General Stoessel. "Ah! so that's it? Wherever we find the war correspondent, we find the commandant, eh?" Any friend of Smirnov's was an enemy of Stoessel's. Two days later the Russian official newspaper *Novoye Krai* was closed for a month on the pretext that it published information that could assist the Japanese. Nojine smuggled out a letter through the consul in Cheefoo addressed to the Tsar, pleading with him to remove Stoessel in the interests of the fortress. "Arthur is enabled to hold out only by the effort of Smirnov and his excellent assistant Kondratenko . . . when I can give you details your hair will stand on end." The letter did not reach the Tsar, and the enmity persisted between the rival commandants.

By issuing orders comparing the gallantry of the soldiers with the ineptitude of the sailors, Stoessel continued to inflame interservice rivalries. The sailors, out of their element on land, were often difficult to handle. Even Colonel Tretyakov, effective and understanding, had to bring pressure to bear on the unwilling sailors. Sometimes when they were on guard in a fort, they would simply take a tea break and walk away from the position. But mostly the faults he found with them were of minor importance. "Sometimes they had no kettles, sometimes they had no warm clothing and had to be supplied from the regiment, at other times they were tired and wanted rest, and so on and so on; but they were splendid fighters, especially if they were led by good officers," he wrote in his memoirs after the war.

Through the early days of September, the Japanese dug through soft topsoil, solid limestone, and quartz rock. Thirteen miles of underground tunnels were carved out and soon the whole country in front of the eastern ridges was an intricate maze of zigzag trenches that were covered over with earth, grass, and stones. The Japanese were under constant attack, and only one or two men at a time could work at the head of the trenches. In time, they shoveled hundreds of tons of earth into more than 1,200,000 bags to build up the breastworks. At a few pence per bag, the Japanese spent more than £40,000 on sandbags alone, or at current values perhaps half a million pounds.

Making his first visit to the Third Army in September, General Kodama* quickly appreciated the shortcomings of Nogi's force. He urgently requested many more heavy guns and ordered the construction of approach trenches, and for the first time drew attention to the importance of 203 Meter Hill, which other officers had disregarded.

In Tokyo, General Nagaoka was inundated with official and unofficial suggestions for capturing Port Arthur. Every mail brought letters containing advice. Cranks invaded his office with inventions and suggestions to be used against the fortress, including the use of hot pepper to be fired into the defenses.

A lively dispute now went on between the Imperial General Headquarters and Oyama over supplies of ammunition and rations. Kodama, who had previously been governor of Formosa, had arranged his own rice supplies, with the help of the navy, which had commandeered a German freighter carrying rice from Formosa to Manchuria. General Nagaoka was critical of Kodama for getting rice from Formosa when there were plentiful supplies to be had from Japan itself.

Planning for the attack on 203 Meter Hill presented many difficulties. The hill consisted of two peaks connected by a razor-backed ridge. The northern peak was slightly higher. Situated northeast of Pigeon Bay, 203 Meter Hill's summit provided a direct view over the waters of Port Arthur's harbor two miles away. Though it was bare of trees, huge outcrops of boulders stretched across the valley between it and Namako Yama, still in Russian hands.

The previous May, General Stoessel had stood, hands on hips, to gaze up through the drifting mists to the summit of 203 Meter Hill, where men could be seen working around the fortifications. "Why are heavy guns being mounted there?" he asked. "They are quite unnecessary. When necessary, I will send a field battery up, and the devil himself will not be able to come

---

*The General had been briefed on the intelligence provided by a Russian civilian defector attached to the general staff, who gave Commander Mori Gitaro in Cheefoo a complete account of the Russian defenses.

near it." For three months nothing had been done to strengthen the position.

Now an upper and lower trench had been constructed. Two six-inch guns were mounted on the northern peak and two field guns in position close to the southern hill. The First Company of the Twenty-eighth Regiment and a company of seamen were stationed on the hill with machineguns, one-pounder guns, and a torpedo tube. The Russian positions, however, were exposed and there were still no permanent installations.

September 18 saw the start of the new attacks. The Waterworks Redoubt, for which the two sides had fought so bitterly a month earlier, was taken with the loss of 500 Japanese. The Temple Redoubt, to the south, also fell to the Japanese First Division after furious fighting in which many Russians were buried alive in the ruins of the works. This time the Japanese lost one thousand men, but the fort was in their hands.

Namako Yama, a long, narrow hill with sheer sides, was attacked by the First and Fifteenth Infantry Regiments under General Yamamoto. The lower slopes were taken below the Russian trenches, and for several hours the defenders tried to dislodge the Japanese hidden among the rocky outcrops. General Yamamoto withdrew most of his men, leaving only enough to hold the captured trench overnight. The remainder of his column returned to lower slopes of the hill, and on the following day the trenches on the northeastern side of Namako Yama were almost destroyed. Out of 150 Russians, only forty-eight remained. The Russian commander was taken prisoner, the few survivors fell back, and Kondratenko was informed that the hill had gone. From the new position on Namako Yama, the Japanese began to fire on 203 Meter Hill as a preliminary to storming it.

On September 19, a Japanese reserve regiment, under the protection of strong machinegun fire from Namako Yama, attacked 203 Meter Hill's upper trenches. The unoccupied lower trench was easily taken and during the night the infantry succeeded in reaching the upper trench. But Kondratenko sent up reinforcements for the hard-pressed defenders, and the Japanese were driven back to the shelter of a deep ravine at the foot of the hill.

The Russians now began to strengthen the strategic hill, building fortifications on the steep section of the southwestern peak and setting up command posts along the traverses, with layers of railway lines and thick stone walls to hide them. On the northern peak, they erected fortifications with six-inch guns and built an underground passage from the foot of the fortifications to the gun batteries on the saddle of the hill. Trenches were deepened, protection provided over loopholes in the gun positions, and wire placed all over the sides of the hill.

Apart from the high casualties on both sides, the Russians and Japanese were suffering from disease. Inside the fortress food supplies were running low. Beef had been supplemented by horse and donkey flesh, and vegetables were scarce. There were many cases of scurvy and typhoid among the wounded from the battlefields and the garrison forces.

In August, the Japanese had 10,000 men incapacitated with beri-beri, dysentery, and typhoid. Latrines were close by the camps and horse lines, and though these were emptied by gangs of Chinese coolies, who used the excrement for manure, their proximity to eating quarters was most unsanitary.

General Nogi was showing the strain of the costly assaults on the fortress, but he hid despondency from the foreign correspondents who had come to the front to see what was to have been the final attack on Port Arthur. The correspondents were permitted—or "compelled," as one correspondent put it—to remain. "They insisted that we should make no effort to send any news to the outside world of what was taking place."

From a journalistic point of view, the scene was not very encouraging, but General Nogi did his best to make life pleasant for the band of foreign newspapermen, often inviting them to his headquarters for a drink or lunch. They found him a kindly host, living simply in his two-room Chinese cottage, under the guns of the fortress. In the tiny white-washed house he had two rooms, one with a camp-bed, the other for his office. In fine weather he preferred to work under an enormous acacia tree in the garden of the cottage, itself a luxury in this treeless land. Goats and pigs, waiting their turn for the cooking pot, wandered around, while Chinese women and children drove blindfolded donkeys round and round a stone that ground millet for their food.

Nogi's meetings with the stranded newspapermen usually took place under the big tree in the garden, where he played host. His short gray beard and closely cropped iron-gray hair reminded an American correspondent of Ulysses S. Grant. He was always dressed in a short black coat, white leather breeches, and high boots. For the entire length of the siege, even at night, he did not change out of his uniform. Sometimes he called correspondents in to discuss the war they could not cover, sometimes to celebrate some quite unconnected occasion, such as the birthday of King Edward of England or the anniversary of battles fought long ago. The invitation was always accompanied by a bottle of champagne, "to keep our hands warm," as the Japanese said.

After lunch one day, Nogi sat in an armchair watching, entranced, as a conjurer swallowed his watch and chain, coins produced from the general's short gray beard, and eventually his samurai sword as well. The sword was rescued just as the hilt was disappearing down the throat of the comedian, Reginald Glossop of Yorkshire, leader of the entertainment troupe. Disappointed at not being permitted to swallow the general's sword, he begged permission to borrow it once more for a sword dance. Nogi was quite unperturbed by the sound of nearby battle. "I wake each morning," he said, "worrying about General Stoessel and what a hard time he must be having inside the fortress. I feel very much for him and his brave soldiers."

The show was over and the correspondents were invited on a tour of inspection to view the engagement—not, of course, for publication.

Standing on a small hill, they looked down on the scene of an earlier battle, where broken rifles and twisted bayonets lay scattered among the old bodies left over from the August and September assaults, little more now than bones and scraps of uniforms. The stench from the dead was unbearable and here and there newly killed men, still burning, lay with the rotting corpses. Though they were sworn to write not a word, the correspondents were taken then to inspect the captured positions, deep into the bowels of forts where thousands of men lived, enemy and opponent, fifty yards or so from each other, separated only by rocks and concrete walls.

Over 400 guns were now facing the Russian forts, including six-inch naval guns worked by survivors of the battleship *Hatsuse* and other larger naval guns. Krupp guns captured from the Russians at Nanshan and other field guns were scattered through the valleys and on captured hills.

By the first of October, Nogi had the further assistance of six of the big eleven-inch siege guns. They were mounted on Namako Yama hill, overlooking the town and the fortress and just below 174 Meter Hill, which had been taken in August. Although it was not possible to see the entire harbor from the new positions, observers were able to direct their fire accurately enough to cause damage to the Russian fleet.

The big shells from the new Japanese guns, weighing nearly 500 pounds each, did their work in Port Arthur as the first half a dozen came whistling in on the flour mill and set it on fire. General Stoessel's own house was hit, and he promptly had bomb shelters built for himself and his staff. Many townspeople now had to build their own shelters, and thereafter a large number of residents spent their days and nights below ground. "The conditions in the besieged fortress—the wearying, trying uncertainty, the want of confidence, and the constant, unavoidable danger began to tell. The younger men lost their nerve, and suicides commenced," wrote Nojine.

The big Russian ships clustered in the basin as close as possible to Quail Hill, while the destroyers went out to sea during the day to escape the Japanese shells. *Peresvyet* was hit nine times in one day, the hospital ship *Mongolia,* which had returned after the battle in the Yellow Sea, was badly damaged, and *Poltava* was set on fire.

As long before as July it had been expected in Japan that Port Arthur would have fallen, but for months now no word of the operations had reached the Japanese public. In Tokyo and Yokohama scaffolding for the victory decorations waited to be hung with lanterns and flags. Storehouses were filled with paper lanterns and other decorations, and in several towns celebrations had already been held, as false reports of victory were received. The Emperor issued an edict asking the people to be patient and to work harder for the war effort instead of wasting their efforts in excessive emotionalism.

Newspapers began to demand the "speedy reduction" of the fortress and clamored for more and more troops to be sent. A new general attack was promised in the near future, so that Port Arthur could be presented to the Emperor on November 3, his birthday.

Outside Port Arthur the Japanese waited for the grand attack on the outer forts. Some spent the time building shrines, made from tent poles and bright red blankets and covered improvised altars with offerings for the repose of the spirits of those who must fall in the coming battles.

For the last six days in October the same useless waste of lives occurred in attacks against the forts on the Chinese Wall, from Erh-lung to Chi-kuan, and to a lesser extent against 203 Meter Hill and Akasaka Yama, slightly to its north. Again, the trenches did not reach far enough up to the Russian forts, but the Japanese were as hopeful as ever of covering the few intervening yards by storm. They now knew that many of the forts were surrounded by deep moats and came provided with bamboo ladders so that these could be crossed. Once on top of the parapets, they believed, they would be able to overrun the defenders by sheer weight of numbers. As Major Shiki had warned in June, it was a mistake to imagine that once the trenches had been brought to within fifty meters of the enemy the fort would fall easily. That final fifty-meter dash over open ground into the teeth of the enemy fire would be the ultimate test.

The attack opened with a bombardment of a "force and vehemence the like of which we had never seen before nor should ever be likely to see again," wrote the Reuters correspondent, hoping that this time success would be sufficient to allow him to send something to his agency. The Japanese swarmed like ants over the hillsides and the Russian infantry blazed at them, killing them by hundreds.

The parties sent off to storm the moats surrounding Erh-lung and Sung-shu forts found that the flimsy bamboo ladders were too short. Trying to fill the deep chasms, they threw sandags in for hours, every now and then probing with a long pole to see what progress had been made. Their poles were forty feet long but could not find the bottom of the Russian moats.

The battle for Fort Chi-kuan, the southernmost fort in the Chinese Wall area, lasted for five days. On October 20 a few Japanese established themselves on one of the parapets. Every man was shot as he reached this position. The bodies lay on the parapet for months until they were buried by an explosion inside the fort.

Alongside Chi-kuan was a small rise, known only as "P," commanding the casemates of Fort Chi-kuan. Here, the Russians had picked off the Japanese as they clambered on to Chi-kuan's parapet. General Ichinobe, commander of the Japanese Sixth Brigade, personally led the attack against this small work. His example inspired his troops and they charged in shouting *"banzai,"* using bayonets, rifle butts, jiujitsu, nails, and even teeth in their attack against the Russian defenders. At the end of the day it was in Japanese hands. Next day the small but important spur called "P" was renamed Fort Ichinobe by the Japanese.

When the Emperor's birthday had come and gone, the besiegers had taken only one ditch of Fort Erh-lung out of the three permanent works attacked, plus three provisional fortifications, including Fort Ichinobe. Their losses for the six days amounted to 4,800.

The dead of both sides lay where they had fallen all along the line in front of the Russian forts, and trenches again overflowed with dead and wounded. No armistice was allowed. At night small groups from either side attempted to drag in their injured, as they had done in August. For a short time the wounded could be distinguished from the dead and attempts were made by both sides to throw food and bottles of water to the men in no-man's land. In a day or so there was no movement left on the rocky plains and slopes.

CHAPTER 23

&&&&&&

Sha-ho

UNTIL THE BATTLE for Liaoyang, most of the Russian forces in Manchuria had continued to fight in the belief of their invincibility. From the highest to the lowest, the retreat came as a fearful shock. Alexeiev, who heard the news in Mukden, stopped the movement of southbound trains for several hours while his own special was made ready to dash back to Harbin, which was filled with "mad debauch."

The Russian newspapers did their best to gloss over the situation. The *Novosti* said there was no reason to despair over a defeat that had never taken place. The *Invalid Russ,* the army journal, insisted that it was Oyama who had suffered a strategic defeat.

The Tsar was kind. "The retreat of the whole army in such difficult circumstances and along such terrible roads was an operation excellently carried out in the face of grave difficulties," he said in a message to Kuropatkin. "I thank you and your splendid troops for their heroic work and continued self-sacrifice. God guide you."

There was no great excitement about the result at Oyama's headquarters. Hamilton asked Oyama whether he was pleased. "Moderately," he replied. "The Russians have managed their retreat too cleverly." Liaoyang had been no Sedan. The Japanese in Manchuria, by dividing their forces between enterprise at Liaoyang and unwanted necessity at Port Arthur, had been deprived of the decisive victory they had hoped for, and needed.

Among those close to Kuropatkin, however, there was no joy. "My heart is sick with him," said one of his oldest and most faithful staff officers. "At Liaoyang, Skobolev would have won, or he would have finished the army,

[384]

for he would have accepted no alternative. My heart is sore with Kuropatkin."

As the Russian retreat went on, there were celebrations of a kind in Liaoyang. Every shop and every house flew a Japanese flag, but even this show of support did not deter the troops in their plunder. "Seldom has any city been looted by three armies in three days, but this is what happened at Liaoyang," Lord Brooke reported in a Reuters dispatch. The Russians plundered the Chinese and European shops, destroying what they did not want or were not able to carry away, ripping open bales, bags, and boxes with their bayonets and scattering their contents over the streets. The liquor, which they found in vast quantities, they drank. The Chinese soldiers and police continued after the Russians had left, and the Japanese finished off what remained. After fighting for five days without food except dry rice, they entered the town and seized anything that remained in private homes.

While continuing to claim a victory of sorts, Kuropatkin blamed his subordinate commanders for the poor showing not only at Liaoyang but in the battles that had preceded it. "In all these combats we did not display the necessary firmness, and we retired before we had even ascertained the real force of the enemy," Kuropatkin wrote. "I consider that it is necessary to place at the head of army corps, divisions, brigades, and regiments that are to be sent to the theater of war leaders of repute and not notoriously incapable officers, as has sometimes been the case hitherto."

Alexeiev and his staff bitterly assailed Kuropatkin. General Sakharov, the minister of war, bluntly termed the battle a defeat. When Kuropatkin asked him to explain, he replied, "According to generally accepted terminology, the side which attains its object at whatever cost has won a victory, while the side which fails to do so has suffered a defeat."

Kuropatkin wanted to continue his withdrawal beyond Mukden to the hills around Tieh-ling, some forty miles to the northeast, where the terrain was much more favorable for defense than the plains around Mukden. This caused another row with Alexeiev, who immediately enlisted the support of Nicholas.

"To the question I put to him relative to Mukden," Alexeiev telegraphed, "the Commandant of the Army has made an evasive reply, saying that he will only make a decision after a detailed inspection of the position, and according to the actions of the enemy. I dare not disguise from Your Majesty that, in my opinion, the continued retreat to Tieh-ling and beyond will not prove favorable to the morale of the army."

For days the flow of reinforcements through Harbin was delayed as the Russian armies sorted themselves out and St. Petersburg reached a decision.

At the best of times, Harbin was a bottleneck. Trains that had made the great journey across the Trans-Siberian Railway were sometimes delayed for forty-eight hours or more due to the congestion on the tracks in Harbin. Alexeiev, with his ninety-eight orderlies, had two trains for his own personal use and his chief of staff had a third. Often, these trains could not be shunted out of the way because their occupants were busy. Because the whistles and the rumbling of the trains disturbed the Viceroy, no trains were allowed to pass at night.

Though there were days when the troops aboard got neither food nor water, the trains eventually got through, and the losses at Liaoyang were made good. The First Army Corps and the Sixth Siberian Corps arrived in their entirety during September, ending Kuropatkin's fears that he was outnumbered. In artillery and in cavalry, which had been used to little purpose at Liaoyang, at the Yalu and at Te-li-ssu, he was especially strong.

In the hope of improving the state of the Manchurian command, the Tsar on September 24 announced the creation of the Second Army under the leadership of General Oscar Casimirovitch Grippenberg, a sixty-six-year-old veteran of the Crimea, who had served as *aide-de-camp* to Nicholas and had recently been promoted to *aide-de-camp* general. Although the Second Army did not function separately, the appointment was regarded as a snub to Kuropatkin. Grippenberg was ten years his senior in age and very much his junior in the army. He had received no formal military education, was deaf, and was known to have suffered a seizure. His highest previous field command was the leadership of a battalion.

Pressure to initiate an early Russian offensive was strong. Kuropatkin's reputation had been called into question. And, since he now had sufficient forces in hand to attack, any delay could only be at the expense of Port Arthur. The rapidly approaching winter was another reason why the decision had to be taken quickly.

Kuropatkin had been pushed into actions he did not favor in the past; now, with the Baltic fleet preparing to sail from Libau, it was even more difficult to advance plausible arguments against switching to the offensive. Hadn't Kuropatkin himself claimed victory at Liaoyang? What, then, was he waiting for? If Nogi succeeded at Port Arthur, his forces would be free to turn north against the Russians, and the numerical advantage Kuropatkin had gained might well be lost.

Confronting Kuropatkin's men were serious problems of morale, apparent in manifold ways. One was an increase in self-inflicted wounds. This aggravated conditions in the hospitals. Doctors and nurses often had to sleep on the floor between the patients' beds. The Russian military, to make matters worse, treated the army doctors as second-class officers, declining to admit them to their clubs and submitting them to all sorts of humiliations. General Ezerski, the chief inspector of hospitals, was a former police chief, and he behaved like one. Doctors were disciplined if they failed to wear their swords while attending patients in the wards. Dysentery was regarded by the military authorities as an undesirable disease that reflected badly on the army and was therefore classified as "influenza."

General Ezerski was nothing if not conscientious. As the number of malingerers increased, he hunted them down personally, galloping from station to station and from train to train to arrange raids among the sick and wounded. Nothing lay beyond his writ. Hospital trains, freight trains, passenger trains all received his attention. "He verified and changed the diagnoses of the surgeons, and put out the sick, whom he declared to be well," Dr. Veresáev wrote. There were no ambulances available to move the wounded from the battlefield. Instead, the wounded were carried over the awful Manchurian roads on small, springless carts, or *dvukolks,* which had been shipped out in large numbers as a convenient vehicle for supplies of all kinds. These were wholly unsuitable for the movement of the wounded. Often even badly wounded men loaded into them begged to be let out. "The groans and lamentations from these vehicles were heartrending to anyone whose sensibilities had not been blunted by the habit of such scenes," Colonel Valery Harvard, assistant surgeon general in the U.S. army, reported. "Frequently men were found dead on arrival."

Military hospitals ran out of soap, bedpans, and mattresses. Dysentery was universal. Venereal diseases became so widespread that they formed the subject of a special order issued by Kuropatkin. "This was mostly directed at the officers," Colonel Harvard noted. More than a quarter of the sick moved beyond Mukden for treatment were suffering from syphilis or gonorrhea. Except in Harbin, which was practically a Russian town, little attempt was made to regulate activities of prostitutes, and neither officers nor troops were subjected to any special examination or restriction.

Brutality was another manifestation of declining morale. No longer were the Russians friendly to the villagers. They suspected every Chinese of aiding the Japanese. Village after village was razed to the ground, and their inhabitants, if they were slow to move, were put to the sword.

"People were killed because they failed to understand what the Russians meant, or because unwilling to give up their animals," wrote Dugald Christie, a missionary in Mukden. "A man was made to lead some Cossacks to a village, and because he could not run fast enough they bayoneted him. A party of eighteen farmers and laborers were accused of being brigands, tied with ropes to some Cossacks' horses and made to run the forty miles to Mukden." Two who fell exhausted were killed. A whole family hiding in a pit were shot because someone suggested they were Japanese spies.

The Cossacks, with their steel-tipped whips, were the worst of the lot.

Though they were a highly colorful addition to the war, their military contribution was negligible. They came with a high reputation for valor and daring, qualities not revealed in Manchuria.

The Caucasian Cossacks, with their bright Oriental costumes, sabers and lances, were detested by the other Russian troops. Traditionally, the principle of Cossack service was that, in return for a grant of land and freedom from taxation, every man should come out when called upon, bringing his own horse, arms, and equipment. This led to great variety in apparel and equipment, to even greater inefficiency, and to an unrestrained tendency to plunder.

As the winter approached, the Chinese saw their villages taken over or destroyed, their cattle killed, and their women raped. One group of Cossacks rode into a village where the inhabitants in their curiosity came out to look at them. Immediately the Cossacks drew their sabers and launched into attack against men, women, and children. They were mutinous, barbarous, and as soldiers all but useless.

The quality of the officers and men was not low only among the Cossacks, however. More than 2,000 officers gave themselves up to the Japanese during the war. Units that left European Russia at full strength arrived at Mukden with their ranks heavily depleted by desertions, and the population of the Siberian settlements increased substantially as the war progressed. The Poles deserted at any opportunity and readily passed on information to the Japanese.

The quarrel between Alexeiev and Kuropatkin was an open scandal, as was the behavior of much of the officer corps. If they had pursued victory with the same determination that they sought out the other sex, the war might have taken a different course.

An Italian correspondent writing in *The Times* on December 3, 1904, quoted one of the "best" Russian colonels as saying that, if he had had his way, he would have hanged fifty percent of his brother officers. "Perhaps this is too much," wrote the Italian, "but it is beyond doubt that many officers were conspicuous by their absence at critical moments, and this applies especially to senior officers."

The army was riddled by graft. Even Kuropatkin hoped to enrich himself. When he was first appointed to command the Manchurian army, he was offered a salary of 50,000 roubles a month. Because the Grand Duke Nicolai Nicolaievitch, the elder, had been granted 100,000 roubles a month and forage money for twelve riding and eighteen carriage horses as commander-in-chief of the European front during the Russo-Turkish War in 1878, Kuropatkin demanded the same. "I tried to demonstrate that a commander-in-chief had to set his entourage an example for accepting a moderate salary, since his salary would be taken as a basis for the salaries of all other military officials," said Finance Minister Kokovtsov.

I begged him particularly not to insist on such a large number of horses for his personal needs, as in reality if there were any such horses at all they would be few in number; besides, to introduce into the appropriations an item for "forage money" for nonexistent horses would not look well and would only be a temptation to his subordinates. My arguments were in vain. . . . although he had no carriage horses at all and only one riding horse, which, as I recall, was presented to him by the city of Moscow at the time of his appointment.

An army of hangers-on, merchants, tradesmen, pimps, and procurers followed the forces to Manchuria, manipulating and stealing. Since vast quantities of goods had to be requisitioned locally, the opportunities for corruption in the army were unlimited. "Against every man's name there was a charge of some kind of scandal," said McCormick.

A hundred and fifty generals had reached the war zone before the fall of Liaoyang. Kuropatkin railed constantly against the type of officer given command. He was no less insistent on the promotion of capable men in the field. Again and again, he was overruled. "When I left St. Petersburg for the seat of the war in March 1904, I saw a friend of mine, who had never done a day's regimental duty except for a short time as a youngster on joining," wrote a British military observer. "When I saw him again, ten months later, he had risen from subaltern to full colonel."

Many fashionable regiments in Russia were officered far above their established ratios. The simple solution was to send the unwanted officers to the war, where some, who lacked any knowledge or previous experience, were immediately given command of regiments in the line. One colonel in the Twenty-second Siberian Regiment did not even know how to read a map.

The trains arriving from Europe brought reinforcements, weapons, and ammunition, but they had little room to spare for other essentials. The September nights were cold. Most of the Russian troops had lost their greatcoats on the retreat from Liaoyang, and there were no stocks available to replace them. Large stocks were in the depots at Harbin, but bottlenecks, corruption, and sheer inefficiency caused long delays in sending them to the front. The Russians either had to freeze or to start wearing Chinese cotton-padded coats. They chose the latter expedient. Lost caps could not be replaced from stocks, either. To their Chinese overcoats, the Russians now added conical straw hats and soon trousers, underwear, and even shoes.

Clothing soon became so short that Kuropatkin announced that the army would not enforce the dress prescribed by military regulations. In any event, the clothing coming from Russia was of the poorest quality. Boots were known to wear out in twenty miles or less. Though supplies of felt-lined boots were made available, the army was still 300,000 pairs short at the beginning of December.

While the Russians were beginning to die from the cold around Mukden, consignments of greatcoats made from woollen blankets and with fur collars began to arrive in substantial quantities for the Japanese. Every Japanese soldier now carried two blankets; the Russian soldier had none.

Distribution of food was no better on the Russian side. The troops clamored for salt during the enervating heat of summer. Only Chinese black salt was available, and it was barely edible. Sugar was even harder to come by, and both fresh and canned meat were rare.

What the Russians lacked in morale, training, equipment, food, and medical attention, they made up for in alcohol, sex, and religious fervor. When there was no vodka or champagne or brandy, there was always the local, and potent, millet spirit. The Russian priests conducted religious services even in the front lines, and Heaven help any unfortunate hospital commander who did not have an adequate supply of ikons on hand when General Ezerski made one of his inspection visits. The privies might be inches deep in excreta: there was nothing an ikon could not cure, including the dose of pox picked up by raping a village girl.

An altogether different situation prevailed in the Japanese ranks. A handful of vendors sold cigarettes, fans, handkerchiefs, soap, toothbrushes, writing paper, and envelopes to the troops near the front. The nearest shop where saké or beer was available was fifty miles to the rear. Drinking tea, smoking cigarettes, and cooling themselves with fans were the Japanese soldiers' luxuries. For entertainment out of the line they wrote letters home or fished. Fighting was their task and their duty, and to this they were prepared to devote everything, including their lives.

It is little cause for surprise, therefore, that Kuropatkin, having been convinced that the time had come to take the offensive, continued to show caution. He called in his generals to seek their advice and received little encouragement. Neither Stackelberg nor Sluchevski was eager to attack. Through the month of September, however, Kuropatkin's staff worked on a series of offensive plans. Their problems were compounded again by the absence of maps. An urgent call had been sent to St. Petersburg for surveyors and draftsmen, but these did not arrive until the end of September. Then, instead of being attached to Kuropatkin's staff, they were sent to Alexeiev's headquarters and thus provided no assistance whatever for the forthcoming battle. Kuropatkin's staff did the best they could and maps of a sort were produced. But, as usual, they lacked detail, failed to show the contours, and were far from accurate.

The general nature of the countryside over which the battle was to be fought had not changed much from Liaoyang, except that nearly all of the millet had been harvested and stacked. The Russians had fallen back from Liaoyang to Mukden, with their front east and west of the Sha-ho, a tributary of the Tai-tzu, which it joined several miles to the west of Liaoyang. The railway line formed the main axis of the Russian communications. Its embankment, which varied from ten feet to thirty feet in height, passed through the flat millet fields. To the east were the hills and mountains.

This time the villages, all of them surrounded by clumps of poplars, willows, and pines, were much more prominent. They had been largely concealed at Liaoyang by the millet. Now they stood out conspicuously on the plains. Since the trees provided cover and some protection, they became the center around which many of the battles were soon to rage.

Unable to muster the momentum to pursue Kuropatkin toward Mukden after the Liaoyang battle, Oyama had not hurried. It was not until the middle of September that he gave the order to concentrate his forces on the northern bank of the Tai-tzu. His reinforcements continued to arrive smoothly, and by the end of the month his ranks were all up to strength. Where Kuropatkin had been strengthened by the arrival of two additional corps, the Second Cavalry Brigade under Prince Kanin was the only notable addition to Oyama's forces. Ammunition was short. Nogi's attack on Port Arthur had made heavy demands both on the Japanese transport system and on the output of the arsenals in Japan. Purchases from abroad, notably from Germany, were far from sufficient to meet demands.

On October 2 Kuropatkin issued a long proclamation that left neither his own forces nor the Japanese in any doubt that he intended to make another attempt to regain the initiative. "The moment has arrived for us to force our will on the Japanese. . . . [W]e will fearlessly advance, firmly resolved to stake our lives in fulfilling our duty to the last. May the will of the Almighty guide us all."

Under his command Kuropatkin had 261 battalions of infantry and supporting troops against Oyama's 170 battalions. Kuropatkin's force was demonstrably too large to be commanded efficiently by one general officer, and of this he was initially well aware. He therefore divided the army into two sections. The Eastern Detachment under General Stackelberg consisted of the First, Second, and Third Siberian corps, a brigade of the Fourth Siberian Corps, and the Siberian Cossack Division under Major-General

Alexander Vasilitch Samsonov.* General Bilderling had the Western Detachment, with the Tenth and Seventeenth Army corps, supported by the Fifty-first and Fifty-second Dragoon regiments, half of the Orenburg Cossack Division, and the Ural Cossack Brigade. The Sixth Siberian Corps, which was in reserve between Tieh-ling and Mukden when the battle began, subsequently fell in to the west of the Mandarin Road and the railway line and eventually came under the command of the Western Detachment. On the extreme west of the Russian position, three infantry regiments, an artillery brigade, a cavalry brigade, and a Cossack regiment guarded the flank.

Bands playing and flags flying, Kuropatkin's armies marched out at dawn on October 5 on a front forty miles long to engage Oyama's armies to the north of Liaoyang. A wide gap separated the Russian and Japanese forces, and the intervening territory had been the scene only of relatively small-scale patrol actions after the retreat from Liaoyang. The day was bright and sunny. In the fields the Chinese peasants were busy with the harvest.

After the nightmare of the millet at Liaoyang, the Russians at first welcomed the changed appearance of the countryside brought about by the harvest. The infantry, in particular, were soon to find the going difficult even here. The stubble was hard and razor sharp, and both Russian boots and Chinese shoes ripped to pieces.

It was not on the plains, however, or on the undulating hills that led to the mountains but in the mountains themselves that Kuropatkin had ordered Stackelberg to launch the major assault. The hills here were so steep that even the infantry had difficulty in moving off the tracks. The maps were useless.

Forty-five miles to the northeast of Liaoyang, deep in the Manchurian mountains and guarding the main Japanese position against a surprise left hook, was the Umezawa Brigade of cavalry. It was here that Kuropatkin's first pressure began to be felt. Umezawa's advanced posts came under heavy attack from strong Russian cavalry forces. Despite reinforcements, which Kuroki quickly pushed out, there was a danger that Umezawa might be cut off.

To Kuroki, the Russian moves in such strength on the right flank indicated that Kuropatkin, however improbably, intended to make his main effort here. Oyama remained unconvinced. Again, when he needed it badly, Kuroki had another stroke of good fortune. On the body of a Russian staff officer killed in the hills the Japanese discovered Kuropatkin's detailed

---

*Samsonov later commanded the Russian Second Army on the Eastern Front in 1914. For a description of his last hours and suicide, see Barbara Tuchman's *The Guns of August*, pp. 298–299.

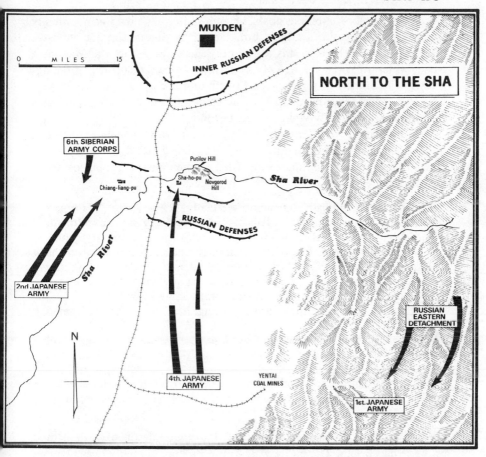

MUKDEN

INNER RUSSIAN DEFENSES

MILES

NORTH TO THE SHA

6th SIBERIAN
ARMY CORPS

Putilov Hill

Sha-ho-pu

Chiang-liang-pu

Novgorod
Hill

Sha River

Sha River

RUSSIAN DEFENSES

2nd JAPANESE
ARMY

RUSSIAN
EASTERN
DETACHMENT

N

4th JAPANESE
ARMY

YENTAI
COAL MINES

1st JAPANESE
ARMY

orders to Stackelberg to turn the Japanese right flank and then to march on Liaoyang.

Characteristically, the Japanese decided to meet the offensive head on. During September, Oyama had strengthened the northern face of the Liaoyang defenses, but instead of waiting passively to be hit he now gave orders to attack.

Caution again opposed daring. While they still had the initiative, Kuropatkin's forces advanced hesitantly, seemingly intent at first on creating defensive positions rather than risking a direct challenge of arms. Oyama's orders, issued at 10 P.M. on October 9, called for a general advance by the three armies, with Oku on the left, Nozu in the center, and Kuroki on the right. Twenty-four hours later the aggressive Japanese command had de-

[393]

cided on even more ambitious goals. Oyama's intention now was not merely to preempt Kuropatkin's attack, but himself to launch a major offensive designed to drive the Russians to the northeast, away from the Mandarin Road, which followed the line of the railway embankment. Using the aggressive First Army as a pivot, the Fourth and Second armies to the west were to wheel around the major Russian assault forces, attacking their lines of communication with Mukden and beyond.

On a hill close to the Yentai mines, Hamilton, with a notebook to record his impressions, watched the massive approach of the Russian forces on Kuroki's army and the ultimate indecision on their part that soon cost them the initiative.

Five miles to the north the enemy were advancing. As far as I could see the ground was alive with Russians. No *kaoliang*, no concealment, and there stood the Russians in solid masses, cavalry, infantry, guns —formations such as I have not seen in recent years except upon the paradeground. . . . These dark masses began a stately deployment into long, continuous lines which made my heart sink with the impression of resistless strength of a tremendous impending blow.

And now the long lines halted. Strange decision. They remained motionless ten minutes, twenty minutes, and then I realized that they were entrenching out of range of the Japanese. In that one moment all anxiety passed. I cannot explain the sensation, or instinct, that possessed me. There it is, and I feel possessed of great calmness and the full conviction that the Russians have, by their failure, parted forever with that moral ascendancy which is the greatest of all assets of an attack.

Hamilton's instinct served him well. Kuropatkin's offensive had died before it had begun. The battle was still in its infancy, but it was Oyama, not Kuropatkin, who was to set its tone and make its pace.

At dawn on October 11 Stackelberg concentrated 100 guns from the batteries of the First and Third Siberian Army Corps on General Inoue's Twelfth Division trenches on the rocky hills three miles to the east of the Yentai mines. Bunched together, the Russian infantry attacked under cover of the barrage and were shot down by the hundreds.

The Japanese were up to their usual tricks. To mislead the Russian gunners, they detonated explosive charges behind the infantry lines and caused the Russian gunners to waste thousands of rounds bombarding nonexistent artillery positions. At noon, Stackelberg personally gave orders to continue the assault, regardless of cost. Six times the Russian infantry gained the extremity of the Japanese lines and six times they were pushed back. By nightfall the Third Siberian Army Corps and attached troops had lost 5,000 men killed and wounded. Though the Twelfth Japanese Division had been unable to respond to Kuroki's order to attack, it had held firm at a cost of nearly one third of its effectives.

Faulty staff work and the lack of proper maps were again part of Kuropatkin's undoing. His orders to Stackelberg, who commanded the Russian Eastern Detachment, required of him an impossible task on October 10. He was to move on Yentai through mountainous country, driving out the First Army in the process, and to establish himself a mile northeast of the Yentai mines. Frontally, the going was easy enough, but the enveloping operation to the east carried his troops into fearful terrain. "The maps in my possession," Stackelberg said in a message to Kuropatkin,

> show nothing but a blank space along my line of march and only one road running from east to west. From the map the country through which we must pass would appear to be as flat as a pancake, but in reality it is extremely hilly and hardly passable for field artillery. . . . I await further instructions. If there are any maps of this part of the country in possession of the general staff, I request that I may be provided with one.

Kuropatkin's reply reached Stackelberg at 8:40 P.M. on October 10. "My orders still hold good," he said. "The time of execution I leave to you. You must not lose a day except under the most urgent necessity, especially as you are opposed only by a weak force." But he enclosed no maps, and the day had already been lost.

Stackelberg's concern about the terrain and the lack of maps was more than justified, but he fell into an old military error and overlooked the difficulties that his enemy was also encountering. To Kuroki, the position on his right flank had once seemed all but hopeless; Stackelberg's caution gave him the time he needed to redeploy and reinforce.

Kuropatkin's orders to Bilderling, who commanded the Western Detachment, did not encourage his field commander to be bold. True, Bilderling had been told to advance, but only as he completed one defensive position was he to move on again, there to build another. Stackelberg's forces were the spearhead of Kuropatkin's offensive; Bilderling's role was to create a diversion, but he was also repeatedly warned to stand upon the defensive should the enemy in their turn attack. Inevitably, Bilderling's contribution was tentative, half-hearted, and so lacking in vigor that Oyama was given no cause for concern.

By the evening of October 12 Stackelberg had been halted in the east, while in the center and west the progress made by Oku and Nozu now began to assume menacing proportions. Under pressure, Kuropatkin's system of command degenerated into chaos. Having created the Eastern and Western detachments for the specific purpose of decentralizing control, Kuropatkin

[395]

revealed once again his lack of confidence in his subordinate commanders. His orders often bypassed the detachment commands and went directly to corps commanders. Since Russian communications were as bad as ever, and messages took hours to reach their destination, the detachment staffs were thrown into utter confusion. The situation was further aggravated when Kuropatkin, to meet tactical threats as they developed, broke up large formations and scattered them from corps to corps.

Neither the Russians nor the Japanese made much use of visual signals, either the heliograph or the flag. Both had field telephones and field telegraphs, but the Russians, whose use of the telegraph was "perfunctory," placed much more reliance on runners, who sometimes spent hours delivering vital messages. When General Stackelberg decided to retreat from Te-li-ssu on June 15, for instance, he sent two of his officers to tell Major-General Gerngross, who commanded his left wing, to retire. It took nearly three quarters of an hour for the message to reach its destination, and, as a consequence, the Russians suffered heavy casualties when they pulled out. Again, at Liaoyang on the second day of the battle, General Stackelberg relied on messengers and a single overworked telephone on Cairn Hill, and it often took him an hour or more to get an answer to a message.

Except during the battle of Liaoyang, when the telephone line linking Kuroki with Oyama's headquarters was cut, the Japanese communication system worked much better. Operators were better trained and more efficient, and messengers were used infrequently and only when no other means of communication was available.

Now because of the appalling state of the communications system, Kuropatkin and Stackelberg were soon at cross purposes. A message from Kuropatkin's headquarters at 10:15 on the evening of October 12 did not reach Stackelberg until 9:40 A.M. on the thirteenth. This message turned over to him the Second Siberian Corps, part of which he sent immediately to help the First Siberian Corps, which was in trouble east of the Yentai coal mines. Then, at 11:05 A.M., he got another message instructing him to send the Fifth East Siberian Rifle Division to help the Fourth Corps in the center. By this time, Stackelberg had decided to abandon his own offensive, and, believing his forces to be in considerable danger, he was most unwilling to part with the last of his reserves. But at noon he learned that one of Bilderling's Corps, the Seventeenth, which had been holding advanced positions to the east and west of the railway, had been forced back over the Sha, leaving the Fourth Corps in grave danger and Kuropatkin's offensive in ruins.

Again, more perseverance on the Russians' part might have radically changed the course of the battle, but, now intent on withdrawing, the Russians were in no mood to exploit the exploitable. General officers fled without orders and without bothering to notify forces on their flanks. Kuropatkin's confidence in his subordinates deteriorated still further.

In response to Oyama's order to reach the Sha as quickly as possible, the Japanese continued their dash to the village of Sha-ho-pu on the south bank.

When they took it, the Japanese were within arm's length of the only two significant features on the plain—One Tree Hill and another rise soon to be known as Putilov Hill, which were no more than eighty feet high, connected by a scarcely discernible saddle running half a mile between them, and less than five miles from the Mandarin Road and the railway. But two small hills were mountains on this flat plain. For the Russians to lose them to the Japanese was to lose all that remained south of the Sha— and to risk overwhelming defeat in an unprotected withdrawal.

Kuropatkin sounded the attack—only to learn that his available forces were already in retreat, or preparing to retreat. To halt a defeated force by command is at any time a difficult task. But Kuropatkin tried and, to some extent, succeeded. He found the Ninth Division, which was bolting to the rear, and turned it back into action. He also found a detachment led by General Mau that had crossed the river with the Fourth Corps and ordered it back into action with General Gershelmann and other Tenth Corps forces. By midafternoon a formidable concentration of artillery and rifle fire was being poured into Sha-ho-pu, where three Japanese regiments were now digging for their lives behind the thick mud walls of the village.

Small groups of reinforcements and some supplies reached the defenders early in the evening. But the outlook to the Japanese defenders seemed utterly bleak. Russian fire continued to be heavy, and at any moment the Japanese expected to be overwhelmed.

General Mau's force was supposed to deliver the *coup de grâce*. General Sluchevski, the Tenth Corps commander, had been told early in the afternoon that he could expect Mau and his men at any moment. He attacked in their absence but could not break through. By nightfall Mau was still missing. Instead of attacking, his force had entered upon "a maze of marching and countermarching from which it was not finally retrieved until 1 A.M. on the following morning by a staff officer sent to locate it." Instead of being ready to join the fight now, Mau's men were exhausted. Out of water, out of food, almost out of ammunition, and surrounded by their dead and dying, the Japanese continued to hold on.

Across the Mandarin Road and railway tracks, another remarkable battle had been fought between the freshly committed Sixth Siberian Corps and Major-General Tsukamato's Fourth Division. All movement across the plain was visible for miles. The Japanese had watched with interest the approach of two Russian columns, each of brigade size. The first column, nearest to the railway, quickly ran into trouble, and Major-General Baranovski, the brigade commander, halted until Major-General Laiming, with the Second Brigade of the Fifty-fifth Infantry Division, came into line.

There then occurred a sight to have warmed the heart of any very old soldier. General Laiming's fresh battalions, facing action for the first time, formed up in parade ground order, officers in front, flags flying, band playing. As the men stood stiffly to attention, company and battalion commanders passed down the lines in inspection. After the officers came the men of God, the long-haired priests carrying sacred ikons for the men to kiss before venturing forward in paradeground order to their death.

With these ceremonies over, the officers dismounted. Though the band had ceased to play, the drummers took over as the Russians marched on the deployed ranks of the astonished Japanese Eighth Regiment. The Russians' target was the village of Chiang-liang-pu, where the Japanese were waiting. As a concession to the dangers that might conceivably lie ahead, the Russians changed formation when they were about half a mile from the Japanese position and advanced now in close single file.

The Japanese opened fire as the Russian formation changed. In a few minutes the Russian Second Brigade had lost almost all its officers. The ranks simply closed up and the column continued to move ahead. Though the stubble was strewn with dead and dying, General Laiming galloped up, reassembled what was left of the force and personally led the troops into the attack. At 3 o'clock he was wounded, and the now well blooded Yukhnov Regiment, which had lost nearly 2,000 men, fell back out of the fight.

Kuropatkin, who had begun the offensive with three full corps in reserve, had now committed every last man. Since the Eastern Detachment had failed in its task and was no longer heavily engaged, he decided to replenish his reserves by taking twenty-five of Stackelberg's sixty-five battalions. Even at this stage of the battle, there was still no telephone or telegraph link between Kuropatkin's headquarters and Stackelberg's. As soon as he received the order, Stackelberg dispatched a staff officer to Kuropatkin's headquarters, requesting that instead of being deprived of his forces he should be allowed to launch an attack to the west.

Stackelberg's messenger left at once. It was 9 P.M. before he returned with the news that the request had been rejected. By this time it was too late to send the battalions as reinforcements before dawn the following morning when the battle resumed with fresh fury.

Little real organization was left on the Russian side. Staff officers galloped about the battlefield trying to ascertain what positions were still held by the Russian forces and a confusion of information and misinformation flowed back to Kuropatkin. Weakened everywhere by the fearful casualties of the past week that had reduced regiments to battalions and battalions to companies, Kuropatkin put together a force of overwhelming size to recapture

Putilov and One Tree hills. To Major-General Novikov, the commander of the First Brigade of the Twenty-second Infantry Division, went the task of attacking One Tree Hill. The Thirty-sixth East Siberian Rifle Regiment was to provide protection on the flank and to the rear of the position. And the Second Brigade of the Fifth East Siberian Rifle Division under Major-General Putilov was to attack the hill nearest the river.

The orders called for a night attack. To the Ninth Brigade of the Fifth Japanese Division, which had a bird's-eye view of the assembling Russian forces, there was no element of surprise in what was being prepared for them. They had no doubt that they were soon to be struck by a sledgehammer.

To Oyama and Kodama, however, it was by no means apparent that Kuropatkin had such limited objectives as the twin hills. A more likely possibility, they thought, was that Kuropatkin intended to launch a major attack along the Mandarin Road and the railway against the Second Army. To meet this threat, Oyama began to gather his reserves in the Second Army area. There were none to spare for the calls for help coming from Major-General Yamada on One Tree Hill.

Although the attack was not scheduled to begin until after dark, the Thirty-sixth East Siberian Brigade had begun earlier to infiltrate across the river in small groups, assembling in the dead ground on the south bank of the river. During this period, the Russian artillery maintained an unremitting barrage against the Japanese trenches on the hill. While this was going on, General Yamada began to evacuate his wounded. To pull out all of his forces during daylight, however, was to run the risk of heavy loss. He decided, therefore, to hold out until nightfall and then to attempt to slip away.

Every moment reduced his chances of success. The Thirty-sixth East Siberian Rifle Regiment, having crossed the river in good order, began its encircling movement, caught the retiring Japanese wounded and baggage on the move, and wiped out the lot. Just at dark one battalion stormed One Tree Hill from the rear, killed the regimental commander and most other officers of the Japanese defenders, and occupied the position.

The rear attack was to prove too successful. For while the victorious Thirty-sixth Regiment was digging in among the dead and dying members of the Japanese, General Novikov opened his own attack on the hill—without knowing the hill had already been taken. And, since the three forces engaged in the whole operation lacked any means of liaison, there was no way of getting the message to him. As Russian fought Russian, the handful of survivors of the Japanese Forty-first Regiment regained parts of the position.

Major-General Putilov launched his assault as soon as he heard that

General Novikov had moved against One Tree Hill. While the Thirty-sixth East Siberian Rifle Regiment had gone far beyond the tasks set for it, both Novikov and Putilov had jumped off ahead of time. Among the Russians the battle had become a contest to see who could achieve the most quickest.

General Putilov was no man to stand waiting on the sidelines. As an intelligence officer, he had fought against the British in the Boer War. During the early months of the Russo-Japanese War, he had rusticated in Harbin. A soldier after Kuropatkin's own heart, he had now been given a field command and this, clearly, was a chance to prove himself.

Colonel Sluchevski, who commanded the Nineteenth East Siberian Rifle Regiment, and Lieutenant-Colonel Zapolski, his chief of staff, splashed their horses across the shallow waters of the Sha at the head of their troops and advanced along a spur toward the Japanese positions. At a range of more than half a mile they came under fire. They replied with a bayonet attack and a bloody hand-to-hand fight ensued. The Twentieth East Siberian Rifle Regiment now joined Putilov's attack. The Japanese were caught between the two Russian regiments and overrun. "By one gun stood a Japanese officer," the *British Official History of the Russo-Japanese War* reported. "Seeing the hopelessness of resistance and determined not to surrender, he rushed to the muzzle and was blown to pieces."

Fierce hand-to-hand fighting continued on the main position and in a village below, but by 9 P.M. it was all over on what was soon to become known as Putilov Hill. Two hours passed before General Putilov learned that the task had been only half-completed and that the remains of a Japanese battalion were still on One Tree Hill. Little remained of the too-adventurous Thirty-sixth East Siberian Rifle Regiment, but he organized a force of some strength from among the survivors, and by dawn on October 17 One Tree Hill and fourteen Japanese artillery pieces were also in the hands of General Putilov—at a cost of 3,000 men killed, wounded, and missing.

On this note of "victory" the battle of the Sha-ho came to its end. The Tsar graciously gave permission for the northernmost hill to be named after General Putilov, who was decorated on the spot, and One Tree Hill in the Russian histories became Novgorod Hill, after the garrison town of the Twenty-second Infantry Division. "We must wish the Japanese some more of these lessons," said Kuropatkin. "We are already somewhat superior in numbers; we are more experienced in the conduct of an action. We must take advantage of the defeat we have inflicted upon them."

The offensive had cost Kuropatkin 41,351 casualties, of whom 10,959 were either killed or missing. Oyama's losses were 3,951 killed and 16,394 wounded.

The Russian army did not lack in courage. Technically, it was incompetent. It made little use of the telephone or telegraph, and it spurned the use of older, but useful, forms of communication, the semaphore and the heliograph. Its much-vaunted cavalry, which heavily outnumbered the Japanese and which might have been used to great advantage on the plains around the railroad and the Mandarin Road, played almost no part in the action. One Cossack brigade on the Russian left flank lost only thirteen officers and men killed and ninety-eight wounded. The rest scarcely saw a shot fired. If the era of the saber had passed, the Russians were singularly slow to appreciate the value of a mounted rifleman.

Above all, however, the Russian failure was the failure of a command. Kuropatkin picked the wrong ground for his offensive. By choosing the mountains for his flanking movement, he sacrificed his heavy superiority in artillery. He lacked nothing in personal courage, but as a commander, he was pusillanimous.

Kuropatkin again blamed others. The troops with which he fought lacked training and military skill, and his senior officers, as he made pointedly clear in a memorandum to unit commanders issued on October 26, were incompetent, or worse. There were no substitutes, Kuropatkin believed, for personal courage and personal example. "While it is conceivable that a corps may be compelled to fall back by superior force, such a course is only justifiable after every means, including the personal example of the commander, has been employed to maintain the positions held."

In St. Petersburg, it was clear at last that the divided authority in the East had to come to an end. Either Alexeiev or Kuropatkin had to go. For better or for worse, the Tsar entrusted Kuropatkin with the full military powers that he had so long sought, and his long and divisive feud with the Viceroy came to an end with the announcement by Alexeiev at Harbin on October 25 that the Tsar had "acceded to my request to be relieved of the duties of Commander-in-Chief." The news was hailed by the army with delight. Five days later, the unlamented Viceroy boarded his special train and headed west for St. Petersburg, where he arrived on November 10, to be received without ceremony and driven from the station without escort.

On November 14, Japan raised a second sterling loan for £12 million issued in both London and New York. With the Japanese out of ammunition and the Russians out of morale, both sides dug in on the Manchurian plains and prepared for the winter.

CHAPTER 24

☙☙☙☙☙☙

On the Dogger Bank

By THE BEGINNING of October 1904, Russia's Baltic Fleet, now renamed the Second Pacific Squadron, was preparing to set out on its long and arduous journey to reinforce the Russian Far Eastern squadrons. Soon after his appointment as commander-in-chief of Russia's naval forces in the Far East, Admiral Makarov had suggested tentatively that more ships should be sent to assist the Port Arthur and Vladivostok squadrons. His death in May led to a conference on June 20 of the Higher Naval Board, with the Tsar presiding. Present at this meeting was the new commander-in-chief of the Baltic Fleet, Rear-Admiral Zinovi Petrovitch Rozhdestvenski, who for the next three months worked tirelessly to prepare his unwieldy armada for its long voyage.

As Rozhdestvenski struggled with the inevitable tangle of Russian red tape, newspapers everywhere speculated about the sanity of sending a fleet halfway around the world with no bases of its own on the way.

Japanese intelligence had alerted Admiral Togo that a large naval force was collecting in Russia to reinforce the fleet in Port Arthur. While the Japanese commander-in-chief built up a supply of mines to lay in the path of the embryonic Baltic Fleet, Rozhdestvenski worked eighteen hours a day, sometimes without sleep for three nights in a row, fitting out fifty ships, of all types and sizes, some new and others that had seen service in the Russo-Turkish War of 1877. Food for the fleet's twelve thousand seamen had to be requisitioned and stowed on board, along with clothing to cope both with Arctic temperatures and life in the tropics. The route chosen would take them through the cold waters of the North Sea, around Africa and the Cape of Good Hope and then across the Equator and into the tropics before reaching Port Arthur, if it still held out—or Vladivostok, if the fortress had, by some awful chance, already fallen.

Since the days of Peter the Great, Russia had endeavored to become a great sea-going nation, but one half of the year in Russia was too cold for training at sea. Because it was a warm-water harbor, Port Arthur was especially important, and now it was fast slipping from Russian grasp.

The ships were manned by mostly raw crews, many of whom had never sailed before and were averse to leaving home for a war that they felt was all but lost. Others among them were plotting revolution. There was a serious shortage of experienced engineers to care for the new boilers, though large numbers had been commandeered from private shipping companies. Most of the Baltic Fleet was made up of land-sailors, whose love of home prevailed over their sense of adventure. Rozhdestvenski's reluctant sailors would have preferred even to stay at Kronstadt, the naval base guarding St. Petersburg, which was known as the hardest post in the country, rather than face the unknown dangers of the long voyage and what lay beyond.

As cattle were being driven aboard the ships to provide meat for the crews, together with crates of boots and clothing, dried biscuits and vegetables, vodka and champagne for the officers, and tons of shells, torpedoes and mines, the biggest task of all was still to be faced. Rozhdestvenski had to provide the fuel for his fifty ships, with no Russian base en route. International law forbade neutral ports to service the ships, and the Admiral had to beg among the few nations on friendly terms with Russia. France decided that she would allow the fleet to take in coal at her ports along the way but would provide only sufficient coal to get the fleet to its next port.

The world's newspapers gave a great deal of space to the suspicious movements of Russian ships from the Baltic Sea to the Red Sea and from the Baltic to the Atlantic. When the passenger ship *Malacca* and other British ships were interfered with by Russian vessels in July, it was widely publicized that neutral ports along the way would be closed to any Russian squadron attempting to reach the Far East.

Coal had been declared contraband, a likelihood the Japanese government had forseen before the war. For years she had been laying in large quantities of Cardiff coal, which, unlike other coals, was smokeless.

Britain, Japan's ally, would not officially offer Russia even a quarter ton of her fine Welsh coal. Kaiser William II, anxious to keep Russia in the war as long as possible, eventually agreed to help. German bases, however, were few and far between on the route to the Far East, but he arranged for a fleet of sixty colliers of the long-established Hamburg-Amerika Line to supply coal between Libau in the Baltic and Port Arthur. The colliers were to be dispatched in succession to meet the slow-moving fleet at prearranged rendezvous. When coal was required in areas where there were no friendly

[403]

or neutral ports, the coal would be loaded at sea direct from the colliers to the ships, but outside the three-mile limit of territorial waters laid down by international law.

Quite apart from fueling needs, the great fleet would require coal, even when at anchor, to keep up steam in the boilers, to produce electricity, and to condense drinking water. Every thousand miles would consume about 17,000 tons of coal, and the ships would need to be full of fuel when they reached their destination and Togo's fleet.

Rozhdestvenski was a tall, handsome man in his middle fifties. He had joined the navy at seventeen and eight years later was promoted to the rank of lieutenant. At thirty-six he had been naval attaché in London, but most of his life had been spent with guns and high explosives. As a young lieutenant in the war with Turkey, under Makarov's command, he had served on various torpedo-carrying ships in the Black Sea. One confusing incident involved Rozhdestvenski, who, as an officer on *Vesta,* an 1,800-ton screw steamer with very few guns, attacked a large Turkish warship. It was said to have fled in flames before sinking. Rozhdestvenski and his commander were acclaimed heroes and presented with the fourth-class Order of St. George and the Order of St. Vladimir.

A year after the incident Rozhdestvenski wrote an article for a Russian newspaper, titled "Ironclads and Auxiliary Cruisers," in which he denied that the Turkish ship had been destroyed. Hobart Pasha, an English aristocrat who served as admiral with the Turkish Navy, agreed that the story was exaggerated and said that the two ships had merely exchanged a few shots. Whatever the truth of the incident, it made no difference to Rozhdestvenski's promotion. After a brief spell organizing the Bulgarian navy and his term in London as naval attaché, he was put in charge of the Baltic Fleet's gunnery training program. The opportunity to lead the new Russian squadron on a spectacular journey across the world was a big chance, and he worked feverishly in the brief time at his disposal to make the fleet strong and efficient.

Never an even-tempered man, the Admiral was in a state of high nervous tension at the end of August when he gathered his warships together at Kronstadt. He fought for what he wanted, roared and raved at his staff, and terrified merchants who came aboard his ships with foodstuffs, machinery, and other supplies.

By September, however, he was as ready as he could be, but the fate of the new squadron was still under consideration. Some high officials advocated the immediate departure of the fleet, but others wanted to hold it back because the army would soon sweep the Japanese before it. Money had been set aside to train the fleet, but when the final decision was reached, haste was more important than quality. Efficiency was forgotten in the hurry to get the ships to sea.

The Admiral's optimism was fading. Returning one day from a visit to the construction site of two light cruisers being rushed through to accompany his fleet, he spoke gloomily to a fellow officer. "What success can there be? We should not have started this hopeless business, and yet how can I refuse to carry out orders when everybody is so sure of success?"

Rozhdestvenski raised his flag on *Kniaz Suvarov,* which, with all the additions given her in recent months, now had a displacement of more than 15,000 tons. As if to invite destruction when she encountered the enemy, she was, like the rest of the fleet, painted black, her two tall smokestacks picked out in bright canary yellow with black rings at the top. In addition to a huge array of smaller arms, she carried four twelve-inch guns and was fitted with a ram for delivering the *coup de grâce.* Her top speed was more than eighteen knots, although she was never to attain it at any time during the coming voyage.

Nothing went right during two weeks of practice in gunnery and maneuvers. Ships collided with each other, and the gunners seemed hopeless. Thirty-year-old Chief Engineer Eugene Sigismondovitch Politovski, a builder of ships and not a sailor, was about to start on his first cruise, desperately unhappy and pessimistic as to the outcome of the "mad" journey. He had just finished building the *Borodino,* sister ship to the flagship, and had hoped he would be released to return to his wife; but at the last moment, with barely time to pack, he had been summoned to *Suvarov* and the care of the fleet. Now he was kept busy with engine room breakdowns on half a dozen ships, not only in the obsolete vessels but in the new warships that had been rushed through for the voyage.

Off Reval, the Admiral sprang a surprise on his fleet. Order 69, issued in early September, said:

Today at 2 A.M. I instructed the officer of the watch to issue the signal for defense against a torpedo attack. Eight minutes afterwards nothing had been done. Everyone was sound asleep except the officers and men of the watch, and even they were not sufficiently alert. Not one of the searchlights was ready. The men told off for torpedo duty were not at their posts. No steps had been taken to light the deck, though it is impossible to work in the dark.

Some of the crew having heard rumors of Japanese in the area, actually believed that a real torpedo attack was taking place. "Officers shouted at the petty officers, and these, in turn, shouted at the men," wrote one of the troublemakers on *Orel*. If it had been an authentic enemy attack, *Orel* would have been sunk before the voyage began.

Orel, one of the new battleships, was repeatedly in trouble. She had caught fire in St. Petersburg while she was still being built and then miraculously survived her launching when she was found to be too heavily armored, so that some of her plating had to be removed. "An unlucky bitch" from the start, *Orel* was now laden to the hilt as she sailed from Kronstadt. All of the ships were overloaded with coal far beyond the limits of safety —a step ordered by the ministry of the navy in case of fueling problems during the voyage.

Five minutes after she had weighed anchor, *Orel* was stuck in the mud, and 400 of her crew were ordered to run back and forth from one side of the deck to the other to dislodge her. The crew wondered, laughing as they ran across the deck, how a collection of men weighing in all about thirty tons could be expected to have much effect on an iron-plated ship weighing 15,000 tons. The men were right. Manpower had no effect, and dredges were called in to deepen the channel. At last, *Orel* was free and moved to Reval, where the official sendoff was to take place.

Next day there were troubles of a different kind, wrote A. Novikov-Priboy, a revolutionary member of the crew of *Orel*, sneering at the inefficiency and pomp of Russia under the Tsar.* He described the "fury of cleaning and polishing" for the full-dress review by Nicholas and his entourage. "Again and again we washed the gangways with soap and water; we scrubbed the bridges; touched up the paint; scoured the brasswork. Engines and stokeholes were not forgotten, though it was most unlikely that the visitor's exalted feet would tread the narrow ladders giving access to the bowels of the iron-clad. Cleanliness became a mania."

Admiral Rozhdestvenski received the Tsar, the Tsaritsa, and the precious baby boy, Alexis, in his full-dress uniform decorated with golden eagles and golden epaulettes and rows of medals on his chest. He was supported by an odd couple—two admirals, Baron Dimitri von Felkerzam and Oscar Adolvitch Enquist, who were to command divisions of the fleet, the former beardless, the latter supporting the longest, bushiest and whitest beard in the navy. Admiral Felkerzam was an efficient seaman, but his appearance was against him. Now, standing beside the towering commander-in-chief, he appeared comical. "He was extremely obese," wrote Novikov-Priboy,

---

*His book, *Tsushima, Grave of a Floating City*, written from notes in prison camp, took many years to come off the presses, and was published, and probably greatly rewritten, after the Russian revolution. It was awarded the Stalin prize for literature in 1941 and, according to the English-language edition, sold nearly a million and a half copies in Russia.

"and walked with short, trotting steps. He ran to fat, and his face was beardless, so that he looked like a eunuch. When he was angry, his tiny mouth became as round as the opening of a thimble; and his treble voice was quite unsuited to his sex and station."

Thousands of spectators lined the waterfront and the piers. Bands played gay music and from the signal masts over the forts fluttered strings of flags spelling out good luck messages. At last Russia, or parts of it, had been whipped up into a state of exhilaration. In spite of the burst of sunshine, the weather was too chilly for Alexandra to stay long with the baby, but she presented each ship with hand-made chalices to be kept in their chapels.

The fleet saluted, and the smoke from the guns was so thick that it was difficult to see anything at all from the shore. The Tsar visited ship after ship, giving the same rousing speech to all the thousands of sailors lined up in their new blue jumpers and black trousers. "His Majesty kept us waiting," said one sailor, "and we wanted our dinners." But he was as impressed as everyone else when the Tsar vowed vengeance on the "insolent Japanese who had troubled the peace of Holy Russia." On each ship, the Tsar finished his oration with the words: "I wish you a victorious campaign and a happy return to your native land."

It was all a repetition of that other day in 1902, also at Reval, when in similar sunny circumstances Tsar Nicholas II of Russia and Kaiser William II of Germany swapped each other's full dress uniforms to watch Rozhdestvenski, then a mere captain, put the Russian ships through an exhibition of gunnery. It was a magnificent performance, as ship after ship fired at fixed targets and then at targets towed by fast-moving boats.

"I wish I had such splendid admirals as your Rozhdestvenski," said William, dreaming of the day when the trident would be in his own hand. The two monarchs embraced and exchanged expensive presents, and when the practice was completed Rozhdestvenski, his future assured, kissed his Tsar's hand. "If only we could fight now, sire," he whispered.

As Germany's monarch left the scene of the successful 1902 celebrations, his ship, *Hohenzollern,* put up the signal: "The Admiral of the Atlantic bids farewell to the Admiral of the Pacific." Nicholas was a little slow in the uptake. The obvious reply was, "The Admiral of the Pacific salutes you," but that day his signal read merely, "Farewell, pleasant journey."

The sun shone brightly again in 1904, as Rozhdestvenski said farewell to the Tsar and took the rest of the royal party below for a banquet. He was willing and able to take his ill-prepared fleet across the world to fight the enemies of his Tsar. But in his heart he held many misgivings.

As the fleet sailed, Nicholas returned to his family and the joy of the long-awaited son. "We must have a strong country for Baby," his wife had urged. And Nicholas that night wrote of the fleet in his diary. "Bless its voyage, Lord. Permit that it arrive safe and sound at its destination, that it succeed in its terrible mission for the safety and happiness of Russia."

Rozhdestvenski's main force consisted of three sister battleships to the flagship—*Borodino, Alexander III* and *Orel,* all new and all carrying workmen still engaged in giving finishing touches to the over-laden, top-heavy warships. Apart from these new ships, Rozhdestvenski had with him the *Oslyabya,** an ugly-duckling, ineffective battleship, flying the flag of Rear-Admiral Felkerzam, and *Sissoi Veliki* and *Navarin,* both of them old, slow battleships. Even more aged were the cruisers *Dmitri Donskoi,* flying the flag of Rear-Admiral Enquist, and *Svetlana,* fast but unreliable. Four other cruisers, *Oleg, Zhemchug, Aurora,* and *Izumrud,* were fast and modern, and the *Admiral Nakhimov* was an armored cruiser. Nine 350-ton torpedo boat destroyers completed the list. Attached to the fleet was a hodgepodge of auxiliary ships, transports, a hospital ship, water-condensing vessel, tugs, a refrigerated food ship, an icebreaker and a repair ship, the *Kamchatka,* which was to prove more troublesome than all the other ships put together.

Chief Engineer Politovski found himself in a cabin previously occupied by an officer who had gone mad—a realization that did little to lift the feeling of deep depression with him from the beginning. "There is no use our fighting," he wrote his wife. "Things have come to such a pass that I can only wring my hands and feel sure that no one can escape his fate, for this is the only possible assurance. Such gloom overwhelms me that I feel inclined to hang myself." Only the constant work, mostly on *Orel,* which was frequently in trouble, kept him sane during the gray, foggy October days.

A good many others also saw little hope in the voyage. Some were already disheartened by the failure of the Port Arthur squadron, and among them were many revolutionaries, "slackers and dangerous elements." A large library of subversive literature went with the fleet and was lent out to sympathetic sailors during the voyage. On board *Orel* a crippled engineer officer distributed this literature, secretly at first but later quite openly.

Also in *Suvarov,* and as troublesome in his own way, was Captain Nikolas Lawrentievitch Klado, forty-three-year-old junior flag officer to the Admiral. He had been decorated for action against Kamimura's fleet and had returned to Russia when Vladivostok was cut off from the Port Arthur squadron, with the express intent of sailing with Rozhdestvenski. Before the

---

* *Oslyabya, Dmitri Donskoi,* and *Aurora* had been on the way to reinforce the First Pacific Squadron when the first naval attack on Port Arthur occurred. They had reached the Red Sea when this news was received and were ordered back to the Baltic.

fleet left he had begged that more ships should be sent, whether they were big or small, efficient or completely inefficient. The more ships there were, the more difficult it would be for the Japanese to hit the *Suvarov* and her sister ships, he argued. Rozhdestvenski said that he anticipated enough trouble with the fleet as it was without adding to it derelicts with old guns that would consume his precious coal. Only a few of the ancient tubs suggested by Klado were eventually included. The Admiral and Klado began the voyage hating each other.

On Klado's list were ships unlaunched and those only fit for the scrap heap. The Tsar's yachts could go, he suggested, and at a pinch could be used as hospital ships or scoutships. His view was that bad sailors and poor engineers sailed with the Second Squadron, men who had "never studied the science of naval history nor naval strategy nor modern naval tactics." He was continually causing trouble among the officers of the flagship, though most of them got on well with him at first, including even Captain Clapier de Colongue, the chief of staff, a handsome, fair-haired, rather effeminate officer of aristocratic French birth who supported his Admiral at all times, taking the blame for errors of judgment and receiving the brunt of Rozhdestvenski's evil temper. It was said that he often came from interviews with the Admiral with tears in his eyes.

Also in *Suvarov* was Commander Vladimir Semenov, who had reached Libau just in time to join the squadron after his ship, the *Diana*, had been interned in Saigon after the battle of the Yellow Sea. Semenov had the full confidence of the Admiral, but no official position. Rozhdestvenski welcomed him: "We shall ply you so much with questions, and you will consequently have to work so hard with your mouth, that you won't be able to think of any other work." It did not turn out that way. Semenov found that the other officers resented his earlier part in the war, and some blamed him for the failure of the Port Arthur squadron, a failure that had led to this marathon journey of rescue.

Novikov-Priboy, in *Orel*, rejoicing that he was not on the flagship, wrote that only one or two officers, apart from Semenov, dared to speak to the Admiral. "The others tremble before him like thieves before the constable. He treats them worse than a bad master treats servants." The men hid from the Admiral as soon as he came on deck, as if he had the evil eye, he noted. Semenov, "tubby, with a face puffed out and ruddy, straggly wisps in place of a beard," was no better. The sailors nicknamed him "the perambulating bladder."

On October 17, the fleet moved out of the Baltic and on toward the narrow waters of the Danish Skaw. Though the weather had improved and the sun shone brightly, the fleet was nervous. The waters were tricky and Rozhdestvenski was troubled, also, by reports that Japanese torpedo boats or submarines might be lurking even so far away from home, eighteen thousand sea miles distant. Orders were given that no outside ship of any sort must be allowed to come among the fleet.

A motor launch sent out to deliver a message to the Admiral had blanks fired under her bow. The Russians would not allow it to come near but launched a boat to which the crew then delivered the dispatch: the notification that Rozhdestvenski had been belatedly promoted to the rank of vice-admiral. Pleased at the honor, he read the message to his ships, but at the same time sent out urgent orders that all merchant ships must hoist their national flags, otherwise they would be fired upon.

Even an intelligent man like Chief Engineer Politovski, worried by the pile-up of repairs, felt the alarm in the fleet. In a spare moment, with a long-needed cup of coffee, he dashed off a note to his wife as the fleet entered the narrows:

> Tonight there will be danger. We shall all sleep in our clothes and all guns will be loaded. . . . we are afraid of striking Japanese mines in these waters. Perhaps there will be no mines; but considering that long ago Japanese officers went to Sweden and swore to destroy our fleet, we must be on our guard . . . panic prevails on board. Everyone examines the sea intently. The weather is glorious. The slightest suspicious-looking spot in the water is carefully watched. The guns are angled. The crew are standing about on deck . . . it is curious that we are so far from the theater of war and yet so much alarmed.

The work piled up. A cruiser broke down, the *Sissoi Veliki* was in trouble again, and three Danish steamers carrying coal needed attention. "I do not take into account minor mishaps such as the torpedo boat which struck her bows somewhere and, of course, bent them," wrote Politovski. *Orel* left the fleet with a broken rudder and the engineer suspected that there was some "scoundrel" on board who was trying to injure the ship. The chief engineer wished more than ever that he had never come to sea with the troublesome, ill-equipped ships. A torpedo boat was sent back with a leaking condenser, and *Yermak,* an old icebreaker, which repeatedly ignored signals from the flagship was brought into line only when a shot was fired under her stern.

The ships passed through the Skaw and steamed through thick fog toward the North Sea. "The world had become nothing but an infinite envelope of mist," wrote Novikov-Priboy on *Orel,* now temporarily repaired and groping through the mist far behind the fleet. "Men looked like phantoms. . . . The impression of mystery was intensified by the noise of sirens . . . the big ships seemed to be trying to outdo one another in the loudness of their stentorian halloos. As a wind-up to each bar of the performance, the *Anadyr* uttered shrieks of agony, as if announce some terrible misfortune."

When the mist cleared away only *Kamchatka,* the repair ship, was missing from the great calm expanse of the North Sea. Steaming along slowly, all alone, she suddenly reported to the flagship that she was being chased by torpedo boats:

SUVAROV: Anxious. How many? From which side?
KAMCHATKA: From all directions.
SUVAROV: How many torpedo boats? Give details.
KAMCHATKA: About eight torpedo boats.
SUVAROV: What distance from you?
KAMCHATKA: A cable length.
SUVAROV: Have they discharged any torpedoes?
KAMCHATKA: We haven't seen any.

On board *Suvarov* everyone was sure that the Japanese were trying to find out from the little repair ship the position of the fleet, and when *Kamchatka* became silent slow panic took over the flagship. For twenty minutes the *Kamchatka* was silent to inquiries from *Suvarov* as to whether the torpedo boats were still in sight but at last she replied. "We cannot see any."

"The sea moaned. Hours passed on leaden feet. This waiting for invisible dangers oppresses us," wrote Novikov-Priboy. Some of the crews were given leave to turn in but few took advantage of it. Commander Semenov went below to his cabin and contemplated his portrait of Admiral Makarov, given to him long before. There had never been time to have it framed and it stood propped up against a bulkhead where a drop of water had stained the strip of narrow red paper around its border, so that smudges of crimson formed a streak across the Admiral's face and breast. "A bad omen," he was thinking, when suddenly there was a sound of action stations: "Torpedo boats! A torpedo attack!" Then: "The destroyers! We're done for!" Men seized lifebelts from the ships' rails. Others, running to their hammocks, tore out the cork mattresses. Some crossed themselves; others cursed. The terrified gunners fired blindly across the dark sea where their searchlights were probing.

Engineer Politovski, on the high afterbridge of *Suvarov,* blinded by the searchlights and deafened by the noise of the guns, admitted to his diary that he put his hands to his ears and bolted below. Before he fled, he saw, to his horror, a tiny red and black-painted steamer rolling helplessly below him, its funnel and bridge clearly visible.

Commander Semenov, passing the wireless office, took a look at the time —12:25 A.M.—and made a note of it before he joined Admiral Rozhdestvenski and his staff on the bridge. Here he could see a number of lights, among which from time to time signals flashed. This, he was told, was Admiral's Felkerzam's division, but closer to the ship he saw in the search-lights a small steamer, with one mast and one funnel. A second small ship was heading right for *Alexander* as if with the intention of ramming her On the starboard side forward. The *Alexander* and *Suvarov* poured a hail of shell on the ship and one after the other the Russian ships opened fire. One steamer sank as Semenov watched. Rozhdestvenski, realizing at last what was happening, seized the gun layer by the shoulder and shouted furiously: "How dare you? Don't you see—fishermen!"

The "enemy" was the gamecock fleet, as the North Sea fishing boats were known in Britain, of forty or fifty 100-ton, single-screw trawlers, each with a crew of eight or nine, out of Hull and fishing on its usual beat at the Dogger Bank. At first the fishermen thought the warships were British and part of the Channel Fleet under Lord Beresford. As the shells fell among them, panic broke out on the trawlers. The crews were dazzled by the lights and feared that they would be run down. "So me and the rest of the crew held up fish to show who we were," reported the boatswain of the *Swift*. "I held up a big plaice. My mate, Jim Tozer, deck hand, showed a had-dock." When this failed, they cut their nets and tried to escape.

On board the *Crane* the skipper and the third hand were decapitated and all the rest wounded except the cook. "I had just turned into my berth when I hear the firing of guns," said Albert Almond, a member of the crew. "Going on deck, I saw several ships, which had covered us with their searchlights, and which were all firing at us simultaneously. I ran below again, and was followed by the boatswain, Hoggart, who had nearly reached the bottom of the ladder when he fell backwards crying, 'I am shot. My hands are off.' "

All this time the battleships fired on the *Crane* while the small son of the dead captain ran about crying for his father. "We feared to tell him that he was dead," said Almond. *Crane* sank under the fierce attack. Others escaped, dragging their nets behind them, but soon the stoic English fisher-men went back to their fishing, as though nothing had happened.

On board the Russian ships the terror died down. Officers dragged men from their guns, cursing and hitting at them. In *Orel* the bosun tried to get his bugler to sound the ceasefire, hitting him across the face, until at last the man, his lips bleeding, managed to obey. *Orel* had fired seventeen six-inch shells and five hundred of smaller caliber. Five of her shells had hit another Russian ship, *Aurora*, belonging to Admiral Enquist's fleet, which was supposed to be miles away. It was not until it was realized that the signals in the distance came from their own ships that firing ceased. On board *Aurora* the chaplain had his hand torn off. Other injuries were slight, but both *Aurora* and *Donskoi* were badly damaged. Engineer Politovski, thinking of the work ahead of him, found the time to write a short note to his wife, begging her to take care of his letters. "They are better than any diary. Perhaps some day I will read them myself and refresh my memory about the present excitements . . . a very, very sad occurrence. The only consolation is that our shooting is so good."

As the fishing fleet returned to Hull, flying their flags at half-mast, crowds gathered at the harbor to inspect the battered boats. "A scene altogether without parallel was witnessed at St. Andrew's dock," wrote a reporter for *The Times*. The paper used the tragedy as its main news story and wrote an editorial denouncing the Russians.

It is almost inconceivable that any men calling themselves seamen, however frightened they might be, could spend twenty minutes bombarding a fleet of fishing boats without discovering the nature of their target. It is still harder to suppose that officers wearing the uniform of any civilized power could suspect they had been butchering poor fishermen with the guns of a great fleet and then steam away without endeavoring to rescue the victims of their unpardonable mistake.

King Edward was deeply moved by the tragedy, which occurred on the anniversary of the Battle of Trafalgar. He summoned the British foreign secretary, Lord Lansdowne to Buckingham Palace and donated two hundred guineas for the victims. "A most dastardly outrage," he penciled on the margin of the report to Parliament.

The Tsar, outwardly sympathetic, wrote privately to his mother of his "mangy enemies," the English. "They are very angry and near to boiling point. They are even said to be getting their fleet ready for action. Yesterday I sent a telegram to Uncle Bertie, expressing my regret, but I did not apologize. . . . I do not think that the English will have the cheek to go further than to indulge in threats. . . ."

When the fleet arrived at Vigo, Edgar Wallace, then a reporter on the *Daily Mail,* interviewed several Russian sailors, including a steward on one of the battleships, who had been in the pantry washing up after dinner, when a midshipman rushed into the mess room, crying, "The Japanese are attacking us!" Officers dropped their playing cards and their glasses and ran on deck in great excitement. Soon afterward a sailor told him that one of the officers wanted him to bring up two glasses of brandy to the deck: "Just as I reached the upper deck I heard shooting. All the sailors on deck were lying down on their faces and the officers were all under cover. I admit that I was very much frightened, for the officers were greatly excited and all talking together at the top of their voices. [A midshipman] was waving his drawn sword, crying 'The Japanese!' " He told Wallace that no officers were

[413]

drunk on board his ship that night, but one had fainted from "sheer excitement." Several days later all crewman were ordered to say nothing of the incident in letters to relatives or friends; anyone offending would be punished. Wallace cabled the story to the *Mail* and was instructed to go on to Tangier, where the Russian ships would call later. When he arrived in Tangier, he found that his informants had been executed and buried at sea.

Britain was on the brink of war with Russia. "The mind of the government, like the mind of the nation, is made up," said *The Times*. Crowds demonstrated in Trafalgar Square demanding that action be taken against the Russian "barbarians." When the dead fishermen were buried at Hull, long processions followed the cortège to the graveside. On the same evening the mayor of Hull received a telegram from the mayor of Tokyo, offering his sympathy and that of the citizens of Japan to the victims of the Russian outrage. "History and human nature are both condensed in this timely and feeling dispatch which shows with curious distinctness how, though East is East and West is West, the twain can sometimes meet," remarked Cassell's *History of the War*. Count Hayashi Tadasu, Japanese ambassador in Britain, publicly denied any Japanese involvement. It would have been beyond even the capabilities of the Japanese navy to bring torpedo boats all the way from the Far East without coaling or taking in food (though they could have been bought in Europe and provided with crews easily enough).

In Manchuria, General Kuropatkin's officers thought that war between England and Russia was likely as the result of the killing of British seamen. "On the whole the majority of the Russians, or the majority of those whose opinions carry weight, would have welcomed a war," wrote Lord Brooke. Most of Kuropatkin's officers shared this opinion. They believed the war was caused by the Machiavellian diplomacy of England, which wanted to use Japan as a tool in order to injure Russia. They could not believe that Japan by herself would have dared to defy Russia.

They were equally sure that torpedo boats had been sent out by England to destroy the Baltic Fleet off the Dogger Bank. Lord Brooke, the Reuter correspondent, wrote that the probable scene of operations would be the northeast frontier of India. "It would be quite easy for Russia to drive England out of India," an infantry colonel told him.

The world's press, including some of the usually friendly German newspapers, sided against the Russians. They recalled that one of their ships, the *Sonntag,* had also been fired on by the Russian fleet a few days before the Dogger Bank incident. The *Berliner Tageblatt* wondered whether the fleet should be permitted to sail the seas. "Rozhdestvenski is known to be an exceedingly nervous gentleman. He gets into a state of boundless excitement over trifles and it is all the more strange that he should have been entrusted with a post so unsuitable to a person of his type."

Russia was unrepentant. One Russian newspaper commented that the Japanese had been too smart to use their own torpedo boats for the attack and had hired English ships for the purpose. "If Great Britain can rely on numerical superiority of the sea and if she threatens with violence and unjustified vengeance, we should remember that it is not in the spirit of the Russian people to yield to menace."

As Rozhdestvenski, still unaware of the sensation he had caused, passed the white cliffs of Dover, crowds of Englishman on shore watched him go, with hatred in their hearts. While Admiral Felkerzam stood off Brighton Pier to take on coal, the British fleet got steam up. Gibraltar prepared for war, and warships were recalled from foreign stations.

Rozhdestvenski and his officers were convinced that there had been torpedo boats, rigged up to look like fishing smacks. Others felt that there had been torpedo boats that had disappeared when the firing started. Engineer Politovski, predicting an international scandal, sympathized with the dead and injured fishermen, but believed that the fishermen had only themselves to blame. They must have known the fleet was on the way and they must as certainly have known that the Japanese wished to destroy it. He put no trust in the English. "There was foggy Albion," he wrote to his wife. "I pondered over this clod of earth—so powerful, so rich, so proud, and so ill-disposed toward us. We are only three hours journey from London and six by rail from Paris. The crew feed birds who come to settle exhausted on the ships. . . ." He was tired of the constant fogs, and the constant work of repairing the ships, and terrified of the rats in his cabin which jumped from the writing table to his bed. "I used to sleep with my feet toward the door but have now put my pillow there. . . . they could easily have jumped on my head."

The bright Spanish sun helped to lift the Russian spirits as the fleet approached Vigo Bay. But once in harbor, Rozhdestvenski discovered that news of the affair in the North Sea had preceeded him. After 1,800 miles his bunkers were almost empty, but now he was told that he could take on only 400 tons for each ship from the waiting German colliers. The Spaniards were sorry, but they were also conscious of the British cruiser division standing close by. The British had warned the Spanish government that it would consider it a breach of neutrality if the Russian ships were allowed to take on coal or even water. Rozhdestvenski, cheered by a large crowd, went ashore to talk to the governor, who with tears in his eyes begged the Admiral to be more patient. A message came from the Tsar:

> In my thoughts I am constantly with you and My Squadron. While there may be temporary difficulties between Russia and a friendly nation, I have given my ministers orders to settle these differences as

[415]

soon as possible. The eyes of Russia are on you, and Our hope and confidence accompany you. May you continue your voyage in the same spirit of confidence.

It was a good message, but it was not coal.

Rozhdestvenski, bristling, read the message to his crews, together with his reply telling the Tsar that they were ready to carry out his wishes to the end. He called for three cheers for the Tsar, but when they came they lacked the old vivacity. Alongside sat the British cruiser *Lancaster,* waiting and watching. From the back ranks of the men lined up on *Suvarov*'s deck came the voice of a young officer: "A pity the war with them did not come off." Commander Semenov asked him why he thought this. "Because then they would have scattered us directly we had got outside. Now we have to go all that distance to meet the same fate," the officer replied.

In the afternoon they began to take on their short rations of coal, and for twelve hours officers and men labored. Everything was black with coal dust and the offer of an extra tot of vodka to the men if the work was well and speedily finished was an added encouragement. Fueling went on all night long as double the allotted amount of coal was surreptitiously stowed away into each ship's bunkers.

Rozhdestvenski sent off a telegram at last, insisting that his attack on the English fishing fleet was accidental. The incident had been precipitated by the presence of two torpedo boats in the area, he said. They had tried to spare the fishing boats and begged "in the name of the whole fleet to apologize for the unfortunate affair, to express our sincere regret for the unfortunate victims of circumstances in which no warship could, even in times of profound peace, have acted otherwise."

It was not completely satisfactory, though the sensation was over in England. An international commission was appointed and Admiral Rozhdestvenski ordered officers from each ship involved to leave at once to give their account of the affair. This was his opportunity to get rid of Captain Klado, though he had been belowdecks when the attack started and had seen nothing. Klado was chosen to represent *Suvarov.* As he went off in the pinnace, another *Suvarov* officer muttered: "It is said that rats leave the ship before she sinks." Long afterward Admiral Rozhdestvenski was to realize his error in sending to the commission the one officer on board his flagship who was capable of causing him harm, though, so far as the Dogger Bank incident was concerned, Captain Klado remained adamant that torpedo boats had been involved. A correspondent from the *Echo de Paris* who interviewed him reported that Klado looked him straight in the eye and said: "I have been in the Navy for the last twenty-six years. I know what a torpedo boat is. I know what a fishing boat is. I know what a torpedo boat disguised like a fishing boat is, too. Well, I saw with my own eyes, and I could not be mistaken—two torpedo boats going toward the *Kniaz Suvarov,* ready to launch torpedoes against her."

The commission, which met in Paris in December, found that *Kamchatka,* "temporarily aroused by her isolation, the damages to her engines, and her own sense of weakness," had fired on several foreign ships before sending the signal to the fleet that she was being attacked by torpedo boats. Admiral Rozhdestvenski, though negligent in not stopping after the English fishing ships had been hit, personally did all he could to stop the attack on the Dogger Bank fishing fleet when he realized his mistake. Soon afterwards, Russia agreed to pay £65,000 in compensation to the families of the dead and injured fisherman and to provide new trawlers to replace those lost.

The fleet sailed from Vigo to the cheers of the Spanish crowds, while ten British warships steamed ahead, "as if convoying prizes of war."

Engineer Politovski was the busiest man in the squadron. *Orel,* the troublemaker, signaled that her steering engine was damaged, and the fleet stopped so that he could go aboard to make repairs. "When our ships stopped, the English probably took it for a hostile demonstration," he wrote to his wife.

They quickly assembled astern of our division and formed in battle order. Horrid folk! They are Russia's eternal enemy. They are cunning, powerful at sea, and insolent everywhere. All nations hate England, but it suits them to tolerate her. If you could only hear how furiously Spaniards abuse the English! They shake their fists and nearly foam at the mouth. If only they could they would gladly play some low trick on them. How many impediments has this "ruler of the sea" put on our voyage? Every impediment has come from Britannia.

From the bridge, Admiral Rozhdestvenski watched with Commander Semenov as the British ships maneuvered. One cruiser went off to the southeast at top speed, the others divided up into two pairs. "All their movements were so regular, all maneuvers were carried out at such speed and with so much precision, that they did not look as if they were due to unexpected orders, but as if a well-rehearsed play were being enacted before our eyes," wrote Semenov.

Behind him a voice asked: "Do you admire this?" He turned and saw Rozhdestvenski. "Do you admire that?" repeated the Admiral, his voice bitter with despair. "That is a real squadron. Those are seamen. Oh, if only we . . ." He broke off in midsentence and hurried down the companion ladder.

CHAPTER *25*

ᘒᘒᘒᘒᘒᘒ

The Long, Long Trail

W HILE GENERAL NOGI'S Third Army was endeavoring to wrap up Port Arthur for the Emperor's birthday, the Russians on land and sea celebrated the tenth anniversary of the Tsar's accession to the throne. In Port Arthur, disease had broken out, and men were dying at the rate of ten a day in the main hospital on Tiger's Tail Peninsula. Shells fell repeatedly on the ships in the harbor and occasionally in the streets of the town. Celebrations for Nicholas were confined to church parades and half-hearted toasts, in vodka or tea, to the long life of the Tsar.

Aboard the ships of the Baltic Fleet, things were more cheerful, despite the ominous news contained in a newspaper from Gibraltar: Stoessel had announced that Port Arthur would be his grave. The ten British warships had fallen back, however, and the men were looking forward to shore leave in Tangier on the following day. Admiral Rozhdestvenski made a short, spirited speech on the subject of the Tsar's anniversary, and vodka flowed freely above and belowdecks while the bands on all the ships played martial music. Afterward, the Admiral entertained the officers of the flagship at a grand lunch, where many of the toasts were not only to their Tsar but to the downfall and ruination of the Royal Navy.

In the middle of the afternoon of the following day, November 3, the three divisions of the fleet met at Tangier for the first time since leaving Libau. Rumors flew about the Dogger Bank incident. Two Japanese torpedo boats were said to be at Hull, probably the ones that had attacked the fleet. Russia was said to have bought seven more cruisers and they were on the way to join up with Rozhdestvenski's squadron. The local paper had the news that another Russian ship had been sunk off Port Arthur, but no name was given. The paper was unreliable, everyone said. For instance, one story reported that Rozhdestvenski had insulted an English admiral at Vigo, that guns were fired, and that the English had fled in disarray. Nobody could believe such lies.

Kamchatka, the repair ship, which had started all the trouble before the affair on the Dogger Bank, turned up, still out of breath, bragging of the 300 shells she had fired at the supposed enemy. Another late arrival was *Esperance,* a cold-storage ship, with a consignment of 1,000 tons of frozen meat. The hospital ship, also called *Orel,* painted white with a big red cross on her funnel, came into harbor with 100 nurses, including a niece of the Admiral, all dressed in white. *Orel*'s first patient was the unfortunate chaplain from the *Aurora,* who died of blood-poisoning. The fleet's first casualty had died from its own fire.

More important was the matter of coaling. In tropical rain, Rozhdestvenski's ships began to take on fuel from the waiting German colliers. Torrents of water poured down upon the mountains of Cardiff coal and flowed in dirty streams over the decks of the ships, while the men toiled to the strains of music from a dozen bands.

The Sultan of Morocco's representative welcomed Rozhdestvenski with great friendliness. He was told that he could stay at Tangier as long as he wished and do whatever he desired. The Sultan had received no official advice about the war between Russia and Japan. Indeed he had hardly heard of Japan and, anyway, the Prophet taught that all strangers were to be given hospitality. If the Japanese ever turned up in his country, he would probably treat them in the same friendly fashion.

The men stripped to the waist for coaling. The Admiral offered a reward of 1,500 roubles to the crew of the ship taking on the most coal in the shortest period of time. To the music of the bands the men lugged the heavy bags, their white teeth gleaming through black-stained faces. *Alexander III* won the prize by loading 400 tons of coal.

Rozhdestvenski prepared his fleet for the next leg of the journey, south to Dakar in French West Africa. Admiral Felkerzam had his flag changed from *Oslyabya* to the *Sissoi Veliki* and was instructed to take his division —his new flagship, *Navarin, Svetlana, Jemchug,* and *Almaz* and some of the auxiliary ships—through the Suez Canal. The ugly-duckling, top-heavy *Oslyabya* was attached to Rozhdestvenski's own division. Nobody but the Admiral knew why this change of plan had occurred, but most believed that he did not care to risk the older warships on the long journey around the Cape of Good Hope.

Admiral Felkerzam left at 9 P.M. with orders to meet the main fleet at Madagascar. The next day Rozhdestvenski's division prepared to leave Tangier. The battleship *Orel* had trouble almost immediately, and Politov-

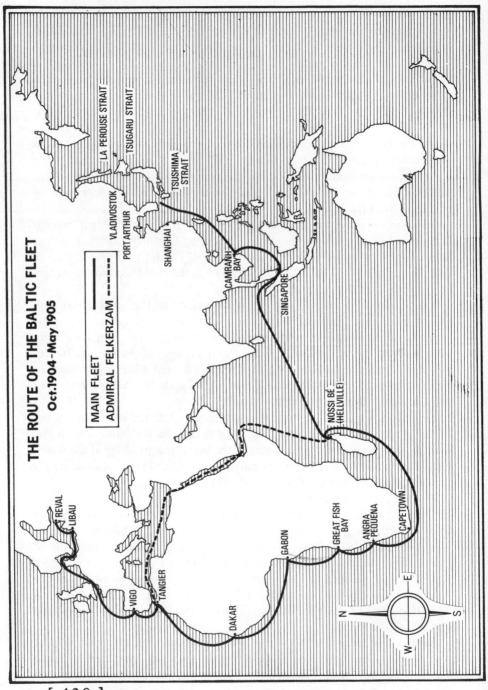

THE ROUTE OF THE BALTIC FLEET
Oct.1904 – May 1905

MAIN FLEET ———
ADMIRAL FELKERZAM -------

LA PEROUSE STRAIT
TSUGARU STRAIT
TSUSHIMA STRAIT
VLADIVOSTOK
PORT ARTHUR
SHANGHAI
CAMRANH BAY
SINGAPORE
NOSSI BÉ (HELLVILLE)
REVAL
LIBAU
GABON
GREAT FISH BAY
ANGRA PEQUENA
CAPETOWN
VIGO
TANGIER
DAKAR

N E S W

ski had to hold up the fleet while he went off in a cutter to make repairs. *Anadyr* caught her anchor chain in the underwater telegraph cable. "Lucky it was a French cable," mused the overworked chief engineer. "Had it been English, the scandal would have been dreadful. They would probably say, anyway, that it was done purposely so that no telegrams could be sent announcing our departure." The ships steamed in all directions after narrowly avoiding colliding with each other. On *Suvarov*, Rozhdestvenski shouted at his officers, stamping up and down the bridge, while his patient flag officer, Clapier de Colongue, tried to sort out the muddle. "Cut the cable!" roared the Admiral to *Anadyr's* captain, thereby interrupting Tangier's telegraphic communications with the outside world for several days. But the flagship was also in trouble. The ships had just begun to sort themselves out when her steering broke down and she bore down on the repair ship *Kamchatka*, which scooted out of the way. An hour later the damage was repaired and the fleet moved out.

In spite of the uprooted telegraphic cable, the foreign newspapermen filed bright stories of the unseemly departure, and details of the fleet's route. Blazing headlines announced: "ROZHDESTVENSKI STEAMS AROUND AFRICA—BALTIC FLEET SEPARATES AND TAKES DIFFERENT ROUTES." Few on board the Russian ships knew why Rozhdestvenski had decided to split up the fleet. All they knew were the long, hot days at sea, through deserted waters, rough and wild. As the white-painted houses of Tangier disappeared in the rain clouds, the homesick sailors thought of their faraway peasant homes, of wives and families, and wondered if they would see any of them again. Some, like Novikov-Priboy, the revolutionary paymaster-steward in the troublesome *Orel*, immersed themselves in the subversive books so lavishly supplied by the ship's engineer officer.

Once or twice British cruisers appeared by night. In the daytime they kept out of sight. By the time the fleet had passed the Canary Islands, all had disappeared. As the fleet approached the Equator, the heat became more oppressive. Politovski wore only a cross when he turned in at night, sharing his cabin with the rats that kept him awake. All portholes were closed and the air was stuffy and damp. It was like living in a steambath.

Ten colliers were waiting at Dakar with 30,000 tons of coal to be taken on board ships already overloaded with the filthy coal. "What are we to do?" asked Captain Nicolai Victorovitch Yung of *Orel*. "What on earth are we to do? I never heard of such a thing. How can I possibly keep the ship clean with a thousand tons of coal lying about in odd corners?"

Each battleship had to take on an additional thousand tons more than her bunkers could hold. The German ships had been waiting for five days with their 30,000 tons, all of which had to be taken on the voyage. Rozhdestvenski knew that at most ports along the 6,300 miles to Madagascar he would have difficulties concerning coaling. He gave orders for the coal to be stowed in every possible space—on upper and lower decks; in bathrooms and engine rooms, workshops and corridors; in bags between the guns and loose on the quarterdeck.

The news that the Russian ships would coal at Dakar spread round the world. The British and the Japanese protested that this was a breach of neutrality. No sooner had Rozhdestvenski's ships anchored than the port commander came aboard the flagship and ordered them out within twenty-four hours. Rozhdestvenski replied that this was most unfair. "I shall continue coaling until your coast batteries stop me coaling," he replied. The Frenchman explained that they had no coast batteries at Dakar. The two men shook hands, toasted each other in champagne, and the coaling continued.

The temperature was now 120 degrees and humidity above ninety percent. During the day it was like working in a furnace. Men stripped entirely and worked with oakum stuffed between their teeth or cloths over their mouths and noses to avoid being choked by the coal dust. They gagged and coughed and sweated, rushing up on deck for air and a hosing down before returning to the coaling. A few cases of heatstroke were inevitable, and the son of the Russian minister to France collapsed and died from the heat. "We are tormented by thirst, hot and unpleasant, but one drinks incessantly. I alone drank six bottles of lemonade today," wrote Politovski, who was not coaling. "Our comings, our goings, our voyage, our success, depend on coal. . . . Coal dust has penetrated everywhere. Into the cabins, the cupboards, onto the tables, the decks are clouded with dust, everyone is so black that you do not recognize people at once. . . ."

The battleships could normally load from 1,100 to 1,200 tons of coal each, but the Admiral knew that this would not last to the nearest port. On the other hand, if they loaded more they might overturn. Politovski pointed out that in a heavy sea everything would depend on whether the ports of the lower battery decks held. Rozhdestvenski decided to take the risk and the ships were all laden with as much coal as would poke into every corner.

In some of the ships that night ices were served to the officers with dinner. The men on night shift were given tots of vodka to keep them going, and enormous quantities of seltzer water and lemon drinks were consumed. After sunset, when the heat of the day had gone, the young officer who had died from sunstroke was buried in the town, with full military honors. The chief engineer, the doctor from *Suvarov,* and other officers went ashore for the funeral, and afterwards wandered around the dreary, dusty town. Politovski asked a Negro waiter for the menu and was presented with cards, dice, and a glass of lemonade. He wrote to his wife that night to tell her of the God-forsaken town where no one spoke Russian, and mentioned the

Japanese spies he had seen in the shops and the naked children and natives bedecked with amulets. On the way back to *Suvarov,* the ship's doctor foolishly picked some unknown fruit from a tree and became violently ill.

The fleet moved out of Dakar, "not up to the neck but over the ears" with coal, carrying sick and dispirited men, unable to eat but thirsting for drinks. They eased their parched throats with everything but water. The little water available for drinking purposes was desalinated and unpalatable. Seltzer water, tea, beer, vodka, and red and white wines were popular, but *kvass,* brewed from yeast, flour, and malt, proved the favorite thirst-quencher on many of the ships.

With over 2,000 miles to their next coaling port, the ships lurched heavily through the high seas. Asked his expert opinion on the fleet's chances, Politovski could say only that if they escaped strong winds things might be all right. "When the maindeck ports no longer hold and the water pours in—then good-bye." He was kept constantly at work on *Malay* as the fleet stopped for five hours while he made repairs. Early in the morning, *Donskoi* signaled that she had sand in her seacocks, and the *Borodino's* engines were not working properly. The fleet halted again.

At Dakar, the sailors had brought birds on board the ships. Since they had not thought to provide food for them, they were dying everywhere. Crews slept on their newly bought native mats on deck to avoid the heat. The floors of the cabins were too hot to walk in bare feet. Perhaps the terrible heat was partly to blame, but on some of the ships the first signs of revolt began to appear. Many of *Kamchatka's* crew, especially the stokers, were civilians. There were constant threats of strikes, and Rozhdestvenski took firm action, promising to put the malcontents in open boats to find their own way to shore. On other ships, men insulted their officers, who retaliated with brutality. The heat got everyone down. Ships ran out of formation, reeling along "like drunken men," and time after time Rozhdestvenski sent out furious signals. "You don't know how to command your ship," he told the captains of *Orel* and *Borodino.* As punishment, the offending vessels were told to break line and steam to starboard of the flagship, like naughty schoolchildren made to stand in a corner.

To make matters worse, the fleet got lost. Gabon was close by but could not be found. The tug *Roland* was sent to investigate, returning to state that they were thirty miles south of their destination. The fleet retraced its steps, crossing the Equator for the second time, and anchoring in an estuary, four miles offshore. At least they had not capsized. St. Nicholas the Just and the newly canonized Seraphim of Serov, the Tsaritsa's favorite saint, had brought them safely to another wild shore.

The governor brought aboard baskets of tropical flowers and fruits, pineapples, bananas, mangoes, and "something else" quite unknown to the

Russian sailors. He was pleased to welcome them, but also delighted that they would be coaling a short distance out to sea. The coaling was completed in a little bay out of sight of the town. While repairs were being carried out, the Admiral put his ships through gunnery practice, maneuvers, and formation changes. Nothing was well done. The fleet was becoming rusty, and the guns had been fired only once since they left Libau—at the Dogger Bank fishing fleet. The exotic tropical shore, with little white houses above the sandy beaches, beckoned the ship-bound men. Three young officers in *Donskoi* borrowed a boat and took one of the nurses from the hospital ship for a visit to the steamy little town. On the return trip the searchlights picked them up, and the three dissolute officers were sent home to Russia to be court-martialed.

Before the fleet left the tempting barren shores of Gabon, some of the officers and men were allowed ashore, most of them for the first time in six weeks. They discovered huge boa constrictors, eighteen feet long, and moths as big as dinner plates and marveled at the natives, many of whom were cannibals. They watched as young monkeys were soaked in bogs to make them tender for the pot. It was whispered that these savages ate their own dead, after cutting off the hands and feet and tenderizing them as they did the monkeys. They bought fruit and bright parrots and baby monkeys back to the ships, and some sailors, starved for female companionship, found the native women attractive. One group of officers escorted some natives back to their ship and treated them to brandy and a tour of the warship. They drank and laughed and sang sad songs, forgetting for a time the voyage and what lay ahead. Politovski and his friends called on the native king, "just a wild nigger," he wrote to his wife. "The king received the officers in an English naval uniform and cocked hat, no trousers or shirt, and introduced them to his several wives."

After crossing the equator, they headed for Great Fish Bay in Angola, a Portuguese colony, and immediately *Malay* signaled that she needed help. More and more ships signaled that they had sickness on board, and the fortunate patients were transferred to the hospital ship *Orel* and the ministrations of the angels of mercy. On through the dark African nights and the burning days the fleet lumbered along in the heavy swell until they reached Great Fish Bay, with nothing to see but sand and sea. The Portuguese, "Britain's oldest allies," were not inclined to permit coaling even outside the three-mile limit. The captain of the Portuguese gunboat *Limpopo* insulted the Admiral and ordered him to leave at once. There was to be no loading of coal or food. Rozhdestvenski, controlling his fury, explained that they were outside the Portuguese territorial waters and that he would take the coal from the waiting German colliers.

"But you are anchored in the bay. That is the point," said the Portuguese.

"In this respect we can only thank the Lord that He made the entrance of the bay wider than six miles, and that between the two strips of Portuguese territorial waters, the neutrality of which is, of course, sacred to me, He had placed a narrow strip of sea, open and accessible to all," replied the Admiral.

Rozhdestvenski took on his coal. Politovski made his repairs to *Malay* and other ships, and they left the unfriendly shores of Great Fish Bay for Angra Pequena in German Southwest Africa, the last stop before Madagascar, which was to be the meeting place with Felkerzam's squadron and the place for refitting before the long trip across the Indian Ocean.

Now it was cooler but the terrors of the trip were taking their toll. An officer was buried at sea and another fell into a coal shute and broke his leg. A sailor in *Orel* went insane, calling and sobbing that the Japanese were after him. "We shall all be sunk, we shall all be sunk," he cried over and over again. He could not be transferred to the hospital ship, which had already gone on ahead, so he was confined to a cabin. His ravings and forebodings of disaster could be heard by everyone who passed by and it had a bad effect on the crew. They had now been at sea for over two months, without news from home, sailing into the unknown.

The Germans at Angra Pequena were fêted on the Russian flagship while Rozhdestvenski waited for the howling wind to die down so that he could begin coaling. The seas were too rough for the colliers to come in and they stood out at sea, crashing against the sides of the war ships in an alarming fashion. The Admiral's temper became worse and he shouted at everyone, especially the long suffering Clapier de Colongue. After two days the storm died down and coaling began.

Rozhdestvenski finished the storm in a bad state. As he climbed down from the bridge, everyone noticed how old and tired he looked after days with little sleep. He had good reasons. During the storm, when he feared for his entire squadron, news had arrived that a flotilla of Japanese sailing schooners had assembled at Durban, armed with torpedo tubes. At the same time the Admiral received a polite note from the British government, mentioning in passing that many fishing ships would be met on the route around Durban. A repetition of the Hull affair was highly undesirable. Rozhdestvenski, terrified of Japanese torpedo boats, sent a reply to the effect that any Durban fishing vessel trying to break through the squadron would be destroyed. He sent it in clear, not code, so that the world would understand.

During coaling, news come that 203 Meter Hill overlooking Port Arthur had been captured by the Japanese. Rozhdestvenski shrugged. The faroff hill had no meaning to him. The fleet was his concern. "203 Meter Hill, and what is that?" he snapped.

Full to overflowing with the filthy coal, the fleet left Africa on December

17, sailing into the South Atlantic, and celebrated St. Nicholas's day, with mass, prayers, salutes, and plenty of vodka. Table Mountain faded behind them and they headed for the Cape, through storm-whipped waves sometimes as high as seventy feet. "If we double the Cape in safety, then thanks be to God," wrote Politovski.

Malay signaled that her engines had broken down and she put up sails in a feeble attempt to make headway, and then disappeared, "drifting in the gale like a wind-blown leaf." Rozhdestvenski ordered searchlights turned on her to show her the course, but there was little else he could do. The fleet passed by the little ship, with her small and wretched sails, without stopping. Politovski watched helplessly as *Suvarov* went by without lessening speed. His own ship, *Borodino,* his pride and joy, left the line for a while, and he sweated till she came back to the fleet without his paternal assistance. Each ship now could think only of herself. Water poured over the decks and cascaded into cabins and galleys. Astern of the flagship the *Alexander III* was tossed like a cork on the mountainous waves. "Sometimes her bows were at the bottom of a wave, and her stern at the top; and then all her deck, from bow to stern, could be seen from *Suvarov,*" Politovski wrote to his wife, adding that the *Borodino,* the ship he had built, was the best-behaved of all—a ship to be proud of.

There was nothing to do but forge ahead through the hurricane. The nearest port was a thousand miles away. For two days and nights they rode it out, pitching and tossing and disappearing in the valleys of the waves. And all the time the streams of water mixed with black coal swirled and slushed over everything.

Everywhere there was trouble. *Suvarov* got a fire in her coal bunkers, though this was quickly put out, and then a little later damaged her steering wheel. Five minutes later a steampipe burst and badly scalded two seamen. The tug *Roland* got out of line and disappeared toward the coast.

The worst ship in the fleet, *Kamchatka,* signaled frantically that her coal was bad, requesting permission to throw overboard 150 tons. Calmly, the Admiral signaled back: "Find the guilty ones and throw them overboard, but not the coal." A little later *Kamchatka* asked: "Do you see the torpedo boats?" Crews were alerted, officers were wakened from their sleep and buglers and drummers stationed to sound off quarters for action—a general alarm. "Sorry," she signaled a little later. The signalman had used the wrong code. What he intended to say was, "We are all right now." *Kamchatka* should never have gone to sea.

CHAPTER 26

ଐଐଐଐଐଐ

The Fall of Port Arthur

B<small>Y THE MIDDLE OF</small> N<small>OVEMBER</small> the big siege guns ordered by General Kodama from Japan arrived at the shattered railway station at Chang-lin-tzu, eight miles from Port Arthur—the last station outside the zone of Russian fire. Each gun, weighing eight tons without its carriage, had to be hauled for several miles up the precipitous hills. Horses or oxen created too much commotion for a task that had to be carried out as silently as possible. Teams of men took their places, 800 to a gun. They moved at night, often in heavy rain, and under constant Russian fire, dragging the siege guns on sleds attached to big black cables as thick as a man's leg. Four abreast, with hemp thongs across their shoulders, they hauled the guns over rocks and crevices and through deep mud toward their positions in the hills.

Thousands of 500-pound shells for the big guns also had to be brought from the railhead to be transported to the emplacements on the hills. Each shell was lugged fifteen miles from the railway and then loaded on small carts drawn by soldiers who pulled three shells at a time up the steep hills.

While engineers cut trenches nearer and nearer to the still-defiant forts, and engineers installed underground mines beneath the Russian positions, the eleven-inch mortars moved slowly up the hills to concrete emplacements eight feet deep, prepared for their installation. From the hills already captured the Japanese could see some of the Russian ships lying in the harbor. But only 203 Meter Hill could provide direct observation to the entire harbor, including the inner basin and the dockyards. Maps of Old and New Town were accurate enough for effective shelling of selected official buildings and storehouses, but the ships moved constantly. Until an observation post could be placed on 203 Meter Hill, the Russian fleet, though practically denuded of men and arms, could not be destroyed, and the Japanese Combined Fleet, urgently in need of repairs for the coming battle with the Russian Baltic Fleet, could not return to Japan.

By November 15, the tunneling was progressing slowly but effectively, though the Russians, creeping into the sap-heads at night, made constant attacks on the Japanese working parties. The saps were being carried much closer to the Russian forts and at the same time shafts were driven beneath some of the permanent defenses and filled with dynamite. As the Japanese burrowed their way through their trenches, the hiding of the excavated earth became a major problem. Sappers in the front lines threw spadefuls of earth and rock between their legs to the men behind, and it was passed backwards through the saps and carried away in bamboo baskets, far beyond the zigzagging lines of trenches.

In Tokyo, the press and the public clamored for news of the fall of the fortress. Rumors reached Japan that men sent to Port Arthur were treated like sheep on the way to the slaughterhouse. Old men and young boys straight from military college were sent to Port Arthur. And for the first time in Japan's history a dozen or more women were sent to join the ranks.* Feeling against General Nogi, "the showoff," became intense. From the armies in the north and from the navy the news that reached Japan was always good news. From Port Arthur there was nothing. The newspapers demanded that 100,000 men should be sent to reinforce Nogi's Third Army, and Marshal Yamagata, who had appointed Nogi as commander of the Third Army, now proposed that he should be replaced. The Emperor was present when his proposal was considered. He put an end to the discussion. "Who would replace him?" he asked and left the room.

Marshal Oyama wanted Kodama to supplant Nogi, however, and again Kodama went to Port Arthur with plans to transfer the central point of attack to 203 Meter Hill. Richard Barry, a young Irish-American correspondent, working for the *Eastern Illustrated War News*, the San Francisco *Chronicle*, and other publications, met Kodama at the residence of the former Russian mayor of Dalny. Barry found the general, dressed only in a kimono, curled up on the red cushions of the ex-mayoral chair. He was smoking a big cigar and cleaning his nails with a knife. "I could hardly

---

*Several Russian women, disguised as men, also fought at Port Arthur. One peasant woman from Siberia followed her lover from the north, borrowed a uniform, and fought alongside him during the siege. She was killed at Fort Chi-kuan. When the Japanese captured the fort they found her body and buried her with the other Russian dead. Ellis Ashmead-Bartlett, who came to Port Arthur at the end of the siege, was shown a letter telling of her heroic deeds and a photograph of her taken in the trenches.

realize on looking at the wee figure that it could be the genius of the great war, the man the whole Japanese empire depended on for the success of the campaign," wrote Barry. Now that he was to direct operations at Port Arthur, Kodama had few doubts about the fate of the fortress. "I hold it here," he said, extending his small cupped palm to the correspondent, "in the hollow of my hand. Port Arthur is strong—very strong, but we will take it. We will!"

He gave Nogi one more chance. From November seventeenth to the twenty-fourth, with limited success and at the cost of many Japanese lives, mines were exploded under some of the Russian forts. The third general attack on the fortress was planned to begin on November 26. Nogi was very depressed. He had not slept for three days and nights. "I don't know what more I can do," he said. "I am willing to hand over the right of command to anyone suitable." Since Nogi was happy to accept advice, Kodama did not oust him, and Nogi pushed ahead with the saps and trundled the big guns into position for the main attack on 203 Meter Hill.

A message from the Emperor, urging him on to victory, and a poem, in classical Chinese and of his own composition, from Yamagata, referring to Nogi's belief in visions and his tardiness in taking the fortress, did little to raise Nogi's spirits. The poem was entitled, "Last night I dreamed of the fall of Port Arthur."

> Like thunder a hundred guns shook the heavens!
> Half a year of siege, and myriad corpses!
> With a will that is stronger than iron,
> At last I have conquered Port Arthur!

The pre-assault concentrated mainly on the forts along the Chinese Wall, from Chi-kuan in the east to Sung-shu in the west, in order to prevent a concentration of the Russian forces on 203 Meter Hill. The usual storm assaults took place, with the Japanese rushing across the open ground under Russian artillery and machinegun fire. Around the foothills and the line of forts the casualties were as heavy as they had been during the two previous general assaults. Inside the fortifications, both sides exploded mines, burying thousands of men and blowing others to pieces. The Japanese dead had to be shoveled into rice bags to make room for the living. Asphyxiating gases, hand grenades, balls of trash, dung, and torpedoes from the ships were all used by the Russians to drive the Japanese from the underground passages.

At Sung-shu ("Pine Tree Hill"), a final attempt was made to take the fort on the night of November 26. General Nakamura called for a kamikaze attack on the fort, and 2,600 men of all ranks, including 1,200 from the newly arrived Seventh Division, set out with instructions not to fire a shot until the troops were inside the fort. Only bayonets were to be used if they met Russian troops. "The object of our detachment is to cut Port Arthur into two," Nakamura told the troops. "No man must hope to return alive. . . . Every officer of whatever rank shall appoint his successor. The attack shall be chiefly effected with the bayonet . . . the officers are authorized to kill those men who, without proper reason, straggle behind or separate themselves from the ranks, or retreat."

For two miles they marched in columns of four, unmolested, until they came to a bridge just above the railway line. Here, one formation of eighty men from the Seventh Division, fresh from Hokkaido, took a wrong turn and ran into a party of 400 Russian scouts. The Japanese were all killed or captured. The remainder crossed the railway line and, within sight of the fort, were caught and held in the Russian searchlights.

A company of Russian seamen held a hill outside Sung-shu and after several hours of hand-to-hand fighting General Nakamura was seriously wounded. More than a thousand men were killed. Many of the survivors were frozen to death in the below-zero temperature and next morning hundreds of closely packed bodies lay on the slopes below the battery.

A ceasefire was called for on November 27 to collect the dead. Russian and Japanese soldiers stood together, while all around lay the dead of both sides. The Japanese and Russians spent a long time looking for signs of life before they returned to their own lines. There were no wounded left. Those who had not been killed in the battle had been frozen to death in the blinding snowstorms of the previous two days.

During the freezing days and nights of winter fighting, the Japanese troops wore dark blue uniforms that stood out starkly against the snow-covered ground. Often on duty in the front lines the men pulled their summer-weight khaki tunics over their dark uniforms or made overalls from sacking as camouflage. Sometimes they wore their dark gray underwear over the dark winter uniforms in order to be less conspicuous.

The Russian soldiers often went into battle wearing heavy greatcoats that weighed them down when they charged over the snow-covered ground. But during these November assaults they fought furiously and bravely. In two days the Japanese had lost another ten thousand men, with nothing gained but a few ditches around Erh-lung and Sung-shu forts.

Port Arthur had won a reprieve. General Kondratenko, now in command of all the land defenses, began to move his men, including sailors from the fleet, and orderlies from the naval barracks, toward 203 Meter Hill. Without observation posts, the Japanese were firing blindly and at random into the town and installations. A civilian told of the conditions within the fortress, where sickness, fear, and lack of proper food added to the misery of the inhabitants of the town and the men of the fortress.

The time will come when there will be no bearing the inconvenience of the siege. . . . no enduring the unceasing hell of bursting shells—shattering houses, killing unfortunate friends, and tearing huge holes in the ground—to say nothing of the miasma arising from a thousand corpses rotting on the hills and in the ravines round the forts. . . .

The conflict among those in authority continued. General Stoessel, though long ago recalled from duty in Port Arthur, was still "the Tsar's ambassador." He countermanded his commandant's orders, encouraging his ally, General Fock, to spread discontent among the garrison. Fock, long dismissed by General Smirnov for disobeying orders, found satisfaction in writing and distributing anti-Smirnov propaganda. Early in November, Fock, with Stoessel's approval, published a memorandum comparing the besieged fortress to a man suffering from gangrene. "In the same way that he must sooner or later succumb, so too, must a fortress fall," it read. "No doctor would torture a patient by attempting to reunite the amputated organs . . . no commandant should waste his men in an attempt to recapture a position once yielded to the enemy, even though it were abandoned through carelessness. . . ."

It was a sure and deadly poison for the fortress defenders, many of them ill with scurvy and other diseases. Fifteen thousand patients filled the hospitals of the town. "They lie side by side on the floor, on the bedboards, underneath them, just as they were placed when they came in," wrote Nojine. "The faces are shapeless, swollen, and distorted, and upon the yellow skin are large blue bruises . . . outside it is freezing; inside, in spite of the musty and sickening stench, the cold is intense. On all sides is filth, nothing but filth, and on it and among it crawl millions of greasy gray lice."

All healthy persons, including women, engaged in some sort of defense work. Only the few remaining children seemed indifferent to the bombardment of the town. Their favorite game was a sort of roulette. They divided the streets of New Town into squares with imaginary lines and bet on which part of the town the next shell would fall, and how big it would be.

Admiral Viren, who had taken over what remained of the fleet after Vitgeft's death in August, had little to do but provide men, guns, and ammunition to the land defense of the fortress and watch his ships being gradually pounded to pieces by the Japanese fire. Port Arthur, enveloped in mist and snow, with biting winds coming in from the sea, was full of misery. Only a few were still hopeful of success, including Smirnov, Tretyakov, and the indefatigable Kondratenko, who from the first attack in February had toiled to complete the fortifications of the sadly neglected line of hills.

The Japanese also had their differences. From the beginning the army and the navy had vied for recognition. Each had its heroes, and when battles on land or at sea were successful, they received publicity at home and abroad. Commander Hirose and Warrant-Officer Sugino, who had died in the blockship *Fukui Maru*, were made "war gods." A colonel who had died at Liaoyang was another. Nogi was a potential "war god," but so far his efforts at Port Arthur had resulted only in the deaths of thousands of men to no purpose. The army was annoyed that the navy had won the two first battles of the war, at Chemulpo and Port Arthur. It was felt, also, that the navy had not cooperated as it should have in the defense of army landings. There was conflict, also, between the Satsumas and the Choshus, though Oyama, if not always cheerfully, accepted Kodama's tactical preeminence.

Port Arthur's western front, which included Akasaka Yama and 203 Meter Hill, was under the command of Colonel Tretyakov. 203 Hill's defenses had again been strengthened. A four-gun battery had been installed on its crest. The main defense consisted of a 600-foot trench, four feet wide and seven feet deep, twisting up toward the breastwork at the summit, and a lower trench that had not been completely fortified. Wire entanglements surrounded the foot of the hill and rifle pits were placed to direct fire on the slope below. Tretyakov's force on 203 Meter Hill consisted of three companies of the Fifth Regiment, one company of the Fourteenth, and one of the Twenty-seventh, engineers, and some seamen machinegunners. Food and water were both short in these positions and the only meat for the forces was horse or mule flesh, occasionally replenished by fish caught in nearby ponds and small birds, mostly nighthawks, which the men shot in the woods.

The Japanese decided now to take 203 by storm and to carry Akasaka Yama at the same time. For the task they used the First Division and a portion of the Thirty-eighth Kobi Regiment. Two battalions of the Twenty-sixth Regiment of the Seventh Division were held in reserve in trenches, and the attack was supported by four eleven-inch howitzers from a nearby hill and field guns and howitzers emplaced on three sides of the Russian position.

For two days the two hills changed hands several times. It was impossible from one side of the hill to see what was happening on the other. Every now and then a new batch of Russians climbed up the perilous slopes to take the place of dead and wounded and to replace the sailors who occasionally deserted their posts under the fearful fire. Tretyakov usually forgave them, ordering the officers to stay with their men. The mixed army of riflemen and sailors responded to Tretyakov's encouragement, and sometimes to being hit over the head with his sword ("the flat, of course"). He found that the sight of a Japanese flag, carried to the crest of the hill by some adventurous volunteer, brought instantaneous response. "Go and take it down, my lads," he would shout, and always his sailor-troops rushed up the slopes to haul down the hated flag waving in the breeze atop the crest.

By November 30 the Japanese realized that the capture of the position by assault was impracticable. Because of the hard, frozen ground, cover could be obtained only by building up parapets of rocks and the bodies of dead or half-dead men to shelter the living. The artillery was brought in and soon 203 Meter Hill was hidden in great clouds of smoke and dust. The Russian position was in ruins, with the sides of the trenches falling in. If a man tried to reach the hill other than along the trenches, he was immediately killed. The Russians were running out of weapons as well as men. With their rifles full of dust and overheated from continual firing, they used hand grenades which were made in the town and in one day they threw more than 7,000 at the Japanese, sometimes at a distance of a few yards.

During these days General Nogi's second and favorite son, Yasusuke, was killed, shot through the head while carrying a message to the front. Nogi was dozing in his chair in his command tent when his staff officer came to break the news. "Was it after he had completed his task or was it before?" he asked. His staff officer replied that Yasusuke had delivered the message and had been on the way back to his regiment when he had been killed. Nogi said that he was pleased that the task had been completed. "I often wonder how I could apologize to His Majesty and to the people for having killed so many of my men. But now that my son has been killed. . . ." Shirai, his staff officer, saw tears in the General's eyes, as he asked what should be done with the body. "Cremate it," he was told. "Turn it into ashes."

Many bodies could not be burned or buried and were left to rot for months where they had fallen. When collection of the dead Japanese could take place, identification cards were removed. Wherever possible, the Adam's apple was cut out so that a small bone, the *nodo-botoke* or "Little Buddha," could be sent home to relatives.*

By November 30 it was impossible for the Russian or Japanese artillery to fire at the crest of 203 Meter Hill for fear of hitting their own men. The Japanese Seventh Division under General Oseko was ordered to support the First Division for a final assault. The troops massed in the valleys to pass

---

*"According to the shape of this little bone when found after the burning, the future condition of the dead may be predicted. Should the next state to which the soul be destined be one of happiness, the bone will have the form of a small image of Buddha. But if the next birth is to be unhappy, then the bone will have either an ugly shape, or no shape at all. At the great temple of Tennojii, at Osaka, all such bones are dropped into a vault. . . . After a hundred years from the beginning of this curious collection, all these bones are to be ground into a kind of paste, out of which a colossal statue of Buddha is to be made."—Lafcadio Hearn, *Out of the East.*

by their ensigns. As each battalion went by, it saluted the flag and swore to take the hill or not return. The Seventh Division surged up the hill in a series of rushes, making for the rear of the fort, but the Russian snipers picked them off as they ran, finishing them off with the bayonet. Very few of the reserves from the mountains of Hokkaido were alive at the end of the day.

On the night of November 30 General Kodama was told that 203 Meter Hill had at last fallen to the Japanese. The next morning at breakfast he learned that the Russians had recaptured the hill. He threw his plate on the ground and walked angrily from the room to see Nogi. This time he came straight to the point and said he wanted to issue the orders. Nogi thought about it for a moment and then agreed. Though he had Oyama's letter in his pocket, naming him as Nogi's successor, Kodama still hesitated to produce it. Nogi might eventually hand over the Third Army by his own decision, but the order from Oyama requiring him to stand down would bring disgrace on the Third Army and on Nogi, and he would kill himself.

Tretyakov's gallant defense was nearing its end, however. With a silver cross around his neck as a charm, he stood in a deep ravine near one of the dressing stations where the slopes of the hill were covered with dead sailors and soldiers. He called the unwounded men together and climbed the road toward the crest to launch a fresh counterattack. In the pitch black night fire from rifles, machineguns, and grenades fell on the Russian attackers. All around, wounded men were calling for help among the piles of dead. At the top, the path was blocked with mangled bodies. Suddenly, he heard shouts. A company of his men paused and wavered and one or two men rushed back in disorder. Soon men were pouring out of the breastworks, tumbling over each other in their hurry to leave the hill. "Stop! Stop!" Tretyakov called to them. "Reinforcements are on the way."

The panic passed and he gathered them in again and led them against the breastwork. Riflemen and sailors rushed together, and in a few moments they had recaptured the place at the point of the bayonet. Once they were back on the summit, it was a simple task to throw their grenades on to the retreating enemy, and the Japanese were driven from the hill. By midnight fire had ceased all along the line, but the Russian defenses had been seriously damaged. During the day more than 1,000 Japanese shells had been fired at 203 Meter Hill and Akasaka Yama, reinforced by hospital personnel, slightly wounded patients, and servants.

The Japanese now concentrated on 203 Meter Hill. The summit was soon covered with smoke and billowing clouds of dust. On the morning of December 1 the Russians clinging to the southern end of the hill were throwing hand grenades at the Japanese from a distance of a few yards. On the northern side of the hill the eleven-inch guns fired continuously, but on the following day all was quiet from the Japanese side. It was soon realized that they were pushing their trenches forward. By the morning of the fourth the Japanese were swarming around the southern hump of the hill.

That evening many of Tretyakov's officers were blown up by fire from the Japanese eleven-inch guns, and he himself was badly injured. The next counterattack failed, and one more piece of Hill 203 fell to the Japanese. Kondratenko was forced to withdraw.

General Oseko's Seventh Division, which had arrived from Japan only a few weeks before, had been reduced to a thousand men. He asked to be allowed to attack again. Kodama looked up at the weeping commander. "Let them do it once more," he said. The Seventh Division fought for the next week, losing almost all its remaining men.

Another truce was called in the east, where hostilities had ceased. General Nogi had agreed to the truce on condition that fighting on other fronts for Hill 203 should not be interrupted. The Japanese truce party produced bottles of saké, beer, and food, and the Russians, not to be outdone, arrived with claret, champagne, and little cakes. For three hours the stretcher parties collected dead and wounded.

By the time the collection of the dead and injured was over, not a single Russian was alive on the western side of Hill 203. On the northern peak, small groups of Japanese were climbing to the breastworks, and soon two battalions occupied the whole ridge. The Russian side of the hill was being swept by artillery fire and reinforcements could not be brought in. About 4 P.M. on December 5 the only Russian officer alive on the hill reported that the Japanese were holding the whole summit on the northern side. He called for reinforcements, and almost immediately the telephone went dead. By 5 P.M. the whole of 203 Meter Hill was in Japanese hands.

On the top of the hill Japanese soldiers could be seen outlined against the sky. Before them lay the harbor and the Russian warships. General Kondratenko organized two desperate counterattacks, but the commanders of the companies were all killed or wounded. The western side of the hill had been pounded by the eleven-inch shells, so that little remained of the Russian entrenchments. Despite the enormous losses, the Japanese infantry alone had been unable to take the hill. The defense was broken down, not by the determination of the Japanese infantry, but by the fire of the Japanese siege guns, which finally converted the works into shapeless heaps of rubble.

Fourteen thousand Japanese soldiers and more than 5,000 Russians had died in the battle for this one small hill. "The mountain after its capture would have been an ideal spot for a peace conference," wrote Ellis Ashmead-Bartlett, a British correspondent. "There have probably never been so many dead crowded into so small a space since the French stormed the great redoubt at Borodino." The faces of the young boys who had fought for the first and last time touched the hearts of the hard-bitten correspondents who had been counting the dead for months. For weeks before the battle they had marched along roads strewn with bodies of men who had fallen before them, knowing that their fate must be the same. "They had stamped on their features all the various emotions that are supposed to animate young soldiers on such occasions. Their look was a mingled one of determination, anxiety, and of immense astonishment. No doubt that is exactly how they felt when the iron storm burst upon them."

On December 6 an observation post had been installed on the hill, and siege guns already erected on the surrounding positions were pounding the harbor. By the next day Admiral Togo could report that not a single ship moved on the harbor—all was quiet. "The enemy seem to have completely abandoned their fleet and given them up to us for targets without an attempt to save them."

Many of the 500-pound shells intended for the Russian ships came over into the town, and some fell on the hospitals. In vain, Stoessel pleaded with Nogi to spare the hospitals, some of whose patients were Japanese wounded. Nogi's reply was blunt: "As we all know, shells cannot necessarily be expected to exactly reach the intended points." He refused to limit the zone of his fire.

Of the Russian ships, only *Sevastopol* was intact. Togo was determined to finish this last ship of the Russian Port Arthur squadron. So long as she remained afloat the Japanese battleships had to remain in the area. Once she had been destroyed the Japanese ships could return to Japan for repairs before meeting Rozhdestvenski's fleet. But, as Captain Pakenham pointed out, there was another reason why *Sevastopol* could not be allowed to escape. So far it had been a military victory bought with the blood, courage, and skill of the army. The sailors realized that if they let *Sevastopol* go, it would be a slur on the navy. "The navy feels that it has been deprived of a glorious opportunity of showing its worth, and is, moreover, not yet assured it can carry out successfully the minor duty that has devolved upon it," Pakenham wrote.

Sevastopol had 120 torpedoes fired at her as she lay in the outer harbor at Port Arthur protected by booms and close to the shore of the Tiger's Tail. For nearly three weeks she fought off the Japanese torpedo boats with the assistance of several Russian destroyers. The Japanese battleships and cruisers stood at sea to prevent her from escaping and guns from the top of 203 Meter Hill tried to fire on her, though she was hidden from sight and protected by a hill. She was badly damaged by the rain of torpedoes and at dead of night on January 2, her commander, Captain von Essen, had her towed out to sea, with only 100 men of her original complement of 600 on board. Then he sank his ship by opening the seacocks, and he and the crew took to the boats. She heeled to starboard and in ten minutes went down in thirty fathoms of water. Of the thirty-five vessels which took part in the attacks, two Japanese torpedo boats were lost and six others badly damaged while thirty-five Japanese officers and men were killed. Another casualty was the protected cruiser *Takasago,* which struck a floating mine while keeping a guard on the Russian battleship. The ship sank with the loss of 274 men.

Sevastopol's valiant fight with the Japanese torpedo boats had shown what the Russian Pacific Fleet was capable of. Now it was too late. Admiral Viren sent his destroyers to sea at night. They were all captured or interned. *Peresvyet* was scuttled by the Russians, but every other ship of the fleet, except *Sevastopol,* was stuck in the mud on the bottom of Port Arthur harbor.

Togo left *Mikasa* and climbed with General Nogi to the crest of 203 Meter Hill. Nogi would have ridden, but, because he knew that Togo had always been terrified of horses, they clambered on foot through the snow strewn with the bodies of the soldiers who had won Port Arthur. "The meeting was as quiet as a still lake," wrote a member of Togo's staff. Satisfied that none of the ships in the harbor below could ever fight against him, he telegraphed the navy department the news of a victory that was not his to relate and for which he claimed no glory. Togo was ordered to Tokyo to report to the nation.

The foreign and Japanese correspondents could now send out to the world uncensored stories of victory. "Of all the news which reached Tokyo during the war, and with hardly an exception it was cheerful," wrote Ashmead-Bartlett, "there was none which caused such intense joy and gave rise to such a feeling of relief as the final destruction of the Port Arthur squadron. To accomplish that result the Japanese had spent millions of money and sacrificed thousands of lives, at this time amounting to over 64,000 men killed and wounded."

On December 30, 1904, Admiral Togo with Admiral Kamimura, commander of the Second Squadron, forgiven now for his failure to catch the Russian Vladivostok Fleet, arrived in Tokyo. Their reception was overwhelming. As they stepped out of Shinbashi station they looked out on to a sea of faces. The people of Tokyo had come to greet their heroes. Togo and Kamimura visited General Nogi's wife and she served them saké and congratulated them on their safe return. Togo expressed condolence on the deaths of her two sons. She replied that she was proud that her children had died for their emperor. "I thought her an heroic woman of rare quality," wrote Togo.

At Port Arthur, after the capture of Hill 203, a council was held to decide the next steps to counter the Japanese attacks. General Smirnov, supported by Kondratenko and other officers, pleaded that the fortress could hold out for several months more. Their main enemy was sickness, especially scurvy. To eradicate this disease, he urged an increase in the ration of meat. "We have about 3,500 horses. According to my calculations, not more than 500 are required for the works. I think that, with luck, we may take for food without harm to the transport of supplies, more than 3,000 horses." He proposed to issue to the garrison an extra half a pound of horse-flesh per man. "I have not worked it out exactly, but roughly, for a garrison of 40,000 men that means fresh meat for forty-eight days at half a pound per day," he said. It was decided to issue half a pound to those in hospital and a quarter of a pound to combatants.

General Stoessel's chief of staff jumped to his feet to ask how long the council considered the fortress should be defended, but Smirnov cut him short: "That question does not permit of discussion." Ammunition was fast running out, but they had enough to repel at least two more heavy assaults. "When the big gun ammunition runs out we shall have more than 10,-000,000 rounds of small-arms ammunition left. When *all* the ammunition is finished we shall still have our bayonets." Of other supplies flour, groats, greens, tea, and sugar would last for another month or so. "In addition to this we have sufficient biscuits for more than a month and a half. The question of surrender cannot at present be considered. I cannot allow any discussion with regard to a capitulation before the middle of January at the earliest."

When the minutes were sent to Stoessel, he gave definite instructions that the fortress should be defended to the last. Too many of the officers had been against him. "I shall know when the time comes, and I will not permit a street massacre," he said.

Smirnov's urgent call for a ration of horseflesh resulted only in a small daily issue, and the numbers of men ill with scurvy grew daily. At this time a cow, all skin and bone, cost a dollar a pound and eggs nearly seventy cents each. Daily rations for the garrison now were: half a pound of biscuit, a quarter pound of horse flesh, and one eighth of a pint of vodka.

On December 15, the much-respected General Kondratenko, the only officer of high rank who stood aloof from fortress rivalries, was in the bowels of Chi-kuan fort pinning decorations for gallantry on a couple of noncommissioned officers. It was eerie in the underground concrete shelter, while above them the sounds of the big Japanese shells never ceased. After the ceremony a depressed Kondratenko sat with his head in his hands without talking. Another shell came over, the fifth since General Kondratenko had arrived, and they all listened to its approach. A moment later it killed

Kondratenko and six of his senior officers and badly wounded seven others.

For the fortress General Kondratenko's loss was as demoralizing as Admiral Makarov's death had been to the navy. Kondratenko had worked tirelessly on the defenses, visiting every position and working with his men day and night.

For General Smirnov this was the loss of his dearest friend and the only man who could smooth things over when Stoessel interfered. Now he was adamant that one of the deposed commandant's men should not be put in Kondratenko's place. The man he feared most for the post was Fock, whom he had dismissed for disobeying orders months before.

"I have already appointed General Fock in place of Kondratenko," said Stoesscl. "The order is published. You should know by now, General, that I never alter my orders. I *never* alter my orders."

On December 29 there was another council of war, called by Stoessel; one by one the assembled officers gave their opinions. Some were for holding out to the very last. Others reported that poor food and diminishing ammunition gave them little chance of continuing the defense. Scurvy was increasing, and there were not enough men to garrison the works. But the majority insisted on holding out. "We have held out until now, and we can hold out longer; and then—God's will be done," was the general opinion.

Of the officers who wished to give in, Fock was the most adamant. "A short time ago I was in the trenches. My God! What did I not see? The suffering, the wounds, the sickness—never shall I forget the sights Who is better or more noble than the private soldier? Who can equal him in gallantry, unselfishness, and endurance? We should not let him die for nothing. We should not let him die unless something is gained thereby."

General Smirnov had the last word. He talked long and earnestly. Russian regulations for the guidance of commanders of fortresses required them to hold out until "all strength and means are exhausted."

The officers were silent, waiting for Stoessel, who had sat with a paper concealed in his hand throughout the meeting. "In my opinion the second line is extremely weak, and it is in no way important," he began. "However, gentlemen, I see that all of you almost are in favor of a further defense, and we will accordingly carry on. Russian soldiers could not act otherwise. I am extremely grateful to all of you for coming to such a resolution."

The paper that Stoessel decided not to read was a copy of a telegram already sent to the Tsar before the council meeting. It read: "We cannot hold out more than a few days; am taking measures to prevent a street massacre."

During the next four days the Japanese captured Fort Erh-lung, Wantai and Sung-shu, along the Chinese Wall, with a loss of nearly 2,000 men. Mines were exploded in these forts and hundreds of Russian soldiers were buried alive in the ruins. Wantai, in the center of the Chinese wall, was the last fort to fall and soon after 5:30 P.M. on January 1, the Japanese flag was flying from its summit.

New Year's Day was the beginning of the end for the fortress. A Russian officer carrying a large white flag passed by. Someone jokingly said, "Looks as if he were taking our New Year greetings to Nogi." It was no joke. He carried a letter from General Stoessel to Nogi, dated December 1904, with no day of the month:

> Being acquainted with the general state of affairs in the theater of war, I am of opinion that no object is to be gained by further opposition in Port Arthur, and so, to avoid useless loss of life, I am anxious to enter into negotiations for capitulation. If Your Excellency agrees, I would ask you to be so good as to appoint accredited persons to negotiate concerning the terms and arrangements for surrender, and to appoint a spot where they may meet my requirements.

Several days before, Stoessel had sent a message to St. Petersburg: "The position of the fortress is becoming very painful. Our principal enemies are scurvy, which is mowing down the men, and eleven-inch shells, which know no obstacle and against which there is no protection. There only remain a few persons who have not been attacked by scurvy." The next day he sent an addendum: "We will only hold out a few days longer. We have hardly any ammunition left. I have now 10,000 men under arms. They are all ill."

To the Tsar he telegraphed on January 1: "Great Sovereign! Forgive! We have done all that was humanly possible. Judge us, but be merciful. Eleven months of ceaseless fighting have exhausted our strength. A quarter only of the defenders, and one half of them invalids, occupy twenty-seven versts* of fortifications without support and without intervals for even the briefest repose. The men are reduced to shadows."

General Nogi wrote his last poem of the war:

> His Majesty's millions conquer the strong foe.
> Field battles and siege result in mountains of corpses.
> How can I, in shame, face their fathers?
> Songs of triumph today, but how many have returned?

---

*1 verst = 0.66 mile

࿐࿐࿐࿐࿐࿐

CHAPTER 27

"The Place of Peace"

AT HOME, THE JAPANESE had a triple celebration. The news of the fall of Port Arthur reached Tokyo on New Year's Day. The streets were already thronged and people were busy decorating their housefronts with pine branches and bamboo, emblems of strength and endurance, and flags, both Japanese and British. Kites and balloons flew high over the city. Then, on January 3, to cap it all, the crown prince and princess announced the birth of a second son, Prince Takamatsu, Hirohito's younger brother.

Men ran with bells calling loudly to announce the Port Arthur news, and special editions of the newspapers appeared quickly on the streets. Bands played military tunes, rockets showered down their stars from the sky, and the streets filled with lantern-carrying processions.

Patriotism was at fever pitch. There was no lack of recruits wanting to share the victories. Among them was Lieutenant Tojo Hideki, who had celebrated his twenty-first birthday in military college the day before Port Arthur fell. He was still waiting to go to war when his father, a major general, returned sick with beri-beri, like thousands of other Japanese soldiers who contracted the disease in Manchuria, and in disgrace in Oku's army for squandering lives in the attack on Cairn Hill during the battle of Liaoyang. Thirty-six years later Tojo Hideki would lead his country to a war with the United States that began without declaration or warning.

General Nogi stayed in Port Arthur to take the surrender from General Stoessel. The surrender formally took place in a tiny Chinese house in the center of the village of Shui-shih-ying, about two miles from the Old Town. The correspondents called it Plumtree Cottage. It belonged to an old Chinese farmer who had refused to leave the home where his family had lived for generations. All through the long months of the siege he had stayed in the one-room house, with its bare floors and mud walls, occasionally taking refuge in his cellar during heavy bombardments.

Over the low doorway of Plumtree Cottage someone had pasted a sign in Chinese characters which read, "The Way to Peace." In front of the house was a large open space, like a village green, with one withered Chinese date tree, older by far than the ancient Chinese who owned the cottage.

The village had once been large and prosperous, but it had been destroyed by both Japanese and Russian fire. Only this cottage remained, and it was here at 11 o'clock on January 2, 1905, that the Japanese delegation, headed by General Ijichi, the Third Army chief of staff, arrived in a sudden burst of sunshine to meet with the Russians. The official Russian party, preceded by a mounted Cossack carrying a white flag on a long pole, consisted of Colonel Reuss, Stoessel's chief of staff, the captain of the battleship *Retvizan*, the Red Cross director from the town, and an interpreter.

The Japanese presented the capitulation terms. These were absolute, they said, but they would be happy to consider any suggestions the Russians might have. At 1:30 P.M. the Russian party went alone into the little mud house, where a couple of tables and cane chairs had been placed on the bare floors and Japanese newspapers pasted over the walls. They deliberated for an hour or more, then asked for some changes. They requested that all soldiers should be released and not taken as prisoners, arguing that, since the garrison was under oath, permission to surrender would have to be obtained from the Tsar. They also requested that officers be allowed to keep their horses and baggage. General Smirnov, who had pleaded to be allowed to hold out to the end, did not participate in the negotiations. He had already sent a message to General Kuropatkin, informing him that Stoessel had arranged for the surrender without his knowledge.

The Japanese insisted that soldiers and sailors could not be released but that officers, civil officers, and volunteers would be given parole. Officers would be allowed to have one orderly each, but horses could not be retained. The conquerors also requested an account of the numbers of wounded in hospitals in Port Arthur.

General Stoessel hoped that the Japanese would soon restore order, and requested a guard for his own house. His message to the Tsar, written in English, as the Japanese had ordered, so that it could be read by his captors was dispatched: "I was forced today to sign the capitulation surrendering Port Arthur. Officers and civil officers paroled with honors of war; garrison prisoners of war. I apply to you for this obligation."

In Russia, the news of the fall of Port Arthur was at first denied by the newspapers. Nicholas's address to his forces dispelled any doubts on the subject. He praised the heroism of the defenders of Port Arthur who had been cut off from the world for seven months.

Deprived of help and without murmuring, the garrison endured the privations of the siege and moral tortures while the enemy continued to gain successes. Unsparing of life and blood, a handful of Russians sustained the enemy's furious onslaughts in the firm hope of relief. With pride Russia witnessed their deeds of heroism, and the whole world bowed before their heroic spirit. . . . Glory be to you the living. May God heal your wounds, and give you the strength and patience to bear your sore trials! . . . With all Russia, I trust that the hour of victory will soon dawn, and pray to God that He may bless my dear troops and fleets, in order that, united, they may overthrow the enemy and uphold the honor and glory of Russia.

Contrary to many reports, the Tsar did not "tuck the telegram in his pocket and go to lunch." His diary, which so often expressed his true feelings, has an entry dated January 4, 1905, referring to the defenders of Port Arthur. "They are all heroes, and have done more than could be expected from them. Therefore, it must have been God's will!"

His return telegram to General Stoessel did not change the surrender terms. It was short: "I allow each officer to profit by the reserved privilege to return to Russia under the obligation not to take part in the present war, or to share the destiny of the men. I thank you and the brave garrison for the gallant defense."

Early in the evening of January 2 the articles of capitulation were signed, and 878 Russian officers, 23,491 men, and 8,956 seamen surrendered their arms, agreeing either to abstain from further part in the conflict or to become prisoners of war. About 15,000 sick and wounded remained in the hospitals.

As soon as the Russian troops heard the news, they flung down their weapons and began to loot the town. "Our men seemed suddenly to change their natures, all discipline went to the winds, and rioting commenced. Some, throwing their arms away, went straight down to the town, which became one vast scene of drunkenness and orgy," wrote Nojine. "The shops and stores were looted, and wholesale robbery was the order of the day. The crowd broke up everything they could, among other things, the library of the *Novoye Krai*. The officers, seeing that it was hopeless to try and cope with their men, hid from the maddened crowds."

With a hundred Japanese soldiers guarding his house, and an orgy of drinking and looting in the town, Stoessel ordered Smirnov to send out patrols. "The strictest steps must be taken at once to deal with the looting

[443]

which has commenced. . . . Reuss tells me that the terms of the surrender are honorable. Please excuse pencil."

Smirnov made no response. Not until the trials in the following year did he reveal publicly his hatred of the man who had thwarted him throughout the siege and then given in to the enemy.

Colonel Irman, who had fought valiantly in the last days of the siege, requested permission from Stoessel to escape to Cheefoo in a destroyer, so that he could fight with the army in the north. Stoessel flatly refused him permission. Then, more concerned about the treasures seized during the march on Peking in the Boxer Rebellion of 1900, Stoessel added: "Good heavens! what are you talking about? What are we to do with all the gold vases? How am I to get them away? Why, the Japanese might get them; we must save them."

"If you want to make certain that the Japanese don't get them, sir, I should throw them into the sea," replied Irman.

Outside Port Arthur the Japanese troops celebrated the surrender around campfires where soldiers gathered to drink, sing patriotic songs, and generally "behave like schoolboys on vacation." War correspondents shared in the saké, the shouting, and the songs. At headquarters Japanese officers toasted victory in beer, brandy, champagne, claret, and saké.

Nogi's plans for the meeting with Stoessel got off to a bad start. He had given orders that no troops were to collect in the streets or to line the approaches to the village. He did not want to turn the meeting into a Japanese triumph, he said, but he, as host, would be waiting at the cottage when General Stoessel and his party arrived. The difference in Japanese and Russian time upset the arrangements.

Stoessel was about to turn away when Nogi's aide came rushing up, "looking as if he wished the earth would open and swallow him." He had ridden into Port Arthur to escort the Russian general to the "place of peace," only to find that Stoessel had already left. Nogi was contacted by telephone and soon came trotting up on a bay pony, accompanied by General Ijichi and three other officers. With an apologetic smile, he jumped from his horse and the two generals shook hands and walked into the cottage.

Nakarai Tosui, an *Asahi* correspondent who had arrived on the village green in time to see the two generals shaking hands, took a photograph of them just before they dismounted from their horses. General Stoessel looked very dignified, he wrote, "truly a warrior." The *Daily Mail* correspondent noticed the contrast between the two leaders, "the one coarse-voiced, coarse-featured, and heavy in person; the other gentle of voice, refined in feature, and keenly alert, with eyes that go into the depths of your soul, bringing out confidence and trust, obedience and admiration; and a man as great in soldierly qualities as he was tender of heart for those he commanded." Stoessel he added, looked for all the world like a "well-fed Boer dopper."

Nogi admired General Stoessel's magnificent Arab horse, and Stoessel presented it to him. "Your kindness is beyond description," replied Nogi, "but I cannot accept your present, because to the army belong all horses, cannon, and other booty, and I have no right to make them my private property; but I will see that great care is taken of your horse, and that he is treated with special kindness." After the war the Arab returned to Japan and Nogi called it Kotobuki ("Long Life"). In years to come he rode it to and from the Peers School in Tokyo, where he became the principal and was for a time tutor to Hirohito, the present emperor.

For the first time since May 1904, trains now ran from the Port Arthur station. Drivers raised their price for the day to £5 for a single-horse carriage and £7 for a two-horse carriage to transport General Stoessel and his staff. Correspondents who went to the station to see them off remarked on the bad behavior of the Russian officers. "Women and children were left to fend for themselves," wrote one correspondent. "The poorer women, some with babies only a few months old, sat on bundles on the railway station and fed their children out of paper bags, while the 'demi-monde' spent the time powdering their noses and arranging the nets on their hats."

When the train pulled in, Russian officers pushed women and children aside to obtain seats. Many women and children who managed to board the train had to sit in trucks with the common soldiers and servants of the officers. "The widow of an officer killed in the siege whose beauty might have aroused some spark of dormant gallantry in the breast of one of the Tsar's chosen warriors, was left wandering about and would have missed the train had not General Nogi's aide cleared out some soldiers and found room for her in a truck," wrote Ashmead-Bartlett, who heard one shocked Japanese soldier whisper, "They treat their women like so many beasts."

The buxom Madame Stoessel emerged from the waiting room, followed by five little boys, sons of officers killed in the siege, and five little dogs, who all got into a special carriage. General Stoessel shook hands with the Japanese party and offered his hand to a group of Russian soldiers. The soldiers, shocked at such familiarity, gazed at his outstretched hand without touching it. The train gave a whistle and General Stoessel, who had sworn to die with the fortress, stepped inside the carriage. The train moved out, leaving most of the women and children still sitting on the platform to wait for the next train. "It was a miserable scene," wrote Ashmead-Bartlett, "and dissipated the last remaining feeling of regret for the misfortunes of the garrison."

The day after the Russians left, General Nogi made his entry into Port

Arthur. He had earlier sent in a force to police the fortress, but no one else was allowed inside. War correspondents and military attachés had been told to wait for the official take-over. The correspondents suffered so many insults from "swelled-headed" Japanese officers that they asked to be relieved of their accreditation to the Third Army. Nogi, as charming as ever, apologized profusely and begged them to be patient for a little longer, but, when at last they got into the fortress and the town, the story was dead. Some newspaper reports said that there was little damage to the town and plenty of food in the stores. Typical of these was a report from Morrison of *The Times* on January 5. He said that he knew Port Arthur well, having been there on four occasions before the siege began. Neither lack of food nor shortage of garrison troops nor cold nor diminished ammunition nor want of shelter had brought about the surrender, he wrote. There was ample food in the town, and the seas teemed with fish. Two thousand horses were still uneaten, and there was an abundance of flour, as well as champagne and medical supplies. "All accounts agree that no man who ever held a responsible command less deserved the title of hero than General Stoessel," he reported.

On his way home Stoessel was interviewed by correspondents at Aden. He insisted that Kuropatkin had sent him a telegram in September saying that in three months he would come to the rescue of Port Arthur. The three months had gone by and he had received word from neither Kuropatkin or Rozhdestvenski. Further resistance, he said, would have resulted in fearful carnage, which was the main reason he had decided to capitulate. "I acted without consulting anybody. I had to reckon with the judgment of the Tsar and of my equals. They will judge me and they will say whether I ought to have accomplished the heroic but criminal deed of blowing up the fortress. I prefer having a small reputation in military records to having 30,000 human lives on my conscience."

When Stoessel was asked his opinion of Russian officers who had gone to Japan as prisoners instead of returning to Russia, he said that he could not understand such action. In Japan they would be useless, he said. Those who returned to Russia could work for their country. "There are other ways of doing so than by fighting."

Conflicting reports described great destruction at Port Arthur especially in the Old Town, with hardly a house intact, and the streets ploughed up by shellfire. But few newspaper reports described the destruction so vividly as Seppings Wright in his book, *With Togo,* published after the war. At the gates of Port Arthur the Russians had built barricades of felled trees and wire entanglements in a last-minute attempt to stop the Japanese, and these were covered with dead soldiers, still clutching swords in their hands. Inside the gateway, he saw bombproof shelters and cave dwellings and many ruined houses. The music hall on Pushkin Street had been wrecked, and huge holes had been torn in the streets of the town. *Retvizan*'s anchor, which had been planted in a roadway near the harbor, had dragged and ploughed through the hard macadam as the ship sank. *Pallada*'s funnels rose from a blackened heap of scrap iron, and the other sunken battleships seemed to fill the harbor.

Great clouds of smoke rose from 203 Meter Hill, where the dead were being burned. "Every inch of the ground had been ploughed by the projectiles, rocks were ground to powder, and the hill was little more than a great mound of soft yielding dust," wrote Wright. "The trenches on the side could scarcely be traced for they were filled to the level of the ground with Russian corpses, burnt beyond recognition. Such a terrible sight I had never looked upon . . . everywhere scorched faces with hideous death grins looked up at us with unseeing eyes from the awful debris."

Nogi's official entry into Port Arthur, through the great Nicholas Gate, was blessed by sunny weather, most unusual for the time of the year. It was a simple affair, wrote Ashmead-Bartlett. "The music was about as poor as one could comfortably stand; the salutes were often badly given, and many of the troops had apparently forgotten their drill . . . their uniforms were shabby, and sadly in need of repair; their boots were much worn, and even the rifles not very clean."

Nogi stood with his staff at the saluting base, near the public gardens where in happier days on Sundays and holidays Russian bands had played their patriotic tunes. Only a few correspondents, naval attachés, the remaining inhabitants of the town, and some nurses attended.

Next day Nogi conducted a ceremony for the souls of the Japanese dead. Standing bareheaded in the rain he read the invocation to the spirits of those who had died for him:

I, Nogi Maresuke, commander-in-chief of the Third Imperial Army before Port Arthur, celebrate with saké and many offerings a fête in honor of you. . . . I wish to tell you that your noble sacrifice has not been in vain, for the enemy's fleet has been destroyed, and Port Arthur has at last surrendered. I, Nogi Maresuke, took oath with you to conquer or seek oblivion in death. I have survived to receive the Imperial thanks, but I will not monopolize the glory. With you, Spirits of the Dead, who achieved this great result, I desire to share the triumph. . . .

Since the Japanese landing in May, Port Arthur had cost the Japanese 57,780 men killed and wounded. Fourteen thousand of them fell to capture Hill 203. Men suffering from dysentery, beri-beri, and other diseases brought the total casualties to 91,549. Often during the siege Nogi had wept for the thousands of men dying under his command. Now that the costly victory was won, he poured out his sorrow in a letter to General Terauchi, the army minister. "The feeling I have at this moment is solely one of anguish and humiliation that I have expended so many lives, so much ammunition, and such a long time upon an unaccomplished task," he wrote. "I have no excuse to offer to my sovereign and to my countrymen for this unscientific, unstrategical combat of brute force. . . . I thank you heartily for your kind condolences on the deaths of my sons and I beg you to forgive my long display of military unskillfulness."

Sabotage, St. Petersburg, and San-de-pu

Cʜɪɴᴀ's "ɴᴇᴜᴛʀᴀʟɪᴛʏ" ʜᴀᴅ sᴇʀᴠᴇᴅ the Japanese well during the siege of Port Arthur. While other officials in Peking made formal protests against Japanese violations, Yuan Shih-k'ai, the Viceroy of Chih-li, continued to cooperate fully. His help farther north in Manchuria had now begun to make the Russian lines of communication uncomfortable and often dangerous. The bands of Chinese mounted guerrillas under Japanese leadership whose activities he had sanctioned were operating with greater impact than ever.

From the beginning of the war the Japanese had used China as an important source of supply for the army in Manchuria. Two hundred thousand sets of winter clothing from north China reached the Japanese force digging in for the cold weather along the banks of the Sha River. Horses, cattle, pigs, and vegetables flowed into Manchuria in a constant stream for the Japanese army.

Under Yuan's instruction, all high-ranking Chinese officials in Mukden, Liaoyang, Hai-cheng, and other important centers cooperated with the Japanese. The Russians were now fully aware of Yuan's role and of his feeling that only their defeat would restore Manchuria to China. One Russian-sponsored attempt to assassinate him was thwarted by Japanese intelligence, and thereafter Yuan was ever more cooperative. Not only did he help the Japanese, but he also worked to prevent Russian smuggling from China.

General Senba upbraided Japanese officials every time they failed to give due courtesy to the Chinese when important issues were not involved. "We should make it a policy to be ruthless when it comes to major matters that affect the interests of our forces and our country," Senba complained to

Tokyo after the local Japanese authorities had refused to allow the Chinese administrator of Newchwang to enter that town. "But in minor matters that do not necessarily concern the interests of our country and armies, we should desist from quarreling with them and show them kindness and give them advantages in order to befriend them." The Chinese administrator of Newchwang, he pointed out, was an old man "of no particular importance." He "would have been pleased to cooperate with us if we had treated him with superficial consideration."

It was good advice and, when adopted, worked well with the espionage system and the Chunchuse "armed bandits," who had now become the plague of the Russian rear areas. No Cossack band, no section of Russian soldiery, felt safe away from any Russian camp. Through the winter of 1904–1905 and the spring that followed, the Chunchuses swooped and plundered on hit-and-run raids that persuaded the Russians that there were tens of thousands of enemy troops operating against them behind the lines.

"To give color to our fears, a whole series of reports, each more alarming than the last, were received from General Chichagov," Kuropatkin wrote. "In these he described the large numbers of the enemy that had appeared behind us with the intention of seizing Harbin as well as of destroying the railway." In reality, the Japanese forces engaged in the commando raids were small. Six squads had been organized in Peking in January 1904 with a total Japanese component of seventy-one. Some of the Japanese squad members spoke Chinese and wore Chinese clothing, including pigtails, but for more effective operations Yuan Shih-k'ai agreed to assign selected Chinese noncommissioned officers to the squads and to provide Chinese cavalry for operations around Liaoyang and elsewhere.

Confronted by these problems, the Russians were also having serious difficulties with the Trans-Siberian Railway. In December 1904, two locomotives were derailed in a collision at Taishet, west of Lake Baikal, cutting the line and access to water and coal. It took three days to re-rail the two engines, and caused an absolute halt to all traffic. Without fuel, the fires in the engines went out and numerous locomotives cracked in the cold. St. Petersburg immediately ordered the cancellation of all eastbound traffic except those carrying warm clothing. By December 15 more than 1,000 wagons carrying troops were held up to the east of Taishet, while about 4,800 wagons had accumulated to the west. Four days later this number had grown to 5,200, and all rail traffic was in chaos. To sort things out, all but urgent troop trains had to be canceled for ten days and all goods traffic for twenty-three days.

This was the worst holdup, but there were many others. To maintain the Russian armies in the field required the services of nearly 900 locomotives, and at the beginning of the war the Russians had fewer than 300. Fuel and labor were inadequate, and more than 2,000 trucks became blocked up in sidings—a situation that was not resolved until March 1905 when sufficient locomotives became available.

While Tokyo's military attaché in Peking was manipulating Yuan Shih-k'ai to Japan's advantage, Colonel Akashi, Japan's brilliant intelligence coordinator in Europe, was up to his ears in intrigue with the Russian, Polish, and Finnish revolutionaries. Every new Russian reverse in the Far East added to the surging wave of discontent that was now enveloping Russia and its protectorates. Plehve's assassination had put a match to the fuse.

Toward the end of July, Akashi and Konni Zilliacus went to Switzerland to organize a meeting of revolutionary Russian exiles. Scores of Russian and Polish exiles were now living there. They painted, read, planned, and fought with each other, united in their determination to bring about changes in Russia but in nothing else. Even Zilliacus, who was now the most adroit campaigner for unification among the dissident groups and factions, had his misgivings about cooperating with some of the revolutionary groups. In particular, he warned Akashi against Lenin.

Through fifty-three-year-old Vera Zasulitch, whose tempestuous student days had reached a climax in 1878 with the attempted assassination of the chief of police in St. Petersburg, Akashi met both Lenin and G. V. Plekhanov, who had been living in Switzerland for more than twenty years. He was especially impressed with the former. "Lenin is considered by other Socialists to be a rascal who uses all kinds of methods to reach his objectives," he wrote. "On the contrary, he is a sincere man and lacks egoism. He gives everything to his doctrine. Lenin is the person who can accomplish the revolution." He backed his confidence with hard cash, though how much no one has ever been able to determine.*

Against Akashi's protests, Zilliacus sent invitations not only to the revolutionary, or potentially revolutionary, parties but also to the Russian Liberal party. A few Liberals finally agreed to attend but only on the condition that the conference was held in Paris, not in Switzerland, which was regarded in St. Petersburg as a hotbed of Russian intrigue and revolution. This condition did not please the Russian Social Democrats. Plekhanov complained that since he was barred from France he could not attend and that, in any event, the meeting was not based on the party's principles. The Socialist Revolutionaries and two Bundist parties also refused to participate. It was nevertheless an impressive group of thirteen parties that assem-

---

*According to one Japanese source, up to 50,000 yen.

bled in Paris on October 1. Zilliacus took the chair. Gathered in the hall were men like Paul Miliukov, the distinguished Russian historian; Prince Paul Dolgoruki; Count Peter Heiden of the Imperial Free Economic Society; and Nicholas Chaykovsky, who had been busy in exile in London since 1884 and had founded the Society of Friends of Russian Freedom. To Akashi's intense surprise, the Liberals were as keen as the revolutionaries to bring about change. While eschewing violence themselves, they appeared to take no exception to the call for revolution that they now heard.*

Having agreed that each party should now move actively in its own way to push the campaign against the autocracy, the conference broke up. After the Liberals had left the meeting, however, the other parties got down to serious discussion about tactics and methods. It was decided, among other steps, to attempt to tie down as many Russian troops as possible, to begin street demonstrations in Poland, and to step up the assassination of senior officials in the Caucasus. Akashi promised financial assistance to all who needed it and left for Stockholm highly satisfied with the results achieved.

The autocracy had not been altogether idle, however. The Okhrana, or secret police, working closely with the French police, kept the conference under close surveillance. One of the delegates was none other than Evno Azev, who, in his role as double agent, had been working closely with Zilliacus. He reported to the Okhrana that Akashi and Zilliacus were buying weapons in Hamburg. They were, in fact, buying them all over. Zilliacus had arranged for a supply of 200 Brownings from America. Mausers came from Hamburg. They bought revolvers and explosives in England. Armenian revolutionaries had tapped another source in France, where old French rifles were available. Three other agents were busy in Switzerland. All of them used Akashi's money. "Half the people to whom Japanese money is distributed don't know where it comes from," said Zilliacus. "The other half don't care."

Since Akashi was obliged to be circumspect in his activities in Stockholm and Zilliacus's personal headquarters were in Copenhagen, the two men settled on London as the best possible center for coordinating their activities. Free from interference by the Russian police, the two men soon had a formidable cache of arms in the cellar of a London bookstore: 16,000 rifles, three tons of bombs, 300 pistols, and three million rounds of ammunition were stored away waiting the opportunity—and the ships—to move

---

*Zilliacus also organized in Paris a society calling itself the Friends of the Russian People. Its members included Anatole France; Jean Léon Jaurès, deputy speaker of the House of Representatives and head of the Socialist Party; and Georges Clemenceau. The society took no part in the violence, but its members campaigned against Russian loans and helped to win sympathy for the revolutionary cause.

them to revolutionaries behind the curtain of the autocracy. Through Aka-shi's purse, the Japanese government had become principal *agent provoca-teur* in a revolution that was, in 1905, to shake Russia to its foundations.

To help with the gun-running, Akashi bought two small steamers, the *Cecil* and the *Cysne,* registered in the name of a wealthy American widow and crewed by young revolutionaries from the Baltic. Revolutions are won with guns but built on words. The first issue of Lenin's newspaper, *Vperyed*, appeared on January 4, 1905, with funds provided by Akashi and others, including Maxim Gorki. "A military collapse is now inevitable," Lenin wrote, "and together with it there will come inevitably a tenfold increase of unrest, discontent, and rebellion. For that moment we must prepare with all energy."

On January 16 the big Putilov ironworks in St. Petersburg went on strike. Major demands were the reinstatement of some workers who belonged to the Assembly of Russian Workers, a union sponsored by peasant-born Father Georges Gapon, and the dismissal of an offending foreman. Like most other unions, the Assembly had now been penetrated by agitators, and, since the Putilov works made guns, railway carriages, and many other articles needed for the army in the field, the target of the strike and its timing so soon after the humiliating surrender at Port Arthur were pecu-liarly sensitive. All strikes were illegal under Russian law, but when Putilov turned down the workers' demands, labor unrest quickly spread to the government shipyards on the Neva and the Obukov metalworks, which were also owned by the government.

The annual ceremony of blessing the waters of the Neva was performed by the Tsar on January 19. As the imperial salute announced that the ceremony was complete, a gun accidentally fired a live round. It landed near the Tsar and a piece of shrapnel cut through the double windows of the Nicholas Hall in the Winter Palace, smashing the electric lamps on the opposite side of the hall.

Next day the city came to a standstill. Armies of men left their jobs and wandered through the city in groups to listen to speeches by their leaders, and, in particular, Father Gapon. The electricity supply failed, and the city went to bed on the night of January 21 with the anxious fear that some sort of crisis was at hand. It was.

"St. Petersburg awoke this morning to find itself in a state of siege," wrote the Reuters correspondent the next day.

A more perfect and lovely day never dawned. There were five degrees of frost. The air was crisp and invigorating and the sky almost cloud-less. The gilded domes of the cathedral and the churches and the frost-encrusted roofs and façades of the houses, brilliantly illuminated by the sun, formed a superb panorama as I looked out of the hotel window wondering what the day would bring forth.

He noticed a significant change in the bearing of the passersby. Instead of flocking up the steps of the cathedral as usual on Sunday morning, they were all silently winding their way, singly or in small groups, in the direction of the Winter Palace. Joining in the steady stream of working men, he proceeded along the Admiralty Gardens in the direction of the Winter Palace. Already a crowd of many thousands had collected but was prevented from entering the square by mounted troops drawn up against each thoroughfare. Angrily, the crowd began to press forward to meet it. The cavalry advanced at a walking pace.

Prince Peter Danilievitch Sviatopolk-Mirsky, the new and liberal interior minister, had received a letter the previous day from Father Gapon, urging the Tsar to meet the people in front of the Winter Palace. His Majesty had nothing to fear, the letter said. Although it was Father Gapon's intention to present the Tsar with a petition demanding sweeping reforms, there was no intention that the demonstration should become disorderly. Gapon saw himself as a man with a mission, entrusted by God with the dual role of helping the workers and the Tsar. He believed that only by the personal intervention of the Tsar could the situation be resolved peacefully.

At the head of the procession next day were two priests in full vestments, carrying crosses in their hands. They were accompanied by others with ikons and large pictures of the Tsar. None of the marchers had weapons. In their path were 50,000 troops.

The trouble began at 11 A.M. The military tried to turn back some thousands of men from the Putilov factory when they crossed one of the bridges connecting the industrial center on an island in the Neva with the main parts of the city and the Palace Square. At 2 P.M. several processions, numbering in all about 200,000 participants, were close to the Winter Palace. In every thoroughfare now they were confronted by lines of infantry and Cossack horsemen.

> The Cossacks at first used their knouts, then the flat of their sabers, and finally they fired [Reuters reported]. The strikers in the front ranks fell on their knees and implored the Cossacks to let them pass, protesting that they had no hostile intentions. They refused, however, to be intimidated by blank cartridges, and orders were given to load with bore.
>
> The passions of the mob broke loose like a bursting dam. The people, seeing the dead and dying carried away in all directions, the snow on the streets and the pavements soaked with blood, cried aloud for vengeance.

[454]

The Times reported that Father Gapon marched with the other two priests but without his vestments, which he had intended to put on when he reached the building of the Council of the Empire. When the troops opened fire, the holy pictures and portraits of the Tsar were pierced by bullets, and one of the priests was wounded. Gapon crawled into a neighboring house and escaped.

Crossing Admiralty Square, Madame Kusa, one of the principal dramatic sopranos at the Imperial Russian Opera and the wife of a leading Russian composer, saw the cavalry fire the first volley into the crowd.

"The Japanese you don't know how to kill, but defenseless people at home you kill," she shouted in anger to an officer in the elite Preobrazhenski Regiment.

"Pass along, imbecile," he answered.

No one knows how many people were killed or wounded in the snow-covered streets of St. Petersburg on "Bloody Sunday." Some accounts listed ninety-two dead and between 200 and 300 wounded. Others put the number of killed at about 2,000 and the wounded close to 5,000. But, whatever the size of the casualty list, it was enough. "The prestige of the Tsarist name has been ruined for ever," Lenin exulted. "The uprising has begun."

Witte, who had no real authority as chairman of the council of ministers, but much residual influence, was furious. "To fire at helpless men going to see their Tsar with portraits and ikons in their hands is a monstrous thing," he said. "Prince Sviatopolk-Mirsky will have to tender his resignation, for he has discredited himself in the eyes of everyone."

Russia had also discredited itself in the eyes of the world and jeopardized the credit it needed to finance the war. Count Kokovtsov, the finance minister, was in the midst of negotiations with the Germans and the French for new loans when "Bloody Sunday" capped the disastrous loss of Port Arthur. The Germans retained their confidence in St. Petersburg, but the French had begun to have serious doubts. Edouard Netzlin, head of the Russian syndicate in Paris and representative of the Banque de Paris et des Pays Bas, traveled hastily to St. Petersburg to warn Count Kokovtsov, Witte, and finally Nicholas himself of the disastrous effect that the unsuccessful military operations and "Bloody Sunday" had had on Russian securities on the Paris stock market.

Nicholas made light of the revolution to Netzlin and promised a change of fortune in the war as soon as the Baltic Fleet reached the Far East. St. Petersburg had not even begun to learn the lessons that by now should have been so obvious. Madame Kusa was discharged from the Imperial Opera. The mighty Chaliapin, the great bass singer and idol of St. Petersburg, resigned in protest. Maxim Gorki was placed under arrest. Police broke up meetings of the Society of Modern Musicians on the ground that no more than five people were permitted to assemble at one time. Nicholas found a letter containing a death threat in his own room in the palace at Tsarskoe Selo (literally, "the Tsar's village"), a small town fifteen miles from St. Petersburg, and Father Gapon fled the country into the arms of Lenin and Akashi.

To Akashi, Gapon seemed heaven-sent. Despite the resolutions of the Paris conference in October, his efforts to create an effective revolution in Russia continued to be hampered by the factionalism of the revolutionary leaders in exile. Zilliacus had proved his ability to get the various groups together, but the splintering process had not ended. The revolution needed a hero. Gapon seemed likely to provide it.

At a meeting between Akashi, Zilliacus, and Nicholas Chaykovsky in Paris, it was decided to ask Gapon to organize a new meeting of revolutionary parties. Gapon was delighted, and out went the invitations. "I summon all the Socialist parties to enter immediately into agreement and to begin the business of armed uprising against Tsarism. . . . Bombs and dynamite, terror by individuals and by masses—everything which may contribute to the national uprising."

The conference began on April 2 in Geneva in the home of a man identified only by the name "Simon." It must have been a large house, since nineteen different parties and groups accepted the invitation, including Russians, Poles, Finns, Letts, Georgians, and Armenians. The Lettish Social Democrats walked out and were followed by the Jewish Bund and, according to some reports, by the Bolsheviks and the Armenian Social Democrats. But again Akashi was delighted with the results of the conference and its decision to continue resistance regardless of cost and to begin the general uprising in the summer. Poland and Finland were to declare their independence, but eventually would federate with Russia after the Russian revolutionary parties had overthrown the autocracy. There were to be concerted plans to assassinate the Russian imperial family.

Not long after Gapon's conference in Geneva, Akashi had gone to London and was staying at the Charing Cross Hotel. His object now was to arrange the shipment into Russia of bombs, guns, and ammunition for the summer uprising. Before Gapon's arrival, Akashi and Zilliacus had been staying in different parts of the hotel to avoid being spied upon. "It was necessary to meet the Russian revolutionaries several times a day," Akashi explained. "We had to get them to do things, to agitate them, and of course we had to do this with the utmost secrecy."

The day after Father Gapon arrived at the Charing Cross, where he registered under an alias, Akashi decided to move elsewhere, and, under the alias this time of "Abazuresu" (which means "to act shamelessly"), he checked in nearby at the Craven Hotel in Craven Street. The dealings with Father Gapon he handed over to a subordinate.

So far as Akashi knew, only one other man, the Japanese military attaché in London, knew his whereabouts. He had been at the hotel for only a few days, however, when a letter arrived addressed to Mr. Abazuresu, written in a woman's handwriting. "Please meet me at 11 A.M. next Thursday at the Champs Elysées *métro,*" it said. "You do not know me, but I know you and I will not have any difficulty in finding you. I have something to tell you of great importance, but you need not be afraid." The letter was signed "Madame Laurent."

Since there was work for Akashi to do in Paris in connection with the shipment of weapons to the Black Sea, he decided to go to France. "The letter made me feel uneasy," he confessed. "It was very strange that the writer was able to find me at my secret address, but thinking that she might eventually prove of use I kept the appointment."

At the *métro* station a Frenchwoman in her forties approached him. She explained that her husband was a Russian agent, that they had parted company, and that she was willing to tell what she knew of his activities for £400. Akashi was receptive. He replied that he did not mind paying any amount of money for information. "Madame Laurent" then confided that he was regarded as a dangerous person by the Russians and that his arrival in Paris had already been reported to the head of the Russian espionage service by an agent who had seen him taking a walk under the Arc de Triomphe at eight o'clock that morning.

Akashi listened with fascination as she detailed his recent activities, his relations with Zilliacus and Russian nihilists who, she said, were greatly feared by the Russian government. She also knew that Akashi had bought part of a shipment of arms from a man named "Frank" in Hamburg and identified the hotel at which Zilliacus had stayed and the contacts he made there.

"Do you not remember as you walked upstairs that you passed a man?" she asked. "He was Springer, the Russian spy. After you left, Zilliacus hurriedly packed his bags and took off."

The woman knew even the contents of a letter Akashi had given to a Russian revolutionary using the code name "George." "If you wish," she said, "I can even quote you the exact words to prove to you that I know. It is known that you people have actively been buying arms. We are investigating to see whether you are buying them in Hamburg." She advised him to take greater care, not to walk to appointments, and to stay only in large hotels where it was difficult for the Russians to keep him under surveillance. Finally, she gave Akashi the news that the Russians had broken the Japanese code. "This," said Akashi, "became very clear later on."

Forewarned now that the Russians were watching their arms dealings and with this new recruit for his team of agents, Akashi set out to cover his tracks with the most elaborate care. To begin with, arms were not easy to buy in Europe at this time, and, once obtained, any value they might eventually have in Russia clearly depended on absolute secrecy.

Several factors helped Akashi in his work: Lenin was now passionately committed to the revolution; a constant stream of revolutionaries from Russia and its dependencies arrived in search of arms and Japanese help; and the Polish revolutionary leader Pilsudski had returned from Japan and started to move guns into Poland. The revolution fed on revolution. Though the Okhrana, through Azev, had penetrated the revolutionary movement and Akashi had been warned of the broken code, the climate was favorable for action, and he set out to take advantage of it.

All through Russia a wave of strikes signaled the people's anger and discontent. Strikes closed down Warsaw for a week, and looters filled the streets. The authorities, after the excesses in St. Petersburg, seemed reluctant to act. On January 29, however, they decided to make up for lost time. "They proceeded to exercise a terrible and blind repression," wrote the Warsaw correspondent of the Paris *Journal*. "While the Grodono Hussars charged through the principal streets, sabering right and left, infantry patrols commanded by noncommissioned officers were shooting at random people who had nothing to do with the strike. . . . When night fell upon these scenes of horror . . . the pillage began again, but this time the soldiers had their share of it." *The Times*'s correspondent reported on February 2: "Three bugle calls were sounded to give the strikers warning, then rifle and sabre did their work, with the result that two hundred persons were killed and about six hundred wounded. This, for the time being, has quieted the disorder." By February 8 the Warsaw hospitals were so full of wounded that all admissions had to be suspended.

General D. F. Trepov became governor-general of St. Petersburg with dictatorial powers. Prince Sviatopolk-Mirsky, who had succeeded Plehve in the interior ministry, accepted Witte's advice and resigned, and the Tsar received a deputation of thirty-four workmen from the striking factories. The workmen made obeisance to the Tsar, who greeted them with the words, "Good day, my children." "We wish Your Majesty good health," they replied. Nicholas lectured them on the "inevitable consequences" of the disorder that had occurred because "you permitted yourselves to be led away and deceived by enemies of the fatherland." Then he gave them tea and sandwiches.

In the search for scapegoats, the English were now widely blamed for the trouble, and placards on the walls of Moscow accused them of having provided large sums of money for the revolutionaries. But neither paternalistic lectures nor untruths nor the iron hand could halt the tide of revolt. On February 8 the procurator-general of Finland was assassinated at Helsingfors. Nine days later, the Grand Duke Serge Alexandrovitch, uncle and brother-in-law of the Tsar, emerged from the gates of the Kremlin in his carriage. At a fast clip, he was passing the Courts of Justice when he was quite literally blown to bits by a bomb thrown by a member of the Battle Organization and provided by Evno Azev.

Against this background of bloodshed and unrest at home, Kuropatkin had to address himself to the thankless task of waging war in the East. After the battle on the Sha, he recognized the inevitability of the fall of Port Arthur. The fortress had held him in its fatal grasp during the long hot months of the summer, dragging him into battles that he wished to avoid. Its fall, though it gave him more freedom to maneuver and greater opportunity to choose the time and place for action, also posed new problems. Nogi's Third Army was now freed from its tasks at the fortress and would soon turn north to reinforce Oyama's force.

It was, however, perhaps the only period in the war that Kuropatkin enjoyed. With Alexeiev's removal from authority, he now exercised for the first time the unchallenged right to command. General Linievitch, the old vodka-tippling Siberian warhorse, who was now sixty-seven, arrived from Vladivostok to take command of the First Army. Grippenberg had already arrived to take over the Second, and vain, blustering General Baron A. V. Kaulbars was appointed to command the Third.

Despite all the reverses of the previous months and the dire news from home, there was a new spirit in the air. Kuropatkin may not have been a good general, but he was popular with the men, and his misfortunes were attributed largely to the interference of the much disliked Alexeiev. Old Linievitch was regarded as a tough fighter, and Grippenberg arrived talking fight. "If any of you retreat, I'll kill you," he told his troops. "If I retreat, kill me."

By December Kuropatkin's reinforcement and supply position had greatly improved. Despite the temperature, which was dropping rapidly all the time, the Russian troops in Manchuria were living better also, if often at the expense of the civil population. As soon as the battle for the Sha had ended, the Russians systematically destroyed all the villages in the area to provide building materials for winter quarters for the army. They stripped every house of its roof and posts to cover and prop up their underground bunkers. They cut down all fruit and other trees for firewood and commandeered all supplies of chickens, pigs, cattle, and grain. Ninety thousand

[459]

refugees fled to Mukden, the clothes on their backs their only possessions.

All of this occurred in the strip of territory between the Sha and the Hun rivers. Between the Hun and Mukden the peasants fared better, though day after day the Russian troops raided Chinese homes for food, drink, fuel, clothing, and women. Religious devotions occupied much of the troops' time when they were not intent on looting or paradeground activities, and on the Hun they erected crosses made of ice decorated with trees and bushes that they had cut down around the peasant cottages.

Japanese psychological warfare teams distributed postcards to the Russians, showing the happy life being led by prisoners in Japan, and, when they found that these were acceptable, they began distributing accounts also of events in Russia and Poland. To the news-starved Russians, dependent for information on the *Official Messenger of the Manchurian Armies,* a Russian army publication, even stories calculated to cause dismay were welcome. The desertion rate, especially among the Poles, increased sharply. One of Colonel Aoki's agents regularly attended Kuropatkin's staff in his capacity as a "Chinese barber," and another, posing as a Chinese businessman, provided supplies for the Russian army and information for his own.

In old, strategically located Mukden, the Tartar capital, which had been the jumping-off place for the Manchus when they captured Peking and also the site of their ancestral tombs, the Russians that winter imposed some of the way of life that they had brought with them to Harbin, Dalny, Port Arthur, and Liaoyang. The city itself, with a population of about 300,000, looked like a small-scale copy of Peking, surrounded by thick brick walls rising to a height of fifty feet. The walls formed a square, each side a mile long, with access to the city through massive gateways.

As at Liaoyang, the population had outgrown the city limits and between the walls and the railway station, which was about two miles from the western wall, the Chinese had spread their tiled cottages. Here, also, the Russians had created their own cantonment.

The imperial tombs, set in thousands of acres of superb parkland, were north and northeast of the city. The whole area was rich in history and legend. Mukden was said to have been built over the tail of a great dragon whose body ran between the imperial tombs for 700 miles to the Ever White Mountains, where its head rested in a lake of quiet beauty. Over the tail of the dragon the Russians, with no regard for the consequences, had built their railway. Legend held that the greatest misfortune that can overtake a man or a regime is to cut a dragon's vein. What effect the constant rumbling of a train might have on a dragon, no one could predict, but the Russians could not be persuaded of the dangers and went ahead with their plans.

The foreign quarter, with the missionary compounds, was just inside the south gate, and here there were well-stocked shops. Filthy, underfed dogs and innumerable large black pigs wandered about the crowded, frozen streets. It was a city of vile smells and innumerable diseases. An outbreak of smallpox took the lives of many of the refugee children. Scarlet fever reached epidemic proportions.

Two days after the fall of Port Arthur, the Russian quartermaster-general revived a favorite old tactical operation. Ever since they had settled in for the winter, Kuropatkin's staff members had been talking about the possibility of an independent cavalry operation along the Japanese lines of communication. With Nogi's army now free to turn north along the railway, the need was demonstrably growing.

"Consider!" said Kuropatkin in a note to the chief of staff on January 4. "Would it not be better for us to make a raid on Newchwang, damaging the railway en route?" Kuropatkin suggested that Mishchenko should take command and that the raid might cause some delay in Nogi's plans to join Oyama and divert some Japanese troops to the rear to avoid a repetition of the raid. Though the circumstances were favorable for a rapid thrust across the flat and frozen plains against the Japanese communications, Mishchenko's force of between 7,000 and 7,500 horsemen was anchored by the weight of an absurdly large supply column. On the first day the troops covered only twenty-three miles. Though the ground was frozen, they kicked up clouds of dust that were visible for miles. Since the possibility of a raid like this had been the subject of café and barber shop gossip in Mukden for months, the Japanese were not surprised.

The need for haste was apparent to Mishchenko but not to his subordinate commanders. On the second afternoon two of his columns wasted hours in a futile village skirmish with a small Japanese force. Even when they reached the railway line, the Russians made only half-hearted efforts to destroy it. As usual, they lacked maps and could not find the target bridges. They succeeded in wrecking a couple of trains, in capturing and destroying some Japanese supplies, and in cutting some telegraph and telephone lines, but these were the sort of results that a dashing commando company might have inflicted.

Instead of slowing down the movement of the Third Army from Port Arthur, the raid gave further warning that Kuropatkin might attempt to regain the initiative and reinforced the assumption that he would try to do this before the arrival of Nogi's army changed the balance of forces along the Sha and the Hun.

As early as the middle of December, Kuropatkin had called in Linievitch, Kaulbars, and Grippenberg to discuss the feasibility of a renewed offensive. When it came to hard discussion, the mood was something less than aggressive. None of the generals wanted to move until the Sixteenth Corps, one of the major reinforcement units, had arrived in its entirety from European Russia.

When the army commanders met again with Kuropatkin after the fall of Port Arthur, they were still hesitant, though Grippenberg put forward an ambitious plan to make a strong right hook to envelop the left wing of Oyama's army. To Kuropatkin and the others this seemed too risky, whereupon Grippenberg suddenly went to the other extreme and became pessimistic. While the Mishchenko raiding party was still outside Newchwang, Grippenberg told Kuropatkin that the whole campaign was lost and that the Russians ought to retire on Harbin, hold on there and at Vladivostok, and from thence move with two armies in other directions.

The prospects of Nogi's early appearance on the northern battlefield had filled Kuropatkin's immediate subordinates with gloom. The Japanese, however, continued to regard Nogi and his staff as incompetent. Kodama had recommended the repatriation of the Third Army command and the appointment of an entirely new command for the march to the north. On January 1, Major Tanaka Giichi, one of Oyama's ablest staff officers (and an original member of the war party group that met at the Kogetsu), submitted a draft telegram to Kodama that again advised the dismissal of Nogi and his staff on the grounds of inefficiency. Colonel Matsukawa, realizing what the telegram contained, persuaded Kodama to cancel it, and a meeting of staff members decided that it was unnecessary, since Port Arthur had already fallen, to humiliate Nogi and his officers. The meeting appointed General Ijichi as chairman of the Port Arthur readjustment committee, an adroit kick upstairs, and replaced him with Major-General Koizumi. Nogi, the figurehead, was to be allowed to keep his command.

Nogi was no figurehead to the Russians. The chief of staff of Kaulbars' Second Army shared Grippenberg's views. It was impossible, he believed, "for us to dream of being successful after Nogi's arrival." Nevertheless, the apprehensive generals finally agreed to take the offensive, and on January 19 Kuropatkin issued his orders. His objective was to drive Oyama back behind the Tai-tzu River at Liaoyang and to inflict as heavy losses as possible on his forces. The plan reversed the tactics employed at the Sha-ho. Instead of trying to outflank the Japanese in the mountains, Kuropatkin decided to attempt a modified version of Grippenberg's original scheme and to outflank Oku's Second Army on the plain.

The action that followed, variously known either as the battle of Hei-kou-tai or San-de-pu, took its name from one of the two fortified villages at the western extremity of the Japanese line. San-de-pu, which was about two miles from Hei-kou-tai, was the larger. Ten miles west of the railway and about thirty miles southwest of Mukden, it consisted of a walled enclosure, containing about a hundred houses and a caravanserai for travelers.

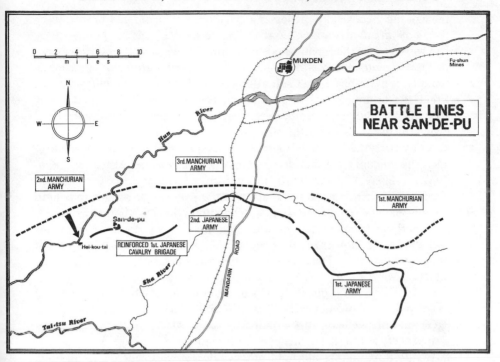

On the Russian side, Grippenberg, deaf, aged, and jittery, compromised the Russian army before the battle had begun. To preserve the element of surprise, Kuropatkin wanted to delay the movement of any troops as long as possible. Yet long before he had even issued his orders, Grippenberg had begun to shuffle his divisions forward. "These movements, of course, at once disclosed our intentions, and information soon came in that the enemy had, in turn, commenced moving their troops westward and fortifying opposite our new dispositions," Kuropatkin noted. He decided, nevertheless, to continue as planned, and on January 25 the First Siberian Corps, at fearful cost, drove two battalions of Japanese troops from Hei-kou-tai. The original plans called for the Fourteenth Division to attack San-de-pu at the same time; but at the last moment it was diverted on false information to cooperate with Mishchenko's detachment in an attack against a nonexistent Japanese position much further to the west.

All the errors and omissions that had been so conspicuously a part of earlier Russian operations were repeated here. Grippenberg failed to mesh his operations with Kaulbars on his left flank. The attack on Hei-kou-tai had been made without preliminary reconnaissance. Officers had no sketch plan of it or its approaches. Kuropatkin himself could not keep away from

[463]

the fighting. Shocked by the losses at Hei-kou-tai, he ordered Grippenberg to call off an infantry attack along the thirteen-mile front until the artillery had worked over the Japanese position. But the message from Grippenberg to lower commands was delayed, as usual, and Kuropatkin personally repeated it to Grippenberg's subordinates on the ground the following day. From the beginning, relations between the two generals were severely strained. Nor did they attempt to conceal their differences as they quarreled openly in the presence of their staffs.

A day later, the Japanese Fourteenth Division drove the Russians out of what they thought was San-de-pu, but which, they soon learned, was Pao-tai-tzu, a different village slightly more than a quarter of a mile to the north. Confronting them now to the south was the real San-de-pu. From behind the fortified and frozen walls and a deep ditch filled with barbed wire that protected the defenders came a withering fire. For the Russian troops this was a crushing blow. Men dropped to the ground in exhaustion and fell asleep in the snow. Their officers could not rally them to continue the attack.

At 3 A.M. when Grippenberg was told of the battlefield error, he refused to believe it and did not pass it on to Kuropatkin.

General Stackelberg, furthermore, ignored twice-repeated orders from Grippenberg and seized a village of no consequence in a bayonet attack. Of its twenty-three officers and 1,500 other ranks, one regiment lost twenty-one officers and 1,150 other ranks killed, wounded, or missing in this attack. In this one action the First Siberian Rifle Corps lost a total of 6,000 men.

Both sides were now more adequately equipped with machineguns. In this sort of fighting, where fortified villages were being attacked and defended, the new guns proved devastating. One machinegun used by the Russians to defend Hei-kou-tai accounted for 180 men in a Japanese reserve company 220 men strong, while in the Russian attack on Pao-tai-tzu one Japanese gun was credited with causing a thousand casualties.

The weather was almost as deadly. A doctor whose hospital was just behind the Russian lines claimed that only those were saved among the wounded who with their own strength could crawl to the dressing stations. All others froze to death. There were not enough carts or stretchers, and the wounded fortunate enough to get back to evacuation centers were taken to Mukden in unheated freight cars. Many failed to survive the journey. The inspector of hospitals in the Second Army shot himself at the end of the battle. Stackelberg, whose unfortunate First Siberian Corps had lost 7,348 men, was relieved of his command. General Grippenberg declared himself ill and took off for St. Petersburg, pausing only long enough at Harbin to denounce Kuropatkin as a traitor.

The Grippenberg scandal, coupled with the failure to achieve any of

Kuropatkin's objectives in the battle, left the Russian forces more thoroughly demoralized than ever before. The quarrel between Alexeiev and Kuropatkin had been the cause of much discontent; the Grippenberg affair blazed through the entire army, and there were many who agreed that it would be better now to retreat beyond Mukden, and even Harbin, rather than risk battle when Nogi's army appeared.

CHAPTER 29

☙☙☙☙☙☙

Mukden

W ITH THEIR LEFT WING anchored in the wild and tangled mountains far to the southeast of Mukden and the center and right stretching for more than ninety miles across the frozen plains beyond the Sha and the Hun rivers, the three great Russian armies recoiled from the buffeting at San-de-pu and readied unsteadily to spring again. General Kaulbars, who had taken over from General Grippenberg, commanded the Second Manchurian Army in the plains on the right of the line. General Bilderling, with the Third Manchurian Army, looked after the massive defense system that had been created around Putilov and Novgorod hills, won so dearly at the Sha-ho. Linievitch, "the Siberian Wolf," had the First Manchurian Army and the mountains stretching away to the east.

No greater force had ever been assembled in the history of war—275,000 infantrymen, 16,000 cavalry, and 1,219 artillery pieces, including sixty howitzers and siege guns. In the five months that had passed since Kuropatkin fell back from Liaoyang much time had been spent fortifying Mukden's defenses. Some Russian officers still thought that they were impregnable. There were not very many, however, who believed that a continuing offensive would now reverse the pattern of previous defeats. The ill-fated sortie to San-de-pu and the bitter dissensions at the top had destroyed too much of what remained of the army's morale for any such ambitious notion as that.

Forty-five miles to the south, trains from Dalny and Port Arthur emptied their men and matériel into the great Japanese dumps at Liaoyang. Day and night the work went on with an impatience that countenanced not the slightest delay. Time had come for a major effort, but time was also running out.

Despite the creation of the Army of the Yalu, consisting of the First Reserve Division and the Eleventh Division, which had marched into the hills from Port Arthur, and the arrival of Nogi's Third Army, Oyama still could not match Kuropatkin man for man. His infantry totaled a shade under 200,000. He had only 7,350 cavalry and 992 artillery pieces, though these included some of the eleven-inch siege guns that had reduced Port Arthur. Only in machineguns was he more plentifully supplied: he had 992 against the Russians' fifty-six.

Just as soon as the Third Army and the newly formed Army of the Yalu were in position, Oyama intended to attack. Only a day after the Third Army had marched to its jumping-off place west of Liaoyang, he issued his orders. They sounded more optimistic than he and Kodama felt. "The object of the battle is to decide the issue of the war. The question is not one, therefore, of occupying certain points or seizing tracts of territory. It is essential that the enemy should be dealt a heavy blow. Since in all our battles hitherto pursuit has been very slow, it is imperative upon this occasion to pursue as promptly and as far as possible."

The orders called for General Kawamura's Army of the Yalu to march on the Russian coal mines at Fu-shun, twenty-five miles east of Mukden, on February 23, and for the other armies to begin their moves three or four days later as Kawamura's forces began to exert some real pressure on the Russians. In fact, the Army of the Yalu had already anticipated Oyama's orders and as early as the previous evening had made first contact with the Russian cavalry.

What concerned Kuropatkin and his fellow generals as they debated the possibility of their own coming offensive was the destination of Nogi's army. They were still uncertain as Kuropatkin issued his orders on the evening of February 21 for his own offensive to begin on February 24. In essence, these orders repeated those issued before San-de-pu. Kaulbars was to batter his way through the Japanese left wing after an intensive artillery preparation.

The war had taken a heavy toll on Kuropatkin. Plagued by interference from St. Petersburg, by the inadequacy of his officers, and by repeated defeats, he had become old and haggard, and his hair and beard turned white. His principal worry was that the Japanese had learned of his battle orders to renew the assault through San-de-pu. Much of February 24 was wasted while he sent a messenger to Kaulbars to ask him whether he thought the infantry attack should go ahead as planned on the following day. After a long council of war at his headquarters, Kaulbars phoned

Kuropatkin to ask him whether the general reserve could be sent to help him.

"Not a bayonet will be sent," replied Kuropatkin, who had now become acutely sensitive about the situation in the east. "Alexeiev [the general commanding the detachment engaged with the Army of the Yalu] is hard pressed."

Kaulbars thereupon exercised his discretion, and Kuropatkin's offensive died before birth. Instead of going into action against San-de-pu, the gallant First Siberian Corps, now commanded by General Gerngross, was detached from Kaulbars' command to march as quickly as possible to the left flank to meet the threat that appeared to be developing southeast of the Fu-shun mines.

From all parts of the Russian line the Japanese Army of the Yalu, with its Port Arthur campaigners, its scarcely blooded troops, and its veterans from the Sino-Japanese War, all but last of the reserves, fighting with blind courage and fanaticism, drew on itself forces—in all 42 battalions and 128 guns—that Kuropatkin had needed for his own offensive and was soon to need even more urgently in the west as Oyama's real plans began to unfold.

Kuropatkin was convinced now that Nogi's Third Army would strike in

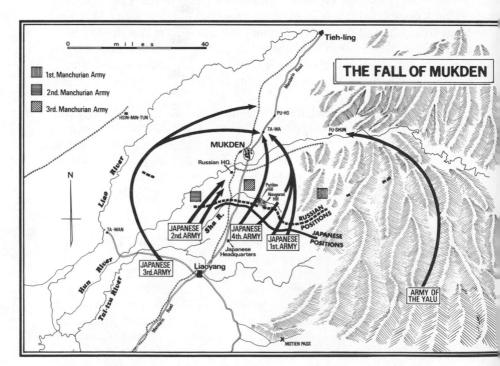

the east, but Nogi had not yet moved from his base west of Liaoyang. When he did move, his orders were to strike for an entirely different part of the battlefield.

Kuroki's First Army, which was in the hills to the west of the Army of the Yalu, now joined the action, and its three divisions started to fight their way forward. All was still quiet in the west, and it was not until February 27 that the Third Army began to move. It crossed the Hun and marched north with the Liao River on its left flank. Nogi expected to run headlong into the Russian cavalry, now led, in the absence of Mishchenko, who had been wounded in the San-de-pu action, by Major-General Pavel K. Rennenkampf. But Rennenkampf had also been rushed by Kuropatkin to the east to help block Kawamura and Kuroki. This was just what Kodama had planned. "I had resolved to attack the Russians by enveloping them apparently in the east, so that they might dispatch their main strength thither, while our main force was to be directed against the Sha-ho–Mukden–Tiehling section of railway, enveloping them from the west," he reported after the battle. "As soon as the first line had been taken by us and evacuated by the Russians, the First and Fourth armies were to advance northward at once to the east of Mukden." The plan worked perfectly, and, while the First and Fourth armies made their way east of Mukden, the Third Army, against negligible opposition, went on its way around the western flank.

Kodama had anticipated that the engagement would resolve itself into two battles fought side by side simultaneously on either side of the railway. He assumed that the Russians would take the offensive in one of these actions and preserve a defensive attitude on the other.

Not all of Kuropatkin's immediate subordinates shared his fears for the eastern front. General Bilderling, who held the Mandarin Road and railway leading to Mukden, envisaged an attack here. And on the evening of February 26, General Sakharov, Kuropatkin's chief of staff, said in a memorandum that the main Japanese concentrations were in the center and on the Russians' right flank.

Six of the eleven-inch howitzers from Port Arthur had been sent north by train and had gone to Nozu's Fourth Army on the plains in front of Bilderling. Here they were set in concrete to provide the thunder in an imposing array of 108 guns, ranging from 3.5 inches to 7.8 inches, with which Nozu was soon to hammer the Russian positions on Putilov and Novgorod hills. All of the early Russian optimism had evaporated, and officers at the second level now fully reflected the defeatism of their seniors.

On February 27, the Japanese guns opened fire with little accuracy but devastating effect on Russian morale. "It is impossible to hold the line now, our position is untenable," said a Russian officer as the first eleven-inch shells crashed among the defenses.

To add to this shock on the central front now came the most alarming news of all. About 11 A.M. on February 27 the Cossacks on the Russian right flank noticed Nogi's cavalry on the move, and throughout the day reports reached Kaulbars' headquarters of new and larger sightings. Hasty conferences set in motion a force consisting of two cavalry regiments and a horse battalion ordered to send patrols to Hsin-min-tun, forty-five miles northwest of Mukden, with the intention of establishing the depth of the Japanese penetration. A second but smaller, cavalry force, consisting of only two squadrons and four guns, was detailed to drive back the Japanese wherever they might be encountered.

Since their assignments were to cut across the face, or even to assault the entire strength of Nogi's Third Army, neither of these moves had the slightest effect on the Japanese advance. General Kaulbars had no doubt now about the nature of the threat that was building up out of sight across the plain, but since his own army had been badly depleted by the removal of forces to meet what Kuropatkin considered to be the threat in the east, he lacked the means to take immediate, effective action. Instead he began to think in terms of retreat. He also instructed that his siege guns and baggage should be sent to the rear.

That night Mukden saw great fires burning to the southwest, and the city buzzed with rumors brought in by the Chinese that they had been stopped by Japanese, not Russians, on the Liao River. Next day the Chinese Imperial Post,* which had run all winter between Mukden and Hsin-min-tun, failed to get through.

Oku's Second Army, which lay between Nogi and Nozu, now threw itself into the fray to prevent any large-scale redeployment by Kaulbars. With the Fifth Division as the spearhead and backed by a heavy concentration of artillery, it launched a furious assault.

Because of his catastrophic miscalculation at the beginning of the battle, Kuropatkin, like Kaulbars, also found himself short of reserves and in no position to respond adequately to Nogi's move. He realized that it would take several days to accumulate a sufficient force for the task. The best he could hope to achieve in the interim was some sort of screening operation that might slow down Nogi's advance. All he could find immediately were the eight battalions of the First Brigade of the Forty-first Division and three batteries of guns—an entirely inadequate force for the task.

February 28 was artillery day, and Putilov and Novgorod hills were the major Japanese targets. Hour after hour the Japanese shells crashed in. A Russian ammunition dump went up in a great cloud of black smoke near

---

*The mail service.

the railway line, and on the next day, when the bombardment resumed, Bilderling also gave orders to send the baggage to the rear. So inaccurate were the eleven-inch siege guns, and so strong were the defenses on the two hills, that the Russians' physical casualties were negligible; but morale sagged with each new incoming round. The reports from the hills grew gloomier and gloomier, and Kuropatkin was now half inclined to believe that the major Japanese attack might yet come from this direction.

Between March 2 and March 7 the battle hung in a state of suspension while Kuropatkin's reserves sought to block Nogi's path and to contain the armies of Oku, Nozu, Kuroki, and Kawamura. Behind the Russian lines there was both demoralization and disorganization. Exhausted troops straggled from one side of the battlefield to the other, their paths blocked by the paraphernalia of the withdrawal—a jumble of carts drawn by oxen, donkeys, horses, and mules, and containing, among other military necessities, heavy tables, beds, baths, cases of champagne, and even dog kennels.

In Mukden itself, rear-echelon Russians were filled with a consuming desire to drink all the city's stocks of vodka and champagne. As supply dumps became vulnerable to the Japanese advance, the Russian troops fell on them hungrily. "Great scenes raged round the vodka cases," wrote Francis McCullagh, reporting the scene from a station close to Third Manchurian Army headquarters, where stocks were being destroyed.

> The barrels had been stabbed with bayonets and hacked open with knives, swords, and axes till they bled from scores of wounds. A frantic crowd of men struggled round these openings seeking to apply their mouths to them or to catch the precious liquids in cups, cans, empty sardine tins, and even the cases of the Japanese shells that were falling conveniently around. A huge red-capped Orenburg Cossack jumped on one of the barrels wielding an axe with which he soon stove in the head of another barrel amid wild cries of drunken delight. . . . The vodka that overflowed from the burst casks collected a foot deep in a depression in the ground. Men knelt down to drink the muddy liquor, scooped it up in the hollows of their hands as one would scoop up water from a well. Some fell into it bodily. Many were wetted by the jets of liquor from the barrels squirting over them. Buriat Cossacks, Mohammedans from the Caucasus, forbidden by their religion to touch drink; riflemen, dragoons, all sorts and conditions of military people, joined in this mad spree and with the dust and the smoke from the burning stores eddying around them, they looked like alcoholic demons struggling in the wreck of hell.

Kaulbars' Second Army was broken up to provide the nucleus of the screen with which Kuropatkin hoped to block Nogi's path. Kaulbars took command of this force, and the rump of his army, which only a week earlier had been ready to launch the offensive, ceased to exist as an organized, disciplined fighting force. Corps, divisions, and brigades which had split up and disappeared finally reemerged as hastily improvised detachments.

A blinding snow storm on March 2 turned into a blizzard, hampering the Russians in their attempts to redeploy and shielding the Japanese as they advanced. For the first time, however, Nogi slowed down, and most of the Fourth Army made little progress. Early in the evening of March 2 a report reached Kuropatkin that Nogi's forces had changed direction and that, instead of moving north, had swung round and headed east toward Mukden itself. Another contradictory report put a division of Nogi's troops north of the Mukden—Hsin-min-tun road. Whatever the truth of the reports, Kuropatkin had to react and to draw on whatever troops he could find, this time on the dwindling resources of General Bilderling's Third Manchurian Army.

Far to the east, General Rennenkampf continued to hold off the Army of the Yalu, but here, at a critical moment on March 3, the supply columns from Fu-shun station failed to get through with artillery and small arms ammunition, and the Japanese, discovering their opponents' difficulties, stormed the key hill that dominated the right section of the Russian defenses. Cooks, bandsmen, and clerks hastily gathered to renew the assault for the Russians; to the strains of the national anthem and with colors flying, they reoccupied part of the hill. For the Russians it was a rare and brief moment of glory in a period of unrelieved disaster.

Aware of the great movement of men and matériel that was taking place behind the Russian lines, Oyama wanted to maintain the illusion that his main thrust might come through the center. Despite the shaken morale on Putilov and Novgorod hills, Bilderling's men were still holding most of their ground. Both the Fourth Army and Kuroki's First Army had assailed the southern rim of the Russian defenses with little to show for their efforts.

In Mukden, the frenzy of the drunken parties grew wilder. Only in Kuropatkin's train was there complete calm. McCullagh, who had earlier lost himself in the torrent of men, horses, guns, Red Cross wagons, transport cars, and commandeered Chinese vehicles that was converging on Mukden from the newly abandoned position in the west, finally found his way to the station on the night of March 3. Both Kuropatkin's and Kaulbars' trains were at the station. He noted that one window of Kuropatkin's train was blocked by the back of a typical waiter

standing in faultless evening dress behind his master's chair, his spine bent at an angle of well-bred attention. On the steps of the carriage stood Kuropatkin's adjutant, smiling, suave, exceedingly well groomed, every brass button and gold tag on his uniform shining like a mirror. He was chatting pleasantly with somebody and seemed as serenely oblivious of the hordes of beaten men who were tramping past as if he were standing in one of the most exclusive drawing rooms in St. Petersburg.

Kuropatkin refused to concede defeat. On the contrary, he wanted Kaulbars to attack on the following morning. Unaware even of the location of some of the units with which he was to make his assault, Kaulbars demurred: it was impossible to do more than hold the line against Nogi on March 4; the attack would have to wait until March 5.

Although his fears appear to have been exaggerated, Oyama also was worried. After its brilliant start, Nogi's Third Army was now not making the progress he hoped for. He responded characteristically by ordering the last of his reserves into the attack with the Third Army.

With the return to his command of the First Siberian Corps, haggard and exhausted but still willing to fight, Kaulbars collected the numerous detachments that had come under his command under the banner of the Second Manchurian Army again. At 2 A.M. on March 5, after hours of work with staff borrowed from Kuropatkin, he issued his orders for the offensive. On the right was General Gerngross with the eighteen battalions of the First Siberian Corps and thirty other battalions. The Twenty-sixth Infantry Division was in the center, and another thirty-two battalions were on the left. The three forces were supported by 199 guns.

Red-faced Tserpitski addressed the troops before they moved. "Men of Minsk," he began, but this was too formal. "Children," he corrected himself, "Russia always conquers. We will conquer now. Advance and sweep these Japanese pagans to hell. There will be no retreat, no coming back."

Like so many other Russian counterattacks, this desperate bid to save Mukden was hesitant and unsure. General Gerngross was slow to move the First Siberians. General Tserpitski himself came under attack, and Kaulbars reinforced him from Gerngross's columns, thereby robbing the offensive of any real thrust. The attempt was that of cautious men, afraid of their flanks, afraid of the enemy, and already convinced that the battle was lost.

That night Kuropatkin studied the reports of the day and concluded gloomily that, though "very little had been done," he would try again on March 6. Military historians have blamed Kuropatkin for taking a too restricted view of his task. It was not enough to have knocked together a sizeable army for Kaulbars and to have ordered it into the offensive; if he wanted to strike with all his might, his other two armies should have been committed to the offensive, thereby forcing Oyama to think twice before continuing with his own hazardous offensive plans. He was quite simply out-generaled. Kaulbars' performance was no better. His plans called for even less aggression than his forces had shown on the previous day.

Kodama now appreciated that his assumptions about Kuropatkin's tactics at the beginning of the battle were in error. Instead of taking the offensive on one side of the railway and the defensive on the other, the Russians had been defensive on both sides. "This greatly simplified matters for us," said Kodama. "It also made the result of the battle far greater than had been anticipated. It was never thought possible by us that we could surround the Russians and bring about a second Sedan."

Discreetly, Kuropatkin questioned Kaulbars' lack of offensive spirit in his orders. In a telephone conversation with Bilderling he was much less discreet. "The Second Army is not acting energetically," he said. "Its orders are wretched."

Whatever improvement Kaulbars might have effected in his planning, Oyama still called the shots. Alarmed now that the retreat of the Russian armies might dangerously expose Nogi's Third Army, he ordered the Second Army to draw on itself the maximum amount of Russian attention during the day. It succeeded at bloody cost. Of the 5,500 men who went out in the morning only 1,300 were not either killed or wounded.

This action was not in any way decisive, but it marked a turning point in the minds of the opposing army commanders. Kuropatkin had seen his offensive wither and die. Oyama girded for the chase.

During the afternoon Kuropatkin decided to pull back the First and Third Manchurian armies secretly after nightfall, leaving only a strong rearguard to hold out as long as possible. The moment of crisis was near. That night a patrol from Nogi's army cut the railway line north of Mukden. Before it was restored, Kuropatkin sent a dramatic message to St. Petersburg: "I am surrounded." This exaggerated the situation, but the escape route was clearly in peril. It was saved only by a savage and effective assault on the First Infantry (Reserve) Brigade, which was closing on the road and railway when it was routed by the Russians. "The long serpent must not be allowed to escape," Oyama's headquarters warned Nogi.

Reviewing the situation with his staff in his train at Mukden station, Kaulbars counted up to see what was still available in the way of combat forces and concluded that there was "only one way out of the difficult situation in which we are now in"—to launch a general attack with 220 of the 321 battalions.

A general attack along the line had also been Oyama's plan early in the evening of March 7. At midnight he learned that Kuropatkin's "secret" move had begun. At 12:20 A.M. on March 8 he sent out new operational orders to his armies, adding: "I intend to pursue in earnest and to turn the enemy's retreat into a rout."

Kuroki received his orders from Oyama as soon as they were issued. Ten minutes later from his headquarters, he issued his own orders. Typically, they began "1) The enemy in our front has begun to retreat; 2) the army is to press the enemy to the utmost."

The Japanese First Army now took off. During the morning, patrols discovered that the Russians had retired all along the Sha. Kuroki amended his orders to give further impetus to the assault. If possible, his forces were to cut the Mukden–Fu-shun line by nightfall on March 8. For days the staff had debated the merits of an all-out frontal attack against the heavily defended Russian positions, but they knew that enormous losses would have resulted and Kuroki had not been ready to squander his forces in such reckless effort. Oyama's order changed his mind. He now told his divisional commanders to race to the Hun, even if they lost half their men in the effort.

The move was slower than Kuroki had hoped and the First Army failed to cross the Hun on the eighth. Still, the retreating Russians had no time to prepare new defenses along the river, and the Guards streamed across the following day without opposition, then headed west to round the circle of fire that Oyama hoped to bring on Kuropatkin's armies in Mukden.

They were helped, as were the attacking Japanese forces all along the line, by one of the worst dust storms in Mukden's history. A warm southerly gale brought with it the fine, loess dust from the plains and hurled it in the eyes of the Russian defenders. It was so thick that in Mukden visibility was no more than a few feet, and along the front until noon on March 10 visibility was never more than a hundred yards.

For the Russian soldiers in Mukden it was too late to loot anything but liquor. Drunken soldiers roamed the streets, threatening anyone in their sight. The imperial northern tombs had become a battleground. To the west of the city no one had time to bury the dead. Thousands of exhausted Russian infantrymen slept among dead saddle and work horses and the debris of slaughtered sheep and bursting shrapnel.

For a time early in the afternoon the wind blew less fiercely and the dust storm subsided. Around 4 o'clock, however, it was blowing as hard as ever and to the dust was now added the smoke of burning Russian supply dumps. When darkness thus closed in more than an hour early, the Chinese in Mukden became filled with superstitious fear that soon communicated itself to the Russians. There was panic at the railway station as train after train, headlights scarcely penetrating the dust and smoke, pulled out with the wounded.

A brilliant contribution to Russian apprehensions was now made by a

Chinese named Yang Chen-tung, who had been working as an interpreter for the Russian Fourth Army headquarters. Yang, who was in the employ of the Japanese, warned the Russians on instruction from the Japanese that the Japanese Second and Third armies threatened the Russians' flank and rear and that, if they did not withdraw, their escape routes would be cut off.

On the evening of March 9, however, Kuropatkin was still unaware of the dangers now posed by the Guards Division. The continuing threat from Nogi's Third Army alone had been sufficient cause for him to order the general withdrawal to Tieh-ling. At 6:45 P.M., he instructed General Sakharov to arrange for the retreat during the night. Kuropatkin's order and the news of the Guards' breakthrough reached Sakharov almost simultaneously. At 8:15 P.M., within half an hour of the receipt of Kuropatkin's message, the orders were signed and fifteen minutes later, with haste and urgency, they were issued.

For ten days Mukden had heard the sound of rifle fire pressing ever closer. That night it was at the walls. For several hours a single great gun pounded out its shells at regular intervals. "No wonder our faces paled with superstitious awe when we heard that funeral note," wrote McCullagh. "It was the death bell tolling for the loss of Mukden, the passing away of Russia's great empire in Manchuria. . . . Nay, who knows but that it was the death knell of the Russian army itself?"

All the private trains of the senior generals, including Kuropatkin's, were now pressed into service in a desperate effort to evacuate Mukden ahead of the arrival of the Japanese. At 11 o'clock the first group of eight trains, each with fifty carriages and trucks and loaded with artillery matériel and other supplies, pulled out. Another group left at 4 A.M. on the tenth and a third at dawn. Vast quantities of matériel nevertheless had to be left behind, and soon after dawn the Russians put a match to the supply depots and ammunition dumps. Mukden was rocked again by the sound of massive explosions, including one soon after 7 A.M. that demolished the great steel bridge across the Hun.

For the retreating Russians, there were days of agony ahead. The military attachés and correspondents had debated for several days whether Kuropatkin could escape again or whether this would not at last be his Sedan. They envisaged Kuropatkin fleeing to the west, attacked not only by the pursuing Japanese but also by Chinese and Chunchuses. Most observers predicted total disaster, and several decided to stay behind in Mukden.

Kuropatkin elected to take the lesser risk and to fall back along his lines of communication, the Mandarin Road and the railway. Dr. Veresáev, who left with his hospital unit ahead of the rout, wrote:

The torrent of cars, wrapped in dust, slowly moved on, stopped, stood still, again began to move. At narrow turns of the road, when entering a village, or near the bridges, the confusion became intolerable. Ten rows of carts could not get by at once, and they hurried on, and tried to cut each other out, came in conflict, and were in each other's way. The red, savage faces slashed through the dust, and the sound of blows, the swish of whips and hoarse curses could be heard. As always, the authorities, forever annoyingly present when they are not needed, were absent here. No one in command gave orders, and the carts struggled on in the rear. The jam was terrible. . . . New baggage trains kept pouring from the crossroads into the Mandarin Road. In the rear the cannon thundered in a broad semicircle and the rifle discharges rattled.

By noon the Japanese, in considerable force, were threatening Ta-wa on the Mandarin Road, only six miles from the walls of Mukden. With the Japanese on both sides of the road and railway, the scene seemed to be set for a mammoth ambush in which the Second and Third Manchurian armies might well be destroyed. As the Second Army began to converge on the village of Wan-tzu-yeh, the Japanese infantry seized the railway embankment and, supported by artillery, began to fire on the densely packed ranks of Russians. Until this point there had been some order in the withdrawal. Though they were not deployed for action, troops were marching in formation, and, on the road, where progress was very slow, the long lines of carts were at least moving. With the first Japanese shots, the Russian troops broke and ran for cover in a ravine near the village, and the carts tried to follow them. For a time some 10,000 troops, without leaders and without formation, hoping without success to escape the Japanese rifle and artillery fire, huddled under the banks of the ravine. Out of the chaos, two generals, Tserpitski and von der Launitz, tried to rally a force to fight. A third had reached the village ahead of his troops and was captured. General Tserpitski received a wound in the leg, which ultimately led to his death. Despite his wound, Tserpitski continued to organize the resistance until two other generals, Dembovski and Vasilev, arrived with other forces.

General Dembovski, taking charge, succeeded in holding off the Japanese long enough to allow the retreat to continue, though throughout the day retreating troops who followed came under attack. One of these was McCullagh, who had joined the retreat after the blowing up of the Hun River bridge. He plodded his way to the north in an ever-growing motley of empty ammunition carts, dismounted Cossacks, wounded men, drunks, and unarmed soldiers "who seemed to be insane." Like most who had gone before them, they kept close to the railway. Ta-wa was in the line of their retreat.

"About a square mile of ground seemed to have been strewn thick with old mess tins, overturned carts, canteens, boots, socks, palliasses, dead horses, bags of flour, rifles, bayonets, cartridge clips, and cartridges," McCullagh noted. He paused to inspect the damage and was showered with bullets. Along with hundreds of others he rushed to the railway embankment and continued his march north on the other side. Repeatedly, other wandering bands of Russians encountered his group and exchanged shots. Each time more men were killed or wounded. For some time the Japanese shadowed them, lacking sufficient strength to move in for the *coup de grâce*. A colonel who refused to get off his horse was shot through the head and died instantly. Other officers, trying to organize the rabble, continued to expose themselves to Japanese fire. The Japanese marksmen shot them down one after another. There could be only one end to this pursuit. It came when Japanese reinforcements arrived and captured those in flight, McCullagh among them.

To the east, Linievitch's First Army retreated in fair order and with some discipline. Bilderling's First Manchurian Army and Kaulbars' Second disintergrated. Kaulbars, gray with dust and fatigue, and with a broken collarbone and rib caused in a fall from his horse, had paused to rest when an officer inquired where he might find the Seventh Regiment. Kaulbars overheard the remark. "The Seventh Regiment?" he repeated. "I do not know what has become of my whole army, and he asks me where my Seventh Regiment is?"

Kuropatkin tried desperately to restore some sort of order to the retreat. He succeeded in organizing two rear guards to follow the railway track and a third to protect the stragglers on the Mandarin Road. But time and again panic swept through the ranks of fleeing men, especially when the Japanese succeeded in blocking their path.

The Mandarin Road looked like a garbage dump. The *British Official History of the Russo-Japanese War* gave a dramatic description. "There were carts in matchwood, wagons with their wheels in the air—some with axles, some with poles smashed to atoms—while valises, haversacks, saddles, cooking pots, bread, forage, and every kind of baggage lay crushed by horses' hoofs or by the wheels of vehicles which had passed over them."

Five miles beyond Ta-wa was the village of P'u-ho, which gave its name to the small stream close by. The Mandarin Road passed through the center of the village and across the stream by a bridge that had been destroyed. Since the river had high banks, it was difficult for the carts to cross, especially since the warm sun had melted the ice for a distance of several feet close to the northern bank. Some troops had used the railway bridge to cross, but scores of Russians gathered at the steep banks, while engineers tried to build a crossing. The Japanese artillery worked on both flanks. With reckless fear the Russians attempted to drive their artillery and carts down the steep banks and across the river. Hours passed in futile frenzy. Then, as the Japanese shells came thicker, the troops abandoned their baggage and fled on foot, leaving behind a mass of carts, guns, and personal belongings.

Frederick McCormick said it all looked like a great fair swept by a hurricane. Four hundred carts and caissons were left in the river, but eventually a crossing place was made and "a vast phalanx of runaways, on foot, on horseback, in carts and wagons, on field soup-wagons, Siberian wagons, tarantasses, and other equipages swept through the little chasm that had caused this undoing, and moving with the dust fell upon the contingents in the path beyond."

A caravan of twenty-five carts carrying the Mukden staff of the Russo-Chinese Bank had struggled to the far side of the river. Its baggage included the bank's deposits of about a quarter of a million roubles and a piano. The sight of the piano was too much for the troops. Wounded were left behind, they said, while officers carted off their musical instruments. With wild fury they fell on the caravan, killing some of the guards and grabbing the money. The manager escaped on the top of an ammunition caisson and his associate fled on a soup wagon, hugging the flue. All discipline collapsed. Troops turned against their own officers, rifled their baggage, stole their horses, threw them out of their carts, and fled. Nightfall brought no relief. Some of the better organized groups stopped and set up perimeter defenses. Others straggled on, got lost, and sometimes even began to retrace their steps. Rumors spread through the ranks, adding to the terror. Fifty thousand Japanese were said to be advancing from the west . . . ten thousand British troops had joined in the fight . . . hordes of Chunchuses were massing. . . .

But Oyama's *coup de grâce* remained undelivered. He had won the battle, but his forces failed him at the last moment. The Army of the Yalu did not exploit its advantage fully and stopped near the Hun River. Nogi's Third Army seemed to feel that it had achieved enough when it reached the railway north of Mukden, and the Second and Fourth armies wasted time in and around the city. Army commanders failed to obey orders. Many of the replacement troops were of inferior quality. The victory was celebrated as Army Memorial Day until the end of World War II, but privately many Japanese senior officers were bitterly critical of their performance. Their armies could win battles, but they could not deliver a decisive blow.

Cold fear drove the Russians across the plains to the safety of the mountains around Tieh-ling. Terror put wings on their feet. Though urged to pursue, Nogi's and Kuroki's men were simply not fast enough to catch them. Oyama's weakest arm had always been his cavalry. It did not fail him now: he just did not have enough horsemen or enough ammunition. His infantrymen were spent.

*   *   *

And so into Tieh-ling, some still on horseback, some on foot, came the Russian generals. Kuropatkin's train awaited them at the station. It was Sunday, and they came, as usual, to pray—Kaulbars, with his broken collarbone and rib; Tserpitski, with the wound in the leg from which he was soon to die; Bilderling and grizzled old Linievitch, on whose shoulders great responsibility was soon to rest.

Kuropatkin had lost one third of his armies in the battle. More than 20,000 had been killed or were missing in action, apart from the 20,000 left behind in Japanese hands. The wounded numbered more than 49,000. The Japanese casualties reflected the ferocity of the action. Oyama lost 15,892 officers and men killed and 59,612 wounded, or more than a quarter of the forces committed to battle.

Rumors and stragglers continued to flow into Tieh-ling for several days, and Kuropatkin could at last make some sort of assessment of the residual fighting strength of his armies. Short of arms and ammunition, with much of his transport lost to the Japanese, with the morale of his troops apparently beyond the point of no return, and convinced that Oyama would now try to outflank him on the Tieh-ling line, he decided to abandon it without a fight and to retreat to Hsi-ping-kai, ten days' march to the north.

His troops put the torch to Tieh-ling and went their way, bands playing and singing hymns, but without maps, into the *terra incognita* of northern Manchuria. Two days later the Tsar directed Kuropatkin to hand over command to Linievitch and to return to Irkutsk.

Kuropatkin's action now was typical. He got only as far as Harbin when he telegraphed St. Petersburg, pleading to be allowed to remain in a subordinate capacity. "I may not be a good general," he said, "but I am at least as good as some of my corps commanders."

Nicholas concurred. Kuropatkin took over from Linievitch as commander of the First Manchurian Army and returned to Hsi-ping-kai, where his troops, free now from the immediate threat of destruction at the hands of Oyama, gave him a hero's welcome.

CHAPTER 30

ଌଌଌଌଌଌ

Journey of the Damned

THE NEWS OF THE FALL of Port Arthur and with it the loss of the First Pacific Squadron had spread swiftly through Rozhdestvenski's ships in January. The mission seemed doomed. "We shall have about as much chance as a gamecock would have in a battle with a vulture," said Engineer Vasiliev* on the battleship *Orel*. Long before Mukden fell, morale had begun to collapse.

Everyday there was blatant insubordination. A sailor in *Orel*, tired of coaling, threw away his shovel and walked toward his quarters. An officer grabbed the man and shook him. "Don't you know, idiot, what I could have done to you for this?"

The sailor, full of potent *kvass*, brewed on all the ships, replied that he was afraid of nothing now. Soon they would all be dead. "Do you think I care a tinker's curse if you draw that pistol and put a bullet through my head?"

The officer turned away. He had lost control.

Rozhdestvenski felt that he had lost control over the movements of the fleet as well. On his arrival at Sainte Marie, a French penal colony, east of Madagascar, he heard from Felkerzam that he was at Nossi-Bé with his ships on the other side of the island and unable to sail for another two weeks.

Rozhdestvenski was furious. "If they are so old that they can't steam,

---

*Novikov-Priboy's pseudonym for V. P. Kostenko, who later occupied an important position in the naval dockyards of the Soviet Union.

then they may go to the devil. We have no use for rubbish here. But no, it is simply the old custom! However, I'll go there myself—I'll drag them out fast enough!" he told Semenov.

Sainte Marie was like all the other tropical ports that the fleet had visited, —hot, steamy, and wet—but the inhabitants were unfriendly and even the French who had made the place into a jail for political prisoners and murderers had little control over them. Two officers had recently been killed in the settlement, and few of the Russian fleet's crew were permitted ashore. Only two colliers were waiting, and it took a very short time to load the inadequate rations of coal.

As the ships were leaving the unfriendly shores of Sainte Marie a tugboat hurried to the flagship with the news that the First Pacific Squadron at Port Arthur had been destroyed. This was disaster enough, but the last part of the message from St. Petersburg was the final straw for Admiral Rozhdestvenski. A third squadron was on the way out from Libau to the Far East.

Captain Klado had won. On his return from the international commission on the Dogger Bank incident in Paris, he had persuaded the authorities that Rozhdestvenski's squadron could not defeat the Japanese without further assistance. In a series of articles in the *Novoye Vremya* he forecast defeat unless reinforcements were sent immediately. His plan was for a third squadron to leave for the Far East, and for hundreds of torpedo boats and midget submarines to be sent in sections by rail to Vladivostok, where they could be assembled. All available ships must leave Russia, he insisted, no matter how old or decrepit. "Don't wait for a third squadron to be completed, just send them as they are ready, one after another. Some could go today. Do not let us worry about defense at home. Nobody can fight the whole world."

On the day that 203 Meter Hill fell, Rear-Admiral Nicholas Nebogatov was appointed commander of the Third Pacific Squadron.* It was made up mainly of ships Rozhdestvenski had rejected as unsuitable for the long voyage and the task at the end of it. They were to help him in the battle against the Japanese Combined Fleet, and he was to await their arrival, in eight or ten weeks' time.

Before retiring to his cabin, Admiral Rozhdestvenski called Clapier de Colongue and instructed him to send a telegraph to St. Petersburg. "Tell them I wish to be relieved of my command," he said. He closed the door of his cabin and locked it.

---

*Yet another squadron was being prepared to come to Rozhdestvenski's assistance. This included three battleships—*Slava,* launched in 1904, but not completed, the *Alexander II,* fifteen years old, and *Pamiat Azova,* which had taken the Tsar to Japan in October 1890. This squadron never left Russia.

"Are they joking or have they quite lost their heads?" asked Chief Engineer Politovski in a letter to his wife. "Everywhere failures, corruption, stupidity, and mistakes. There is not one bright spot. All around is hopeless darkness."

Christmas day came as the flagship made its way to Nossi-Bé, with the temperature crawling up into the nineties. After Mass, the crew of *Suvarov* was called to the quarterdeck for an unheralded address by the Admiral, who had not been seen since the signal arrived telling him of the dispatch of Nebogatov's fleet. Rozhdestvenski looked depressed and exhausted as he climbed to a gun turret, champagne glass in hand, but there was little sympathy in the faces of the ship's company lined up to hear his speech.

He began with platitudes, wishing them safe return when the job was done. "You as well as I serve our country side by side. But it is my right and my duty to report to the Tsar how you are doing your duty, what fine fellows you are, and he himself will thank you in the name of Russia."

His tone was quiet and listless, but as he went on a tremor crept into his voice. His audience, at first hostile, fell under his spell. Men now listened intently as he continued, his shoulders straight but his voice breaking so that they could hear the sobs. "Always remember that the whole of Russia is looking upon you with confidence and in firm hope. May God help us to serve her honorably, to justify her confidence, not to deceive her hopes." He raised his glass to his lips, emptied it, and waved it like a flag above his bare head: "To you, whom I trust! To Russia!"

The Admiral's voice was drowned out by cheers as men threw their caps in the air and crossed themselves. Men who had come to scoff found themselves in tears. "We'll do it! We won't give in!" "Lead us! Lead us!" Their cries were lost in the thunder of a thirty-one-gun salute, but the men took a long time to calm down. "Oh, if we could go into action now!" Commander Semenov wrote in his diary.

The big island of Nossi-Bé and the dozens of smaller islets clustered around it, formed the harbor in which the fleet anchored. Officers who had been there said the harbor, dotted with the white houses of the European residents and the rough, red clay huts of the natives set against the vivid green of the surrounding jungle, was more beautiful than the Bay of Naples. The town was called Hellville, after the French admiral who had taken it for France in 1841. As time went by, it seemed to many in the fleet that no better name could have been found for it. For a time after the long journey it was Heaven. The reunion of the ships with Admiral Felkerzam's ships was a joyful one. Bands played on the flagships of all three admirals. The meeting of the admirals at lunch in the *Suvarov* was nevertheless cool. Rumors spread quickly that the spontaneous goodwill of other officers did not carry over into the highest circles.

Even the brief enthusiasm of the crews of Rozhdestvenski's squadron died with the announcement that there was no mail awaiting them. Coaling was now the main concern. For four days they labored in the heat, their faces and clothing blackened by the dust that turned to sooty liquid with the perspiration from their bodies. Several cases of sunstroke were reported, and two sailors in *Borodino* died from the poisonous coal fumes.

Sickness spread throughout the fleet. Men contracted malaria, dysentry, typhoid, and ear diseases, but the worst complaint of all was a tropical eczema, accompanied by frightful irritation. Those affected scratched themselves raw, adding to their agony by pouring vodka, kerosene, and eau de cologne over the inflamed spots.

The ships were also decaying. Barnacles and moss covered their sides and hulls and everything on board grew slimy and filthy. On deck, animals bred and increased—porcupines, hares, pigs, monkeys. Small crocodiles—kept in the officers' wardroom—helped to turn the warships into floating menageries. Monkeys swung from the riggings and bright tropical birds perched everywhere, uttering wild, never-before-heard cries. Rats increased in number and inflicted painful bites. The ships stank, and bad meat thrown overboard from *Esperance,* whose refrigeration plant had broken down, attracted swarms of sharks.

The Admiral remained in his cabin, seen by few. All about him the fleet was rotting. Rumors of conditions at home reached the ships in newspapers and the few letters that got through. There were barricades in the streets of St. Petersburg. Two thousand people had been killed and many more wounded. "They lie," wrote Engineer Politovski without conviction, "but there is never smoke without fire." The constant repair work, sometimes underwater, surrounded by sharks, was taking its toll. He wrote: "How I curse that I have come with the fleet. Here I sit chained, seeing the mistakes of others. I have already feared that I shall go mad."

Complaints began to come in from the town. The lack of rain and failure of the crops were blamed on the visit of the Russian ships. Gangs of sailors had wrecked some shops in Hellville and money had been stolen from the offertory box of a church.

Rozhdestvenski was roused from his sick bed to deal with the chaos that had increased during his breakdown. He closed the gambling centers and allowed shore leave to men only on feast days. "You men and your ship are a disgrace to the fleet," he told one captain. All pets had to be thrown overboard or put on shore.

Rozhdestvenski decided that, despite the shortage of ammunition, the ships should put to sea for exercises. These proved completely unsuccessful. Ships nearly collided, the gunnery was wild, and formations became very confused. On one of the battleships a munition hoist jammed. On investigation, a cobra's nest was discovered, with the snake coiled around the rope of the hoist. Apparently it had come aboard in a bale of hay for the livestock.

Rozhdestvenski's orders to the fleet were full of contradictory instructions. One day he appealed to captains to work their men harder, the next he reminded them of the shortage of ammunition. Target practice and maneuvers continued to fall short of his expectations. Every day bitter sarcasm crept into his orders.

If we have not learned to work together during the four months we have been in company, we are hardly likely to do so by the time we may, under God's will, expect to meet the enemy . . . by day the entire squadron did not score *one single hit* on the targets which represented the torpedo boats, although these targets differed from the Japanese torpedo boats to our advantage, inasmuch as that they were stationary. . . .

Several ships that were continually breaking down were dismissed and returned to Russia, including the *Malay*, laden with sick and insane men, and the *Esperance*, whose refrigeration plant had finally collapsed. Over 700 tons of bad meat were thrown overboard from the *Esperance*, adding to the filth around the ships and attracting still more sharks.

As the food became poorer, discipline of many of the ships deteriorated still further. Often the offenses were of a kind that would normally have carried a death sentence. But Rozhdestvenski would not listen to those who regarded him as being too lenient. "How can I intimidate men ready to follow me to the death by condemning them to be hanged?" he asked. "Before going into action all prisoners are to be released, and—who can tell? perhaps *they* will prove to be the heroes."

All disturbances on the ships were attended to by Rozhdestvenski personally, and, after every visit to an offending ship, his nerves suffered. It seemed to *Suvarov*'s staff that the Admiral had had a slight stroke. Every now and then he retired to his cabin, to reappear a day or so later, thinner and more haggard, a small pulse near his temple twitching and his left leg dragging.

After the telegram from St. Petersburg in January his condition deteriorated. He confided in few of his staff, but everyone knew that he had been ordered to keep going and to gain command of the sea, after which he was to force his way to Vladivostok, bringing with him supplies and ammunition to reinforce the ships already there. All this was to be accomplished with the help of God.

The "fresh water" sailors in St. Petersburg said that if Rozhdestvenski felt his squadron was not strong enough for the job, every available ship remaining in the Baltic would be sent to his assistance. He was asked for his views and replied tartly that he had no prospect of gaining command of the sea. The addition of old and inefficient ships would not strengthen his squadron but hamper it, he said.

The food situation was becoming desperate. Cattle were brought alongside the ships and hauled aboard by their horns, but fresh vegetables were scarce and expensive. Casks of pickles and salt meat which had traveled with the squadron from Libau exploded while being opened and the putrid contents had to be thrown overboard. Mutiny broke out on several of the ships because of the poor food. Politovski visited the *Gromki,* a torpedo boat, to carry out repairs. "It was time to eat but they did not think of laying a table. They brought the crew their cabbage soup and my appetite left me. There were only four sausages for the officers. . . . Life on board a torpedo boat is sufficiently penal but in this one they starve as well," he wrote.

Clothing and boots were almost worn out and some officers had their uniforms tailored from sheeting since no other material was available. Officers sat around drinking tea or vodka out of jam jars, because on most ships the glassware had been broken. They were barefooted and often in only vests and trousers. "I cannot become accustomed to such a sight somehow," wrote the meticulous Politovski, who complained if his laundry came back unstarched.

Drink became the ruling passion. Though shore leave was restricted, officers could draw whatever they wanted from their canteens. Men stole from the officers, or bought supplies from bumboats* that visited the ships. Wild parties took place on many ships, officers and men joining together in drunken orgies which usually resulted in one or two of the participants going overboard. It was as though a wind of lunacy had blown across the squadron, wrote Novikov-Priboy.

Politovski, long a teetotaler, could find no ice for the desalinated water which made him ill. Beside himself with despair, he began to drink. "I indulged myself and drank some *kvass,* which is made of rye flour and malt," he wrote to his wife. *Borodino* gave a party in his honor, laying the dining table in the shape of the letter "P," with flowerpots and blossoms scattered over the cloth. The band played, and wine flowed in streams. "At first I drank nothing," he wrote, "but, having eaten my fill, and sitting listening to the band and hearing my beloved little Russian march, I began to drink champagne . . . and with each glass I remembered how you feared that I should take to drink . . ."

Only the arrival of the mail saved Politovski. A large bundle, tied with

---

*Originally a scavenger boat in the Thames. Later, the name was given to small craft offering goods and services to ships at anchor.

a ribbon, was brought to him. He ran to his cabin and read the letters over and over again. Everywhere it was the same. For the living, the mail brought salvation. But there were also letters from home for men who had despaired and killed themselves and for those who had become insane. Toasts were drunk and the bands played. Many men were crying—all their letters had come at once, after months without a word.

Rozhdestvenski decided not to wait for Nebogatov's ships, which were proceeding to the Far East through the Mediterranean. The fleet should go on while it was still capable of sailing. Everywhere men were writing home, scribbling furiously, to mail letters ashore before the departure. Politovski took his own letters into Hellville, feeling calmer now that he had heard from his wife. In a month they would be in Vladivostok—"that means that if nothing happens and if the fleet leaves here soon we shall see each other at the beginning of May."

Back from mailing letters to his wife, Politovski found that *Kamchatka* was sinking, with the men up to their chests in water in the engine room. *Aurora* was in trouble with her davits, and both *Orel* and *Anadyr* reported machinery defects. At the very last moment two lost supply ships turned up from Russia with supplies, including badly needed boots. Ships, already overladen with coal in every available corner, now stowed on board extra boxes of biscuits, butter, tea, salt meat, engine spares, and hundreds of cases of champagne and vodka.

Rozhdestvenski steamed out of Nossi-Bé harbor on March 17 after two months of idleness. French torpedo boats, flying "Bon Voyage" signals, escorted her, and the flagship's band played the *Marseillaise*. It was a relief to be moving again at last. Some in the fleet said that they were running away from Nebogatov and his floating "tubs." Across the world the route Rozhdestvenski would take was predicted. Most newspapers reported that he would go through the Sunda Straits between Sumatra and Java. A British admiral declared that if he were in Rozhdestvenski's place he would steam south of Australia, a long but safe route, which would allow a stop at the German Carolines. Far out at sea, the fleet heard with relief that Rozhdestvenski had chosen the shorter route through the Straits of Malacca.

For more than three weeks the ships steamed on, lost to the world, thousands of miles from shore. "Anxiety wrings my heart," wrote Politovski to his wife. "I have lost all interest in everything."

One third of the officers in *Suvarov* were suffering from illnesses of various kinds. The chief of staff, Clapier de Colongue, who had to contend with Rozhdestvenski's tantrums, had a brain hemorrhage during the journey and was partially paralyzed. Several senior officers were suffering from bowel disturbances. Food for them had to be specially prepared, and the ship's doctor prescribed sedatives containing opium and morphine.

The chief engineer, overworked and depressed, often labored underwater in a diving suit, while men stood by with guns to fire at the sharks that surrounded the ships. One day he finished a job on *Buitri,* which had constant mechanical breakdowns. Wet, tired, and barely able to stand, he returned to *Suvarov* in a whaler. Standing on deck was Rozhdestvenski, shaking with rage. "Shameful!" he cried. "You serve on the staff and cover yourself with filth and return at five o'clock instead of three." Though it was the first reprimand he had received in seven months of work, Politovski vowed he would never forget the Admiral's reproach. He stumbled to his cabin, changed his clothes, and fell into a deep sleep. For a long time he had wondered why his sleep was so heavy. Now, far out at sea, without the chance to buy fresh stocks, he realized that the 2,000 cigarettes he had bought at Nossi-Bé were filled with opium.

This part of the journey was the most remarkable of the whole voyage. Rozhdestvenski brought his ships 4,700 miles across the Indian Ocean without touching at any port. Every four or five days he stopped to coal in the open sea and on more than a hundred occasions the whole fleet, strung out across the ocean for nearly seven miles, lay at anchor while repairs were made. The destroyers, towed by transports to preserve the precious coal, were continually in trouble as the tow ropes snapped like threads in the heavy swell that swept in from thousands of miles away.

Whenever weather permitted, officers and men labored from sunrise to dark, loading the coal from the colliers and pouring it sack by sack on to their ships. In broken shoes or no shoes at all, their heads wrapped in cloths to keep out the dust, they worked like galley slaves in the fearful heat. "Our lungs were choked with the dust," wrote a sailor on the battleship *Orel.* "We swallowed it with our food and it blocked the pores of our skin . . . we thought only in terms of coal which had become a sort of black veil hiding all else. . . ."

For the first two weeks no ships were seen on the route but Rozhdestvenski and the fleet were continually on the lookout for Japanese vessels. If any had appeared it would have taken nearly an hour to call the scattered ships into line. Even then the guns would have been useless until tarpaulins used to protect them from the coal dust had been removed.

On April 8 the fleet passed Raffles Light, off Singapore. Thousands of excited people lined the shore and piers to see the long line of ships, steaming seven miles out to sea, with streamers of black smoke trailing overhead and foot-long seaweed showing at every waterline, the *Straits Times* reported. "Forty-seven ships steaming slowly at eight knots an hour, four abreast, presented a striking spectacle," wrote *The New York Times.*

Vessels, however, bore evidence of the effects of their long sea voyage . . . the decks of the warships were coal-laden while the colliers and the former Hamburg-Amerika liners were light of draft . . . tally men and submarine mariners were kept at their positions all day manning the guns and mines. As the fleet did not touch the harbor limits, no salutes were fired. The squadron disappeared about five o'clock in the afternoon, still smoking black on the eastern horizon.

The Russian consul at Singapore approached the fleet in a launch, calling through a megaphone that Japanese ships had been off Singapore three days before; Mukden had fallen and Nebogatov had left Djibouti in French Somaliland near the Gulf of Aden on January 18. The ships did not stop, but from official papers taken aboard, Rozhdestvenski also learned that he was to proceed to Camranh Bay in Indochina and wait for Nebogatov and the Third Squadron. He was then to proceed to Vladivostok and hand over the fleet to Admiral Birilev, commander of the Baltic Fleet who had already left on his way to the Far East.

The appearance of the Russian fleet off Singapore revived interest in Rozhdestvenski's fate. *The Times* believed it to be an event worthy of reluctant commendation. "It was a splendid spectacle," wrote a correspondent, two days after Rozhdestvenski had paraded past the port. "We have suffered many things at the hands of the Russian navy during this war. Nevertheless, the news that Admiral Rozhdestvenski and the Baltic Fleet, scorning evasion and concealment, have stood on down the Straits of Malacca, have passed Singapore, and have sailed proudly into the China Seas, will send a thrill of admiration through all Englishmen who read it."

Rozhdestvenski had also felt a thrill of excitement as he brought his ships before the eyes of the world, but now the brief moment of optimism had been driven away by the orders to wait for Nebogatov and, if he reached Vladivostok, to hand over his fleet to Birilev, a man who called himself a "fighting admiral" but had never been in action.

"What has happened to the Admiral?" asked an officer. "Has he been stung by a fly, or has a louse run over his liver?" Rozhdestvenski was restless and irritable, going from ship to ship, issuing orders and finding fault with officers and men. "The Admiral is so odd today, so restless, so taciturn . . ." wrote Semenov in his diary when the fleet was about sixty miles from Camranh Bay. "He is running about nervously, dragging his leg, appearing first on one bridge, then on the other, then disappearing for a short time in his cabin; after that he moves about again on deck, looks through his notebook, notes down something in it; now he is frowning, now again smiling (but the former more frequently), and finally he starts talking to himself."

Admiral Rozhdestvenski had decided to disobey orders. At lunch that day he spoke to no one and went to his study immediately after it was over. At one o'clock he appeared again on the bridge of *Suvarov* and signaled to all ships to report the exact amount of coal on board and then to begin coaling. When the loading was completed, each captain was asked to furnish the amount of coal it now carried in its bunkers. Most had 100 to 150 tons more than they had reported earlier.

Only *Alexander III,* the ship manned by sailors of the guard of which Empress Marie was honorary commander, hesitated in making a reply. *Alexander III* had given the least trouble on the long journey, had won the prize for the fastest loading, and had carried out coaling more efficiently than any other ship in the fleet. At last she signaled her estimate of coal. "We see it, but can't understand it. Is there not a mistake in your signal?" asked *Suvarov.* There was no mistake. *Alexander* had miscalculated. Instead of 900 tons she had less than 300 tons on board. There was now no hope of going straight on to Vladivostok with one of the best battleships short of coal. Rozhdestvenski stared unbelievably at *Alexander*'s signal. He signaled to the fleet to proceed to Camranh Bay, and retired to his cabin.

Several days later the fleet anchored in Camranh Bay. The second-in-command of the French Far East Squadron, Rear Admiral de Jonquieres, called on Rozhdestvenski. He regretted that under international law it was not possible for the fleet to remain in the bay for more than twenty-four hours. Rozhdestvenski was too tired to argue. Day after day he withdrew his fleet to a bay beyond the sight of the charming French commander, returning again on the following day. Angrily, he cabled St. Petersburg that he would wait for Nebogatov. "I will not telegraph again before the battle. If I am beaten you will learn it from Togo. If I defeat him I will announce it to you."

The Russian ships were now desperately short of food and other supplies. St. Petersburg had sent instructions to all Russian offices in Asia to procure supplies, and a consular official in Shanghai left for Indochina on a buying mission. The only meat available now was salted. "Gradually everything is coming to an end," Politovski wrote. "There is neither vodka nor coffee at the Admiral's table . . . cigarettes and matches are scarce. I obtained a piece of soap today and there is only one other left." He was so tired that he could hardly see, he wrote, and could not be bothered to hide his possessions, as most of the officers and men were doing. Reports that Japanese ships were in the area added to the tensions and misery.

Day after day men committed suicide. Several deserted on the wild shores. Coal filled every corner of the ships. To make more space, the partitions between the officers' cabins were removed, the bunks were taken away, and mattresses laid out on the floor. The Russian consulate in Singapore hired a Chinese cook for *Suvarov* and joined in the quest for food to refurbish the hungry fleet.*

A week or so after the fleet reached Camranh Bay, Politovski wrote to his wife that, though the Admiral's Chinese cook had not turned up, the food had improved somewhat. He added that the men who sorted the newly arrived supplies behaved like "wild wolves." The crew of *Orel* broke open a box of liquor and got drunk. One of the drunken sailors attacked a doctor who was standing by. Officers lost control and nearly killed him. "They beat his face into a pulp. It was horrible."

The improvement of the food situation did not last very long. Much of the meat went bad quickly, and only the advent of Easter and fasting for Lent saved men from further sickness.

Easter brought more troubles, this time over a cow. In a letter home, Politovski said that the cow had broken her leg, but in the battleship *Orel* the sailors believed that it was diseased. One man overheard the ship's butcher say: "Slaughter her at once—she'll do for the men's dinner tomorrow."

When dinner was served, the men threw their dishes overboard. "Feed us on carrion, would you?" a seaman shouted. The Captain confined several men in the brig and reported the incident to Rozhdestvenski.

"Traitors! Rascals! Mutiny, would you?" he shouted when he addressed the crew. He called for the ringleaders. No one knew who had begun the riot, and officers picked out eight men at random. Rozhdestvenski towered over them, his chest heaving and his words spilling out so rapidly that it was difficult for other sailors, lined up on deck, to understand what he was saying. "Look at them, these enemies of Russia. They are more like beasts than men. Hangdog faces. What price did you get for selling your country . . . take a good look at these traitors—at the men who sold our country to the Japanese . . . their pockets bulge with Japanese gold." He jerked one of them toward him, a small pock-marked sailor. "See how God has written a curse upon his face. Own up! How much did you get from the Japanese?" Turning to the other officers and men lined up before him, he spoke derisively. "As for you, only in a sea fight and in your own blood can you wash out your sins. If you don't I'll skin you alive, you dirty dogs!"

Rozhdestvenski's intention of evading Nebogatov and his derelict fleet was thwarted by an ordinary seaman, Vasily Fedorovitch Babushkin. Babushkin's ship had been destroyed in Port Arthur harbor and he had been

---

*It succeeded in buying 370 tons of refrigerated meat, butter, and other foodstuffs from Brisbane; this had become impregnated with tar that had melted on the roof of the Singapore Cold Storage's newly installed refrigerated godown.

set to work on the strengthening of the trenches surrounding the forts. Badly injured in a Japanese bombardment, he had been sent off to Russia on a neutral steamer that called en route at Singapore. Here Babushkin met the Russian consul who explained that somehow or other he had to get a message to Admiral Nebogatov, informing him that Rozhdestvenski was looking for him, and he was afraid he might miss him when the fleet passed Singapore. Before leaving Port Said on April 7 Nebogatov had telegraphed to St. Petersburg asking for instructions. The reply was vague: "You are to join up with Rozhdestvenski, whose route is unknown to us." Nebogatov called a meeting of commanding officers at which it was decided to make for the Straits of Malacca, hoping to meet Rozhdestvenski somewhere along the way. Seaman Babushkin came to the rescue.

Still weak from his wounds, he persuaded the consul to allow him to take a launch and wait for the Third Squadron in the narrow straits of Malacca between Malaya and Sumatra. Dressed in a white suit and a topee, so that he looked like any other tourist, he walked to the harbor and took off in a launch with his crew, a Frenchman and a Hindu engineer. Babushkin was the captain.

After one day at sea in the open boat his wounds had opened and he was badly burned by the scorching sun. The Hindu and the Frenchman were all for turning back. On the third day they ran out of water and had so little fuel left that it was impossible to return to Singapore. Babushkin's crew mutinied. "Are we going to stay here much longer?" they asked. "As long as necessary," said Babushkin. "We're going to wait for the detachment."

When they saw the smudges of smoke in the distance, they threw the last logs of wood on the boiler and steered towards the ships, praying that they were Russian and not British or Japanese. "If you make any trouble," said the Russian sailor, "I'll open the scuttle, and sink the lot of us."

Nikolai I, flying the Admiral's flag, saw them first. As the launch drew up, Babushkin climbed on board and produced the letter from the consul with the information that Rozhdestvenski would be waiting at Camranh Bay. He went on with the fleet while the Frenchman and the Hindu, supplied with fuel, returned to Singapore.

The meeting of Rozhdestvenski and Nebogatov at Van Fong Bay, near Camranh Bay, on May 9 raised the spirits of men in both squadrons and, on the surface, the reunion between the two admirals was genial. Rozhdestvenski's order of the day praised the crews who had overcome the tribulations of the long and difficult journey, without the use of friendly ports. Both fleets had suffered hardships but now that they had joined forces he foresaw success against the enemy. "The Japanese possess far speedier vessels than ours," he said, "but we do not propose to run away from them." He offered his men some grim reminders: the Japanese had many more torpedo boats and submarines and floating mines that could be dropped in the path of the Russian ships, and they already had battle experience against the First Pacific Squadron. "The loyalty of the Japanese to Throne and country is unbounded," he said. "They do not suffer dishonor and they die like heroes. But we also have sworn before the Most High Throne. God has inspired us with courage. . . . God will strengthen our right hand. He will bestow upon us His blessing so that we may carry out the will of our Sovereign and wash away the bitter shame of our country with our blood."

He and Nebogatov embraced before going aboard the *Suvarov,* but, once inside Rozhdestvenski's quarters, all affability faded. Nebogatov later wrote that after an hour's conversation Rozhdestvenski dismissed him. "We never discussed a plan of campaign. He gave me neither instructions nor advice . . . I handed over my squadron to Admiral Rozhdestvenski, and from this moment I played the part of a subordinate, obliged to carry out precisely every order of my chief." Nebogatov said that he had no part in the composition of his squadron and that many of the men who sailed with him were thieves and drunkards. Others were recruits and old men who had never been to sea. Nebogatov added that one of the few orders he received from Rozhdestvenski was to paint the funnels of his ships yellow, in keeping with the rest of the fleet.

Chief Engineer Politovski packed away his ikons, his wife's letters, and all her photographs in his sea chest. He had written to her every day during the seven-month voyage, telling her all that happened; of the Admiral's rages and his occasional bursts of kindness; his own secret worries; and the pleasure he obtained from the ship's dogs, until they went mad. Any bird that alighted on board was described in his letters—the big heron and the dove that fell exhausted on the deck. He talked of strange birds whose names he did not know, of gulls and albatrosses, and the canary that once perched on *Suvarov*'s rail.

He wrote, finally, about the gossip of the ships, including how somebody had tried to sell him a small boy for a few francs, "far cheaper than a pig." He packed the letter full of interesting items, describing the wild goats at Camranh Bay, the tigers and panthers that prowled the beaches at night, and the elephants that pulled up telegraph poles on the shore. He did not mention the many suicides or the deep depression that had overtaken the fleet. He found himself a new notebook and promised to post the next letter in Vladivostok. "Vladivostok seems like the promised land. Vladivostok! Vladivostok! . . . if I reach there a distance which can be passed over in fourteen or fifteen days will separate you from me. How microscopic it will seem in comparison to what we have already passed. It will seem quite close to me."

It was his last letter home.

[493]

CHAPTER *31*

&&&&&&

The Battle of Shadows

WHEN TOGO CLIMBED HILL 203 at Port Arthur and looked down on the remnants of the Russian First Pacific Squadron, his relief had been mixed with regret that he had played so small a part in its final destruction. The Third Army, with General Kodama's assistance, had destroyed the Russian First Squadron. The unsuccessful pursuit of the *Sevastopol* had been a further slur on the Japanese navy. Togo determined that the defeat of Rozhdestvenski's Second Squadron would add glory only to the Combined Fleet.

His home leave lasted three days. He then went to work supervising the refitting and repair of ships, attending naval conferences, reshuffling his staff, and completing his battle orders. Ships were dismantled and new parts fitted. Guns were overhauled, engines inspected, and bottoms cleaned. The battleships and armored cruisers were attended to first. As soon as these were repaired, the cruisers, destroyers, and torpedo boats went into naval dockyards or to private yards for intensive overhaul and repair. There was not time to salvage the sunken Russian ships at Port Arthur, but three new destroyers were added to Japan's fighting force as well as the *Ryeshitelni,* which had been captured at Cheefoo. Now renamed *Akatsuki,* after the Japanese destroyer that was sunk on May 17, 1904, she was refitted and prepared for action against her sister ships.*

One important change had been made in Admiral Togo's staff. Captain

---

*Twenty-five new destroyers were being rushed through in Japan's dockyards in Yokosuka, Nagasaki, Kobe, and Kure. Ten were almost completed in March 1905 but were not ready in time for the coming battle against the Baltic Fleet.

Shimamura Hayao, hitherto his chief of staff, was made a rear-admiral and given command of a division in the Second Squadron under Admiral Kamimura, with his flag in the cruiser *Iwate*. Rear-Admiral Kato Tomosaburo* replaced him as Togo's chief of staff.

The failure of the Japanese fleet to destroy the Russians at the battle of the Yellow Sea was probably the reason for Shimamura's replacement, for Shimamura and Togo always appeared to be on good terms. There seemed to be complete affinity between the two admirals, but others felt that Togo should have closed in earlier in the afternoon of August 10. Togo had wanted to close, but Shimamura had talked him out of it. They had killed the Russian admiral but had not sunk a single ship. This time, without Shimamura at his elbow and with his fleet stronger than it had been in August, he would be likely to take more risks.

Togo went aboard *Mikasa* on February 6. On February 21 he took the First and Second squadrons to Sylvia Basin, the secret base between Koji Island and Masan on the Korean coast, a deep, sheltered bay which the Russians had long coveted and where, a year earlier, Togo had prepared the fleet for war. The Third Squadron, under Vice-Admiral Dewa, was sent to a naval station at Tsushima Island, and Admiral Kamimura, with part of the Second Squadron, mined the entrance of Peter the Great Bay at Vladivostok between Askold and Korsakovsk islands, for a distance of thirty-five miles. Kamimura put down 715 mines—one mine for about every hundred yards—not only insuring that the Russian fleet would remain in the port and that Rozhdestvenski would have trouble entering it, but also trapping in the minefield the cruiser *Gromoboi*, the one ship that tried to venture out.

Only the battleship *Asahi*, with the impatient Captain Pakenham aboard, was left behind at Kure on Japan's Inland Sea. *Asahi* had been hit by a twelve-inch shell near her waterline in the battle of the Yellow Sea, and damage to her armor had to be repaired and guns replaced. When the ship was sent to Kure dockyards her repairs were delayed by frantic welcome-home activities. If Rozhdestvenski's ships had been faster, Togo would have faced the Russians minus *Asahi*'s big guns.

It was assumed that Rozhdestvenski would try to reach Vladivostok now that Port Arthur had fallen. He had three alternatives—the Straits of Tsushima between Japan and Korea, the Tsugaru Straits between Honshu and Hokkaido, or La Pérouse Strait between Hokkaido and Sakhalin. The Tsugaru Straits were closer to Vladivostok than the others, but the entrance to the strait is narrow and ships passing through it could not escape observation from the shore. The current in the channel is exceptionally strong,

---

*Prime minister in 1922–1923.

occasionally up to six knots, so that the Russian ships would have taken at least eight hours to pass through the strait. To approach by way of La Pérouse Strait meant a much longer journey for the tired ships.

The most direct route was through the Tsushima Strait. This course, however, would bring the fleet close to the Japanese coast and its naval bases. Rozhdestvenski rejected La Pérouse because of the fogs and difficulties of coaling in the open sea. Tsugaru Strait was too narrow to maneuver his unwieldy fleet. Rozhdestvenski did not consider this route. Commander Semenov wrote: "The armada only managed with difficulty to maintain something in the shape of a formation even in clear weather and under the most favorable conditions for navigation."

Togo was fairly sure that Rozhdestvenski would not risk the Tsugaru Strait or take the long passage north and east of Japan to skirt Sakhalin. But he was gambling, and he knew it. Apart from a few torpedo boats to guard the home ports, he had left the entire Japanese coast, including the capital, unprotected. If Rozhdestvenski chose either of the two northern routes, Togo believed that he would still be alerted in time to intercept him. As a precaution, he decided on a secondary base, 300 miles north of Masan, to which he could move his fleet against Russian ships entering La Pérouse or Tsugaru Straits.

He stayed at Masan, exercising his ships in the unfrequented waters, where no merchant ship would be likely to discover his whereabouts and pass on the information to the Russians. Togo's speech to the fleet on May 15 reiterated what he had said at the beginning of the war before the attacks on Chemulpo and Port Arthur: "If your sword is too short, take one step forward." The fleet had waited long for this battle. It would be successful if each man remembered always to be on his guard. When disaster struck their own ships, they must realize that the same sort of thing would be happening on the Russian ships. "When we are fighting there is no need to think of defense. A positive attack is the best form of defense . . . the vital point in actual warfare is to apply to the enemy what we do not wish to be applied to ourselves and at the same time not to let the enemy apply it to us . . . we must always forestall them."

The Combined Fleet's navigational officers had divided the waters of Tsushima Strait, between the Island of Quelpart and Vladivostok, into squares like those of a chessboard, with each square representing ten minutes of latitude and longitude. Japanese scout ships patrolling the entrance to the strait needed merely to give a single number to indicate the location of the enemy.

A cold, fine mist hung over Masan on the night of May 22, adding to the tension in the Japanese Fleet. Almost a week had passed without news of Rozhdestvenski. He had been sighted passing between the northern Philippines and Formosa, and, even if his vessels were as barnacle encrusted as reports had suggested, he was due, and overdue, if he intended to force the Straits of Tsushima. Togo had gambled everything on his judgment. If he waited too long, and Rozhdestvenski found his way unmolested through one of the northern passages, the whole character of the war would change again. The victories on land and sea would perhaps have been in vain, since Japan's vital lines of communication would again be dangerously threatened.

On May 17, while he was coaling at sea, Rozhdestvenski stopped a Norwegian steamer under contract to a Japanese firm and with a heavy-handed attempt at deception told her captain that he was going through the Tsushima Straits, hoping that Togo, when he learned of this, would think that he was heading for one of the northern passages. Exhausted by his long, nerve-wracking voyage, Rozhdestvenski apparently did not even consider the use of a decoy force before entering the Tsushima Straits. In a further effort to persuade Togo to divide his forces, however, he sent two armed merchant ships round the eastern shores of Japan and two cruisers into the Yellow Sea on the pretext that they were heading for Port Arthur.

By the evening of May 23 no Japanese ship had reported the Russian fleet entering the squares of the checkerboard. On May 25 Rozhdestvenski sent off his six supply ships, with orders to proceed to Shanghai. He had no scouts out. He also forbade the dispatch of wireless messages. *Ural,* which had powerful telegraphic equipment, reported that messages were being picked up between Japanese ships, but Rozhdestvenski was determined to maintain absolute telegraphic silence in the hope of avoiding detection. Early the next day he sent two signals to the fleet: "Prepare for action," and "Tomorrow at the hoisting of the colors battle flags are to be sent up."

With the dispatch of the supply ships to Shanghai Rozhdestvenski made the worst of his early errors. Togo was becoming impatient. He could not wait indefinitely for the Russians to appear—another day or two, perhaps, but after that he could no longer afford to take the risk that Rozhdestvenski had outwitted him and gone north. A report that reached Masan on May 25 persuaded him to remain there for another night. Rozhdestvenski's ruse, if it could be called such, had failed. The message Togo received that day told him of the arrival of six Russian auxiliaries, including colliers, at Shanghai. If Rozhdestvenski had planned to take either of the longer routes, he would have kept the colliers with him.

On the night of May 26–27 the moon rose about midnight but broke only fitfully through the heavy overcast. The Russians blessed the fog. Every hour that it enveloped them was an hour closer to Vladivostok. With lights showing only toward the flagship, the fleet sailed on.

On board the *Suvarov,* the senior navigating officer concluded that Togo was waiting for them off the northern point of Tsushima. "I think that we have reached the culminating point of our adventures," he announced.

It is absurd to think of steaming victoriously into Vladivostok, or of getting command of the sea! The only possible chance is a dash through, and having dashed through, after two, three, or at the most four sallies, we shall have burnt all our supplies of coal, and have shed our blossoms before we have bloomed. We shall have to prepare for a siege, take our guns on shore, teach the crew to use bayonets.

Later that night the Russians picked up disjointed Japanese messages. All that could be made out was, "Last night" . . . "nothing" . . . "eleven lights . . . but not in line" . . . "bright light . . . the same star." The Japanese had found their location, but the observer was obviously signaling to the fleet from a great distance.

It was dark on *Suvarov*'s decks as Commander Semenov made a tour of the ship, walking softly so that he would not disturb men not yet on duty, sleeping fully dressed at their guns. Officers and men peered into the darkness of the sea, seeing torpedo boats in every ripple. There were signs of strain now, from the Admiral stooping over his charts on the bridge to the sailors manning the guns. In the wardroom, usually crowded and noisy, there were only one or two off-duty officers asleep in their chairs. Semenov also fell asleep and was wakened at three in the morning to find the ship hushed and eerie, her funnels, masts, and riggings standing out darkly against the mist-streaked moonlight.

Admiral Rozhdestvenski was dozing in a chair on the forebridge and Captain Ignatzius, the commander of the flagship, was padding up and down the bridge in carpet slippers. Captain Ignatzius was glad of the mist, which hid even the rear ships from *Suvarov*. The Japanese would never be able to find them in such weather, he told Semenov. "If it's the same tomorrow, we'll give them the slip! . . . My! what a stew they must be in!" He stuffed his handkerchief in his mouth so that his laughter would not wake the sleeping Admiral, but everyone on the ship knew that Captain Ignatzius, despite his outward gaiety and his faith in St. Nicholas, had little hope of survival when the battle began. The Japanese would be after the *Suvarov*.

The mist lifted momentarily at 3:30 A.M. and a strange-looking ship with two funnels was seen fleetingly by the lookout man on the Russian hospital ship *Orel,* astern of the other ships. Men ran to the rails as she turned sharply away from the ship and disappeared into the gray of the morning. *Shinano Maru* of the NYK line, serving as an armed merchant cruiser, transmitted the long-awaited news to Japanese cruisers in the area, which passed on the information to the Japanese flagship: "The enemy sighted in number 203 section. He seems to be steering for the eastern channel." If no one else in the Japanese fleet realized its significance, to Togo the coincidence of the number was the happiest of omens. It was a hill called 203 that he had climbed at Port Arthur to see the Russian First Squadron sunk deep in the mud of the harbor.

An hour and a half later the *Mikasa* steamed out of Masan, followed by the *Shikishima, Fuji, Asahi*, the battleships of the First Division, and the armored cruisers *Kasuga* and *Nisshin*. Vice-Admiral Kamimura followed with the five ships of the Second Division, the flagship *Izumo, Azuma, Tokiwa, Yagumo*, and *Iwate*. Then came the Fourth Division with four ships, the flagship *Naniwa, Takachiho, Akashi*, and *Tsushima*. At least one of Togo's division commanders was taken unawares. Admiral Kamimura was once again out fishing in a small boat when the signal came in. Not even his wife's prayers, which he believed had turned the tide months before when he was chasing *Rurik*, could have saved him from the wrath of his commander-in-chief if he had been unable to return to the fleet that morning.

The Japanese ships had taken on fuel in anticipation of a chase after the Russians to Vladivostok. Now, all the good Welsh coal was tossed over the side. Coal was still going over the side of the battleship *Shikishima* when *Mikasa* came proudly past the rest of the line, her band playing the navy march, to take her place at the head of the line.

Meanwhile in the Russian ships there was a tot of vodka or rum for every man to conclude the festivities in honor of the ninth anniversary of the Tsar's coronation. On *Suvarov*, the Admiral and his senior staff had already gone to the bridge, but champagne was provided in the wardroom for other officers. Glasses were raised high for the dual toasts: "On this, the great anniversary of the sacred coronation of Their Majesties, may God help us to serve with him our beloved country. To the health of the Emperor! the Empress! to Russia!"

The crew of the battleship *Orel* took their places sullenly on the main deck where the ship's red-bearded chaplain stood in front of the ikons and hurried through prayers. "The men's faces were sour and rigid as in a cataleptic trance," wrote Novikov-Priboy. "They crossed themselves as if flapping away flies." The call to action stations sounded before the prayers had finished and the priest's thoughts and those of the men were far from the palaces of the Tsar.

In the Japanese ships the main-brace was spliced, according to the best British traditions, decks were wetted and sprinkled with sand, and the men, freshly bathed after the dirty business of disposing of the coal, changed into clean uniforms and underclothing. Before any important event one must always be pure, to be sure, but there was more to it than this. Clean clothing next to the skin prevented infection from wounds. Bandage packages were distributed and gun battery crews issued with boracic solution to bathe their eyes (to prevent injury from powder fumes) and cotton wool plugs for their ears.

Around the decks men read books, listened to the phonograph, or played deck quoits. One man sang a little song:

> And raging storms dispel the morning dew,
> So shall the triumph by our vessel won
> Scatter the Russian ships and all their crew. . . .

On *Asahi,* a big box of cigars, a present from the Emperor, was passed around among the officers. One non-smoker declined the honorable offer. "If you don't take it gladly," said another young officer, "perhaps you will be the first to fall today."

The news of the approach of the Russian ships had been, in Togo's own words, "received with enthusiastic joy by the whole fleet." He stood on the bridge of his flagship, with his black active service uniform buttoned high up under his chin. He and his staff officers surrounded the compass, now padded with hammocks to protect it from splinters. With him were Rear-Admiral Kato Tomosaburo, his new chief of staff, who had replaced Shimamura; Captain Ijiichi Hikojiro, the commander of the flagship, and Commander Akiyama Masayuki, the officer in charge of plans and operations.

In a famous painting of Togo and his staff, and almost completely hidden by the range-finder in front of the padded mast, stands Ensign Hasegawa Kiyoshi (later admiral, who died in September 1970). Hasegawa regarded Commander Akiyama, who had studied under Mahan at Annapolis and had been an observer in the Spanish-American War, as "the single brain of the Japanese navy."

Then the most junior officer on *Mikasa,* Hasegawa recalled Togo as a strict disciplinarian, always properly dressed, always correct. Everyone had to follow his example. "We never took our coats off until we were in our cabins. However, Akiyama behaved as he wished, often appearing in the Admiral's presence wearing a shoe on one foot and a slipper on the other. Sometimes his buttons were all set in their wrong holes. He was absent-minded about everything but his job—I have seen him drink beer with flies in his glass."

Akiyama had worked out a battle in seven distinct stages, covering the Russian fleet's entry into Tsushima through to Vladivostok. Rozhdestvenski had not been discovered in time for Togo to include steps one and two

—destroyer and torpedo attacks—and Suzuki Kantaro, commander of the destroyers and torpedo boats, who became prime minister at the end of World War II, reluctantly withdrew. Even if his services had been required now, the seas were too rough for torpedo attacks. All the little ships were ordered off to shelter at Tsushima Island until further notice. The third step was a direct engagement between the two fleets, the fourth a torpedo attack during the following night, and the fifth the meeting of the surviving ships on the morning after the torpedo attack. Steps six and seven were to be mopping-up operations.

Wireless telegraphy was in its infancy, but the Japanese had occasionally received signals from ship to ship at a distance of more than five hundred miles with their "modified Marconi" apparatus. Early in the morning of May 27 the two fleets were only forty miles apart and telegraphic messages kept Togo constantly informed of the Russian movements. "In spite of the thick mist which confined the vision to within five nautical miles, the information thus received enabled me at a distance of several tens of miles to form a vivid picture in my mind of the condition of the enemy," Togo later reported. "I was thus able, before I could see the enemy with my own eyes, to know that the enemy's fighting sections comprised the whole of the Second and the Third Squadrons; that they were accompanied by seven special service ships; that the enemy's ships were disposed in a double column formation . . . and so forth." Togo made a "mental resolution" to meet the enemy at about two o'clock in the afternoon—step three in Akiyama's careful plan.

The weather cleared about 7 A.M., and Rozhdestvenski's fleet caught sight of a Japanese cruiser, the *Izumi.* She shadowed the Russians for several hours. Rozhdestvenski ignored her. If the Japanese fleet appeared, he wanted every gun available. At 9 A.M., abreast of the southern tip of Tsushima Island, the Russian fleet altered course to N23°E. They were in the homestretch. At the end lay the closed waters of the Golden Horn and the safety of Vladivostok. Forty-five minutes later Kataoka's Third Division, with three cruisers and the *Chin-Yen,* which had been stationed off Tsushima Island overnight, steamed around the southern end of the island.

Rozhdestvenski, fearing an attack from the port side, began to alter his formation into battle order by increasing the speed of the First and Second Battleship divisions to eleven knots and placing them ahead of the port column. This took some time because the Third Division, which headed the port column, maintained a speed of nine knots. *Dmitri Donskoi* and *Vladimir Monomakh* were ordered to protect the transports to starboard, and the *Izumrud,* which had been on the port beam of the *Nikolai,* Nebogatov's flagship, steamed round the head of the fleet and with the destroyers of the

First Flotilla took station astern of the *Zhemchug*. The fleet was ready for attack from port side. At 11 A.M. the Japanese Third Division under Admiral Dewa began to close in to a range of eight or nine thousand yards.

At about the same time, Captain Nikolai Yung of *Orel* tired of the shadowy shapes of Japanese cruisers and destroyers hovering in the distance and opened fire. Almost immediately Admiral Rozhdestvenski signaled that ammunition was not to be wasted, but about thirty rounds had been fired and the crews were elated that they had scared off the enemy. The men of *Orel* lost their glumness and talked a great deal at lunch that day, and afterward sat in corners to discuss their first shot of the battle and everything else under the sun. Among *Orel*'s unruly crew the revolutionary engineer, Vasiliev, remained a pessimist. He was torn both ways. If the Japanese finished off their fleet, his cause would be advanced. It would have much more effect than bombing a minister of state or some distinguished nobleman. "Still, I cannot think without horror of the sinking of our ships, with the loss of life this will entail," he said.

After lunch the Russian fleet steamed safely past Tsushima Island, where long before, in 1861, Russian marines had landed to secure freedom of navigation in the straits, only to be unceremoniously pushed out by the British.

When the Japanese cruisers disappeared, Rozhdestvenski, realizing that they had gone to report his movements, changed into fighting formation, with his ships line abreast. His First and Second Battleship divisions were to turn eight points to starboard in succession and then to resume the original course together, while the Third Division was to form line abreast independently, a maneuver in which the fleet had had some practice. *Suvarov* began to turn to starboard, but before she could complete the eight point turn, the Japanese cruisers reappeared. Rozhdestvenski countermanded his order to the Second Division and himself resumed his original course, followed by the ships of his own division in succession. Confusion set in. The First Division was now in a separate column some distance to starboard of the Second and Third divisions. "The enemy continued to turn to port and lay parallel to our mob, since this is the only adequate word to express our formation at the time," Admiral Nebogatov later wrote. "The First Division continued to steam, but the Second and Third divisions reduced speed, and even stopped to avoid collision."

Having maneuvered once to meet the attack from the port which had failed to materialize, Rozhdestvenski now believed that Togo would come from the mists to the north, and he again gave orders to change to line abreast. This was not a difficult maneuver. The faster ships of the First and Second Battleship divisions were to swing hard to port in succession, while the Third Division changed course independently. As soon as the First and Second divisions had all completed their ninety-degree turn to port they would make a simple simultaneous ninety-degree turn to starboard, thus changing from line ahead to line abreast. Rozhdestvenski signaled the change of formation, altered course in the *Suvarov*, and immediately sighted the Japanese cruisers again.

Disconcerted at the reappearance of the cruisers, he canceled his order before the Second Division ships had begun their turn. The First Division followed the *Suvarov*, with the result that, instead of meeting Togo's ships when they appeared in conventional formation, either line abreast or line ahead, the Russian fleet was now sailing north in two columns, with the First Division to the starboard of the Second and Third divisions. This is the formation the fleet had been following early in the morning, the same disposition that Togo believed he had to contend with tactically. The Russians were strong on the starboard side, weak to port. His attack would be made from the port side.

When the Russian ships came out of the fog at 1:19 P.M. and Togo at last sighted his quarry, he was to the north and starboard of Rozhdestvenski. At a speed of twenty-four knots the two fleets were bearing down on each other, with Togo badly out of position if he was to follow his original plan and attack the Second and Third divisions.

From *Suvarov*, Commander Semenov, standing with Rozhdestvenski and other staff officers on the upper forebridge, saw the Japanese coming, far ahead. He recognized his six Port Arthur acquaintances and cried: "There they are, sir—all six of them—just as on August 10." Without turning his head, the Admiral corrected him: "No, there are more—they are all there," and descended to the conning tower.

On the Japanese flagship, Kato tried to persuade Togo to leave the bridge and seek the protection of the conning tower, but the Admiral shook his head. "I am getting on for sixty," he said, "and this old body of mine is no longer worth caring for. But you are all young men with futures before you, so take care of yourselves and continue living in order to serve your country." This was the opportunity he had dreamed of. He would not miss it.

To the Russians, it seemed that Togo would soon turn south and close the gap, bringing his battleships with their broadsides to bear on the weaker Russian divisions. This tactic, though conventional enough, would have left the Russians heading in the direction of Vladivostok, while the Japanese sailed in the opposite direction. Though this might have been responsible for heavy damage to the weaker Russian ships, it left the way open for Rozhdestvenski's First Division to escape. That had no part in Togo's plans. His intention was to execute a bold maneuver that would bring the Japanese

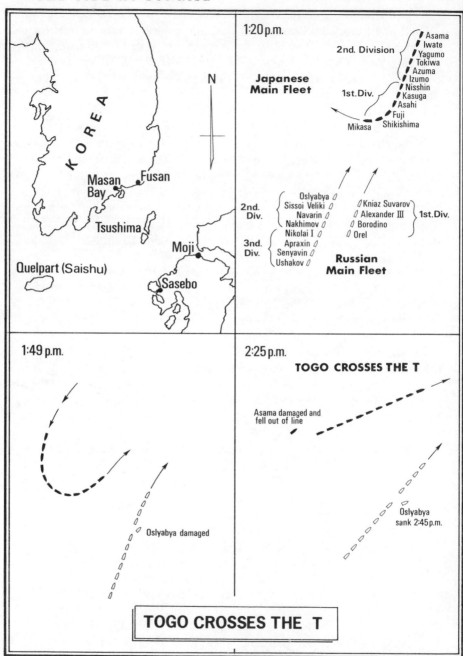

1:20 p.m.

2nd. Division

Japanese
Main Fleet

1st.Div.

Mikasa

Asama
Iwate
Yagumo
Tokiwa
Azuma
Izumo
Nisshin
Kasuga
Asahi
Fuji
Shikishima

KOREA

N

Masan
Bay
Fusan

Tsushima

Moji

Quelpart (Saishu)

Sasebo

2nd.
Div.

3nd.
Div.

Oslyabya
Sissoi Veliki
Navarin
Nakhimov
Nikolai I
Apraxin
Senyavin
Ushakov

Kniaz Suvarov
Alexander III
Borodino
Orel

1st.Div.

Russian
Main Fleet

1:49 p.m.

Oslyabya damaged

2:25 p.m.

TOGO CROSSES THE T

Asama damaged and
fell out of line

Oslyabya
sank 2:45 p.m.

TOGO CROSSES THE T

[504]

battleships and armored cruisers back across the path of the oncoming Russian fleet.

The maneuver was no surprise to Captain Pakenham, who had predicted Togo's precise use of the tactic in a message to the Admiralty on April 17. Nor was it a surprise to Britain's First Sea Lord, Admiral Sir John Fisher, who had urged on Togo the tactical advantages he would enjoy and could exploit, if he went into action against the slower Russian ships, overloaded with coal, while carrying only enough himself to see his ships through the action.

There were fearful hazards to be faced in making the turn in the manner Togo had in mind, but once it was made he could bring the full weight of his broadsides to bear on the Russian ships, sweeping Rozhdestvenski's columns from end to end with enfilading fire, or concentrating the fire from the entire Japanese line on the foremost Russian ships in classic execution of the tactic known as "crossing the T."

"Speed is the factor of maritime efficiency least understood," wrote Pakenham in his April 17 dispatch. "The meeting fleets promise a difference in this respect sufficiently marked to demand careful notice should be given to its effect." Speed and gunnery, too, Akiyama believed, and he was confident that the Japanese gunnery was far superior to the Russians'.

At 1:55 Togo raised his right hand and drew a semicircle in the air, and the command went out to Captain Ijiichi, "Hard to port!" He hoisted his battle flags with a signal so very like that of Nelson's just a hundred years before: "The rise or fall of the empire depends upon the result of this engagement. Do your utmost, everyone of you." He turned northwest, then west, across the face of the two columns of Russian ships.

The maneuver brought him across the face of the oncoming Russian fleet. In a sense, therefore, he had already crossed the T, but the range was too great to bring his broadsides into play. Togo had more ambitious plans for the T, so long known to the pirates of the Inland Sea and the mariners of Satsuma. The line was joined by the six armored cruisers, *Izumo, Asama, Azuma, Tokiwa, Iwate,* and *Yagumo,* so that it was now twelve ships long, steaming at right angles to the Russians.

Captain Pakenham, in *Asahi,* was wearing a new white uniform. He perched on the very edge of the cane chair where he had been reclining comfortably, "taking notes like an official at a yacht race," and, with awe, looked straight down the Russian lines. "At the head of the right column the four big battleships loomed enormous, dwarfing all others to insignificance. It was not easy to credit that the Japanese battleships were probably producing the same impression on the minds of the Russians."

Rozhdestvenski realised that, whatever maneuver the Japanese now attempted, he was caught with his columns down. In a last-minute attempt

[505]

to protect the Second and Third divisions, he turned the First Division to port, and increased speed with the intention now of adopting a line-ahead formation.

What followed after Togo passed in front of the Russian fleet was breathtaking. *Mikasa* threw the wheel hard to port and, to the astonishment of the Russians, executed a full circle, leaving herself and all the ships of the First and Second divisions that followed exposed, open, and vulnerable, and a stationary target for the battleships. "I looked and looked," wrote Semenov, "and, not believing my eyes, could not put down my glasses."

"How rash!" exclaimed another officer. "Why, in a minute we'll be able to roll up the leading ships." Within seconds *Suvarov* opened fire on *Mikasa* at a range of 6,400 yards. Only two out of the twelve Japanese ships had made the dangerous turn. As each ship followed *Mikasa* into the turn it became a sitting duck. The Russians were using shells with smokeless powder, and they burst only when they hit a target. "A hit could only be detected when something fell—and nothing fell!" lamented Semenov. Shells rained around the Japanese ships, drenching them in spray, but there were few direct hits, and these mostly from six-inch batteries.

Togo took a calculated risk. If he had ordered his fleet to turn "together," the Second Division with Admiral Shimamura in command would have led the fleet into action. As Togo's chief of staff during the battle of the Yellow Sea, he revealed his timidity when the Russian ships had been within their grasp. By turning "in succession," with *Mikasa* out in front, Togo now led the fleet in person. There was to be no timidity this time.

The turn completed, Togo now recrossed the T, but this time within range. Akiyama, the tactician, dismissed the maneuver as not particularly new to the Japanese navy. "I do not know how well they are known in Europe and America but they were well known formations in our country some 700 years ago."

Togo held his fire as 300 Russian shells fell on and around his ships. Minutes passed like hours, reported Pakenham on *Asahi*, but all his unstinted praise of the Japanese admiral had been no exaggeration. Months before he had written to the British Admiralty, extolling the virtues of his hero, comparing him more than favorably with famous men of the past. Napoleon, he called "a lecherous scoundrel," Caesar and Moses, "sly casuists," and Nelson, "a grovelling snob." He explained carefully that it would be unreasonable to look for perfection in the Japanese admiral "or to expect to discover a dazzling meteor, but that of a useful star may be found, whose exact magnitude only posterity can accurately determine."

When *Fuji* and *Asahi* had also turned, the Japanese opened fire. As they came out of the turn they headed northeast with their main batteries blazing. They had put on speed and were now making fifteen knots, sprinting

[506]

across the head of the much slower Russian columns. Most of their fire fell on *Suvarov* and *Oslyabya.*

Rozhdestvenski made his last attempt to regain control of the battle at 2:24 P.M. when he turned slightly to port, thus reducing the range. But this maneuver only increased the fire of the *Mikasa* and minutes later *Suvarov* turned back to starboard, on fire.

It was a battle of shadows. In the Yellow Sea in August it had been possible to identify the enemy ships. This time the Russian Fleet was never seen as a whole, and was sometimes lost sight of altogether in the heavy seas and fire and smoke of battle. Pakenham said many strange-looking vessels came into view and vanished again before their names could be ascertained. When the two long lines of ships were firing at each other, the fate of the day seemed to hang on every shot.

Nebogatov's Third Division concentrated on the Japanese armored cruisers at long range. Afterward, he complained that Rozhdestvenski had given him no instructions, except that his division would be in the rear of the general line but might be moved to the center of the column during the battle. He had seen Rozhdestvenski only once when the two fleets had met at Van Fong Bay. "We talked about matters in general in the presence of his staff, but not a word was mentioned of the coming action. We have not seen each other since." Now, in the first minutes of the battle, his old ships, manned mostly by men who had never before been to sea, damaged three of the enemy's ships, hit many others, and forced the *Asama* out of the fighting line.

Nebogatov was later criticized for not giving more assistance to the two burning battleships, but his squadron did more damage to the Japanese that day than any other ships of the three Russian squadrons. From *Nikolai* he watched the *Suvarov,* "burning like a peasant's hut," and saw the huge hole in *Oslyabya's* side.

The Japanese shells, huge four-foot long "portmanteaus," flew over the Russian ships. The Japanese had used these at Port Arthur and the Russian crews watched them turning head over heels through the air, emitting long, wailing sounds before they hit. Semenov, slipping and sliding in the pools of new blood on the deck of the flagship, set the men to fighting the fires. Most of the Russian crews had never been in action before and gazed at the smoke and flames as though mesmerized. "Wake up! Turn the water on!" he shouted. It seemed to be raining shells. Semenov had prepared to take notes as he had done in other battles, recording the times and places where hits were made. "But how could I make detailed notes when it seemed impossible even to count the number of projectiles striking us? I had not only never witnessed such a fire before, but I had never imagined anything like it. Shells seemed to be pouring upon us incessantly, one after another."

In their shells the Japanese were again using the powerful "Shimose" powder, now being manufactured in large quantities at Takinogawa, ten miles from Tokyo. It had been used with great success in the eleven-inch siege guns that bombarded Port Arthur. Many of the men on the Russian ships soon carried multiple wounds from shells charged with Shimose powder.

Five hundred Japanese guns were firing on *Suvarov* and the great, unwieldy *Oslyabya*, flying the flag of Admiral Felkerzam. But Felkerzam was dead. On the long voyage out from Libau he had been desperately ill and on May 25 had died suddenly. His body was lying in its coffin still awaiting burial because Rozhdestvenski thought the report of his death might upset the fleet. Even Nebogatov, who would now be in command of the fleet if anything should happen to Rozhdestvenski, had not been told. The Japanese believed that Felkerzam still commanded *Oslyabya*, and with *Suvarov* she shared the brunt of their fire. With her great stacks towering into the sky, she was a good target for Kamimura's heavy cruisers, which opened up on her with their main armaments. The cumbersome ship had been included in the Russian list as a battleship "to frighten the enemy," according to Novikov-Priboy. She had been built in a hurry and her armor was not as strong as the original plans had indicated. She made the best of her disadvantages. If she was not an attractive-looking vessel, she was probably the cleanest ship in the fleet. Her captain was a strict disciplinarian, never satisfied until the ship gleamed and sparkled. After coaling, the men not only swabbed the decks until they were pristine clean, but he also insisted on washing the bags in which the coal had been stored. Before the battle he gathered the men on deck and, with little conviction in his voice, bade them give their "hides" for the Tsar. "You will show yourselves to be true Russian sailors," he said as the men scowled. Their Admiral was dead, lying in a coffin on the quarterdeck—a very bad omen. Captain Baer's pep talk had no effect on the crew of *Oslyabya*.

Suvarov was also on fire, though her guns remained in action. *Asama*, bringing up the rear of Kamimura's Second Division, was the first Japanese casualty, and the first ship on either side to drop out when three shells struck her near the waterline and disabled her steering gear. She was down but not out, however. Two hours later, having fought off attacks from several Russian ships, she was back in her station.

Suvarov continued to receive a fearful battering from the Japanese broadsides. The range-finders had been destroyed and she refused to answer to the helm, though the gunners stayed at their places and continued to fire. She was badly hurt, but *Oslyabya*'s wounds were more quickly fatal. Admiral Kamimura, the handsome commander of the Second Division who had once been so bitterly criticized by the Japanese public and press for his failure to dispose of the Russian Vladivostok squadron, brought six cruisers in close to the top-heavy, ugly-duckling Russian battleship and poured fire and flame across her decks.

Under the sea lay the thousands of Japanese soldiers of *Hitachi Maru* and two other transports who had died because he could not stop the Russians in the previous year. It was suggested that Kamimura should commit hara-kiri, as so many of the doomed men on the transports had done. Now Kamimura showed no mercy. *Osylabya* died horribly. Men crawled up from below on broken legs to get to the lifeboats that were no more. The commander of one of the gun batteries shot himself in the head as the ship's nose turned downward into the sea.

Other Russian ships passing her saw hundreds of white-clad men swarming over her side and bilge keel, like moths on a wet windowpane. Her huge yellow funnels lay flat on the water, shooting smoke and steam over the men in the water. Captain Baer was calling to them to get away from the ship. "The devil take you! You'll go down with the suck!" She sank at 2:45 P.M., the first ship sunk at Tsushima and, for a short space of time, the only armored battleship ever to have been sunk by gunfire alone. Four destroyers came in and picked up about a third of her officers and crew, including one sailor who was clinging to Admiral Felkerzam's coffin, which had floated off the quarter deck.

At least a dozen shells had fallen on *Mikasa,* one of them coming perilously close to Togo as he watched through his telescope. He did not look around, according to Captain Ijiichi, the commander of the flagship, who collected the splinter which had touched the master and pocketed it as a souvenir. The second ship in line, *Asahi,* received much heavier fire. An explosion under her afterbridge sent wood and splinters flying everywhere. The first man to die was the sub-lieutenant who had refused the Emperor's cigar.

With brisk efficiency sailors cleaned up the blood and scraps of flesh on *Asahi.* "I was puzzled to know where to step as the shattered deck was bestrewn with pieces of human flesh and besmeared with fresh blood, while mutilated hands and feet and human bowels were scattered everywhere," wrote an officer. He found his men loathe to remove the remains and set the example with his own hands.

Captain Pakenham was hit by one of the flying fragments. "It was the right half of a man's lower jaw, with teeth missing," he wrote. "Everything and everybody for twenty yards round was bespattered with tiny drops of blood and minute particles of flesh that adhered to whatever they struck. A six-inch shell had exploded against a twelve-pounder gun, killing the officer and crew and some of the by-standers. In spite of the quantity scattered, the amount of blood left on the deck looked sufficient to fill a big

[509]

cask." Drenched in blood, Pakenham left his chair and disappeared below. This was too much even for the indomitable Englishman, the Japanese thought. Five minutes later he reappeared in a new set of immaculate whites and resumed his seat and his notetaking.

Suvarov was experiencing the same sort of terror on a greatly magnified scale. Commander Semenov raised his glasses and marveled at the perfection of the Japanese maneuvering before turning to look at the decks where debris was piled high among the dead. "Signaling and judging distance stations, gun-directing positions, all were destroyed . . . the officer commanding the fire parties had had both legs blown off and was carried below. Men fell faster and faster." Astern he could see *Alexander III* and *Borodino* also enveloped in smoke and flame. He reached the conning tower where Rozhdestvenski and Captain de Colongue were peering out between the slits in the steel walls at Kamimura's cruisers firing into the confused mass of battleships. Two officers lay face downward close to the wheel and Captain de Colongue was pleading to Rozhdestvenski to shorten the range. "They're all being killed—they are on fire!" It was still too early, said the Admiral. "Wait a bit," he added. "Aren't we all being killed, also?"

Suvarov was enveloped in red-brown flames, one mast had gone, and she was often completely obscured by the gun-fire from a dozen Japanese ships. The captain of *Asahi* found a sailor with a camera standing alongside him and encouraged him to get a picture of *Suvarov*'s agony. It was not surprising that the cameraman's focus was unsteady. When the plate was developed, all that could be seen were the burning hammocks packed around the Russian flagship's bridge.

Captain Thomas Jackson, aboard *Azuma,* though not endowed with Pakenham's gift for words, wrote cold, precise accounts of the battle, mixed with an obvious sympathy for the death of men and ships. Through the haze of mist and battle he watched the vague shapes, their yellow funnels standing out in startling contrast against the gray of sea and sky, all blurred into a confused gray smudge.

A dense cloud of black smoke now enveloped the sea. Unaware of what had happened to *Oslyabya* and unable to grasp the depths of *Suvarov*'s troubles, Togo saw only that the principal Russian ships were heading north toward Vladivostok. He signaled the First Division and headed northwest to cut them off. If he had obeyed instructions to the letter, Kamimura would have followed, placing his armored cruisers on the tail of Togo's battleships. Instead, he chose to risk combat alone and held to his southeastern course, every one of his ships raking the Russian ships from a range of only about 3,000 yards. The maneuver was brilliantly successful. Having completed it, Kamimura turned to follow the First Division, which had again brought the Russians under fire. There was now a wide gap between the First and

Second divisions, however, and Togo's battleships were out of range. Admiral Kamimura again chose to interpret standing orders in a liberal manner and closed in on the dying *Suvarov*.

The Russian flagship had received a direct hit on the conning tower. Rozhdestvenski, already wounded and in great pain, received a sliver of shell in his brain. The upper deck was ablaze and while trying to squeeze through into the six-inch turret with the assistance of some of his officers, he received another splinter in his leg, which paralyzed the ball of his foot. Rozhdestvenski lost consciousness. When he revived, his first words were for the battle. "Why isn't the turret firing? Fall in the crews immediately."

Suvarov was dying, even as a torpedo boat, the *Buini*, came alongside to take the Admiral aboard. Neither ship had a boat that could be launched, and *Suvarov* was so aflame and the waves so high that the smaller vessel could not come in close enough to take on the injured commander-in-chief. The flagship was burning from one end to the other. Her hoses were broken and her lifeboats smashed. In the dressing stations there were now no wounded. The ship's ikons still stood behind unbroken glass, candles burning brightly before them. But only the dead lay among the wreckage of spilled bottles, stretchers and operating tables. "She was a most striking and awful sight. . . . covered with dense smoke, through which her one remaining mast was just visible," wrote Captain Jackson as his own ship joined the four destroyers that had arrived with the torpedo boats to pour on more fire and destruction. Explosions rocked the *Suvarov* as the coal, with which she was so overloaded, caught fire. She was unable to signal from her battered superstructure, but the captain of *Alexander III* took over command of the fleet without instructions, and turned sharp to the north toward Vladivostok. With their superior speed, the Japanese headed her off and pushed her southward.

The two big battleships followed by *Orel* endeavored to come to the flagship's assistance, but were forced into confusion by the Japanese fire. "They've given it up." "They are going off." "They couldn't do it." All over *Suvarov* similiar expressions were heard. Kamimura's armored cruisers circled her, firing again from a range of only about 3,000 yards.

When *Buini* arrived, the Admiral refused to leave, continuing to sit on a box in the gun turret where he had received his last injury, eyes turned to the floor, half-conscious. "Collect the staff," he called when they came for him but of his staff only two could be found. The engines had stopped working and down below men suffocated in the smoke. "Of the 900 men composing the complement of *Suvarov*, it would not be far wrong to say that, at this time, there remained alive only those few who were gathered together in the lower battery and on the windward embrasure," wrote Semenov.

Sailors carried the Admiral, protesting until he again lost consciousness, through the narrow doorway to where *Buini* rose and fell on the waves, and rolling him down over the backs of other sailors to the waiting hands on the destroyer. "Push off quickly!" shouted Midshipman Werner von Kursel. "Push off—push off—don't drown the Admiral!" Captain de Colongue, Semenov, and the flag lieutenant went with their Admiral, but Midshipman von Kursel refused the chief of staff's plea to leave the flagship. "No, sir," he shouted. "I shall stay by the ship."

The repair ship *Kamchatka,* seeking protection from the bombardment now battering both ships, swung close in against the burning flagship. "One felt pity for her and admiration for the *Suvarov* who was still on fire and still fighting," wrote Captain Jackson on *Azuma.* "As from time to time the bursts of shell were seen there were some shouts of *'banzai'* from the upper deck gun crews, the only cheering heard throughout the two days and the sound jarred unpleasantly."

The little *Kamchatka* was the first to go. Her sole surviving officer, dying from his wounds, refused an offer to surrender. *Kamchatka,* always in trouble on the long voyage out from Libau, went down at 6:50 P.M., her flag still flying.

Midshipman von Kursel and a couple of sailors manned *Suvarov*'s last gun as the armored cruisers tore her apart. *Suvarov* fired slowly and defiantly, only to become the target of a torpedo attack from the *Chihaya* and the Fifth Flotilla of destroyers. She had started firing at 1:48 P.M. At seven o'clock she went down.

Twenty-two-year-old Hasegawa Kiyoshi, in charge of the range-finder on *Mikasa,* said that it was impossible to tell which Japanese ship had sunk the *Suvarov.* He watched the Russian sailors jumping from the burning ship and felt a momentary stab of pity for them. They had come so far for the battle and now there was no chance of saving them. Hundreds of men were struggling in the water, grasping at pieces of wreckage and drowning each other in attempts to save themselves. One huge sailor pulled himself high up out of the water, his arms flung above the waves, and calling for help. "It was a piteous sight," wrote one of the British naval attachés. "A marine Verestchagin will have no difficulty in finding subjects for his canvas."

The battleship *Borodino* also turned over with the last of the day. "Though sudden, this was not dramatic," wrote Pakenham. "While all watched, the unfortunate ship disappeared, her departure only marked by a roar not greatly louder than that of one of her own bursting shells, and, until dispersed by the wind, by a great increase in volume of the dense cloud that brooded over the place she had occupied." There was only one survivor from *Borodino,* the pride and joy of her designer, Chief Engineer Politovski, who had ministered to the needs of the Second Pacific Squadron on its long journey out from home. Politovski died with the ship. "Those who were below were not called," his wife wrote bitterly. "They saved the 'valuable life of Admiral Rozhdestvenski.' "

Alexander III probably sank a little after 7 P.M. Kamimura's cruiser squadron, while chasing the Russian cruisers toward the north, saw a battleship of her description turn over and sink about that time. Of her 900 officers and men, about sixty survived.

After five hours of battle the day's fighting was at an end and the Japanese battleships and cruisers retired, leaving the night to the torpedo boats, which closed in like "jackals gathering around a carcass."*

On the Japanese ships a flurry of cleaning up took place. The crews made temporary repairs and washed the blood from the decks, while the ships' doctors busied themselves with the wounded. Loud hammering was heard on many of the ships. In *Asahi* eight coffins were made that evening for the men who had been killed. The captain personally tried them out for size, complaining that he could not lie with his feet stretched out: "If I am killed tomorrow, you must make a longer one for me," he told the carpenters.

The Russians had only an hour or so to clean their decks before the Japanese torpedo boats started their three-hour attack. The seas were still rough, but the wind had died down as Akiyama's step four began. According to Admiral Togo's report, the Japanese torpedo boats came in so close that the Russians could not bring their guns to bear on them. This was according to plan. In the Yellow Sea battle the torpedo boats had fired at very long range, without hitting a single Russian ship. This time Togo's instructions were clear. Six hundred yards was to be the maximum range.

Almost every torpedo boat behaved with suicidal bravery, dashing in to within 300 yards before releasing its torpedoes, blinded by the spray and with the skin of their faces burned and peeling from the wind and snow. Later it was suggested that Admiral Togo, a student of Admiral Makarov and Admiral Mahan, may also have been impressed by a paper, "The Tactics of Fast Craft," written by Captain Reginald Hugh Spencer Bacon of the Royal Navy, which appeared in *Brassey's Annual* in 1900: "During the night," Bacon asked, "would not the admiral keep his fast craft at the enemy? Would they be kept for future scouting work which might never prove necessary? Would they not be let loose like hell-hounds to tear into the enemy's fleet—torpedoeing, ramming, destroying, and using every nerve and knot to destroy, and so pave the way for the morrow's visitors?"

Captain Bacon was suggesting kamikaze tactics to a nation well aware

---

*At 6:50 P.M., just as the day's action was ending, a shell struck *Nisshin*, removing two fingers from the left hand of Midshipman Takano Isoroku, who later took the family name of Yamamoto and planned and led the Pearl Harbor attack in 1941.

of such procedures, and his mythical battle, to illustrate his paper, had actually been placed in the China Sea, with Admiral Togo in command of the Japanese fleet. "He who sends them forth to attack large and worthy prey must do so with the full knowledge that they may never return."

Whoever sowed the seed, the Japanese torpedo flotilla became a suicide squadron on the night of May 27. "We ought to be able to close within twenty yards of the target before she is sunk. . . . If we hit we shall go down with the Russians; if we are hit the Russians shall come with us, for the last man alive will steer the spare torpedo in the water," wrote an officer in one of the Japanese boats to a friend. "What is life but a summer night's dream?"

The fifty-eight destroyers and torpedo boats met Admiral Nebogatov's ships during the night and faithfully obeyed Togo's instructions. With his flag in *Nikolai I*, Nebogatov fought off a series of vicious attacks, during which destroyers and torpedo boats closed in at point-blank range. After the daylight battle only *Nikolai*, *Orel*, and *Izumrud* and two old coast defense ships were together. *Navarin* and *Sissoi Veliki* were lost and *Monomakh* and *Nakhimov* disabled. *Navarin* was alone during the night and was hit by three torpedoes. Everyone was ordered to jump overboard, but only three men were saved. They reported later that, when they were in the water and cried out for help, Japanese torpedo boats fired on them. When they stopped calling, they were left alone. At noon the next day, sixteen hours after *Navarin* had sunk, they were picked up by an English steamer and taken to Tientsin.

Monomakh and *Sissoi Veliki*, after many attacks, limped alongside each other but neither could help the other. *Monomakh* was approached by a Japanese cruiser next day and lowered her flag. Most of her crew were picked up by the Japanese cruiser. Others escaped in their own boats. When the boarding party arrived, they found that the seacocks had been opened and the ship went down.

During the night Admiral Enquist in the *Oleg* parted company with *Svyetlana*, *Dmitri Donskoi*, and *Monomakh*, and with his flagship and *Aurora* and *Zhemchug* made several attempts to break through to the north. He was surrounded by Japanese ships, however, and in desperation steered for the southern exit from the Tsushima Straits. He reached Manila at the beginning of June, where the ships were interned by the American authorities. *Dmitri Donskoi*, another of the trouble-makers on the journey from Russia, was ordered to sink the foundering destroyer, *Buini*, where Rozhdestvenski lay in a hammock in the captain's cabin. The little ship had been badly damaged and was overloaded with men from *Suvarov* and hundreds of half-drowned survivors from *Oslyabya*. Her engines failed on

May 29 and it was decided to transfer Rozhdestvenski to *Bedovi*, another destroyer.

The slow old *Dmitri Donskoi* was practically out of ammunition and fuel. She had six holes above her waterline and her boilers had been penetrated by shells. Her captain was dying, and it was decided to abandon ship. While the crew was being put overboard into boats or to swim to shore two Japanese torpedo boats and four cruisers appeared. *Dmitri Donskoi* covered herself with glory, damaging two of the torpedo boats and repelling attacks by the cruisers, before crawling off to scuttle herself on the shore.

Admiral Nebogatov's squadron was exhausted when the Japanese ships appeared at 5 A.M. next day. Vladivostok was still 300 miles off. A thousand stories have been told of the last hours of what remained of the Russian fleet. Those concerning *Orel*, split by dissention and insubordination, are perhaps only half-true. The ship was a mess, but other ships in worse physical state sank themselves and their crews rather than surrender. Stories of bribery, corruption, mutiny, and massacre filled the newspapers of the world for months afterward.

Only two of *Orel*'s twelve-inch guns were working by the morning of May 28. Thirty men had been killed and about a hundred injured. Her masts were down and her funnels had been pierced by hundreds of shells so that they looked like huge nutmeg graters. Coal filled cabins, wardrooms, and corridors and spilled across the decks. Hundreds of tons of water filled the ship, adding to her overweight. *Orel* was a battleship in name only. The armor of her deck was inadequate and she did not have the armored protection of battleships of the day. Water, coal, and heavy superstructures made her sit so low in the water that the little protective armor she possessed was below sea level.

Despite the revolutionary elements aboard, many of *Orel*'s crew did not want to surrender. A few men went below to scuttle the ship before the Japanese boarding party arrived. They were hunted out by the Japanese and shot. Half of the surviving crew was taken aboard *Asahi* and the remainder were left aboard the ship which was then taken in tow by the *Asama* for the journey to Japan. Her captain died of wounds on the way to Sasebo and was buried at sea, stitched in sailcloth with weights at his feet.

Novikov-Priboy was ordered aboard the *Asahi*. Before he left, he bade farewell to the crippled engineer of *Orel* who had contributed much to the revolutionary spirit on the voyage out from Russia. "Take good care of yourself," said Vasiliev. "We are on the eve of great things today. A new chapter opens in the history of the Russian empire."

What was left of the Russian Fleet was now under Admiral Nebogatov's command, but this he did not know. His men could fight no longer. The lights were out. His lifeboats were useless. The shore was distant, and 2,000 men waited for him to decide their destiny. He called the officers of his flagship together and among them they voted for surrender. He looked down on the faces of his crew to address them. "Gentlemen, I propose to surrender as the only means of saving our crews from destruction. Please give orders to run up the white flag."

By 11:15 A.M. the Japanese battleships, cruisers, and destroyers had formed a great circle around the Russian ships. Feverishly, Nebogatov's staff searched for a white flag. At last they found a large tablecloth, double damask with a pattern of flowers and leaves, and ran it up on the flagship. On *Azuma* Captain Jackson saw the signal "Surrender" and the reply "Will send a message." "Everyone laughed," he reported, "not derisively, but from sheer happiness."

Only Togo refused to accept the evidence. Akiyama stood beside him on the forebridge of *Mikasa* and waited for the Japanese firing to stop. But Togo would not give the order. The insignificant little *Izrumrud* pulled down her surrender flag and scurried off with Japanese cruisers and destroyers in pursuit.

Togo maintained his fire on *Nikolai I* and the other Russian ships flying the surrender flag. "Sir, the enemy has surrendered," said Akiyama. "Shouldn't you give the order to cease fire?"

Togo made no reply. In desperation, the Russians on *Nikolai I* and the other ships hoisted the Japanese flag. Still, the ceasefire order did not come. "Sir, doesn't the code of *bushido* compel us to stop firing?" asked Akiyama with tears in his eyes. Coolly, Togo replied that the Russians had not yet stopped their engines. When they had done so he would order the ceasefire. It was some time before *Nikolai I* understood that Togo was prepared to be as ruthless now as he had been when he sank the *Kowshing* eleven years before.

Akiyama was sent by Togo with another officer to bring Nebogatov to the *Mikasa*. He waited while Nebogatov went to his cabin to change into full dress uniform. Before the Russian admiral went to the Japanese flagship to accept the surrender terms he asked his sailors to behave themselves and not to get drunk. Many ignored this final order.

On *Orel* they scooped the rum from the scuppers, where it had been tipped, and rifled the officers' wardroom. According to Novikov-Priboy, who wrote his book so long after the war had finished and won the Stalin Prize, the officers had almost all been bad and the men disinclined to fight. Other ghastly stories told when the ship reached Sasebo were cabled around the world, and many people believed them. "The awful story from the battleship *Orel* must fill the world with horror," wrote the *Manila American*. It said:

. . . Hopeless Russian wounded men for whom every provision should have been made even in the thickest of the fight were thrown into the sea, defenseless and dying, while others were shot to still their cries for relief from their tortuous wounds. Then to cap the climax of these horrors, the feeding of the bodies of the dead to the furnaces to get them out of sight before they were cold was the ghastliest story that has come out of this savage war. We are not surprised that the world shuddered and almost everywhere people are crying for the war to cease.

Admiral Rozhdestvenski's pennant and the Red Cross flag had both been run up on *Bedovi,* where he lay unconscious. Almost immediately a Japanese destroyer approached and ordered the ship to stop. To the amazement of the Japanese captain who boarded the destroyer, he was told that the wounded Russian Admiral was aboard. "I won't disturb your Admiral," he said, "but at least I must see him with my own eyes." Convinced that he had indeed captured the commander-in-chief of the Russian fleet, he posted a sentry at the cabin door and returned to his ship. *Bedovi* was escorted into Sasebo naval base under tow, the Japanese flag flying on the last ship Rozhdestvenski was ever to command.

Admiral Togo and a young officer, Lieutenant Yamamoto Isoruko, called on him in hospital a few weeks later. Togo and the officer, who thirty-seven years later was to mount the attack on Pearl Harbor, were met by Captain de Colongue, who took them to the Admiral's room. Rozhdestvenski raised himself slightly from his pillow and saluted the Japanese Admiral. Then the two admirals shook hands. "Defeat is a common fate of a soldier," said Togo. "There is nothing to be ashamed of in it. The great point is whether we have performed our duty." Rozhdestvenski, overcome, merely bowed his head.

Later he was transferred to a temple in Kyoto with other prisoners. He refused to sign a pledge not to drink while in internment and spurned invitations to geisha parties. When the time came for him to return to Russia his hair was white and he was skeleton thin. "His nerves are of iron," said a Russian doctor, as he was leaving Japan. "He will outlive all of us."

Courts-martial in St. Petersburg failed to tell the whole story. Some men lied to save their own reputations, and the truth remained elusive. In evidence, many men said they had demanded that the ships should be blown up, and others vowed that they had volunteered for the task. A seaman from the flagship said that only one third of the crew could swim. "The crew consisted of stablemen, cooks, boot-makers, tailors, etc., but very few sailors," he said. Quartermaster Babushkin, who had made the extraordinary boat trip from Singapore in an effort to acquaint Nebogatov of Rozhdestvenski's whereabouts, was an unexpected, and highly suspect, witness. He said that this time he had swum from *Nikolai I* to the destroyer on which Rozhdestvenski lay unconscious. He assured the court that he had seen the Admiral, who had told him that the Japanese had been defeated. He then swam back to *Nikolai I* and reported this information.

Priests gave evidence that crews had wept when told they were to surrender. Others told of weak men who had been brave at the end, like the captain of *Ushakov* who went down waving his hand, and of brave men turned coward.

At his trial in the admiralty building in St. Petersburg, in 1906, Admiral Nebogatov said that Rozhdestvenski had given him few instructions before the battle and had not informed him of Felkerzam's death. He had been given only one order: to take his ships out to join Rozhdestvenski, which he did.

In a clear voice he told the court that he had been entrusted with the lives of thousands of men. "I am not by any means a soft-hearted man and I assure you that I would not have hesitated to have sacrificed 50,000 men if it could have been of the least use, but in this case why should I sacrifice the lives of young men? It would only have been suicide. If I had said: 'Ivan, drown yourself!' 'Petrov, shoot yourself!' 'Nikolai, blow your brains out!' they would have done so, but what right had I to sacrifice their lives to no purpose?"

Nebogatov insisted that he alone had raised the signal to surrender. "Whatever may have been said with regard to the protests made by officers against the surrender, I can only say that I would not have allowed any such protests. I was in command and therefore invested with the power to give such an order, otherwise what kind of a commander should I have made?"

Admiral Rozhdestvenski, called for the defense of Nebogatov, took full blame for his fleet's defeat. He had given the orders for Nebogatov to proceed to Vladivostok. None of his subordinates would have dared to disobey his orders. Asked had he been in Nebogatov's place, under the same duress, would he have surrendered, Rozhdestvenski answered, "Yes, most certainly."

"Tell me, Admiral," asked the prosecutor, "if among your staff of officers one would have been found who, contrary to your order to surrender, would have tried to persuade the crew to disobey and to continue the battle, what would you have done?"

"I would have shot him," replied Rozhdestvenski.

News of the battle filtered out to the world slowly. The Tsar's diary told of contradictory reports from Tsushima, "which only speak about our losses and do not mention theirs at all. This is very annoying and terribly disturbing." The weather was fine. He rode his horse around the palace grounds, rowed on the lake and walked with Alexandra, who was about to celebrate her thirty-third birthday. On June 2, the final and overwhelming news of the loss of the fleet reached him: "Rozhdestvenski himself is wounded and has been taken prisoner!!! The weather was lovely, which added to one's depression . . ."

His message to Rozhdestvenski stressed his belief in the will of God. "From my heart I thank you and all the officers of your squadron who have honorably done their duty unselfishly for Russia and for me. By the will of the Almighty success was not destined to crown your endeavors, but your boundless bravery will always be a source of pride to the country. I wish you a speedy recovery. May God console you all." The restriction of his thanks to those who had "honorably" done their duty was duly noted. Nebogatov and other commanders who had surrendered their ships were in disgrace.

Of the twelve Russian ships that made up the battle line, eight were sunk and four captured. Of the cruisers, four were sunk, one scuttled, three were interned at Manila, and one, the *Almaz,* formerly Viceroy Alexeiev's yacht, ran undetected along the Japanese coast and arrived in Vladivostok, to be greeted by an enthusiastic crowd, peering into the distance for the remainder of the fleet. Two destroyers followed her into port. Four others were sunk, one captured, and one interned in Shanghai. Three special service vessels were sunk, two interned in Shanghai, and one reached Diego Suarez on the northern tip of Madagascar at the end of June.

Russian casualties amounted to 4,830 men killed or drowned, just under 7,000 taken prisoner, and 1,862 interned by neutral countries.

The Japanese lost three torpedo boats. Several other ships were badly damaged, but all were fit for further service. Japanese losses in men were 110 killed and 590 wounded.

Commander Akiyama, his steps successfully taken, wrote Togo's long report of the battle in one night. In his own memoirs, published several years later, he defended Admiral Nebogatov's surrender to the Japanese fleet. Resistance would have been as useless "as sweeping the sea with a broom," he said. Naval war was not as simple as playing chess on a table. "I have full sympathy with the enemy's commander and am inclined to think that those who treat the surrender of the commander with contempt are guilty of ignoring the troubles and efforts which Admiral Togo and our officers went through in creating this psychological change in the enemy's commander." He did not regard the victory of May 27 as so strange and wonderful. The Japanese gunnery was no more efficient than at the battle of the Yellow Sea, the fire no fiercer. The Russian ships were overloaded with coal and their armor was deficient.

"We won the victory where it was easy to win and not over something that was hard to conquer. . . . each division of the combined squadrons did its work well and not more. There was nothing remarkable in our bravery. We regard ourselves as a fit example of good fight. . . ."

Togo summed up the battle thus:

> The enemy opened fire at 2:08 and our First Division bore it for a few minutes and replied at about 2:11. The number of enemy shells fired during these few minutes exceeded 300 and the *Mikasa* was damaged and had casualties before she had fired a shot. About a half hour later the enemy's battle formation was entirely out of order, so that the fate of our empire was really settled within this first half hour. The *Mikasa* and the eleven others of the main force had taken years of labor to design and build, and yet they were used for only half an hour of decisive battle. We, too, studied the art of war and trained ourselves in it, but it was put to use for only that short period. Though the decisive battle took such a short time, it required ten years of preparation.

Admiral Togo became the "war god" of the Japanese navy, just as General Nogi had been made the hero of the fighting for Port Arthur. Though the breathtaking maneuver at the beginning of the battle became known as the "Togo turn," other Japanese officers at the Battle of Tsushima contributed much to its success. Their names have been forgotten. Kamimura, who took his own initiative and closed in on the Russian battleships, was regarded by some as the real hero of the battle. Yet in November 1905, when a list of promotions in the Japanese navy was issued, alongside Kamimura's name, the second-last on the list, was written, "Not occupied."

Akiyama, who had worked out the seven steps for the destruction of the Russian Fleet and had stood with Togo and the rest of the senior staff on the bridge of *Mikasa* during the battle, was at heart not a fighting man. Just before he died, at the age of fifty, he wrote in his memoirs: "The scene of the shambles made me feel life's tragedy as a warrior and made me repeat the very words—'bows and arrows I shall give up.' "

CHAPTER 32

ﾓﾓﾓﾓﾓﾓ

Portsmouth

THE BATTLE OF TSUSHIMA left Russia grief-stricken, angry and rebellious. Crowds of *mujiks* surrounded those who were able to read the news bulletins in the streets and wept while they listened to the sorrowful details of the disaster. "Those guilty of Russia's disgrace should be overwhelmed with shame," wrote *Russ,* the country's largest newspaper. "The death of half a million men and the loss of billions of money is the cost of the rejection of progress and Western civilization. Sevastopol struck the shackles from the serfs, and Port Arthur, Mukden, and Tsushima should free Russia from the slavery of the bureaucracy."

"Enough blind folly for 200 years," said another newspaper.

The Russian people have been marching to the brink of destruction but the bandages are now torn from their eyes. They will neither be led nor driven over the precipice. Let the people speak. The bureaucracy has had its say and has crowned its work with national shame and humiliation. Our only consolation in this bitter hour is the consciousness that it is not the people but the government which has suffered a defeat. Enough.

Even Admiral Alexeiev's mouthpiece, *Slovo,* commented that Russia had had calamities enough. It demanded peace.

"Peace cannot be a disgrace, as many wrongly imagine," wrote Leo Tolstoy's wife, in a letter published in *The Times.* "A lost war is not a disgrace but a misfortune. A spiritually undeveloped, un-Christian nation such as the Japanese was bound to conquer, for among them is rife the principle of patriotism, which is opposed to the principle of love of one's neighbor and therefore of opposition to war."

"What's the difference?" Tolstoy asked. "What does it matter if they burn us too as well as my works? We have to die sooner or later."

Maxim Gorki, under house arrest after his release from prison, had a different view. "The war has been a good school for those who precipitated it," he said. "The lessons are beginning to tell."

A visitor to Moscow was taken by his driver to look at the spot where Grand Duke Serge had been killed. Pointing to the place, the driver said: "Look, that's where that dog was blown to pieces. A fine sight it was. And all they found of him was a few fingers. Where do you think they found those? In the Red Cross box. They were accustomed to be in that box. He had four hundred million roubles when he died, and he stole it from the poor soldiers in Manchuria."

Deeds increasingly accompanied words. On June 4, 5,000 demonstrators at a summer resort nineteen miles from Tsarskoe Selo clashed with police when they demanded a funeral march for the sailors who had lost their lives at Tsushima. "By rising let us show respect for the victims," cried the former mayor of Baku. "Down with the war. We have had enough blood."

Poland was in a state of ferment. May Day in Warsaw had been marked by bombs and Cossack charges, and a hundred people were killed or wounded in the streets. Mutiny threatened in the Black Sea Fleet. Western Georgia threw out its Russian officials and prevented the mobilization of more troops. In the Caucasus, the mobilization of the First Army Group was abandoned. "It makes me sick to read the news," said Nicholas. "Strikes in schools and factories, murdered policemen, Cossacks, riots. But the ministers instead of acting with quick decision only assemble in council like a lot of frightened hens and cackle about providing united ministerial action."

Antiwar demonstrations in St. Petersburg spread across the country. "Conditions in Russia are overshadowing the war," wrote *The New York Times* on June 6. "There is fear of revolution."

Rioting broke out in Warsaw again on June 19. About 2,000 Socialists carrying red flags were stopped by Cossacks. The Socialists opened fire with their guns and the Cossacks charged with drawn swords into the thick of the procession. Three days later troops stormed the barricades at Lodz. In the ensuing fighting an estimated 2,000 were killed or hurt. According to *The New York Times,* soldiers killed innocent men, women, and children, and the rioters replied by throwing sulfuric acid on the troops.

Colonel Akashi provided the kindling for many of these fires. The Georgian revolutionary, Dekanozi, one of Akashi's closest collaborators, left Switzerland after the meeting with Father Gapon with an advance of 40,000

yen from Akashi to create a mutiny among the crews of the Black Sea fleet.*
The execution fell short of expectations, but it brought bloodshed to the
streets of Odessa and mutiny to the battleship *Potemkin,* the most powerful
ship in the Black Sea Fleet, and, until the provocateurs went to work,
manned by a crew that exhibited little interest in the revolution.

A boat came ashore bearing the body of a sailor named Vakulintchuk
who had been shot by an officer, according to a note pinned to his chest,
for having expressed dissatisfaction with the food. The note added that the
officers aboard the battleship had been killed and that the *Potemkin* would
bombard Odessa if the port authorities caused the body to be removed or
approached the battleship.

Thousands of workers gathered around the body to listen to inflammatory speeches by Socialist Revolutionaries. With the troops afraid to open
fire because of the presence of the *Potemkin,* the mob pillaged the warehouses and other vessels tied up alongside, broached casks of wine and
spirits, got drunk on the contents, and threw quantities of goods into the
sea.

At nightfall they set fire to the godowns and shipping offices, and destroyed three ships. They also reduced the port area to rubble. Next day the
local authorities declared a state of war, and troops surrounded Odessa. The
Potemkin pulled away to about half a mile from the shore and fired three
blank shots as prescribed by the naval code for the funeral of a sailor. The
sounds of the blanks had just died away when two live shells came crashing
into the city from the *Potemkin*'s guns. With civilian representatives of the
Socialist Revolutionaries aboard, the *Potemkin* then sailed for Rumania
and there surrendered to the authorities.

Akashi exulted, especially since the *Potemkin* incident had been created
by such a minor incident as a seaman's complaint about maggoty meat in
the borscht. Well might Akashi exult. While Togo and Oyama were bent
on the destruction of the Russian fleets and armies, Akashi was striking at
the heart of the Russian empire. To his fleet of two steamers, *Cysne* and
Cecil, he now added a third, the *John Grafton,* soon to be known to
newspaper readers around the globe as a "mystery ship." At the end of July
she left Flushing in Holland for a rendezvous in the English Channel with
another boat carrying the collection of bombs, guns, and ammunition that
had been stored in London by Zilliacus and Akashi. The seas were rough
and the transshipment difficult. The changeover took three days, but finally,
with its cargo aboard, the *John Grafton* sailed for the Baltic Sea. Her orders

---

*Akashi received secret funds of one million yen from the Imperial General
Headquarters, of which he spent 750,000, or around $30 million at today's value.

were to pass through the Straits of Denmark on the night of August 14, to land arms and ammunition for the use of Lithuanian revolutionaries and others for shipment to Moscow by August 18. Having delivered this cargo, she was to anchor off a small island south of Vyborg, there to await the arrival of the *Cecil* into which she was to discharge the rest of her cargo for use at St. Petersburg, seventy-five miles away.

After discharging only the first part of her cargo, things went badly wrong and the *John Grafton* ran aground off the Finnish coast. When St. Petersburg received the report of the wreck from provincial officials, it dispatched a cruiser to investigate. She loaded 8,400 rifles still stacked on the beach and returned with them to St. Petersburg, where, according to Akashi, the pervasive revolutionaries bought them back readily and swiftly.

The news reaching St. Petersburg from the front was filled with gloom. Linievitch's first step after his appointment to succeed Kuropatkin was to ask General Sakharov, his chief of staff, for an assessment of the military situation. Sakharov submitted a bleakly pessimistic report concluding that there was no hope of overcoming the Japanese and that it was impossible to continue the war with forces so badly trained, lacking in intelligence, and fighting at the far end of the Trans-Siberian Railway. The morale of the armies had been lowered to such an extent by their successive defeats, he believed, that there was not only no desire to win but not even any inclination to fight.

Japan also had grave problems. Mukden had been a great and enormously costly victory, but not the Sedan that Oyama needed. At best, the Imperial General Headquarters reckoned that it could form no more than one or one-and-a-half divisions from the replacement units still available, and there were strong disagreements in Tokyo about how these troops should be used. Against a foe superior in numbers and arms and with a long military tradition, Oyama had won a series of magnificent, if inconclusive, victories. But to go deeper into Manchuria or into the Siberian wastelands was to risk the fate that had overtaken Napoleon when he marched on Moscow. Though there were men like Dr. Morrison of *The Times,* offering gratuitous advice to the Japanese about the problems of supply that would confront the Russians once they had been pushed back into the grainless lands beyond Harbin, the military leaders were extremely conscious of the exhaustion of their reserves and of the dangers that would confront them, even if operations went no farther than Harbin.

Vital decisions had to be made, and the central figure once again was Kodama. After planning the strategy of the war and helping it to unfold brilliantly but without crowning success in Manchuria, he now returned on a secret visit to Tokyo. The hawk of 1903 had become a 1905 dove. "I have come to Tokyo for the express purpose of stopping the war," he told Major-General Nagaoka, vice-chief of the Imperial General Staff, when he met him at the Shinbashi station. "Why aren't you doing something?" Kodama asked him. "Don't you know that if you light a fire, you must also know how to put it out."

Kodama arrived unannounced on March 28. Four days earlier Japan had negotiated its third foreign war loan, this time for £30 million sterling at 4½ percent, raising her total foreign war debt to £52 million. This was a large sum for the times. In part, her ability to borrow so largely could be related back to the massacre of the Jews at Kishinev. Jacob H. Schiff, of Kuhn, Loeb and Company, the New York bankers, was furious about the treatment of Russian Jews and did all he could to help the Japanese raise the finances they needed. No amount of goodwill on the part of Schiff and others would have been sufficient, however, if Japan had proved unable to establish her claims by her performance on the field of battle. Kodama wanted to maintain this situation and to negotiate from strength. Japan, he knew, could not win if the war continued, though the nation carried away by repeated victories, was shouting for a march across the Urals and on to St. Petersburg.

Though Kodama brought news that most did not want to hear, the message quickly began to spread, and on April 2 Count Inoue, the elder statesman, told Hara Takashi of the Seiyukai party that Kodama had informed the government any further advance by the army was impossible. Not all of Kodama's colleagues agreed with him. Independent-minded General Nozu was all for continuing the war, but Kodama found an immediate supporter in Ito, still the country's most influential man, who warned that finance would not be easily obtained if the war continued indefinitely.

Peace had been considered at many levels and in many countries, including Japan, as soon as the first shots had been fired. Viscount Kaneko Kentaro had left for the United States with the specific purpose of persuading President Roosevelt, with whom he had been a fellow student at Harvard, to mediate at the appropriate time. Informal discussions on peace began as early as July 1904 when Witte, angry at the terms of a commercial treaty that Germany had forced on Russia, visited London and privately sounded out Hayashi. After the fall of Port Arthur, Japanese diplomats in the United States and Europe had again raised the possibility of peace. Mukden gave further impetus to the peace movement. On March 20 Kaneko saw President Roosevelt and Secretary of War William Howard Taft. Roosevelt, whose sympathies during the war had been strongly with the Japanese, was beginning to fear an expansionist Japan if Russia collapsed. He told Kaneko on March 20 of his willingness to act as a mediator and of his discussions with the French and the Germans on the question of peace.

Kaneko cabled Tokyo the gist of his discussion with Roosevelt. The cabinet was already considering peace terms when his cable and the weight of Kodama's arguments, and those of the military department generally, were thrust into the discussion. On April 21 the cabinet decided upon the terms that it intended to demand if the war could be brought to the conference table. Tsushima capped all its war expectations, and on May 31 Komura wrote to Takahira Kogoro, the Japanese minister in Washington, instructing him to express to Roosevelt the hope that

> he will see his way directly and entirely of his own motion and initiative to invite the two belligerents to come together for the purpose of direct negotiations, and you will add that if the President is disposed to undertake the service, the Japanese government will leave it to him to determine the course of procedure and what other power, or powers, if any, should be consulted in the matter of the suggested initiative.

Just before Mukden, the Kaiser had urged Nicholas to continue the war and to fight for victory. Tsushima changed his mind. On June 4, the U.S. minister in Berlin cabled Roosevelt to inform him that William now considered the situation in Russia so serious that "when the truth is known in St. Petersburg in regard to the recent defeat, the life of the Tsar will be in danger and the gravest disorders likely to occur."

Nicholas was filled with conflicting opinions and emotions. The Tsaritsa urged him to continue the struggle. General Linievitch, supported both by Kuropatkin and the other commanding generals, reported that the Manchurian armies had recovered from the low point reported in March and were now in first-class fighting order. Very much better reinforcements in vast numbers had now not only made good all the Mukden losses, but were adding each day to the size and capacity of the armies. Deficiencies in the armament and equipment had been remedied; the Manchurian armies were ready to go. On the other hand, Linievitch reported, the Japanese armies after a year and a half of continuous struggle showed signs of reaching the breaking point. The will to fight was notably absent, and, in increasing numbers, deserters were crossing to the Russian side. The war weariness, Kuropatkin confirmed, was general and the early fanaticism had disappeared.

Peter the Great would have fought on.

Nicholas, as Prince Lobanov-Rostovski remarked, was not a Peter the Great. On June 6 he called a conference of military leaders to set the stage for Russia's participation in the peace talks, at the same time approving the dispatch of additional forces for Linievitch. "You have come at a psychological moment," Nicholas told American minister George Meyer, when he saw him that day. "As yet no foot has been placed on Russian soil; but I realize that at almost any moment they can make an attack on Sakhalin. . . . Therefore it is important that the meeting should take place before that occurs."

On June 9 the White House made public a note it had sent to St. Petersburg and Tokyo. It explained: "The President feels that the time has come when, in the interests of all mankind, he must endeavor to see if it is not possible to bring to an end the terrible and lamentable conflict now being waged." The identical notes from Roosevelt invited both Russia and Japan to meet for direct discussions without any intermediary. He offered to help arrive at a mutually acceptable time and place for the meeting. Japan accepted the offer the following day, and on June 12 Russia also agreed.

Nicholas's fears for the island of Sakhalin were fully justified. Kodama was in favor of peace, but he also saw the need for strengthening Japan's bargaining position. In Tokyo he gave active support to the plans pushed with singleminded purpose by General Nagaoka to launch an invasion of Sakhalin, which flanks the Maritime Province of Siberia and was therefore of great strategic value to Russia. To begin with, the cabinet, Yamagata, Terauchi, and the navy were all either lukewarm or resolutely opposed. The reserves were desperately low and no one, except Nagaoka and Kodama, saw much point in sending them off to the island of fog and ice when there might be more urgent tasks to perform in Manchuria. Yet Kodama's influence proved decisive, and on July 7 landing operations began aimed at bringing maximum pressure on the Russians and forcing them to negotiate. So far, Russia had not lost a square mile of its own territory.

A month later, Sakhalin was in Japanese hands. As Kodama had intended, this neat little military operation had important political significance. It caused Russia's only territorial loss of the war, and it implied a direct threat to Vladivostok. Japan's bargaining position was notably improved.

No less important for Japan was the renewal of the Anglo–Japanese Alliance for a period of ten years. England explicitly gave Japan a free hand in Korea, subject only to the maintenance there of trading opportunities for all nations. The early alliance had been purely defensive; the new alliance went much further and required the military cooperation of both if either was attacked by even a single other power. And to cap this diplomatic coup, Japan, in exchange for assurances that it harbored no designs on the Philippines, also reached a secret understanding with the United States, the Taft-Katsura Agreement, that recognized Japanese suzerainity over Korea "to the extent of controlling her foreign relations and thus obviating future trouble."

[527]

Events were moving altogether too fast for the Kaiser, who had seen so much profit to be gained by urging Nicholas to war. The growth of the Entente Cordiale between England and France had been viewed with marked disfavor in Germany. William now decided to test the strength of the entente by precipitating a crisis in Morocco, and on March 31 his forces landed at Tangier, with the intention of preventing the country from becoming a French protectorate. While this crisis was still simmering, he and Nicholas met aboard their yachts in the Baltic. Without preliminary warning, William produced a treaty under which Germany and Russia agreed to lend each other mutual help in case either was attacked in Europe by a third power, and to ask France to be a cosignatory. To Nicholas, floundering in the distress of the disastrous war, it seemed that Willy was throwing him a lifebuoy. Without consulting any of his advisors, he signed it, only to learn from Witte and Lamsdorf that, though the treaty was directed primarily against England, France would react violently and with grave prejudice to the finances that Russia so desperately needed.

The despised Witte, who had been kicked upstairs as chairman of the council of ministers, had now become indispensable. "Anyone but Witte," Nicholas said when the question of the leadership of the peace delegation was first under discussion. But nobody else wanted the thankless task. Witte it had to be. "When a sewer has to be cleaned, they send Witte," Witte told Count Kokovtsov, the finance minister, "but as soon as work of a nicer kind appears, other candidates spring up."

Ito was the obvious choice as leader of the Japanese delegation. Witte, who remembered Ito's peace mission to St. Petersburg before the signing of the Anglo–Japanese Alliance, even took the unusual step of seeking through an intermediary to persuade the Japanese that the best prospects for a satisfactory peace for all depended on Ito's presence. But Ito, unsure that the conference would bring peace, did not want the job, arguing that Katsura should retain responsibility for the war, and Foreign Minister Komura was named as chief Japanese delegate.

The choice of a site for the conference was the subject of repeated diplomatic exchanges. Roosevelt had preferred Switzerland. The Japanese wanted somewhere in the Far East. The Russians preferred Paris. Eventually Portsmouth, New Hampshire, rich in American historical associations, with winding, narrow, and tree-shaded streets, was selected on the grounds that a city in the United States was more or less acceptable to both countries. Since the conference was to be held in midsummer, Washington was ruled out because of the climate. Remote, quiet, cool, Portsmouth seemed ideal.

Komura, Harvard University's first Japanese graduate, slight of stature but an experienced and able diplomat who had strongly favored the war, left Tokyo on July 8. Crowds of spectators greeted him in America with cheers, firecrackers, and banners proclaiming, "Right is right. Our compliments to the bravest of the brave." Most of the enthusiasts on the West Coast were Japanese. American opinion had begun to swing away from the Japanese toward the Russians. There was so much talk of the "Yellow Peril" that Komura felt constrained to say at St. Paul, Minnesota, where he paused on his way across the United States by train, that the "so-called 'Yellow Peril' is a creation of the imagination on the part of some interested people in Europe. Not only Japan and China but the entire civilized world has gained immeasurably from our conflict with Russia."

Witte, sailing from Cherbourg aboard the German liner *Wilhelm der Grosse,* was well received in New York when he arrived on August 3. Conscious of the need for good public relations and that his own lack of knowledge of English would prove a handicap, he had enlisted the support of Dr. E. J. Dillon, the St. Petersburg correspondent of the London *Daily Telegraph,* an old friend and adviser. Witte was already persuaded to abandon formal diplomatic precedents and customs, and his speech on arrival, ghosted by Dr. Dillon, set the pattern for an extremely well-conducted Russian campaign in psychological warfare. It referred to Russia's "brave antagonist" and spoke about strengthening the bonds of friendship between the United States and Russia. There was just a hint that Witte's mission might prove unproductive, but this was couched in expressions of utter reasonableness. Roosevelt was viewed, of course, as a "gifted leader."

The journalists were not merely impressed; they applauded. Large numbers of friendly letters and telegrams arrived for Witte at the St. Regis Hotel in New York. One, from the publisher of the *American Miner* in Philadelphia, said: "Seven tenths of the people of the Pacific Coast are with you in refusing Japanese impertinent territorial demands."

Despite the seeming good will, the prospects for peace were discouraging. Yamagata visited Manchuria late in July for a series of briefings by Oyama and Kodama and returned to Tokyo alarmed at the state of the Japanese armies, now led mostly by elderly reserve officers (since most of the others had been killed), and by the size of the Russian buildup and the expressions of optimism emanating from Linievitch's headquarters. Yet the war party in Japan, loudly and insistently, demanded the imposition of the most humiliating terms on the Russians. St. Petersburg, on the other hand, was finally moved to question whether Linievitch and Kuropatkin were not right after all. Linievitch now had half a million men under his command. Oyama's heavily outnumbered forces, desperately short of reserves and reinforcements, faced the most dangerous situation of the entire war.

Witte (privately as pessimistic as ever about the military situation) and other members of his delegation spread the word that the situation had

[529]

changed in Manchuria to Russia's advantage. Russia had not been conquered—and could not be conquered. Therefore, if the Japanese insisted on
demanding vast sums of money, the Russians would have no alternative but
to go on with the war.

The idea was to persuade the world that Japan was fighting for material
gain. As soon as it was established that the Japanese did in fact want money,
their case would be gravely prejudiced in the eyes of independent observers.
The brave little Japanese would become avaricious and dangerous little
"Japs." Of Witte's tactic, the Japanese were acutely aware. Suddenly, they
were on the defensive.

To Teddy Roosevelt fell the exacting and thankless task of trying to
persuade the Japanese not to make what the Russians would regard as
unreasonable demands, while also persuading the Russians that they needed
peace. On August 6 he received the opposing plenipotentiaries and introduced them to each other aboard the U.S. navy yacht *Mayflower*.

The formal negotiations began at the navy yard in Portsmouth on August
8 in the middle of a heat wave. "Not only is it fearfully hot, but the
humidity, sultriness, and stickiness are a revelation to the New Yorkers,"
The New York Times correspondent complained. "There is a deluge of
mosquitoes of a viciousness which puts New Jersey insects to the blush.
They have speckled legs, great industry, and no gift of singing to warn the
unwary of their approach. They leave behind not just ordinary lumps but
great welts and bars." The Japanese were also plagued by droves of girls
holidaying in New Hampshire. One Japanese official tired of all the attention and asked an American correspondent for an explanation of the girls'
behavior. "The girls look on you as toy dolls," said the correspondent.

Witte had his personal troubles as well. He was so big that he could not
fit into his bath at the Wentworth Hotel on Newcastle Island. He found the
food dreadful and was unable to persuade the staff to provide him with tea
in the quantities and at the times he demanded. Smoking was not permitted
in the hotel dining room—another irritant to Witte, who, since he insisted
on smoking with his coffee, was required to take it in a small, hot anteroom.

Public opinion was much in the minds of both delegations. Sunday,
August 13, provided a rare opportunity to influence it. Because he liked to
attend church, the far from devout Witte told the Japanese, he wanted the
morning session canceled. Fearing that this might put them in a position
of pagans, thereby affecting their standing, the Japanese decided that for
appearance' sake Ambassador Takahira Kogoro should also attend church.
He was up against hopeless odds in a Christian country. Witte and two of
his staff set off for Christ Church in a motorcar followed by the rest of the
Russian delegation in a large omnibus. The rector of Christ Church, who
conducted the service, left no doubt about where his sympathies lay: one

of the psalms, with reference to victory over the heathen, was sung to the tune of the Russian national anthem.

Both the Russian and the Japanese governments had prepared briefs for their delegations. For obvious reasons, the Japanese were primarily concerned with what they could extract from the Russians, while the Russians were more interested in what they could properly concede and the limits beyond which they could not go.

Count Lamsdorf, the Russian foreign minister, in his first draft report to the Tsar, recommended that Russia abandon the idea of exercising any influence in Korea. He envisaged the Japanese demands for an indemnity but expressed no views on it. Finally, he discussed the limitation of Russian naval and military forces in the Far East.

Nicholas read the report through and added his own comments: "I am ready to terminate by peace a war which I did not want, provided the conditions offered us befit the dignity of Russia," he wrote at the top of the report. "I do not consider that we are beaten; our army is still intact, and I have faith in it." He was ready to abandon Russian interests in Korea, since it was not Russian territory. As for the indemnity, he was adamant: "Russia has never paid an indemnity: I shall *never* consent to this." He underlined "never" three times.

There was no surprise in the Russian delegation when Komura presented the peace plan to the Portsmouth conference—the acknowledgment of paramount Japanese interest in Korea; the Russian evacuation of Manchuria; Japanese rehabilitation of Manchuria; reciprocal Russian and Japanese agreement not to obstruct "any general measure common to all countries, which China may take for the development of commerce and industries in Manchuria"; the cession of the island of Sakhalin and all public works and property thereon to Japan; the transfer of Port Arthur, Dalny, and other adjacent territory to Japan; the Russian transference to Japan of the railway between Harbin and Port Arthur, together with the coal mines belonging to or worked for the benefit of the railway; Russian retention of the Trans-Manchurian Railway for commercial and industrial purposes only; an indemnity to reimburse Japan for the costs of the war; the surrender to Japan of all Russian ships of war that sought asylum in neutral ports or surrendered to Japan; the limitation of Russian naval strength in the Far East; and full fishing rights for Japan along the coasts, bays, and rivers of all the Russian Far East.

The Russian delegation settled down to a private detailed point by point study of the Japanese draft. Witte had been wholly out of sympathy with Russia's policy in Korea, and there was immediate acceptance of Japan's demands there, with the stipulation that no action should be taken which would threaten the safety of the Manchurian border. Having pledged to

[531]

evacuate Manchuria under the Russo–Chinese Agreement of 1902, there was no Russian objection to surrendering the railway but only to the point where the Russian troops were holding their positions. Witte's view was that the Russians should act as broadmindedly as possible on questions that were of no material importance and "stand out for those conditions that are really important and show our compliance, so that in case of a rupture the blame should fall on the Japanese."

The two points on which the Russians had to dig in their toes were the indemnity and the cession of Sakhalin. It was late in the evening when the cutter returning from the navy yard took the Russians back to their hotel. The two delegations had agreed that their negotiations would be kept secret, but next morning the Boston newspapers had detailed accounts of the Japanese draft proposals. The Associated Press picked up enough from Witte and J. J. Korostovetz, the Russian spokesman, to write a clear account of the demands. The Japanese were furious, asserting that the Russians wanted to make the terms known so as to appeal to public opinion against them.

The following day Witte replied point by point. With minor qualifications, he agreed to most Japanese demands, but on Sakhalin and the indemnity he was adamant. Russia was not prepared for peace at any price. But Japan wanted, and needed, money, and, in any event, the payment of indemnities had become the traditional way of bestowing tribute on the victor. The war was costing a million dollars a day and Japan had no more than $200 million to her credit in London and New York. The Japanese public was being taxed unmercifully to pay for the war. No less than 53 percent of the budget went toward war expenses. Chances of further foreign loans seemed poor.

Since it had been decided on the advice of President Roosevelt to deal with each item separately, so that the more difficult problems might be isolated, the crisis in the negotiations was not immediately apparent and until August 15 there was appreciable progress.

Sakhalin came up for discussion on August 15. The Japanese made a proposal to ransom it for a sum variously said to be £120 million to £150 million. Since both sides were far apart in their views, it was agreed to defer further discussion until later in the conference. Two days later, however, other stumbling blocks had developed over the problems of interned ships and Japanese demands for the limitation of Russian naval forces in the Far East, and the conference seemed set for collapse. Advised of this by Count Kaneko, and alarmed at messages from St. Petersburg that Russia would neither cede Sakhalin nor pay an indemnity, President Roosevelt decided to intervene personally, and in a message to the Tsar on August 21 urged him to accept a compromise solution based on the partitioning of Sakhalin and the payment of a substantial sum by the Russians for the northern half, which was now in possession of the Japanese. Two days later he reinforced his appeal, after warning Count Kaneko that he did not think Japan's case for an indemnity was a good one. These interventions seemed to have served no purpose. The Tsar had decided against further concessions and was not prepared to pay anything for Sakhalin. On the contrary, he was ready to take to the field himself rather than pay an indemnity.

Witte filled Komura with dismay when he told him that there was no hope of compromise on the Russian side and that the military were pressing vigorously for the continuation of the war. There seemed to be no way out of the deadlock. Komura reported that the conference was on the point of collapse and so advised Tokyo. The Russians were packing their bags in anticipation that the meeting on August 28 would be the last and that the war would go on.

A message from Tokyo instructed Komura to seek a postponment of the final session of the conference for twenty-four hours. Witte agreed, but indicated that the meeting would be the last. As the Russians left for the navy yard on August 29, reporters asked Korostovetz about the chances of an agreement. He replied that it was "almost sure" there would be a rupture.

Like the rest of the Russian delegation, he was unaware of the agony that had overtaken the Japanese government when Komura's messages arrived. The cabinet, together with three of the elder statesmen, Ito, Yamagata, and Inoue, met on August 28. Yamagata, who had been to Manchuria, was as concerned as Kodama about the arrival of two new Russian army corps from Europe. The bottlenecks on the Trans-Siberian Railway had been removed and the Russians were now generously supplied. On the other hand, by straining all resources, the Japanese could put no more than another division and a half into the field. A decisive battle was beyond the capacity of the Japanese forces: only the Russians could envisage a Sedan now.

That afternoon the Japanese leaders met again in the presence of the Emperor. At 8:30 P.M. Komura was instructed to abandon the demand for an indemnity. The message also instructed him to give up the claim to Sakhalin if it threatened to endanger the chances of peace, though this was modified subsequently when the British tipped off the foreign office in Tokyo that the Tsar was willing to settle for the northern half of the island.

Though hints of the changes in Tokyo had already appeared that morning in *The New York Times* and there had been some private exchanges between the leaders of the two delegations, the formal meeting of the peace delegates on August 29 took place in an atmosphere of high drama.

Komura, his face composed and expressionless, opened the session with

[533]

the statement that the Japanese had not yet received an answer to proposals they had made on August 23: the partition of Sakhalin at the 50th parallel on condition that the Russians paid 1,200,000 yen for the cession by Japan.

Witte replied by reading a note rejecting the compromise.

For a few seconds there was absolute silence. Witte's strain showed as he tore up pieces of paper on the table.

Then Komura rose again. "We make you another offer," he said. "To withdraw the money payment and give you half of Sakhalin."

"I accept your offer," said Witte.

Komura broke down and wept after Witte had left the conference room, fending off the congratulations of admirers, newspapermen, hotel clerks, and holiday makers who converged on the Russian annex at the Wentworth Hotel.

"What about the indemnity?" a reporter asked.

"Not a sou," Witte cried.

"Vive la Russe," shouted a French correspondent. The crowd took up the shout and repeated it three times. Witte, beaming, bowed to the crowd and, followed by wild cheers, disappeared into his quarters. Several young American women called later in quest of Witte's autograph and were ushered into the presence of the man who had just won for Russia its only victory of the war.

At 3:45 P.M. on September 5 the two delegations and a small group of Americans, including Captain Cameron Winslow, *aide-de-camp* to Roosevelt, and Governor John MacLane of New Hampshire, gathered for the official signing of the treaty, which, though falling far short of the anticipations of the Japanese public, fairly represented the situation in the field.

While the secretaries were busy applying the seals to the treaty, Witte and Komura both lit cigarettes. Standing near the table with the Japanese, Constantine Nabokoff, the secretary to the Russian delegation and the most passionate partisan of peace, exclaimed, "Oh, what a blessing!"

"You think it is a blessing for Russia?" the Japanese asked him.

"I think," said Nabokoff, covering up his *faux pax,* "that peace is a blessing for Japan as well as for Russia, but I did not mean peace, I meant tobacco."

Russia recognized Japan's "paramount political, military, and economical interests" in Korea, and pledged itself "neither to obstruct nor interfere with the measures of guidance, protection, and control which the imperial government of Japan may find it necessary to take in Korea."

The Russians also agreed to transfer the lease of Liaotung Peninsula that they had negotiated with China in 1898 to Japan, together with the Chinese Eastern Railway between Port Arthur and Chang-Chun beyond Mukden and the regional coal mines that provided the railway with fuel. Both countries agreed to evacuate Manchuria, except, of course, for the Japanese lease of Dalny, Port Arthur, and the rest of the Liaotung Peninsula. Along with the southern half of Sakhalin, Japan also got fishing rights along the Russian coast in the Japan, Okhotsk, and Bering seas. The treaty paid lip service to China's proprietary rights in Manchuria, and both countries agreed to obtain the consent of the Chinese government.

At 3:49 P.M. the two principal delegates signed. Nabokoff was standing close to Komura's chair and beside another member of the Japanese delegation. As the Japanese reached for the inkpot, apparently about to take it as a souvenir, Nabokoff remarked sarcastically, "I would like very much to carry away this armchair, but it is far too heavy."

Any embarrassment was masked by the nineteen-gun salute in the navy yard and by the bedlam of church bells and the whistles of tugboats and ships in the harbor.

"The judgment of all observers here, whether pro-Japanese or pro-Russian, is that the victory is as astonishing a thing as ever was seen in diplomatic history," wrote *The New York Times.* "A nation hopelessly beaten in every battle of the war, one army captured and another overwhelmingly routed, with a navy swept from the seas, dictated her own terms to the victors."

Witte reached across the table and seized Komura by the hand. His fellow delegates followed their example and for a few seconds both sides clasped hands. Everyone then adjourned to toast the peace in the dining hall, where there was plenty of champagne, but no champagne glasses. Waiters hurried off by automobile to bring some from the Rockingham Hotel.

Witte became the conquering hero, showered with invitations and congratulations. At a dinner party given by *Harper's Magazine* at the Metropolitan Club in New York the ices were served in heart-shaped dishes on which the American and Russian flags were intertwined with the dove of peace. The Metropolitan orchestra played Russian airs between the speeches. The chairman who introduced Witte called him "the most prominent maker of peace and love and harmony in the civilized world." Diners gave Witte a standing ovation before and after his speech, which he delivered in French, waving their napkins and even their handkerchiefs to show the warmth of their appreciation.

While Witte was being fêted, Komura had fallen ill in the Waldorf-Astoria. The rest of the Japanese delegation sat around dismally, refusing invitations with growing concern and reading the news from Tokyo, where there were few toasts to peace.

All the national frustration that had been exhibited at the time of the peace treaty after the Sino-Japanese War reappeared. The Japanese public had expected an indemnity big enough to meet the entire cost of the war.

When they did not get a penny and, worse, acquired only half of Sakhalin, they felt that they had been cheated of the just spoils. Their fury was directed at Ito, Komura, the government generally, and the United States. The Anti-Russian League, which had played its part in whipping up popular support for the war, now went into action to create popular frenzy against the peace. Agitators spread leaflets throughout Tokyo denouncing the peace terms, which had not then been published, as humiliating. The only flags hung in the city streets were draped with crepe. Newspapers published caricatures of Katsura, Komura, Ito, and others surrounded by skulls and skeletons and what Baroness d'Anethan described as "other ghastly and obscene objects." Children showed their contempt when they swam and fished in the palace moat.

A mass meeting in Hibiya Park on September 5, timed to precede the signing of the Treaty of Portsmouth, led to mass demonstrations and repeated attacks on the official residence of the interior minister. One mob tore down the newly erected statue of Ito in Tokyo and dragged it through the streets. Others wrecked hundred of police boxes. Another mob headed for the American legation where 400 troops were needed to keep them off. Seventy percent of the police boxes, fifty-three residences, thirteen Christian churches, and fifteen streetcars were burnt. Killed and wounded numbered more than a thousand.

With one exception—the *Kokumin*—the metropolitan newspapers rallied to the side of the outraged populace. The *Nichi-Nichi* called the treaty "an insult to the nation." The *Nippon* said it was the "bitterest dose the nation has ever been compelled to take" and advised the people to "take a lesson from it, to gain wisdom and strength and to prepare against a similar contingency in future." The *Kokumin* suffered for its moderation: the mob burned it down. When streetcars were set ablaze, the government introduced martial law. This violent upsurge of national passion was crowned at 12:30 A.M. on September 11 with one of the worst disasters of the entire war: the sinking of the *Mikasa* in Sasebo harbor. An explosion ripped her apart, and she sank to the bottom, taking with her 251 members of the crew, 141 more men than had been lost by the entire fleet during the Battle of Tsushima. Had she committed *seppuku* to wipe out the stain of the dishonorable peace? There were many in Japan who believed that this samurai among ships had chosen a samurai's death.

The cause was more prosaic. Togo and his staff had left Sasebo that night for Tokyo to congratulate the Emperor. Sailors remaining in the *Mikasa* were drinking industrial alcohol in the powder room. To remove the smell they had set it on fire in a washbasin in a passage. The burning fluid spilt on the floor and the fire quickly spread.

E. H. Harriman, the American financier, accompanied by his sons Averell and Roland, arrived on the eve of the riots with plans to work with the Japanese government to take over and expand the railways of southern Manchuria. Harriman had close links with Jacob H. Schiff, who had helped so much to finance Japan's war effort. This did not prevent his party from coming in for some mob attention. Nevertheless, Harriman and his party went to Manchuria and reached agreement with the Japanese only to have it vetoed by Komura, who returned from the United States sick in health and heart, and in danger of assassination. His veto was hailed as a great victory, but from Japan's point of view it was a great blunder. The history of the Far East might have followed a very different course if the Americans and the Japanese had become partners in the Manchurian railway scheme and the commercial adventures that accompanied it.

Though the flame of ill-temper, xenophobia, and anti-Americanism, fed by the Black Dragon Society and others, flickered dangerously in the next few months, the British Far Eastern Fleet arrived in October to receive a tumultuous welcome. Geisha girls served free beer to the British sailors in Hibiya Park. "The consequences of the unwise proceeding being that the sights later in the day were hardly seemly," Baroness d'Anethan noted. The Emperor received Admiral G. H. Noel at luncheon and turned over the Shiba Palace to the Admiral and his staff as a guest house. Balls, dinner parties and garden parties for the officers followed in dazzling succession. The fleet was decorated by day and illuminated by night. Admiral Noel reported enthusiastically that the popularity of the alliance had been expressed by thousands of people and children from all the schools waving the Union Jack.

For Roosevelt and the United States, the Japanese had feeling of an entirely different order. If the Treaty of Portsmouth marked the real emergence of the United States as a great Pacific power, it also earned for it the bitter enmity of Japan. The Japanese people wanted a scapegoat for the loss of the Russian indemnity: the United States was the obvious choice. By December 16, 1907, when Roosevelt's Great White Fleet set sail from Hampton Roads, there were many in Europe, in America and elsewhere who thought that it was going to teach the Japanese a lesson. The Japanese, who issued a formal invitation to the fleet, were by no means intimidated, and laughed at America's "pretty battleships" and the "men of pleasure" who manned them. The visit began in an atmosphere of great tension but passed off without serious upset.

In contrast to Tokyo, St. Petersburg received the news of the Portsmouth treaty calmly. There was much more concern with the onrush of revolution than there was about the fate of the unpopular war far away in the east. "The hostilities were much too far removed from us," Count Kokovtsov wrote. "The war was too feebly reflected in everyday life." The threat of revolution was direct and immediate. "The Baltic region was in an uproar, and even at the threshold of St. Petersburg, so to speak, attacks upon the police and the army became increasingly common." Violence flared in Moscow. The Lithuanians in the Baltic declared their independence. Poland was in revolt. There were bloody incidents in Kiev, Odessa, and the Caucasus.

"All this is trifling compared with what is going to happen one of these days," said Witte, who had come home pessimistically and prophetically to be honored with the title of count and to nudge Nicholas into grudging constitutional reforms, which created an elected legislative Duma but failed to satisfy those who wanted revolutionary changes.

Colonel Akashi sailed for home on November 18, aware that he had not only helped to win the war but to create the Russian revolution. Uprisings along the Baltic coast had caused St. Petersburg to dispatch the Twentieth Army Group to the area. The Finns flew the Finnish flag at the gate of the governor-general's home, and a shipment of 8,500 rifles and 1,200,000 rounds of ammunition were on their way aboard the merchant ship *Sirius* to the Black Sea. More than 8,000 of the guns lost on the *John Grafton* had been bought back by the revolutionaries and distributed, and of Akashi's network of agents in Russia he had lost only three—a military officer who was arrested and committed suicide in prison, another who was exiled just before the peace treaty was signed at Portsmouth, and a third who was arrested and not heard of again.

"There is much hope for the future," one of Akashi's Russian revolutionary friends wrote to him after his return to Tokyo. "Though we could not overthrow the government all in one fell swoop, we are invading its fortifications step by step. The Tsarist government will fall soon."

V

THE
AFTERMATH

CHAPTER *33*

🐉🐉🐉🐉🐉

Unfinished Business

Asia CHEERED THE JAPANESE VICTORY. Artemio Ricarte, the Filipino nationalist leader—"the viper," as the *Manila American* used to call him —fled from the Americans in the Philippines to Japan, and there became a living shrine of Filipino revolt, holding court for students returning from America and preaching the doctrine of independence in close association with Toyama. Phan Boi Chau and Prince Cuong De of the Royal Family of Annam in Indochina made their way to Tokyo and called upon their countrymen to rise in revolt against the French. India's Pandit Nehru remembered the war as one of the most important events of his early life. "Japanese victories stirred up my enthusiasm. . . . Nationalistic ideas filled my mind. I mused of Indian freedom and Asiatic freedom from the thraldom of Europe."

"A stir of excitement passed over India," an English observer wrote. "Even the remote villagers talked over the victories of Japan as they sat in their circles and passed around the *huqqa* at night."

Kuroki's maneuvers on the Yalu and at Liaoyang and Nogi's at Mukden had no less of an impact on tactics. To turn the enemy's flank became a staff officer's obsession. When this tactic failed in Europe ten years later, the opposing armies fell back on the stalemate of trench warfare with all of its bloody consequences.*

---

*"An army forced to take the defensive must defend itself by incessant counterattacks," General de Negrier, former inspector-general of the French army and a member of the Supreme Council of War, solemnly concluded in his *Lessons of the Russo-Japanese War*. Acting on his advice, Allied and German commanders on the

[541]

To what extent Akashi's activities in Europe ultimately contributed to the Russian revolution in 1917 can be nothing more than conjecture, though twenty years after the war Marshal Pilsudski remembered the Japanese efforts with enough affection to decorate fifty-one of the top Japanese officers of the war with the highest Polish award, the *Virtuti Militari.*

In the case of the Chinese revolution it is easier to be more specific. Yuan Shih-k'ai identified himself with the Japanese war effort for the purpose of stimulating the reform movement in China. The Treaty of Portsmouth had not yet been signed when he presented a memorial to the Chinese Throne calling for the establishment of constitutional government within twelve years. In September, the Dowager Empress agreed to abolish the rigorous examination system, by which candidates were selected for government appointment, and three months later a high-ranking Chinese delegation left to study the art of constitution making in Europe. Chinese students had begun to flock to Japan during the war. There were no more than a hundred in Tokyo in 1900: in 1905 there were about 8,000 and the following year a peak of 15,000 or more, including Chiang Kai-shek. Many openly talked revolution and helped to provide an organized base for Sun Yat-sen when he arrived in July 1905 from Europe.

If Yuan Shih-k'ai expected that his wartime collaboration would be rewarded with the coming of peace, however, he was gravely mistaken. Warned by the bitterness of the reaction in Japan to the Treaty of Portsmouth, Komura, with British and American approval, now traveled to Peking to win Chinese concurrence for the new "rights" in Manchuria that Japan had acquired as a result of the war. Reluctantly, but with no real option, Yuan gave way, and the Chinese placed their stamp of approval on Japan's acquisition of the Liaotung Peninsula. They had no choice, but they expected that their services during the war might be better rewarded.

The Koreans were even easier to handle. Wartime exigencies had facilitated the extension of Japanese controls. Though Syngman Rhee, then twenty-nine years of age and already prominent in the Korean nationalist movement, had turned up in the United States on the eve of the peace conference to plead the cause of his country with President Roosevelt, the secret Taft-Katsura Agreement had already been signed and Japan had won American approval for its free hand in Korea. Messages expressing the Korean Emperor's concern about Japanese activities had been transmitted to Washington during the war by Dr. H. N. Allen, the American minister. But these and other efforts by the Emperor to invoke the initial Treaty of Amity in defense of Korean interests proved unavailing. Marquis Ito ar-

---

Western Front sent millions of men to death on futile, ill-conceived attacks.

rived in Seoul to persuade the Emperor, who had been forced to accept Japanese financial and diplomatic advisers, to sign an agreement giving control of Korean affairs to a Japanese resident general.

Since the Emperor was regarded as having been pro-Russian during the war, Japanese troops paraded through the streets of Seoul and surrounded the palace in the established manner. At gunpoint, the Emperor agreed that Korea should become, in effect, a Japanese protectorate. The Emperor's final *cri de coeur,* a cable smuggled out of the country and dispatched from Cheefoo to Homer B. Hulbert, who had been sent with a letter from the Emperor to Roosevelt, failed to win Washington's sympathy. "I declare that the so-called treaty of protectorate recently concluded between Korea and Japan was extorted at the point of a sword and is therefore null and void," the Emperor cabled. "I never consented to it and never will. Transmit to American Government." By this time Korea had, in the eyes of the American government, ceased to exist as a sovereign independent state. "We cannot possibly interfere for the Koreans against Japan," Roosevelt had written to secretary Hay in January 1905. "They could not strike one blow in their own defense." Plans were now made to withdraw the U.S. legation from Seoul to Tokyo. Britain also shrugged her shoulders at Korea's impending loss of independence.

Refused official American sympathy and support, the Emperor in July 1907 appealed to the government of the Netherlands and the Hague Permanent Court of Arbitration to examine the regime imposed on Korea by the treaty of November 17, 1905. When his appeal failed, he spurned further Japanese coercion and abdicated. The Japanese, pleased to see him go, found the Crown Prince much more pliable material.

Ito, who had taken the post of resident-general, was liberal and his rule was light—but not light enough to curb the sense of outrage among the Koreans who had lost their nationhood to the Japanese "dwarfs." When his old foe, Katsura, again became prime minister, Ito, now bearing the title of prince, resigned, planning to revisit St. Petersburg with the concept of close Russo–Japanese cooperation still uppermost in his mind. He was met at Harbin by a Russian guard of honor and had just finished reviewing it when he was confronted by a young Korean clutching a Browning pistol. Struck by three bullets in the chest and abdomen, he died half an hour later. With little further ado, Japan ceased to trifle and annexed Korea.

Witte, like Ito, also hoped that with the adventurers out of the way the Treaty of Portsmouth might facilitate a rapprochement, even an alliance, between Russia and Japan. In this he had the concurrence of Alexander Izvolski, who became foreign minister in 1906. The transfer of the southern branch of the Chinese Eastern Railway did not take place until August 1,

[543]

1906, but it provided an opportunity for negotiations that led, in 1907, to the amicable decision by the Russians and the Japanese to carve Manchuria into spheres of influence, the Russians taking the north and the Japanese the south.

Yuan Shih-k'ai's loyal friends, Major-General Senba and Colonel Aoki, the Japanese officers responsible for coordinating Chinese and Japanese intelligence activities in Manchuria, thought that "a new Japan" should be established in the three Manchurian provinces (and that this should eventually be extended to include all of China) and that Chinese forces there should be under Japanese supervision. General Senba wanted to use Yuan Shih-k'ai as the Japanese puppet, extending his authority for Chih-li under the supervision, or course, of Japanese "advisers." "If necessary," Colonel Aoki wrote, "the Japanese officers should wear disguises, or special uniforms." Major Idogawa recommended that police schools under Japanese instruction and supervision should be established in Manchuria, and that Japanese should hold supervisory positions in the building of roads, schools, and hospitals "because of the corruption and inefficiency of the Chinese."

In all solemnity, Togo, Oyama, Nozu, Kuroki, and the other Satsuma leaders went to Kagoshima at the end of the war to report their victories before Saigo's statue. Nogi, the Choshu, made obeisance in an entirely different, if similar, way. At the great victory parade in Tokyo, he took an obscure place mounted not on Stoessel's magnificent Arab but on a decrepit nag. When the triumphant admirals and generals arrived at the ceremonial reception given by the Emperor, Nogi appeared in the battle dress that he had worn every day and night at Port Arthur. Furtive chuckles greeted his appearance. As he read his report to the Emperor, tears streamed down his cheeks so that he could not continue for a time. When he had finished his report, he sat on the floor of the throne room and bowed his head, begging the Emperor to allow him to die. This was not the time, replied the Emperor. "If Your Excellency wishes to die, wait until I am gone."

For Nogi the task was not yet completed. He still wanted to serve—and to atone. Service was the message he instilled into his students at the exclusive Peers School in Tokyo where, as a reward for service, he had taken over as principal. Sometimes his material was unreceptive.

"What do you want to be when you grow up?" Nogi asked the infant Saito Tarao* when he was introduced to the school by his mother.

"I want to be a general," replied Saito.

---

*Better known to western friends as "Tiger" Saito, gifted editor of the now defunct annual, *This Is Japan*. He died in 1971.

"Like whom?" asked the flattered Nogi.

"Like General Booth" [of the Salvation Army], replied the ingenuous Saito.

When the Emperor died in 1912, Nogi ended his service and made full atonement. On September 12, the night before the Emperor's funeral, he took some sponge-cakes to his horses in their stables and wrote ten letters to relatives, friends, and government officials. One began: "I am now going to kill myself and follow my Emperor. Pardon me, please. Ever since losing my regimental flag in the civil war I have always intended to sacrifice myself."

Just after the gun sounded to announce the departure of the Emperor's hearse from the palace gates on September 13, Nogi, in full-dress Japanese military uniform, disemboweled himself. A moment before, his wife pierced her throat with a short sword, the traditional method of suicide for a high-born woman.

The concept of following one's lord to the grave had been regarded as an inestimable virtue among the samurai class. For centuries, however, it had been forbidden by law. Symbolic clay dolls were a sufficient token of a retainer's loyalty. That Nogi should have taken his own life, therefore, and assisted in killing his wife excited a storm of comment in Japan. There were critics, but eventually Nogi was not merely admired but deified. He became a divine warrior, a "war god." His errors at Port Arthur were not merely forgiven but, for many years, not even admitted. Nogi was a feudal anachronism: but he also became the symbol not only of the Japan that died with Meiji but of the new, ever more ambitious Japan that emerged after the Russo-Japanese War.

"Japan is the pioneer of the new age: she is the hope of a new Asia," wrote Kawai Tatsuo, author of *The Goal of Japanese Expansion*. Toyama, patron of the Black Dragon Society, concurred. His list of sedulously cultivated Asian friends included Sun Yat-sen; Chiang Kai-shek; Wang Ching-wei, later head of a Japanese puppet government at Nanking; Ras Bihari Bose and Subhas Chandra Bose, Indian nationalists who worked with the Japanese during the Second World War; and many others. Just as the Sino-Japanese War caused an industrial revolution in Japan and prepared the way for fresh conquests, the Russo-Japanese War generated dramatic economic, industrial, and military growth. As early as the mid-twenties the invasion of the Philippines was discussed at the war college.

For Russia, the situation was radically different. The search began for scapegoats. Kuropatkin continued to hold high office under the Tsar. (He fought in World War I and died in 1923 after working as a village clerk and schoolteacher under the Bolsheviks.) The unfortunate Rozhdestvenski,

Clapier de Colongue, Nebogatov, Stoessel,* Fock and Smirnov were all tried by court-martial in St. Petersburg during the winter of 1906. Though exonerated on the grounds that he had been unconscious when the *Bedovi* surrendered, Rozhdestvenski insisted on being tried with his fellow officers. Rozhdestvenski was acquitted. Nebogatov tried to take all the blame for surrender on his own shoulders, and both he and Clapier de Colongue were sentenced to death. The sentences were never carried out but they spent long years in prison. Though privately Nicholas defended him—*"il reste et il restera toujours héros"*—Stoessel was found guilty of surrendering Port Arthur without assembling the council of war and knowing that the previous council of war was against it. He was also charged with having knowingly permitted Fock to circulate subversive notes. He was found guilty and sentenced to be shot. Fock was found guilty of distributing the subversive notes but was released without punishment. Smirnov was acquitted on all charges. Like Clapier de Colongue and Nebogatov, Stoessel escaped the firing squad but was imprisoned for many years.

To Nicholas and his ministers, encouraged by Witte, postwar cooperation with Japan suggested itself as the best way of preserving Russia's Far Eastern interests. The agreement of 1907, with its secret clauses on the allocation of spheres of influence in Manchuria, was followed by secret conventions in 1910 and again in 1912, which extended the line of demarcation to Mongolia, where the Russians, taking advantage of the Chinese revolution, managed to convert what had been a de facto Chinese colony into one of their own. As for the United States, they were shut out of Manchuria in both trade and investment, a major factor in the now rapidly deteriorating U.S.–Japanese relations.

Kuropatkin, who had become Russian administrator of Central Asia after the Russo-Japanese War, continued to warn St. Petersburg of the need for expansion at China's expense. "As for China, the danger menacing Russia in the future from that empire of 400,000,000 people is not to be doubted," he advised Nicholas in 1916. "The alteration of our frontier is absolutely imperative. By drawing the border line from the Khan Tengri range [27,000 feet high and the highest in the Tian Shan mountain range] in a direct line to Vladivostok, our frontier will be shortened by 4,000 versts [2,640 miles] and Julja, northern Mongolia and northern Manchuria will be included in the Russian empire."

By 1918, however, as the flames of revolution licked across all Russia,

---

*Nogi did his best to save Stoessel from death and was the inspiration for articles that appeared in Berlin, London, and Paris, justifying the surrender of Port Arthur as inevitable. When Nogi committed suicide, "a priest in Moscow" sent the family incense.

even Siberia was in danger, and not merely from internal threat. Britain and France, fearful of the effects of the Bolshevik revolution, sought U.S. approval of the Japanese occupation of Siberia along the Trans-Siberian Railway as far as the Urals. British officers in the field strongly encouraged the scheme. Brevet-Major R. B. Denny, assistant British military attaché in Peking, in a long report on March 13, 1918, on the situation in northern Manchuria, wrote: "If Japan is not given a free hand in some part of the Far East, there is a danger that she might actually go over to the enemy. With Russia a prostrate neutral between them, Japan and Germany would form an extremely strong combination, which would threaten the whole of the allies' possessions in Asia and even in Australasia."

The United States had no wish to see Japanese expansion in any direction. As soon as world war had broken out, Japanese troops invaded Shantung Province and, ignoring Chinese neutrality, seized Tsingtao from the Germans. Their next step was to inform the Chinese that they were taking over German possessions in China, including the Tsingtao–Tsinan railway and a strip of territory protecting the track, which, they said, needed to be defended by Japanese troops. These preliminaries were followed by the notorious Twenty-one Demands, which extended to all of China the blueprint for annexation that General Senba had once proposed, thus rewarding Yuan Shih-k'ai with final betrayal.

The United States had protested vigorously and successfully against the Twenty-one Demands, and it now denied Japanese claims to have "special interests" in China and Siberia. To forestall an exclusively Japanese occupation of Eastern Siberia, the United States proposed a joint Japanese–American occupation of Vladivostok. In the end, Japan contributed 72,000 troops of the allied force of less than 100,000 designed to rescue a force of former Czech prisoners of war who were trying to make their way east along the railway. The Japanese earned for themselves a reputation for excessive brutality and remained long after their allies had gone home. Not until 1922 did they take their leave of Siberia, and they stayed in northern Sakhalin until 1925. So long as they saw any hope of a Bolshevik defeat, they intrigued with White Russian bands for concessions. Major Denny reported that the leader of a White Russian Cossack force had told him that the Japanese were trying to obtain rights in the region of Lake Baikal in exchange for money and guns. Toyama's Black Dragon Society agents turned up to offer their encouragement and their money.

Japan's military and imperialist ambitions led to hardening American attitudes. The basic cause of American concern was Japan's territorial expansion of which the Twenty-one Demands, which would have turned China into a Japanese "protectorate," were a classic example. Japan, in turn, was outraged by legislation in the United States restricting Oriental immigration and by the treatment of Japanese living in the United States. As early as October 1906, the San Francisco school board ordered the segregation of Japanese schoolchildren. The storm at this time was resolved by a gentleman's agreement under which Japan cut down on the numbers of Japanese migrating to the United States in exchange for the U.S. decision not to exclude Japanese immigrants. It was soon to be raised again by U.S. laws relating to citizenship and state land-ownership and by Japan's demonstrable and increasing power. American apprehensions were also shared by Britain, and both had refused to recognize Japan's demand for recognition in the League of Nations of the principle of racial equality.

To check Japan's military expansion the United States called the Washington conference in 1921. It resulted in a naval treaty that fixed the capital ship tonnage between Britain, the United States and Japan on a 5 : 5 : 3 ratio. This marked the end of the Anglo–Japanese Alliance. When Britain started to build the Singapore naval base there was an uproar in Japan, which saw it as an Anglo-American threat to Japanese interests in the Pacific.

For Japan, however, the diplomatic climate had changed very much for the worse. Supported by the British and the Americans, and with the friendly assistance of Yuan Shih-k'ai, it had had to worry only about Russia in 1904–1905. Now it had enemies everywhere. Attempts to find a *modus vivendi* with the Soviet Union in 1925 failed to produce results. Whether Japan was drawn into Manchuria and China by the new threat of Communism or by economic imperialism or by military conspiracy is now irrelevant. It was very relevant, however, that Japan, without the protection of the British alliance, found herself in a position in which her military power had to be directed against China, with which she was at war; against the United States, whose people and government were becoming extremely antagonistic; and increasingly against the Soviet Union, which had challenged the Japanese army's plans for all of Mongolia by signing a mutual assistance pact with the Mongolian People's Republic. Despite its meager natural resources, Japan had to scatter its military potential against these numerous real and hypothetical enemies. Eventually, the alliance with Nazi Germany seemed the only way out.

Japan's defeat in World War II saw the eclipse of Britain as a significant Pacific power and the emergence now of the United States as the dominant power. It also provided the Soviet Union with the opportunity to recover much that it had coveted and lost in the Russo-Japanese War. No Plehve, no Bezobrazov, no Abaza, no Tsar could have been more imperialistic in his demands than Stalin when he stated his terms for entering the war against Japan. Unlike Lenin, who had accepted Akashi's money and help,

Stalin believed that the Russian defeat in 1905 "had left grave memories in the minds of our peoples. It was a dark stain on our country. Our people trusted and awaited the day when Japan would be routed and the stain wiped out." Averell Harriman, saw him on the night of December 14, 1944, and on the following day described the meeting in a top secret dispatch to President Franklin D. Roosevelt.

> He [Stalin] went into the next room and brought out a map. He said that the Kurile Islands and lower Sakhalin controlled the approaches to Vladivostok, that we considered that the Russians were entitled to protection for their communications to this important port and that "all outlets to the Pacific were now blocked by the enemy." He drew a line around the southern part of the Liaotung Peninsula, including Port Arthur and Dairen [Dalny], saying that the Russians again wished to lease these ports and the surrounding area. Stalin said further that he wished to lease the Chinese Eastern Railway.

In exchange for entering the war, the allies gave Stalin what he wanted: the preservation of the *status quo* in Outer Mongolia; the restoration of former rights "violated by the treacherous attack of Japan," including the southern part of Sakhalin and the islands adjacent; the internationalization of Dalny together with safeguards for the "preeminent interests of the Soviet Union"; the lease of Port Arthur as a naval base; the joint operation of the Chinese Eastern Railway by a Soviet–Chinese company on the understanding that the "preeminent interests of the Soviet Union should be safeguarded"; and the Kurile islands.

Vast changes have occurred since. Having defeated and occupied Japan, the United States found itself obliged, as the Cold War developed, to assume the role of protector of Japanese interests. After August 1945, and in conformity with the agreement reached at Potsdam, the Russians began to take the surrender of the Japanese troops north of the 38th parallel in Korea, while the Americans took the surrender in the south. The line of demarcation followed no social, economic, or geographical perimeter. It cut through farms and villages and was not intended to be permanent, though it quickly became so.

Instead of getting the independence they had been promised at the Cairo Conference of 1943, the Koreans found their land divided into two ideologically opposed camps. All heavy industry was in the north. The south had most of the food. No trains ran on the tracks across the frontier. No message passed along the telephone lines, and no one traveled across the border. Until the Americans brought in LSTs in 1946 and stationed them in the ports where their generators supplied light and power, South Korea depended on the North for its supply of electricity. The Northerners frequently threw the switches, plunging the South into darkness, discomfort, and economic disadvantage.

On December 30, 1948, after an occupation lasting for nearly three-and-a-half years, the Soviet Union announced the withdrawal of all its forces from Korea. Six months later the United States, its hand forced by the Soviet move, withdrew from the South, leaving only a military advisory group of 500 men. On June 25, 1950, the Northern army, with a spearhead of Russian tanks, invaded the South. The United States, acting as a proxy for Japan—which had no armed forces to resist what it clearly regarded as much as a threat to its own interests as it regarded China and Russian activities there in the latter part of the nineteenth and the beginning of the twentieth century—came to the rescue, along with supplementary forces from the United Nations.

What began as an extension of the Russo-Japanese War quickly developed overtones of the Sino-Japanese War as China, seeing itself threatened again from Korea, moved its troops across the Yalu. If the war was initiated or encouraged by the Soviet Union in the expectation that advantages would follow, Moscow must have been bitterly disappointed with the results, though this was far from obvious at the time.

For the next decade it seemed that ideology might take precedence over national interests and that the Soviet Union and China, united by the common bonds of Communism, would forget past differences, ambitions, and betrayals and form an alliance so powerful that the whole world might tremble. Mao Tse-tung visited Moscow in December 1949. Out of his nine weeks' stay in the Soviet Union came the Sino-Soviet Treaty of Friendship, Alliance and Mutual Assistance, an agreement on the joint use of the Chinese Eastern Railway and of Port Arthur, either until the end of 1952 or the signing of a peace treaty with Japan, whichever came first. Along with these agreements went a Russian loan of $300 million at an interest rate of one per cent a year.

So had the stage been set for the Korean War. A quick breakthrough to Pusan by the North Korean forces in the summer of 1950 would have presented the United States, which earlier had seemed ready to wash its hands of South Korea, with a *fait accompli* and would have notably complemented Russia's arrangements with China. Instead, Kim Il-sung failed to break the Naktong Riverline, Mao Tse-tung's forces stole the glory, and the United States, more conscious than ever before of Japan's strategic importance as a counterbalance to the Soviet Union and China, concluded, despite strong Russian objections, a peace treaty with Japan and the U.S.–Japan Mutual Security Treaty.

With its full sovereign status now restored and its defense assured by the

United States, Japan used American offshore procurement as a lever to start off a new industrial and technological revolution that has now carried her to third place behind the United States and the Soviet Union among the world's industrial powers.

In 1954, Russian Premier Nikita S. Khrushchev visited Peking for the October 1 celebrations and agreed to the final abandonment of Port Arthur, Dalny, and the Chinese Eastern Railway. Although relations between Russia and China appeared to be friendly, the great schism soon appeared. Signs were discernible early in 1958. By 1960, despite continuing protestations of friendship, the break was in the open. Chinese and Russian spokesmen clashed in various organizations around the globe, and both sides began actively to recruit supporters against the other in the world Communist movement. Ideological differences soon led to much deeper troubles and, in March 1969, to bloodshed on Chenpao Island in the Ussuri River, a hundred miles south of Khabarovsk. Chinese troops invaded the island and Russian rockets burned them and all their equipment. In June, July, and August there were further clashes, some of them on the Ussuri, others in Central Asia.

The Communist party of the Soviet Union addressed a letter to friendly parties around the globe, setting out the details of the Soviet charges against the Chinese. The letter accused China of making "practical preparations for war" and warned that the "Soviet Union cannot permit events to develop in such a way as to bring about protracted frontier war, and will undertake additional measures to safeguard the interests of the Soviet Union and the frontiers of our country."*

On August 28, 1969, in response to this letter, the Central Committee of the Chinese Communist party issued a directive exhorting the population to prepare for war. On the same day, a *Pravda* editorial warned China of the danger of a nuclear war. A surprise visit by Premier Alexei Kosygin to Peking after he had attended the funeral of Ho Chi Minh in Hanoi in 1971 led to the resumption of talks in Peking between China and the Soviet Union. These proved fruitless, though they served to reduce some of the tensions that the incidents earlier in the year had created. They did not deter the Soviet Union from continuing its military buildup along the China border. "It is more than ten years since the leaders of the People's Republic of China have taken the line of fighting the U.S.S.R. and, in effect, the entire socialist community, which they continue to regard as the main obstacle to their great-power designs," said Leonid I. Brezhnev, general secretary of the central committee of the Communist party of the Soviet Union on Decem-

---

*From a copy of the letter in the possession of the authors.

ber 21, 1972, in a major review of Soviet policies. He listed the Russian complaints against China and insisted that the Soviet Union had neither territorial nor economic claims to Chinese territory, but added: "Nothing will make us depart from our principled Marxist–Leninist line, from our firm defense of the state interests of the Soviet people and the inviolability of Soviet territory, from our determined struggle against the divisive activities of the leadership of the People's Republic of China in the socialist world and the liberation movement."

When the row first flared up on the Ussuri, the Chinese appeared to want nothing more than the settlement of relatively minor border disputes, including navigational rights on the rivers and the admission that large tracts of Soviet territory had been acquired from China as a result of the unequal treaties. As late as October 1969, the Chinese government stated unequivocally that it "never has demanded the return of territories which the Soviet government occupies as a result of the treaties." Yet, on May 13, 1970, Dmitri Petrov, a leading Russian expert on Japan, speaking to the Asia Research Association in Tokyo, also stated unequivocally that "an especially strange demand is its [China's] territorial demand for an area exceeding one million square kilometers." Petrov's speech, which was mostly concerned with the need for increased Soviet and Japanese cooperation, led to angry criticism by Peking on all points except the charge that China was actually demanding the return of territory.

How serious China is on this point is unclear. After more than a century of Russian control of the "lost" territories, it is unrealistic to expect that they will be returned. China is, however, no less concerned than she was in 1898 with the preservation of the territorial integrity of Manchuria. Manchuria developed rapidly under Japanese control and the cities of Shenyang and Anshan are important industrially. Taching, China's biggest oil field, discovered by the Russians in 1959, is immediately south of the Amur River.

In real military terms, China is not a threat to Russia. Although all military advantages, manpower alone excepted, favor the Soviet Union, the Russians can scarcely have failed to note, however, from the American experience in Vietnam the difficulty in fighting a limited war against a dedicated and determined people in their own country. The Russians, moreover, are extremely sensitive south and east of Lake Baikal, where the Trans-Siberian Railway, now laid on double tracks, runs through a long, narrow, and highly vulnerable defile. To defend it, Russia might be forced back on nuclear weapons, with grave consequences to its standing in the Communist and nonaligned worlds. Yet what China demands, by implication if not directly, is all the territory east of the Ussuri River and running through Vladivostok to the Korean border, so skillfully filched from the

Manchus by Count Ignatiev when he persuaded them to sign the Treaty of Peking in 1860. Without this territory Russia would find itself confined to Sakhalin and the lands north of the Amur and would, in effect, cease to be a Far Eastern power.

It is against this background that the Soviet Union's decision to become a leading world naval power must be viewed. Russia has neither the global trade nor the global territories traditionally associated with the development of great naval power. The Cuban missile crisis forced upon her an awareness of her maritime weaknesses, but it was the desire to contain the spread of Chinese influence and the fear for her land communications with the East that took her back through the Indian Ocean and into the Pacific.

Long before it reached its present proportions, the crisis between the two great Communist states had already had worldwide consequences. While the Vietnam war and the need to supply Haiphong brought a rapid expansion in Russia's merchant navy, the need to open quicker communications with the Far East also spurred it to take the initiative in the Middle East. The Suez Canal used to be the lifeline of the British empire: it may become the lifeline of the Soviet empire.

Concern with China also led Russia to help India on a generous scale with military equipment and economic aid. Southeast Asia threatened to become a Russo–Chinese ideological battleground, with Russia urging on the free nations of the region a collective security system obviously directed against China.

Prince Norodom Sihanouk established himself in Peking after his ouster in Cambodia; the Russians continued to recognize the Lon Nol government. The Vietnam war, some Western observers thought, would help to bring China and the Soviet Union together in common purpose; instead, it drove them farther apart. Russian propagandists sound almost like the late John Foster Dulles when they discuss China's ambitions in Southeast Asia, and Moscow has become the latest proponent of the domino theory. "Peking's desire to lay hands on the countries of Southeast Asia and South Asia is so obvious that it is worrying even those who sincerely want to cooperate with the Chinese People's Republic and receive assistance from it in their revolutionary struggle," said an article in the Moscow magazine *New Times* on June 9, 1970. "Their apprehension is all the more justified, since the evidence is that China is being turned into an armed camp, that a war psychosis is being whipped up there, that China's youth is being injected with the poison of great-power chauvinism and the cult of brute force, and is being prepared for war." Mao, we were told, was more treacherous than Hitler.

By the end of 1970, it was apparent, however, that Russia had abandoned or shelved any plans that it might have had for a preemptive war with

China. Superficially, it appears to have embarked on a long-term policy of containment. Move is matched by countermove from Korea through South and Southeast Asia. Whether Russia will be able to persist indefinitely with such a policy is open to question. After the easing of the Cold War, the Soviet leaders succeeded in ameliorating the Russian way of life. A protracted policy of containment, though accompanied by a major effort to increase its share of world trade, would probably mean new austerities and put added strains on the still far from rugged Russian economy. Each successive Chinese nuclear development, even though China is pledged not to use nuclear weapons first, each new indication that China is gaining in strength and in confidence, must lead to a reexamination of plans and policies in Moscow. It is also axiomatic that if Russia is confronted by the possibility of war in the East, she must be secure in the West. The détente with West Germany in August 1970 that preceded a series of agreements with the United States can be seen, therefore, as a sign of preparation, not of relaxation.

China has not been idle. Prince Norodom Sihanouk's fortuitous arrival in Peking in March 1970 led to swift new initiatives, which reestablished Chinese leadership in the Asian revolutionary and Communist family. Sino–North Korean relations, which had deteriorated to the point where shots were fired across the border, began to pick up after Ho Chi Minh's funeral and a visit to Pyongyang by Prime Minister Chou En-lai in April 1970. He proposed that the two states "unite closely and enhance preparedness against war in our common fight against the enemies." This marked the foundation of a united front of the Indochinese, Chinese, and North Koreans, which Sihanouk helped to cement on his visit to Pyongyang in July 1970.

Far more important is the increasing cordiality between the United States and China and the additional room for maneuver that China now enjoys because of it. The United States might not intervene on China's side if Peking and Moscow become involved in war, but the possibility that it might is in itself a deterrent.

Logically, both the Russians and the Chinese should appreciate the unique and exploitable opportunities that would be theirs if the two great Communist powers were to resolve their differences and agree to act in tandem. The reasons at this time for continued hostility between the two countries, however, are many and valid. When the Chinese call the Russian leaders the "new Tsars," they are not without evidence to support their claim. The Russians show no fraternal interest in divesting themselves of the spoils of the unequal treaties of the past. The Chinese were shocked by the implications of Russian ruthlessness in Czechoslovakia and alarmed by the ominous and constantly increasing Russian military buildup along their common frontier.

As for the Russians, they see the Chinese as a threat to the Russian Far Eastern empire. They also have had the temerity to challenge the Russian leadership of the world Communist movement. Leadership cannot be divided or shared. One side must concede supremacy, and neither is willing. After all these years the people of both countries have become involved. From the embers of the first Cold War, this second Cold War emerged.

Only relatively less important for the security of northeast Asia are the divisions that still exist between North and South Korea, the future role of Japan, its relations vis-à-vis the two Koreas, China and the Soviet Union.

Of all the countries in the region, including the Soviet Union, Japan reacted with undisguised shock to the visit of Dr. Henry Kissinger to Peking in July 1971, and the invitation to President Nixon that arose from it. That the United States should not have bothered to forewarn its major Asian ally of such a dramatic, and dramatically mounted, shift in policy caused deep unease in Japan. "I doubt that the Japanese will ever completely trust the United States again," said Prime Minister Lee Kuan Yew of Singapore. With this judgment it is difficult to disagree.

In its own efforts to establish meaningful relations with China, Japan was inhibited by Peking's deep distrust of its economic motives in Asia, and by its own diplomatic and commercial entanglement with Taiwan. Sentiment and commercial prospects, whether real or imaginary, demanded a move toward Peking, but the realities of conflicting national interest dictated caution. When President Nixon visited Peking, however, Japan was left with no alternative but to move rapidly toward the establishment of relations with China. This eased the tensions between China and Japan and apparently resulted in greater understanding in Peking of Japan's incipient military revival, which is, in large part, stimulated from outside by events over which it has no control. It was not entirely Japan's wish, but at least in part that of the United States that caused Japan to accept renewed responsibility for its conventional defense.

It remains to be seen how quickly, or how far, the United States will withdraw from Asia or, as some Japanese fear, be drawn into closer association with China at Japan's expense. The likelihood is that Watergate and the withdrawal from Vietnam will generate further pressures at home for wider and faster disengagement. Even such traditional friends as Australia and New Zealand were content to support the American effort in Vietnam only with tokens and, when a change of government took place in both countries late in 1972, quickly denounced the United States for its conduct of the war.

Just as the psychological shock of the 1968 Tet offensive in Vietnam helped to father the Nixon Doctrine of helping only those who help themselves, so the doctrine led Nixon to Peking. That this will result in improved relations between China and the United States is patent. But it will also erode American influence in other parts of Asia and both American will and capacity to shape the course of events.

The Chinese and the Russians may exaggerate their mutual suspicions and fears. The North and South Koreans may continue to live indefinitely in a state of neither war nor peace while they spar over reunification. The Taiwan problem may be resolved without recourse to arms. And Japan's bid to become the world's preeminent industrial power may suffer no more than a temporary setback because of trade and fiscal difficulties with the United States. Nevertheless, there are obvious dangers in the unfinished business that began when Perry and Putiatin pushed their way into Japan and Ignatiev sped homeward from Peking on his palanquin bearing the Maritime Province of Siberia as a new jewel in the crown of Tsar Nicholas II. Russia's ambitions are still unsatisfied. Japan, described as long ago as the early thirties as "a high-powered steam engine with a particularly stout gang of stokers shoveling fuel into the boilers," has developed an even more remarkable head of industrial steam; and China, unified by the discipline of Maoist Communism, has ceased to be the "sick man" of Asia. There is an old Chinese saying that it is wise to take advantage of an enemy to ward off another enemy. For most of the past century this view has prevailed in China. From 1860 until the Boxer revolt China turned in desperation to the Russians to protect it from the predatory European powers. Betrayed in Manchuria by Russia, it helped Japan in the Russo-Japanese War, and, betrayed again, sought the friendship of Britain and America. With the defeat of Japan in 1945 and the rise of Mao, China leaned again to the Russians, only to find that the new tsars were all too like the old. Now China leans, however imperceptibly, toward the United States and, even more cautiously, Japan.

The difference today is that China is no longer a minus factor, but a significant force in determining the equilibrium in what is now the center of the world power balance. But whether it will find firm support in the United States, no longer motivated by the spirit that sent the adventurous Commodore Perry and his "black ships" to Tokyo Bay, or in a Japan unsure of its own role, only the future will determine. As Ruth Benedict once wrote, Japan "will seek her place with a world at peace if circumstances permit—if not, within a world organized as an armed camp." The energy crisis late in 1973 hastened its hour of decision.

As for Russia, the most perceptive comment was made nearly a century and a half ago by Lord Palmerston, perhaps Britain's greatest foreign secretary. "The policy and practise of the Russian government have always been to push forward its encroachments as fast and as far as the apathy or want of firmness of other governments would allow it to go," he said, "but always to stop and retire when it met with decided resistance and then to wait for the most favorable opportunity to make another spring on its intended victim." The Russo-Japanese War changed much in the world, but it did not eliminate the chauvinism that brought it about.

Acknowledgments

We would like to emphasize the debt we owe to the late Lieutenant-General Tani Toshio, whose secret lectures at the Japanese War College in the 1920s have thrown much new light on the war. Tani was cultured, intellectual, and brilliant. After studying in Britain and serving as military attaché in India, he devoted himself to a study of the Russo-Japanese War. Twenty years after the war, his lectures, based on interviews with participants and the documents, were considered too sensational for all but the most exclusive audience. His course was restricted each year to ten specially selected officers at the lieutenant-colonel level. The only others with access to Tani's material were a small group of the highest ranking staff officers and top officials in the War Ministry. After he left the War College, Tani resumed his active military career and later became commander of the Sixth Division. He was tried as a war criminal by the Chinese at the end of World War II and executed on charges arising from the Rape of Nanking. His lectures were preserved for his bereaved family and have now been published in Japanese by the Hara Bookstore in Tokyo for the use of historians. We have found his material invaluable.

Many people have helped us with source material, and in other ways. We cannot name them all, but, in particular, we would like to thank Esther Parrott, who was responsible for much of the long, tedious, and difficult work of research in London, and those in the Public Record Office and the Admiralty Library who helped her; James Oki spent many months translating our Japanese source material, checked, and rechecked the manuscript for errors, and, in the process, directed us to many sources that would otherwise have escaped us; M. Iwata, Japanese librarian, the Far Eastern

Collection of the Baillieu Library of the University of Melbourne; Professor Kimura Ki, who helped to guide our initial research in Tokyo; Dr. Oyama Azusa (grandson of Field Marshal Oyama) of the Historical Section of the Ministry of Foreign Affairs; Hata Ikuhito of the Defense Bureau of the Japanese Defense Agency; Nishimura Susumu, head of the War History Office of the same agency; the late Admiral Hasegawa Kiyoshi, who was on the bridge of the *Mikasa* during the battle of Tsushima and whose vivid recollections of this battle, and of the Yellow Sea battle, were of great value; Vice-Admiral Fukuchi Nobuo, commandant of the memorial battleship *Mikasa;* the late Saito Torao, and Takeda Shin-ichi; Chihaya Masataka, a former Japanese naval officer, who was helpful with technical details; Serge Nabokoff, for permission to quote from Constantine Nabokoff's unpublished diary of the Portsmouth peace conference; Max Bell, for details of the victualing of the Russian Baltic Fleet at Camranh Bay; Ted Weatherstone, for assistance with source material in Tokyo; Mark Garner of the Russian Department, University of Melbourne; Mrs. Peter Taylor, for permission to quote from the diary and papers of her father, Brevet-Major R. B. Denny, written when he was assistant British military attaché in Peking; and Mrs. M. Ashburner for letters from Japanese naval officers.

Phil Garrett and the research staff of the State Library of Victoria provided us with assistance far beyond the call of duty. Mrs. H. J. Kovalevsky produced vital biographical material when all others had failed. Kuwabara Makato of the National Diet Library, the *Toyo Bunko,* the Reading Room of the British Museum, the National Library in Manila, the library of the Siam Society in Bangkok and the *Straits Times* in Singapore also gave us their time, patience, and source material. In London, *The Times* gave access to their archives for material relating to the exploits of Lionel James and the *Haimun.* David Sissons guided us in the right direction in Japan. Don Coutts drew the maps. Major-General Charles Long, Professor Norman Harper, Professor Harry Simon, Dr. T. B. Millar, Geoffrey Fairbairn, Cedric Bright, Joseph Sherman and the late Dyce Murphy lent us rare reference works. Stephanie Warner worked long hours transcribing tape recordings of material gathered around the globe, and Sally Daly and Joan Morris typed and retyped the manuscript. Finally, we owe a special debt to our editor, Richard Kluger, who conceived the book, commissioned it not once but twice, and helped in a thousand ways to sharpen our account of the war, its causes, and its consequences.

We encountered unusual difficulties in the spelling of Chinese, Korean, Japanese, and Russian names. According to modern practices of transliterating Japanese, we should have written Tōgō or Toogoo and ōyama or Ooyama, but we finally elected for simplicity and used the more familiar spellings, Togo and Oyama. To our more specialized readers, we apologize, but the general reader may find the system we have adopted an easier way of coping with difficult names. In dealing with Russian names, we hoped to be no more than consistent, but even this proved impossible. Having decided to use *v* instead of *ff* at the end of proper names, for instance, we were asked by one of our sources to write "Nabokoff" and not "Nabokov." We call the former Russian finance minister and peace negotiator Serge Witte, but others have referred to him as Sergei or Sergius, and when we have borrowed quotations we have also adopted the spelling adopted by previous writers. If we may seem to be consistently inconsistent, therefore, it is deliberate.

Readers will find important source material listed in the notes for each chapter. We have usually given detailed page references only in cases where the material seems unusually important, controversial, or new to history. When referring to the detailed sources, readers are asked to consult the bibliography. Where possible, books are identified by the names of the authors listed in the bibliography.

Bibliography

Academy of Sciences of the U.S.S.R., Institute of History, *A Short History of the U.S.S.R.*, 2 vols., Moscow, 1965.

Ackroyd, Joyce, *Women in Feudal Japan*, The Transactions of the Asiatic Society of Japan, November 1959.

Adachi Kinnosuke, *Probable Japanese Terms of Peace*, North American Review, May 1905.

Adler, Cyrus, *Jacob H. Schiff: His Life and Letters*, vol. 1, New York, 1928.

Admiralty Reports: Reports from British naval observers with the Japanese forces in the archives of the Public Record Office, London.

Admiralty War Staff (I.D.), translators, *Japanese Official Naval History of the Russo-Japanese War*, 2 vols., London, 1913–1914.

Akashi Motojiro, *Rakka Ryusui* ("Fallen Blossoms—Flowing Water"), memoirs of Colonel Akashi on his espionage work before and during the Russo-Japanese war. Comments by Inaba Masao and Kuroba Shigeru, *Gaiko-Jiho*, (Current News of Diplomacy), Japan, Tokyo, 1966.

Alcock, Sir Rutherford, *The Capital of the Tycoon*, 2 vols., London, 1863.

Allan, C. W., *Makers of Cathay*, Shanghai, 1936.

Allen, H. N., *Korea: Fact and Fancy*, Seoul, 1904.

Almedingen, E. M., *The Empress Alexandra, 1872–1918, A Study*, London, 1961.

Andrews, C. F., *The Renaissance of India*, London, 1912.

Anon., *Before Port Arthur in a Destroyer*, translated from Spanish, London, 1907 (purporting to be the diary of "Hesibo Tikouvara").

———, *Life of Gordon*, London, undated.

———, *The Russo-Japanese War*, Tokyo, 1904.

Arahata Kanson, *Hitosujino Michi* ("A Straight Road"), Tokyo, 1954.

Arima Yoriyasu, *Shichijunen-no Kaiso* ("Recollections of Seventy Years"), Tokyo, 1936.

Asahi Shimbun, *Nichiro Taisen Hishi* ("Secret History of Japan-Russian War"), 2 vols., Tokyo, 1938.

Asakawa, K., *The Russo-Japanese Conflict: Its Causes and Issues,* London, 1904.

Ashmead-Bartlett, E., *Port Arthur, The Siege and Capitulation,* London, 1906.

Asiatic Society of Japan, *The Transactions of . . .,* Tokyo, November 1959.

Australian Army Public Relations, *A Brief History of the Australian Army,* Melbourne, 1973.

Avrich, Paul, *The Russian Anarchists,* New Jersey, 1967.

Ballard, Admiral G. A., *The Influence of the Sea on the Political History of Japan,* London, 1921.

———, *Rulers of the Indian Ocean,* London, 1927.

Banno Masataka, *China and the West,* Cambridge, Mass., 1964.

Barr, Pat, *Foreign Devils: Westerners in the Far East,* London, 1970.

Barry, Richard, *A Monster Heroism,* New York, 1905.

———, "How Port Arthur Fell," *Fortnightly Review,* March 1905.

———, "Port Arthur, Its Siege and Fall," *Cornhill Magazine,* May 1905.

———, "The New Siege Warfare at Port Arthur," *The Century Magazine,* March 1905.

Bausman, F., *Let France Explain,* London, 1922.

Bemis, S. F., *A Diplomatic History of the United States,* New York, 1964.

Benedict, Ruth, *The Chrysanthemum and the Sword,* Boston, 1946.

Bérard, Victor, *The Russian Empire and Czarism,* London, 1905.

Bing, E. J., ed., *The Letters of Tsar Nicholas and Empress Marie, Being the Confidential Correspondence Between Nicholas II and His Mother, Dowager Empress Maria Feodorovna,* London, 1937.

Bird, W. D., "An Account of the Battle of Liaoyang," *The Army Review,* July 1912.

———, *Strategy of the Russo-Japanese War,* London, 1911.

Bishop, I. B., *Korea and Her Neighbors,* 2 vols., London, 1898.

Bland, J. O. P., and Backhouse, E., *Annals and Memoirs of the Court of Peking,* London, 1913.

———, *China Under the Empress Dowager,* London, 1910.

Blond, Georges, *Admiral Togo,* London, 1961.

Bodley, R. V. C., *Admiral Togo: The Authorized Life,* London, 1935.

Boorman, H. L., and others, *Moscow–Peking Axis,* New York, 1957.

Borst-Smith, E. F., *Mandarin and Missionary in Cathay,* London, 1917.

Borton, Hugh, *Japan's Modern Century,* New York, 1955.

Bridge, Sir Cyprian, "Naval Warfare Today: What Japan Has Done," *Cornhill Magazine,* September 1904.

Brindle, Ernest, *With Russian, Japanese and Chunchuse,* London, 1905.

Brinkley, Captain F., *Historians' History of the World, A History of the Japanese People,* New York, 1914.

Brogan, D. W., *The Development of Modern France, 1870–1939,* London, 1940.

Brooke, Lord, *An Eye-Witness in Manchuria,* London, 1905.

Broomhall, M., *The Chinese Empire*, London, 1907.

Browne, Courtney, *Tojo: The Last Banzai*, New York, 1967.

Busch, Noel F., *The Emperor's Sword*, New York, 1969.

Bywater, Hector C., *Sea-Power in the Pacific*, London, 1921.

Callwell, C. E., *The Effect of Maritime Command on Land Campaigns Since Water-loo*, London, 1907.

Cantlie, Sir James, and Jones, C. S., *Sun Yat-sen and the Awakening of China*, New York, 1912.

Carmichael, J., *A Short History of the Russian Revolution*, London, 1966.

Cassell's History of the Russo-Japanese War, 5 vols., London, undated.

Chamberlain, Basil H., *Things Japanese*, London, 1891 and 1905.

Chamberlin, W. H., *Japan Over Asia*, London, 1938.

Chen, Jerome, *Yuan Shih-k'ai*, London, 1961.

Chiang Kai-shek, *Soviet Russia in China*, London, 1957.

Chirol, Valentine, *The Far Eastern Question*, London, 1896.

Christie, Dugald, *Thirty Years in Mukden, 1883–1913, Being the Experiences and recollections of Dugald Christie, C.M.G., F.R.C.S., F.R.C.P.*, London, 1914.

Chuo-Koron-Sha (Central Review Publishing Company), *Nihon-no Rekishi* ("A History of Japan"), Tokyo, 1965–1967, 26 vols.; maps, chronological charts, 5 vols.:

vol. 11, *Sengoku-Daimyo* ("Feudal Lords of the Period of Internecine Wars"), Sugiyama Hiroshi, 1965.

vol. 19, *Kaikoku-to Joi* ("Opening of the Country and Expulsion of the Barbarians"), Konishi Shiro, 1966.

vol. 20, *Meiji-Ishin* ("Meiji Reformation"), Inoue Kiyoshi, 1966.

vol. 21, *Kindai-Koxka-no Shuppatsu* ("Start of a Modern State"), Irokawa Daiki-chi, 1966.

vol. 22, *Dai-Nippon-Teikoku-no Shiren* ("Trials and Tribulations of the Great Japanese Empire"), Sumiya Mikio, 1966.

Churchill, Winston S., *World Crisis*, 1931.

Clyde, Paul Hibbert, *The Far East, A History of the Impact of the West on Eastern Asia*, New York, 1948.

Collbran, Christine, *An American Girl's Trip to the Orient*, New York, 1899.

Collier's Weekly, "Russo-Japanese War, A Photographic and Descriptive Review," New York, undated.

Conger, Dean, "Siberia, Russia's Frozen Frontier," *National Geographic Magazine*, March 1967.

Conroy, Hilary, *The Japanese Seizure of Korea, 1868–1910*, Philadelphia, 1960.

Cordonnier, E. L. V., *The Japanese in Manchuria*, 2 vols., London, 1912 and 1914.

Cowen, T., *The Russo-Japanese War, From the Outbreak of Hostilities to the Battle of Liaoyang*, London, 1904.

Cowles, V., *The Russian Dagger*, London, 1969.

Crankshaw, E., Introduction, commentary, and notes, *Khrushchev Remembers,* London, 1971.

Creswell, Hiraoka, and Namba, *A Dictionary of Military Terms, English-Japanese–Japanese-English,* Tokyo, 1932.

Crouch, R. A., "An Australian View of the War," *The Contemporary Review,* August 1904.

Dai Jinmei-Jiten ("Comprehensive Encyclopedia of Personal Names"), 10 vols., Tokyo, 1953–1955.

Dai-Jiten ("The Comprehensive Lexicon"), Tokyo, 1954.

Dallin, D. J., *Soviet Russia and the Far East,* London, 1949.

———, *The Rise of Russia in Asia,* London, 1950.

d'Anethan, Baroness A., *Fourteen Years of Diplomatic Life in Japan,* London, 1912.

de Custine, *The Journals of the Marquis de Custine: Journey for Our Time,* New York, 1951 (first published in Paris, 1843).

de Négrier, General, *Lessons of the Russo-Japanese War,* London, 1906.

Dening, Sir E., *Japan,* New York, 1960.

Dennett, Tyler, *Roosevelt and the Russo-Japanese War,* New York, 1959.

Denny, Brevet-Major R.D., Unpublished papers and diaries during his period as assistant military attaché in Peking.

Der Ling, Princess, *Old Buddha,* London, 1929.

Dillon, E. J., "Sergius Witte," *The American Monthly Review of Reviews,* New York, September 3, 1905.

———, "Sergius Witte and Jutaro Komura," *Harper's Weekly,* New York, September 2, 1905.

———, "Japan and Russia," *The Contemporary Review,* London, March 1904.

———, "What the Peace of Portsmouth Means to Russia," *Harper's Weekly,* New York, September 16, 1905.

———, "The Story of the Peace Negotiations," *The Contemporary Review,* October 1905.

———, "A New Grouping of the Powers," *The Contemporary Review,* August 1904.

———, *The Eclipse of Russia,* Paris, 1918.

Diósy, Arthur, *The New Far East,* London, 1904.

Dua, R. P., *The Impact of the Russo-Japanese War (1905) on Indian Politics,* New Delhi, 1966.

Dunn, R. L., *Collier's Weekly,* "The Russo-Japanese War," New York, undated.

Ebisawa Arimichi, "Crypto-Christianity in Tokugawa Japan," *Japan Quarterly,* July–September 1960.

Eckel, P. E., *The Far East Since 1500,* London, 1948.

Edie, J. M., and others, *Russian Philosophy,* vol. 11, Chicago, 1965.

Elegant, R., *The Centre of the World,* London, 1963.

Ellison, Herbert J., *History of Russia,* New York, 1964.

Elsbree, W. H., *Japan's Role in South-East Asian Nationalist Movements, 1940–45,* Cambridge, Mass., 1953.

Ennis, T. E., *Eastern Asia,* New York, 1948.

Essad-Bey, M., *Nicholas II,* London, 1936.

Ex-Counsellor of Legation in the Far East, *The Problem of Japan,* Amsterdam, 1918.

Fairbank, J. K., *The United States and China,* Cambridge, Mass., 1962.

Falk, B., *Bouquets for Fleet Street,* London, 1951.

Falk, E. A., *Togo and The Rise of Japanese Sea Power,* New York, 1936.

Feldmann, Constantine, *The Revolt of the Potemkin,* London, 1908.

Firth, C. B., *From Napoleon to Hitler,* London, 1955.

Fischer, L., *The Life of Lenin,* New York, 1965.

Fitzgerald, C. P., *Revolution in China,* London, 1952.

Fleming, P., *The Siege at Peking,* London, 1959.

Fraser, D., *A Modern Campaign of War and Wireless Telegraphy in the Far East,* London, 1905.

Frumkin, J. G., et al., *Russian Jewry, 1860–1907,* New York, 1950.

Fujiwara Ginjiro, *The Spirit of Japanese Industry,* Tokyo, 1940.

Fujii Shoichi, *Nisshin-Nichiro Senso* ("Japano-Chinese and Japano-Russian Wars"), Tokyo, 1969.

Fujisawa Rikitaro, *The Recent Aims and Political Development of Japan,* New Haven, 1923.

Fukushima Yasuko, *Kawahara Misaoko* ("Kawahara Misaoko"), Biography of the woman espionage agent and Chinese language expert, Tokyo, 1934.

Fuller, Major-General J. F. C., *The Conduct of War, 1789–1961,* London, 1962.

Furuya Tetsuo, *Nichi-Ro Senso* ("Japano-Russian War"), Tokyo, 1966.

Futrell, Michael, *Northern Underground,* London, 1963.

Gapon, G., *The Story of My Life,* London, 1905.

Ganz, H., *The Land of Riddles: Russia of Today,* New York, 1904.

Gardiner, A. G., *Prophets, Priests and Kings,* London, 1917.

German General Staff, *The Russo-Japanese War,* 5 vols., prepared by the Historical Section, authorized translation by Karl von Donat, London, 1909–1910.

Golownin's Captivity in Japan, 3 vols., London, 1824.

Gorki, Maxim, *Letters,* Moscow, 1966.

Great Britain, *Parliamentary Papers,* "*Blue Books,*" *China No. 2 (1904). Correspondence Respecting the Russian Occupation of Manchuria and Newchwang,* London, 1904.

Greener, William, *A Secret Agent in Port Arthur,* London, 1905.

Griffis, W. E., *The Mikado's Empire,* New York, 1866.

Griswold, A. W., *The Far Eastern Policy of the United States,* New York, 1938.

Gubbins, J. H., *The Progress of Japan, 1853–1871,* Oxford, 1911.

[567]

Gurko, V. I., *Features and Figures of the Past,* translated by Laura Mateev, Stanford, 1939.

Hahn, Emily, *China Only Yesterday,* London, 1963.
Haldane, A. L., *Reports From British Officers Attached to the Japanese and Russian Forces in the Field,* London, 1908.
Hamada Kenji, *Prince Ito,* Tokyo, 1936.
Hamilton, Lord Frederic, *My Yesterdays: The Vanished Pomps of Yesterday,* London, 1920.
Hamilton, Lieutenant-General Sir Ian, *A Staff Officer's Scrap Book During the Russo-Japanese War,* 2 vols., London, 1906.
Hamilton, Ian B. M., *The Happy Warrior, A Life of General Sir Ian Hamilton,* London, 1966.
Hanabusa Nagamichi, *Meiji Gaiko-Shi* ("Diplomatic History of the Meiji Era"), Tokyo, 1966.
Hardy, O., and Dumke, G. S., *A History of the Pacific Area in Modern Times,* Cambridge, Mass., 1949.
Hargreaves, R., *Red Sun Rising: The Siege of Port Arthur,* London, 1962.
Harrington, Clifford V., *The Silent Samurai of the Sea,* Tokyo, 1964.
Harris, Townsend, *The Complete Journal of . . .,* New York, 1930.
Hart, R. A., *The Great White Fleet,* Boston, 1965.
Hart, Sir Robert, *These From the Land of Sinim,* London, 1901.
Hart-Synott, Captain, *Reports From British Officers Attached to the Japanese and Russian Forces in the Field,* London, 1908.
Hayakawa Teisui, *Nogi Hyaku-Wa, Ijin-no Omokage* ("A Hundred Anecdotes about Nogi, the Image of a Great Man"), Tokyo, 1925.
Hayashi Fusao, *Midori-no Nihon-Retto* ("The Green Japanese Archipelago, Torrentially Flowing, A Hundred Years of Meiji"), Tokyo, 1966.
Hearn, Lafcadio, *Out of the East,* London, 1927.
————, *Kokoro,* Leipzig, 1907.
Hedin, Sven, *My Life as an Explorer,* London, 1926.
Hekirurien (Watanabe Kahei), *Nogi Taisho* ("General Nogi"), 2 vols., Tokyo, 1913.
Heusken, H., *Japan Journal, 1855–1861,* New Brunswick, 1964.
Hildreth, Richard, *Japan As It Was and Is,* Tokyo, 1902.
Hill, C., *Lenin and the Russian Revolution,* London, 1947.
Hingley R., *The Russian Secret Police,* London, 1970.
Hirata Kossen, *Kokai Dai-Kaisen* ("The Great Sea Battle of the Yellow Sea"), Tokyo, 1896.
Hiroshi Mizuo, "Abodes of the Gods," *Japan Quarterly,* July–September 1968.
His Majesty's Stationery Office, *The Russo-Japanese War, Reports from British Officers Attached to the Japanese and Russian Forces in the Field,* 3 vols., and 2 vols. of maps, London, 1908.
Historical Section of the Committee of Imperial Defense, *The Official History of the Russo-Japanese War (Naval and Military),* 3 vols., and 3 vols. of maps and appendices, London, 1910–1920.

History Research Rooms, Faculty of Liberal Arts and Sciences, Tokyo University, *Nihon-Shi Gaisetsu* ("An Outline of Japanese History"), Tokyo, 1961.

Ho Kan-chih, *A History of the Modern Chinese Revolution,* Peking, 1959.

Holtom, D. C., *Modern Japan and Shinto Nationalism,* Chicago, 1942.

Honma Tsuneji, *Ah, Hitachi Maru!* ("Ah, Hitachi Maru!"), Tokyo, 1930.

Horiuchi Keizo and Inoue Takeshi, *Nihon Shoka-Shu* ("A Collection of Songs of Japan"), Tokyo, 1958.

Hough, Richard, *The Fleet That Had To Die,* London, 1958.

House, Colonel, *The Intimate Papers of . . .,* vol. 11, London, 1926.

Hozumi, N., *Ancestor-Worship and Japanese Law,* Tokyo, 1912.

Hsiung, S. I., *The Life of Chiang Kai-shek,* London, 1948.

Hulbert, Homer B., *The Passing of Korea,* London, 1906.

———, *History of Korea,* 2 vols., London, 1962.

Hummell, A. W., *Eminent Chinese of the Ch'ing Period,* 2 vols., Washington, 1943.

Hutchison, John de M., Captain, British naval attaché, Admiralty reports in Public Record Office, London.

Ikejima Shinpei, ed., *Rekishi-Yomoyama-Banashi* ("Sundry Talks on History"), 4 vols., Tokyo, 1966.

Inoue Kiyoshi, *Nihon-no Rekishi* ("A History of Japan"), Tokyo, 1950.

Institute of Strategic Studies, *The Military Balance,* London, 1973–1974.

Ishii Takashi, *Meiji Ishin-no Kokusaiteki Kankyo* ("International Environment of the Meiji Reformation"), Tokyo, 1957.

Ishimitsu Makiyo, *Bokyo-no Uta* ("Songs of Nostalgia"), Tokyo, 1958.

———, *Koya-no Hana* ("Flowers of the Wild Plains"), Tokyo, 1958.

Iswolsky, A., *Memoirs,* ed. and translated by C. I. Seeger, London, 1920.

Ito Hirobumi, *Commentaries on the Constitution of the Empire of Japan,* Tokyo, 1906.

Ito Masanori, *Dai-Kaigun-o Omou* ("Thinking of the Great Navy"), Tokyo, 1956.

———, *Kokubo-Shi* ("History of National Defense"), Tokyo, 1941.

Ivanovich, "The Russo-Japanese War and Yellow Peril," *The Contemporary Review,* August 1904.

Jackson, T., Captain, British naval attaché, Admiralty reports, Public Record Office, London.

James, D. H., *The Siege of Port Arthur, Records of an Eye-witness,* London, 1905.

James, Lionel, *High Pressure,* London, 1929.

Jane, F. T., *The Imperial Japanese Navy,* London, 1904.

———, *The Imperial Russian Navy,* London, 1904.

Jansen, M. B., *Sakamoto Ryoma and the Meiji Restoration,* Princeton, 1961.

Japan Foreign Office, *Nihon Gaiko Bunsho* ("Japanese Diplomatic Documents"), vols. 37 and 38, Tokyo, 1904–1905.

———, *Komura Gaiko-Shi* ("History of Komura Diplomacy"), vols. 1 and 11, Tokyo, 1953.

————, *Nichiro Kosho-Shi* ("History of Japano-Russian Negotiations"), 2 vols., Tokyo, 1944.

Japan Ministry of the Army, *Meiji Gunji-Shi* ("A History of the Military Affairs of Meiji Era"), vols. 1 and 2, Tokyo, 1965. (Part of 35 vols. of "Historical Materials for the Biography of Emperor Meiji, Military Affairs," ed. by Takeuchi Hideyoshi.)

————, *Meiji-Tenno Go-Denki-Shiryo* ("Historical Materials for the Biography of the Emperor Meiji"), Tokyo, 1966.

Japan Naval General Staff Office, *Meiji 37–8-nen Nichiro-Sensoshi* ("History of the Japano-Russian War of 37–8th Years of Meiji"), Tokyo, 1912.

Japan Times, *Man-Shu Chimei-Jinmei-Jisho* ("A Dictionary of Manchurian and Chinese Proper Nouns"), Tokyo, 1931.

Japanese National Commission, *Japan, Its Land, People and Culture,* Tokyo, 1958.

Jordan, R. B., *Born to Fight,* Philadelphia, 1946.

Jukes, G., *The Soviet Union in Asia,* Sydney, 1973.

Juttikala, E., with K. Pirinen, *A History of Finland,* translated by Paul Sjoblon, London, 1962.

Kada Tetsuji, *Ishin-Igo-no Shakai Keizai Shiso Gairon* ("Outline of Social and Economic Thought since the Reformation"), Tokyo, 1934.

Kahn, H., *The Emerging Japanese Superstate, Challenge and Response,* New Jersey, 1970.

Karnow, S., *Mao and China,* New York, 1972.

Kashimura Eiichi and Yano Koji, compilers, *Chukoku Tairiku Shobetsu Chizu* ("Provincial Atlas of Continental China"), Tokyo, 1971.

Kawai Tatsuo, *The Goal of Japanese Expansion,* Tokyo, 1938.

Kawasaki Ichiro, *Japan Unmasked,* Tokyo, 1969.

Kazutoshi Ueda, ed., *"Togo Gensui" Hensankai* ("Society for the editing of *Fleet Admiral Togo"*), Tokyo Imperial University.

Keeling's Guide to Japan, Yokohama, 1890.

Keeton, G. W., *China, The Far East and the Future,* London, 1949.

Kennan, G., "Russian Views of Kuropatkin and His Army," *The Outlook,* February 1905.

Kennedy, J., *Asian Nationalism in the Twentieth Century,* New York, 1968.

Kennedy, M. D., *Some Aspects of Japan and Her Defence Forces,* London, 1928.

Kimura Ki, "The Japanese 'Mayflower,' " *Japan Quarterly,* July–September 1960.

————, "A Brief History of Tokyo," *This Is Japan,* 1964.

Kimura Shohachi, "Birth of the Ginza," *This Is Japan,* 1959.

Kinai, M., *The Russo-Japanese War, Official Reports,* 3 vols, Tokyo.

Kinkodo Publishing Company, *The Russo-Japanese War,* 3 vols., Tokyo, 1904.

Klado, Captain N. L., *The Russian Navy in the Russo-Japanese War,* translated by L. J. H. Dickinson, London, 1905.

————, *The Battle of the Sea of Japan,* translated by L. J. H. Dickinson and F. P. Marchant, London, 1906.

[570]

Kobunsha, publisher, *The Memorable Battles in the 37th and 38th Years of Meiji*, Tokyo, 1911.

Koempfer, Engelbert, *An Account of Japan*, London, 1853.

Kokovtsov, Count, *Out of My Past: The Memoirs of Count Kokovtsov*, Stanford, 1935.

Kokuruyukai (Amur or Black Dragon Society), ed., *Toa Senkaku Shishi Kiden*, 2 vols., ("Biographers of the Loyal Pathfinders of East Asia"), Tokyo, 1933.

Komai Gonnoské, *Fuji from Hampstead Heath*, London, 1925.

Komori Tokuji, *Akashi Motojiro*, ("Akashi Motojiro"), 2 vols., Tokyo, 1928.

Korostovetz, J. J., *The Diary of . . .*, London, 1920.

Kotoku Shusui, *Selected writings in Nihon-no Meicho* ("The Great Books of Japan"), vol. 44, Tokyo, 1970.

Kublin, Hyman, *Asian Revolutionary: The Life of Sen Katayama*, Princeton, 1964.

Kurihara Hirotaro, *Ningen Meiji-Tenno* ("Emperor Meiji the Man"), Tokyo, 1953.

Kurita Tomitaro, *Recollections of Lushun Blockade*, Tokyo, 1912.

Kurohane Shigeru, *Sekaishijoo-yori Mitaru Nichiro-Senso* ("The Japano-Russian War as Seen from the Viewpoint of World History"), Tokyo, 1960.

Kuropatkin, A. N., General, *The Russian Army and the Japanese War*, 2 vols., New York, 1909.

Ladd, G. T., *In Korea with Marquis Ito*, London, 1908.

Latourette, K. S., *A History of Modern China*, Yale, 1954.

Lattimore, O., *Manchuria: Cradle of Conflict*, New York, 1932.

Lecky, H. S., *The King's Ships*, London, 1913.

Lederer, Ivo J., ed., *Russian Foreign Policy*, New Haven and London, 1962.

Lenin, V. I. *The Revolution of 1905*, London, 1931.

———, *Selected Works*, vols, 1, 2, 3 Moscow, Leningrad, 1934.

Lensen, G. A., ed., *Korea and Manchuria Between Russia and Japan, 1895–1904, The Observations of Sir Ernest Satow, the British Minister Plenipotentiary to Japan (1895–1900) and China (1900–1906)*, Tallahassee, 1960.

———, *The Russian Push Toward Japan*, Princeton, 1959.

Lerski, J. J., "A Polish Chapter of the Russo-Japanese War," *The Transactions of the Asiatic Society of Japan*, Tokyo, 1959.

Levine, I. D., *The Kaiser's Letters to the Tsar*, London, 1921.

Lloyd, A., *Every-Day Japan*, London, 1909.

———, *Admiral Togo*, Tokyo, 1905.

Lobanov-Rosktovsky, Prince, *Russia and Asia*, Ann Arbor, 1951.

Lockhart, R. H. Bruce, *The Two Revolutions*, London, 1967.

MacNair, H. F., *China*, Berkeley, 1946.

———, *Modern Chinese History: Selected Readings*, Shanghai, 1946.

McCaul, E., *Under the Care of the Japanese War Office*, London, 1904.

McCormick, Frederick, *The Tragedy of Russia in Pacific Asia*, 2 vols., New York, 1907.

McCullagh, F., *With the Cossacks, Being the Story of an Irishman Who Rode with the Cossacks Throughout the Russo-Japanese War,* London, 1906.

McCune, S., *Korea's Heritage: A Regional and Social Geography,* Tokyo, 1956.

McKenzie, F. A., *From Tokyo To Tiflis,* London, 1905.

———, *The Tragedy of Korea,* London, 1908.

———, *Korea's Fight for Freedom,* London, 1920.

Mahan, Captain (later Admiral), A. T., *The Problem of Asia,* London, 1900.

———, *The Influence of Sea Power upon History,* London, 1892.

———, *On Naval Warfare,* ed. by Allen Westcot, Boston, 1942.

Malozemoff, A., Russian Far Eastern Policy, 1881–1904, Berkeley, 1958.

Many War Correspondents, In Many Wars, Tokyo, 1904.

Maraini, Fosco, *Meeting with Japan,* London, 1959.

March, Captain Peyton C., *Reports of Military Observers (U.S.) During the Russo-Japanese War,* Washington, 1906.

Martin, W. A. P., *The Awakening of China,* New York, 1907.

Marx, Karl, *Marx on China, Articles for the New York Daily Tribune, 1853–1860,* Bombay, 1952.

Massie, R. K., *Nicholas and Alexandra,* New York, 1968.

Mateaux, C. L., *Peeps Abroad,* London, Paris and New York, undated.

Matsudaira Narimitsu, "Summer Festivals," *Japan Quarterly,* July–September 1960.

Matsui Masato, "The Russo-Japanese Agreement of 1907: Its Causes and the Progress of Negotiations," *Modern Asian Studies,* vol. 6, part 1, 1972.

Matsuoka Yosuke, *Building Up Manchuria,* Tokyo, 1937.

Matsushita Yoshio, *Meiji-no Guntai* ("The Army of Meiji"), Tokyo, 1963.

———, *Nogi Maresuke* ("Nogi Maresuke"), Tokyo, 1960.

———, *Nisshin-Senso Zengo* ("About the Time of the Japano-Chinese War"), Tokyo, 1939.

Maynard, J., *Russia in Flux,* New York, 1962.

Military Correspondent of *The Times* (Charles A'Court Repington), *The War in the Far East, 1904–05.*

Minogue, K., *Nationalism,* London, 1967.

Miyagi Eisho and Oi Minobu, *Nihon Josei-shi* ("History of the Japanese Woman"), Tokyo, 1959.

Mizuno Hironori, *Kono Issen* ("This One Battle") Tokyo, 1911.

Molloy, F., *The Russian Court in The Eighteenth Century,* vol. 1, London, 1905.

Montgomery, Field-Marshal Viscount, *A History of Warfare,* London, 1968.

Morison, S. E., *"Old Bruin," Commodore Matthew Calbraith Perry,* London, 1968.

Morisue Yoshiaki, *Nihon-Shi-no Kenkyu* ("A Study of Japanese History"), Tokyo, 1955.

Morris, J., *Makers of Japan,* London, 1906.

Mosley, Leonard, *Hirohito, Emperor of Japan,* London, 1966.

Murdoch, James, *A History of Japan,* 3 vols., London, 1949.

Murray, David, *The Story of Japan,* London and New York, 1894.

Nabokoff, Constantine, *Unpublished Memoirs of the Portsmouth Peace Conference*, in the possession of Nicholas Nabokoff.

Nakamura, K., *Prince Ito*, New York, 1910.

Nehru, Jawaharlal, *Glimpses of World History*, London, 1959.

———, *An Autobiography*, London, 1936.

Nichi-nichi (Tokyo) and Mainichi (Osaka), *Nichi-Ro Dai-Kaisen-o Kataru* ("Talking of the Japano-Russian Great Sea Battles"), Tokyo, 1933.

Nicholas II, *Journal Intime*, translated by A. Pierre, Paris, 1925.

———, *Archives Secrètes de l'Empereur Nicholas II*, Paris, 1928.

Nicolaievsky, Boris, *Aseff: The Russian Judas*, London, 1934.

Nihon Rekishi Dai-Jiten ("Comprehensive Dictionary of Japanese History"), 23 vols, Tokyo, 1961–1964.

Nihon Jinbutsu-Shi Taikei ("An Outline History of Personalities of Japan"), Tokyo, 1950, vol. 5, *Kindai* ("Modern Era") 1, ed. Konishi Shiro.

vol. 6, *Kindai* ("Modern Era") 2, ed. Okubo Toshinori.

vol. 7, *Kindai*, ("Modern Era") 3, ed. Inoue Kiyoshi.

Nihon-no Hyakunen ("One Hundred Years of Japan"), Tokyo, 1962, 10 vols.

Vol. 7, *Meiji-no Eiko* ("Glory of Meiji") (1900–12).

Vol. 8, *Kyokoku-o Mezashite* ("Towards a Strong Power") (1889–1900).

Vol. 9, *Wakitatsu Koron* ("Surging Public Opinion") (1877–87).

Vol. 10, *Go-Isshin-no Arashi* ("The Storm of the Great Reformation") (1853–77).

Nihon-Rekishi ("Japanese History"), Iwanami series of lectures, 23 vols., Tokyo, 1964–1968, vols. 17 and 18.

Nippon Dempo Tsushinsha (Japan Telegraphic News Service), *Japan Illustrated*, Tokyo, 1938.

Nish, I., *The Anglo-Japanese Alliance: The Diplomacy of Two Island Empires, 1894–1907*, London, 1966.

Nitobé, I., *The Intercourse Between the U.S. and Japan*, Baltimore, 1891.

———, *Bushido, The Soul of Japan*, Tokyo, 1935.

Nojine, E. K., *The Truth About Port Arthur*, translated and edited by Captain A. B. Lindsay, and Major E. D. Swinton, London, 1908.

Norman, E. H., "The Genyosha, Origins of Japanese Imperialism," *Pacific Affairs*, vol. 17, September 3, 1944, 261–284.

Norregaard, B. W., *The Great Siege, The Investment and Fall of Port Arthur*, London, 1906.

Novikov-Priboy, A. S., *Tsushima, Grave of a Floating City*, New York, 1937.

Numata Ichiro, *Nichiro-Gaiko-shi* ("A History of Japano-Russian Diplomacy"), Tokyo, 1943.

Numata Takazo, Lieutenant-General, *Nichi-Ro Riku-Sen Shinshi* ("New History of the Japano-Russian Land War"), Tokyo, 1924.

Ogasawara Nagayo (Naganari), *Life of Admiral Togo*, Tokyo, 1934.

———, *Kokoku Kaijo-Kenryoku-Shi, Mikasa Monogatari* ("History of the Empire's Maritime Power, A Story of Mikasa"), Tokyo, 1938.

————, *Nihon Teikoku Kaijo Kenriku-Shi Kogi* ("Lectures on the History of the Maritime Power of the Empire"), Tokyo, 1902 and 1904.

————, *Togo Gensui Shoden* ("Detailed Biography of Fleet Admiral Togo"), Tokyo, 1926.

Ogawa Gotaro, *Expenditures on the Russo-Japanese War,* New York, 1923.

Okamoto Shumpei, *The Japanese Oligarchy and the Russo-Japanese War,* New York, 1970.

Oka Yoshitake, *Kindai Nihon Seijishi* ("Political History of Modern Japan"), Tokyo, 1962.

Okuma Shigenobu, *Fifty Years of New Japan,* New York, 1909.

O'Laughlin, J. C., "The Russo-Japanese War," *Collier's Weekly,* New York, undated.

Oliphant, E. H. C., *Germany and Good Faith,* Melbourne, 1914.

Ono Sanenobu, ed., *Gensui Koshaku Oyama Iwao* ("Field Marshal Prince Oyama Iwao"), 2 vols., Tokyo, 1935.

Ookhtomsky, Prince, *Travels in the East of His Majesty, Tsar Nicholas II of Russia,* 2 vols., translated by Richard Goodlet, London, 1896.

Osatake Takeshi, *Meiji Seijishi Tenbyo* ("Sketches of the Meiji Political History"), Tokyo, 1936.

Otomo Sakuo, ed., *Nogi Taisho* ("General Nogi"), Tokyo, 1913.

Oyama Azusa, *Nichiro-Senso-no Gunsei-Shiroku* ("Historical Records of the Military Administration of the Japano-Russian War"), Tokyo, 1973.

Ozaki Chikara, compiler, *Wa-Ei Kaigo-Jiten* ("A Japanese-English Dictionary of Nautical Terms"), Tokyo, 1929.

Pakenham, Captain W. C., British naval attaché, Admiralty reports, Public Record Office, London.

Palmer, Frederick, *With Kuroki in Manchuria,* New York, 1904.

————, *With My Own Eyes,* New York, 1933.

Pares, Sir Bernard, *A History of Russia,* London, 1926.

Pascal, R., *The Growth of Modern Germany,* London, 1946.

Payne, R., *Lenin,* London, 1964.

————, *Marx,* New York, 1968.

Pearl, C., *Morrison of Peking,* Sydney, 1967.

Peffer, Nathaniel, *Japan and the Pacific,* London, 1935.

Penkala, Maria, *A Correlated History of the Far East,* Tokyo, 1969.

Pokrovskii, M. N., *Russia in World History,* ed. by Roman Szporluk, Ann Arbor, 1970.

Politovsky, E. S., *From Libau to Tsushima, A Narrative of the Voyage of Admiral Rojestvensky's Fleet to Eastern Seas,* translated by Major F. R. Godfrey, London, 1906.

Pooley, A. M., ed., *The Secret Memoirs of Count Tadasu Hayashi,* London, 1915.

Possony, Stefan F., *Lenin: The Compulsive Revolutionary,* Chicago, 1964.

Potter, J. D., *Yamamoto,* New York, 1965.

Price, E. B., *The Russo-Japanese Treaties of 1907–16, Concerning Manchuria and Mongolia,* Baltimore, 1933.
Price, W., *Key to Japan,* London, 1946.

Quested, R. K. I., *The Expansion of Russia in East Asia, 1857–1860,* Singapore, 1968.

Radziwill, Catherine (Princess), *Nicholas II: The Last of the Tsars,* London, 1931.
Rappoport, Dr. Angelo S., *Fair Ladies of the Winter Palace,* London, 1914.
"Raucat, T.," *The Honorable Picnic,* Tokyo, 1954.
Red Archives (Krasni Arkhiv), *C. E. Vulliamy,* translated by A. L. Hynes, London, 1929.
Redesdale, Lord, *Tales of Old Japan,* London, 1915.
Rekishigaku Kenkyukai ("Society for the Study of Historical Science"), compiler, *Nihonshi-Nenpyo* ("Chronological Chart of Japanese History"), Tokyo, 1966.
Rhee, Syngman, *Japan Inside Out,* London, 1951.
Richardson, T. E., *In Japanese Hospitals During War-time,* London, 1905.
Romanov, B. A., *Russia In Manchuria* (1892–1906), translated by Susan Wilbur Jones, American Council of Learned Societies, Ann Arbor, 1952.
Rosen, Baron, *Forty Years of Diplomacy,* New York, 1922.
Ross, Colonel C., *An Outline of the Russo-Japanese War,* 2 vols., London, 1912.
Russian Ministry of Ways and Communication, *Guide to the Great Siberian Railway,* St. Petersburgh, 1900.

Sadler, A. L., *A Short History of Japan,* Sydney, 1946.
Sakamaki Teijiro, *Shina Bunkatsu-Ron* ("On the Division of China"), Tokyo, 1913.
Sakurai Tadayoshi (Chuon), *Human Bullets,* Tokyo, 1907.
Salisbury, H. E., *The Coming War Between Russia and China,* London, 1969.
Sanseido Publishing Company, *Sekai Rekishi Nenpyo* ("Chronological Chart of World History"), Tokyo, 1927.
Sansom, G. B., *Japan: A Short Cultural History,* New York, 1943.
Sasebo Kaigun Kunko Hyoshokai ("Sasebo Society for Commendation of the Meritorious Services of the Navy"), *Nichi-Ro Kaisen-Ki* ("Chronicles of the Japano-Russian Sea Battles"), Tokyo, 1906.
Sasaki Nobutsuna, *Meeting at Shui-Shih-Ying,* Tokyo, 1910.
Satow, E., *A Diplomat in Japan,* London, 1921.
Sawa Kannojo, *Kaigun Shichijunen Shidan* ("Talking of the History of the Navy"), Tokyo, 1942.
SCAP, *Education in the New Japan,* 2 vols., Tokyo, 1948.
_____, *Religions in Japan,* Tokyo, 1948.
Scherer, J. A. B., *Three Meiji Leaders,* Tokyo, 1936.
_____, *Japan's Advance,* Tokyo, 1934.
Schiffrin, H. Z., *Sun Yat-sen and the Origins of the Chinese Revolution,* Berkeley, 1968.

[575]

Schram, S., *Mao Tse-tung,* London, 1966.

Schurmann, F., and O. Schell, *China Readings 1, Imperial China,* London, 1967.

Seaman, L. L. *From Tokyo Through Manchuria With the Japanese,* London, 1905.

——, *The Real Triumph of Japan,* London, 1906.

Selle, E. A., *Donald of China,* New York, 1948.

Semenov, Captain V. I., *Rasplata* ("The Reckoning"), London, 1909.

——, *The Battle of Tsushima,* translated by Captain A. B. Lindsay, London, 1906.

——, *The Price of Blood,* London, 1910.

Seton-Watson, H., *The Decline of Imperial Russia,* London,·1956.

——, *The Russian Empire, 1801–1917,* London, 1967.

Shigemitsu Mamoru, *Japan and Her Destiny,* London, 1958.

Shinobu Seizaburo and Nakayama Jiichi, *Nichiro Sensoshi-no Kenkyu* ("Studies of the History of the Japano-Russian War"), Tokyo, 1959.

Simpich, F., "Manchuria, Promised Land of Asia," *National Geographic Magazine,* October 1929.

Smight, G., *Supremacy in the Far East,* London, 1905.

Smith, W. R., *The Siege and Fall of Port Arthur,* London, 1905.

Stead, A., ed., *Japan by the Japanese,* London, 1904.

——, "The Far Eastern Problem," *The Fortnightly Review,* January 1904.

——, "The War in the Far East," *The Fortnightly Review,* March and June 1904.

——, "The War and International Opinion," *The Fortnightly Review,* October 1904.

——, "Port Arthur and After," *The Fortnightly Review,* February 1905.

Steer, A. P., *The "Novik" and the Part She Played in the Russo-Japanese War,* London, 1913.

Steevens, G. W., *Naval Policy, With Some Account of the Warships of the Principal Powers,* London, 1896.

Steiner, J. F., *Behind the Japanese Mask,* New York, 1944.

Stewart, A. M., "The Revelation of the East," *The Contemporary Review,* August 1904.

Storry, R., *The Double Patriots,* London, 1957.

——, *A History of Modern Japan,* London, 1960.

Story, Douglas, *The Campaign With Kuropatkin,* London, 1904.

Street, J., *Mysterious Japan,* London, 1923.

Sumner, B. H., *Tsarism and Imperialism in the Middle and Far East,* London, 1940.

——, *Survey of Russian History,* London, 1944.

Sun Yat-sen, *Memoirs of a Chinese Revolutionary,* London, 1918.

Suyematsu Kencho, *The Risen Sun,* London, 1905.

Tae Hung Ha, *Folk Tales of Old Korea,* Seoul, 1959.

Takada Hideji, *Tokudane Hyakunen-shi* ("One-Hundred-Year History of Scoops"), Tokyo, 1968.

Takayanagi Mitsutoshi and Takeuchi Riichi, *Kadokawa Nihon-shi Jiten*

("Kadokawa Dictionary of Japanese History"), Tokyo, 1966.

Takeyama, Michio, "The Secularization of Feudal Japan," *Japan Quarterly*, January–March 1959.

———, "Traditions and Japanese Youth," *Japan Quarterly*, July–September 1960.

Talbot, H. M. S., Log of . . ., February 1904.

Tamon Jiro, *Dan-u-no Shita-o Kugurite* ("Going Under the Rains of Bullets"), Tokyo, 1927.

Tamura Kinya, *General Nogi*, London, 1912.

Tani Toshio, Lieutenant-General, *Kimitsu Nichi-Ro-Sen-shi* ("Intelligence History of the Japano-Russian War"), lectures at the War College, Inaba Masao, ed., Tokyo, 1966.

Taylor, A. J. P., *The Course of German History*, London, 1945.

Teng Ssu-yu and Fairbank, J. K., *China's Response to the West*, New York, 1963.

Thiess, F., *The Voyage of Forgotten Men*, New York, 1937.

This Is Japan, Tokyo, 1954–1969.

Thomas G. S., *Catherine the Great and the Expansion of Russia*, London, 1947.

Thomas, R. C. W., *The War in Korea*, Aldershot, 1954.

Togo Kichitaro, *The Naval Battles of the Russo-Japanese War*, translated by J. Takakasu, Tokyo, 1907.

Togawa Yukio, *Nogi-to Togo* ("Nogi and Togo"), Tokyo, 1969.

Tokutomi Roka, *Yadorigi* ("Mistletoe"), Tokyo, 1909.

Tokutomi Soho, *Soho Jiden* ("Autobiography of Soho"), Tokyo, 1935.

Tolstoi, L., "Bethink Yourselves," *The Times*, July 16, 1904.

Tretyakov, Lieutenant-General N. A., *My Experiences at Nan-shan and Port Arthur With the Fifth East Siberian Rifles*, London, 1911.

Trotski, L., *The History of the Russian Revolution*, 3 vols., London, 1967.

Tsukamoto Yoshitane, *Asahikan-jo-yori Mitaru Nihonkai-Kaisen* ("Sea Battle of the Japan Sea Seen from the *Asahi*"), Tokyo, 1907.

Tuchman, Barbara, *The Guns of August*, London, 1962.

Uchida Roan, *Omoidasu Hitobito* ("People I Remember"), Tokyo, 1925.

Ular, Alexander, "North-Eastern Asia after the War," *The Contemporary Review*, February 1907.

Unger, F. W., and C. Morris, *Russia and Japan, and a Complete History of the War in the Far East*, Philadelphia, 1904.

U.S. State Department, *The Conferences at Malta and Yalta*, Washington, 1955.

U.S. War Department, Office of the Chief of Staff, *Reports of Military Observers Attached to the Armies in Manchuria During the Russo-Japanese War*, 2 vols., Washington, 1906.

———, *Epitome of the Russo-Japanese War*, Washington, 1907.

Van Bergen, R., *The Story of China*, London, 1902.

Varè, D., *The Last of the Empresses*, London, 1936.

Veresáev, V., *In the War*, translated by Leo Wiener, New York, 1917.

Villiers, F., *Port Arthur, Three Months With the Besiegers*, London, 1905.

Vorres, I., *The Last Grand Duchess, The Memoirs of Grand Duchess Olga Alexandrovna,* London, 1964.

Wada Teijuhn, *American Foreign Policy Towards Japan During the 19th Century,* Tokyo, 1928.

Warner, Marina, *The Dragon Empress: Life and Times of Tz'u-hsi (1835–1908), Empress Dowager of China,* London, 1972.

War Office, Intelligence Division, *Handbook of the Russian Army,* London, 1889.

War Office, *The Russo-Japanese War,* 4 vols., London, 1906.

Watanabe Ikujiro, *Mutsu Munemitsu-Den* ("Biography of Mutsu Munemitsu"), Tokyo, 1941.

Watts, A. J., and B. G. Gordon, *The Imperial Japanese Navy,* London, 1971.

Washburn, S., *Nogi,* New York, 1913.

Waters, Colonel W. H-H., *Reports From British Officers in the Field With the Russian and Japanese Forces,* London, 1906.

Weale, B. L. Putnam (Bertram Lenox Simpson), *With Manchu and Muscovite,* London, 1904.

————, *The Coming Struggle in Eastern Asia,* London, 1908.

————, *The Truth About China and Japan,* New York, 1919.

Weizmann, Chaim, *Trial and Error,* London, 1949.

Wellesley, F. A., *With the Russians in Peace and War,* London, 1905.

White, J. A., *The Diplomacy of the Russo-Japanese War,* Princeton, 1964.

Williams, A. Rhys, *The Russians,* London, 1943.

Williams, H. S., *Tales of the Foreign Settlements in Japan,* Tokyo, 1959.

Wilson, C., *Rasputin and the Fall of the Romanovs,* London and New York, 1964.

Wilson, H. W., *Ironclads in Action,* 2 vols., London, 1896.

Witte, Count Serge, *Memoirs,* translated and edited by Abraham Yarmolinsky, New York, 1921.

Wittfogel, K. A., *Oriental Despotism,* London, 1957.

Wolfe, B. D., *Three Who Made a Revolution,* Boston, 1955.

Woodward, D., *The Russians at Sea,* New York, 1965.

Wortham, H. E., *Chinese Gordon,* Boston, 1933.

Wrangel, Count Gustav, *The Cavalry in the Russo-Japanese War,* translated by J. Montgomery, London, 1907.

Wright, H. C. Seppings, *With Togo, the Story of Seven Months Under His Command,* London, 1906.

Wu Yung, *Flight of an Empress,* London, 1937.

Wyatt, H. F., and L. G. H. Horton-Smith, *The Passing of the Great Fleet,* London, 1909.

Yokoyama Kendo, *Taisho Nogi* ("Nogi the General"), Tokyo, 1912.

Yamaguchi Osamu, *Nihon-no Rekishi* ("A History of Japan"), Tokyo, 1953.

Yomiuri Shimbun, Jinbutsu: Nihon-no Rekishi ("Personalities: History of Japan"), 14 vols., Tokyo, 1966;

Vol. 10, *Ishin-no Gunzo* ("Group Statues of the Reformation") by Toyama Shigeki;

Vol. 11, *Nihon-no Ninaite* ("Bearers of Japan," 1) by Toyama Shigeki;

Vol. 12, *Nihon-no Ninaite* ("Bearers of Japan," 2) by Konishi Shiro.

———— *Nihon-no Rekishi* ("A History of Japan") Compiled by Inoue Kiyoshi, *et al.*, 13 vols., Tokyo, 1966–1968.

Yoshida Shigeru, *The Yoshida Memoirs*, London, 1961.

Zilliacus, Konni, *The Russian Revolutionary Movement*, New York, 1905.

Newspapers and Periodicals

Authors of important magazine articles will be found in the preceding pages of the bibliography. The Japan Publications Trading Company has prepared microfilm of the *Asahi* from July 1888; *Mainichi* from February 1872; and *Yomiuri* from November 1874.

American Magazine
American Monthly Review of Reviews
Army Review
Asahi Shimbun, 1904–1906
Baltimore Sun, November 22, 1852
Blackwood's Magazine, January 1897
Collier's Weekly
Contemporary Review
Cornhill Magazine
Cosmopolitan
Daily Mail, 1904–1906
Daily Telegraph, 1904–1906
Eastern World
East Orient
Fortnightly Review
Harper's Weekly
Illustrated London News
Japan Daily Herald
Japan Quarterly
Japan Weekly Mail
Jiji Shimpo, June 21, 1895
Kobe Chronicle, 1904–1906
Korea Review
Mainichi, 1904–1906
Manila American
National Geographic Magazine, October 1929; March 1967
National Magazine
National Review

New Times, January 1973
New York Daily Tribune, 1904–1906
New York Times, 1904–1906
Nineteenth Century
North American Review
Novoye Krai
Novoye Vremya
Outlook
Pacific Affairs, September 1944
Peking Review, April 10, 1970
Straits Times
The Times, 1904–1906
This Is Japan
Yomiuri, 1904–1906

Notes

Abbreviations Used in the Notes

BFO   British Foreign Office.

BOHRJW   The Official History of the Russo-Japanese War (Naval and Military), 3 vols., and 3 vols. maps and appendices. It is listed in the bibliography under Historical Section of the Committee of Imperial Defense.

GOARJW   *The Russo-Japanese War,* 5 vols. This is listed under German General Staff in the bibliography.

JFO   Japanese Foreign Office.

JONH   Japanese Official Naval History of the Russo-Japanese War, 2 vols, listed under Admiralty War Staff in the bibliography.

NTM   *The Letters of Tsar Nicholas and Empress Marie.*

RBO   Reports from British officers attached to the Japanese and Russian forces in the field, listed under His Majesty's Stationery Office in the bibliography.

WNL   *The Letters of Kaiser William to the Tsar.*

Introduction

ix "humbug": *Baltimore Sun,* November 22, 1852

ix Edo reaction: Nitobé, *The Intercourse Between the U.S. and Japan,* 46; Morison, 325–326

xi Forty-five divisions: *The Military Balance,* 1973–74, 6

CHAPTER 1.
The First Pearl Harbor

For an account of Port Arthur and Dalny at the beginning of the war we have drawn from eyewitness accounts, notably Ashmead-Bartlett's *The Siege and Capitulation;*

[581]

Brindle's *With Russian, Japanese and Chunchuse;* Greener's *A Secret Agent in Port Arthur;* McCormick's *The Tragedy of Russia in Pacific Asia;* Norregaard's *The Great Siege;* Seaman's *From Tokyo Through Manchuria with the Japanese;* Nojine's *The Truth About Port Arthur;* W. R. Smith's *The Siege and Fall of Port Arthur;* Steer's *The "Novik" and the Part She Played in the Russo-Japanese War; The Times,* April 7, 1904; "Putnam Weale's" *Manchu and Muscovite.* For the attack on Port Arthur we have relied on JONH, BOHRJW, *Nihon-no Hyakunen* ("One Hundred Years of Japan"), Vol. 7 ("Glory of Meiji"); Sasebo's *Nichi-ro Kaisen-ki* ("Chronicles of the Japano-Russian Sea Battles"); *Before Port Arthur in a Destroyer,* Nojine, Steer, and *The Times.* Alexeiev's character is drawn variously in many publications. We have placed principal reliance on the writings of Dr. E. J. Dillon, Baron Rosen, Witte, Nojine, Tani, and Ashmead-Bartlett. Nojine and Greener have much to say about Stoessel. Togo has been the subject of numerous biographies. Our material draws principally on Morris's *Makers of Japan;* Ogasawara's English edition of *Life of Admiral Togo* and his Japanese-language books, *Detailed Biography of Fleet-Admiral Togo, History of the Empire's Maritime Power, A Story of Mikasa,* and *Lectures on the History of the Maritime Power of the Empire;* Lloyd's *Every-Day Japan;* Bodley's *Admiral Togo: the Authorized Life;* and H. W. Wilson's *Ironclads in Action, 1855–1895.* Descriptions of ships of both navies come from BOHRJW, JONH; Jane's *The Imperial Russian Navy* and *The Imperial Japanese Navy;* Watts and Gordon's *The Imperial Japanese Navy;* Bywater's *Sea-Power in the Pacific;* Woodward's *The Russians at Sea.*

3 Mori Gitaro: JONH, vol. 1, 103
5 "to take such . . .": Komura to Kurino, No. 48 JFO, Tokyo, 2:15 P.M., February 5, 1904
5 Forty-four years earlier: H. S. Lecky, *The King's Ships,* vol. 1, 68–69
6 Kansas barnyard: McCormick, vol. 1, 35
7–8 Effiemov's: *ibid.,* 28–39; Greener, 42–43
9 "He was not an army man . . .": Witte, 127
10 Stark's hospitality: McCormick, vol. 1, 41; Greener, 56–57, JONH, vol. 1, 103; BOHRJW, vol. 1, 57; Smith, R., 36

11 "It is desirable . . .": White, 165; also see Radziwill, 138
12–13 The mayor: *New York Times* Sunday magazine supplement, June 10, 1904
14 Stark's orders: BOHRJW, vol. 1, 57
15 "Make the attack": JONH, vol. 1, 88
18 "To expose my fleet . . .": *ibid.,* 14
19 "Treat the white flag . . .": *ibid.,* 30
20 Japan would shorten its negotiating period: Tani, Chapter 1, 1
20 Akagi flag flown on Mikasa: Woodward, 147

CHAPTER 2.
Rising Sun Rising

The account of the early history of Japan and the character of the Japanese draws on many sources. These include Alcock's *The Capital of the Tycoon;* Benedict's *The Chrysanthemum and the Sword;* Brinkley's *History of the Japanese People;* B. H. Chamberlain's *Things Japanese;* Diósy's *The New Far East;* Golownin's *Captivity in Japan;* Griffis's *The Mikado's Empire;* Harris's *Complete Journal;* Hearn's *Out of the East* and *Kokoro;* Heusken's *Japan Journal;* Hildreth's *Japan As It Was and Is;* Inoue Kiyoshi's *Nihon-no Rekishi* ("A History of Japan"); Keeling's *Guide to Japan;* Kimura Ki and Kimura Shohachi, *This Is Japan;* Koempfer's *Account of Japan;* Lloyd's *Every-Day Japan;* Japan Ministry of the Army's *Meiji Gunji-Shi* ("A History of the Military Affairs of Meiji Era"); Murray's *The Story of Japan;* Nitobé's *Bushido* and *The Intercourse Between the U.S. and Japan;* Okuma's *Fifty Years of New Japan;* Sansom's *Japan: A Short Cultural History;* Stead's *Japan by the Japanese;* Storry's *A History of Modern Japan;* Wada's *American Foreign Policy Towards Japan During the 19th Century;* and Wilson's *Ironclads in Action,* vol. 2. Biographical sources included Bodley, Ono Sanenobu's *Gensui Koshaku Oyama Iwao,* Hamada, Morris, Ogasawara, Lloyd, Togawa Yukio's *Nogi-to Togo* ("Nogi and Togo"). Storry has an excellent account of the activities of the ultranationalistic societies in *The Double Patriots.* Norman's article in the September 1944 issue of *Pacific Affairs* details the creation of the Black Ocean and Black Dragon Societies, and *Kokuruyukai's* (The Black Dragon Society's) *Toa Senkaku Shishi Kiden* ("Biographers of the Loyal Pathfinders of East Asia") gives an inside Japanese account. Tani in Japanese and Okamoto in English provide excellent accounts of the working of the Japanese oligarchy. The best account of the *zaibatsu's* origins is in Sumiya's *Dai-Nippon-Teikoku-no Shiren* ("Trials and Tribulations of the Great Japanese Empire") published by Chuo-Koron-Sha. Chamberlain's *Things Japanese* is also useful.

Education in the New Japan, published by General Headquarters, Supreme Commander for the Allied Powers, Civil Information and Education Section, Education Division, in 1948 provides a good account of the historical background of Japanese education. The various Japanese-language histories of Japan give by far the most detailed accounts of the problems of Japanese adjustment after the arrival of Westerners.

23 Japan's progress: *The Times,* Financial and Commercial Supplement, September 4, 1905

24–26 Westernization: *This Is Japan,* 1959, 197–199; 1964, 182–184;

Hearn, *Out of the East,* 144–149;

Japan Quarterly, July–September 1960, 295–301;

Morris, 34–36

26–28 Christian persecutions: Murray, 248–268;

Hildreth, Chapters VIII, XVII, XXIII, XXIV;

Murdoch, vol. 2, 236 *et seq.*

Brinkley, 540–549;

Griffis, 247 263;

B. H. Chamberlain (1891), 298–302;

Inoue, *Nihon-no Rekishi,* (Yomiuri series) vol. 7, 142;

Japan Quarterly, January–March 1959, 13–22, and July–September 1960, 288–294

28–35 Perry: Hildreth, 513–523; Murray, 309 *et seq.;* and Morison, 318–326

28–34 American policy: Wada, 63–164

30–34 Putiatin: Quested 1–55

34 Threat to Townsend Harris: Harris, 509–512

35 Richardson affair: Lloyd, 362; Murray, 342–345

37 hara-kiri: Redesdale, 115, 281–285

CHAPTER 3.
Russia, the Boiling Pot

There is a vast literature on Russia during the period under consideration and the bibliography lists only the books on which we have drawn. For the earlier period, there is nothing more illuminating than de Custine's *The Journey of Marquis de Custine*. Seton-Watson's *The Decline of Imperial Russia* and *The Russian Empire, 1801–1917*, are standard reference works. Bérard's *The Russian Empire and Czarism*, Ganz's *Land of Riddles*, Hamilton's *Vanished Pomps of Yesterday*, Wellesley's *With the Russians in Peace and War*, and Wolfe's *Three Who Made a Revolution* provided many insights. For more intimate observations of the court of Nicholas II and the attitudes of the Tsar and his associates we relied on Almedingen's *The Empress Alexandra*, Bing's *The Letters of Tsar Nicholas and Empress Marie*, Levine's *The Kaiser's Letters to the Tsar*, Ookhtomsky's *Travels in the East of His Majesty Tsar Nicholas II*, Essad-Bey's *Nicholas II*, Massie's *Nicholas and Alexandra*, *Archives Secrètes de l'Empereur Nicholas II*, Radziwill's *Nicholas II: The Last of the Tsars*, and Vorres' *The Last Grand Duchess*. In this chapter, and in others, we have also drawn heavily on Witte's *Memoirs*. The English translation of Romanov's *Russia in Manchuria (1892–1906)*, though extremely difficult to read, was invaluable. Hingley's *The Russian Secret Police*, Cowles's *The Russian Dagger*, Nicolaievsky's *Aseff: The Russian Judas*, and Avrich's *The Russian Anarchists* shed important light on the revolutionaries and the attempts of the secret police to cope with them.

57 Guards' rebellion: de Custine, 122
58 "Things are moving . . . :" Payne, *Marx*, 361
59 "We are consuming our capital . . .": Wolfe, 58
61 "Long Live the Russian Emperor": Bausman, 140–141
61 Tolstoi: *ibid.*, 140–141
62 Alexander Ulyanov: Wolfe, 60–65
65 Bitter hatred for Japan: Radziwill, 132
66 "Poor, unhappy Emperor . . .": Witte, 181
68 Witte's conversation with Li Hung-chang: Witte, 182
69 "merely possessed of an unreasoned desire . . .": Witte, 83

69 "would be well to consider . . .": Romanov, 52
69 "for Russia a year-round . . .": Romanov, 53
69 "join in any step": Romanov, 53
69–70 Witte's speech: Romanov, 54
70–71 Council decisions: Witte, 84
74 "An Englishman is a *Zhid*": Witte, 189
75–76 Skobolev and Kuropatkin: Sven Hedin, *The Times*, November 1, 1904
79–80 Marie's letter and Nicholas's reply: NTM, 162–166
80 Evno Azev: Essad-Bey, 115; Hingley, 90–92

CHAPTER 4.
Korea, the Cockpit

Allen's *Korea, Fact and Fancy;* Bishop's *Korea and Her Neighbors;* Brinkley's *A History of the Japanese People;* Conroy's *The Seizure of Korea, 1868–1910;* Griffis' *The Mikado's Empire;* Hulbert's *History of Korea* and *The Passing of Korea;* Ladd's

In Korea With Marquis Ito; Lensen's *Korea and Manchuria Between Russia and Japan, 1895–1904,* and *The Russian Push Toward Japan;* McCune's *Korea's Heritage;* McKenzie's *The Tragedy of Korea,* and *Korea's Fight for Freedom;* Romanov; and Stead's *Japan by the Japanese* were the principal sources for this chapter.

85 "The earth is the earth's earth . . .": Griffis, 242

85 Hideyoshi's invasion: Hulbert, *History of Korea,* vol. 1, 350

86 Deaths attributed to Queen Min: Ladd, 284

87–88 "In great hurry . . .": Stead, 183

90 Lucius Foote: *ibid.,* 193

92 Tong Haks: Hulbert, *History of Korea,* vol. 2, 203–204, 248, 276; also Norman, "The Genyosha," *Pacific Affairs,* September 3, 1944, 281–282; McKenzie, *Korea's Fight For Freedom,* 44–46

93n Dwarf myths: Hahn, 193

94 "we know the extreme of her wickedness . . .": McKenzie, *ibid.,* 56–57

97 Bryner concession: Romanov 130–131, 268–269, and Witte 116–117

97 Yalu company charter: Romanov, 269

97 Yalu company charter: Romanov, 269

97 "We suffer not . . .": Romanov, 273

97n Bryner: Letter from Catherine Brynner to authors.

CHAPTER 5.
Carving Up China

A vital book on the historical associations between Russia and China is Quested's *The Expansion of Russia in East Asia, 1857–1860,* an enlargement and revision of her doctoral thesis. Though ideology briefly papered over the deep national differences that grew out of this period, much of the recent past history of the Sino-Soviet split has its origins in the events covered by this book. Lattimore's *Manchuria: Cradle of Conflict* and Fairbank's *The United States and China* (72–82) explain the complicated relationship between China and Manchuria, both ruled by the Manchus, who sought to keep the Chinese out of Manchuria by building a ditch several hundred miles long beyond which no immigrant could pass. Bland and Backhouse's *Annals and Memoirs of the Court of Peking* and *China Under the Empress Dowager;* Borst-Smith's *Mandarin and Missionary in Cathay;* Broomhall's *The Chinese Empire;* Fleming's *The Siege at Peking;* the two lives of General Gordon, one written by Wortham and the other anonymously; Hahn's *China Only Yesterday;* Latourette's *History of Modern China;* Pearl's *Morrison of Peking;* Sun Yat-sen's *Memoirs of a Chinese Revolutionary;* Teng and Fairbank's *China's Response to the West;* and Varè's *The Last of the Empresses* provide much color and background. For the Russian version of events, we drew principally on Kuropatkin's *The Russian Army and the Japanese War,* Romanov, and Witte. For the Japanese version, we relied mainly on Tani.

100 "We have admitted you . . .": Romanov, 125

105 Ignatiev's role in Peking: Quested, 240–258

105 "It covered an area of many miles . . .": *Life of General Gordon,* 26; also Wortham, 54

CHAPTER 6.
The Wedding of the Moon
and the Mud Turtle

Pooley's *The Secret Memoirs of Count Tadasu Hayashi* is the best primary source on the Anglo-Japanese Alliance. Nish's *The Anglo-Japanese Alliance: The Di- plomacy of Two Island Empires, 1894–1907,* complements this very well. At the Tokyo end, Tani provides his usual insights into Japanese official attitudes and decisions. Pascal's *The Growth of Modern Germany* and Taylor's *The Course of German History* provide first-class German background. Brogan's *The Development of Modern France, 1870–1939,* is a standard work on France. On the relationship between the powers we found Bausman's *Let France Explain,* Bemis's *A Diplomatic History of the United States,* Dennett's *Roosevelt and the Russo-Japanese War,* and White's *The Diplomacy of the Russo-Japanese War* most useful.

133 "However disagreeable . . .":
NTM, 128
133 "He was as rude . . .": Massie, 82
133–134 "It is certain . . .": Witte, 105
135 "A war in which we were not actively concerned . . .": White, 116

136 "benevolent neutrality": Dennett,
27
136 "promptly side with Japan": Dennett, 2, Roosevelt letter to Spring-
Rice dated July 24, 1905

CHAPTER 7.

The End of the Mangy Triumvirate

This chapter leads us into conflict with some of our otherwise most valued sources.
The modern view is that the role of Bezobrazov and his clique played only a fairly
minor part in the events that finally led to war. On the evidence available, it seems
that the earlier view of the importance of Bezobrazov, and especially of Abaza, is
nearer the truth. In his diary (pp. 13–14), J. J. Korostovetz says he was casually
a witness to a conversation between Witte and Lamsdorf which he believed took
place in October 1903 at a dinner at Lamsdorf's house. He quotes Lamsdorf as
saying that the Tsar listened only to Bezobrazov, who had persuaded the Tsar of
the necessity for a strategic screen on the Yalu River. As late as December, when
Bezobrazov was already ill, or at least sick at heart with the reverses suffered by the
lumber company on the Yalu, Lamsdorf told Kuropatkin: "They are pushing the
Emperor toward war even from the German side. William keeps on asking whether
Bezobrazov is still well, for he is their reliable ally." (Kuropatkin diary entry
December 24, 1903, *Krasny Arkhiv*, 2, 94.) Evaluating the drift toward war in his
lectures more than twenty years later, Tani saw confusion on both the Russian and
Japanese sides, but ascribed a large share of the blame to Abaza.

The Russian Ministry of Ways and Communication and *Blackwood's Magazine*
of January 1897 give the best account we have found of the building of the Trans-
Siberian Railway, but much other material is contained in BOHRJW and
GOARJW. Romanov and Witte provide detailed, but sometimes conflicting, evi-
dence of the Russians' "new course" that led to war. White's *Diplomacy of the
Russo-Japanese War* is a splendid secondary source.

138 "So far as I have read . . .": Kuropatkin, vol. 1, 150
138–139 Trans-Siberian Railway:
*Guide to the Great Siberian
Railway,* and *Blackwood's
Magazine,* January 1897
139–140 "When the road for sledges is
not yet": GOARJW, vol. 1,
53–54
140 "the feeling of gratitude cherished . . .": Romanov, 71
140–141 Badmaev: Witte, 86; Romanov, 46–48
141 "a railroad to Peking": Witte,
86

141 "who was entirely ignorant": See
Witte, 82 and 87
142 "My God, I forgot to tell my
secretary": Witte, 93
142 "For his signature to the treaty as
such . . .": Romanov, 84
144 "Japanese government, in order
to correct . . .": Tani, Chapter 1,
Section 2
144 "unconditionally and forever
lost . . .": Romanov, 294
144 "The report failed to impress His
Majesty . . .": Witte, 118
145 "In all the discussions . . .": Witte,
119

146 Madridov: See White, 43
146 Kishinev: Avrich, 16–17, Frumkin, 31–33
147 new course: Romanov, 284
147 Troops to Yalu: Kuropatkin, vol.
1, 167 et seq.
147–148 Strategy conference, Witte,
120; Romanov, 285–286
148 Russian Lumber Company float:
See White, 62–63; Kokovtsov,
20–23

149–150 Reports from China: Tani,
Chapter 1, Section 3, 36–37
150–151 Kuropatkin's visit to Japan;
Kuropatkin, vol. 1, 216–222
152 "I do not dare conceal . . .": Witte,
121; Radziwill, 136
152 Vital telegram: White 68, citing
Abaza to Bezobrazov, June 24,
1903; also Malozemoff, 179–186
and 208 et seq.

CHAPTER 8.

And So to War

Basic biographical material about Oyama is contained in Ono's *Gensui Koshaku
Oyama Iwao* ("Field Marshal Prince Oyama Iwao"). Kodama's career is given in
Yomiuri's *Jinbutsu: Nihon-no Rekishi* ("Personalities: History of Japan"). Tani's
lectures reported Japanese war preparations and Kuropatkin's visit to Japan. Kuropatkin's *The Russian Army and the Japanese War* gave his own version of his visit
to Japan and of general Russian lack of awareness of Japanese capabilities. Akashi's
own document *Rakka Ryusui* ("Fallen Blossoms—Flowing Water") and Tani described his intelligence gathering activities in St. Petersburg on the eve of the war.

157 "The question of peace and war in
the Far East": Scott to Lansdowne, BFO No. 244, Very Confidential, St. Petersburg, August
20, 1903
158 "The Chinese troops are drilling
day and night": WNL, 99–101
159 Bezobrazov's reports: Tani,
Chapter 1, Section 2, 31–34
160 Abaza's intrigues: Tani, Chapter
1, Section 2, 33
160 Akashi's activities: Akashi,
Rakka Ryusui; Tani, 255–277
161 Japanese intelligence in Manchuria: Tani, Chapter 7, Section 2,
251–253
168 "How are things going": *Chuo-
Koron-Sha, Dai-Nippon-Teikoku-
no Shiren* ("Trials and Tribulations of the Great Japanese
Empire"), quoting *Koya-no Hana*
("Flowers of the Wild Plains"),
276–277; Tani, 288–289
171 "Yes": Satow diary entry April

12, 1907, quoted in Lensen, *Korea
and Manchuria Between Russia
and Japan*
171 Aoki and Yuan: Tani, Chapter 7,
Section 2, especially 279; also
Chapter 20, 669 et seq.
173 "I can do nothing . . .": Kurino to
Komura, No. 70, January 30,
1904, JFO
174 Kuropatkin's appreciation:
BOHRJW, vol 3, Appendix 5
175 "if Russia is left alone . . .": From
a talk given at the general meeting
of the officers' group of the Azabu
and Hongo Regimental Districts,
March 25, 1923, by Viscount
Kaneko Kentaro, cited by Tani,
Chapter 1, Section 3, 44–48
175 "Finally, we are going to fight
Russia . . .": Togawa, *Nogi-to
Togo,* 296
175–176 "It is suicidal folly": Christie,
165

CHAPTER 9.
One Hundred Victories
in One Hundred Battles

JONH and BOHRJW have been used as the basis for the account of the attack on the Russian ships at Chemulpo. Eyewitness accounts come from various sources, notably Sasebo's *Nichi-Ro Kaisen-Ki* ("The Chronicles of the Japano-Russian Sea Battles"); *Nihon-no Hyakunen* ("One Hundred Years of Japan"), vol. 7, *Meiji-no Eiko* ("Glory of Meiji") and *The Times*. Other eyewitness accounts come from Togo Kichitaro, captain of the battleship *Asahi*, and Pakenham, who was on board the same ship as a British observer. The log of *H.M.S. Talbot* was valuable, as were reports from Hulbert in *Korea Review* and Dunn in *Collier's* pictorial history of the war, both on shore when the battle took place. We have also called on Togawa, Morris's *Makers of Japan*, Ogasawara's *Life of Admiral Togo*, Bodley's *Admiral Togo: The Authorized Life*, and books by Lloyd, McKenzie, Thiess, Unger, and with caution, the anonymous writer of *Before Port Arthur in a Destroyer*.

184 Standing Squadron dissolved: JONH, vol. 1, 3
185 "They will collect . . ." : *ibid.*, 10
186 "The time of . . .": *ibid.*, 13
186 "It has been decided . . .": *ibid.*, 14
189–190 First shot: *ibid.*, 57, 60, Appendix: 536

194 "This would stir up trouble . . .": JONH, vol. 1, 71
194 ". . . a sort of suicidal . . .": *The Times*, March 17, 1904;
195 Togo's report, February 10, 1904, Kinai, vol. 1

CHAPTER 10.
"A Place of Honor
in the Naval Annals"

Port Arthur had few historians. Three foreign war correspondents were in Port Arthur when hostilities began and others based at Cheefoo came in almost daily before the war. Frederick McCormick wrote that he and other newspaper men were regarded by the Russians before hostilities began as "vultures hovering over prospective carrion." Those who stayed on during the siege were often regarded as spies, censorship was strict, and stories more often than not were smuggled out of the town. We have used in this chapter Nojine, McCormick, Greener, Brindle, and McKenzie. Otherwise we have relied heavily on JONH and BOHRJW, newspaper reports that managed to reach the outside world, and Steer aboard the cruiser Novik. Sasebo's *Nichi-Ro Kaisen-Ki* ("The Chronicles of the Japano-Russian Sea Battles"), Dennett's *Roosevelt and the Russo-Japanese War* and Matsushita's *Meiji-no Guntai* ("The Army of Meiji"), *Nihon-no Hyakunen* ("One Hundred Years of Japan"), vol. 7, *Meiji-no Eiko* ("Glory of Meiji"), and Inoue's *Nihon-no Rekishi* ("A History of Japan"), *Yomiuri* edition, provided valuable material in this and other chapters.

198 "I consider . . .": JONH, vol. 1, 94
200 "The entire . . .": Steer, 17

201 Damage to Japanese ships: JONH, vol. 1, 533–535

203–204 no declaration: Asakawa, citing Japanese Government report in press of March 3, 1904, 351–362; *The Times*, February 10, 1904; *New York Times*, April 13, 1904

203 Illegal landing: Matsushita *Meiji-no Guntai* ("The Army of Meiji"), 145

204–205 re Kaneko: Matsuoka, 24–26

205 "I have done all . . .": Roosevelt: Dennett, 160–161

205 Roosevelt, concern over Philippines: *ibid.*, 162

205 "No human beings . . .": *ibid.*, 119

205 "only walks like a man": *ibid.*, 119

206 "I don't know . . .": Okamoto, 95

206 Japanese declaration: Asakawa, 346–348

207 "They attack us . . .": *The Contemporary Review*, August, 1904, 290–291

209 Russian declaration: *The Times*, February 11, 1904; Suyematsu, 92

209 "We have heard . . .": BOHRJW, 398; JONH, vol. 1, 102–103

CHAPTER 11.
Practical Joke

Details of Port Arthur's defenses were found in BOHRJW, reports from British observers, and Norregaard, David James, Greener, Ashmead-Bartlett, McCormick, and Nojine. Tani supplied reports of poor Japanese intelligence at Port Arthur. Details of the blocking expedition are mainly from JONH and the reports of captains of the blockships. Sasebo's *Nichi-Ro Kaisen-Ki* ("Chronicles of Japano-Russian Sea Battles"), Togawa, Ishimitsu Makiyo, and Kurita Tomitaro, who took part in blocking expeditions, give personal details. Semenov and Steer, who were aboard Russian ships, are used for eyewitness accounts. Sources on *bushido* include Nitobé's *Bushido: The Soul of Japan*, Benedict, Sansom, and Maraini's *Meeting with Japan*. Maraini agrees with other writers that the name *bushido* appears to be modern but says even if this is true its basis is ancient. Maraini's fascinating book on the Japanese character quotes Chamberlain's *Things Japanese* (1939) as saying "the very word appears in no dictionary, native or foreign, before the year 1900." Our copies of *Things Japanese* were published in 1891 and 1905. The earlier edition makes no mention of *bushido* and the later edition scoffs at Nitobé's *Soul of Japan* as being written by a Japanese educated abroad "who has taken not mediaeval Europe, but modern America as his standard of comparison with feudal Japan." Perhaps Benedict (who had never been to Japan) and Maraini best explain *bushido* and its connections with *giri* ("moral obligations") and *chugi* ("loyalty").

213 Order to sink ships: JONH, vol. 1, 30

214 Bishop Montgomery: *Illustrated London News*, June 4, 1904

215 "It is a pity . . .": JONH, vol. 1, 12

215–216 *bushido:* Nitobé, *The Soul of Japan*; Benedict, 175–176 and chart 116; Holtom: 103–109; Maraini, 273–277

220–221 Port Arthur planning: Tani, Chapter 6, 196 *et seq.*

CHAPTER 12.
Little Grandfather Arrives

Details about Makarov are drawn from JONH, vol. 1, Togo Kichitaro's *The Naval Battles of the Russo-Japanese War,* Wilson's *Ironclads in Action,* vol. 1, and Woodward. For this chapter we also used Kurita Tomitaro's *Recollections of Lushun Blockade* and Sasebo's *Nichi-Ro Kaisen-Ki* ("Chronicles of the Japano-Russian Sea Battles"). Semenov, who had worked with Makarov in Russia, provides penetrating insights into his character. An account of the second attempt to block Port Arthur harbor is found in JONH, vol. 1, and BOHRJW. Sources on Hirose include Tani, Sumiya's *Dai-Nippon-Teikoku-no Shiren* ("Trials and Tribulations of the Great Japanese Empire") in the *Chuo-Koron-Sha* series, Ishimitsu Makiyo's *Bokyo-no Uta* ("Songs of Nostalgia"), and Togawa's *Nogi-to Togo* ("Nogi and Togo"), citing Jirocho Shimazu, a famous swordsman of the Emperor's court.

222 Makarov in Turkish war: H. W. Wilson, vol. 1, 293 *et seq.;* Woodward, 113–116, 126; Togo Kichitaro, 21

223 "Often there was no . . ." Semenov, *Rasplata,* 2

225 "Experience up to . . .": JONH, vol. 1, 167

226 boarding party: JONH, vol. 1, 173–174; and *Before Port Arthur in a Destroyer,* 68–74

228 Makarov's moves to improve the Russian fleet: BOHRJW, vol. 1, 85; Semenov, *Rasplata,* 81 *et seq.;* JONH, vol. 1, 196–197

229 Woodward, 129, 163; B. Falk, *Bouquets for Fleet Street,* 102

231 "A good way to find out . . .": Togawa, *Nogi-to Togo,* 322–323

232n "gunshin": Togo reported to the Emperor that Hirose was not only a model warrior in peacetime but in his last hours had proved himself a model "imperishable for ten thousand years."

CHAPTER 13.
. . . And Fights

Makarov and Togo had both studied Mahan's *The Influence of Sea Power Upon History,* in which he wrote: "Granting the meeting of two fleets which represent practically the whole present strength of their two nations, if one of them be destroyed, while the other remains fit for action, there will be much less hope now than formerly that the vanquished can restore his navy for that war; and the result will be disastrous just in proportion to the dependence of the nation upon her sea power" (47). Neither admiral overlooked Mahan's warning. JONH, vol. 1, details Togo's ruse to draw out the Russian fleet, while making sure that his own limited supply of ships did not suffer. Makarov's task was even greater. He was cut off from the Vladivostok squadron and the Baltic fleet and the ships and men under his command were both rusty after a long period of inaction and bad leadership. Semenov's *Rasplata* and BOHRJW show the strenuous attempts he made to overcome the "risk nothing" policy, without unnecessarily endangering his fleet. Semenov and Steer give graphic eyewitness reports of the sinking of the *Petropavlovsk* and the death of their "master." Pakenham's reports to the Admiralty would make a short book on this disaster and its importance to the Japanese.

[591]

CHAPTER 14.

On to the Yalu

Russian defeats and the Japanese determination to wrap the war in secrecy did not make it easy for the world to follow the land battles. Although both armies permitted large numbers of foreign military observers and correspondents to accompany the forces, they all fretted constantly under the restrictions placed on their movements. In the early days of the war, neither observers nor correspondents were permitted to accompany the troops in action, and since official reports were either inadequate or deliberately misleading there was an early credibility gap. There were some first-class reporters with Kuroki's First Army, however. General Hamilton's reports, reports from other British officers in the field, and Hamilton's Staff Officer's Scrap Book, though written with an eye to Japanese sensitivities, are good guides to the Yalu and ensuing battles. David Fraser, when he escaped from his tedious radio duties with *The Times* at Cheefoo, proved to have a better eye for military detail than his bureau chief, Lionel James. Colonel Cordonnier's *The Japanese in Manchuria* brought French military experience to bear on the war. Ross's *An Outline of the Russo-Japanese War* and Cowen's *The Russo-Japanese War, From the Outbreak of Hostilities to the Battle of Liaoyang* are also useful. BOHRJW and GOARJW, especially the former, are standard references. Kinai's *The Russo-Japanese War* contains the official Japanese reports of this and other battles. Color, often heavily tinged with Japanese propaganda, is provided in the several volumes of *The Russo-Japanese War* produced by the Kinkodo Publishing Company.

261 "His Majesty has made me . . .": Cordonnier, vol. 1, 110

262 "the very trees . . .": General Hamilton, vol. 1, 109

262 "Thus in an easy triumph . . .": General Hamilton, vol. 1, 110

262 "unbearable . . .": BOHRJW, vol. 1, 122

263 Kashtalinski's message: Cordonnier, vol. 1, 116

268 Japanese and Russian losses: BOHRJW, vol. 1, 443, 444

CHAPTER 15.
Russia's Day

To Russia the loss of a battleship mattered less than the death of Makarov. To Japan the loss of two-thirds of the country's main fighting strength was even more disastrous. Throughout the war, as Pakenham reported, the Japanese admiral fought "with a rope around his neck." He was expected to win battles without losing ships. Hasegawa, who was on Yashima when the battleship went down, told us that the lower ratings felt that Japan was finished. Only Togo's calmness encouraged them. Pakenham agreed. As the battleship *Asahi*'s representative he visited Togo on *Mikasa* and reported the "anguish of mind" of the Japanese admiral. Pakenham denied that he ever advised Togo but it is possible that on this occasion the man who was to become Britain's Fourth Sea Lord gave more than condolences to the Japanese Commander-in-Chief. Togo may have thought he would be dismissed but he would not have considered committing *seppuku*. To kill himself now would have been a fool's courage. "It is true courage to live when it is right to live, and to die only when it is right to die," the laws of *bushido* taught.

Sources for this chapter include Tani, *Nihon-no Hyakunen* ("One Hundred Years of Japan") and Nichi-nichi's *Nichi-Ro Dai-Kaisen-o Kataru* ("Talking of the Japano-Russian Great Sea Battles"), BOHRJW, JONH, Togawa, Ogasawara, Honma Tsuneji's *Ah, Hitachi Maru!*, and Pakenham's long and detailed reports to the Admiralty.

271 Criticism of bombarding of Port Arthur: Pakenham, ADM. 1/7840—3244

272 *Kinshu Maru* sunk: BOHRJW, vol. 1, 98

274ns (1) JONH, vol. 1, 261–262, (2) *seppuku,* variation of hara-kiri: Benedict, 317

275 "none of the ships . . . (closer) . . .": JONH, vol. 1, 267

278 "I am no leader . . .": Semenov, *Rasplata,* 151

283 Decision to hide loss of *Yashima:* JONH, vol. 1, 308–310; Pakenham's report ADM 1/7840, May 15 and 19, 1904

284 Suspicion of submarine use: JONH, vol. 1, 379; Togo's telegram, May 16, 1904, Kinai, vol. 1, 48

284 Search for steamer carrying gold: Woodward, 138

CHAPTER 16.
Nanshan

Colonel Tretyakov's own account of this battle is an invaluable supplement to reports by Colonel Haldane in RBO. Cordonnier, Ross, Cowen, BOHRJW, and

Nojine deal with the battle and Tani discusses Japanese intelligence agents among the Chinese workers.

296 Japanese losses: BOHRJW, vol. 1, 448

298 "You are a wretched, undisci-

plined corps of traitors . . .": Nojine, 84

CHAPTER 17.
The Siege Begins

Most of the war correspondents who covered Nogi's Third Army outside Port Arthur came prepared to describe the courage of the "little Japs." They were treated generously at Nogi's headquarters. They could go everywhere and see everything. But they were not permitted to send news to the outside world, unless it was good news. At this time all news for the Japanese was bad news. Sources on the fighting outside Port Arthur include Ashmead-Bartlett, McCormick, W. R. Smith, Norregaard and Barry, who put their experiences into books after the war.

Our sources on Nogi are numerous. In Japanese, we drew especially on Tani, Togawa, and Matsushita Yoshio. Books in English include Washburn's Nogi, Scherer's *Three Meiji Leaders,* Morris, Benedict, and B. H. Chamberlain.

Background to the chapter comes also from Nojine, BOHRJW, JONH, vol. 1, and Greener. Our sole participant eye-witness account of the land battle in this chapter is from Sakurai's *Human Bullets.* At sea we draw on Steer and Semenov.

300 Nogi's attempt to kill himself in 1877: Matsushita Yoshio, *Nogi Maresuke,* 28; "I will open the seat . . .": Nitobé, *Bushido,* 120

303 "Say, Shiki . . .": Talk by Lieutenant-General Shiki Moriharu, "Thoughts of One Who Served on the Frontline in the Lushun-encircling force," Tani, 239

303 "You will remain commandant": Nojine, 86

304 Togo's knowledge of fitting up of Baltic Fleet: JONH, vol. 1, 287

308 June 23 sortie and Pakenham's defense of Togo: "Can it be denied," Admiralty Report 7840, 14

308 "they will destroy the ships . . .": citing Makino, JONH, vol. 1, 419

309 Tsar's message to Alexeiev re fleet: BOHRJW, vol. 1, 302–303

309–310 Vitgeft: "The squadron cannot go out . . .": *ibid.,* 302, and Alexeiev's reply: "I again reiterate . . .": *ibid.* (published in *"Russkaya Starina"*)

CHAPTER 18.
Te-li-ssu and the Motien Pass

By the time the battle for Te-li-ssu was fought, the fundamental strategic differences between Alexeiev, who wanted to hold Port Arthur at all costs, and Kuropatkin, who would have preferred to have concentrated on an army for offensive operations at Harbin, was no longer a secret, and both official observers and correspondents in the field and at St. Petersburg were reporting on it. Fresh observers had arrived with the Russians, one notable addition being that of Lord Brooke for Reuter's, who was initially sympathetic, arguing that Stackelberg's cow was necessary to provide milk, since he was in ill health, and that the presence of his wife and a maidservant in no way inconvenienced operations.

Disenchantment with the Russian performance set in gradually, but Brooke remained an excellent and dispassionate observer of the scene. Cordonnier notes that Stackelberg's Order 194, which was issued on June 14, was received by none of his subordinate commanders and, since communications improved little during the battle, Stackelberg was largely in ignorance of its developments. Haldane in BFO, Ross, and GOARJW add useful interpretative reports to the basic accounts in BOHRJW. David Fraser, Palmer, and Ian Hamilton were on hand for the battle of the Motien Pass.

312 Council of war, *The Times*, June 2, 1904, quoting St. Petersburg dispatch for Paris Matin

312 Kuropatkin's and Alexeiev's telegrams: Kuropatkin, vol. II, 217

316 Russian and Japanese losses: BOHRJW, vol. 1, 455–456

317 Doctors: *The Times*, March 11, 1904

317 "selfish interests . . .": *The Times*, March 28, 1904

318 "too apparent not to be noticed": *The Times*, June 17, 1904

321 "Destruction was as simple . . .": Palmer, *With Kuroki in Manchuria*, 169–170

322 "mounted bandits . . .": Tani, Chapter 7; Seaman's *From Tokyo Through Manchuria with the Japanese*, 161; RBO, vol. 1, 234

CHAPTER 19
The Yellow Sea

The battle of the Yellow Sea has been described as a stokers' battle. After five anxious hours the stokers on both sides took over, shoveling coal into the furnaces in appalling heat and under appalling conditions. Togo, as always, believed that the gods were on his side, and in this battle they were. However, he was overcautious, conscious of the fact that he could not afford to lose more ships. When at length he decided to chase the Russians darkness was falling, and in those days night fighting was unknown. The three lucky hits on the Russian flagship, Tsarevitch, were a turning point of the war. BOHRJW provided background to the battle which has been called the fastest sea battle ever fought.

For eye-witness accounts on the Japanese side we drew on the two British naval observers, Pakenham (in *Asahi*) and Jackson (in *Asama*), JONH, vol. 2, and reports contained in it from officers on board the Japanese ships. Togo's own reports of the battle in JONH, the Official Japanese Reports (Kinai) and interviews with Hasegawa who was rangefinder on *Mikasa* were valuable. Sixty-six years after the battle Hasegawa still remembered the excitement of the fight and his disappointment when the Russian ships escaped. We drew heavily on Russians who took part in the battle, including Steer, Semenov, and survivors from other Russian ships. Seaman's *From Tokyo Through Manchuria* with the Japanese gives insight into the capture of *Ryeshitelni* at Cheefoo.

Kamimura's reports, Tani, Nichi-nichi's *Nichi-Ro Dai-Kaisen-o Kataru* and *The Times*' correspondent at Cheefoo were used for the account of the destruction of the ships of the Russian Vladivostok Squadron.

[595]

325 Vitgeft: "My orders are to go . . .": Nojine, 151

328–329 Russian accurate fire: Pakenham Report to Admiralty, August 11, 1904

329 "Such things as the breakage of an enemy's mast . . .": Report from Captain Oi of the *Kasuga*, August 15, 1904, JONH, vol. 2, 132

334 *Ryeshitelni:* JONH, vol. 2, 201; BOHRJW, vol. 1, 352–353; Seaman, *From Tokyo Through Manchuria with the Japanese,* 174 *et seq.;* Togo's official reports, August 11 and 12, 1904, Kinai, vol. 1, 89–90; *The Times,* August 13, 1904 (interview with captain); Tani, Chapter 20

335 *Rurik* destruction: Vice-Admiral Kamimura's official report, received in Tokyo August 14, 1904, Kinai, vol. 1, 92–94

CHAPTER 20.

The Disastrous Frontal Assault

Details of the defenses outside Port Arthur have been drawn from correspondents and observers with Nogi's Third Army, some of whom had been in the area during and after the Sino-Japanese war. Greener and Nojine provided conditions inside the fortress itself. Tretyakov and Sakurai, the former Japanese intelligence agent, provided eyewitness accounts of these early assaults. Tani, *Chuo-Koron-Sha's Dai-Nippon-Teikoku-no Shiren* ("Trials and Tribulations of the Great Japanese Empire"), and Ikejima's *Rekishi-Yomoyama-Banashi* ("Sundry Talks on History," vol. II), talks by Lieutenant-General Shiki Moriharu, give material on Japanese lack of knowledge of the defenses.

339 "In truth, barren results . . .": Mahan, *The Influence of Sea Power upon History* (footnote 4)

341 "It is not surprising . . .": Hutchison Report Adm. 1/7775, October 27, 1904

344 Truce offered by Japanese: Nojine, 158–162; JONH, vol. 2, 202

345 "The condition of the fortress . . ." (Nogi): Tani, Chapter 6

346 Western-style house as fort: Tani, Chapter 6

347 "I saw that . . .": Tretyakov, 131–132

349 Smirnov's defense of Gorbatovski: Nojine, 171

350 Japanese mutineers: Smith, W. R., 209

CHAPTER 21.

Liaoyang

The Russians had relaxed their restrictions on the movements of observers by the time of the battle of Liaoyang and McCormick and Brooke were among those to give firsthand reports of the fighting. Hamilton and Palmer were with Kuroki, who was again to play a vital part in the battle, repeating his tactical right hook that proved so successful on the Yalu. Kuropatkin failed to concede that the battle resulted in his defeat and wrote a strong defense of his generalship, coupled with a sweeping denunciation of many of his subordinates. Ross, Bird, Cordonnier, and Haldane add insights to the work of BOHRJW, GOARJW, and Japanese official reports.

353 Azev-Plehve: Hingley, 92

353–354 Kuropatkin's message to Tsar: Kuropatkin, vol. II, 227

355 Armed quickly: Tani, *Activities of Special Task Personnel and truth about the use of mounted banditry*, Chapter 4, Section 3

363 Maps: RBO, vol. 2, 207

364 Ishimitsu Makiyo: Quoted in *Bokyo-no Uta* ("Songs of Nostalgia")

366 Disposition No. 3: Cordonnier, vol. 2, 300; BOHRJW, Appendix 5, vol. 2, 714

372 "Most unfortunate": BOHRJW, vol. 2, 152

373 Manju Yama: General Hamilton, vol. 2, 127

373 Russian and Japanese losses: BOHRJW, vol. 2, 721 and 723

CHAPTER 22.

Nogi Fails Again

For the first time the Japanese and the Russians began to realize the importance of 203 Meter Hill. Japanese sources come mainly from Tani. The correspondents waiting for news fit to send to their newspapers watched from vantage points the frenzied Japanese attacks on the forts. One reporter, Ashmead-Bartlett, wrote that he felt like a kind-hearted Roman emperor "gazing from his box on a gladiatorial show." Eyewitness and background reports come from Tretyakov, Nojine, BOHRJW, and military observers.

374 "A fresh wave . . .": Nojine, 184

376–377 "Everyone here knows me . . .": Nojine, 174

378 Kodama's first visit to Port Arthur: Japan Ministry of the Army's *Meiji-Tenno Go-Denki-Shiryo* ("Historical Materials for the Biography of Emperor Meiji"), 1425

378–379 "Why are heavy guns . . . ?": Nojine, 243

CHAPTER 23

Sha-Ho

A new, highly critical observer of the Russian war scene arrived soon after the battle of Liaoyang. He was Dr. Vikenti Vikentivitch Smidovitch, who wrote under the pseudonym of Veresaev. He quickly observed the poor morale of the troops and the high incidence of self-inflicted wounds. Colonel Valery Harvard, an American Army observer, was no less critical, as was Dugald Christie, longtime medical missionary in Mukden. The Russian Finance Minister Kokovtsov, who detested Witte and disliked Kuropatkin, added his bitter comments. BOHRJW gives the best account of the battle, but we also made extensive use of the supplementary sources drawn on during the battle of Liaoyang, including Hamilton, whose stay in the war theater was now drawing to a close.

384 "mad debauch": Veresaev, 64

384 "Moderately": General Hamilton, vol. 2, 143

384–385 "My heart is sick . . .": McCormick, vol. 2, 184

385 "In all these combats . . .": Cordonnier, vol. 2, 315; see

also Kuropatkin, vol. I, 300

385 "According to generally accepted terminology . . .": Cordonnier, vol. 2, 314; BOHRJW, vol. 2, 177

385 "To the question I put to him . . .": Ross, vol. 1, 455

386 Self-inflicted wounds: Veresaev, 316

387 Ezerski: Veresaev, 316

387 "People were killed . . .": Christie, 189–190

387–388 Cossacks: McCormick, vol. 1, 266–267

388 Kuropatkin's salary: Kokovtsov, 19

389 Kuropatkin railed: Cordonnier, 315; Kuropatkin, vol. 1, 300

389 "When I left St. Petersburg . . .": RBO, vol. 1, 176

390 A different situation: The Times, September 19, 1904

392–393 Stroke of good fortune: General Hamilton, vol. 2, 175

394 "Five miles to the north . . .": ibid., vol. 2, 184–185

400 Casualties: BOHRJW, vol. 2, 736 and 737

CHAPTER 24.
On The Dogger Bank

The Dogger Bank incident, which almost brought England into the war, was reported throughout the world. Our main sources are BOHRJW, newspaper reports from America, England, Japan, Germany, Russia, and France. Rozhdestvenski's own reports and diaries kept by Semenov, Politovski, Novikov-Priboy, and Klado are used for reactions to the "incident." Russian background is drawn from Massie, Colin Wilson, Kokovtsov, and Bing's The Letters of Tsar Nicholas and Empress Marie. "The Report Upon the Dogger Bank Incident of the International Commission," held in Paris from December 1904 to February 1905, is in Appendix 30, BOHRJW, vol. 3, Maps and Appendices.

404 Conflicting reports on Rozhdestvenski: Woodward, 113–116; Hough, 17–18; Novikov-Priboy, 140

405 "Today at 2 A.M. . . .": Novikov-Priboy, 38

407 "The Admiral of the Atlantic . . .": Pares, 472

409 Klado's efforts to take more ships . . . : Klado, The Russian Navy in the Russo-Japanese War (from articles printed in Novoye Vremya)

413 Reaction to Dogger Bank incident: The Times, October 21, 24, 25, 1904; Cassell's, vol. 3, 284; vol. 4, 290; Semenov, Rasplata, appendix, 479 et seq.

413 "They are very angry . . .": NTM, 178

413–414 Edgar Wallace reports: Cassell's, vol. 4, 302–303, and Colin Wilson, Rasputin and the Fall of the Romanovs, 81

414 Russians would have welcomed war with England: Lord Brooke, An Eye Witness in Manchuria, 238–239

415 Russian reaction: Novoye Vremya, St. Petersburgh, October 28, 1904

415–416 Tsar's message; "In my thoughts . . .": Thiess, 156

416–417 International Commission report: BOHRJW, vol. 3, Appendices and Maps, Appendix 30

416 "It is said that rats . . .": Semenov, Rasplata, Part 2, 303

416–417 Klado: The Times, December 21, 1904, citing Echo de Paris.

417 "Oh, if only we . . .": Semenov, Rasplata, Part 2, 304

CHAPTER 25.
The Long, Long Trail

Men who made the long journey with Rozhdestvenski provide most of the material for this chapter, including the revolutionary Novikov-Priboy on *Orel,* Semenov on the flagship *Suvarov,* and Politovski, chief engineer for the fleet. We relied on BOHRJW Naval Comments, Hough, Thiess, Klado, and the military correspondent of *The Times* for background.

421 Rozhdestvenski Steams Around . . . : Thiess, 158

424–425 "But you are anchored in the bay . . .": Semenov, *Rasplata,* Part 2, 321

425 Message re Durban fishing boats: *ibid.,* 326

425 "203 . . . and what is that . . . ?": *ibid.,* 325

CHAPTER 26.
The Fall of Port Arthur

Ashmead-Bartlett, Norregaard, David James, Barry and W. R. Smith, Japanese correspondents, and military observers all saw the final assaults on Port Arthur and its fall. Tretyakov, official histories Tani, Togawa, Nojine, Numata, Matsushita, and Seppings Wright provided background.

427 Arrival of the heavy guns: Barry, *Century Magazine,* March 1905, 682 *et seq.;* David James, 70–71, Ashmead-Bartlett, 168.

428 Reaction in Japan to slow fall of Port Arthur: Ashmead-Bartlett, 272; David James, 302–303; Numata Takazo, 140–142

428n Women in Russian and Japanese forces: Ashmead-Bartlett, 341–342; Japanese women spies, Nihon-Josei-shi ("History of the Japanese Woman"), vol. 7, 218

429 Emperor's message to Nogi: Numata Takazo, 165–167

429–430 Nakamura and kamikaze attack: Nojine, 240; Ashmead-Bartlett, 301

431 Fock's memorandum re gangrene: Nojine, 227 *et seq.* (dated November 3, 1904)

434 Kodama asks to take over: *Chuo-Koron-Sha,* Sumiya, *Dai-Nippon-Teikoku-no Shiren,* 267

435 "Let them do it once more . . .": *ibid.,* 268

436–437 *Sevastopol's* fight: An account of her last days, by Captain von Essen (translated from *Novoye Vremya,* April 6, 1905); Pakenham's reports, December 13, 1904, April 19, 1905, and May 13, 1905.

CHAPTER 27.
"The Place of Peace"

More than twenty-eight correspondents had waited for the fall of Port Arthur. One was Nakarai Tosui of the *Asahi* who, with the other reporters, could now send the great news to the world. We have also used reports from Ashmead-Bartlett, Barry, David James, Norregaard, and Seppings Wright. The background comes from BOHRJW, Japanese official reports, Nojine, and *The Times* military correspondent.

Japanese sources were most valuable, including Ogasawara, Tani, Sasaki, and Togawa. The capitulation terms are drawn from Appendix F of BOHRJW, vol. 3, Maps and Appendices.

441–442 Surrender: BOHRJW, vol. 3, 692–693; Nojine, 322–335

443 Nicholas' address to his forces: *The Times,* from articles published in January 1905

443 N i c h o l a s : T h e y a r e a l l heroes . . .": Diary, January 4, 1905, cited in Radziwill, 142

443 "I allow . . .": Ashmead-Bartlett, 398

444 "What are we to do with the . . . vases?": Nojine, 333–334

446 Interview with Stoessel at Aden: *The Times,* February 13, 1905 (citing Le Matin)

447 Nogi's official entry into Port Arthur: Ashmead-Bartlett, 408

447 "I, Nogi Maresuke . . .": Ashmead-Bartlett, 419–420

447–448 Casualties at Port Arthur: BOHRJW, vol. 2, Appendices 21 and 22, 750–751

CHAPTER 28.

Sabotage, St. Petersburg, and San-de-pu

In Chapter 20, Tani describes in considerable detail Chinese collaboration with the Japanese, and the activities of the mounted guerrillas operating in the Russians' rear areas. Among the youthful Chinese recruits to the Japanese cause was Wu Pei-fu, who later briefly enjoyed power in Peking. Tani's account of Akashi's activities in Europe is supplemented from Russian and European sources by Futrell's *Northern Underground* and by Possony's *Lenin: The Compulsive Revolutionary.* Seton-Watson's *The Decline of Imperial Russia,* 219–221, Gapon's *The Story of My Life,* Ellison's *History of Russia,* 257 *et seq.,* Kokovtsov's *Out of My Past,* and Lenin's *The Revolution of 1905* describe the events and the impact on the Russian government of Bloody Sunday.

449 Yuan Shih-k'ai: Tani, Chapter 20, 669 *et seq.*

449–450 "We should make it a policy . . .": Tani, Chapter 20, 677–678

450 T r a n s - S i b e r i a n R a i l w a y : BOHRJW, vol. 3, 816

451 *et seq.* Akashi and Zilliacus: Tani, Chapter 7, 260 *et seq.*; Possony, 78–79

451 "Lenin is considered . . .": Komori, vol. 1, 142

452 Azev: Futrell, 69

453 *Cecil* and *Cysne:* Akashi, *Rakka Ryusui;* Futrell, 70

453 *Vperyed:* Possony, 80–81; Tani, Chapter 7

455 "To fire at helpless men . . .": Kokovtsov, 36

456–457 Abazuresu *et seq.:* Tani, Chapter 7; Akashi, *Rakka Ryusui*

459 "If any of you retreat . . .": Veresaev, 285

459 Destruction of property: Christie, 186

CHAPTER 29.
Mukden

Christie, McCullagh, McCormick, Veresaev, and the foreign military observers with the Russian armies awaited Oyama's assault on Mukden and contributed detailed eyewitness accounts to amplify those available from the official histories.

469 "It is impossible to hold the line now . . .": McCormick, vol. 1, 381

470 Chinese Imperial Post: Christie, 178

471 "and containing, among other military necessities . . .": citing Lieutenant R. Ulrich, *The Trial Under Fire of the Russian Army in 1904–5, An Eyewitness Description*, BOHRJW, vol. 3, 415

473 "very little had been done": BOHRJW, vol. 3, 501

474 "The Second Army is not acting energetically . . .": BOHRJW, vol. 3, 511

474 "I am surrounded": Christie, 179; *New York Times*, March 11, 1905

474 "only one way out . . .": BOHRJW, vol. 3, 541; also vol. 3, Maps and Appendices, Appendix 21

475 Kuroki's orders: Report by Lieutenant Colonel C. V. Hume, RBO, vol. 3, 249

476 Yang Chen tung: Tani, Chapter VII

476 haste and urgency: BOHRJW, vol. 3, 631

477 "The torrent of cars . . .": Veresaev, 268–269

478 "The Seventh Regiment . . .": Veresaev, 228–229

478 garbage dump: BOHRJW, vol. 3, 674

CHAPTER 30.
Journey of the Damned

Many books have been written of this momentous journey, including Hough's *The Fleet That Had To Die*, Novikov-Priboy's *Tsushima: Grave of a Floating City*, and Thiess's *The Voyage of Forgotten Men*. All are as graphic as the titles of the books. We have drawn on them for background, using the same sources, including Politovski's *From Libau to Tsushima*; Semenov's *The Battle of Tsushima*, *The Price of Blood*, and *Rasplata*; Rozhdestvenski's fleet orders; BOHRJW; and Klado.

481–482 "if they are so old . . .": Semenov, *Rasplata*, 341

483 Rozhdestvenski's Christmas-day speech: *ibid.*, 343

483 Hellville: Thiess, 214–220; Novikov-Priboy, 79

484 Animals and birds aboard: Thiess, 217–218; Politovski, 168

485 Rozhdestvenski's stroke: Semenov, *Rasplata*, Part 2, 378

488–489 Singapore: *New York Times*, April 9, 1905; *The Times*, April 15, 1905

490 "If I am beaten . . .": *Echo de Paris*, April 15, 1905

491n Cold Storage food: as told to Max Bell by Jack Etlin

492–493 Rozhdestvenski's Order of the Day, "The Japanese possess . . .": BOHRJW, vol. 3, 738–739

493 "We never discussed a plan . . .": Précis of Rear-Admiral Nebogatov's explanatory statement, translated from *Novoye Vremya*, February 23–24, 1906

CHAPTER 31.
The Battle of Shadows

The numerous sources cited in the bibliography were used in this chapter, including observers Pakenham and Jackson aboard Japanese ships and Hutchison, in Tokyo. Pakenham's report to the Admiralty, No. 7, dated June 1, 1905, (written on April 17) was particularly interesting. Copies were sent to the King, the cabinet, the Prince of Wales, and the Prime Minister—endorsed "this is truly excellent." Our eyewitness accounts come from Akiyama Kazutoshi's *(Togo Gensui Hensankai);* Hasegawa; Novikov-Priboy; Politovski; Semenov's *Rasplata* ("The Reckoning"), *The Battle of Tsushima,* and *The Price of Blood;* Togo Kichitaro's *Naval Battles of the Russo-Japanese war;* and witnesses at the trial of Nebogatov and officers of his squadron (reported by Captain Hon. Victor A. Stanley, R.N., Naval Attaché, St. Petersburgh, December 29, 1906). Background is drawn from BOHRJW, Japanese Official Military Reports, vol. 2, Bodly, Busch, Hough, Lloyd, Ogasawara, McCormick, Thiess, Seaman, Rozhdestvenski's orders of the day, letters translated from *Novoye Vremya,* January and February 1906, and Togo's reports.

495 Kamimura lays mines: BOHRJW, vol. 3, 725

495–496 Prediction of Rozhdestvenski's route: BOHRJW, vol. 3, 729, 742; Pakenham, ADM I/7840, June 1, 1905

496 Waters of Tsushima divided into squares: Translation of *Azuma*'s signal log, ADM report, CAB 45/I-5929; and *The Times,* August 22, 1905

499 "The enemy sighted in number 203 . . .": Togo's report published by Imperial Naval Headquarters Staff, ADMI I/7842

500–501 Akiyama's seven stages: *The Times,* August 22, 1905

501 Togo's resolution to meet the enemy at two o'clock: Togo's report of the battle, ADM I/7842

505 Crossing the T: Sasebo's *Nichi-Ro Kaisen-Ki,* Chapters 5 and 6, 467 *et seq.;* Pakenham, ADM I/7840, 3244, April 17, 1905

505 Fisher: Colonel House, diary entry, February 17, 1916, *The Intimate Papers*

506 Napoleon—"a lecherous scoundrel . . .": Pakenham, ADM I/7840, 3244, February 8, 1905,

report 5/05, *Togo, The Admiral of Today,* 3

509–510 "It was the right half . . ." (Pakenham): ADM report, June 1905

513 Captain Bacon re torpedo boats: *Brassey's Annual,* 1900, cited in *The Times,* April 7, 1905

514 ". . . the last man alive . . .": Kobunsha, *Memorable Battles,* 35

515 shooting of survivors: Woodward, 152

516 "Everyone laughed": ADM report, CAB 45/I 5929, Captain Jackson's report of the battle, Section I, 9

516 "Sir, the enemy has surrendered": Togawa, *Nogi-to Togo,* Part 2, 448

518–519 Tsar's diary entry of the battle: Radziwill, 143, Almedingen, 106

519 Russian losses (ships): Togo's *Supplementary Report on the Battle,* June 14, 1905, Admiralty Reports I/7842; BOHRJW, vol. 3, 788

519 Casualties: BOHRJW, vol. 3, 788; Russian losses are taken from official sources; Japanese from the *Japanese Medical History of the War*

CHAPTER 32.
Portsmouth

Korostovetz's diary provides the most illuminating account of the Portsmouth treaty from the Russian side. As usual, Tani is rich in Japanese insights. Okamoto, White, and Dillon's articles in *Harper's*, *The American Monthly Review of Reviews* and the *Contemporary Review* are all important. Dennett's documentation of Theodore Roosevelt's role is invaluable, as is White on the diplomatic history generally. *The New York Times* devoted much space to the treaty negotiations. Witte's own comments are useful, and Baroness d'Anethan was, as usual, an interesting observer of the Tokyo scene.

521 Russian newspaper comment: *The Times*, June 1, 1905

522 "By rising let us show our respect . . .": *The Times*, June 6, 1905

522 "It makes me sick . . .": NTM, 183

522–523 Akashi's finance for revolution and *John Grafton:* Tani, Chapter 7, 270; Futrell, 66–67

524 Sakharov's report: BOHRJW, vol. 3, 822

524–525 "I have come to Tokyo . . .": Tani, Chapter 8, 314–315

525 Jacob H. Schiff: White, 168–169

525–526 Roosevelt to Kaneko: White, 203

526 "he will see his way directly . . .": Dennett, 215

526 "when the truth is known . . .": Dennett, 191

526 Linievitch reports: *New York Times*, June 7 and 20, 1905

526–527 "You have come at a psychological moment . . .": Dennett, 194

527 Taft-Katsura Agreement: Bemis, 493; White, 268–269; Dennett, 112–114

528 Witte to Kokovtsov: Kokovtsov, 53

529 "Right is right . . .": *New York Times*, July 24, 1905

530 *Mayflower:* BOHRJW, vol. 3, 844

531 "Russia has never paid an indemnity . . .": Kokovtsov, 55

532 Witte's view: Korostovetz, 54

532 Sakhalin ransom: BOHRJW, vol. 3, 844

532–533 Roosevelt message to Tsar: Dennett, 265–267

533 Korostovetz on rupture: Korostovetz, 100

534 "We make you another offer . . .": *New York Times*, August 30, 1905

534–535 Nabokoff anecdotes: The unpublished diary of Constantine Nabokoff, secretary to Russian delegation

535 Witte's standing ovation: *New York Times*, September 6, 1905

536 Tokyo newspaper reaction: *New York Times*, September, 1905

537–538 "The hostilities were too far removed from us . . .": Kokovtsov, 58–59

538 "All this is trifling . . .": Kokovtsov, 60

538 "There is much hope for the future . . .": Tani, Chapter 7, 273

CHAPTER 33.
Unfinished Business

This chapter covers a vast time span, and to indicate even a fraction of the references consulted would require the repetition of much of the bibliography. On postwar relations, however, the following works were especially helpful: Andrews' *The*

Renaissance of India; the Denny papers; Dua's *The Impact of the Russo-Japanese War (1905) on Indian Politics;* Kennedy's *Asian Nationalism in the 20th Century;* Prince Lobanov-Rosktovsky's *Russia and Asia;* McKenzie's *Korea's Fight for Freedom;* Nish's *The Anglo-Japanese Alliance, 1894–1907;* Price's *The Russo-Japanese Treaties of 1907–1916 Concerning Manchuria and Mongolia;* Schiffrin's *Sun Yatsen;* and Tani for his insights into Japanese attitudes toward Manchuria and China.

541 "Japanese victories . . .": Nehru, *Glimpses of World History,* 401; and *An Autobiography,* 16

541 "A stir of excitement . . .": Andrews, 4

542 Chinese in Japan: Schiffrin, 256; Kennedy, J., 19

543 "I declare that the so-called treaty . . .": McKenzie, *Korea's Fight for Freedom,* 100–101

543 Britain also shrugged her shoulders: see Nish, 351

544–545 "What do you want to be? . . .": Saito to authors

545 "Japan is the pioneer of the new age": Kawai Tatsuo, 114

545 Toyama's friends: Norman, *Pacific Affairs,* September 3, 1944

545–546 Trials: BOHRJW, vol. 3, Appendix 26, 760–769

546 *"il reste et il restera":* Nicholas II, Archives Secrètes, 18 (Nicholas wrote these words in French in a letter to his mother)

546 As for the United States: Matsui, 36

547 "If Japan is not given a free hand . . .": The Denny papers

547 Toyama's agents: The Denny papers

547–548 U.S. Japan relations: Bemis, 681

549 Harriman's message to Roosevelt: Foreign Relations of U.S., The Conferences at Malta and Yalta, Department of State, 1955, 389, 894–897, 984

551–552 Brezhnev's speech: *New Times,* Moscow, January 1973, 1

552 Petrov statement: *Mainichi,* Tokyo, May 14, 1970

554 United fronts: *Peking Review,* April 10, 1970

556 "high-powered steam engine . . .": Marshall Green, U.S. Assistant Secretary of State, cited in *Bulletin of Japan-America Society of Washington,* vol. 17, No. 10

556 Japan's future: Benedict, 316

557 Palmerston: Wolfe, 13

THE AUTHORS

Denis and Peggy Warner have been closely involved with Asian affairs since the end of World War II when they lived for several years in Japan. Later, they made their headquarters in Singapore for many years and traveled extensively in the Far East. Mr. Warner, who fought in the Australian army in the Middle East during the earlier part of World War II, later served as a correspondent with the American forces in the Central Pacific. He covered the Korean War, the Indochina War, and the Malayan Emergency for the *Daily Telegraph*, London, and Australian newspapers. After an interlude at Harvard University in 1956–1957, where Mr. Warner was an associate Nieman Fellow, the Warners settled in Australia but continued to work on Asian affairs. Both reported the beginning of the Second Indochina War in Laos in 1959. Until 1968, Mr. Warner was the Far Eastern correspondent of *The Reporter* magazine and a frequent contributor to the *Atlantic Monthly*, twice winning citations from the Overseas Press Club in New York. Later, he became *Look*'s Asian correspondent. His newspaper dispatches appear in many countries, including the United States, Britain, and Japan. Both have written other books on Asia: *Out of the Gun, Hurricane from China,* and *The Last Confucian*—one of the first warnings of the Vietnam dangers—by Mr. Warner; and the light-hearted *Asia Is People* and *Don't Type in Bed* by Mrs. Warner.

This book is the product of many years of travel and research in nine countries. From Admiral Togo's wardroom on the *Mikasa* to Inchon in Korea, to London, Bangkok, Manila, Hong Kong, Moscow, Peking, and Singapore, the Warners traveled in quest of documentation for their account of the war.